GAUDEAMUS IGITUR

"Therefore Rejoice"

THE CAMPAIGNS
OF
THE CANADIAN ARMY
IN
THE SECOND WORLD WAR

A. DONALD MCKAY

*To Peter Unsworth,
A new neighbor but already
a valued friend
With best wishes
Donald McKay   2005*

© Copyright A. Donald McKay 2005

All rights reserved. No part of this publication my be reproduced, stored in a retrieval system, or transmitted in any form or by any means, electronic, mechanical, photocopy, recording or any other method without the prior written permission of the author.

ISBN 1-894255-53-4

Library and Archives Canada Cataloguing in Publication

McKay, A. Donald, 1925-

**Gaudeamus Igitur - Therefore Rejoice:
The Campaigns of the Canadian Army
in the Second World War / A. Donald McKay.**

**Includes bibliographical references and index.
ISBN 1-894255-53-4**

1. Canada. Canadian Army - - History - - World War, 1939-1945.
2. World War, 1939-1945 - - Campaigns. I. Title

D768.15M334 2005   940.54'1271   C2005-905469-7

Published by:
Bunker to Bunker Books,
Calgary, Alberta, Canada

Printed in Canada

CONTENTS

Preface and Acknowledgments   v

List of Maps   viii

Part I - Overview and Setting   1

Chapter I : Overview and Setting   1

Part II - Hong Kong and Dieppe   9

Chapter II : Hong Kong 8 - 25 December 1941   9

Chapter III : Dieppe 19 August 1942   23

Part III - The Italian Campaign   45

Chapter IV : The Campaign in Sicily   45

Chapter V : From Reggio to Ortona   71

Chapter VI : From Winter to Diadem   87

Chapter VII: The Gothic Line and After   101

Part IV - The Northwest Europe Campaign   127

Chapter VIII : Normandy - From D-Day to Caen   127

Chapter IX : The Road Past Falaise   151

Chapter X : The Channel Ports and Scheldt   181

Chapter XI : The Rhineland   207

Chapter XII : From the Rhine to the North Sea   225

Part V - Paratroops - Special Forces and Canloan   245

Chapter XIII : First Canadian Parachute Battalion   245

Chapter XIV : The First Special Service Force   257

Chapter XV : Canloan   271

Part VI - Results and Conclusions   277

Chapter XVI : Results and Conclusions   277

Reference Notes   287

Appendices   311

Appendix I   Order of Battle   311

Appendix II   Nomenclature   315

Sources and Bibliography   320

Index   322

PREFACE AND ACKNOWLEDGMENTS

Raison d'Etre

To those who still recall their Third Form Latin (whose numbers like those of Canada's veterans are steadily vanishing) the choice of title ("Therefore Rejoice" - from a rousing medieval student song) may seem singularly inappropriate for a treatise on the Canadian Army at war. However the choice may be defended on several grounds.

First, as should become manifest in this and subsequent chapters, what our army accomplished in that titanic conflict of long ago should truly bring pride to all Canadians. We should indeed rejoice that our youth of that era were of such a mettle as to put their very lives and futures on the line for their country and for those shared ideals and beliefs to which an overwhelming majority of their countrymen subscribed.

Second, the closing words of that song are an anthem to the youth of that time:

Post jucundam juventutem
Post molestam sinecure
Nos habebit humus

(After happy youth and tiresome old age the earth will claim us.)

For far too many of those Canadian youths (over 40,000) there would be no tiresome old age, and precious little happy youth--the earth did indeed claim them - in the very flower of their lives. A.E Housman put it thus:

Here dead lie we because we did not choose
To live and shame the land from which we sprung.
Life, to be sure, is nothing much to lose;
But young men think it is, and we were young.

Finally, it was the survivors among those same men and women who on their return fashioned for us many of those aspects of Canada that we so treasure today - tolerance, freedom from want, universal education, medicare, old age security and the opportunity to advance to wherever our talents and ambition take us. And that is surely something for which we can rejoice.

Prelude

Over half a century has elapsed since the end of the Second World War (WW2) since when the world's consciousness, if not conscience, has been benumbed by a seemingly endless procession of lesser wars - some deemed just, many more unjust and most simply boringly unpleasant, soon-to-be-forgotten, news bites of the time.

Against such a setting, and given the average, especially average young, Canadian's lamentable (so we are told) knowledge of history it is little wonder that their grasp of what their forebears did in the Second World War is hazy at best and badly skewed at worst. It is bad enough that their perception is clouded by the constantly bad-pressed state of the current military. But when such perception is reinforced by the recent spate of scholarly presentations which endlessly harp on the perceived command and performance deficiencies of the army in WW2 it would be miraculous if their views were not seriously biased.

Admittedly a great many balanced and, at least in the early post-war era, some embarrassingly over-glowing, accounts of our army's achievements in WW2 have been published over the years. But outside of the small coterie of professional historians and military history buffs anything more than a few years old has disappeared from the screen of today's audience who consider events beyond the pale of CNN's current sound and video bite as boring ancient history. In the hope of somewhat redressing the balance this book will attempt to outline every significant action in which the Canadian Army participated in that war. An effort has been made to limit detail to that necessary for the reader to form a balanced judgement of events. While its avowed thrust is to accentuate the positive, the negative receives its due and Part VI especially will try to evaluate what, from a military sense, came out of it all.

Although intended as a scholarly treatise, its hope is to also counterbalance some of the more narrowly focused of these and to appeal to a wider field. Accordingly, despite the previous denigration of the news flash approach, its thrust is probably closer to that of Bernstein and Woodward than to Toynbee. However while not aimed only at the professional historian, some of the notations and occasional unorthodox conclusions may provide targets for their future scholarly delving or scornful counterattacks. If it has a target audience it would probably be budding student historians in the hope that it may stimulate some of these to further pursue the matter and instil pride in future generations of Canadians over what their forefathers, themselves just young Canadians, achieved in that gigantic conflict of the distant past. We would of course also hope that the general public will find interest in these pages. And if some find all of this too much to digest we suggest that they skim through the introductory and concluding paragraphs of each chapter in the hopes that their appetites may thereby increase.

Acknowledgments

Over the years I have had the acquaintance, to a greater or lesser degree, of many of the principal players of this drama - from Prime Ministers and generals to colonels and lesser ranks galore. Although I have had discussions with many of these, some meaningful some not, much of which has emerged already exists in print some place or other. Accordingly this history is based principally on the printed words of many others as filtered by these conversations and my own recollection of the events of the time. The primary sources have been the official Canadian and British histories. The many other sources are listed in the bibliography.

The six parts of this study are as follows:

Part I---Overview and Setting
Part II-- Hong Kong and Dieppe
Part III- The Italian Campaign
Part IV-The Northwest European Campaign
Part V--Paratroops, Special Forces and Canloan
Part VI-Results and Conclusions

DEDICATION

To the 82 names on the Indian Head Cenotaph,
may their number never increase
and
To my wife Louise whose advice,
help and encouragement have been indispensable.

List of Maps

Hong Kong and New Territory	10
Hong Kong Island	14
Dieppe	22
Sicily	44
Italy	70
Canadian Landings and Advance to Potenza	74
To Campobasso and Beyond	75
The Moro and Ortona	80
Liri Valley	91
Gothic Line (1)	102
Gothic Line (2)	105
Gothic Line (3)	109
The Last Hurrah (1)	121
The Last Hurrah (2)	122
Normandy - D-Day to Carpiquet	128
Caen to Tilly and Verrieres	146
Road Past Falaise	150
The Falaise Gap	176
The Channel Ports	182
Boulogne	186
Calais and Cap Gris Nez	191
The Scheldt	193
The Rhineland	210
Holland and Germany	224
Canadian Parachute Operations	244
Operation Varsity	245
1st Special Service Force - Winter Line	256
Anzio and Rome	258

OVERVIEW AND SETTING

CHAPTER I

OVERVIEW AND SETTING

Let us therefore...so bear ourselves that, if the British Empire and its Commonwealth last for a thousand years, men will still say: "This was their finest hour"

Winston Churchill, House of Commons, 18 June 1940

Genesis - World War I 1914-1918 - The Canadian Corps

From Vimy Ridge onwards in World War I the Canadian Corps was the most effective fighting formation in the British Army, indeed probably the most effective of all Western Front formations allied or enemy.(1) And General Sir Arthur Currie, its commander after Vimy, and subsequently often maligned or ignored, was the most successful of all Allied generals.(2) The magnificent Australians came close but too often laboured under commanders, including Birdwood and Monash, who were not up to the high standards of Byng or Currie.(3)

The instrument which was to become the superb Canadian Corps was painstakingly forged. Following a brilliant stand in the face of the world's first major gas attack at 2nd Ypres in April 1915, where the flanking French Colonials bolted, the Canadian performances at Festubert, Givenchy and St. Eloi were painful learning experiences. The corner was turned at Mount Sorrel (May/June 1916) a major Canadian triumph. The Corps' bloodbath on the Somme (August/October 1916) ended in bitter victory at Courcelette and Regina Trench. Thereafter it was ever victorious.

Vimy in April 1917, with the Corps under the British Lt Gen Julian Byng, was a superb success and Hill 70 in August, with the Corps now commanded by Canadian Lt Gen Arthur Currie, was another. The Canadian Corps was inserted late at 3rd Ypres in October 1917 but brilliantly overcame the unparalleled horrors of mud, blood, shot, shell, concrete pillboxes and mustard gas to finally, in November, capture an almost obliterated Passchendaele, that grim and elusive final objective which had defied, thwarted and taunted the best efforts of two full armies since July. Passchendaele still haunts the annals of the armies of Empire and Commonwealth as the ultimate horror.

Despite these magnificent successes the Corps achieved even greater glories in the war's final Hundred Days. At Amiens (August 1918) the Canadian and Australian Corps, "matchless attacking troops "in the words of Liddell Hart, attacking side by side achieved so complete a victory that Ludendorff the German commander characterised it as "the Black Day of the German Army".(4)

Amiens was followed by equally brilliant successes at Arras and the Drocourt-Queant Switch, the latter of which has been singled out by some historians as "the British Army's single greatest achievement on the Western Front".(5) These were followed by signal successes at Canal du Nord, Bourlon and Cambrai culminating with the capture, on the war's last day, of Mons where for the British Empire the land war had begun in August 1914.

All of these battles were won through a combination of meticulous planning, preparation, all-ranks briefings, overwhelming densities of artillery and machine guns and, above all, the superb elan of the Canadian infantry. The infantry attacked with flexible platoon and section tactics under the leadership of first class and resourceful junior officers and NCOs. And, most important, the attacking formations wherever possible employed the maximum number of battalions simultaneously assaulting the entire objective. Unfortunately these unparalleled achievements were marred by a vitriolic campaign of hatred against Currie by his onetime champion, the ex-Minister of Militia, Sir Sam Hughes. Hughes' accusations, refuted too late, when coupled with the Corps' heavy "Hundred Days" casualties, led many Canadians to wrongfully accept the libel that Currie had been an uncaring butcher from the same mold as the host of other publicly disdained generals from Haig down. Currie was thus denied his just laurels as the Allies' outstanding commander and one of the great generals of all time.(6)

The Second World War 1939 - 1945

Comparative Performance

For a variety of reasons, many of which have been enunciated in searing detail in learned journals and elsewhere, the Canadians of the Second World War never attained the successes, recognition or pre-eminence of their First World War forebears. Indeed it is difficult to see how it could have been otherwise. Much was expected of them, often of exaggerated proportions, and when they did not quite meet their critics' high expectations there was a tendency to belittle their achievements or damn them with faint praise. There were however some special factors which contributed to this sense of under-achievement, a few of which are treated below.

Late Commitment to Action

Except for the sad one-shot disasters of Hong Kong in December 1941 and Dieppe in August 1942 the Canadian Army was only committed to action in July 1943, nearly four years after the war's outbreak and after the tide had clearly turned in favour of the Allies.(7) The great, and some not-so-great, battles of Norway, Belgium/France, North and East Africa, the Balkans, Crete, South East Asia and early Burma had been fought with Canada on the sidelines, first as a supportive cheerleader then increasingly as an embarrassed onlooker. Guadalcanal in the Pacific, Stalingrad in Russia, El Alamein in Africa, all in 1942, had marked the beginning of the end of both Japan and Germany and pushed Italy to the brink of total collapse.

The embarrassing spectacle of hundreds of thousands of Canadians sitting under-employed in Britain while climactic battles raged elsewhere was largely, but by no means solely, the handiwork of two men - though for quite different reasons. Mackenzie King, the Prime Minister, would go to any lengths to prevent the army from suffering the heavy casualties which might force conscription on him and thus threaten his fragile home-front compromise. Meanwhile his army commander, General A.G.L. McNaughton, influenced by the First World War example, strove to keep his entire army together until he could lead it into action as a "dagger pointed at the heart of Berlin". Both men

OVERVIEW AND SETTING

were to be disappointed. Mackenzie King would eventually have overseas conscription forced upon him, albeit too little and too late. McNaughton would see his command divided and the "dagger" wielded by others while he was to suffer the personal indignity of being denied permission to even visit his erstwhile troops in action.

By not committing one or more divisions to earlier combat, probably in North Africa, the Canadians were denied the chance of gradually honing their craft, possibly against less than resolute opposition, and reaping early kudos as did the Australians at Bardia or the South Africans in East Africa. Or, if committed later, they may have shared in the glories of Alamein or the capture of Tunis. By the same token of course they were spared the humiliations of the Balkans, Crete and such North African debacles as "the November Handicap" and second Tobruk.(8) This meant, of course, that they thereby missed the chance of seasoning their troops at more acceptable casualty levels.(9) At least equally important it denied Canadian commanders the opportunity of acquiring on-job training on a gradual, continuing basis as well as gaining at least associate membership in the chummy Desert Army club of hunting, shooting old boy commanders.

Thus by the time the Canadians were finally committed on land the Russians were well out of danger and threatening to win the European war by themselves.(10) Meanwhile, in the Pacific, the Americans had long since turned the corner at Midway and Guadalcanal and were well on their island-hopping way to Japan. So it was with a certain ennui and a feeling of, "what, you've actually decided to get fully into the war?" that the world yawningly greeted Canada's entry into the land lists.

Designation of the First Canadian Army

The fact that Canada fielded a nationally named army in Northwest Europe gave a false impression of both the composition of that army and the size of the Canadian combat component. An Army is a powerful formation of at least two, and often three or more, corps perhaps including a dozen or more divisions. Thus when citing Dempsey's British Second, Bradley's US First or Patton's US Third Army one rightly conjures up the image of an immense national force bearing on the enemy. However this would convey an incorrect image when one refers to Crerar's First Canadian Army.

Until the final campaign in Holland, in the last two months of the war in Europe, the Canadian combat element of what was entitled the First Canadian Army consisted of just a single corps, comprised of, at most, three divisions and an armoured brigade. The rest of the so-called Canadian Army consisted of British formations, a Polish division and elements of other national formations or units. Indeed, in the early stages of the climactic Rhineland campaign the battle element was overwhelmingly British.

This led to some embarrassing misconceptions, as when the US General Bradley, despairing of First Canadian Army's slow advance to Falaise and beyond, complained to Field Marshal Montgomery, Commander 21 Army Group, that perhaps he should replace the green Canadians with seasoned British troops. Apart from the fact that the Canadian Army had a very sizeable British combat component, the all British Second Army was equally struggling in its Operation Bluecoat. Indeed, some of the most underachieving divisions in the Anglo-Canadian 21st Army Group were the famed, and most seasoned, veterans of the Desert Army- the 7th Armoured and 51st Highland.

Meanwhile, from Carpiquet onward, apart from the shared capture of Caen and the ill-starred Operation Goodwood, the main 21 Army Group thrust from Caen to Falaise and Trun was spearheaded by a mere handful of Canadian divisions and the armoured brigade. Of these only one division (3rd Canadian Infantry-3CID)-then part of Second British Army - led to Caen; then only two (2 CID and 3 CID) to Verrieres and Tilly; and finally three (2 and 3 CIDs and 4th Armoured (4CAD))to close the Falaise pocket and beyond. In all of these operations they were, of course, joined by several British formations and, in the later stages, one Polish division. Meanwhile, because of the designation Canadian Army, the world's perception, such as it existed at all, was that a vast number of Canadian divisions were slowly stumbling their way to Falaise and the gap.

How different might that perception have been had the Army borne some other designation - perhaps something such as "First Commonwealth Army". Then the leading edge role played in it by the painfully few Canadian divisions might instead have been lauded for contributions far beyond the number of formations they employed. *Sic Transit Gloria.*

Denigration by Commanders and Historians

The self-serving criticisms of their own troops by, especially, Generals Simonds and Foulkes have been well documented in military journals and elsewhere but have been only weakly refuted. They warrant a full rebuttal which, one hopes, will someday be forthcoming and widely promulgated.

On the other hand, criticisms by such British commanders as Montgomery, Crocker and Tedder fall under the once familiar, but now happily rarer, arrogant British upper class denigration of the real or imagined shortcomings of anyone or anything not of their ilk, while overlooking or evading their own less than glorious performances.(11) In an aside not intended for a wider audience former Prime Minister Pearson, himself an Oxford old boy, once delightfully parodied this trait as one of "inbred Carleton Clubbers peering haughtily down their Balliol College noses...", while sniffily dismissing the deeds of lesser breeds.(12)

Field Marshall Montgomery's put-downs are legion such as his fatuous, and palpably ridiculous, comments on General Crerar's alleged before and after lunch errors on the very day the latter assumed his command. However Montgomery was equally scathing of everyone else, including Eisenhower and Patton, who were outside his own coterie of personal, and constantly shifting, acolytes and myrmidons. But this was part and parcel of the Monty mystique and, to give the devil his due, he was as often lavish in his praise of his Canadian's deeds as he was critical of what he sometimes saw as their failure to follow his infallible plan to certain fruition.

Lieutenant-General Crocker, the commander I Corps under whom the Canadian 3rd Division initially served in Normandy, made snide comments on the Canadians' so-called "failure" at Carpiquet and was admired by the McKenna brothers for his criticisms of Major-General Keller, the commander 3CID(13). Crocker's comments should be considered in the light of his own early shortcomings which led Crerar to attempt to sack him at one stage. Crocker had a history of loose lippery including his infamous sneering remark on the Americans at the Fondouk Gap in Tunisia. "Tell the American division commander not to attack. I will do the job with a battalion of Guards." In the event, the subsequent Tunisian performances, at Green and Longstop Hills, *et al*, of his Guards, his Corps and he himself could most charitably be characterized as stodgy. The

OVERVIEW AND SETTING

rankled Americans gained sweet revenge at Massena, Normandy and thereafter. Again, to balance the ledger, Crocker, whose Corps served in the 1st Canadian Army from Normandy to the Rhineland, became a loyal and most effective subordinate of Crerar and his magnificent Corps significantly contributed to the successes of the Canadian Army.

Air Marshall Tedder's criticisms centred on what he perceived to be a reluctance on the part of the Canadians to mount a major attack without calling on the help of Bomber Command. Given the often limited value of heavy bomber support (Boulogne and Walcheren excepted) there may have been some validity in Tedder's remarks. However, as Eisenhower's Air Deputy, Tedder would have been better advised had he devoted more of his efforts to vastly improving air support in all aspects, including communications, response times, close support control and heavy bomber targeting than in carping at those who expected more of air support than he was able to deliver.

More damaging, because of the source, are the works of Canadian historians, writers and academics who, in attempts to find something new to write about, have tended of late to focus on Canadian shortcomings instead of accomplishments. These authorities (whose comments are uncritically accepted and echoed by their foreign peers), almost alone among their contemporaries seem almost masochistically reluctant to trumpet the successes of their nation's forces. Contrast this with the way our wartime allies have chronicled their nations' triumphs and tragedies.

The Wartime Annals of our Allies

The following is in no sense a criticism or denigration of the very real achievements of our former allies. It is simply to show how these allies have treated their triumphs and disasters in the most positive of lights.

United Kingdom

The first three years of the Second World War featured a sordid succession of humiliating disasters- Norway, Belgium/France, North Africa, the Balkans, Crete, Hong Kong, Malaya, Burma. Poor generalship, tactical ineptitude and disgrace abounded. Singapore and the early Arakan campaigns were miserable failures while performances in other theatres were often quite ordinary. Yet all of these are subsumed in the national British conscience, which rightly focuses and celebrates the true triumphs of Beda Fomm, Alamein, Tripoli, Tunis, Centuripe, Sangro, Admin Box, Imphal/Kohima, Mandalay, D-Day, Arnhem, Rhineland and the race to the Baltic. These are the true measures of a nation's pride and remembrance

USA

Few would dispute that, in the grand scheme of things, the Americans and Russians between them won the Second World War. In the Pacific the American island hopping campaign was a superb continuum - New Guinea, Solomons, Tarawa, Saipan, Philippines,, Iwo Jima, Okinawa. In Europe their great Normandy victories at Cherbourg, St Lo, Avranches and Argentan were in marked contrast to the plodding Anglo/Canadian advance. Their sweep through France, airborne drops in Market Garden, the Saar, Colmar, Bastogne, Remagen and the drive across Germany were the stuff of legend - and Hollywood. Yet their Aachen and Hurtgen Forest battles were as plodding as anything for which 21 Army Group was reviled as were their early Bulge actions where they lost 7000 prisoners and gobs of real estate. The first Philippines and New Guinea were barely fair and Kasserine in Tunisia a near disaster. Their Italian performances, especially at the command level, at Salerno, Anzio, the Rapido and the Winter Line were sub-par by any measure. But all of these pale, as they should, in story, legend and truth beside their unparalleled victorious achievements.

Australia

No veteran who has visited Australia can fail to be impressed by the magnificent manner in which that country pays tribute to the achievements of its military. The memorial at Canberra is the supreme example but other superb memorials tug the heartstrings in Sydney, Melbourne and Perth. While in nearly every town the war memorial is a proud and poignant centerpiece. The Aussies are rightly proud of their fine achievements in both world wars. They justly celebrate their Gallipoli Calvary with solemn pride - Anzac Day is a venerated rite. Yet despite heroic efforts their Gallipoli battles were almost universal failures - but for Australians it is the heroism, not the failure, that is celebrated. Their Second World War battles at Tobruk, Alamein and Milne Bay are rightfully trumpeted. Yet MacArthur carped at their New Guinea performance while their celebrated early successes at Bardia, et al, were against a feeble foe. Their campaigns in the Balkans and Crete were total defeats, Syria (against the Vichy French) was undistinguished, Darwin a panic and Singapore a complete disaster. Yet always only the positive is accentuated - as it should be.

New Zealand

The 2nd New Zealand Division has sometimes been cited as the Allies' finest - it was certainly one of the best. Yet it failed in the Balkans and its loss of Maleme airport to lightly armed German paratroopers was a critical failure which sealed the fate of Crete. Sidi Rezegh was at most a saw-off, Enfidaville, Orsogna and Cassino all failures. Yet it is their valour which is remembered, as is right.

South Africa

The annihilation of its 5th Brigade at Totensonntag and the collapse and surrender of its 2nd Division at Tobruk are largely forgotten.(14) But South African successes in East Africa and by its 6th Armoured Division in the late stages of the Italian campaign are well remembered.

These examples are merely to show how other countries look beyond less than glorious episodes and focus on the valour and heroism and success. How different the recent Canadian experience which seems obsessed with failure and where even brilliant victories such as Ortona are labelled failures by foreign experts and treated with disdain by

OVERVIEW AND SETTING

the government.(15) Let us now wipe the slate clean and return to the war years to see what the Canadian army really did accomplish.

The Canadian Army in Battle

Although committed late to battle the Canadians, once committed, participated in full measure in, and often spearheaded, some of the most gruelling, ferocious and critical campaigns of the war. And, as will be shown in subsequent chapters, their performance was nearly always good, often excellent and, except for the special cases of Dieppe and Hong Kong, in the end prevailing. Later chapters will cover the part played by the Canadians at Dieppe and Hong Kong, by our airborne and special forces and especially in the climactic Italian and Northwest Europe campaigns. So, while leaving battle details to these later issues, a few general points will be made here.

Combat Milieu

Except for a very brief period at the outset in Sicily the Canadians were never accorded the luxury of meeting a second class foe. Almost without exception, for two long years, they were hurled again and again against an absolutely first class, superbly led and resolute enemy, often over appalling terrain and in abominable weather. Despite minor setbacks, terrible casualties and occasional lapses in leadership they always, in the end, won through. And that is the *raison d'être* of an army and the true measure of its worth.

POW to Casualty Ratio

Note should be taken of the fact that of all the allied forces the Canadians had, often by far, the lowest ratio of prisoners to other battle casualties(16). Admittedly they missed the debacles and wholesale surrenders of the Balkans, Crete, Malaya, Burma and the Western Desert. But they had their Dieppe and Hong Kong. While too much should not be read into POW to other casualty ratios it does say something about the determination of the troops to continue to journey's end.

Potpourri on Things to Come

Paratroops. After dropping on D-Day, fighting in the Bulge and dropping over the Rhine the 1st Canadian Parachute Battalion advanced 500 kms to the Baltic - the deepest advance into Germany of all 21 Army Group.

Special Forces. The superb actions of the joint US/Canadian First Special Service Force at Difensa, Majo, Anzio and the capture of Rome are largely unknown. They deserve much more.

Hong Kong. With his Headquarters overrun, Canadian Brigadier Lawson was killed when he went "outside to shoot it out". Even the Japanese were impressed by his valour. In the entire Hong Kong campaign the Japanese only reported meeting very severe resistance and suffering heavy casualties on two occasions - both against Canadians.

Dieppe. This resulted in Canada's heaviest one-day casualties of the war - the dead alone amounted to one-fifth of the force. The number of prisoners was also high - largely because they could not be brought off in the face of heavy fire.

Italy. Ortona was Canada's finest division strength battle of the Italian campaign. The breaking of the Gothic Line by I Canadian Corps, under the oft-maligned Lt Gen Burns, was Canada's greatest victory of the entire war and ranks as one of the finest actions of the entire Italian Campaign by anyone.

Northwest Europe. 3rd Canadian Division's battles of D-Day, Bretteville, Buron, Authie, Abbaye Ardenne, Leopold Canal and Moyland Wood rank as some of the war's finest actions. 2nd Division's assaults on Verrieres, Walcheren and the Hochwald were among the most ferocious. Denied the glamour of the long advance, 4th Armoured plugged the Falaise Gap and fought well in the Scheldt and the last hundred days.

The Netherlands. Finally, in our proudest moment, the now united Canadian Army fought a grinding, bloody campaign to liberate the heroic and long suffering Netherlands - and launch an ongoing chapter of mutual admiration between the two. It is ironic that remembrance and heartfelt appreciation of what our army accomplished is today remembered more by the Netherlanders than by our own citizens. It is time to redress the balance.

Canadian Troops arriving at Hong Kong.
They are the Winnipeg Grenadiers 16th. November, 1941. (I. W. M.)

HONG KONG and DIEPPE

CHAPTER II

HONG KONG 8 - 25 DECEMBER 1941

Yesterday, December 7, 1941
-A date which will live in infamy-

President Roosevelt - *Joint Session of Congress, 8 December, 1941*

Eastern Sunset

The defence of Hong Kong, Canada's first major land battle of the Second World War was, like Dieppe which followed it, a dismal failure and library shelves are replete with accusatory and finger pointing publications concerning Canada's role in the defeat. However, unlike Dieppe, the general, and even usually informed, public remains largely ignorant of the course of the battle and especially of the part played by the two Canadian battalions and their commanders. What little impression most persons retain is often based on biased and even misleading presentations such as that of the oft-reviled "The Valour and the Horror"(1) or on occasional journalistic reportings which usually deal with the suffering of Canadians in Japanese prison camps and their resulting efforts to gain compensation.

Prelude to Disaster

The defence of Hong Kong must be viewed in the light of the overall British pre-war plans drawn up for the possibility of war with Japan. These plans were anchored on two key pillars - the defence of Malaya as part of ensuring the invincibility of Singapore, and, the concentration of a large British fleet in the Far East which, in concert with the US Navy, would defeat any Japanese moves against British, Dutch and USA possessions. Indeed the British had used these plans, with solemn assurances of their fulfilment, as the basis of their arguments to convince Australia to denude its own defences in order to provide forces for North Africa and elsewhere.(2)

In the event these plans proved to be a chimera of the wildest sort. The battles of the Atlantic and the Mediterranean precluded the timely dispatch of a major fleet. Instead, in the all too dreary repeat of "too little and too late", the British sent to Singapore, at the last minute, only two capital ships, the Prince of Wales and Repulse. Here they were promptly mishandled by their commanders and sunk by the Japanese within days of their arrival. Meanwhile, before Hong Kong was invaded, the Japanese had destroyed most of the US Pacific Fleet at Pearl Harbour and largely eliminated US air power in Hawaii and the Philippines and British air power in Malaya and Singapore. The fumbling defence of Malaya and the Dutch East Indies then progressed from fiasco to ignominious disaster. Therefore from the outset Hong Kong was totally cut off and isolated.

In such a setting the defence of Hong Kong must be considered for what it actually became - a sacrificial campaign to which no outside help or hope could be extended. It was into this forlorn scenario - the very worst and most hopeless conditions under

GAUDEAMUS IGITUR

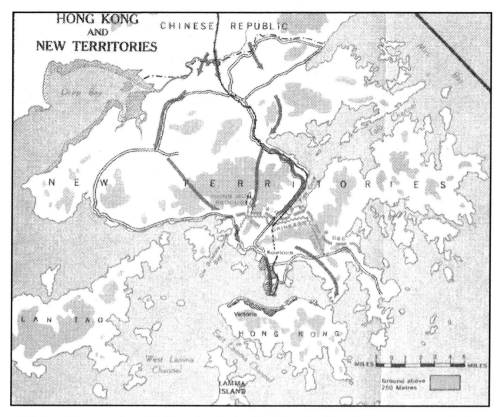

which soldiers can be asked to give their all - that the Canadians were committed to action. And once committed there could be no way out save death or captivity. It is one thing to fight well when there is the possibility of victory or relief or even withdrawal. It is quite another to fight well without hope. Yet the green, under-trained, under-armed, under-equipped, under-supported Canadians did just that. They fought with courage, determination, valour and incredibly even with some success to the very end. And it is in this context that the Canadian performance must be viewed

But all these things were yet to come to pass and prior to 8 December 1941 in Hong Kong such possibilities were not forecast nor even seriously contemplated. In their place wishful thinking, complacency and appalling bad intelligence prevailed.(3) Tea dances in the Peninsula, race meets at Happy Valley and the minutiae of colonial society occupied the hours of the Hong Kong expatriates to the very end. And the band played on.(4)

The Canadian Requirement

The late 1941 requirement to augment the existing four battalion Hong Kong garrison with one or two additional battalions was recommended by the Commander-in-Chief Far East, Air Chief Marshal Sir Robert Brooke-Popham.(5) After much consideration, vacillation and changes of course it was agreed by the British Chiefs of Staff and their Prime Minister Winston Churchill.(6) As the British, in view of their overstretched world-wide commitments, felt that they could not spare any of their own units for this purpose a request was directed to Canada and was willingly accepted.

So as not to interfere with the ongoing build-up of Canadian forces assembling in England for an eventual continental invasion the Canadian authorities looked elsewhere. The battalions eventually selected were the Royal Rifles of Canada (RRC) under Lt-Col W. J. Home and the Winnipeg Grenadiers (WG) under Lt-Col J.L.R Sutcliffe. To these were added signals, medical (including two nursing sisters), dental, chaplain, provost, postal and auxiliary services elements making a total force strength of 96 officers and 1877 other ranks. The force was commanded by Brigadier J.K. Lawson with Colonel P. Hennessy as Officer in Charge Administration.

The battalions, of necessity, were chosen from those whose state of training, due in large part to the nature of their erstwhile garrison duties, was not of the highest level. Much has since been made of this by critics of Canada's involvement. However at that time, although the Japanese government had clearly embarked on a course of aggression, it was not widely expected that Japan was contemplating war with the USA or UK in the near future.(7) Indeed one of the thoughts behind the British *volte-face* on the size of the Hong Kong garrison was that, "A small reinforcement of one or two battalions would increase the strength of the garrison out of all proportion to the actual numbers involved ... provide a stimulus to the garrison and the Colony.... have a very great moral effect in the Far East and show Chiang Kai Shek that we really intended to fight it out in Hong Kong."(8) This last was a most important consideration as, at the time, it was hoped that the Chinese Nationalist Army, the closest elements of which were within striking distance of nearby Canton, might attack the Japanese in rear if the latter attacked Hong Kong. While with 20/20 hindsight this was clearly "pie in the sky" the British, at the time, held the strong opinion that war in the Far East, beyond the ongoing incursion into China, was unlikely in the near term. And, if Japan did attack, it was expected that Russia rather than the British Commonwealth would be the target.

The formal British request to Canada was made on 19 September 1941, was accepted, and on 11 October the final decisions on the force were taken. The component parts were warned, prepared, assembled and left Vancouver on 27 October, arriving in Hong Kong, via Honolulu and Manila, on 16 November - an incredibly rapid response under any circumstances

Unfortunately the force's transport, 212 essential vehicles, left later on a second ship which only reached Manila on 12 December, four days after the outbreak of war with Japan. With Hong Kong now effectively cut off, the vehicles were, quite properly, diverted to the USA forces defending the Philippines. This loss was to severely hamper the Canadians who, after arriving in Hong Kong, had to make do with just two universal carriers and a hodgepodge of, at most, 40 other vehicles which they borrowed locally. The units also lacked anti-tank weapons and mortar ammunition. The latter deficiency, in the light of the subsequent paucity in artillery support, was an extremely serious defect.

The Defence Plan

The defence of Hong Kong envisaged two phases - a delaying action on the mainland (New Territories and Kowloon) followed by a prolonged defence of the island. (See Map). Until the nomination of the Canadian reinforcements the delaying action on the mainland was to be undertaken by only one battalion whose task was "to cover a comprehensive scheme of demolitions and act as a delaying force."(9) It was expected that this phase would perhaps last only 48 hours .With the arrival of the Canadians the GOC Hong Kong, Maj Gen C.M. Maltby, reverted to a 1937 defence plan which envisaged defending the mainland with three battalions along a ten mile long "Gin Drinkers Line".(10) This line consisted of entrenchments and pillboxes anchored on the west by the key Shing Mun Redoubt. The three manning battalions were 2nd Royal Scots (2RS) (left), 2/14th Punjab (centre) and 5/7th Rajput (right) in an *ad hoc* Mainland Brigade under British Acting Brigadier C. Wallis. Supporting mobile artillery consisted of only four troops: one of 6 inch, one of 4.5 inch and two of 3 7 inch pieces. The expected delaying action on the mainland was thus raised to a minimum of seven to twelve days.

The ensuing perimeter defence of the Island would be conducted by two battalions defending the dangerous north coast fronting Kowloon from Victoria Harbour to Lye Mun Passage, and two battalions defending respectively the south-east and south-west shores against a feared Japanese seaborne landing. A reserve was to be formed from the Hong Kong Volunteers and other detachments (including naval and a few Free French) along with elements of units returning from the mainland. The Island was ringed with 72 concrete pillboxes manned by machine gunners of the Middlesex Regiment (MX) and Hong Kong Volunteer Defence Corps (HKVDC) backed by numerous searchlights. Unfortunately, in a scenario eerily reminiscent of the poorly sited French pillboxes at Sedan nineteen months previously, many of these were sited in undefiladed positions facing the front where they could be readily located and engaged from across the narrow harbour.(11) The lack of air support combined with a serious weakness in artillery and mortars was to severely limit the defence capabilities.

Due largely to their unfamiliarity with the local geography, existing defence plans and friendly forces the Canadians were initially assigned to the perimeter defence of the Island's south coast -the RRC on the south-east and the WG on the south-west. They were to retain these defensive responsibilities throughout - long after the Japanese real lines of advance had been determined. As a result the Canadian commitment to battle was all too often to take the form of attacks by individual platoons and companies hastily called forward from their main positions. The Canadians were seldom to fight as complete battalions or with both battalions in concert - indeed co-ordinated actions above company level were the exception. This fact must also be considered when assessing the Canadian performance. Although originally billeted on the mainland the Canadians played a negligible part in its defence, despite inferences which the uninformed may have drawn from the Hong Kong episode of *The Valour and the Horror.* But they were to participate in the fullest measure in the climactic battles on the Island .

The Mainland Battle

The Japanese plan, which presumed serious resistance by the defenders of the Gin Drinkers Line, called for a deliberate, methodical advance by the reinforced 38th Division over many days. However, after rapidly closing up to the line in only one day, the Japanese 228th Regiment, whose commander Colonel Doi showed outstanding initiative and tactical ability, attacked the key Shing Mun Redoubt on the night of 9 December.(12) The Redoubt, manned by a single platoon of the 2nd Royal Scots, was quickly subdued after sporadic tough fighting - the Japanese were astonished at the ease of their victory.

Surprisingly, given the absolutely critical status of the Redoubt, the British mounted no counter-attack to restore the situation although troops could have readily been found, even earmarked in advance, for this vital role. But passivity reigned - even the Royal Scots own reserve company remained inactive and uncommitted.(13)

After one day's respite the redoubtable Japanese again attacked the Scots and "easily broke through the British line."(14) At this stage "D" Company WG was brought forward to cover the gap caused by the breakthrough but experienced no serious fighting and was never used to counter the Japanese advance. The British command was now determined to get back to the Island as soon and as intact as possible, despite all the serious consequences that such a move implied to friend and foe alike. On 11 December General Maltby withdrew his force to the Island, except for the 5/7 Rajput who were to hold the dominating Devil's Peak peninsula. The strength of this position and the possibilities that might have been had Maltby steeled himself to really contest the mainland were demonstrated on 13 December when the Rajputs beat off a Japanese attack and inflicted considerable casualties in the process. Despite this success Maltby withdrew the Rajputs to the Island the next day.

The Battle for the Island

On the night of 18 December the Japanese, after heavy shelling and the destruction or neutralisation of key northern beach defences, assault landed on the Island's north eastern sector held by the recently returned Rajputs. The Rajputs and Middlesex machine gunners inflicted considerable casualties but could not stem the invaders who landed on a wide front and, with their customary elan, rapidly pushed inland. On the Japanese left their 229th Regiment went for Boa Vista and Mount Parker, in the centre the 228th aimed for Jardine's Lookout while the 230th on their right moved on Wong Nei Chong. Again no serious pre-planned or well co-ordinated counter-attacks were launched although the British had had many years to prepare for just such an eventuality. Even the defensive artillery fire, such as it was, was poorly co-ordinated and largely ineffective. Left largely to their own resources and with their front pierced in many places the Rajputs, who had fought so well on the mainland, soon ceased to exist as an effective fighting unit.

The Island's defenders were now organised, if such a word can apply in the chaos ensuing, into two brigades roughly divided by the north-south road linking Causeway and Repulse bays via Stanley Gap. The two Canadian battalions were split one to each brigade. The East Brigade, under British Brigadier Wallis, which was the sector of the Japanese main effort, consisted of only one full battalion, the RRC, two companies of MX, elements of the HKVDC and naval detachments. The West Brigade, under Canadian Brigadier Lawson, comprised the WG, the remaining parts of the RS, Punjabs and Rajputs, two companies MX and HKVDC elements. Lawson's Headquarters was at Wong Nei Chong with Headquarters Fortress Artillery.

The defence consisted almost entirely of individual company, and often platoon, counter-attacks hastily planned and over-hastily mounted, poorly co-ordinated with other actions and very weakly supported, if at all, by a mishmash of artillery pieces. The

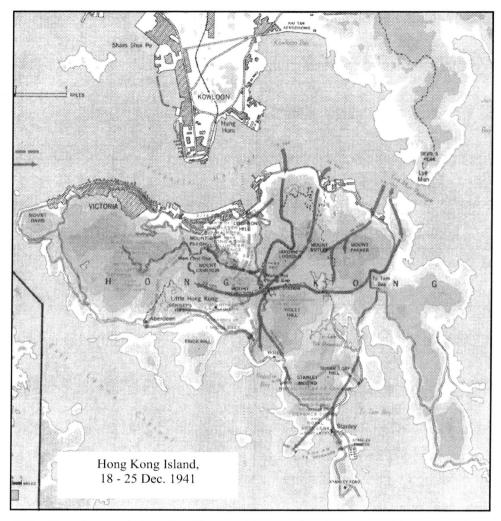

Hong Kong Island, 18 - 25 Dec. 1941

MX still retained a number of medium machine guns but these were seldom grouped for effective counter-attack covering fire while the hilly nature of the ground precluded realistic MMG defensive fire tasks using the gun's excellent beaten zone.

The East Brigade

The RRC were the first Canadians into heavy action when its "C" Company under Maj W.A. Bishop was called forward on the first night to counter the penetration of the Rajputs. The company launched vigorous attacks against strong Japanese forces on the key Sai Wan area but despite some initial successes failed to seal off the enemy. It did, however, beat back a succession of Japanese attacks with considerable casualties to both sides. A second RRC company attacked the enemy who had, with a remarkable display of initiative and fitness, captured the dominating Mount Parker. The RRC counter-

HONG KONG and DIEPPE

attack was repulsed with heavy casualties. The indomitable Japanese continued their relentless advance and after only the first night had captured Mounts Parker and Butler and approached Wong Nei Chong Gap - hard by Brigadier Lawson's West Brigade Headquarters. So much for the strategy of not fighting hard for the mainland lest it jeopardise the defence of the Island

In an effort to group his dwindling resources and form an effective counter-attack force Wallis decided to withdraw his East Brigade to a line Repulse Bay - Red Hill. While this was a reasonable enough plan it had the effect of losing contact with the West Brigade. In accordance with this redeployment the RRC, considerably reduced after the first night's fighting, took up positions at Stanley Mound, Sugar Loaf Hill, Palm Villa and Stone Hill. The already thin defences of the brigade were further worsened by the abandonment of coast batteries at Capes Collinson and D'Aguilar and mobile guns at Red Hill .

On 20 December Wallis ordered the RRC to advance on Violet Hill with a view to making contact with the West Brigade. The advance was hampered by a total lack of artillery support and the loss by the HKVDC of a covering position at Gauge Hill. Meanwhile the Japanese had already seized Violet Hill and reached the Repulse Bay Hotel. "A" Company RRC under Maj. C.A. Young drove the enemy from the hotel but could not advance farther and took up defences around the hotel and Castle Eucliffe. "D" Company pushed on to Violet Hill , were repulsed and withdrew to Stanley View.

With progress stopped on his left Brigadier Wallis ordered a right hook on Ty Tam Tuk Reservoir for early 21 December. The RRC, against strong resistance, drove the enemy from south of the Reservoir and with a few of the HKVDC captured a key crossroads. Now widely dispersed, weakened by casualties and out of mortar ammunition they could advance no further. Accordingly Brigadier Wallis ordered the Royals back to their main position

Later that day Fortress Headquarters ordered another try to reach Wong Nei Chong via Repulse Bay. The attempt, under British command, included "A" Company RRC and proceeded via The Ridge which the company had taken previously. The attack failed and after another unsuccessful engagement resulting in heavy casualties the company withdrew to Repulse Bay. The next day Maj. Young was ordered back to The Ridge. "A" Company returned and with some British troops held throughout the day, withdrawing after dark With the Japanese barring the way to Stanley, "A" Company split up and part succeeded in returning to Stone Hill. The remainder, after an adventuresome trek via Round Island and the beached HMS Thracian, only returned some hours after the Island's surrender.

Back in the main position covering Stanley things were rapidly deteriorating with the sleep deprived and exhausted Royal Rifles at the end of their endurance. On the 22nd "C" Company retook Sugar Loaf Hill but "B" Company lost Stanley Mound and failed to retake it the next day. With the RRC down to nearly one third strength the Brigade withdrew to the narrow neck at Stanley with "B" Company RRC detached to Chung Hum Kok. Since his battalion had gone five days without any rest, Lt Col Home insisted they be relieved and after some unpleasantries with Brigadier Wallis they were, although this did nothing for the detached "A" and "B" Companies. At 0230 on the 25th "C" Company was roused to defend Stanley Village. That morning "D" Company, unsupported, counter-attacked Stanley Village and failed with the loss of 100 men. A reconstituted "A" Company lost a further 18 to shellfire. The Governor surrendered shortly thereafter.

Throughout, the Royals had mounted a series of determined attacks and stout defences at Repulse Bay, Ty Tam Tuk Reservoir, The Ridge, Sugar Loaf Hill and Stanley Village. After five days of continuous fighting, heavy casualties, sleep deprivation and constant gruelling moves to and fro over appalling terrain they were utterly exhausted physically and mentally. This fact appears to have been lost on Brigadier Wallis who expected this single over-committed, green, exhausted and ill-equipped battalion to perform miracles and do what his full brigade had been unable to accomplish on the mainland. Much misunderstanding and acrimonious comment, on both sides, regrettably ensued. (15)

The West Brigade

The West Brigade was initially deployed with 2/14 Punjab in Victoria City fronting the harbour, a company each of RS and MX at Leighton Hill, 2RS less a company in force reserve and the WG covering the south-west coast with its "D" company as Brigade reserve at Wong Nei Chong. Headquarters Company WG, positioned at Wan Chai Gap, was organized into platoon flying columns for immediate counter-attack. These preparations pointed to a higher degree of planning by the defenders than had heretofore been in evidence.

When the Japanese landed on the evening of 18 December the WG flying columns were immediately ordered forward to back up positions covering the landing areas. Lt G.A. Birkett's platoon occupied Jardine's Lookout but was attacked by strong elements of the Japanese 230th Regiment and was forced off. Birkett was killed while heroically covering with a Bren gun the withdrawal of his men. A second platoon under Lt C.D. French attacked Mount Butler but was forestalled and repulsed by enemy of the 229th Regiment. Lt French died of wounds received in the action. A third WG flying column platoon secured the road junction above Wong Nei Chong.

After midnight on 18 December "A" Company WG under Maj A.B. Gresham was ordered to clear Jardine's Lookout and advance on Mount Butler. Part of the company, against all odds, actually captured the summit of Mount Butler and held it for several hours before being driven off. The remnants of the company attempted to retire to Wong Nei Chong but were cut off, surrounded and overrun. All of the officers and most of the warrant officers and NCOs were killed or wounded. One of these, Company Sergeant Major J. Osborne, won a posthumous Victoria Cross for his heroism in this action.

By 1000 hrs on 19 December the Japanese closed up to Brigade Headquarters at Wong Nei Chong, completely destroying three Royal Navy platoons in the process. With his headquarters surrounded, Canadian Brigadier Lawson reported to General Maltby that he was "going outside to fight it out" and was killed along with several of his staff in so doing. Even the hard bitten Japanese were impressed. Colonel Shoji, Commander 230th Regiment, ordered Lawson's burial, in the blanket of the company commander who captured the position, "on the battleground on which he had died so heroically".(16)

Also heroic was the defence of nearby shelters by "D" company WG. After two of its platoons had been overrun the rest of the company, augmented by another platoon and a few individuals, held this vital position blocking the island's only major north-south road for four days of extremely severe fighting. The Japanese reported meeting heavy opposition and suffering many setbacks and casualties in this major action. The Grenadiers, ably assisted by machine gunners of the HKVDC in two nearby pillboxes, inflicted some 800 casualties on the 230th Regiment and severely disrupted the Japanese timetable. The small force of defenders was successively commanded by Capt A.S. Bowman (killed),Capt R.W. Phillip and Lt. T.A. Blackwood (both wounded). The shelters were only overcome when the Japanese brought up a light gun and blew in the doors and shutters.(17)

After failed counter-attacks by the RS, "B" Company WG attacked Mount Nicholson but was repulsed with heavy casualties including all officers and seven WOs and NCOs. At about this time Colonel P. Hennessy the senior Canadian administrative officer was also killed.

On 21 December a scratch company of WGs and Royal Engineers took Mount Cameron and held out under heavy enemy pressure. On the 22nd the force retired under cloudy circumstances - the Grenadiers believing they were so ordered by Brigade Headquarters, the latter denying this. Given the prevailing confusion - a natural product of the fog of war - such misunderstandings, however regrettable, are understandable.

On 24 December the WG with naval elements held a general line Bennet's Hill-Mount Cameron. One company MX was at Little Hong Kong with another still miraculously holding Leighton Hill. The RS were on the slopes of Mount Cameron with the remnants of the two Indian battalions to their north. That day the Japanese finally captured Leighton Hill and drove the Scots off Mount Cameron. The Grenadiers beat off a night attack on their part of Mount Cameron and aided by the naval detachment succeeded in repulsing an attack on Bennet's Hill after one WG platoon had been pushed back.

Finale

On Christmas Day the Japanese captured Mount Parrish and Wan Chai Gap and threatened Fortress Headquarters. At 1515 hrs, on the advice of General Maltby, the Governor, Sir Mark Young, surrendered. Nearly 300 Canadians had been killed in action and 500 wounded, a further 250 were to die in captivity. In the words of the brilliant soldier/author Sir David Fraser, "The colony, but little honour, was lost."(18)

Despite some recriminations which have been pointed at the Canadians from time to time it should be noted that only in areas defended by the Canadians did the Japanese attest to meeting the severest difficulties and suffering their heaviest casualties - a fitting tribute indeed. And this to a force which was only partly trained, was new to the island, lacked vehicles and supporting arms and had been divided into separate brigades.

An Assessment

With hindsight it is obvious that without adequate air cover, strong artillery and mortar support and ironclad assurances that the Chinese would vigorously take from the rear any Japanese invaders of Hong Kong, there was no justification whatsoever to reinforce the colony. Churchill's initial analysis was bang on.(19)

However once the British had taken the decision to reinforce and had requested Canadian assistance the latter was quite right to accept. We had certainly been standing on the sidelines quite long enough and both Japan and Hong Kong shared the Pacific rim with Canada. Also, at the time of acceptance, available intelligence appreciated no Japanese attack in the near term. If this assessment had come about the Canadians would have had time to become familiar with the terrain, battle plans and friendly forces. They would also have received their full complement of vehicles, support weapons and ammunition and possibly even been reinforced to brigade group level.

This latter prospect would have given Brigadier Lawson more influence in defence plans and, most importantly, allowed the Canadians to fight as a homogeneous, well armed and supported brigade group. The results could only have been better - although, since Hong Kong once invested could not be relieved, the end result would have inevitably been much the same. But a better show in Hong Kong may have resulted in a stiffening of spines elsewhere. And while the foregoing is purely speculative the facts and events as they actually unfolded permit the formulation of a number of cogent observations.

No End of a Lesson

The Canadian's arrival encouraged the British commander to adopt a 1937 plan calling for the use of three battalions for the defence of the mainland rather than the one battalion screening force heretofore envisaged. Although this enabled the development and manning of the potentially strong Gin Drinker's Line in force no concomitant change was made to the defence concept. The commanders at both Headquarters Far East in Singapore and the Hong Kong Garrison feared that any attempt to fight a determined battle on the mainland could lead to such heavy losses as to militate against the defence of the Island and therefore the Colony. Thus the strong *ad hoc* Mainland Brigade was just expected to delay the enemy advance for a slightly longer time than could the one battalion screen.

Such a policy, falling between the twin stools of forward and back, was fraught with peril to the morale and future effectiveness of the troops. It is one thing for a one battalion screen to withdraw under a predetermined plan at a measured pace while exercising long-range delaying tactics. It is quite another for a brigade occupying a strong position to be forced out and hustled to the rear with no real attempt to stem the tide. This leads to a natural tendency for the troops in future to be looking over their shoulders for a way out instead of doing their utmost to stand firm and stop the enemy on the spot. Apart from the loss of morale by the defenders it results in a tremendous boost in morale and confidence to the attackers. And the initiative once surrendered is extremely difficult to wrest back. And in Hong Kong and indeed throughout most of the Far East this never, in the near term, happened.

By failing to properly defend the mainland the defenders threw away the chance of stemming the enemy advance on ground of their own choosing with pre-arranged fields of fire, pre-recorded defensive fire tasks and well rehearsed counter-attack plans. Both the Gin Drinker's Line and the Devil's Peak peninsula provided excellent defensive positions. The latter in particular proffered two superb defensive lines anchored on deep water and well supported by fire from the Island. They could have given the enemy no end of a problem. Indeed Devil's Peak did, in fact, lead to the Japanese suffering a bloody nose when they attacked the Rajputs in that position before the final pull out.

Once the mainland was abandoned the Japanese could, and did, close up to the harbour at will and systematically destroy beach defences - pillboxes, searchlights and fixed batteries on the Island. They were also handed a protected and easy approach to the narrow Lye Mun Passage where they, in fact, made their first crossings. It should be noted that at this time the Japanese military was not clothed in the all-conquering mantle it thereafter assumed. Indeed the British had regarded the Japanese serviceman with considerable disdain as a non-thinking automat, lacking initiative who was inherently inferior to the white colonial master. All this took a 180 degree turn with the collapse of the mainland.

Had the defences of Hong Kong and Malaya been conducted with vigour, initiative and courageous determination from the outset the Japanese soldier could have been denied the near superman image he thereby acquired. Subsequent determined actions by the Australians at Milne Bay and Kokoda Trail and by the US Marines at Guadalcanal (the latter against the very division that so easily conquered Hong Kong) stripped away the myth of Japanese invincibility and showed that with proper leadership and determination he could be beaten. Of course no amount of leadership and determination would have saved Hong Kong in the end. But a better showing there might well have translated into better showings in Malaya and Burma, a dislocation of Japanese plans and provided a real fillip to Allied morale - just the opposite to what actually happened.

The Gin Drinker's Line, and with it the mainland, was lost when the Japanese overran a single platoon holding Shing Mun Redoubt. Despite the fact that there were a total of three reserve companies available neither the Commanding Officer Royal Scots nor the Brigade Commander made any attempt to counter-attack and restore, or at least seal off, the position.(20) Instead indecision, funk and passivity reigned supreme and when, after a day's respite, the Japanese attacked and routed the remainder of the Scots the fate of the mainland and the Colony was sealed.

The near paranoid fear of getting over-involved on the mainland availed the garrison naught for the seeds of defeatism rapidly flowered. The Royal Scots never fully recovered from the debacle of Shing Mun and the Indian battalions, who had stopped the Japanese cold on the mainland, were effectively destroyed on the Island's beaches during the first night's landings.(21)

The Shing Mun disaster calls into question the British and Canadian tactic of holding defensive positions with widely separated platoon localities with minimum mutual support and with no promise of the immediate counter-attack model which was so successfully employed by the Germans throughout the war. This tactic of wide platoon dispersion and weak mutual covering fire was to prove for the British a frequent recipe for disaster throughout World War Two. And the Canadians were certainly not immune as Putot-en-Bessin in Normandy, and even Hill 187 a decade later in Korea, were to show. Admittedly there were other mitigating circumstances but the point is that the defensive tactics were essentially flawed.

The Hong Kong battles on both mainland and Island were conducted by the defenders on a piecemeal company and platoon basis throughout. There was seldom any co-ordinated action involving several companies in concert and only rarely after the initial landings was a battalion to be employed as such. Instead of concentrating on the big picture senior commanders - of brigade and even garrison - too often tried to order the deployment of individual companies. While the hands-on direction of a battle by divisional and corps commanders is an admirable, even essential, facet of command (the failure of which will be the subject of criticism in future instalments) there is a fine difference between the forward control of resources and opportunities and interference in subordinate command. That is not to say there is no place for a senior commander on the spot to seize the moment and intervene, or for the mounting of sudden, small, violent counter-attacks by whatever forces can be scratched together. There certainly is, as the Germans proved again and again. Unfortunately, the defenders of Hong Kong lacked the resources, training and skilled leaders at all levels to effectively employ these concepts.

The constant fear of being cut-off and surrounded, which happened often enough, frequently led to the over hasty abandonment of good positions in the seldom realized hope of finding something better in rear. When the troops did stay and fight, as did the Rajputs at Devil's Peak, the Middlesex at Leighton Hill, the HKVDC at Jardine's Lookout and the Winnipegs at Wong Nei Chong, serious reverses were inflicted on the enemy. It took the British commanders several years to learn this hard lesson. In Hong Kong, Malaya and Singapore they never did. And in Burma a succession of fumbling Arakan offences inevitably ended in hasty retreats until, at the Admin Box, they finally found that by standing firm they could, and did, beat the Japanese.

General Maltby's fixation with a never realized Japanese seaborne invasion led him to tie up the two Canadian battalions (one third of his infantry) on sterile beach defence duties far from the main threat. This violation of the principles of concentration of force and economy of effort ensured that the units defending the critical north shore were too thinly spread to prevent successful Japanese water crossings followed by rapid penetrations and advances inland. Had the two Canadian battalions instead been sited as immediate counter-attack forces behind the north beaches and reconnoitred their roles in the brief time available, the initial Japanese landings could have been seriously discomfited.

In fairness to Maltby a near total lack of aircraft precluded his gaining early warning of a seaborne approach. And had he totally ignored the threat and had the Japanese sea landed he would rightly have been excoriated.. But he could, and should, have adopted a middle course and employed his limited naval resources for screening purposes, instead of frittering them away on fruitless channel actions, and employed sea watchers on nearby islands. The actual defence of the southern beaches should have been left to the stout HKVDC and Middlesex gunners. In the event the Japanese never seriously contemplated a seaborne landing and when they did fake a seaborne approach as a diversion no one noticed it.

From the outset, indeed from long before, Allied Pacific command, control, communications and intelligence were deplorably bad. Commanders at all levels first contemptuously dismissed their opponents until, surprised and outmanoeuvred at every turn, they virtually capitulated to them. Grit and determination to hold at all costs were replaced by blue funk and *sauve qui peut*. Intelligent pre-planning and battle improvisation were largely non-existent. Once initiative was surrendered to the enemy no concerted effort was made to wrest it back. Higher command was a near total failure. Its sole tools were over optimistic plans with hasty and ill-considered orders, followed, when these failed, by the exhortation of exhausted and bewildered troops to do the impossible.

HONG KONG and DIEPPE

Conclusion

Despite these failings the defence of the Colony was bitter and courageous. Only against the Canadians did the Japanese report severe resistance and heavy casualties. But all of the national forces performed magnificently in turn - the Royal Scots redeeming themselves on the Island. The heroic valour of Canadian Brigadier Lawson at journey's end was nearly unique among commanders anywhere and should be the source of pride and legend amongst all Canadians. Anywhere else it would be, but "Only in Canada ,pity!"

Fighting against a strong, well supported enemy, and in the knowledge that there was no ultimate hope, the defenders of Hong Kong did their duty to the end. They inflicted some 3000 casualties on the enemy and suffered over 3000 themselves, including some 700 killed of which the Canadian share was about one-third. They were to suffer many more in the nearly four years of horrible captivity which followed. It is the prisoners' terrible and residual suffering and the fifty years of government and Japanese indifference to their plight that lives in the minds of most Canadians - if they think of Hong Kong at all.

This should now change. It is time to exorcise the ghosts of the prison camps and to remember and revere our Hong Kong veterans for their valour in action and the truly magnificent fight they fought against hopeless odds. In a campaign doomed from the outset they brought everlasting glory to themselves and honour to their country. They should have our everlasting thanks and remembrance. They deserve no less.

A Calgary Tank being abandoned on the Dieppe beach.
An original painting by Robert Sharp.

GAUDEAMUS IGITUR

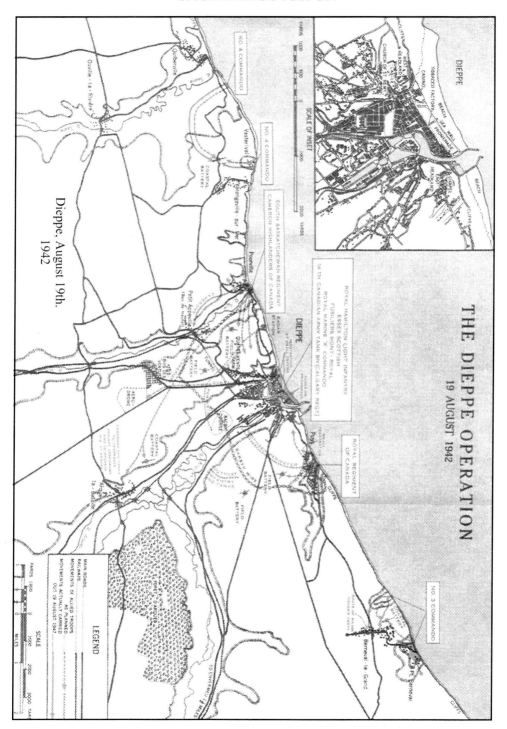

HONG KONG and DIEPPE

CHAPTER III

DIEPPE 19 AUGUST 1942

Once more unto the breach, dear friends,...
Or close the wall up with our...dead.

Shakespeare, *King Henry V.*

Prologue

The story of Dieppe has been told, rehashed and analysed so extensively that little new can, or need, be added. Hardly a year passes without some "new" denouement alleging failures in concept, intelligence, planning, direction or conduct. And letters to the editor commenting on these have become a near cottage industry especially in such venerable publications as The Times and the Journal of the Royal United Services Institute.

Dieppe, like Hong Kong of eight months before, was certainly a failure and a very bloody failure indeed. Yet, insofar as individuals and units were concerned, it was in many instances a magnificent failure. The gallantry of often unsupported infantry charging the beaches under murderous fire ranks alongside other heroic and foredoomed charges such as Balaclava, Gallipoli and the First Day on the Somme. Its memory deserves the same veneration.

Casualties were appalling - over 3300 from a total Canadian force of under 5000. Nearly one-fifth of the Canadians who embarked for Dieppe, 907 in all, were killed or died of wounds - an extremely high proportion indeed and rendered even higher since many hundreds were not able to land at all.(1) Another 1154 were wounded. Also high was the number of prisoners of war - 1946 of whom 568 were wounded. This number, similar to what the Canadians were to suffer in either of the entire Italian or Northwest Europe campaigns, was largely due to the inability to re-embark the troops under near impossible conditions

Dieppe - The Genesis

Having been hustled from the Continent in May/June 1940, the British were, quite naturally, initially concerned with the possibility of a German invasion of Great Britain. This became the principal focus of British battle plans in which the Canadians were allotted a key role. It was not until the Germans invaded Russia in June 1941 that the prospect of their invading Britain virtually disappeared.

Throughout this period inchoate ideas percolated for a British return to the Continent. The first of these came soon after Dunkirk with an abortive attempt to re-enter the lists via Normandy and Brittany, in which the 1st Canadian Division participated.(2) The impending French surrender put paid to this endeavour and the troops were withdrawn.

The British next embarked on a series of small commando(3) raids on the occupied coasts. These had the multi-faceted aims of imbuing the forces with offensive spirit, harassing the enemy, gaining insight into invasion techniques and, on occasion, seeking intelligence (as at Bruneval) or denying some facility (as at St. Nazaire). With its army rebuilding at home and heavily committed in Africa, the Balkans, Syria and, after December 1941, in the Far East the British were in no position to contemplate any grand adventures on the Continent.

All of this changed with the entry of the United States into the war following Pearl Harbour in December 1941. Despite the fact that by July 1942 the US was only able to muster three divisions in the UK, they lobbied hard from the outset for an early return to the Continent. At this time the German invasion of Russia, after a winter check, had resumed apace and there was a very real possibility that Russia would be defeated and forced from the war. Stalin, not unnaturally, clamoured for a second front and found considerable sympathy in the west.

The Americans, led by Presidential Advisor Hopkins, Generals Marshall and Eisenhower and, somewhat equivocally, Admiral King pressed for a Second Front in 1942. Only the dogged opposition of Churchill and the British Chiefs of Staff [COS] later decisively joined by President Roosevelt, put paid to what could only have been a half-baked disaster. Instead Churchill's plan for an assault on the "soft underbelly" of the Axis, in the Mediterranean, was adopted. This culminated in Operation Torch, the North African landings, which commenced in November, 1942.

Meanwhile a series of plans were formulated, or more frequently conceptualized, for a return to the Continent on a limited basis. The principal driving force behind these plans was aid to the hard pressed USSR although there was considerable dichotomy over what would trigger them. Most commonly the trigger would be forlorn-hope relief to a Russia on the verge of collapse. Alternatively it would be a hasty "get on board" in the event of a sudden Soviet victory.

The principal of these plans was *Sledgehammer* which passed through many guises from a Second Front proper, through a bridgehead around Le Havre in the event of a German collapse, to a relief operation if Russia collapsed. Others included *Wetbob* to gain a foothold around Cherbourg, *Roundup* a full scale invasion of the Pas de Calais - Seine area, and *Imperator* an armoured raid on Paris. The raid on Dieppe did not form part of these plans but grew parallel to them from a requirement by the Combined COS to keep pressure on Germany via a series of raids.

The Concept

The initial plan for the Dieppe operation, first code-named *Rutter* later changed to *Jubilee,* was framed by Headquarters Combined Operations [HQCO] under Lord Louis Mountbatten in April 1942. The plan was heavily influenced by the need to try out a large scale combined operations landing, of a sort not attempted since Gallipoli 27 years before, in rehearsal for the launch of a future Second Front. Apart from the experience to be gained from performing an actual assault landing *Rutter/Jubilee* would try out new techniques, equipment and concepts. One such requirement was the immediate capture of a port which, at that time, was deemed essential for the successful lodgement of a full scale invasion force.

The selection of Dieppe, as a less obvious target than the Pas de Calais, was influenced by a number of factors apart from possessing the requisite port facilities. Chief of these was the need to operate within the limited range of the fighter aircraft of that day.

Furthermore, in order to avoid discovery while still at sea, the objective had to be within one night's sailing of the departure harbours. The selection of a beach suitable for landing and the deployment of tanks and with egress to the interior was a major requirement. Dieppe met these criteria although the primary beach offered only one mile between flanking headlands while cliffs and the town itself were problems to egress.

. Two alternative plans were considered. The first of these envisaged a direct assault on Dieppe proper with supporting flank attacks at Puys and Pourville. The second, which aimed at the indirect approach, planned landings on the flanks leading to an envelopment of the town(4). Since the use of tanks was integral to the plan the frontal option was selected as the planners believed that the two rivers on the west flank were formidable tank obstacles. They also believed that landing the tanks directly in front of the main objective offered better prospects of surprise. Both of these assumptions proved to be off target. The feared rivers, the Saane (which being four miles west of Pourville was not even a factor) and the Scie were hardly formidable obstacles - only some 30 feet wide and three feet deep. Tanks could readily have negotiated them, if necessary by using fascines. They were no obstacle at all to infantry. All this information could have readily been obtained from the French underground or by clandestine reconnaissance. Not to do so was a major intelligence failure - one of many as things transpired.

Planning by HQCO was well advanced before any Canadians were brought on board. At the end of April, 1942 General B.L. Montgomery, GOC Southern Command, under whom the Canadians then served, briefed General A.G.L. McNaughton on the plan and proposed that Canadians provide the main force.(5) Canada, whose troops had been on the sidelines for nearly three years and whose principal actions, apart from Hong Kong, comprised a series of aborted operations, readily agreed.(6) 2nd Canadian Division (2CID) under Major-General J.H. Roberts, whom Monty considered to be the best Canadian formation, was selected for the task.

The outline plan which had been prepared by HQCO was reviewed and generally approved by HQ 2CID. The Canadians considered HQCO (whose feet of clay had not yet become apparent) to be the experts in such matters. Also they did not wish to jeopardize their eagerly awaited initial action by appearing too negative or overly cautious on too many details. The 2CID staff appreciation seemed overly concerned with the employment of tanks and insufficiently concerned with the provision of adequate fire support, the beaches and their outlets, and with optimum tactics to be employed at each landing site. Had it done so it might have converted the headlong dash at Puys into a more imaginative and stealthy operation and allotted tanks to Pourville and even to Puys. It should also have come up with better intelligence on the terrain and enemy strong points and with an infinitely better fire support plan.

But even on the employment of tanks the staff work was badly flawed. Apart from grossly exaggerating the river obstacles, the staff badly underestimated the difficulties in breaching the obstacles which blocked entry into Dieppe. And if they considered the Scie and the harbour to be obstacles to entry into Dieppe they overlooked them, and the built up town, as obstacles to exit the town to link up with the flank battalions As refined by HQ 2CID Operation *Rutter*, as it was then still coded, called for frontal assaults on Dieppe, Puys and Pourville by the combat elements of 4 and 6 Canadian Infantry Brigades (CIBs) supported by tanks, engineers and other elements. British commandos were tasked with silencing flanking coastal batteries and providing part of the floating reserve.

2CID meanwhile commenced specialized combined operations training. After intense training on the Isle of Wight the division underwent two dress rehearsal landings in Dorset. The first was something of a shambles and showed the problems faced by the Navy in trying to land large numbers of different craft at the proper place and time. After a number of navigational and control improvements the second went somewhat better.

The operation was scheduled for early July and the troops were duly embarked on the 2nd and 3rd of that month. A series of weather delays ensued during which time elements of the assembled force were bombed by German aircraft without serious damage or casualties. The operation was finally cancelled due to poor weather and the deeply disappointed troops debarked and returned to barracks. It all seemed just a dreary replay of many past disappointments. The equally disappointed HQCO set about reviving the plan. In this they were encouraged by Churchill who was being constantly chivvied by the Russians for some direct supporting action. In the end the operation, now renamed *Jubilee*, was revived, almost entirely by HQCO on its own initiative, for August or September 1942. After further preparations, training and revision of plans the force re-embarked on the 16th and 17th and set sail on the evening of 18 August. They were due at Dieppe at dawn the next day.

A critical change from the original *Rutter* concept eliminated the opening heavy air bombing, something that later operations were to show to be of mixed value. But nothing meaningful was substituted in its place. The change of date compacted perforce the operation into a one, as opposed to two, high-tide time frame. This resulted in a shortening by five hours of the original time frame for the completion of the operation. This was to have serious implications on the planned deep penetration and withdrawal but again the objectives were not altered. This time contraction also resulted in allotting only one-half, instead of one, hour between flank and main landings. But the plan's most critical failure remained its totally inadequate provision for fire support both from the sea and on land. Close air support was now largely limited to initial fighter strafing and smoke laying. The provisions for calling, providing and controlling close air support on a meaningful short time frame remained abysmal.

The Plan

The revised plan still envisaged the capture of Dieppe by a tank supported frontal assault covered by flank attacks on the headlands and Pourville leading to operations against a German airfield/airstrip at St Aubin and a mistakenly suspected German divisional headquarters at Arques-la-Bataille (which in fact was located at Envermeu six miles east). This intelligence error should not be too severely criticized, the German Headquarters (O.K.H.) in Berlin made the same mistake. Extensive demolitions were to be employed against the harbour and other installations. The detailed plan (See Map) called for landings on eight beaches: Yellow 1 and 11 (Berneval), Blue (Puys), Red (Dieppe East), White (Dieppe West), Green (Pourville), and Orange1 and 11 (Varengeville).

The flank attacks, slotted for 0450 British Summer Time, comprised stealth operations by No 3 Commando on the eastern German battery at Berneval (Yellow), by No 4 Commando on the western battery at Varengeville (Orange) and a frontal attack by the

HONG KONG and DIEPPE

Royal Regiment of Canada (RRC) (Lt Col D.E. Catto) on the dominating Puys headland (Blue). The South Saskatchewan Regiment (SSR) (Lt Col C.I. Merritt) would land simultaneously at Pourville (Green) to the west to link up with the main Dieppe force and establish a bridgehead through which the Cameron Highlanders of Canada (CHC) (Lt Col A.C. Gostling) would pass to link up with tanks landed at Dieppe and capture the airstrip and believed German Divisional HQ.

The main assault on Dieppe proper had the Essex Scottish (ES) (Lt Col F.K. Jasperson) on the left (Red) and the Royal Hamilton Light Infantry (RHLI) (Lt Col R.R. Labatt) on the right (White). The 14th Army Tank Regiment, The Calgary Tanks, (CT) (Lt Col J. G. Andrews), equipped with the new Churchill infantry tank, would land in support of the main beach assault with two troops landing with the first wave. A floating reserve comprised Les Fusiliers Mont-Royal (FMR) (Lt Col D. Menard) and the Royal Marine "A" Commando (RMA) (Lt Col J.P. Phillipps). The FMR were to land once the town was secured and form a perimeter defence to cover the force's withdrawal. RMA were to remove or destroy enemy barges in the harbour or be otherwise employed as directed by the force commander.

The assault would be covered by eight Hunt class destroyers and several gunboats and sloops. The entire naval force comprised thirteen groups totalling some 250 vessels sailing from five different ports - a most complex operation. The Naval Commander Captain J. Hughes-Hallett and the Force Commander Maj Gen Roberts sailed in the destroyer HMS Calpe, designated and equipped as the Headquarters Ship. Brigadier C. Mann the military deputy sailed on HMS Fernie, the alternative headquarters.

Air support would be provided by some 75 squadrons of the RAF, RCAF, USAAF and several allied nations. These comprised 56 fighter and fighter/bomber squadrons, four tactical reconnaissance squadrons, two intruder, three smoke laying and six light bomber squadrons and USAAF Fortress squadrons to attack Abbeville airfield. The Air Commander, AVM T.L Leigh-Mallory, controlled air operations from RAF Uxbridge near London and was represented in the headquarters ship by an Air Commodore. Admiral Mountbatten and Lt Gen H.D.G. Crerar, the Canadian Corps Commander, were also at Uxbridge.

The Enemy Forces

The entrance of the United States into the war along with Russia's continual insistence on a Second Front led the Germans in 1942 to focus on, and greatly strengthen, their Channel and Atlantic defences. Command was unified under the formidable Field Marshall von Rundstedt and extra armour and infantry formations were moved to the west. Work was intensified to create "an impregnable fortress along the Atlantic and Channel coast."(7)

The Dieppe sector was allotted to the 302nd Infantry Division with its Headquarters at Envermeu some ten miles inland. The controlling 81 Corps Headquarters was at Rouen with German Headquarters West at St. Germain-en-Laye near Paris. The powerful 10th Panzer Corps was at Amiens while four infantry battalions were positioned in Army Reserve at Barentin, north-west of Rouen. The German Army was well supported by its air force from a variety of nearby airfields in France.

The actual defence of Dieppe was entrusted to the 571st Infantry Regiment with a battalion on each of the East and West Headlands and one in reserve. They were supported by divisional and coastal artillery, engineers and the formidable German mortars. The sector was backed up by artillery batteries and protected by strong points and barbed wire. Pill boxes concealed under the headlands at Puys, the main beach and Pourville and on the harbour mole covered the beaches with machine guns firing in enfilade. The artillery comprised fourteen 155mm guns and howitzers, three 177mm guns, twenty 105mm and eight 75mm guns and anti-aircraft batteries. The town was covered by nine anti-tank guns, mostly of insufficient hitting power to penetrate the tough Churchills, and was protected by concrete anti-tank obstacles which would require special effort to overcome.

The Approach

The revised plan called for the flanking forces to land at 0450 BST with the main assault set for 0510 BST. The time difference was largely due to a lack of sea room for the large force, consisting of vessels of different speeds and handling characteristics, to go in at once. The hour of "go - no go" was 0300 hrs this being the time that infantry landing craft would be lowered and head for the beaches.

At 0347 hrs occurred the first of many reverses for the assault force. The eastern Assault Group 5, carrying No. 3 Commando in 23 landing craft heading for Berneval covered by three gunboats/launches and the destroyers Slazak and Brocklesby, collided with a German coastal convoy and firing broke out. Vessels on both sides were sunk or damaged and the craft carrying No. 3 Commando were totally scattered with only seven continuing on to their objective. Subsequently much was made of the loss of surprise engendered by the encounter. However post-war evidence indicates that it had a negligible effect in warning the German defenders. Its effect on the eastern covering attacks at Yellow I and II and Blue beaches is more difficult to assess.

The Commando Operations

Three commandos, two army and one Royal Marine, were employed at Dieppe. No. 3 Commando at the Yellow beaches was to neutralize the eastern Berneval battery, No. 4 at Orange was tasked with the western Varengeville battery while the Marines were part of the floating reserve. Things started badly for No. 3 when, as noted above, it collided with a German convoy and was dispersed - only seven of its 23 landing craft actually landing its troops. Six craft, carrying 120 commandos, landed at Yellow I at 0510 hrs (20 minutes late) and encountered enemy opposition which was soon reinforced. The commandos were unable to advance and were overwhelmed with over 80 taken prisoner. Only a single craft managed to land some 20 commandos at Yellow II. Landing unobserved and not fired upon the party climbed a narrow gully to within 200 yards of the Berneval battery. They took cover and sniped at the battery for about an hour and a half thus preventing the battery from firing. The commandos then withdrew without loss and re-embarked.

The No. 4 Commando operation at Varengeville was perfectly executed and totally successful. One-third of the party landed at Orange I at Vasterival north of the enemy battery. Moving comparatively unmolested into position they fired at the battery with small arms and two inch mortars. Through incredible good luck a mortar bomb hit stacked gun charges and blew them up(8). At 0620 hrs RAF Hurricanes made an effective low level attack. At this point the main commando body, which had landed at Orange II to the east near Quiberville and had managed to outflank the battery unobserved, assaulted from the rear. After a short battle the enemy was destroyed with some 60 killed or wounded for a loss of 45 commandos. The six coastal guns were destroyed and the commando withdrew at 0730 hrs.

These superb operations, which prevented the two batteries from firing on the invaders, illustrate the vital importance of landing unobserved and moving into attack positions unmolested. Where this happened at Varengeville, and to a lesser extent at Yellow II, success was attained and friendly casualties minimized. Where it did not happen, as at Yellow I, Blue and the main beaches, disaster followed. It seems a simple and self-evident lesson but was one which the Canadians - and the British - seldom applied throughout the war. When it was, as at Assoro in Sicily or the Melfa in Italy (by Lt. Perkins' troop) crowning success followed.

Puys - the Eastern Flank

One critical place where the lesson was not applied, with predictable disastrous results, was at Puys on Blue Beach, the objective of the Royal Regiment of Canada. And in a classic case of "for want of a nail..." the failure contributed in large measure to the failure of the entire Operation Jubilee. The small village of Puys lay about one mile east of Dieppe harbour in a narrow gully dominated by cliffs on each side. The beach was backed by a formidable ten to twelve foot high sea-wall surmounted by barbed wire. Although Puys was defended by only a mixed army/luftwaffe company it occupied extremely well sited and hidden pill boxes and bunkers which completely commanded the beach with flanking fire. The east cliff defences in particular were totally dominant. All were backed by artillery and the deadly German mortars.

The HQCO plan for Blue Beach called, somewhat optimistically, for the RRof C to secure the Puys headland, destroy local posts, flak installations and a gun battery southeast of the town and then move west to protect the demolition by engineers of the Dieppe gas and power plants. Success thereby hinged on three actions - surmounting the sea-wall, penetrating the gully and moving inland all before the German gunners could commence their murderous enfilade fire. These actions in turn were predicated upon surprise in landing and moving off the beach in sufficient darkness and dash to deny accurate enemy observation and observed fire. Since all of these factors were highly problematical, prudence would indicate that special steps be taken to surmount the cliffs and gully by stealthy commando style tactics. At a minimum, the killing ground nature of the beach called for the troops to be protected by at least some tanks and be liberally equipped with mortars to smoke off the headlands(9) and PIATs for the anti-bunker and mini-artillery role.(10) None of these requirements were met, if indeed they were ever even considered. Instead, as if the first day on the Somme had never happened, the planners, both HQCO and HQ 2CID, relied on a headlong Balaclava - style rush with the same paucity of fire support as was accorded the poor Light Brigade.

The Royals' plan called for the battalion to land in three waves - three companies and tactical battalion headquarters (Bn HQ) at 0450, the fourth company at 0500 and three attached platoons of the Black Watch of Canada to land where and when called for by Bn HQ. An artillery forward observation officer (FOO) would accompany the second wave.

GAUDEAMUS IGITUR

The first wave landed some twenty minutes late due to a series of misadventures which is not surprising given the extreme complexity of an assault sea landing on a narrow beach in darkness. The effect of darkness and an air laid smoke screen were thus lost - not the first nor last time that rigidly timed programmes went awry without superb communications to correct things. And on Blue Beach, indeed throughout Jubilee, good communications were almost totally absent. In the event the German defenders were fully alert and opened fire when the Royals' landing craft were still some hundred yards off shore. As the first wave touched down and ramps were lowered enemy fire intensified and heavy casualties ensued, many infantrymen being machine gunned as they clambered down the ramps. Despite this the troops with dash and courage charged out of their craft into the water and over the beach all in the face of withering fire. The Royals displayed gallantry in full measure that day.(11)

At the top of the narrow beach the troops collided with the high sea-wall and soon piled up close to the wall or the cliffs while German machine gunners from defiladed positions on the east headland poured down a hail of fire upon their unprotected foes. (12) The beach soon became littered with dead and wounded. The Royals employed bangalore torpedoes and scaling ladders to try and breach the barbed wire and clear the wall but few managed to get through. The second wave, also taking heavy casualties, bravely charged in at about 0530 hrs and met the same fate as the first. Then, in the absence of any signals from ashore, the three Black Watch platoons were sent in and only thickened the targets along the wall.

It seems that only two parties of Royals succeeded in getting past the wall and moving up the gully and inland. In a display of valour and dash fully the equal of any of the deeds of that day the Commanding Officer, Lt Col Catto, led some twenty men in gapping the wire at the western end of the wall and pushing up the cliff inland. Heavy enemy machine gun fire then closed the gap and prevented anyone from following. Catto's party cleared two houses at the top before noting an enemy platoon moving towards them. Catto made the snap decision to move westward to contact the Essex Scottish advancing from Red Beach. But the Essex never got off their own beach and no contact was made. The Royals' party then took up positions in a small wood until 1630 hrs - long after the battle and evacuation had ended and there was no possibility of withdrawal.

In retrospect Catto's decision to move on Red Beach after encountering the German patrol may appear to have been the poorest of the choices open to him. The best course, almost certainly, would have been to engage the enemy patrol from ambush. The prospects of success were good and, if successful, could have had a most negative effect on the other German defenders in that area. The second best choice may have been to move east and attack the enemy pillboxes that were decimating his men from the east headland. This course would probably still require taking out the German patrol first And while it is easy to second guess from the safety of 60 years, Catto had no such opportunity. He made the decision that seemed best at the time. In this context it is one thing to snipe from 200 yards at a clearly visible and meagrely protected battery as at Berneval. It is quite another to try and locate, then neutralize, hidden and well protected pill boxes. And at the time Catto did not know that the Essex had failed. Had they succeeded the Essex could conceivably have turned east and eliminated the enemy at Blue Beach.(13)

A second party of some 25 Royals also succeeded in getting over the wall and through the wire and mines and advancing forward up the cliff. Then, according to German sources, this party was totally destroyed by enemy troops lying in wait. Thus ended the charge of the Royals. *Sic transit gloria.*

Despite several urgent radio calls from the beleaguered troops on the possibility of evacuation it proved virtually impossible for the Navy to remove anyone from Blue Beach.(14) Indeed one enquiring call from the beach was so garbled in reception that it led Maj Gen Roberts to understand that the RRof C had not even landed as a result of which he directed them to Red to aid the Essex. Such unreality would have been farcical had it not been so tragic. In the end, in the face of murderous fire, only one rescuing landing craft succeeded in beaching and, overloaded with troops, it soon capsized. Other craft which tried to approach the beach were driven off. The surviving Royals, strung along the sea-wall amid hundreds of dead and wounded and under continuous fire could no longer advance or be evacuated. They were thus left with only the bitter necessity of surrender at about 0830 hrs.

As a result only 65 of the Royals returned to England - most from a craft that had been unable to land its troops. Of 550 who did land 227 were killed or died of wounds - a staggering 50 % of the total. The fact that most of the rest became prisoners, of whom over 100 were wounded, was due almost entirely because they could not be brought off. The subsequent smug comment from one German source of "Canadians surrendering in swarms..." can only be viewed in this context. Other informed Germans reported quite differently.(15)

Throughout the operation communications with Blue Beach were abysmal and Force Headquarters, as noted above, never knew what was happening there. One of the few working radio links was that of the artillery FOO who passed messages to HMS Garth, the nearest destroyer, from second wave touchdown at 0530 to 0730 hrs. Most of these messages dealt with news of heavy casualties and of being pinned down along the sea-wall. The garbled message at 0630 hrs that led Roberts to believe that the Royals had not yet landed was really an attempt to say that it was impossible to further land troops. The final messages from shore enquiring about the possibility of evacuation were met only with stony silence.

Pourville - The Western Flank

Green Beach at Pourville some two miles west of Dieppe was, compared to Blue, fairly long and open but it too was dominated by cliffs on each side. It was bisected by the River Scie, an only moderate obstacle, which flowed north into the Channel at the town. A radar station, one of the objectives, was near the coast half way to Dieppe. Another objective, Quatre Vents Farm, lay a mile inland near Dieppe's outskirts. The hamlet of Petit Appeville was a mile and a half inland on the left bank of the Scie near to where a railway tunnel emerged from Dieppe. The airfield objective lay three miles inland and a mile east of the river. Arques-la-Bataille, wrongly believed to be German divisional HQ, and over optimistically assigned as a final objective, was a further mile and a half to the south-east. The river which was fordable in many places, although this simple fact seems to have escaped the staff's notice, was bridged at Pourville and Petit Appeville.

The plan called for the South Saskatchewan Regiment (SSR) to land astride the Scie, secure Pourville, clear the east and west headlands and Quatre Vents Farm and capture the radar station. The Cameron Highlanders of Canada (CHC) would pass through and capture the airfield/landing strip in company with tanks landed at Dieppe. If all went well they would proceed on to the believed German HQ at Arques.

The SSR landed on time (0450 hrs) achieved initial surprise and were pushing forward when the enemy opened fire and casualties ensued. Due either to a navigational error or a misunderstanding the battalion was landed entirely west, instead of astride, the River Scie. This meant that the two companies ("A" and "D") tasked with securing the eastern headland, the radar station and Quatre Vents Farm (where a link-up with troops and tanks from Dieppe was expected) were seriously delayed. Heavy fighting was experienced in Pourville and in trying to cross the Scie by the road bridge. Nevertheless led personally by their Commanding Officer (Lt Col C.I. Merritt) they succeeded in clearing a number of pill boxes and positions and crossing the bridge. However, lacking heavy weapons support, they failed to clear the eastern high ground or capture the radar station and Quatre Vents Farm. Their artillery FOO was in contact with a supporting destroyer but was unable to pinpoint either the advanced SSR troops or specific enemy targets. He was thus reduced to firing at targets from the map with unknown and generally ineffective results. The SSR also, for whatever reason, failed to silence one enemy pill box which covered the beach from the east By contrast the western company ("C") was landed in the correct place and promptly secured all of its objectives wiping out many enemy in the process. Another example of what might have been had the landing gone as planned.

The Camerons, partly due to a decision by their Commanding Officer, landed at 0550 hrs - nearly one-half hour late. Despite enemy shelling the landing craft successfully touched down and the men rushed out. At this point the eastern pill box which the SSR had failed to neutralize opened up and inflicted casualties, including the killing of the Cameron's CO, Lt Col Gostling. His second-in-command (2 IC) Major A.T. Law took over.

The CHC had expected to operate east of the Scie and advance south-east to the airfield. But it was landed astride the river with most of three companies landing to the west. With remarkable speed and initiative Maj Law switched to an alternative plan and led this main body in a wide arc west of the river towards Petit Appeville. Under fire from both flanks the Camerons advanced slowly but surely. At Petit Appeville a considerable body of enemy was encountered but there was no sign of any Canadian troops or tanks coming from Dieppe. Since time was short and other information virtually nil, the Camerons wisely abandoned their advance to the airfield and at about 0900 hrs decided to turn and clear Quatre Vents Farm. However increasing enemy forces and the appearance of enemy field guns against which the Camerons, their own three inch mortars now knocked out, had no counter led to this plan being cancelled. At 0930 hrs, on receiving information to return to Pourville, the CHC withdrew under pressure and rejoined the SSR.

At about 1100 hrs, heroically covered by a rearguard under Lt Col Merritt, the SSR and CHC began to re-embark. Due to a misunderstanding "C" Company of the SSR, the company that had done so well on the assault, prematurely withdrew from the western headland allowing the Germans to move up into excellent fire positions. Both battalions lost heavily and the rearguard could not be brought off. Evacuation was completed by 1330 hrs - just in time as the enemy reserves were preparing a major counter-attack.(16)

In common with everywhere else that day the Pourville force operated under a near higher command and communications vacuum. The Camerons were unable to contact brigade or force headquarters at any time during their advance and withdrawal until returning to Pourville at 1000 hrs. And force headquarters had no information on the Camerons except that they had penetrated inland. However even had communications and information been adequate little else could have been done as the main force was stymied at Dieppe and the floating reserve had already been committed elsewhere.

Of equal, or greater, significance was the lack of heavy weapons support to the Pourville force. Without artillery, medium mortars, anti-tank guns and, above all, tanks, the force was at a terrible disadvantage moving through the open against a resilient foe. The addition of a squadron, or even a single troop, of tanks to the Pourville force could have made a quantum difference against the lightly armed enemy forces initially arrayed against it.(17) The failure of the FOO to be able to direct effective naval support fire has already been noted.

Despite their inability to attain their over-ambitiously planned objectives, and in the absence of adequate fire support and support from the main Dieppe landings, the Pourville force did a very credible job, inflicted considerable casualties on the enemy and caused him extreme concern. Their re-embarkation under heavy fire and pressure was well conducted, despite misunderstandings and the inability to remove the entire force, again emphasizing the hazardous nature of that type of operation.

The Pourville force paid for its successes with high casualties - some 340 for the SSR including 84 fatal and 166 wounded. The CHC suffered 344 casualties, 76 killed and 103 wounded. As was the case at the other beaches, most of the prisoners, one-third of whom were wounded, were lost along with numbers of enemy prisoners taken, simply because the Navy, under heavy fire and a shortage of armoured landing craft, could not bring them off.

Dieppe - The Main Beaches

The main attack on the town of Dieppe was conducted by two battalions supported by the 14th Army Tank Regiment (The Calgary Tanks) landing on a frontage of about one mile. The left battalion, The Essex Scottish (ES), was to land on Red Beach, just west of the harbour mole and across from the East Headland. It was expected to capture the Tobacco Factory and advance to the proposed defensive perimeter near the Race Course clearing enemy from the city as it went. The right battalion,. the Royal Hamilton Light Infantry (RHLI), was to land on White Beach, capture the Casino, telephone exchange and City Hall and advance to the proposed perimeter. It was expected to link up with the Pourville force at Quatre Vents Farm.

The assault infantry would be supported by tanks and assault engineers. A floating reserve comprised Les Fusiliers Mont-Royal and Royal Marine "A" Commando. The Fusiliers were to man the eventual defensive perimeter and cover the force's withdrawal. The Marines had a special small boat capture/destruction operation. The troops were to be supported by the fire of four destroyers and one gunboat. Although these seem to provide good support the ships, mounting four inch guns, only had the equivalent firepower of two field batteries while lacking the high angle and fire control capabilities of the latter. The Air Force provided light bomber, smoke and fighter bomber direct support. These gave excellent service on pre-planned missions but lacked the communications and procedures necessary for close on-call targets.

GAUDEAMUS IGITUR

Dieppe was protected by a low sea-wall behind which was a broad promenade. All entrances from beach to town were blocked by concrete anti-tank obstacles and wire. The enemy had pill boxes, machine and anti-tank guns on the mole and both headlands. Snipers, machine gunners and light anti-tank guns operated from the Casino and other buildings along the promenade. Several field and mortar batteries supported the enemy infantry. However the German mobile reserves were many miles back and could not be expected to effectively intervene for several hours.

The assault went in at 0520 hrs - some half hour after the flank attacks and after the enemy had been fully alerted. The Navy supplied supporting fire from one mile out to touch down. The RAF smoke screened the east headland and five minutes before touch down five squadrons of cannon firing Hurricanes made a most effective, albeit temporary, attack on the beach defences. From this point on support would mainly come from the infantry's own weapons and from the tanks, of which nine were supposed to land with the first wave.

Unfortunately, due to a navigational error, the craft carrying the first nine tanks landed some 20 minutes late. During this absolutely critical time the infantry were on their own. Bereft of any fire support they were at the mercy of the enemy gunners who opened up as the landing craft neared and who swept the beach with murderous fire. Despite all this the infantry charged from their landing craft and up the beach with incredible dash and spirit. But, as at Blue Beach, when they hit the sea-wall things ground to a halt. Robert Prouse, C Pro C, who was captured at Dieppe, described the landing, "As the ramp...lowered at about 0540 the men in the front row started to fall....Finally I ran to the front, stepping over all the bodies, and jumped into the sea...threw my body on the coarse gravel and squirmed towards the concrete sea-wall." Prouse describes the heavy casualties and carnage ashore and the unsettling experience of the wounded as the tanks moved back and forth among them stopping every few yards to fire.(18)

The Essex landed on a naked beach under heavy fire from machine guns on the east headland, the mole, a dug-in tank near the mole and from buildings fronting the beach. Several determined rushes were made to cross the sea-wall but were repulsed with heavy casualties. The Essex then took what cover and defensive positions they could find behind the sea-wall and tried to engage an enemy they could not see. Unable to capture the Tobacco Factory they set it on fire with grenades. At least one small platoon of Essex stormed across the sea-wall and promenade, cleared the enemy from several buildings and advanced to the harbour. They were finally forced back about 0800 hrs. Despite these minor successes the majority of the Essex lay pinned along the sea-wall taking casualties. The battalion attained none of its planned objectives. The failure of Lt Col Catto's party from Puys to effect a link-up was one, albeit unplanned, consequence.

The RHLI on the right at White Beach fared somewhat better although it too failed to take its main objectives. White Beach offered the "Rileys" some small advantages principal of which was the protrusion of the Casino onto the sea-wall. Although manned by the enemy the Casino afforded the troops some flank protection and offered a place through which they could infiltrate into the town. White Beach was also farther removed from the harbour mole from whence German machine gunners were able to enfilade the unfortunate Essex.

However these small advantages were counterbalanced when the Riley's right-hand company was largely wiped out on its approach and landing. And, of course, the failure of the tanks to land on time was another blow. Despite these problems the battalion succeeded, after sharp fighting, in clearing the Casino and taking a number of prisoners. And at least three or four parties advanced through the Casino and pushed on into the town. One captured the theatre and moved on engaging several bodies of enemy en route. This party only withdrew back to the Casino at about 1000 hrs, just before the evacuation began. A second party, covered by a single tank from beside the Casino, advanced into the town clearing several houses of the enemy. It too withdrew just before the general withdrawal. The third succeeded in reaching the Hotel de Ville before being eliminated. But in the end the RHLI, like the Essex, failed to attain any of their main objectives except the Casino and their troops suffered a similar fate.

Due to the continuing communications problems and lack, or misunderstanding, of information on the true situation on the beaches General Roberts ordered the reserve, Les Fusiliers Mont-Royal, to land in support on Red Beach. Under complete German observation and a hail of fire Les Fusiliers landed around 0700 hrs and dashed across the pebbly beach. Although intended for Red Beach Les Fusiliers' landing craft were scattered over a wide area, some coming in on Red others on White Beach. Consequently the FMR simply became intermingled with the Essex and RHLI and suffered heavy casualties. Only one party is known to have succeeded in penetrating some distance into town before being eliminated.

Still under the misinformation blanket, Roberts around 0820 hrs ordered his final reserve, the Royal Marine Commando, to land on White Beach in support of the Essex and to swing around and attack the eastern headland from the south. As the Marines approached the beach under a withering fire their Commanding Officer realized the hopelessness of the situation and ordered a withdrawal into a smoke screen. Only three Marine craft briefly touched down before turning back. The CO was killed.

The Calgary Tanks fared only marginally better. Their initial late landing has been noted. In the event of 29 tanks that left the landing craft two, including that of the CO, sank and 27 got up onto the beach. About one and one-half squadrons never landed. Of those tanks that did at least 15 crossed the sea-wall onto the promenade. Here their advance was blocked by formidable anti-tank obstacles. Gallant attempts by the engineers to blow the obstacles failed with heavy casualties. Unable to enter the town the tanks roamed the beach as mobile pill boxes. The heavily armoured Churchills were nearly immune to the light calibre German anti-tank fire and they provided excellent support to the infantry throughout. But they too suffered from the difficulty of finding suitable targets among the well hidden enemy. They remained in action, covering the withdrawal, until nearly 1230 hrs by which time most of the tanks were immobilized due to fire on their track systems or by bellying up in the shingle. By this time the evacuation had virtually ceased and thus only one trooper from the landed tanks made it back to England.

The Evacuation

By 0900 hrs, even without adequate communications between ships and shore, it was obvious that Operation Jubilee had failed. The battalions on Blue, Red and White beaches had achieved only minor penetrations beyond the beaches. Most of the troops lay dead, wounded or pinned along the sea-wall. The tanks, although still very much in action, had been unable to break through the anti-tank obstacles behind the sea-wall. The landing of the FMR reserve had achieved nothing beyond compounding confusion and casualties ashore. The attempted landing of the Royal Marine Commando had been a bloody fiasco. The Germans remained firmly in control of the headlands, the mole and the town of Dieppe. They dominated the beaches with undiminished fire. Only temporarily at Berneval and more firmly at Varengeville and Pourville had there been success. And at Pourville there was now danger that the withdrawal of the Camerons was in jeopardy.

The Naval commander, Captain Hughes-Hallett, advised General Roberts that the situation was serious and it was becoming extremely difficult for ships and landing craft to approach the beaches. He advised the evacuation as soon as possible of personnel only. Roberts agreed and after adjustments to allow the Camerons more time to get back and the Air Force to provide additional cover the withdrawal was set for 1100hrs. Much improvisation was necessary. It was originally planned to evacuate the entire force in tank landing craft from the main Dieppe beaches. Enemy positioning and fire ruled this out and small infantry landing craft had to be used instead. And the Pourville force would be evacuated from its own beach. Under heavy enemy fire but with strong Calgary Tank support and RAF cover and smoke the craft went in.

The few remaining Royals at Puys had been forced to surrender beforehand. And only a handful of landing craft succeeded in reaching the Essex on Red Beach. Indeed, some of the craft intended for Red were diverted to Pourville and six of the eight other Red Beach craft were lost. Despite heroic efforts by the tanks and Navy, only some 350 men were taken off Red and White beaches. The tank crews, fighting to the last to cover the withdrawal, were lost. Great heroism was shown in the evacuation including by the chaplain of the RHLI, Captain J.W. Foote, who along with Lt Col C.I. Merritt SSR and Captain P. A. Porteous No. 4 Commando won the Victoria Cross for valour. The Pourville evacuation went slightly better owing in part to the heroic SSR rearguard and the bonus landing craft inadvertently diverted from Red Beach. In the end only 2211 out of 4963 Canadians who had embarked on the raid returned to England and of these nearly 1000 had never been landed and many of the rest were wounded.

At 1250 hrs the Headquarters ship HMS Calpe, with landing craft lashed to the bow, approached the shore and shelled the breakwater but did not bring anyone off. Twenty minutes later Brigadier Southam, the senior officer ashore, reported that the survivors had surrendered. At 1358 hrs the German artillery ceased firing. The fighting was over; the collection of dead and wounded begun.

Comments

Command and Control

A frequent refrain in any report on Dieppe is the gross inadequacy of communications between ships and shore resulting in the Force Commander receiving little or, even worse, misleading information on what was happening. The artillery FOOs similarly seemed unable to see what the troops were doing or to adequately control the naval fire support. Of the two brigade headquarters involved only one, HQ 6 CIB, landed and it reported via the scout car of the senior signals officer. This rear link functioned reasonably well which would indicate a problem with the brigade forward links. Another working network that appears not to have been fully utilized was that of the

Calgary Tanks. Throughout the battle the regimental net remained in operation. The tanks were certainly in a position to see as well as anyone what was going on yet little relay information reached HMS Calpe from this source.

Although communications between ships and within the air force worked well, the intervening layers of command, especially in the latter case, made response times very sluggish. For example a request at 1144 hrs from HQ 6 CIB for an air strike was routed via the Headquarters Ship and reached RAF Uxbridge at 1217 hrs. Uxbridge issued the necessary orders to the airfields at 1243 hrs - a one hour lag time. The strike finally went in at 1330 hrs - after the last troops had been evacuated or left behind.

Results Achieved and Losses Suffered

Virtually none of the aims of the force were attained so in the ultimate sense the operation was a failure and a very bloody failure. Casualties to all three services were unacceptably high. Of some 6100 troops embarked over half, 3642, became casualties of which the Canadian share was 3367 out of 4963 embarked. Of these a staggering 907 were killed, 586 wounded and evacuated, 568 wounded and prisoners of war (POW) and 1306 unwounded POW. The figures become even more numbing when one considers that about 1000 Canadians, for a variety of reasons, never were landed. Thus the dead and wounded amounted to about 50% of those who landed, a very high percentage.

As noted before the large number of prisoners was almost entirely due to the inability to evacuate them. One measure of the problem is that of seven COs who landed only one, and he badly wounded, returned to England. Two were killed on landing, one penetrated inland and stayed in action long after the battle had ended and one commanded the Pourville rearguard for which, among other deeds, he received the VC. The only brigadier to land was also wounded and captured.

The other services also grievously suffered. The navy lost one destroyer, 32 landing craft and 550 sailors of whom 75 were killed and 270 missing. The RAF suffered its heaviest one-day aircraft losses of the war as the Luftwaffe came out in large numbers to meet the challenge. One hundred and seven aircraft and 67 pilots were lost. These casualties attest to the valiant efforts of the Navy and Air Force to help their Army kindred. Dieppe was a combined operation in the fullest sense of the words.

As would be expected, the German casualties were much less. Forty-eight aircraft were lost and 24 damaged. Losses from the intercepted convoy on the run-in were one submarine chaser, with all hands, and one merchant ship. German personnel casualties were 591 of which 175 were killed. Materially they lost six 5.9 inch guns to No 4 Commando plus numerous beach defence and anti-tank guns. Although numbers of Germans were taken prisoner few could be taken off and only 37 were brought back to England. For many of the prisoners who thus escaped it was a mixed blessing as numbers of these were to meet a worse fate in Russia or one of the other fronts.

The German Assessment (19)

The Germans were scathing in their assessment of the Allied plan for the battle. HQ 81st Corps criticized its overly meticulous planning down to minute details and for the fact that it left no room for initiative. For example the plan had 13 diagrams for withdrawal and evacuation, especially ironic when in the event the evacuation was extemporaneous.

The responsible division, the 302nd, commented on the inadequacy of the Allied naval and air forces for the neutralization of the defenders and the disruption of communications. They expressed surprise that a single division was sent against a well protected and supported regiment (brigade). In fact the actual situation was worse as only two Canadian brigades and commandos were involved. Nevertheless the German CinC West warned that the allies would learn from their mistakes and do things differently next time. Which is about what happened.

German assessments of the quality of the Canadians and the reasons for their failure varied widely. HQ 81 Corps scathingly remarked on the Canadians fighting badly and surrendering in droves afterwards. This glib assessment was refuted in spades by the German division actually involved. This division, the 302nd, stated that the Canadians "attacked with great energy" and "with good offensive spirit" and "did not lack spirit". They correctly attributed the large number of prisoners to the troops being trapped by heavy fire on a beach which offered no cover and little possibility of escape

This assessment was furthered by HQ 15th German Army which reported that, "The Canadian soldiers fought - so far as he was able to fight at all - well and bravely." They attributed the heavy Canadian casualties to four factors:
- The lack of artillery (and by inference mortar) support for the assault troops,
- Poor planning which underestimated the strength of German defences and which at Puys and Dieppe chose landing beaches which placed the assault troops in a hopeless position from the outset.
- The superiority of German defensive weapons,
- The inability, because of defensive fire, of the landing craft to evacuate the troops.

The Dieppe raid had a profound effect on the thinking of the German high command up to and including the Fuhrer Adolf Hitler. Consequently great effort was expended in strengthening the Atlantic Wall and elite divisions were brought west to bolster the limited forces heretofore available. Dieppe also confirmed for them the concept that any invasion should be smashed on the beaches the first day. After Dieppe German assessments of likely invasion areas centred on Normandy and Brittany. Thus, in a sense, the Germans could be said to have profited from the lessons of Dieppe at least as much as did the Allies. Despite these correct appreciations when the actual invasion took place the Germans became wrongly fixated on the Pas de Calais. So much for good staff work!

The Allied Assessment

Many layers of Allied command, including HQCO, HQ Canadian Army and the Royal Navy also devoted much study to the results of Operation Jubilee. And despite the current common sentiment that Normandy owed nothing to Dieppe the facts would seem to indicate otherwise as the following conclusions from these studies show:
- A major invasion must be based on overwhelming naval, air and army fire power and not, as at Dieppe, in seeking success through tactical surprise. This assessment finally put paid to the overoptimistic opinions of those who, led by the Americans (including Eisenhower), had clamoured for a Second Front in 1942 on the basis of surprise and a paucity of fire support.

- Specialized armoured engineer equipment would be needed to destroy enemy fortifications and obstacles such as had thwarted the tanks at Dieppe.
- The planning and conduct must be concentrated in the fewest headquarters possible and not be diffused among several layers as for Jubilee.
- Tri-service intelligence must be better planned, conducted and coordinated.
- Frontal attacks on a major port to be avoided.
- Much improved communications, command and control was now self evident.
- More flexibility needed in both planning and execution.
- Greater care was required in topographical studies for the selection of landing sites.
- The army must have protected self-propelled artillery for immediate availability on landing.
- The Navy must maintain permanent assault landing forces and constantly train with the army and air units with which they would operate.
- The need for air support with better control and response times was now manifest.

Conclusions

Many recent works harp on near "conspiracy theories" of the throwing away of Canadian lives by callous British commanders, of intelligence bungles(20) and of cover ups in high places. While Dieppe certainly had its share of bungles the causes were diffuse and cumulative rather than sinister and cynical.

Much of the post-raid and post-war soul-searching tried to pin responsibility for the planning and ordering of the raid. And if there was a cover up it related to this aspect with Mountbatten, Montgomery, Hughes-Hallett and even Churchill as the principal suspects. Perhaps the most thorough research on this angle was by Brian Loring Villa as covered in his book *Unauthorized Action, Mountbatten and the Dieppe Raid.*(21) Villa, rather convincingly, pins much of the blame on Mountbatten and copiously documents his vain self-glorification, fudging of the record and shifting blame to others. Villa also shows that Churchill, while writing his 1950 memoirs, attempted to get to the bottom of responsibility for the disaster. But in the end the old school circled wagons and Churchill, Mountbatten, Montgomery, Ismay, Hughes-Hallett *et al* had convenient selective memory failures, loss of key records and an eager pursuit of self-exoneration. (22) Churchill's own memoir, apart from getting the raid's date wrong, is incredibly uninformative and bland thereby compounding the high command whitewash.(23)

Although Mounbatten had his apologists, principally his biographer Admiral McGeogh, most analysts including John Hughes-Wilson(24), Saul David(25) and Nigel Hamilton (another of Mountbatten's biographers) are clearly on side with Loring Villa. Perhaps the most authoritative word on the matter is that of the esteemed Admiral Sir Bertram Ramsay, "Dieppe was a tragedy and the cause may be attributed to the fact that it was planned by inexperienced enthusiasts."(26) While Ramsay does not finger the culprits, he obviously meant HQCO and HQ 2CID. But all of this merely disguises the fact that Dieppe was largely a failure due to over optimistic, half-baked, planning assumptions, incredibly poor intelligence and faulty appreciations on the part of HQCO and an over ready willingness by HQ 2 CID to believe that HQCO knew what it was doing and had produced an outline plan that should be accepted at face value.

The fact that Canadians were selected for the operation was a near given and had nothing to do with theories of cynical foredoomed assignments by the British High

GAUDEAMUS IGITUR

Command. The long suffering Canadians in Britain were chafing at the bit for action and could not be once more excluded. Almost alone among the Commonwealth nations they had, for three long years, been denied any part in the land fighting. And in the forthcoming Torch operation they were to be denied again because of Churchill's fear of England being charged with fighting its battles with Dominion and Colonial troops - which up to now, at least in respect of North Africa, had a ring of truth to it. The Canadians had had enough disappointments and aborted affairs. The Army could not accept being left once again at the altar.

The career of Major-General Roberts was ruined by Dieppe which was a most unfair, if necessary, rap. He was handed control of an operation which had largely been planned in detail by others and which he had only limited choice to change even had he so wanted. Once the operation was launched the lack of information and means of exercising decisive control denied him the ability to make effective interventions. Time and chance both conspired against him. Had Dieppe succeeded he might have emerged as a second Currie and garnered great honours for himself and the Canadian Army. It was not to be. But to his everlasting credit he never tried to duck responsibility or shift the blame to where it really might belong.(27)

The single greatest failure of Dieppe was its deplorable choice of main landing sites, Pourville excepted. Dieppe and especially Puys beaches were bottlenecked killing grounds. If success was at all possible in these places it needed exquisite timing in landing men and tanks, enough surprise for the troops to clear the beach and boundless good luck. It got none of these. The 1944 Normandy landings profited from these errors where of the five main beaches only Omaha was a poor choice.

A second major failure was the feebleness of supporting fire. The near paranoid fear of the admirals of risking capital ships in the Channel limited naval support to eight under-armed destroyers plus a few gunboats, sloops and armed landing craft. Again the lesson was learned for Overlord which was supported by no less than five battleships, two monitors, 19 cruisers, squadrons of destroyers, mine sweepers, anti-aircraft ships and specialised gun and rocket firing landing craft. Air support was also vastly increased with Bomber Command and 8th USAAF dropping 11,000 tons of bombs in support of the invasion in the previous 24 hrs. And the Army helped itself with duplex-drive tanks and self-propelled artillery capable of firing from their landing craft.

However even the weak destroyer force available at Dieppe could have been much more effectively employed than it was. The pill-boxes at Puys and the mole and the Tobacco factory, Casino and Castle at Dieppe and possibly even the tank obstacles at Dieppe could have been excellent visual targets for the flat trajectory armour piercing shells of the destroyers. And the ships could and should have been employed much more extensively as radio relay links from shore to Headquarters. They also needed a much more effective fire control network with the troops ashore. As for the missing battleships, while they can bring decisive fire on hard targets they can identify they are much less effective as infantry support weapons. Carpiquet [where too much was expected from the Rodney's 16 inchers], Anzio, Tarawa, Saipan, Iwo Jima and Singapore(28) all showed the strengths and weaknesses of battleship guns against land targets. Which should not be too surprising since the Dardanelles had shown much the same 27 years before.

While much has been made of the cancellation of heavy bomber support (apart from the American attack on Abbeville airport) too much stock should not be placed on this either. As Goodwood, Tractable, *et al* were to show the bombers can have an initial pulverizing effect in depth but are otherwise limited in the tactical land battle. Own troop safety, difficulty in target recognition, visual impairment due to smoke, cratering and collateral casualties to friendly civilians all militate against bombing except in special cases. It is difficult to see what air bombing could have achieved at Dieppe apart from turning a city full of friendly civilians to rubble and ruining whatever slight chance there was of surprise.

Once the troops hit the beach they were largely on their own. Lack of adequate communications with the ships precluded meaningful naval fire support. And even had communications and forward observing worked the ships' flat trajectory weapons were not well suited for hitting defiladed targets - especially amid the fog and smoke which often prevailed at Dieppe.

The soldiers were sorely lacking in their own fire support - artillery and mortars especially. This lack was critical at Pourville where sighted enemy forces, including artillery, could not be adequately engaged making battlefield movement most difficult and slow. The tanks which were expected to fill this role were all grouped in front of Dieppe where the sea-wall and buildings limited visibility and obstacles blocked their entry into town. A squadron, or even a troop, could have played a crucial role in securing complete success at Pourville. And a single troop might have turned the tide at Puys by engaging the hillside pill boxes which so decimated the defenceless infantry. The armoured corps mantras - "tanks should not be used in penny packets" and "tanks - the more you use the fewer you lose" played their part in the Dieppe debacle.

Pre-planned air support was superb - especially at Varengeville where devastating sweeps by cannon firing Hurricanes were exquisitely co-ordinated with the Commando assault. And at Dieppe they may have saved lives in the initial dash ashore. But despite hordes of aircraft being available thereafter the procedures for calling and co-ordinating close air support on targets of opportunity were slow and cumbersome in the extreme. This is one clear lesson that should have emerged from Dieppe but the improvements made for Italy and Normandy were still far short of adequate. The Americans did in fact develop much better procedures after the Normandy landings but these improvements can hardly be credited to Dieppe.

The failure of communications crops up again and again in the analyses of Dieppe. This single failure was the major factor in three other critical failures:
- It denied unit and company commanders the means of controlling the actions of their commands and of exchanging critical information;
- It denied units and FOOs the ability to quickly call down and properly control the available naval firepower;
- It deprived the Force Commander of the accurate and timely information he needed to control the battle.
- A fourth failure involving air support has already been discussed.

Certain army communications links did operate fairly effectively throughout the battle - the 6 Brigade rear link, certain FOO links from time to time and the Calgary Tanks' regimental net. But these were exceptions which were often under-utilised. Much more could have been done with what was available. Much post-operation analyses was devoted to this matter but the problems were never properly resolved. Indifferent communications were to plague Canadian operations to the war's end.(29)

GAUDEAMUS IGITUR

The adoption at Dieppe of First World War type frontal assaults was a recipe for disaster in the absence of strong, well controlled fire support and the communications capability to enable the commander to control events. At Dieppe neither condition applied. In their absence the only feasible alternative is to rely on surprise, stealth and the indirect approach. The success at Varengeville shows what should have been tried at Puys.

This frontal attack concept remained a Canadian bête-noir throughout the war, although normally with infinitely better fire support than was available at Dieppe. Yet when novel and imaginative things were tried as by the Hasty Ps at Assoro, the Argylls at Point 195 and the Lowland Division, under Canadian Command, at Walcheren the rewards were great. Admittedly the Pourville operation was an attempt at outflanking. But operating without tank, artillery or heavy mortar support in open country in broad daylight - after having been landed on the wrong side of a river - is seldom a recipe for success. And at Pourville it was not.

As for command and control, the options open to Maj Gen Roberts were most circumscribed. Once the troops went in he was really limited to two actions - the launching of the reserve and the method and timing of the withdrawal. Plus, of course, the usual "get on with it" exhortations that commanders are wont to make in the absence of anything better to offer. On these he scores 50%. The communications failures resulted in his launching the reserves in the wrong place which only resulted in more needless heavy casualties. But his, and the Navy's, improvised withdrawal, though far from perfect, went about as well as anyone could have hoped under the chaotic prevailing circumstances.

The fact that Dieppe was a raid and the troops knew that they would only be ashore for a few hours psychologically militated against energetically persisting in trying to push deep inland after the initial checks on the beach. After all who wants to be marooned inland when the evacuation fleet sails away? Had the assault been a real invasion the troops would have known that success and safety would lie in getting inland, digging in and being supported. Such an advance was partly achieved at Pourville, despite the fact that the shortening of the raid's time frame put the lead troops in serious jeopardy. And at Puys, the most murderous beach of all, a number of energetic men did succeed in forcing beach and sea-wall and pushing inland and holding out. But for most the sea-wall became their cross and the beach their Calvary.

This psychological bloc may have contributed to what at times appeared to be a failure of junior leadership. This perception was not of a failure of courage but a sometimes failure of leaders at all levels to try everything to get the men - any men, not just their own commands which may have been shattered or dispersed - forward, over or around the obstacles and into town or up the cliffs. Much, of course, contributed to this - primarily the heavy casualties to officers, NCOs and signallers and the intermingling of often leaderless sub-units and even units. But it is in just such seemingly chaotic, even hopeless, situations that junior leaders can, and must, take charge and turn defeat into victory.(30)

But again too much should not be made of this. There were any number of heroic acts performed by leaders at all levels on that day. Tales abound of WOs and NCOs on their own initiative assembling and leading small groups up the cliffs or into the city where they engaged the enemy however they could - some returned many others did not. There were many other instances of junior officers taking out enemy posts under terrible odds or of sappers boldly rushing the obstacles they were to destroy only to be incinerated when their demolition laden back packs were hit and ignited.

Among a host of other decorations three VCs were won that day, two by Canadians - Lt Col C.I. Merritt, SSR and H/Capt J.W. Foote RHLI. The third went to Capt P.A. Porteous of No. 4 Commando. The total of three was equal to the total won by Canadians in two long years of brutal combat in Italy, two more than they won in Normandy and only one less than they won in all of Northwest Europe. While the Dieppe VCs were clearly merited many more should have been awarded to Canadians in the other campaigns. It is a matter to which we shall return in later chapters, but for now all honour to the heroes of Dieppe.

How much Dieppe influenced subsequent allied landings is moot. We have already alluded to defects that were corrected for D Day. Whether or not these improvements would have been made in any case is a matter of conjecture. However the disasters at Tarawa and Makin seem to indicate that at least in the Pacific the Dieppe experience was largely ignored. Elsewhere future planning was certainly much more thorough, controlled and cumulative. The needs of better tri-service training and co-operation, overwhelming controlled fire support and beach selection were addressed as was the importance of hitting the right beach on time.

Yet inter-service co-operation remained imperfect as witness the Navy's shooting down of friendly gliders over Sicillian waters. While Salerno and Anzio showed that the necessity of getting off the beach and striking rapidly inland were lessons not yet absorbed. Beveland and Walcheren were to show that the Allies still did not properly utilize the excellent network of occupied country intelligence. The assumed need for heavy bomber support was apparently learned and often applied yet Cassino, Caen and Cleve were to show that the application had not yet been mastered. And the Dieppe bugbear of C4 remained just that throughout the war which is lamentable because solutions lay at hand and the rewards for their use would have been great.

And so at long last the Canadians had entered the land combat lists in Europe and to paraphrase Kipling "If blood be the price...Lord God they had paid in full". They had suffered the highest one day casualties they were to suffer throughout the war in which they were destined to endure some of the most ferocious battles of the western fronts. They fought the good fight and merit a nation's remembrance and gratitude. Churchill in his usual memorable style wrote their epitaph, "Honour to the brave who fell. Their sacrifice was not in vain."(31)

It was to be eleven long months before the Canadians were again committed to battle, in Sicily, July, 1943. Thereafter they were to be constantly in action, often in the forefront, of many of the most savage battles to be fought in Italy and Northwest Europe. And they were to be nearly always successful. But that is another story.

GAUDEAMUS IGITUR

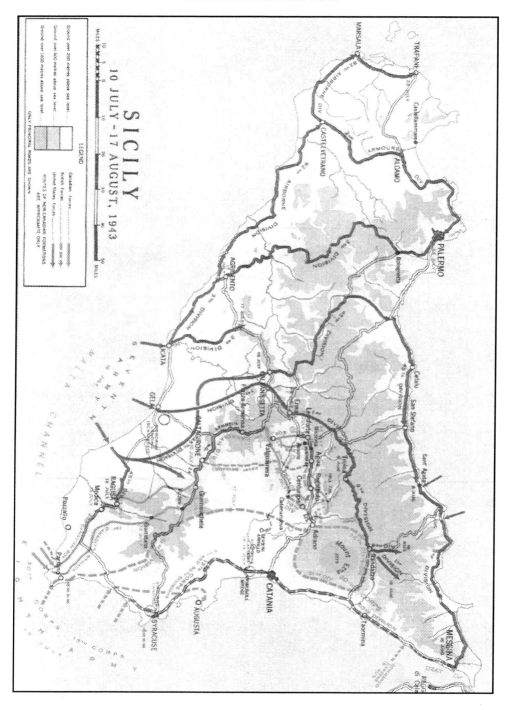

THE ITALIAN CAMPAIGN

CHAPTER IV

THE CAMPAIGN IN SICILY

*Then fare weel, ye banks o' Sicily,
There's no Jock will mourn ...ye.*

--The Highland Division's *Farewell to Sicily*

Prologue

The assault landing on Sicily on 10 July 1943 by the First Canadian Infantry Division (1 CID) and the First Canadian Army Tank Brigade (soon renamed First Canadian Armoured Brigade) (1 CAB)(1) marked the entry of the Canadian Army into continuous action in the Second World War. Thereafter, in growing strength and for much of the time in two separate theatres, the Canadians would be at the forefront of the liberation of Europe. See Appendix 1 for the composition of the Canadian forces in Sicily.

Although considered a preliminary, even minor, operation the six week Sicilian campaign cost the Allies over 19,000 casualties of which 60% were suffered by the British 8th Army to which the Canadians belonged. Canadian casualties in their four weeks of continuous action totalled 2300, including 560 dead. These are very considerable figures.

Despite this being their first long term action the Canadians performed very well indeed. Slotted on the western flank of the 8th Army, adjacent to the American 7th, the Canadians were originally allotted only a secondary flanking role to the major British push up the east coast. However the coastal push soon floundered and the British Commander, General B.L. Montgomery, switched his emphasis to the left flank with the Canadians becoming his main striking force. They were not to disappoint.

The Canadian road to battle in Sicily had been long and frustrating. For three-and-one half years, apart from the one-shot efforts of Hong Kong and Dieppe, they had sat on the sidelines while their Commonwealth and American cousins and many others had campaigned around the world. This was partly due to circumstance - first preparing to join the BEF in France, then defending Britain during its darkest hours. It was also partly due to Canadian Prime Minister W.L. Mackenzie King's efforts to maintain national unity by avoiding conscription, which to him meant avoiding casualties by avoiding battle. It was also partly due to the desire of the Canadian Army Commander General A.G.L. McNaughton to keep his army intact for the grand invasion and not risk losing control by dispersing its formations elsewhere under British command.

But now all of these negative factors had been washed away. There would be no invasion of Northwest Europe before 1944 hence the Army was free for employment elsewhere. Mackenzie King, the quintessential political animal, had come to realize that remote side-shows should mean fewer casualties than the certain bloodbath of a cross-channel invasion. He also realized that the Canadian people, the omnipotent voters, were increasingly demanding action by their Army. McNaughton, by the same token, finally accepted that his Army and his subordinate commanders were clamouring for action and that it was high time for Canada to join the show.

GAUDEAMUS IGITUR

With pressure mounting from all sides Mackenzie King, in March 1943, finally cabled the British Prime Minister Winston Churchill requesting Canadian involvement which, at that stage, still meant North Africa. In response, one month later, the British CIGS General Sir Alan Brooke formally requested to General McNaughton that Canada commit, "one Canadian infantry division and one tank brigade together with necessary ancillary troops" for "certain operations based on Tunisia." Canada agreed and, after a forlorn attempt by McNaughton to limit the undertaking to this specific operation, committed Canadian troops to the biggest amphibious assault of the war.

Selected for the operation were 1 CID and 1 CAB. Maj Gen H.L. Salmon the commander of the First Division was killed in a plane crash en route to a Cairo briefing at General Sir Harold Alexander's headquarters and was succeeded by Maj Gen G.G. Simonds. The division and armoured brigade departed for Scotland for final training and re-equipment while the commanders and staff prepared for the complex movement to the Mediterranean.

The Canadians were to travel directly from Britain in four convoys - a Fast Assault Convoy containing troops for the actual landing, sailed on 28 June. A Slow Assault Convoy containing second wave elements sailed on 19 and 24 June with the follow-up convoys going at the end of June and early July. The sea-landing part of the invasion was a most complex operation. Apart from the Canadians coming non-stop from the UK, other combatants sailed from Malta, Tunisia and Algeria. All had to rendezvous off Sicily on the night of 9/10 July. The Fast Assault Convoy made the trip without loss, despite a scary encounter with a German U-Boat. The Slow Assault Convoy was not so lucky - three of its troop and cargo ships were torpedoed and sunk with a loss of 58 men, 500 vehicles and 40 guns. Divisional headquarters lost 22 of its 26 vehicles with key signals equipment. These losses were to impose severe restrictions on the mobility of the Canadians in the days to come. They would simply have to make do on foot.

Sicilian Genesis

When the North African campaign finally ended on 13 May 1943 with the surrender of the Axis forces in Tunisia, a casual observer would almost certainly, and with little hesitation, have selected Sicily as the next logical battleground for the victorious Allies. Situated only 90 miles from Cap Bon in Tunisia, a scant two from the Italian mainland and weakly defended, it was a tempting prize to the powerful Allied forces with their near total control of the Mediterranean sea and skies and a large victorious army ready to move on.

Alas, things in the ethereal reaches of higher command were not so simple. Long fixated on a cross-channel invasion of northwest Europe, the Americans were deeply suspicious of side-shows which would detract from the main effort. Only when it became manifest that there could be no invasion in 1942 did the USA reluctantly agree to Operation Torch - Churchill's grand plan to invade western North Africa in November that year and attack the enemy via their "soft underbelly". Led by General George C. Marshall, their army commander, the Americans regarded the clean-up of North Africa as an end in itself and not a stepping stone to further grandiose ventures in the Mediterranean.(2) Churchill and the British Chiefs of Staff (COS) were however not so easily deterred. Showing, once again, that a cross-channel invasion was not feasible in 1943 they plunked for an invasion of Italy. In this they were supported by two factors.

THE ITALIAN CAMPAIGN

The first was the need to show the USSR's Joseph Stalin, who was clamouring for a second front, that the Allies were doing something significant in attacking and tying up main German forces thereby materially helping Russia. Secondly, the rotting Fascist regime of Italy's Mussolini was clearly on its last shaky legs. Its armed forces were everywhere beaten and demoralized, its fed-up people war weary and Mussolini's own policies and prestige totally bankrupt. A stout shove would almost certainly knock Italy out of the war and lead to all kinds of glittering possibilities. All that would be required was a strong, cohesive, well planned and controlled Allied operation with clearly defined objectives. Unfortunately in the Mediterranean all of these were then lacking. It was not until the Casablanca Conference of January 1943 that a decision was finally taken.

As Mediterranean theatre commander, US General Dwight D. Eisenhower established a joint planning staff (JPS) at Algiers. Concurrent planning, if it can be so termed, was carried out by the British in London and the Americans in Washington. Eventually two plans emerged - "Brimstone" for an invasion of Sardinia and "Husky" for Sicily. Sardinia was less strongly defended hence easier to capture. It offered excellent air bases for operations against mainland Italy but lacked good harbours and beaches. The JPS and Lord Louis Mountbatten's Combined Operations Headquarters feared the defences of Sicily and opted for Sardinia. While senior British officers wavered their CIGS General Alan Brooke, no fan of Mountbatten,(3) supported by US General Marshall, pushed for Sicily and won the day.

Sicily - Geography

Sicily is a dry, mountainous island lying two miles off Calabria the toe of Italy and some 100 miles northeast of Tunisia and north of Malta. It has the approximate shape of an isosceles triangle - 175 miles along the north and south coasts and 75 miles along the eastern base. The interior is barren, rocky and unstable with hills of eroding sandstone featuring steep, cutting hillsides and dry tortuous gullies. The towns are often perched on hilltops - a legacy of the geography and centuries rife with invading armies and marauding brigands. The roads in 1943 were poor, winding and usually unpaved, resulting in long, dusty, jolting travel to advance short crow-fly distances. Cross country travel, even on foot, was exhausting and confusing.

All of the main cities are on the coast - Trapani in the west, Palermo the capital and largest city in the northwest, Messina in the northeast, with Catania, Augusta and Syracuse along the east coast. All have reasonable harbours. Messina is the key to Sicily providing entrance to and egress from the island via Calabria on the mainland. Within this hilly country are three major plains - around Catania in the east, Gela-Biscari in the south and Trapani in the west. Here were located the principal Axis air bases. North of Catania the massive volcanic cone of Mount Etna dominates the island's northeast quadrant. Its bulk funnels any approach on Messina from the south onto either the narrow, marshy eastern coast or the mountainous hinterland to the west. It similarly channels any advance from the west into the rocky northern sweep between Randazzo and Patti.

The weather which can be wet and cool in winter becomes dry and extremely hot in summer. July is the hottest month with 40 plus Celsius temperatures the norm. Dust, flies and foul smells are endemic. It was into this month that the Canadians, sans most of their transport, were thrust directly from Britain's green and pleasant land. The other Allied formations had at least some acclimatisation in North Africa.

Enemy Forces

At the time of the invasion Sicily was defended by the Italian 6th Army under General d' Armata A. Guzzoni with headquarters at Enna in the interior. Sixth Army comprised two Italian corps with ten divisions of which six were coast defence divisions of very low quality. The four Italian field divisions were the 28th Aosta and 26th Assietta in the west with 4th Livorno and 54th Napoli in the east.

Two German divisions provided the mobile reserve and principal strike forces. These were the 15th Panzer Grenadier Division (Maj Gen E. Rodt) in the west and the Hermann Goring Panzer Division (Lt Gen P. Conrath) in the east. During the course of the campaign they were reinforced by the 1st Parachute Division (Lt Gen R. Heidrich) and the 29th Panzer Grenadier Division (Maj Gen W. Fries). The Germans were controlled by Headquarters XIV Panzer Corps under General Hans Valentin Hube a superb commander who gradually assumed de facto command over all of Sicily. The German Commander-in-Chief South was Field Marshal Albert Kesselring with Colonel General H. von Vietinghoff commanding 10th Army in southern Italy. The German air forces operating from bases in Sicily and south Italy were under Field Marshal W. von Richthofen commander Second Air Fleet.

General Guzzoni's plan for the defence of Sicily intended to keep both (initial) German divisions together in the east as a powerful mobile reserve. He envisaged that the Italian field divisions would delay and blunt the enemy thrusts and hold them up for German counter-attacks. Only Guzzoni appears to have realized that successful counter-attacks would only be possible after the Allies were ashore but before their beachheads were linked up. He correctly appreciated that the critical front would be in the east where the major Axis forces should be concentrated. Unfortunately for his command, but fortunately for the Allies, he was overruled by Kesselring who split the German divisions between east and west. It was to be one of the very few tactical mistakes which the Germans would make.

The Allied Plan

The Casablanca Conference, which confirmed Sicily as the next objective, failed to look beyond this and prescribe an agreed, coherent joint strategy for the Mediterranean thereby denying Eisenhower a mandate for future operations in 1943. A rather loose command structure then evolved. This had General Eisenhower in Algiers as supreme commander. General H.G. Alexander, then located in Cairo, would be the land force and overall commander for Sicily. His future Headquarters 15th Army Group would be based on a planning staff for Sicily which was to be formed initially in Algiers. Air Chief Marshal Sir Arthur Tedder, also then in Algiers, would be Air Commander and Admiral Sir Andrew Cunningham in Malta would command Allied naval forces. With the war still raging in Tunisia the designated commanders had scant opportunity to concentrate on future operations. However it seemed a foregone conclusion that the British 8th Army (Montgomery) and the US Second Corps (Lt Gen George S. Patton) would comprise the major land forces for Sicily.

THE ITALIAN CAMPAIGN

In early February 1943 General Eisenhower established a joint planning staff under British Maj Gen C.H. Gairdner, later succeeded by Maj Gen A.A. Richardson, to prepare initial plans for Sicily. Due to lack of space at Allied Headquarters in Algiers the staff was located in nearby Bouzarea. For security cover it took its name from the hotel room where it first met, becoming "Force 141". Force 141 eventually produced eight plans of which the front runner involved a multi-pronged invasion at several widely separated points from Palermo in the west to Catania in the east Inexplicably the best, and to a layman obvious, option seems never to have been seriously considered. Landings along the Messina and Calabrian coasts, coupled with landings elsewhere, would have cut off the Axis forces from either reinforcement or evacuation and placed them in a hopeless situation. The German generals were incredulous that this was not attempted and scornful of the adopted plan.

The adopted plan was not the aforementioned front runner. Its multi-front approach was scornfully rejected by General Montgomery who proposed instead a concentrated assault in the east, largely by his 8th Army with the Americans in merely a supportive role. He also proposed himself as the overall commander. Not for the first, nor indeed last, time Monty overreached himself. Not only did Alexander remain as overall commander but the American element was upgraded from a corps to the 7th US Army with Patton, its commander, elevated to equal status with Montgomery.

However, despite equal status, the US 7th Army was still relegated to a secondary role by the Monty/Alex tandem who downgraded American capabilities because of Kasserine and the then prevalent British arrogance towards "lesser breeds without the Law." In the final plan the Americans were to assault southern Sicily from Montechiaro to Pozzallo on the 8th Army's left flank with three divisions (3rd, 1st and 45th) supported by 2nd Armoured, Rangers and a para drop by 82nd Airborne. Their objectives were the Gela airfields and a general line Canicatti - Piazza Armerina - Grammichele.

The 8th Army assigned its main effort to Lt Gen Sir Miles Dempsey's 13th Corps whose 5th and 50th Infantry Divisions and 4th Armoured Brigade would land on Sicily's east coast south of Syracuse. Supported by para/glider landings by 1st Airborne Division 13 Corps was then to push rapidly north through Augusta and Catania and on to Messina. The British 30th Corps of Lt Gen Sir Oliver Leese, to which the Canadians belonged, was assigned the secondary role of left flank support to 13 Corps and linkage with the US 7th Army to the west. Comprising the 51st Highland and 1st Canadian Infantry Divisions, the 231st (Malta) Infantry Brigade and supporting armour, including the Three Rivers Regiment (TRR), Leese's corps was to assault Area Bark on the Pachino Penninsula and advance north towards Enna. The 78th Infantry Division in North Africa and 1st Canadian Armoured Brigade(-) were in Army reserve.

1 CID supported by the TRR was to land on the west side of the Pachino Penninsula on the 8th Army's left flank. They were to capture Pachino airfield then advance north along a general axis Caltagirone, Enna and Leonforte. All fine and large except that the only decent road to Enna, Route 117, lay in the American sector. This planning failure was compounded by lack of proper planning in joint-service cooperation. The Navy wanted to avoid the narrow east coast waters and favoured the now discredited multi-prong landing approach. On the air side Tedder and his tactical deputy Air Vice Marshal Arthur Coningham eschewed close air support of the army in favour of achieving long-range air superiority and the interdiction of deep targets. They, in effect, were

re-fighting the independent air arm campaign started by Trenchard in 1917 and still pursued by RAF commanders in England. Patton for one was furious with Coningham for his refusal to provide assurances to the army and navy over what close air support they could expect on D-Day.(4) This resulted in such absurdities as Tedder's and Coningham's later criticisms of Montgomery for failing to cut-off the enemy while they failed to use their overwhelming air superiority to achieve the same end.(5) Instead of knocking heads together to obtain an agreed valid approach General Alexander, the nominal commander, maintained his super-detached non-involvement first from far-off Cairo then from his English country-manor style villa on the Tunisian sea-side.

The Canadian Assault on Bark West - 10 July 1943

The Canadian assault sector, Bark West, was the Costa dell'Ambra bay on the west side of Pachino divided into brigade objectives Sugar left and Roger right. Sugar was assigned to 2nd Brigade (2 CIB) (Brigadier C. Vokes) with the Seaforth Highlanders of Canada (Seaforths) (Lt Col B. Hoffmeister) left and the Princess Patricia's Canadian Light Infantry (PPCLI) (Lt Col R. Lindsay) right. The Loyal Edmonton Regiment (L Edmn R) (Lt Col J. Jefferson) was in reserve. Roger was assigned to 1st Brigade (1 CIB) (Brig H. Graham) with the Hastings and Prince Edward Regiment (Hast PER) (Lt Col B. Sutcliffe) left and the Royal Canadian Regiment (RCR) (Lt Col R. Crowe) Right. The 48th Highlanders (48 H) (Lt Col I. Johnston) was Brigade reserve. The assault brigades were supported by tanks of the TRR (Lt Col L. Booth) and mortars and machine guns of the Saskatoon Light Infantry (Sask LI). 3rd Brigade (3 CIB) (Brig M. Penhale) was in divisional reserve.

The Canadian sector was defended, if that is not too strong a word, by the Italian 206th Coastal Division. Although the division's resolve was questionable it was backed by a formidable array of pillboxes, machine guns and two 6 inch coastal batteries. The Canadian's D-Day objective, Pachino airfield, was some three miles inland.

At 0135 hrs the Canadians boarded their landing craft and commenced their run-in to hit the beaches at H-hour - 0245 hrs. They were supported by strong air cover and the naval support of one monitor, one cruiser and three destroyers.(6) The 2nd Brigade landing went about as well as expected although the Seaforths were landed on the right instead of the left of the PPCLI as planned. Both units hit the beaches against light opposition and by 0400 hrs were everywhere successful and ready to push inland. Graham's 1st Brigade was not quite so lucky as the navy encountered an uncharted sandbar on the way in. This resulted in much shuffling of the troops from Landing Craft Assault (LCA) to Landing Craft Tank to amphibious DUKWs (7) as generals and admirals fumed. Graham, finally taking matters into his own hands, re-boarded the LCAs and commenced the run-in at 0335 hrs. Despite one company of Hast PERs (Hasty Ps) being landed three miles west of their beach both battalions were firmly ashore by 0530 hrs and by 0645 had secured all initial objectives.

Throughout the day the Canadians steadily advanced against weak opposition but in scorching 45 deg C heat and choking clouds of fine white dust. The first serious resistance was against the RCR who, after clearing Pachino airfield, encountered a battery defended by a determined Italian company supported by numerous machine guns. The RCR attacked, cut their way through barbed wire, destroyed several machine gun posts and forced the surrender of the defenders. The first decorations of the campaign - a

THE ITALIAN CAMPAIGN

Distinguished Conduct Medal (DCM) and a Military Medal (MM) - were awarded to Privates Grigas and Gardner for this spirited action. The Canadians pushed on to the Ispica road and dug in for the night. It had been a fine day's work - at a cost of 32 casualties, including seven dead, they had taken all of their objectives, killed or wounded over 100 enemy and captured hundreds more.

The Canadian success was duplicated elsewhere on the 8th Army's fronts. The US 7th had a more sticky day as they met up with spirited counter-attacks by the Hermann Goring Division which seriously disrupted the US 1st Division's progress and inflicted heavy casualties on the paratroopers of 82nd Airborne. A combination of staunch small unit resistance, artillery support and timely naval fire intervention saved the day. But it was a foretaste of what was to come when all of the Allies would collide with the Germans.

The Advance To Contact

The Canadians continued their northward march on the 11th, mostly on foot or on scrounged rides on universal carriers or Three River's tanks - a legacy of their lost transport at sea. In succession they took Ispica, Scicli and Modica capturing thousands of Italians on the way including the commander of 206 Coastal Division, Maj Gen d'Havet.(8) At Ragusa the marching Canadians found that the US 45th Division, which had landed at Gela and was brimful of transport, had already taken the town via a lateral road. The footsore Canadians could only gaze with envy at the jeep riding Americans.

By the evening of 12 July 1 CID had taken Giarratana at which junction they were given a day's rest by Montgomery who fully appreciated the exhausting conditions they were undergoing. They were also treated to a series of Monty's "hood of the jeep" (or, more correctly, "bonnet (or floorboard) of the staff car") pep talks. At the end of the day Montgomery confided to his diary his confidence in his new Canadians.

The 12th also marked another day of controversy between Montgomery and the Americans with the unsuspecting Canadians caught in the middle. In the absence of firm direction from above Montgomery advised his nominal superior General Alexander how he saw the campaign should be fought. He "suggested" that 8th Army's 13 Corps mount a coup-de-main on Augusta (which fell on 13 July), Catania and crossings of the Straits while 30 Corps would operate northward along a line Caltagirone - Enna - Leonforte to cut the island in two. The role he allotted to the Americans was to hold defensively on the line Caltanissetta - Canicatti - Licata, facing west, to cover the 8th Army's left flank.

For this plan Montgomery needed the north - south Highway 117 and the western part of Highway 124 both of which belonged to the Americans. Alexander meekly acquiesced so Montgomery imperiously ordered the Canadians to pass through 51st Division and advance westward to Vizzini - Caltagirone at the same time that the US 45th Division proposed to advance on the same axis. Since speed of advance was of the essence the decision to take one of the few good roads from the vehicle rich Americans and give it to the vehicle poor Canadians was a strange one to say the least. But such were the musings of higher command in Sicily that year.

On 14 July Alexander visited the US 7th Army and ordered the change made. This necessitated that the US 45th Division about face and return towards Gela. The US was told not to fire within one mile of the disputed route. Patton, Bradley and the other

GAUDEAMUS IGITUR

American generals were dumbfounded and furious but obeyed orders and acquiesced.

Montgomery's egotistical plan put paid to a quick US thrust on Messina and an early end to the campaign. It was also a violation of his own principal and pre-Husky rantings on concentration of force. Hereafter his 13th and 30th Corps would be operating on two widely separated thrust lines with virtually no mutual support.

On 15 July the Canadians became the unwitting "beneficiaries" of Monty's route grab when the Hasty Ps and a squadron of Three Rivers tanks reached Grammichele, midway between Vizzini and Caltagirone, and for the first time collided with serious German opposition. Battle elements of the Hermann Goring division had dug in on the town's 250 foot high ridge overlooking Route 124 and opened a hail of fire when the Canadians, in a classic advance-to-contact column, reached the outskirt. Several carriers and tanks were brewed up as the Canadians deployed.

Reacting swiftly the Hasty Ps sent two companies in a wide outflanking hook while the tanks and infantry fire base, decisively joined by British self-propelled guns of the Royal Devon Yeomanry (a territorial cavalry regiment converted to artillery) pounded the position. The Germans, in danger of being cut-off, skillfully withdrew as they were to do so many times in the future. The furious three hour battle cost the victorious Canadians 25 casualties and several tanks and carriers. It cost the enemy much more - three tanks, several flak guns and many troops including 30 single-handedly wiped out by a Mohawk descendant of Joseph Brant who won the MM for his valour. It was a superb, if costly, initial real battle for the eastern Ontarions and the Quebec tankers who owed their victory to initiative, dash and clever tactics. Meanwhile the grounded American 45th Division could only watch and fume. Not only had they been in a much better position than had the Canadians to attack Grammichele and Caltagirone but their artillery was in an excellent position to support the Canadians but was forbidden to do so by the no-fire rule.(9)

The battle contained an eerie hint of things to come. Friction had brewed for some time between Simonds and his 1st Brigade Commander Howard Graham. As the battle for Grammichele started Simonds arrived at the Hasty Ps' command post and criticised Lt Col Sutcliffe's plan of attack and wanted the action stopped. Graham supported Sutcliffe, Simonds backed off and the result of the battle was a resounding success. However the incident incensed Graham who tendered his resignation. The dispute was skilfully resolved by, of all people, General Montgomery who effected a reconciliation between the two.(10) The incident revealed yet another fascinating contradiction in Monty's character. He was ruthless and callous in his own sacking of subordinates and in criticising or scheming against others. But he could not stand to see his subordinates, or peers, play these games and inevitably went out of his way to smooth things over. Ironically he played the conciliator between Simonds and Graham at the very time that he rudely and needlessly denied General McNaughton, who had flown to the Mediterranean for this very purpose, permission to visit his own troops in Sicily.(11)

However the eerie aspect of Grammichele had nothing to do with Monty's venture into conflict resolution. Rather, in criticizing the Hasty P's battle plan Simonds gave an inchoate indication of his future change of Canadian tactics from the innovative and clever toward the First World War type of head-on assaults behind overwhelming artillery fire. His "new" tactics were soon to constrain the Canadian Army's operations for the rest of war. But at least for the next few battles Canadian initiative was to be displayed in all its glory.

THE ITALIAN CAMPAIGN

However these accomplishments were soon overshadowed by tumultuous events occurring elsewhere on the island. In the east Monty's colossal crack up the coast by XIII Corps had come to a grinding halt. German Colonel William Schmalz, commanding Battle Group Schmalz of the Hermann Goring Division, fought one of those brilliant and skilful battles for which German commanders were renowned. With less than a regiment of Germans and small elements of the Napoli Division, with no reserves and a huge gap on his right flank, Schmalz fought XIII Corps to a standstill. Using every trick from the German battle book and leading from the front, Schmalz blocked the British 5th Division at Lentini. It is no exaggeration to say that his superb leadership saved the Axis forces in Sicily.(12) Had he failed XIII Corps could have surged to Catania and Messina and sealed off the island. But he held and the war ground on.

On the night of 13 July Schmalz was reinforced by a newly arrived regiment of the 1st Parachute Division plus two other just-arrived battalions. On 15 July, the date of the Canadian victory at Grammichele, he linked up with the rest of Conrath's division on a general line Leonforte - Catania. For the Axis forces the crisis had passed. Even an heroic parachute and glider assault by the British 1st Airborne Division on Primosole Bridge over the Simeto River south of Catania failed to save the stalled 8th Army.(13) Montgomery now had to look elsewhere.

The German defenders of Sicily were also aided by General Patton's impetuosity which was fuelled by General Montgomery's imperious intransigence in ordering the campaign's direction. Blocked by Alexander's order from driving east on Messina and scornfully rejecting the Alex/Monty idea to merely provide flank protection to the 8th Army, Patton looked westward. Extracting agreement from the pliable Alexander that he conduct a reconnaissance in force to Agrigento on the southwest coast, Patton quickly converted this into a full scale overrunning of the Island's western half. So while the 8th Army bogged down and Montgomery belatedly looked to the Americans for help, the US 7th Army had turned its back and was going pell-mell for Marsala, Trapani and Palermo.

Once more General Alexander's timid exercise of command had led to a gross error. With no clear plans of his own Alexander caved in to Patton's Palermo swan instead of finally orchestrating a concerted drive on Messina. Even US General Omar Bradley roundly condemned the drive on Palermo as grandstanding. The incredulous Germans were scathing in their assessment of this latest Allied cock-up which materially aided them in their escape. And so back to the Canadians.

The Delaying Battles

Following the sharp action at Grammichele 1 CID continued westward on Route 124 and reached Caltagirone at midnight only to find that the Germans had flown the coop. Early on 16 July the 2nd Brigade took over the advance with the L Edmn R and a squadron of Three Rivers tanks in the van. At the junction of Routes 124 and 117 they reached Piazza Armerina perched on a hill half a mile above sea level.

Just short of the town the Loyal Eddies came under heavy artillery, mortar and machine gun fire. The Edmontons swiftly deployed companies to left and right, as if in battle drill, and moved on the heights. The enemy positions were too high and close for the Three Rivers' tank guns to gain sufficient elevation to engage so fire support came from the Loyal's own mortar platoon and, once more, from the British SPs. The battle comprised a series of platoon and company hill-taking attacks until, by last light, the Germans were driven from the town. They decamped by night and Piazza Armerina was secured by first light. The Loyal Edmontons had thus duplicated the Hasty P's excellent encounter battle tactics with equally superb results at a cost of 27 casualties. To give credit where due the battle was also a good piece of work by the German 104th Panzer Grenadiers who had delayed the Allied advance for a full day, in a foretaste of things to come. But no matter how frustrating the German delaying tactics the Canadians, with equal determination, kept advancing and dislodging the enemy hill by hill and town by town.

Brig H. Penhale's Third Brigade took over the advance on the 17th with the Carleton and York Regiment (CYR) (Lt Col D. Tweedie) in the vanguard again assisted by a Three Rivers squadron. Some ten miles north of Piazza Armerina Route 117 forks left to Enna and right to Valguarnera. The tough 104th Panzer Grenadiers held the surrounding hills and the approaches to the fork. Skilfully using fire and demolitions, then disappearing when attacked, the Germans turned the Canadians northward drive, in unbearably hot weather, into a frustrating slog. The Royal 22nd Regiment (R 22er) (Lt Col P. Bernatchez) took over the lead at last light and fought a sharp night time encounter with a German cut-off party.

The next day, on 18 July, the Canadians fought their first full-scale divisional battle of the war. Maj Gen Simonds proposed to engage the enemy frontally with the already committed 3rd Brigade while sending the 1st cross country to outflank and attack Valguarnera from the side. Brig Penhale directed the R22er - the Van Doos - to secure Portello Grottacalda, a narrow pass on the road, while the Carleton and Yorks and the West Nova Scotia Regiment (WNS) (Lt Col P. Bogert) outflanked the dominating ridge, Monte della Forma. Supported by the full weight of the divisional artillery, Three Rivers tanks and Saskatoon Light Infantry (SLI) mortars and machine guns the assaulting Carletons and West Novas struggled forward in the scorching heat. By late afternoon they had taken their objective.

Brig Graham planned that his RCR and Hasty Ps would then cut off Valguarnera by a cross country approach. This required his troops to make a gruelling night march to get into position astride Route117 by dawn. As they reached the road a German halftrack and several trucks appeared and were quickly knocked out by the Ontarions. They then ambushed several trucks carrying German reinforcements to the battle. In this action the Hasty Ps killed over 100 of the enemy and captured 18 before withdrawing to keep contact with their brigade.

At this juncture the RCR attacked and cleared Valguarnera's southern approaches driving the Germans back in confusion. Graham then committed his reserve the 48th Highlanders who swept ahead in a wide outflanking of the town. En route they encountered a sizeable German force which was wiped out by a single six-man section of the Highlanders at a cost of three dead. Cpl Kay the Section Leader, who was wounded, won the DCM for this superb action. After dark the 48th completed the capture of the town. The battle had cost the 1st Division 140 casualties but they had won a resounding victory, capturing their objective and 250 prisoners. They were also paid a compliment by the supreme German commander in Italy, Field Marshal Kesselring, who wrote, "Near Valguarnera troops trained in fighting in the mountains have been mentioned. They are called the Mountain Boys and probably belong to the 1st Canadian Division."(14) He was right about the division but the sobriquet must have come from the

THE ITALIAN CAMPAIGN

Germans themselves.

With his coastal thrust at Catania going nowhere and the Americans running wild in the west General Montgomery abandoned his original grand plan, and his oft-preached principle of concentration, and tried to mount four separate thrusts. Except for the one mounted by the Canadian division they universally floundered. On XIII Corps' sector the exhausted 50th Division were barely holding onto the Primosole bridge while the 5th tried and failed to pass the Simeto River to Misterbianco. On XXX Corps' front the Highland Division's attempt to cross the Dittaino River below Gerbini was repulsed with heavy loss. On the 18th Montgomery halted the Highlanders and continued his left hook with the Canadians alone. He instructed Oliver Leese, the Commander of XXX Corps to direct the Canadians on Enna, Leonforte and Adrano. He also summoned the 78th Division from Tunisia but it would not be available for some time. The placing of the entire load on the shoulders of the Canadian division was, in the words of the American historian Carlo d'Este "a tall order for a division in its first combat and largely bereft of transport in mountainous country."(15) Once more the First Division was up to the challenge.

However before this could happen the Canadians were to be the hapless middlemen in yet another stupid boundary dispute between the 8th Army and the Americans. The walled city of Enna, formerly Headquarters Italian 6th Army, was inclusive 8th Army along the US/British inter-army boundary. In their northward advance the Canadians bumped strong opposition below Enna and were directed by Lt Gen Leese to bypass the stronghold to the east and move directly on Leonforte. This uncoordinated move resulted in the exposure of the right flank of the Americans who were forced to divert a division to attack and clear the town. The Americans, still annoyed over the Vizzini boundary dispute of the previous week, protested vigorously forcing Leese to apologize to Bradley.

Assoro and Leonforte

For the Canadians the long series of advances interspersed with sharp encounter battles against withdrawing rearguards was coming to a close and the main event was at hand. Passing Valguarnera the division slowly made its way northwards through a frustrating succession of demolitions, minefields and enemy rearguards. On reaching the now dry River Dittaino they were ready to move onto a long, snaggly, steep ridge which held the key twin strongholds of Leonforte and Assoro. The two strongholds, about two miles apart, dominated any approach along Route 121, the Island's main east-west road.

Simonds directed the 2nd Brigade on Leonforte and the the 1st on Assoro. Once the ridge was taken the division was to continue through Nissoria, Agira and Regalbuto to Adrano. But first the ridge and its strongholds had to be taken and since they were held in strength by the redoubtable 104th Panzer Grenadier Regiment this was to be no small order. The advance began at midnight on 20 July.

On the 1st Brigade front the 48th Highlanders secured a bridgehead over the dry, but still formidable Dittaino torrent. The crossing was difficult due to the abominable terrain which had to be negotiated in darkness under a rain of pre-registered enemy artillery and mortar fire. With the crossing negotiated by the 48th the RCR and a Three Rivers tank squadron attempted to pass through. In short order the Three Rivers Regiment lost nine tanks to mines and the RCR were pinned down by heavy fire. Dawn

GAUDEAMUS IGITUR

found the craggy Assoro still tantalizingly far away with the Germans using the crest as a perfect observation post (OP) which overlooked the country for miles around. It was manifest that the attack on the summit would have to wait until dark.

Brig Graham spent the morning preparing for the assault which was to be undertaken by the redoubtable Hastings and Prince Edwards. The summit of the high, cliff-ringed ridge was crowned by the ruins of a castle built by Roger II, a Norman ruler of the 12th Century. The site totally dominated the twisting, rising road to Assoro. Graham believed that while a frontal attack would be near suicidal the extremely steep south face of the ridge offered the possibility of a stealthy night assault similar to that pulled off at Quebec by Wolfe's Fraser's Highlanders nearly 200 years before.(16)

While the CO Hast PER, Lt Col Sutcliffe, and his Intelligence Officer(IO) were making their reconnaissance for the night's operation they were hit by an enemy shell. The CO died at once, his IO later of his wounds. Sutcliffe was succeeded by his second-in-command, Major Lord Tweedsmuir, son of the British author and former Canadian Governor-General John Buchan. Farley Mowat, the future author, would soon become the IO.(17)

Graham briefed Tweedsmuir who conducted his own reconnaissance and devised his plan. This called for a special stripped-down platoon from each company to be taken that night, by universal carriers, as far forward as possible. The force would then move cross-country to the base of the cliff and scale it before dawn. Easy to say, but the terrible terrain and near vertical cliffs made for an extremely hazardous undertaking at any time. In wartime at night against a resolute foe it was a long shot indeed.

At 2100 hrs, under a diversionary artillery bombardment of Leonforte, the Hasty Ps left the carriers and started their night march led by a special company under Capt A. Campbell. The approach was a nightmare described by Mowat as "The going was foul through a maze of sheer sided gullies, knife-edged ridges and boulder-strewn water courses"(18) En route they met a young goat-herder and his flock but to everyone's relief no alarm was sounded. The battalion reached the foot of the cliff just before dawn where Tweedsmuir split his command. He would lead the party on the left while Capt Campbell took two companies on the right ascent. The harrowing 40 minute climb, grippingly described by Mowat in *And No Birds Sang*,(19) was nearly completed when, on the left flank, Private A. Long stumbled into an enemy OP. Long killed one man and captured three, along with a superb telescope which the Canadians converted to their own use. Miraculously the Germans were not alerted by this encounter and daybreak found the Canadians in complete control of the summit and its castle ruins.

From the hilltop the Picton unit poured down fire with devastating effect on German convoys attempting to use the road below. Now themselves under heavy artillery and mortar fire the Hasty Ps used the captured telescope and an enormous No 22 radio set, which they had somehow manhandled up the cliffs, to good advantage. Their new 2IC, Major B. Kennedy, was a former artilleryman who skilfully used the telescope to locate enemy guns and the radio to pass this information to the Canadian guns. In short order the enemy guns were either silenced or driven out of range. However the Hast PERs were not yet out of the woods as they were running dangerously low on water, food and ammunition. Their RSM Angus Duffy and Captain W. Stockloser made a dangerous daylight return down the cliff to Brigade Headquarters to summon help.(20) Guided by the redoubtable pair, two companies of the RCR humped the necessary supplies to the base of Assoro and delivered them to the Hasty Ps.

THE ITALIAN CAMPAIGN

While this relief effort was underway Brig Graham, knowing that the enemy's attention was now firmly fixed on Assoro, sent the 48th Highlanders by night up Route 121 to seize the crossroads. The 48th silently moved into their assault position and as dawn broke they attacked behind a thunderous barrage by the division's 25 pounders, the 4.2 inch mortars of the Sask LI and the Highlanders' own 3 inchers. The 48th were soon on their objective as the engineers worked furiously to open the route for tanks. The Canadians held firm against several German counter-attacks. With the battle lost the enemy gave up the struggle and rapidly withdrew by foot to the north, leaving vehicles, weapons and equipment behind. By noon the 48th Highlanders and the Hastings and Prince Edwards had linked up in Assoro capping one of the most brilliant Canadian feats of arms of the war. Major General Rodt, commander of the superb 15th Panzer Grenadier Division, with Assoro in mind, later commented on men of the Canadian Division "In fieldcraft superior to our own troops. Very mobile at night, surprise break-ins, clever infiltrations at night with small groups between our strongpoints."(21)

After less than two weeks in action the Canadians had mastered their craft *magna cum laude* and were ready to build on their successes. Alas, under Major General Simonds' rigid mindset they were soon to abandon their mastery of "Indian Craft" in favour of replays of the First World War Battle of Arras. To paraphrase a prescient Mother Goose, it would soon become a bloody repetition of "High diddle diddle - right up the middle." It usually worked but in so doing the Canadians abandoned their mastery of the innovative, indirect and unexpected and aped other less gifted troops in the stodgy and predictable. Only in Canada (would one jettison such a gift). Pity !

Leonforte, the second of the division's twin objectives, was to prove a more difficult nut to crack. A town of some 20,000 inhabitants Leonforte, like Assoro, was on a high ridge dominating Route 121 which took a sinuous course across a ravine leading into the town's southern borders. The route was totally exposed to the aimed fire from two battalions of the 104th Panzer Grenadiers who were dug-in on the ridge.

The action started on the night of 19 July when the L EDM R crossed the dry Dittaino and established a bridgehead some four miles south of the town. At dawn on 20 July the Seaforths passed through and advanced to within a half mile of Leonforte which they attempted to outflank. When their outflanking failed the Seaforths that night sent a fighting patrol into town. The patrol was soon hemmed in and was withdrawn with difficulty on the 21st. While the Seaforths were holding an Orders Group (O Gp) to detail plans for their next move a salvo of Canadian shells intended for Leonforte came down short on the group inflicting 30 casualties to key members of the unit. As a result Brig Vokes suspended their attack and ordered the Loyal Edmontons to take over and mount a night assault on the town.

The attack started with a heavy artillery bombardment and at 2130 hrs the Loyals crossed the Start Line. They soon penetrated into Leonforte but due to the town's size were forced to commit all four of their rifle companies. They eagerly waited for the Engineers to bridge the Dittaino so they could receive urgently needed tank and anti-tank gun support. Alas, they were pre-empted by the enemy who, in what was to become an all too familiar response, launched an armour supported attack near midnight.

Under heavy pressure the Edmontons withdrew outside the town covered by the Seaforths. However Battalion Headquarters and one rifle company were trapped inside and took up defensive positions in the town. As the engineers strove to bridge the dry torrent under fire their commander, Major K. Southern, led a handful of Eddies in an impromptu counter attack on a tank supported German probe and held them off. As this action ended Major G. A. Welsh OC 90th Anti-Tank Battery came forward with two of his six pounders and had them manhandled across the ravine. They made it just in time to destroy one enemy tank and a machine gun post which were threatening the crossing site. Both Welsh and Southern received DSOs for their night's work; Southern was to be killed later in Italy. At 0430 hrs the engineers succeeded in bridging the gap.

Meanwhile the trapped Loyal Eddies under their CO, Lt Col Jefferson, were reduced to Bn HQ and one platoon surrounded in one house. With radio communications inoperative, Jefferson sent a young Italian boy who had been found in one of the houses back with a note for help. The young boy performed his dangerous job to perfection and the note reached Brig Vokes. Vokes swiftly organized a force of a company of PPCLI, a troop of Three Rivers tanks and a battery of anti-tank guns, under Capt R. Coleman PPCLI (the son of the then president of the CPR) to rescue the Eddies. The first attempt at 0645 hrs failed, the second at 0900 succeeded in a wild dash into town. After a brief tank duel, from which the Three Rivers troopers emerged victorious, the trapped Loyals were rescued. Further heavy fighting followed and the Princess Pats only finished clearing the town at nightfall. Leonforte, like a miniature Waterloo, had been a near run thing.(22)

The brilliant twin victories of Assoro and Leonfonte cost the Canadians 275 men. But they had routed an extremely tough, resolute and well supported enemy brigade-size force fighting from skilfully prepared defences on difficult terrain. The vicious battle for Leonforte also resulted in the first of the Canadians' "denied VCs" along with twenty other decorations. The equally superb action at Assoro garnered none - probably because the commanders, due to the press of ongoing actions, did not write up the citations. This was to be a recurring and unfortunate theme.

During an attack on a hill outside Leonforte a company of PPCLI were pinned down by machine gun fire. A Bren Group trying to get at the enemy was knocked out except for one man, Private S.J. Cousins. Cousins grabbed the Bren and, single-handed, charged the nearest enemy machine gun post killing its five defenders and taking the position. He then, in the absolute open and contemptuous of danger to himself, charged and wiped out a second post. This action unlocked the enemy's position enabling the company to capture it. Cousins was recommended for the VC, for which his heroism met every criterion, but for some inexplicable reason it was turned down. He was killed a short time later and since, in those days, only the VC could be awarded posthumously he received only a mention-in-dispatches - a very poor recognition indeed for such an outstanding action.(23)

Agira

While the Canadians were taking Assoro and Leonforte, General Montgomery was eating crow - although in typical Monty fashion he masked his indigestion by claiming it was all really part of his master menu. With his much touted coastal drive stuck in neutral he came up with a new plan to save face. On 25 July, at Montgomery's behest, General Patton flew to Syracuse to meet with him and General Alexander to discuss the final phase of the Sicilian campaign. Montgomery, with Alexander's connivance and to Patton's fury, had previously fobbed the Americans off with a flank protection role to

THE ITALIAN CAMPAIGN

Monty's main event. Now with his main effort stonewalled, except for the Canadian advance, Montgomery magnanimously proposed to let the Americans in on the final drive. In a scenario to be repeated in Normandy, he proposed that his stalled XIII Corps' erstwhile main effort would hold firm at Catania while XXX Corps to the west would launch "a strong hard left hook" around Mt Etna. The Americans, fresh from "victory" at Palermo, would now be allowed to turn east and advance down the north coast on Messina. Alexander meekly rubber-stamped the plan. Patton, still deeply suspicious of British motives as well he may have been, also agreed.

Impressed with the Canadians' performance, Montgomery instructed Lt Gen Leese to direct the 1st Canadian Division onto Nicosia, Nissoria and Agira preliminary to XXX Corps' drive on Agira and left hook around Mt Etna. The push on Agira would involve the 1st Canadians, the 231st (Malta) Brigade and the 78th Division just arriving from Africa.

On July 21st, prior to his meeting with Patton, General Montgomery had already taken the first step. Noting that of his four plus divisions only the Canadians were making substantial progress, Monty directed that the rest of his army go into a holding pattern while the Canadians advanced. Due to acute supply, transportation and route management problems the 8th Army was rationed to an artillery expenditure of 30 rounds per gun per day. Because they now carried the hopes of the 8th Army the Canadians alone were excluded from this restriction.

In retrospect this decision was a two-edged sword for the Canadians. It gave Maj Gen Simonds, himself an artilleryman, the opportunity to go over to the massed artillery supported attacks that had worked so well for Currie in the First World War. But there was a quantum difference in the two situations. After 1914 the continuous trench lines of the First World War offered scant, or no, chance to turn the enemy's flank. But in Sicily the Germans just defended the main approaches and principal towns. It was a situation ideally suited to the gruelling, mountain climbing, outflanking moves such as the Hast PER had shown at Assoro and the French Expeditionary Corps was to so brilliantly exploit at the Hitler Line in Italy the next year. It was something that the Canadians were to attempt all too infrequently in the battles and campaigns to come.

In accordance with Leese's implementation of Montgomery's directive the 1st Canadian Division, with the 231st Brigade under command, began to move on Agira. Under Simonds' direction the Canadians were to advance eastward along Route 121 while the Malta Brigade approached from the south. The eight miles of Route 121 from Leonforte to Agira were dominated by a series of low hills with the village of Nissoria at about the half-way point.

1st Division moved off late at night led by the 1st Brigade with the 48th Highlanders in the vanguard. At the junction of Routes 117 and 121 the Germans sprang an ambush but were driven off. Then the 4th Princess Louise Dragoon Guards, the divisional reconnaissance regiment, took over and led to near Nissoria where their advance was checked. Although the check was only a minor one Simonds seems to have gotten cold feet. Instead of keeping the momentum going by launching an immediate outflanking assault he paused to mount a full scale coordinated attack. It was the first of a number of questionable decisions that the Canadian general was to make.

H Hour was set for 1500 hrs on 24 July with the RCR as the assault battalion supported once more by Three Rivers tanks. They were to move behind a barrage of seven field and medium regiments from the division and the Army Group Royal Artillery (AGRA) of XXX Corps. Fighter bombers were to strafe ahead of the attackers while medium bombers targeted Agira and approaches. The fire plan called for a creeping barrage lifting forward 100 yards every two minutes. A series of report lines were supposed to coordinate the barrage with the infantry advance and help to control the attack.

As was to happen so often in the future the Forward Observation Officers (FOOs) and brigade and divisional staffs failed to control the barrage which moved inexorably ahead while the infantry struggled far behind. The now unsupported RCR and Three Rivers tankers still managed to capture Nissoria by 1615 hrs knocking out an enemy tank and two guns in the process. However as the attackers moved beyond Nissoria they came under heavy fire from the tenacious 104th Panzer Grenadiers who, as usual, were skilfully dug-in on the surrounding hills. As the RCR companies dispersed and went to ground the Three Rivers squadron found itself exposed to a hail of anti-tank fire. Ten Shermans were knocked out in rapid succession.

Undaunted the lead RCR company commanders took the initiative and planned a wide outflanking movement through a gully to the right. The advance went beautifully and three RCR companies were soon in position close to Agira; it was theirs for the taking. Unfortunately, at this critical time, radio communication uncertain at the best of times failed once more. In order to regain control the battalion commander, Lt Col R. Crowe, went forward and mistakenly walked into an enemy position and was killed. His successor, the 2IC Major T. Powers, was out of touch with the situation and, as he did not know what had happened to his lead companies, confusion reigned. At this juncture Brigadier Graham ordered the Hastings and Prince Edwards to pass through and take Agira by a night time outflanking manoeuvre. Thus, while Simonds slept,(24) and the division lay under the control of the GSO 1, Lt Col G. Kitching, the Hasty Ps advanced into near disaster.

Advancing over an exposed forward slope the Hasty Ps blundered onto a German machine gun post which opened fire. At this the Germans lit up the battlefield with flares and decimated the Ontarions with small arms and mortar fire. By dawn the attack had failed with the loss of 80 men and the battalion was withdrawn. Inexplicably the three RCR companies, sitting secure and unobserved before Agira, were also ordered to withdraw, to the furious consternation of their company commanders.

Simonds, having had his seven hours of sleep, ordered Graham to attack again. Thus, at 1800 hrs on 25 July, the 48th Highlanders behind strong artillery, mortar and machine gun support moved off to the left and soon ran into trouble. After a confused fight the 48th shook off their foe and were in a position to continue their advance. But the German commanders, forward as always, read the situation perfectly and reoccupied hill positions around Nissoria. The 48th, like the RCR the night before, were ordered back from the verge of success. Thus ended in failure the first Canadian divisional crack at Agira at a cost of 170 casualties.(25) Simonds, as he was to do too often in the future, blamed his troops for the failure, which had really been due to a failure of command, control and communications of which the first two could be laid at Simonds' own doorstep.

The next crack at Agira was given to the 2nd Brigade who undertook the attack in three phases, each securing an intermediate objective. The first of these was the high ground east of Nissoria; the second, a ridge 1200 yards further east; and finally, the ridges west of Agira, straddling Route 121, between Montes Crapuzza and Fronte. The

THE ITALIAN CAMPAIGN

PPCLI opened the attack at 2000 hrs on 26 July behind another thunderous artillery barrage. The going was abominable and some platoons wandered off course in the darkness. But after a brisk fire fight the first ridge soon fell to the lead company. The two follow-up companies passed through but en route to the second objective they too became misdirected in the dark.

Lacking clear information on what the Patricias had done, Brigadier Vokes sent for the Seaforths to take the second objective. Part of the Seaforth's Start Line, which ran through the first objective, was still held by the enemy. As a result the Vancouver regiment had to clear its own Start Line before proceeding - something that is a No-No in Staff College teachings but not uncommon in war. Largely due to the leadership of their commander, Major H. Bell-Irving, "A" Company outflanked the objective and by first light had reached the summit. The enemy strenuously fought back but Bell-Irving was reinforced and by 1100 hrs the second objective was firmly in Canadian hands.(26)

At 1400 hrs the next day the Seaforths were directed on Monte Fronte under strong artillery, mortar, machine gun and air support. The tough 104th Panzer Grenadiers had finally been ground down and were replaced by a battalion of the no-less formidable 15th Panzer Grenadiers. Major Bell-Irving again won the day. His, by now, much depleted company was blocked on its frontal approach by withering fire from the new German company holding the hill. Bell-Irving then pulled a mini-Assoro. Using a stealthy approach masked by fire his company outflanked the position and scaled the precipitous south face of Monte Fronte onto the objective. The enemy fiercely resisted and the Seaforths only cleared the position by first light on the 28th. At a cost of seven men "A" Company had captured a very difficult objective along with 15 enemy prisoners, killed 75 (left on the battlefield for the Canadians to bury) and wounded many more. It was a superb action which owed little to the Simonds/Somme concept of "occupy ground won by the artillery" and everything to inspired leadership, initiative, clever sub-unit tactics and the courage and resolution of individual soldiers.

With the Seaforths occupied at Monte Fronte, the Loyal Edmontons were ordered to take the flanking Monte Crapuzza. Due to darkness and the extremely difficult terrain the Loyals only crossed the Start Line at 0300 hrs on 28 July. As per normal for those learning days, and indeed for much of the war thereafter, the artillery barrage had long since run ahead and left the Eddies, except for Sask LI mortars and machine guns, on their own. Nevertheless the Eddies soon occupied Mount Crapuzza and then fought a macabre battle for an adjoining ridge containing the town cemetery. Despite bitter resistance from a numerically superior foe the Loyal Edmontons captured their final objective. The PPCLI then advanced into Agira and cleared the city by 1800 hrs capturing 50 enemy and killing many others in the process.

The battle of Agira cost the 1st Canadian Division 440 casualties and five frustrating days. The casualties could be replaced but the lost time never.(27) Although the so-called divisional battle (really just a succession of individual battalion attacks under brigade control) had been mishandled at the top, the battalions had performed magnificently. Despite appalling terrain and vicious resistance from a tough, determined, well-led and well armed enemy the Canadians had emerged victorious - a testimonial to the superb leadership of field and junior officers and the determined courage of NCOs and men. In beating, in succession, two Panzer Grenadier Regiments, the Canadians killed between three and four hundred and captured some 450 good soldiers. The unit officers, NCOs and men could take just pride in a job they had done extremely well. The end of the battle also marked the deposition of Mussolini. Perhaps, after all the Mediterranean war would "be over by Christmas."

The Germans had now consolidated on the Etna (Hube) Line with strong points from San Stefano - Troina - Adrano to Fossa Bottaceto. They held from east to west with the 1st Parachute, Hermann Goring and 15th Panzer Grenadier Divisions, backed by elements of the Napoli and Livorno Divisions and the newly arrived 29th Panzer Grenadiers.

Regalbuto Adrano and the End

For the final push on Messina the 7th US Army would advance eastward through San Stefano on the north coast and Troina in the interior. With the 7th Army loosening enemy defences from the rear the 8th Army would finally resume its northward advance along the coast with XIII Corps tasked with taking Catania, Taormina, Santa Teresa and, hopefully, Messina. In the centre of the two armies, to the west of Mt Etna, Lt Gen Leese's XXX Corps, using his 1st Canadians, 231st Maltas and the newly arrived 78th British Division would take Regalbuto, Centuripe and Adrano. The XXX Corps operation was code-named "Hardgate". It was an apt name as attempts to crack the gate were to prove.

To ring up the curtain the 3rd Canadian Infantry Brigade under Brigadier H. Penhale was temporarily attached to the newly arrived 78th Division for its drive on Centuripe. The role of the Canadians was to capture Catenanuova, as a firm base for the British advance. The Royal 22nd Regiment led off by capturing 3000 foot high Monte Scalpello which dominated the Dittaino dry torrent. On the night of 29/30 July the West Nova Scotia and Carleton and York Regiments, behind a heavy artillery bombardment, attacked Catenanuova, which was held in strength by the 923rd Fortress Battalion. For one of the few times in the entire Sicilian and Italian campaigns the Germans lost their nerve and bolted - an act which resulted in the dissolution of the unit and numerous courts-martial. Subsequent strong German counter-attacks were beaten off by the Maritimers with heavy casualties to the enemy. The very smartly executed action at Catenanuova was selected by both the R22eR and West Novas as one of their ten colour-emblazoned battle honours of the Second World War.

With Catenanuova secure the 78th moved on to Centuripe while the 3rd Brigade moved cross-country on the Briton's left flank via Montes Peloso and Criscina to hit Route 121 east of Regalbuto. The going was difficult and slow to Monte Criscina which was held by a part battalion of German paratroops. The initial attack on the hill on 2 August by the West Novas was repulsed with heavy casualties and the assaulting companies were pinned all day in the open under murderous fire. As 3rd Brigade was preparing for a fresh night attack on the hill the defenders, learning of the loss of Regalbuto and Centuripe in their rear, adroitly withdrew to avoid entrapment.

Meanwhile the main Canadian assault on Regalbuto, with the 231st Brigade under command, began on 30 July. The Hermann Goring division held the city with its veteran combat engineer battalion supported by tanks, SP guns, artillery and the superb German mortars. The naturally strong Regalbuto ridge was covered by troops on the nearby Tower Hill and Monte Tiglio. The approaches were treacherous, necessitating the crossing of numerous steep ravines and rocky spurs. The 231st Maltese, who had moved into position after a very tough cross-country approach, launched the attack on

THE ITALIAN CAMPAIGN

the night 30 - 31 July. Their objectives were a series of hills north and west of the city. After a bitter fight the Malta Brigade took their objectives on 31 July at a cost of 100 casualties. The stage was now set for the entry of the Canadians.

First Brigade opened the attack on 31 July when the RCR, after a six mile approach march, staged a night assault on Tower Hill. The lateness of the Royals arrival precluded anything more than a cursory reconnaissance in the dark, which is seldom a harbinger of good things to come. Then the Start Line was found not to be secure which imposed a further delay to the opening kick-off. When the assault companies blundered into a steep ravine which guarded the enemy position things really went awry. Here they were halted under heavy fire and when dawn broke they were trapped and spent the entire day lying under a glaring sun without food or water. They withdrew that night having accomplished nothing other than to lend credence once more to the adage, "time spent on reconnaissance is seldom wasted."

The Hasty Ps who, unlike the RCR, had had time for a thorough daylight reconnaissance and proper preparation, attacked after last light on August 1st. Carefully moving from one intermediate hill to another the Hast PERs charged at dawn and swept over Tower Hill. At the same time a patrol of the 48th Highlanders worked into Regalbuto only to find that once again the chickens had flown the coop.

With Regalbuto in the bag the 2nd Brigade headed north towards Adrano along the now dry bed of the Salso River. The going was extremely difficult in addition to which the troops had to capture three major positions - Hill 736 and Mounts Revisotto and Seggio - on the way. The Loyal Edmontons started the tough advance using pack mules to carry their food, water, ammunition and mortars. Virtually cut off from their division by the rugged terrain the Edmontons took four days to reach Hill 736 which was strongly held by a well entrenched enemy company. Under excellent covering fire the Eddies rushed across 300 yards of open ground to close with the enemy. After a brutal battle they seized the hill as the few surviving defenders fled.

With the fall of Hill 736 and Centuripe, Lt Gen Leese ordered the British 78th Division to push along Route 121 to Adrano while the Canadians to the north advanced eastward along the dry Salso to capture Montes Revisotto and Seggio en route to Adrano. Taking a page from the German book on forming ad hoc Kampfgruppen for specific tasks, Simonds organized his own battle group of Three Rivers tanks, Seaforth infantry, PLDG Scout Cars and supporting SP and anti-tank guns all under Lt Col L. Booth. On 5 August Booth's force drove rapidly down the Salsa Valley to the high ground overlooking the flowing Simeto River. By 1100 hrs the Canadians' wild rush had carried them onto their objective which was held by the seasoned 3rd Paratroops. At a cost of 45 casualties the Canadians captured the position in a brilliant action.

The next day the Loyal Edmontons, after a sharp fight, took Monte Revisotto while the PPCLI, despite companies again getting lost on the dark night approach, captured Monte Seggio. Simonds then pushed through his 3rd Brigade as the R22eR grabbed a bridgehead over the Simeto and headed for Adrano. The Capture of Adrano marked the end of the campaign for the hard charging Canadians.(28) They were literally squeezed out between the Americans driving east through Troina and the 78th Division moving northeast along the lower reaches of Mt Etna.

Although they did not know it at the time the Canadians had played a key role in the capture of Troina by the US 7th Army. Troina proved to be the toughest battle which the Americans were to fight in Sicily. Here the supremely tough German 15th Panzers had thwarted the best efforts of the US 1st and 45th Divisions to break through toward Messina. However once the Canadians had cleared the Salsa and taken Adrano the German General Hube realized that the Canadians were now in a clear position to drive north along the Adrano - Troina road and cut off his 15th Panzers from the south. This, more than anything prompted Hube to abandon the Etna - San Fratello - Troina Line and move back to a line Randazzo - Cape Orlando. Thus by their very success in forcing the enemy withdrawal the Canadians removed themselves from the line of battle. Strangely, none of Montgomery, Leese nor Simonds saw what was so evident to the Germans and failed once more, as they would fail so often in the future, to seize the golden opportunity to cut off a large enemy force and score a major victory.

The remainder of the Sicilian campaign was anti-climatic. Continuing his superb delaying tactics against the ponderous Allied advances, General Hube succeeded brilliantly in evacuating his entire force, and a substantial number of Italians, across the Strait of Messina. And all this was in the face of total Allied sea and air superiority.

While Montgomery blustered and stalled and Patton strutted over finally winning the race to Messina, the brilliant Hube established himself as one of the outstanding generals of the war. For 38 days his XIV Panzer Corps had held up two full Allied armies who had enjoyed almost total air and naval supremacy, and in the end he and his force got away Scot free. Even Admiral Cunningham, the same man who had refused to risk his ships in the narrow Messina waters, castigated Montgomery for his failure to use "the priceless asset of sea power" to cut off the German retreat on the east coast highway. The air commanders Tedder and Coningham were equally critical of Montgomery's failure to cut off the enemy while they themselves were more than culpable. The air plan and campaign never came close to fulfilling the claims made by the airmen. Raids against Messina and Reggio Calabria failed to even slow the flow of men, supplies and equipment to Sicily and failed dismally to hinder the withdrawal. The Germans thanked their stars for having such dull opponents and were scornful of the pitiful results.

Assessment and Lessons

a) *The Plan and Its Development*

The planning for Operation "Husky" was bedevilled from the outset. First off the Americans wanted nothing to do with a Mediterranean quagmire which would suck needed resources from a cross-channel Second Front. Then once the British had talked the Americans into a Sicilian venture their own commanders, mainly due to ongoing operations in North Africa, displayed a marked reluctance to get involved in any detailed planning for the island.

Thus it was left to an ad hoc staff at Eisenhower's Algiers Headquarters, under British Maj Gen C. Gairdner, to develop the "Husky" plan.(29) And once tasked with the job the unfortunate Gairdner was bombarded with conflicting suggestions and critiques from all sides Despite this his staff "Force 141" produced a very credible initial invasion plan which called for the US 7th Army to land near Trapani and Palermo in the northwest while the British 8th Army assaulted the southeast from Gela to Syracuse. The plan pleased Admiral Cunningham as it exploited the traditional British use of sea power while sparing him the horrors of a repeat Dardanelles in the Messina Strait. Eisenhower and Alexander were, as usual, non-committal. Not so General Montgomery who was at his vitriolic best in scotching the plan that he had eschewed any part in formulating. In his august view the dispersion of forces around the island violated the principle of concentration of force and his own predilection for one mighty crack. Unspoken was his desire to hog the main effort for himself and to deny the Americans equal billing and a chance to share the limelight. Patton, still a novice at high command machinations and inter-Allied intrigue, accepted the change to the final (Montgomery) version, as he felt a good soldier should, although inwardly seething over the relegation of the US part to secondary status.

The final Monty plan of landing the entire force between Gela and Syracuse and then pushing northward played completely into enemy hands. It enabled the Germans to fight the only battle which their limited resources allowed - to hold and delay and inflict maximum casualties then withdraw behind extensive demolitions and finally to evacuate the island in good order to fight another day. Had the initial (Force 141) plan been pursued it is likely that the German forces would have been trapped between two armies and prevented from escaping across the Strait.

Despite this, and the failure to exploit the Messina option, there was still a chance for a quick victory had the Americans been allowed to keep Routes 117 and 121 and been encouraged to dash for Messina by the quickest way. There was still a third chance had Montgomery availed himself of the "priceless asset of sea power" and conducted a series of behind-the-lines landings up the east coast. It is ironic that, despite the naval operation being largely British, it was the small American fleet supporting Patton that proved most adept at helping the army in its land battles. Its intervention was decisive in thwarting the German counter-attacks at Gela on D day and D+1 and it supported Patton all around the island, culminating in some outflanking landings on the north coast. They did not always succeed but at least they showed what could have been had Alexander, Montgomery and Cunningham played from the same score.

The fact that the British commanders were seldom in synch owed something to the ridiculous dispersion of their respective headquarters. Montgomery was in Syracuse, Alexander first in remote Cairo then Tunis, Cunningham in Malta, Tedder in Tunisia and Eisenhower, the Supreme Commander, was a bystander in Algiers.

Once battle was joined on the island planning degenerated into uncontrolled ad hocery. Alexander, the nominal land forces commander, exercised no control whatever, except to throw a rod into the spokes by meekly acquiescing in Montgomery's demands to limit US involvement and to steal main routes from them - despite the fact that only the vehicle-rich Americans were in a position to fully exploit these. Only after a stalled Montgomery summoned Patton to Syracuse on 25 July, and gave him *carte blanche* to go for Messina, was there any semblance of a coherent and sound strategic plan. Perhaps the final word on planning for Sicily should go to General Omar N. Bradley, later commander of US troops in Northwest Europe, "Seldom in war has a major operation been undertaken in such a fog of indecision, confusion and conflicting plans." (30)

b) *The Commanders*

As has been pointed out ad nauseam the performance of the Allied commanders, in sharp contrast to that of their German opponents or even the Italian Guzzoni, was almost universally poor. Eisenhower, the nominal supreme Mediterranean commander, acted with almost catatonic detachment throughout and had no real part in the proceedings. The same could almost be said of Alexander, the nominal commander for Sicily, who freely let his subordinates take over from him and only intervened, usually with disastrous results, when pushed by Montgomery. Monty was Monty - egotistical, domineering and demanding while blaming others for the failures. Patton, who was shoved into a secondary role by Alexander and Montgomery, can hardly be blamed, as many have since tried to do, for swanning off to Palermo and then racing to be first into Messina. He could hardly be expected to sit twiddling his thumbs while others floundered. Indeed, had he been given a firm mandate to swing on Messina from the outset the outcome of the campaign would have been vastly different and almost certainly much better than what actually happened.

Of minor commanders, the Americans Bradley, Truscott and even the sacked Terry Allen were good. Dempsey the commander of XIII Corps did nothing special to justify his subsequent appointment to command 2nd Army on the Continent, nor, on the other hand, did he make any meaningful mistakes. Leese, the commander XXX Corps and of the Canadians, probably did as well as could be expected given his secondary role over terrible terrain. The boundary foul-ups with the Americans could only partly be laid at his feet. He was also a Monty acolyte and when the master left the theatre his own performance would stagnate. Simonds was a saw-off. He certainly exercised an iron grip over his division and yet, except for the final dash to Adrano, turned out to be a stodgy, predictable commander who orchestrated the rigid, artillery heavy, frontal attacks which were to bedevil the Canadians thereafter. He also fathered the "divisional" attacks which were only a succession of individual battalion actions - a tactic which was also to frustrate future excellence. The three Canadian brigadiers were all adequate but none displayed the fire, battlefield acumen or hands-on leadership which were a staple among enemy commanders and which would stamp them as future stars.

Sicily also did little for the reputations of the senior air and naval commanders. On the navy side Admiral A.B. Cunningham (ABC) vacillated between fear of getting his battleships trapped in narrow waters and boldness in chastising Montgomery for not using sea-borne operations more. ABC, the brother of one of the Desert Army's failed commanders, only succeeded to C-in-C Mediterranean on the deaths of three seniors. He badly underestimated the value of aircraft and submarines. Taranto, a victory for air power, was planned without him and he only won at Matapan because his denigrated Fleet Air Arm torpedoed two major enemy ships. His sniffy dismissal of submarines only underwent a conversion after losing four of his capital ships to underwater attack within a ten month period- including two at anchor at supposedly secure Alexandria. (31)

Air Chief Marshal Tedder, Eisenhower's deputy to war's end, failed utterly to use air power to either prevent German reinforcement of, or withdrawal from, Sicily. His policies and direction, seconded by his tactical commander Air Marshal Coningham, regarded air superiority and interdiction as the true use of air power and failed to deliver adequate close air support to the armies. Like ABC they were quick to criticize Montgomery for failing to cut off the enemy while doing little themselves to destroy enemy transport and roads and block his retreat to and from Messina. Close air support (CAS) during the critical invasion days was very poor. On D Day the US requested six CAS missions and received none. On D+1, during the perilous German counter attacks, the 1st US Division requested five and received one. Only Broadhurst, Coningham's deputy, appeared to realize the value, and championed the use of, battlefield CAS and he was often overruled. Patton was furious at the poor support that Coningham, with 400 aircraft at his disposal, gave to the ground forces.

c) *Joint Forces Co-operation*

Much of this topic, chiefly on the lack thereof, has been covered above as has the deleterious effect on operations of the 600 mile dispersal of the various headquarters. Much of the blame for the failure of co-operation affixes, of course, to General Alexander, who had no strategic vision nor tactical master plan for the campaign. He started the campaign with little faith in American abilities, even when proven wrong, and was too quick to heed Monty's advice on such things. His guiding policy, like that of Asquith in the First World War - and with equally disastrous results - was to "wait and see."

Lacking direction from above the military, naval and air commanders went their separate ways. Initially the air forces refused to even provide the navy with the flight paths of airborne forces destined for Sicily. ABC, in turn, refused to provide assurances that the navy would not fire on airborne forces. The air force finally gave in but too late. Not only were the airborne craft fired on by the navy with devastating results but all too often the hapless paratroops were jettisoned into the sea. It was a sad and stupid exercise in petulant intransigence on the part of the navy and air force for which army soldiers paid with their lives.

The failure of Tedder and Coningham to promise that they would provide CAS to the army and navy soured relations at the outset and fostered mistrust among the services. The air commanders often seemed more intent in pursuing the First World War *idée fixée* of ensuring air force independence than in formulating a common strategy against a common foe.

d) *Battle Tactics*

On the Canadian side these started out in excellent form. The early Canadian actions, starred by Assoro, featured clever innovative tactics, intermediate command initiative and resourceful improvisation. Their final action at Adrano featured more of the same. But in between disturbing tendencies appeared which were to hamper the effectiveness of Canadian formations thereafter. The first of these was a failure of many commanders at battalion, brigade and division to get forward and actively control the battle from the front. Poor communications played a part in this but rather than this leading to a passive rear-area generalship it should have been a prod for commanders to get forward, find out and take action. At the division level this tendency reached its apogee in Simonds' insistence on sleeping undisturbed at night, battle or no. At the battalion level the failure of the acting CO of the RCR to know the true situation of his companies on the road to Regalbuto is a prime example.

Second was Simonds development of the rigid set-piece, single battalion attack behind a mighty artillery barrage which inevitably ran away, far ahead of the attacking infantry, leaving them naked to an unscathed enemy who popped up as soon as the barrage passed. This problem should have been a relatively simple thing to fix, yet it was to be repeated again and again as far in the future as Verrieres. Admittedly, the rolling barrages, much falling on open ground, were to be replaced by timed concentrations on likely enemy positions. But even these failed to be properly controlled for any of a host of valid reasons which should never have been called into question in the first place.

That constant bugbear of poor communications, or the failure thereof, continued through Sicily to the war's end. Much blame was attached to poor radio sets but this should only have intensified efforts to produce other means of getting the message through on time. Seldom was this to be realized.

Army/air cooperation was generally sub-standard in Sicily. This improved as the campaign progressed but the air force's marked preference for pre-planned targets, or pre-planned missions of opportunity, continued to be favoured over immediate close support on-call targets. Again there were many reasons for this but the fact remains that the provision of close air support remained cumbersome throughout.

e) *Battle Efficiency*

The combat efficiency of the Canadians in Sicily was excellent, probably as high as at any time throughout the war. Deprived of transport by submarine sinkings, initially relegated to a secondary role over terrible terrain and always facing a resolute foe the Canadians triumphed despite the odds. Alone of the 8th Army's formations they continuously advanced, continuously beat their foe and always took their objectives. Indeed their success was instrumental in leading Montgomery to switch his emphasis to the inland flank and to exempt the Canadians from the Army's artillery ammunition restrictions. The Canadian actions at Pachino, Grammichele, Piazza Armerina, Valguarnera, Assoro, Leonforte, Agira (despite the foul-ups), Regalbuto and Adrano were superbly executed especially at the company and battalion levels.

Even the British, then often reserved in bestowing accolades on others, voiced approval. Alexander informed Churchill that "the Canadians have made a successful debut and are fighting well." While Montgomery opined "The Canadians are going great guns….they learn very fast; they will be one of the best divisions I have." On Simonds he commented "He will be a 1st Class Div. Comd. in due course, and he will have a 1st Class Division."(32) The Germans were also impressed as noted previously in their comments on Assoro and Agira.

Some authorities have opined that the 1st Canadian Division did so well in Sicily because they were better trained than those who assaulted the Continent a year later. But this is a dubious claim given that the Normandy formations had even more hard training than had the Sicily force, and they had the added benefit of 1st Div's experience and a good leavening of Sicilian veterans. The opinion also implies that the Normandy troops performed somewhat less well than their Mediterranean brethren, which later chapters will show to be decidedly moot. If, in fact, their was a qualitative difference it probably lay in the battle readiness and numbers of reinforcements. Casualties in Sicily were replaced by fresh, equally trained and determined troops. With only one division and part of an armoured brigade in action it was possible to do so. But after the blood baths of Ortona, the Liri and Normandy the pool of highly trained and motivated infantry reinforcements declined alarmingly. Thus the Canadians in Sicily maintained their high standards to the end. But from early 1944 heavy losses led to noticeable declines in efficiency which could only be recouped by rest and rebuilding after each major battle. Excellent leadership by officers and NCOs from the top down was also a prerequisite. And in the vast majority of cases these things prevailed.

Conclusion

And so the 1st Canadian Division had joined the ranks of the world's premier formations. Raw and untested on 10 July, four weeks of constant action had stamped it as one of the very best - Allied and enemy alike. Handicapped by terrible terrain, shortage of

THE ITALIAN CAMPAIGN

transport and an initial secondary role they had prevailed against the cream of the German Army. They were ever victorious. But all of this came at a price. The campaign cost the Canadians 2310 battle casualties of whom 562 rest forever in the Canadian Military Cemetery at Agira.

The 1st Canadian Division, maligned by some as the "D-Day Dodgers", was to maintain its high reputation to the end of the war. Many other once fine formations grew stale or faltered. The 1st Canadian was one of a mere handful which started high and stayed high, they well deserved the designation of "First". At the end of the division's time in battle, as they passed from under the command of XXX Corps, Lt Gen Leese the Corps Commander wrote to Maj Gen Simonds, "I...congratulate you and your Division on your magnificent fighting since you landed in Sicily. The landing operations...reflect the greatest credit on your planning and training....The division marched many miles inland to...Ragusa...fighting its way forward in great heat....For three weeks, with the Malta Brigade under your command, you have fought continuously against stubborn German resistance. Your battle training has stood up extraordinarily well to the high tests demanded...Finally, you forced your way from Regalbuto to the River Salso... under the most difficult physical conditions...in time for the attack. I cannot thank and congratulate you enough on all these performances.....My whole staff tell me how extraordinarily well their opposite numbers in your division have done....We are all very sad that you are leaving the Corps. We hope you will soon come back to us, and in the meantime we wish you a great success and the very best of luck in your next venture." (33) It was a fitting tribute.

Canadian manning an anti-tank gun in Italy. (DND)

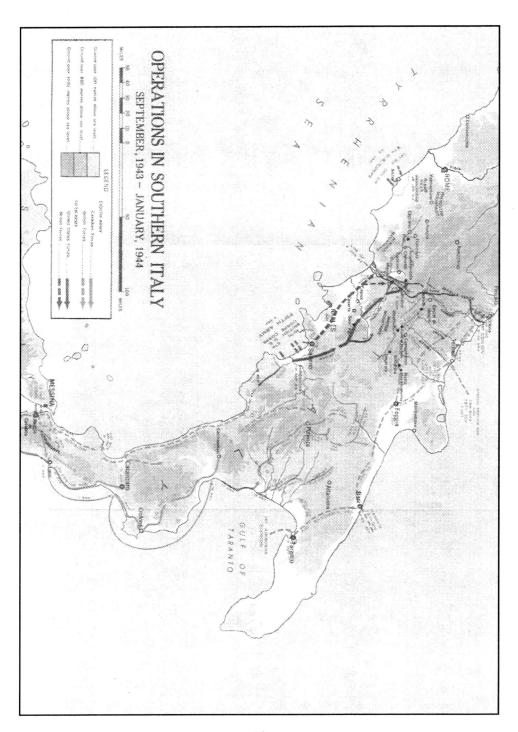

THE ITALIAN CAMPAIGN

CHAPTER V

FROM REGGIO TO ORTONA

Why dost thou stay, and turn away?
Here lies the road to Rome.

Macaulay - *Horatius*

Return to the Mainland

On 26 May 1943 the Combined Chiefs of Staff (COS) in Washington instructed General Eisenhower to prepare for post - Husky operations. Since the headquarters of General Alexander, the nominal land forces commander, was fully engaged in preparations for Sicily the planning for subsequent operations was undertaken by Eisenhower's own Allied Force Headquarters (AFHQ).

Although the Americans still mistrusted getting bogged in a Mediterranean quagmire there was some agreement amongst the Allies on the prospect of operations into south Italy to secure the Foggia group of airfields and the port of Naples. Churchill, always the Mediterranean champion, also promoted the important strategic and symbolic advantages that could accrue from the capture of Rome. Strategic considerations aside the planners were, as always, limited by a number of tactical factors. Foremost of these was the usual need to operate within range of air cover. Assuming Sicily as the base this meant a general area of operations within an arc from Salerno, a small port south of Naples, to Taranto on the Italian heel. A second limitation was the looming loss of a significant number of divisions, air squadrons and scarce landing craft to the forthcoming invasion of Northwest Europe.(1)

As a result of these and other considerations most of AFHQ's plans focused on Calabria, at the toe of the Italian boot, with other options such as Taranto, Crotone and Salerno as additions. The British 8th Army was considered the prime formation to undertake at least the initial operation. All of this underwent a dramatic change on 25 July with the sudden fall of Mussolini and the prospect of Italy's imminent departure from the war. Reacting quickly the Allies now made Salerno the prime target and instructed American General Mark Clark, commander of the US 5th Army, to prepare for an amphibious landing at Salerno to be followed with exploitation to Naples and beyond. The operation, code named "Avalanche", was scheduled for 7 September and would involve the US VI and British X Corps.

The 8th Army's Calabria operation now received second billing but was still deemed essential and was expected to effect a rapid link-up with the Salerno landing. General Montgomery assigned the Calabrian operation, code named "Baytown", to Lt Gen Miles Dempsey's XIII Corps which would consist initially of the British 5th and Canadian 1st Infantry Divisions.

The task of Operation Baytown was "to secure a bridgehead on the toe of Italy to enable our naval forces to operate through the Straits of Messina and to follow up the enemy to aid Avalanche."(2) On 14 August Lt Gen Dempsey issued his instructions to XIII Corps. The 5th Division would land on the left with two brigades to take Villa San

GAUDEAMUS IGITUR

Giovanni and exploit inland and northwest via the coastal road. The 1st Canadians on the right with one brigade, the 3rd, would capture Reggio and its airfield and exploit north and east. D-Day would be 3 September 1943, four days in advance of the proposed Salerno landing.

Calabria

The Calabrian peninsula forms the toe and instep of the Italian boot. It extends 130 miles from Cape Spartivento on the tip of the toe to the Castrovillari isthmus on the Bay of Taranto. Halfway the narrow Catanzaro neck connects the toe and the instep. Calabria features three great granite plateaux with steep terraced sides - Sila in the north, Serre in the centre and Aspromonte in the south. Aspromonte forms a rough square 25 miles per side rising 6400 feet to Mt. Montalto. The very rugged country has few flat areas and these are narrow and hugging the coast. The only towns of importance are Reggio and Crotone.

The state highway and a railroad encircle the peninsula squeezed in between the steep mountainside and the sea. Two "major" lateral routes traverse the Aspromonte - Route 112 from Bagnara to Bovalino (covering 26 air but 63 road miles) and Route 111 from Gioia Tauro to Locri. These roads have the steepest gradients and turns south of the Alps .A minor road from Melito to Gambarie on the Aspromonte connects with another minor road to Reggio. The going is painful and difficult at the best of times but when subject to the extensive and cleverly placed demolitions for which the Germans were renowned it would become a nightmarish chamber of horrors.

The Enemy

The Germans did not intend to concentrate many troops in Calabria, relying instead on a slow delaying withdrawal behind endless demolitions covered by long range fire thus inflicting maximum delay and frustration with a minimum of effort. The main defence of Calabria was entrusted to the Italian XXXI Corps with one field and four coastal divisions. The 211 Coastal Division defended the Reggio area backed by Blackshirt militia and a parachute battalion of the Nembo Division. Apart from the beach defences of machine guns and a few anti-tank posts there were several coastal batteries whose guns could not be sufficiently depressed to engage the beaches. Point 305 in the Canadian sector was defended by two forts and a battery of 280 mm howitzers.

The German 10th Army under the redoubtable Colonel General Heinrich von Vietinghoff, with headquarters at Polla southeast of Salerno, would defend south Italy with 15 divisions in the XIV and LXXVI Corps. The only German troops in Calabria were two battalions of the 15th Panzer Grenadiers and combat engineers covering the main routes north. They would be quite sufficient to serve the German purpose.

The Assault

On 3 September 1943 the Allies returned for good to the mainland of Europe for the first time since the dark days of early 1940 when they had been so unceremoniously hustled from the beaches of Dunkirk. It was an especially poignant experience for those,

THE ITALIAN CAMPAIGN

such as General Montgomery, who had personally suffered the debacle of the Battle of France. It was also a moment of honour for the Canadians to have been selected to spearhead the return.

The assault was preceded by many days of naval bombardment and heavy air raids on Calabria and airfields near Naples. It was opened by a colossal artillery bombardment from the Sicilian shore at 0330 hrs accompanied by naval gunfire. The assault battalions of the Canadian 3rd Brigade had embarked at 0230 hrs for the two hour crossing. The Canadian sector, designated "Fox", extended from Torrente Torbido (Fox Amber) on the left where the West Nova Scotia Regiment landed to Reggio (Fox Green) the area of the Carleton and York Regiment. The Royal 22nd Regiment was in reserve.

Heavy smoke made navigation difficult and the West Novas, in particular, were badly dispersed with some landed in 5th Division's sector and others amid the Carleton and Yorks. Nevertheless they rapidly regrouped in the face of weak opposition and captured Pt 305, its two forts and the coastal battery from whence the crew had precipitately decamped. The Carleton and Yorks did equally well capturing Reggio and its airfield and sending a patrol, accompanied by Saskatoon Light Infantry machine gunners, along the eastern road to Melito taking 1000 prisoners en route. The R22er passed through to the hills on the Reggio - San Stefano road.

At noon the 1st Brigade took over with the 48th Highlanders advancing up the Aspromonte via the San Stefano road. On the right the Hastings and Prince Edwards took the 3300 ft high Mt. Callea. By day's end the bridgehead had everywhere been successfully enlarged and the port and airfield would soon be in operation. The Italian D-Day and return to Europe had been most successfully achieved at a cost to the Canadians of only nine casualties. The Calabrian opening night had been a smash success, unfortunately the rest of the run would be considerably less entertaining.

The 8th Army's first major objective was the Catanzaro neck. To get there the British 5th Division, supported by the armoured Ontario Regiment, had the luxury of moving along the west coast road. The Canadians, in a grinding replay of Sicily, were ordered to advance inland over the road challenged Aspromonte. Montgomery apparently feared that the enemy might try to turn the mountains into a redoubt that once established would be difficult to reduce. And since the enemy, as he had done in Sicily, might contest the coastal route more vigorously than inland Monty would try both and take whatever opportunities would be presented. He also seems to have thought that the eastern coastal road would be difficult to force if contested. Though why it could be more difficult than the rugged mountains is difficult to comprehend.

For the next week the Canadians struggled forward in a frustrating, exhausting, stop-and-go advance over terrible terrain in the face of endless skillful enemy demolitions. The engineers performed near miracles to force a rough route open through which the Service Corps was somehow able to keep the forward troops supplied. The advance was punctuated by a series of sharp actions. The 48th routed the Blackshirt Militia while the Carletons did the same to the Nembo paratroops. Then on 8 September the West Novas fought Italians for the last time, killing six and capturing 60 at a cost of seven Canadians. The public at home, from the comfort of their living rooms, perceived the 8th Army's advance as foot-draggingly slow. To get from Reggio to Naples seemed from the perspective of their sketchy, non-topographic, newspaper maps to be a walk in the park. Why don't the soldiers get a move on? Yet to the soldiers actually doing the

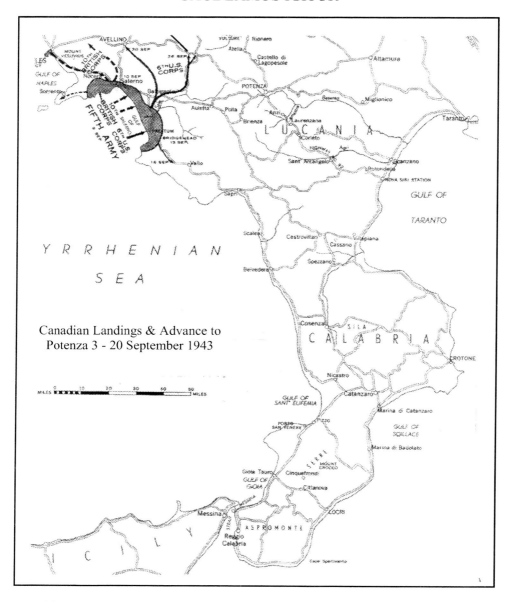

Canadian Landings & Advance to Potenza 3 - 20 September 1943

agonizing marching, climbing, fighting and dying it took superhuman effort just to keep going.

Then on 9 September Mark Clark's 5th Army landed at Salerno and the public eagerly waited for his drive north to Naples and east to Foggia. Nothing of the sort happened of course and the Salerno landers were soon in deep trouble partly due to the ineptitude of the American corps commander on the spot and partly due to the usual energetic German response. With Salerno bogged (at one time Clark even contemplated evacuation) Montgomery redoubled his efforts to effect an early link-up. He finally

THE ITALIAN CAMPAIGN

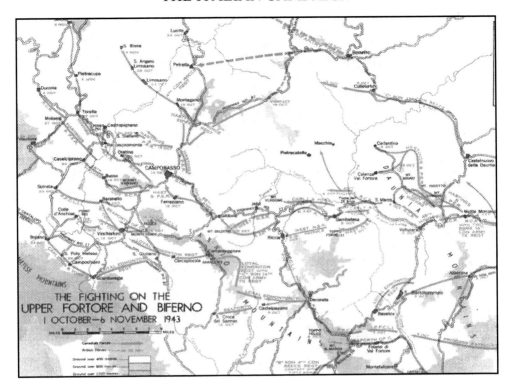

To Campobasso & Beyond 1 October - 6 November 1943

gave the Canadians the go-ahead to use the east coast road and even arranged for a couple of landing craft to provide re-supply. Meanwhile the 1st British Airborne Division was sea-landed without opposition at Taranto. After an essential halt to bring up supplies and its administrative tail the Canadians concentrated at Castrovillari on 17 September the day after 5th Division linked with Salerno.

Potenza

On this date Alexander nominated Potenza as the next key 8th Army objective and Dempsey gave the job to the Canadians. Simonds, taking a page from the German book on *Kampfgruppen*, organized an *ad hoc* battle group based on the West Novas (and called "Boforce" after Pat Bogert the battalion's CO) including a squadron of Calgary Tanks, a battery each of field, anti-tank and AA guns, platoons of Sask LI, engineers and a field ambulance. Boforce kicked-off from Villapiana along the Gulf of Taranto then turned inland to harbour at Sant' Arcangelo. Overcoming severe demolitions and a tough fight against the Germans Boforce reached the hills above Potenza at last light on the 19th.

Wasting no time Bogert attacked at 2300 hrs and daybreak on the 20th found his force battling the 3rd Paras on the city's outskirts. The rest of 3rd Brigade now closed up and Brigadier Penhale sent the R22er on a wide outflanking move. The Calgary

GAUDEAMUS IGITUR

Tanks then moved on the city and resistance crumbled. The West Novas, who suffered 27 casualties, captured 16 paratroopers. The Carleton and Yorks passed through and seized a key road junction two miles beyond. The Canadians had thus brilliantly fulfilled Alexander's directive for which Lt Gen Dempsey, the GOC XIII Corps, sent a very flattering note to Maj Gen Simonds, "I hope you realize what a great achievement the capture of Potenza in sixteen days has been and what a very big effect it has had on Avalanche."(3) Although the accolade was well merited it stretched things just a bit as Salerno had been relieved several days before.

On the 20th the Canadians linked up with the 5th Division and by the 21st the Allies held a line from Salerno to Bari. At this point the 8th Army had so outrun its administrative tail that it had to halt and reorganize its maintenance. The link-up of the 5th and 8th Armies, instead of being the cause of rejoicing, resulted in yet another inter-Allied brouhaha. Mark Clark opined that Montgomery had timidly dragged his feet coming up and avowed that 5th Army had been forced to save itself. While Montgomery, ever the pot stirrer, crowed that he had saved 5th Army's bacon. Clark was incensed.(4)

Following the link-up Clark's army took Naples, which was first entered by the armoured cars of the King's Dragoon Guards. The 5th continued its advance west of the Apennines crossing the Volturno on 15 October and the Garigliano on 2 November On the 8th Army front the 78th Division and 4th Armoured Brigade had landed at Bari and taken the Foggia airfields by the end of September. The Canadians for their part tidied up the line by pushing on to the Ofanto River. After initial rebuffs at Spinazzola the Canadians cleared Atella and captured Melfi in a neat pincers in which the Princess Pats advanced frontally while the Princess Louise's made a wide hook via Canosa. Thus ended the first phase of the Italian campaign. Canadian casualties for the agonizing month long advance over appalling terrain had been surprisingly light - only 32 killed and 146 wounded. However the days of light casualties due to spasmodic enemy opposition were drawing to a close, the Germans were now to contest every Allied advance. September's end also marked changes in command within the 1st Division. Maj Gen Simonds was invalided with jaundice and was replaced by Chris Vokes who was succeeded at 2nd Brigade by the Seaforth's Bert Hoffmeister.

The Allied failure to agree on a strategic plan for Italy now bore bitter fruit. Hitler's intention at the start of the Allied invasion had been to slowly withdraw Von Vietinghoff's 10th Army northward behind a Pisa - Rimini line (later to become the Gothic Line) under Rommel's Army Group "B". However the slow pace of the Allied advance convinced him instead that Kesselring should now hold a winter line from the Garigliano in the west to the Sangro in the east. This decision was to force the Allied armies into a gruelling, miserable and bloody winter campaign which the Canadians were to share front and centre.

The Canadian Corps

While the next phase of operations was unfolding the Canadians in Italy, to the surprise of many and the consternation of some, were being augmented to a full corps with the dispatch from England of the 5th Canadian Armoured Division and the headquarters and corps troops of I Canadian Corps under Lt Gen Harry Crerar.

The augmentation, unwanted by Eisenhower, Alexander and Leese, et al, and opposed by McNaughton, largely happened through the lobbying of Canadian Defense

THE ITALIAN CAMPAIGN

Minister J.L. Ralston and his CGS Lt Gen K. Stuart who sought two things - action for more Canadians and the squeezing out of McNaughton. They were actively and decisively aided and abetted by Prime Minister Mackenzie King for a quite different reason - his continued desire to minimize Canadian casualties in the forthcoming cross-channel invasion.(5) To his reasoning if the troops were in Italy they could not become casualties on the French beaches. All fine and large but his crystal ball failed to reveal the coming Italian bloodbaths of Ortona, Liri Valley, Gothic Line et al and the complications these would pose to volunteer reinforcements and the dreaded specter of conscription.

Despite British opposition(6) King's lobbying with Churchill won the day but it came at a price. The Canadian Army in England was now reduced to single corps strength and would have to be augmented with a British corps.(7) Secondly, due to the chronic shipping shortage, the British CIGS Brooke only agreed to the reinforcements if the incoming 5th Canadian Armoured and the outgoing 7th British Armoured would swap tanks and equipment. Due to the sorry worn-out state of much of 7th Armoured's equipment it was a very poor deal for the 5th. In the event the augmentation, code named "Timberwolf" was undertaken in three phases from November '43 to January '44. It would be well over a year before the Canadian Army would be reunited - in March '45 for the liberation of Holland.

To Campobasso and the Sangro

The ensuing period could best be described as bitter and frustrating for the Canadians who were once more assigned to the road-scarce mountain hinterland. Eighth Army's next " tidying -up" phase had the 78th Division moving along the coastal highway to Termoli while the Canadians were sent west along the twisting Route 17 to Campobasso and the Biferno River. For the advance along the sinuous, switch-backed, Route 17 Vokes, taking a leaf from Boforce, organized a Jock Column(8) of PLDGs, Calgary Tanks, RCR and artillery under Lt Col C. Neroutsos the Calgary's CO. The column started on October 1st and soon bumped enemy positions astride the road. An attack was delayed by one of the traffic jams which were becoming a feature of movement in Italy and insufficient infantry were available to back up the tanks. The attack failed. A heavier attack that night succeeded and the Germans withdrew - to their next delaying position. An attack on this position resulted in the loss of six tanks before the Germans again withdrew behind a chain of demolitions and mines.

It took Neroutsos' column five days of constant advance, encounter and attack - always surmounting obstacles and shellfire - to move 18 air miles to the Fortore River where 3rd Brigade took over. To the Canadians the going was painful and slow. Their opponents from the tough 26 Panzer Division thought otherwise commenting, "the First Canadian Infantry Division had appeared again, which explains the rapid advance of the enemy."(9) However Montgomery apparently did not share the German viewpoint and suggested that the American 5th Army might cooperate by taking the Germans in the rear - a suggestion that the 5th Army, having multi problems of its own, was in no position to agree. So the Canadians, now opposed by the redoubtable 29th Panzer Grenadiers, slogged on through Gambatesa, Jelsi and Gildone where the road branched to Campobasso and Vinchiaturo.

Lt Gen Dempsey considered Campobasso of such importance that he visited Brigadier Graham to press his case for a 15 October capture. Graham needed no pressing and kicked off early on the 13th with the 48th Highlanders in the vanguard. The familiar pattern of skillful enemy rearguards, heavy shelling of the only road and pre-registered targets on any flat areas where Canadian vehicles or guns might harbour delayed an attack on Campobasso until the next morning. Then the RCR, assisted by an outflanking move by the Hasty Ps, took the town as the enemy decamped. A grateful and gracious Dempsey presented Graham with a bottle of Marsala for meeting the target date. Meanwhile 2nd Brigade captured Vinchiaturo and advanced to the Biferno. On the coast the 78th Division took Termoli assisted by tanks of the Three Rivers Regiment who had borne the brunt of Canadian tank work in Sicily.

On the Biferno the RCR drove the enemy out of Busso taking 20 prisoners in the process. Pushing across the Biferno the Carleton and Yorks made a gruelling six day cross-country advance to Boiano which they captured on 24 October. North of Route 17 the 2nd Brigade after a stiff battle established a bridgehead at Colle d' Anchise. Further north 1st Brigade used some daring scout and sniper patrols to capture the crag-perched villages of Roccaspromonte and Castropignano. In equally hard fighting the 48th, at a cost of 20 casualties, took Torella while the Hasty Ps, after a grim 12 mile cross-country slog, captured Molise.

At the end of October the Germans withdrew over the Sangro and the Canadians were relieved by the British and went into reserve to recoup and rebuild. The endless grinding small-unit actions of October had cost the Canadians 650 casualties - four times the number of the previous month. As part of the reorganization Maj Gen Simonds moved to command the incoming 5th Armoured Division leaving Chris Vokes in command of the First Infantry. Third Brigade's Penhale was replaced by Brig T. Gibson. While in reserve 1500 sorely needed reinforcements were absorbed.

But, ominously as the Canadians rebuilt, the impending arrival of the Italian winter was heralded by November's cold relentless rains. The conditions to come would dispel any lingering illusions the troops might have concerning "sunny Italy."

While most of 1st Division was moved to the coast Gibson's 3rd Brigade was tasked with clearing the enemy along the Sangro. It was soggy, rough work in the face of skirmishes, demolitions, ruined villages and streaming refugees. At Castel di Sangro on Point 1009 the West Novas fought a bloody three-day battle against a platoon of paratroopers defending the hill top monastery. After an initial repulse which cost over 30 casualties the Scotians used cliff-scaling, mule transported machine guns, and the fire of nine field regiments to capture the monastery. Its virtually undamaged four foot thick stone walls showed why the Germans had been so difficult to evict. This marked the Division's last inland battle for a while and 3rd Brigade left at the end of November for the coast.

Monty's "Colossal Crack"

The Allies now realized that the Germans were determined to hold south of Rome along their winter position comprising the Bernhard and Gustav Lines from roughly Gaeta to Pescara, anchored on Monte Cassino. Alexander's plan to break through these lines and capture Rome involved both of his armies. In the west Clark's 5th Army was to force the Mignano Gap, cross the Rapido, breach the Gustav Line and advance down the Liri and Sacco Valleys to Frosinone south of Rome. At this point an amphibious landing would take the enemy in the rear.

Montgomery, as always, had a better idea. Once the 5th Army got hung up in the mountains (as he was sure it would) his 8th Army in the east would cross the Sangro to Pescara. Here he would turn west, get behind the enemy, and personally enter Rome at the head of the New Zealand Division. In an Order of the Day to his Army Montgomery concluded, "The Germans are...in the very condition in which we want them. We will now hit the Germans a colossal crack."(10) But as Monty himself admitted he must have fine weather since continuous rains could ruin his plans. Alas, winter in Italy is not the place to find fine weather as even the most casual tourist could have affirmed. And the winter of 1943/44 was, if anything, even more abominable than usual.

Montgomery entrusted his newly arrived V Corps, under Lt Gen C.W. Allfrey, with opening the offensive. On 19/20 November the redoubtable 78th Division crossed the swollen Sangro and was beaten back. Under heavy cold rains the "colossal crack" soon degenerated into a grinding, sloshing, slogging match. Using brute force and overwhelming artillery V Corps established a bridgehead over the Sangro and pushed on to the Moro. But the rains teemed on, the Sangro rose still higher and off-road vehicle movement became nigh impossible. Inland the large, powerful, armour- heavy, New Zealand Division drove on the key town of Orsogna. After a two week battle into which the 8th Indian Division was added the attack failed and Orsogna remained firmly in German hands. General Allfrey now called upon the Canadians to take over from the sodden, bone-weary 78th.

The Canadians' principal objective was the small Adriatic port of Ortona, some two miles north of the Moro. But to advance these two miles and take the town the First Division was to be forced to fight three major battles - the Moro, the Gully and Ortona itself. They were to become Canadian epics - and Canadian Calvarys.

The Moro

Two main routes lead to Ortona from the south. The most direct is the coastal Highway 16. Inland a secondary road via San Leonardo links with the Orsogna - Ortona lateral. Between the Moro and Ortona four 500 foot high east-west ridges intersect the approaches. The region is studded with hamlets, farms, olive groves and wire-laced vineyards interspersed with sunken farm roads and blind switches - a difficult place for a weekend hike let alone an advance into the teeth of a skilled and determined enemy.

Since Highway 16 was wide open to aimed fire the Commander 1st Canadian Division, Maj Gen Chris Vokes, quite sensibly opted for a multi-pronged approach to Ortona. He proposed to cross the Moro at three points on a four mile front - along Highway 16, at San Leonardo and at Villa Rogatti. His division's intermediate objective was the Orsogna - Ortona road junction, code named "Cider". Vokes assigned the coastal route to 1st Brigade and the two inland crossings to the 2nd. H Hour for the planned silent crossings was midnight on 5/6 December. Meanwhile the swollen River Sangro continued to rise and flood, threatening to cut off the division from behind.

The Moro crossings started at midnight. On the right the Hast PER gained only a precarious foothold as did the Seaforths at San Leonardo. Both were driven back. However on the extreme left at Villa Rogatti the PPCLI were completely successful. Crossing by an unguarded ford the Patricias, after a tough battle with the 200th Panzer Grenadiers, captured the Villa by dawn. The expected German counter-attacks started at 0900

GAUDEAMUS IGITUR

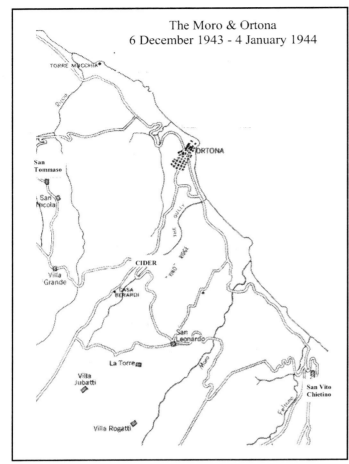

The Moro & Ortona
6 December 1943 - 4 January 1944

hrs on the 6th. The Pats furiously fought back as tanks from the 44th Royal Tank Regiment struggled to cross in support. Eight finally made it by noon.

When the Panzer Grenadiers resumed their attacks in the early afternoon the PPCLI and 44 RTR were ready. After a savage battle against a strong tank supported battalion Cameron Ware's mixed force prevailed. At a cost of 70 casualties and two tanks the PPCLI/RTR combo had accounted for some 100 dead, five Mark IV tanks and taken 40 prisoners. It was a fine victory with honours equally shared by the Canadian infantry and British tankers. Unfortunately, in one of those maddening quirks which so often result from the fog of war, the victory was to be negated by a mistaken engineer and command decision.

While the Villa Rogatti battle raged the Hasty Ps took a second crack at the coastal crossing. Two companies got across but both were pinned down under heavy fire as radio communications failed - again! With half his rifle strength trapped on the far bank Major Bert Kennedy the acting CO led his two remaining companies across in relief. Against strong opposition and under a hail of fire the Eastern Ontarians somehow succeeded in carving out a perilous bridgehead by last light. When supporting tanks were unable to cross the Moro the Hasty Ps manhandled two of their own six-pounders over. Like the US Cavalry in an old movie they arrived just in time to help beat back a German tank supported attack. The Hastings and Prince Edwards endured a night of horror under constant fire but by dawn's early light they still held on, albeit in a precarious position.

Vokes now decided to exploit the PPCLI's success by shifting his attack to the Villa Rogatti bridgehead. At this critical juncture, for one of the very few times, Geoff Walsh's engineers let Vokes down. Their dangerous riverbank reconnaissance revealed that bridging was not possible at either of the existing bridgeheads - only at the failed

THE ITALIAN CAMPAIGN

San Leonardo site. Reluctantly Vokes switched his emphasis back to the coast. This meant he had to give up his advance from the west on Ortona with the grain of the land in favor of a frontal advance against it. Accordingly he turned over his Rogatti bridgehead to the 8th Indian Division and moved to the east. The Indians promptly succeeded in bridging the Moro but it was too late for Vokes to turn back. His new plan called for a two- phase attack. In Phase 1 the RCR would attack west out of the Hast PER bridgehead to take San Leonardo while the 48th Highlanders would cross the Moro to La Torre to the west of Leonardo. In Phase 2 the 2nd Brigade would attack out of the newly enlarged bridgehead and seize road junction Cider.

Phase 1 opened at 1530 hrs on 8 December with a massive artillery bombardment. At 1630 hrs H Hour launched the infantry out of the bridgehead and across the Moro. In the west the 48th were totally successful and by last light had captured La Torre. The RCR were not so lucky as their advance took them across the front of a German battalion. Half way to San Leonardo their lead company was decimated by the deadly German mortar fire which the second company swung to avoid and got lost in the tangled vineyards. The two follow-up companies were soon hit by heavy fire and a tank supported counter-attack. The Royals with strong artillery cover consolidated on a small knoll, known afterwards in regimental annals as "Slaughterhouse Hill", and dug in as they awaited the desperately needed tank support. The raging Moro was the problem.

To this end the divisional engineers, under constant fire, labored through the night. Here a bulldozer operator, Sapper McNaughton, became the second Canadian "denied VC" of the Italian Campaign. Working under heavy fire McNaughton took matters into his own hands. Grabbing his rifle he jumped off the dozer crossed the river, engaged the enemy and returned with two prisoners. He remounted the dozer and finished the job. Recommended for the VC he received only an MM - good but not good enough. Thanks to his and his colleagues' efforts a crossing was opened by 0600 hrs, just in time to get a squadron of Calgary Tanks across.

The Calgary's squadron commander, Major Ned Amy, was given a company of Seaforths and told to take San Leonardo. Amy did just that. Under intense fire his battle group charged on, losing three tanks and two infantry sections en route, and crashed into San Leonardo. The town was taken in large part due to the heroism of a Seaforth subaltern, Lt J. McLean, who led his platoon in a wild sweep of the town, killing eight and capturing 18. McLean was awarded the DSO, a rarity for a subaltern and for this reason highly prized. But while a subaltern with a DSO means an "almost VC", if he survives and becomes, say, a major it becomes just another good gong - something awarded to senior officers for much lesser, and for generals often no, dangerous deeds. San Leonardo had fallen now it had to be held in the face of fierce enemy tank-backed counter-attacks. With only four tanks and 40 surviving infantrymen Amy was equal to the task. Two enemy tanks and many Germans were knocked out and the enemy grudgingly withdrew leaving the Canadians masters of the battlefield.

Once again things were a lot more dicey in the Hasty P's tenuous bridgehead. Of the four RCR companies sent across, one had been virtually destroyed, one had been withdrawn back over the Moro and one had been sent to reinforce the Seaforths in San Leonardo. "A" Company alone, with really just one platoon in position, held "Slaughterhouse Hill" when the enemy struck. Holding a two story stone house this single platoon, under Lt Mitch Sterlin, fought an incredible battle against all odds.

GAUDEAMUS IGITUR

When it ended at least 30 German bodies - many killed by Sterlin's sergeant - littered the battlefield. With their ammunition gone Sterlin led his platoon back into friendly lines. Both Sterlin and his platoon sergeant, R. W. Menzies, deserved VCs. Not surprisingly they got nothing, although two mortarmen who aided them from outside received MMs.

While Sterlin was performing heroics on Slaughterhouse Hill the Hasty Ps were winning their own glories back in their bridgehead. Again and again the Ontario farmboys met and repulsed vicious enemy attacks. When the Germans finally gave up and withdrew they left behind some 175 dead and fifty prisoners. And the Hastings and Prince Edwards solidified their reputation as one of the world's premier infantry battalions.

The battered 90th Panzer Grenadiers withdrew to a new defensive line. And the German 10th Army now knew that they were in for a real fight on the Adriatic. To deny Ortona to the Canadians they ordered the vaunted 1st Parachute Division into the line. The next act - the battle for the Gully was about to unfold.

The Gully

Just south of the Ortona - Orsogna road a deep, narrow gully runs inland from the coast some three miles. The Gully, as it came to be called, provided the enemy with a natural defensive position. A vine-covered ridge on its south side was dubbed Vino Ridge. The road junction nick-named Cider lay on the north side, opposite Vino Ridge. Vokes called on 2nd Brigade to capture Cider and Vino Ridge.

Second Brigade's plan was for the Loyal Edmontons and Calgary Tanks to first seize Cider Junction and for the Princess Pats to then capture Vino Ridge. The Loyals advanced from San Leonardo at 0900 hrs on 10 December in wet, dripping weather behind a thunderous artillery barrage. At 1300 hrs the Eddies reported Cider was theirs. Unfortunately it was not - they had become misdirected and were far from their objective. The Patricia's CO, Cameron Ware, clearly saw this error but Brigade HQ did not and over Ware's vociferous objections ordered the Patricias to clear Vino Ridge. The result was a foregone disaster. Taken in flank and rear by murderous fire Ware's battalion was soon badly shot up and the attack failed. The Patricia's colonel was livid.

Maj Gen Vokes stayed with his plan to capture Cider and advance north. He opened his second attempt on 11 December again with 2nd Brigade. It also failed despite the fact that Hoffmeister committed all three of his battalions. Vokes then ordered up 3rd Brigade who were still weary from their three weeks fighting on the Upper Sangro. The West Novas were directed on Casa Berardi, a three story stone farmhouse west of Cider crossroads. The West Novas attacked at 1800hrs and reached near the edge of The Gully where they dug in for the night. Before they were able to advance the next morning they were hit with a series of strong counter-attacks. The West Novas held firm but suffered 60 casualties including their CO. They were unable to advance further and 12 December ended with Cider still in enemy hands. Vokes tried again.

At 0600 hrs on the 13th the Carleton and Yorks attacked behind a strong barrage but after some initial successes, including the capture of 20 tough paratroopers, they too were halted. One company advanced too far across the Gully and was cut off. All rescue attempts failed and after nine hours of heroic resistance the remnants of the company, out of ammunition and reduced to platoon strength, were forced to surrender. It was a most bitter pill.

THE ITALIAN CAMPAIGN

Meanwhile a series of probing attacks to the northwest achieved considerable success - knocking out three tanks and capturing 100 enemy. A tenuous start line was also secured for an advance on Casa Berardi. The next attack would be made by the R22er, as yet not committed beyond the Moro. As the Van Doos moved into their Assembly Area the remainder of the badly mauled 90th Panzer Grenadiers were relieved by the elite 1st Paras - the Quebecers were to have a real fight on their hands.

The R22er attacked at dawn on 14 December behind a massive artillery barrage and supported by a half-squadron of Ontario Tanks. The battalion advanced across The Gully in a classic two-up formation with "C" and "D" companies in the van. The Canadiens, leaning closely on the barrage, smartly crossed The Gully taking 30 prisoners in the process. However, in the cold pre-dawn twilight, "D" Company took a wrong turn and effectively took itself out of the battle. Captain Paul Triquet's "C" Company was now on its own, its strength reduced from 80 to 50. The supporting Ontario tanks had not yet arrived when "C" Company bumped a German tank. Unsupported but undaunted Sgt JP Rousseau coolly dispatched the tank with a well directed PIAT for which he won a well-earned MM.

The Ontario's tanks, led by Maj HA Smith, now rumbled onto the scene where one was promptly knocked out. Their dander up the Ontarios quickly brewed up four enemy tanks in return. Then, as the advance continued, they knocked out three more Mark IIIs and IVs for a loss of two of their own. Triquet's company was still a mile from its Casa Berardi objective and he was now down to 30 men. As shellfire smashed around him he reorganized the remainder of his company into two small platoons, each under a sergeant, and pushed doggedly on. Triquet was a man possessed. His superb courage, leadership, determination and constant upbeat encouragement kept his rapidly dwindling force going in what appeared to be an impossibly mad endeavour. Pinned down 200 yards short of the objective and now reduced to four tanks and 14 men Triquet led a wild charge which, against all odds, somehow reached and breached the Casa. Les Canadiens made short work of the defending paratroops as Smith's tanks worked up losing one and getting one in return.

By 1530 hrs, after a perilous, hair-raising, eight hour advance through Hell, Casa Berardi was in Canadian hands. With his handful of men and tanks Triquet organized his defence - going everywhere, siting weapons and encouraging his gallant few. It was only after dark that the rest of the Van Doos arrived in his relief. For his unbelievable valour Triquet won a very well merited Victoria Cross. But the Van Doos were now isolated and Cider was still far away. Attempts at a link-up by the PPCLI and Hasty Ps again failed and the Carleton and Yorks were stopped short of The Gully. The remnants of the West Novas, now just 175 strong, made another desperate, tank supported, attempt on The Gully and were virtually wiped out.

Maj Gen Vokes was now under intense pressure from Corps and Army to get going and take Ortona. Such exhortations were all very fine and large to trumpet from the safety and comparative dry comfort of headquarters far in the rear but quite another story to Vokes on the rain-lashed spot with his entire force committed and no worthwhile reserves to conjure up. But if anyone could pull it off it would be Vokes who devised yet another plan to break the deadlock by attacking with 1st Brigade in two phases. Phase One, code-named "Morning Glory", called on the 48th to advance across The Gully and capture Villa Grande. In Phase Two, code-named "Orange Blossom", the RCR would pass through to take Cider crossroads.

GAUDEAMUS IGITUR

Behind a beautifully planned, pre-registered, barrage "Morning Glory" kicked-off at 0800 hrs on 18 December. Leaning close onto their barrage the Highlanders with a squadron of Three Rivers tanks ploughed on through thick mud to reach their objective inside of 20 minutes. At a cost of 25 of their own casualties the Canadians killed most of the defenders and captured 25 more. "Morning Glory" was a brilliant success and a text-book example of infantry-tank-artillery cooperation. Alas, "Orange Blossom" would be quite another story and a very bitter one.

For starters, the artillery had been unable to pre-register their "Orange Blossom" targets and had to engage with predicted fire from maps which turned out to have a whopping 500 yard grid error. Consequently when the attack started at 1145 hrs friendly fire blasted our own troops and left the enemy comparatively unscathed. The paratroop machine gunners made the most of their good fortune. The lead RCR companies suffered over 100 casualties - including all of the company and platoon commanders. One who died was young Lt Sterlin the unrewarded hero of Slaughterhouse Hill. The remnants of another company ended up commanded by a corporal, Red Forrest, who won a well earned DCM. Even the acting CO, Maj W. Mathers, was wounded and was replaced by Maj I. Hodson who was so wracked with malaria and jaundice that he too should have been evacuated. But no such luck. The acting brigade commander, Lt Col D. Spry, ordered the RCR to mount a fresh attack in the morning.

This time the gunners had the time and observation posts to pre-register their targets. Behind an excellent barrage two weak companies of RCR, under Maj Strome Galloway, surged forward at mid-morning on 19 December supported by Three Rivers tanks. By 1630 hrs Cider was theirs. The Royals, now down to 200 effectives, held the crossroads, although much trench and house clearing would continue for several days. But the road to Ortona had now been pried open.

Ortona

There are a few place names which to Canadians, indeed to the informed public, conjure up images of the ultimate overcoming of incredible odds and the horrors of shot, shell, mud and blood to achieve victory. Vimy, Ypres, Passchendaele, D-Day, Falaise and the Hochwald are members of this select company. Ortona is another, although few thought of such a ranking when the 1st Canadian Division stood poised to take the town following its grim victories on the Moro and Gully in late December 1943.(11)

The Ortona of that era was a small Adriatic port dominated by the Cathedral of San Tommaso plus an ancient cliff-top castle and a minor artificial harbour formed by breakwaters. The principal entry to the town square, the Piazza Municipale, was the Corso Vittorio Emanuele - a continuation of Highway 16. As the Canadians approached the Germans demolished the harbour, sealed off the side streets and channeled attackers into the Piazza Municipale which they had turned into a killing ground.

Second Brigade started its advance at noon on 20 December. The Loyal Edmontons, supported by Three Rivers tanks, Sask LI machine gunners and the 17 pounders of the 90th Anti-tank Battery closed up to the town's outskirts where they came under fire and dug in for the night. The Loyal Eddies, due to losses from previous battles and a lack of reinforcements, were now reduced to three companies of 60 men each instead of the established four companies each of 130 - a severe handicap at the outset of a major

THE ITALIAN CAMPAIGN

battle.

Two battalions of very tough and determined German paratroops had turned Ortona into one vast fortress liberally interspersed with prepared killing zones. Stone houses were turned either into blockhouses or mini-Martello Towers - almost impervious to fire from the front but, if taken, vulnerable to German fire from the rear. Others were heavily mined or booby-trapped. Anti-tank and machine guns dominated every approach and concealed ways were constructed to enable the paratroops to infiltrate into the rear of an advancing enemy. Tank approaches were clogged with rubble.

To counter this the Canadians literally wrote the book on street fighting as they went. They sub-divided the town into company and platoon objectives - sometimes just one house, parts of which the platoon would, in turn, allocate to sections. Eschewing roads and open killing grounds the Eddies, soon to be joined by the Seaforths, worked from house to house, mouse-holing(12) or breaking through the clay-tile roofs or upstairs windows. Liberal use was made of grenades, explosives, 2 inch mortars (fired at close range into windows or breaches in walls) and PIATs. The Sask LI heavy mortars were invaluable as were the anti-tank guns, especially in breaching, or demolishing, stone buildings.

Using such tactics the troops advanced methodically into town and by last light on the 21st were within 500 yards of the central Piazza Municipale. Patrols that night reported that the Corso Vittorio Emanuele was clear for 300 yards. Using this information Major Jim Stone proposed sending the Three Rivers tanks at speed straight down the road with claxtons blaring and all guns firing. The gambit, early on the 22nd, almost worked but failed when the lead tank overcautiously halted at a rubble barrier causing the drive to lose its momentum and enabling the Germans to recover their poise. By such narrow margins are the prospects of quick victories won or lost. Stone's infantry then took over and fought their way to the central plaza as darkness came. At this juncture the Seaforths came up and the two battalions divided the town between them along the Vittorio Emanuele road.

The two western battalions slowly but inexorably fought through the battered town, house by house, road block by road block, with some welcome pauses. The Eddies celebrated Christmas dinner in relays near battalion headquarters while the Seaforths did so in somewhat better style by using the Santa Maria church. War returned with a vengeance on Boxing Day when the Germans blew up an entire platoon of Loyal Eddies in a booby-trapped house. Only one man survived and he lay buried in rubble for three days. The Eddies retaliated by blowing up perhaps 50 Germans in another building as the savage company and platoon fighting raged on.

Suddenly on 28 December it was all over, the Germans had withdrawn during the night, leaving over 100 of their dead behind. The week's fighting had cost the Edmontons and Seaforths 275 casualties which represented half of their available combat strength. It had been a magnificent but costly and somber victory.(13) Ironically it was a battle that neither side wished to fight. The Canadians, for their part, expected the city to fall once its approaches had been cleared in the bloody Moro and Gully battles. While Kesselring, the German CinC, stated, "we do not want to defend Ortona decisively, but the English have made it as important as Rome...you can do nothing when things develop in this manner; it is only too bad that...the world press makes so much of it."(14)

While the world's attention was focused on Ortona the rest of the division, led by 1st

GAUDEAMUS IGITUR

Brigade, was trying to outflank and cut off the city from the west. The acting brigade commander, Colonel Dan Spry, called on the Hastings and Prince Edwards to establish a firm base along the Tollo road through which the 48th Highlanders would advance to capture San Nicola and San Tommaso. The RCR would take over and push to the Adriatic coast.

The Hasty Ps jumped off, in a driving rain, at 0930 hrs on 23 December behind a strong barrage but with their supporting tanks bogged behind in the mud. The battalion was initially repulsed but finally joined by the Ontario's tanks they took their objective by dark, although it took another 12 hours to winkle out infiltrating paratroopers and establish a firm base. The 48th passed through on a hair raising night advance which netted them a dozen enemy prisoners. To the relief of everyone dawn found them exactly on their first objective. The woefully under strength RCR now tried to pass through but failed. As 2nd Brigade observed a brief respite within Ortona the three battalions of 1st Brigade endured a miserable Christmas Day stuck in the mud and under constant fire west of the town.

The 48th, in particular, were in dire straits with the Germans trying to encircle and eliminate them and re-supply almost stopped. Early on Boxing Day the Germans commenced their attacks. Three times they hit the 48th and three times they were driven back. Just when things looked blackest three Ontario Shermans squelched up and turned the tide. It was now the turn of the 48th to strike back. The Highlanders drove the enemy, who left 100 dead and prisoners behind, to San Nicola and San Tommaso where they consolidated on their final objective.

It was now the turn of 3rd Brigade. It took Major Allard's R22er until 30 December and three attempts to capture the high ground along the Riccio north of San Tommaso. The Carleton and Yorks in turn waged a grim three day, see-saw battle for Point 59 on the coast. It finally fell when the enemy withdrew from Ortona. With its fall the bitter campaign for Ortona and the coast finally came to its bloody conclusion.

The battle continuum from Moro to Ortona had cost the Canadians 2400 battle casualties and 1600 sick. High figures in themselves but higher still when noting that most of the casualties fell on the poor bloody infantry and mostly on the rifle companies at that. Since the rifle companies at Ortona had a maximum strength of 100 each and there are 36 of these in a division the crippling effect of these casualties becomes a stark reality. As Maj Gen Vokes pointed out it would take months to rebuild the division to its former superlative state. The absorption and integration of reinforcements, always inadequate in numbers and usually in training, can only be effectively accomplished out of action.(15) And this would be the division's principal task until spring came north again and with it a new campaign.

Meanwhile the Canadians could take pride in a job extremely well done. In his farewell to the 8th Army General Montgomery, referring to the six months since the opening of Husky, stated, "We have been successful in everything we have undertaken." And Maj Gen Vokes, referring specifically to the just concluded Ortona battles could justly claim, "We smashed the 90th Panzer Grenadier Division and we gave the 1st German Parachute Division a mauling which it will long remember."(16) Of all five divisions which had launched Montgomery's "colossal crack" in November only the Canadians had succeeded. The 78th stalled on the Sangro, the 2nd New Zealand and 8th Indian failed at Orsogna and the 5th British made only limited gains. The Canadians alone, after a terrible fight, emerged triumphant at Ortona.

THE ITALIAN CAMPAIGN

CHAPTER VI

FROM WINTER TO DIADEM

I have a rendezvous with Death
When spring comes north again this year
And to mine own self I am true
I shall not fail that rendevous

Alan Seeger   *I have a rendezvous...*

The Interregnum

Following Ortona the winter period was anti-climactic and miserable. Bad weather virtually halted all operations on the Adriatic front, but there was still some tidying up to do. On 4 January 1944 the Carleton and Yorks, who had earlier been repulsed at Point 59 above Ortona, gained sweet revenge on the German paras. By Point 59 the Germans had established two heavily armed and protected strong points. Behind a powerful bombardment the C&Ys attacked and completely routed the enemy, capturing the positions and killing over 40 paratroops.

On 12 January the 11th Infantry Brigade of the newly arrived 5th Armoured Division relieved the veteran 3rd Brigade on the Adriatic. In order to distract attention from the forthcoming Anzio landings 11 Brigade was directed to take the high ground east of the River Arielli, without incurring heavy casualties - a rather strange caveat. The Perth Regiment went in first at 0545 hrs on 17 January and immediately came a cropper as they advanced straight into a valley that had been carefully pre-registered by the enemy artillery. Only one platoon, under Lt R. Chamberlain, got onto the objective and no one seems to have known he was there. Accordingly the 11 Brigade commander, Brigadier George Kitching, launched the Cape Breton Highlanders at 1345 hrs. The Cape Bretons had just made it into a river in the valley when the enemy opened up. The Highlanders were repulsed and were withdrawn, along with the Perths, after dark. For this bloody and unnecessary operation the Perths had 137 casualties, 47 fatal. The Cape Bretons lost another 46. The Germans reported total casualties of 63.

On 30 January, their second last day under Lt Gen Allfrey's V Corps, the Hastings and Prince Edwards were committed again to clear the high ground between the Riccio and Arielli. Successive attacks on the 30th and 31st cost over 90 casualties and accomplished nothing. Thereafter the Adriatic front degenerated into a cold, sodden, sector in which harrowing patrolling became the principal activity. Determined to "dominate no-man's land" and "keep the troops on their toes"(1) Corps Headquarters prescribed a strong patrolling policy. Much of it accomplished nothing apart from the numbing fatigue of the few sharp- end troops intimately involved. There were just enough successes to convince the staffs of the wisdom of their policy. The Carleton and Yorks, Van Doos and Cape Bretons all staged raids which netted prisoners and the Bretons, in turn, annihilated a 40 man German patrol leaving 17 casualties behind. The Germans retrieved their dead and wounded under a white flag by agreement with a Canadian sergeant who loaned the Germans stretchers and morphine. True to their word the

GAUDEAMUS IGITUR

Germans returned the stretchers and morphine under another white flag along with a gift of schnapps. On another occasion a single mortar bomb hit a group of men assembled for dinner on a seemingly safe reverse slope, killing or wounding nearly 40. But for most front-line soldiers in was just a cold, dreary, nerve-wracking winter.

On the wider canvas, while the 8th Army bogged on the Adriatic, Mark Clark's 5th stalled west of the Apennines. After establishing a bridgehead over the Garigliano, the 5th was repulsed at San Ambrogio and San Angelo (Bloody River). Offensive operations then came to a squishing halt.

Preparing for Spring

At a series of conferences (Teheran and Cairo in November/December, 1943), cables and indiscrete trans-Atlantic telephone calls, Churchill pressed his case for continued emphasis on Italy against unimpressed Americans who remained fixated on the coming "Overlord". It was finally agreed that, in January 1944, there would be a new amphibious landing, code-named "Shingle", at Anzio below Rome.(2) Clark's 5th Army would then smash the Gustav Line at Cassino, link-up with Anzio and capture Rome. The 8th Army would remain on the Adriatic.

For the Canadians 1 February saw I Canadian Corps become operational on the Adriatic under Lt Gen Harry Crerar. The Corps' activation was marked by those petty animosities which seem to afflict persons in high places. In short order Crerar managed to antagonize both Montgomery, his superior, and Simonds, his subordinate and Monty's protege, who was the newly-appointed commander of 5th Armoured Division. The equipping of both Corps Headquarters and 5th Armoured had proceeded most slowly and bumpily in the face of the apathy and surly foot-dragging of British commanders and the ongoing Crerar - Simonds feud. Crerar also did little to endear himself with either the First Division or its commander Chris Vokes by his insistence on petty dress regulations and spit and polish under less than ideal conditions.

The winter of 1943/44 witnessed a large number of other command changes. General Eisenhower left for England to command the Allied Expeditionary Force for "Overlord". He was succeeded by British General Sir Henry Maitland Wilson with US General Devers as his deputy. Monty also departed to command 21 Army Group for the invasion of France. He was succeeded at 8th Army by Sir Oliver Leese. Crerar and Simonds would both soon follow Montgomery - Crerar to command the 1st Canadian Army and Simonds the II Canadian Corps. Crerar's operational command of I Corps would thereby be limited to 36 days.

In the ensuing rapid shuffles Simonds was succeeded at 5th Armoured by Lt Gen ELM Burns who within seven weeks would take over the Ist Canadian Corps from Crerar. At first blush the choice of Burns to command the Canadian Corps seems ill considered - an opinion still held by a number of Canadian historians. He was certainly an unloved, dour, humourless, meticulous, intellectual introvert in stark contrast to his extroverted off-the-cuff British colleagues of the Desert Army old boys club. He was disliked by the gruff, blunt, thrusting Chris Vokes and by the veteran 1st Division whose members viewed with coolness his lack of combat command experience and personal warmth (a characteristic which, unlike Leese, he did not try to fake). And he commanded a corps headquarters and armoured division which the British generals had not wanted in the first place and were ungracious in having thrust upon them. He thus did not form close relationships with either his subordinate Canadian generals or British superiors and peers. He would therefore be starting his command with two strikes against him. The fact that, despite this, he would lead his corps to two great victories is all the more to his credit.

Other changes saw newly promoted Maj Gen Bert Hoffmeister assume command of the Fifth Armoured Division, finally bringing stability of command to that fine formation. Second Brigade went to G. Gibson, the Third to P. Bernatchez, Eleventh to E. Snow and First Armoured to W. Murphy as successor to Wyman who left for Northwest Europe. Several battalions also received new commanding officers.

On the battlefield things went from bad to worse for the Allies. Three major attacks were made on Cassino - all failed. On 22 January the US 6th Corps landed with high expectations at Anzio, the birthplace of Nero and site of the Apollo Belvedere, and promptly succeeded in getting itself bottled up by the Germans and would remain so until May. Churchill with his gift for trenchant prose decried an Anzio that was expected to become a wildcat tearing at the German belly, "Instead we have stranded a vast whale with its tail flopping about in the water."(3)

Meanwhile Alexander, or rather his brilliant COS Sir John Harding, was planning a new major attack to break the Gustav and Hitler Lines and capture Rome. This involved shortening 5th Army's front to some 15 miles from the coast and moving most of 8th Army over the Apennines to the Liri Valley, on the 5th's right flank, as the main striking force for the attack. The operation, code-named "Diadem", was scheduled for 10 May 1944 to preclude the withdrawal of German forces to face the coming invasion of Northwest Europe. The Canadian Corps would initially be held in reserve to exploit the expected breakthrough --in a role somewhat analogous to that of X Corps at Alamein.

Operation Diadem

While 11 Brigade and the Westminsters of 5th Armoured Division endured an exhausting and frigid month long tour of duty in the line near Cassino under New Zealand command, most of the Canadian Corps was concentrated in the Liri Valley. A comprehensive deception plan to mask the Canadians' move was successful as the Germans misidentified the location of both divisions. The 8th Army concentrated an enormous force about the Liri Valley - II Polish Corps at Cassino, the huge XIII Corps in the valley and the Canadian Corps in reserve. The force was backed by 1200 field and medium guns, nearly one-third more than were employed on a similar front at Alamein. While 8th Army attacked at the Liri, Clark's 5th would strike through the mountains to the south with the Corps Expeditionnaire Francais (CEF)(4) and his VI corps would break out from Anzio.

H Hour for the 8th Army's attack was 2300 hrs on 11 May 1944. Following a thunderous artillery barrage XIII Corps surged over the Gari River and into the Gustav Line. The battle for Rome was underway.

Although the Canadian Corps was held in reserve for exploitation its 1st Armoured Brigade was heavily engaged from the outset in support of 8th Indian Division. Due to yet another silly personality clash between senior officers - this time between Maj Gen Vokes and Brig Wyman of 1 CAB before the latter's departure- the Canadian Armoured Brigade would only occasionally serve with other Canadian formations thereafter. Instead the Canadians would be supported by British armour while the Canadian brigade would brilliantly support other formations of the 8th Army. Frequently the Canadians would be served by the British 25th Army Tank Brigade which added a white maple leaf to its black diablo formation sign in commemoration of the association. They, and later the 21st Tank Brigade, were to prove worthy successors to the Canadian tankers.

In the initial assault on the Gustav Line the Canadian armoured brigade, following a tricky crossing of the Gari River, performed extremely well. The Ontario Regiment decisively aided in the capture of Sant' Angelo in Teodice, an action fierce enough to be selected as one of the unit's ten principal battle honours. The Calgary Tanks captured Panaccioni along with a German headquarters and 125 prisoners. While the Three Rivers Regiment distinguished itself in the capture of Pignataro - an action which precipitated the German withdrawal to the Hitler Line. Following the Gari battles General Leese called the Canadian Brigade, "the best armoured formation in the Mediterranean" - a well merited encomium indeed.

While fierce battles raged along the Gustav Line the Corps Expeditionnaire Francais achieved spectacular successes to the south. Moving swiftly through the mountains against light German opposition the CEF, along with 5th Army advances on the coast, threatened the entire German 10th Army. The French success showed what could be achieved by doing the imaginative and unexpected instead of the plodding and predictable. In two days the CEF, with very light casualties, achieved more than had three major battles of attrition at Cassino or the sanguinary 5th Army battles on the Rapido.

8th Army hurried to exploit these developments by entering into the next phase of the Liri battles. On 13 May I Canadian Corps was moved to the south of the valley and with XIII Corps prepared to break the Hitler Line.

The Hitler Line

On 16 May the 1st Canadian Infantry Brigade passed through the 8th Indian Division near Pignataro with the RCR on the left and the Hastings and Prince Edwards on the right. Both units found the going very difficult and slow. The Royals took Point 59 and 50 prisoners but came under intense fire and suffered 56 casualties. Sir Oliver Leese, under the mistaken impression that the Canadians were being unnecessarily held up by only light opposition, voiced his opinion to Lt Gen Burns and ordered a more determined effort on the morrow. Burns, somewhat hastily, passed these comments on to Vokes who was infuriated that the Corps Commander had not first ascertained the facts. Burns has been roundly criticized for merely post-officing Leese's criticisms. But part of the problem rested with Vokes and his staff who failed to formulate and transmit sound and timely SITREPs (Situation Reports) to enable Burns to properly assess the situation and, in turn, keep his superior informed.

On the 17th Vokes inserted 3rd Brigade into the line on the right of the 1st. The R22er, supported by TRR tanks, made excellent progress and took 120 prisoners. On the debit side seven Three Rivers tanks were disabled by mines and others were bogged. The West Novas and Carleton and Yorks then took over and by last light had established a strong bridgehead over the Forme d'Aquino. Eschewing his headquarters Brigadier Bernatchez, taking a leaf from the German book, commanded from the front and was thus able to take advantage of the fluid situation. On his left 1st Brigade had difficulty against fresh Panzer Grenadiers but also crossed the Forme. Here the 48th Highlanders distinguished themselves in savage night fighting. Their Anti-Tank Platoon

THE ITALIAN CAMPAIGN

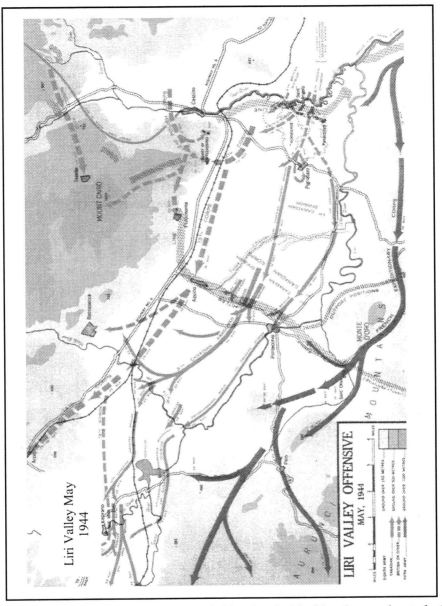

Liri Valley May 1944

LIRI VALLEY OFFENSIVE
MAY, 1944

skillfully knocked out two SPs crossing a bridge thereby blocking the crossing to further armour while their machine gunners blasted the enemy infantry. The next day both Canadian brigades closed up to the Hitler Line itself.

Since intelligence indicated that the Hitler Line was as yet only lightly manned 3rd Brigade was ordered to try and bounce the line. Bernatchez ordered the R22er to do the job but with limited support as most of the corps artillery was then committed to British forces. The Van Doos attacked at 0630 hrs on 19 May in a dense fog which maddeningly lifted an hour later exposing the troops, who were now in the open, to terrible fire. Fifty-seven Van Doos fell as the attack stalled. On the right flank the British 78th Division also failed. A proper set-piece attack was now required.

Sir Oliver Leese issued his directive for the breaking of the Hitler Line on 20 May. On the right XIII Corps would attack between Aquino and Piedmonte. The Canadian Corps on the left would break the line centered on Pontecorvo and exploit north-west to the Melfa River. D-Day for the attack, code named "Chesterfield", was 23 May 1944. The Canadians would thus have two days to make ready. Meanwhile events were moving fast and furious on either side. Alarmed by the rapid advance of the French and the breaking of the Gustav Line the Germans at last withdrew from Cassino on the 19th with the Poles occupying the monastery and the British the town. On the 20th the CEF reached the vicinity of Pontecorvo.

Maj Gen Vokes had reason to hope that this flanking pressure would loosen German resolve along the Liri. But resolve was something the Germans had in full measure and the Hitler Line defences in this sector were extraordinarily strong. The defences were covered by an effective anti-tank ditch and massive barbed wire entanglements liberally interspersed with anti-tank and anti-personnel mines. The main position was based on mutually supporting concrete bunkers backed by dismounted tank turrets (eight on the 1st Division's sector) called *Panzerturm*, housing 75mm guns, MGs and rocket projectors. Self-propelled guns and the superb German artillery and mortars supported the whole.

Vokes' original plan called for a one brigade (the 2nd) assault on a 2000 yard front from Pontecorvo north. The attack would be supported by two British tank regiments and 800 field and medium guns. After endorsing the plan, Lt Gen Burns was overruled by Gen Leese who insisted that the front be widened. Burns, already in Vokes' bad books for his previous post-officing of Leese's wishes, got his reluctant subordinate to widen the assault front by 1000 yards and put 3rd Brigade on the left of 2nd. It was to be a most fortunate decision, for which Leese deserved full marks. Meanwhile, as in Ecclesiastes, time and chance again happened to all. Several successful patrols, and especially a reconnaissance-in-force by the PLDG which netted 20 prisoners, convinced Vokes to attempt something else. Prior to Chesterfield he would try to bounce the line below Pontecorvo and, if successful, exploit from there.

The bounce attack, undertaken by the 48th Highlanders and 142nd Royal Tanks supported by maximum artillery, was twice delayed and finally got underway at 1030 hrs on 22 May. The attack succeeded in penetrating the line, initially with light casualties. The 142nd then lost three tanks to a single *panzerturm* which was itself destroyed at a mile range by a 17 pounder of the 1st Canadian Anti-Tanks. Extensive minefields prevented the British tanks from joining the 48th, who now held a precarious bridgehead surrounded by the enemy on three sides. Meanwhile the redoubtable Plugs almost did it again. At 0700 hrs, supported by tanks of the 142nd, they broke 400 yards into the line and captured 60 prisoners before being stopped by the minefields which knocked out their tanks. It was now apparent that the bounce attempt had failed and Burns would have to re-apply Chesterfield.

Vokes' attempted bounce attack, an excellent idea despite its failure, meant that 2nd Brigade which had been moved in hopes of exploiting the 48th attack, now had to countermarch back and assault at dawn without time for adequate preparation or reconnaissance. As the CO PPCLI remarked it was a case of "order, counter-order, disorder."

THE ITALIAN CAMPAIGN

Breaking the Hitler Line

In one sense the breaking of the Hitler Line could be credited to Sir Oliver Leese. As noted before, it was due to his intervention that Maj Gen Vokes reluctantly widened his front and inserted 3rd Brigade on the left. And it was 3rd Brigade which decisively and magnificently won the day.

The attack opened with a creeping barrage(5) by the corps artillery at three minutes before H Hour - 0600 hrs on 23 May. The main Canadian effort was on the right, below Aquino, where the 2nd Brigade attacked two-up with the Seaforths left and the PPCLI, followed by the Loyal Edmontons, on the right. Both were supported by Churchill tanks of the North Irish Horse. On their right flank the British 78th Division was supposed to neutralize the enemy in Aquino. On the left of 1st Division the 3rd Brigade attacked with the Carleton and Yorks up and the West Novas following up. They were supported by the 51st Royal Tanks.

Eighth Army expected, and corps headquarters planned, that the 1st Canadian Division would punch through the Hitler Line and rapidly advance to the Pontecorvo - Route 6 road. Here 5th Armoured would pass through and exploit the break to the Melfa, Frosinone and beyond. Things did not work out quite as planned.

For starters the 78th Division, for whatever reason and there were many, failed to neutralize the enemy in Aquino who flanked the Canadian line of advance. Unaware of this the 2nd Brigade attack started well enough with both Patricias and Seaforths keeping close to the barrage and rapidly mopping up enemy pockets en route. Then things started to go bad. A thick oak woods separated the infantry from the barrage which ran on ahead. The woods also caused the companies to lose direction with the right hand company passing in front of the left. On leaving the woods they were taken in the flank by the unneutralized paratroops in Aquino and suffered severely. Then the North Irish Horse ran into an undiscovered minefield sited as a killing ground for the *panzerturm*. Stripped of tank support the Patricias were decimated by coordinated enemy fire and were unable to reach their objective. The Loyals followed too close behind the Patricias and soon were intermingled with them and trapped in the same hail of fire. The advance ground to a halt with the Eddies' CO among the casualties.

The Seaforths on the brigade left fared only marginally better. One company under Major J. Allan, after taking heavy casualties and seeing all its supporting tanks knocked out, actually reached the Pontecorvo - Aquino road. Allan collected the survivors of the other companies and dug-in east of the road. With only their PIATs and small arms they knocked out a *panzerturm,* an SP gun and numerous infantry. But no reinforcements or re-supply could get through to them and they were soon cut off.

The day was saved by the added-on 3rd Brigade on the left flank. Their lead battalion, the Carleton and York, unlike the unfortunate PPCLI and Seaforths, had been in position for several days and had thoroughly reconnoitered the enemy defences. As the assault began they leaned closely onto their barrage and were undeterred when their supporting armour brewed and fell behind. Within 75 minutes they had breached the Hitler Line and dug in on the Pontecorvo - Aquino road. By day's end they had killed scores of enemy and captured 200 at a cost of 62 casualties.

Reacting swiftly to the situation Maj Gen Vokes switched his main effort to the left. While Aquino was finally being neutralized by a Canadian generated and most uncommon "W" target,(6) the West Novas, R22eR and Three Rivers tanks would widen the breach and take the division's final objective - the Pontecorvo - Route 6 road. The West Novas and Three Rivers surged ahead and although the tanks were blocked by the San Martino gully the Maritimers secured their objective by last light. They then spent most of the evening beating off a succession of enemy counter-attacks. On their right the R22eR had a comparatively easy time in securing its objective and widening the breach.

While 3rd Brigade was performing its heroics the 1st set about relieving the gallant 48th who were isolated deep inside the Hitler Line near Pontecorvo. The indefatigable PLDGs started things by locating a lane through the minefields leading to the 48th. A squadron of the 142nd RTR then moved up reaching the beleaguered Highlanders that night. Thus reinforced the 48th attacked Point 106 but were repulsed with heavy casualties. Once more it fell to the Hastings and Prince Edwards to save the day. Starting at 1400 hrs one Hasty P company attacked via the route taken by the 48th while a second swung wide through gaps cut in the wire to catch the enemy flank. It went like clockwork Supported by the determined 142nd RTR, "B" and "D" companies slashed through wire, mines, shot and shell to relieve the 48th and secure their objective. "A" Company then charged through to capture Point 106. At a cost of only 30 casualties the Hasty Ps had killed or wounded 100 Germans and captured 300 more. Sgt J. Loshaw of "D" Company personally captured 19 enemy for which he won the MM. In the opinion of their IO, and later author, Farley Mowat it was "probably the most brilliant single action fought by the Regiment in the entire course of the war."(7) Given the number of superb actions which this gifted regiment fought Mowat's opinion is high encomium indeed. The Hitler Line had now been broken everywhere in the south half of the Canadian front.

Major General Vokes called the 3rd Brigade battle "the 1st Division's most outstanding tactical success in any single day of fighting in the war" and termed the Hitler Line "the best battle I ever fought or organized."(8) It was a sentiment shared by the Army Commander Sir Oliver Leese who generously wrote to Vokes, "I would like...to thank and congratulate you and all ranks of your great Division on your breach of the Adolph Hitler Line...Your attack was extremely well laid on, very well supported and brilliantly executed. Your Infantry attacked with that same dash and determination that I have grown always to expect of them since your first operations with me in Sicily. Your action played a decisive part in our initial victory. The Adolph Hitler Line will always be a worthy battle honour...of the 1st Canadian Division..."(9) But the great victory which virtually destroyed the enemy opposing them was bought at a terrible cost. In one day the division suffered 890 casualties of which 2nd Brigade took 543 - the largest single day's total by the Canadians in the entire Italian Campaign. In a magnificent supporting role the British 25th Army Tank Brigade lost 44 tanks.

While Vokes was rightly proud of the superb success of his division others were less charitable of the work of the British XIIIth and Canadian Corps in the Liri. Both Mark Clark of the 5th Army and Alphonse Juin of the highly successful CEF were critical of the 8th Army's ponderous move through the Liri and its slowness in organizing an attack on the Hitler Line.

Vokes in turn was critical of 8th Army's trying to squeeze two full corps into the narrow Liri Valley. He felt, probably rightly, that one corps could have handled the job much better, lessened the deadening congestion and prevented the Aquino fiasco. But if only one corps were used - which one? It would have been unthinkable for the Canadians not to share in this momentous battle and the British would have been loath to give the task to the newly arrived Canadian Corps Headquarters. For his part Lt Gen Burns, himself later to be the recipient of Oliver Leese's criticism, blamed Vokes' attempt to ad hoc with the failed left flanking attack by 1st Brigade resulting in 2nd Brigade being launched with inadequate preparations on the right. But this is hindsight and at the time a coup-de-main seemed like a very good idea.

With the Hitler Line broken, the way now lay open for the 5th Armoured Division to exploit to the Melfa and beyond. Meanwhile the Americans had finally broken out at Anzio and threatened to cut off the Germans from the rear. Speed by 5th Armoured was therefore of the essence.

The Melfa and the Road To Rome

This was 5th Armoureds first action as a division and its lack of battle experience was a factor in its slow getaway. The Corps' plan called for the 5th to pass through the 1st Division as soon as the Hitler Line had been breached. Fifth Division's 5th Armoured Brigade would lead to the Melfa where the division's 11th Lorried Infantry Brigade would pass through to Ceprano on Route 6. Since 1st Division had originally planned to break through with 2nd Brigade on the right Maj Gen Hoffmeister, GOC 5th Armoured, had positioned his troops accordingly. When, instead, 3rd Brigade's successful break-through on the left became the point of exploitation Hoffmeister had to hustle his division to the new front. This meant using new and unreconnoitered Assembly Areas, Forming-Up Places and Start Lines.(10) A more experienced formation may have planned beforehand for just such an eventuality. But even if it had, 5th Armoured's relocation was hampered by a heavy rain which turned the few tracks into quagmires and made vehicle movement a nightmare.

But even this was of secondary importance to the principal bugaboo of the Liri - traffic congestion. This was partly the fault of Burns and his inexperienced corps staff. In its hasty relocation 5th Armoured became entangled with the British 25th Tank Brigade which was trying to recover tanks and regroup after the Hitler Line battles. A more experienced staff would have had plans in place for just such a schemozzle. The green Ist Corps staff was caught off base. But while Burns would take steps to prevent a repetition, the other corps of 8th Army would continue to blunder in this vital matter.

However the principal culprit in the congestion fiasco was Oliver Leese and his supposedly experienced 8th Army staff. Sir Oliver decided to exploit the Hitler Line breakthrough with two corps, the XIIIth of two armoured and three infantry divisions and the Ist Canadian of one of each. Both corps were also supported, or at this stage encumbered, with independent armoured brigades and a plethora of corps' administrative and supply vehicles. Thus in a restricted area of only 25 square miles some 20,000 vehicles and countless foot soldiers were milling about, crossing and recrossing and creating monumental traffic jams at each. Leese and his minions made things even more difficult for the Canadians by allotting the only decent road, Route 6, to XIII Corps thus relegating the Canucks to churned-up, secondary tracks of doubtful utility. This in itself was understandable since only one corps could get Route 6 and XIII, due to its larger size, had as much need as anyone. But General Leese then compounded the problem by decreeing that, if need be, either corps could use roads and tracks in the other's sector. This informality may have been acceptable in Leese's desert experience where good going was seldom a problem and, to give the good general his due, may have been intended primarily to help the route-poor Canadians. But in the rain soaked, ground churned, Liri Valley it was madness without an elaborate traffic control system and organization. And in the Liri these were in very short supply. On at least two occasions British units passed into the Canadian sector generating king sized congestion and confusion.

With all these problems 5th Armoured, "The Mighty Maroon Machine" (so nicknamed from its maroon formation patches)(11) could not start until the morning of 24 May. Hoffmeister based his advance on two battle groups - the equivalent of the highly successful German *Kampfgruppen*. The dash to the Melfa would be led by the British Columbia Dragoons (BCD) and the Irish Regiment (IRC) under the BCD's commander Lt Col Fred Vokes the brother of Chris. Half way to the Melfa Vokes Force would be passed through by Griffin Force of Lt Col P.G. Griffin's Lord Strathcona's Horse (Ld SH) and the Westminster Regiment (WR(M)). The flanks would be covered by the division's reconnaissance regiment the Governor General's Horse Guards (GGHG).

Vokes Force made good going until mid-morning when it collided with the famed 1st Panzer Regiment equipped with superb 50 ton Panther tanks whose armour was almost impervious to the Sherman's short barreled 75s. Fortunately the operative word was "almost" for in the ensuing action the Dragoons and Irish, with great dash, destroyed three Panthers and an SP gun and captured 90 enemy paratroops. Vokes Force lost 33 men and four tanks.

Griffin Force then passed through and headed for the Melfa led by the Strath's Recce Troop under Lt Edward Perkins. Perkins' small command was mounted in three American M3 Stuart light tanks(12) from which, as often with recce units, the turrets had been removed to lower silhouette. Compensating for the missing turret guns was an arsenal of MGs, PIATs and Hawkins grenades. After an encounter with an enemy tank and half-track Perkins' force reached the Melfa and located a crossing. By mid-afternoon his 15 man troop had eliminated an enemy held farmhouse, captured eight paras and established a small bridgehead. Perkins sent the prisoners back with a guard which would double as guides for the following Straths and Westies.

Unfortunately the following Straths were not so lucky. They were spotted by a strong enemy tank, SP and infantry force and a furious tank battle ensued which raged until last light. When the battle ended the Strathconas and Westminsters were masters of the field but at a cost of 55 men and 17 tanks. The Germans lost 11 tanks, nine SP guns and 25 prisoners. They left 36 bodies on the battlefield.

While the tank battle raged the indomitable Perkins performed incredible deeds of reckless daring going here, there and everywhere - inspiring his men, organizing defences, repulsing enemy probes and desperately trying to get the main body forward. It was 1700hrs before reinforcements arrived in the form of a company of Westminsters who left their White scout cars on the far bank and waded across to Perkins' relief. The Westies company commander, Major J. Mahony, was a valorous clone of Perkins and quickly organized a fighting defence. In short order his force attacked and captured 20 Germans defending a fortified house, with a PIAT destroyed an SP gun and repulsed several counter-attacks. Against a tank supported probe they knocked out a second tank with small arms and grenades. A second Westminster company got across by night and the bridgehead was at last secure. For their valour Mahony was awarded the VC and Perkins a DSO, although he too clearly merited the higher decoration.(13)

The Germans were in difficulty and von Vietinghoff issued stern orders to hold the

THE ITALIAN CAMPAIGN

Melfa line. But things were disintegrating everywhere with the Americans half way to Valmontone. While XIII Corps was held up by strong defences at Aquino and maddening traffic jams the Canadian advance resulted in a dangerously exposed right flank. The GGHGs were assigned flank guard and did a super job - bluffing superior enemy armour into withdrawal and capturing 100 prisoners.

On 26 May the 11th Brigade of Perths, Cape Bretons and Irish took over the advance supported by tanks of the 8th Hussars. Against wicked rearguard actions and over appalling terrain the force reached Ceprano the next day, despite its tanks being immobilized for lack of fuel - a legacy of the suffocating traffic congestion. A collapsed Bailey bridge delayed crossing the river until the evening of the 28th and once rebuilt it was allocated to XIII Corps. So 5th Armoured once more had to relocate and spent the night getting over to a bridge on 1st Division's front.

Moving over terrible terrain the BCDs and Westminsters groped forward constantly having to recover tanks and the Westies' White Scout Cars (which had limited mobility in this poor area). By the time the Dragoons entered Pofi they had lost five tanks to enemy action and 20 to bogging down. While 11Brigade ground on to Ceccano the Strathconas fought a major engagement at Torrice Crossroads on Route 6. The 26th Panzer Division fought desperately to keep this vital crossing open while the rest of its corps withdrew. By last light, after a see-saw battle, the Straths secured the crossroads. They had knocked out four panzers and an SP gun for a loss of five Shermans. More ominously, they captured a Panther with its radio tuned to a Canadian frequency. It was a technique that the Germans used to great advantage throughout the war to gain on-the-spot details of Allied actions. And one whose effectiveness could have been markedly degraded had the Canadians made better use of aboriginal and other little known linguistic groups as radio operators. But, maddeningly and incomprehensibly, this simple countermeasure was seldom tried. Similarly, despite the large number of German speakers in the Canadian forces, we seldom attempted to emulate the tactic on the battlefield. More the pity!

Primarily because of the awful terrain Burns switched the 1st Infantry Division for the vehicle encumbered 5th Armoured on 30 May. The next day, after a sharp action, 2nd Brigade took the key centre of Frosinone. Ferentino fell to the RCR and Princess Louises on the 1st of June and Anagni was taken two days later. On that day contact was made with the Americans near Valmontone and with the French at Colleferro. This marked the end of the Diadem campaign for the Canadian Corps which was halted to allow the CEF to cover the 5th Army's flank for the drive on Rome.

Rome fell on 4 June, with the Canadian battalion of the joint Canada/USA Special Service Force in the vanguard of the liberating 5th Army. The Ist Canadian Corps went into reserve somewhat miffed at being halted and denied the "glory" of capturing the Eternal City which they felt had been well within their grasp. At the same time they were happy to be out of the fighting and still alive.

As it was, the capture of Rome was somewhat tainted when Mark Clark, in defiance of Alexander's orders, turned his Army into a race for Rome instead of penetrating inland to cut off the retreating German 10th Army. Perhaps most of the enemy would still have escaped but it was certainly a chance that should have been taken. Failure to do so spoke volumes on the egotistical modus-operandi of the various higher commanders of 18 Army Group. In any event the capture of Rome made news for only one day for on the 6th of June the long-awaited invasion of Northwest Europe began. The Italian campaign was thus permanently relegated to back-page news, even as further severe fighting loomed ahead.

Diadem Revisited

With the Gustav and Hitler lines broken and Rome captured the performance of I Canadian Corps came under scrutiny from within and without. All agreed that the performance of the Canadian combat troops had again been superb. First Division had broken the Hitler Line in one day and 5th Armoured had forced the Melfa in another. At a cost of 3368 casualties the Corps had, in two weeks, killed or captured several thousand enemy, broken two strong lines and advanced 45 straight line miles to within 25 of Rome. It had severely mauled three crack German divisions (26th Panzer, 90th Panzer Grenadier, 1st Parachute) plus other elements of the German LI Corps. For its size it had done wonders.

However the Corps' approach to the Hitler Line and its pursuit after the Melfa had sometimes been tentative and slow. Burns afterwards, in his systematic and thoughtful manner, put his finger on some of the major problems and, unlike most generals, did not exclude himself. Because it was the first full action for both Corps HQ and 5th Armoured their staff work was, inevitably, not up to par. In particular their obtaining, verifying and passing on information and situation reports (SITREPS) left much to be desired. Burns accepted responsibility for not going forward often enough and gingering, even driving, his subordinates harder. But this is a sometimes thing and commanders in Normandy, as we shall see, too often just gingered and exhorted without offering anything concrete to help things along - with predictable meager results.

Sometimes the errors were cumulative, as living examples of the "for want of a nail" adage. One such was the premature collapse of 5th Armoured's Bailey over the Sacco on 27 May. The collapse itself wasted a day then faulty staff work failed to switch the division in time to another functioning Canadian bridge thereby wasting another. Opportunities were also squandered by the slowness of 5th Armoured's 11th Infantry Brigade to exploit its own river crossing and push on to Ceprano when enemy resistance was, for once, weak. There was no shortage of reasons why. One was loss of armoured support when the tanks ran out of fuel due to rear area traffic congestion. Then came the collapsed bridge preventing tank crossings of the Sacco. All very real and valid reasons. But it is in just such situations that more resolute and driving leadership, at all levels, can achieve much with little - even turn defeat into victory.

The oft-mentioned traffic congestion was another major problem that could have been greatly diminished if both Corps and Army had done a better job of route selection and traffic control planning and management. In commenting on this aspect of the Liri the great British general cum author Sir David Fraser observed, "The British had come to rely on...a very large train of mechanical transport. In North Africa with its huge distances this had been the lifeline of the army. In Italy...where advances were measured in a few miles and roads were few and constricted, so great a mass of transport tended to impede rather than promote mobility, and to pose a movement problem which British Staffs were not always sufficiently ruthless or skilled to resolve."(14)

Things were not helped by the informal Desert Army habit of Leese and his staff making casual changes to routes and boundaries with insufficient provision for sorting out the consequences. Sometimes, such as in allocating the Canadian Sacco bridge to the XIII Corps flanking operation, such improvisation was a good idea which became half-baked when the implications to the losing formation were not thought out. British, and Canadian, commanders never did master the common German technique of improvising combat control from the front as the battle developed.

Sir Oliver Leese delivered a sharp rocket to Lt Gen Burns for the slowness of the Canadian pursuit after the Melfa. While such a reprimand is certainly the prerogative of any commander Burns felt, probably rightly, that Leese's outburst was triggered by his disappointment at losing out to Clark in the race for Rome. Although Leese vented his spleen largely on Burns he did acknowledge that the much larger British XIII Corps had done no better.

Leese and Alexander were now intent on sacking Burns and in either replacing him with a British general or breaking the Corps up and placing its divisions in a British corps. Although most British generals were no better than Burns the idea was mainly a non-starter because of the Canadian unity of command principle. Part of the problem was Alexander and Leese's petulant resentment at having an unwanted corps headquarters foisted on them and they now sought a way to get back at this decision. A lesser problem was Burns' dour, starchy personality and his inability to ingratiate himself with others. The British commanders were probably also reacting to what they knew was an antipathy towards Burns by his division commanders. Crerar, Burns' predecessor, identified possibly the major cause as the then prevalent condescending attitude of the British upper class towards non-Britishers and their resentment at the cohesiveness of the Colonials. This opinion was echoed, in another context, by British General David Fraser who, in referring to Greek troops attached to the defenders of Crete stated that the Greeks', "fighting potential tended to be underestimated, in a way not uncommon among British military men..."(15)

In their attacks on Burns both Alexander and Leese paid high tribute to the Canadian troops, although Alexander's was somewhat backhanded, "The choice is either giving the Corps tasks beyond the capability of Corps Headquarters, or tasks below the fighting capacity of their troops."(16) Leese, as quoted by Burns, was even more flattering stating, "the 1st Canadian Division was the best infantry division in Italy, the 1st Canadian Armoured Brigade the best armoured brigade, and that he expected that the 5th Canadian Armoured Division would be in due course the best armoured division."(17) High praise indeed and echoed by Graham and Bidwell in their excellent study, *Tug of War*, "Subsequently the Canadian staff made a thorough and self-critical analysis of the whole operation, but the historian patiently following ...events in the Liri valley ...need say no more than that it established the 1st Canadian Division as the equal of any of the formations in the armies of Italy."(18)

In the end, after a visit by Lt Gen K. Stewart of CMHQ in London who interviewed all the principals including Vokes and Hoffmeister, Burns stayed on. His retention would be validated in spades at the Gothic Line that fall. Meantime Burns, at Leese's prodding, did some of his own housekeeping replacing his COS, Chief Engineer and Commander 11 Brigade. Desmond Smith became COS being succeeded at 5th Armoured Brigade by Ian Cumberland of the GGHGs. Ian Johnston of the 48th replaced Snow in command of 11 Brigade.

Burns, learning from the Liri experience, took steps to improve things within his corps. He directed Brig Lister, his senior administrative officer, to devise a new traffic control system and organization. The result was an excellent solution based on the railway block system and augmenting the provost companies with special traffic control platoons. To answer the valid criticism that his small corps lacked balance Burns was receptive to the idea of converting his two divisions to hybrid armoured/infantry formations in the New Zealand mode. In this he was prompted by Leese who was encouraging similar transformations among his British formations, usually by tapping in the resources of independent brigades.(19)

Lacking independent infantry brigades to draw on Burns first tried to get a new trained infantry brigade from Canada. This request was firmly endorsed by General Alexander but, with delicious irony, was scotched by the CIGS Brooke, hitherto the champion of Mediterranean augmentation, as it might detract from the Overlord build up. Burns then sought to incorporate 1st Armoured Brigade into 1st Division and transfer one of First's infantry brigades to 5th Armoured thus creating two balanced divisions. This was thwarted by 8th Army, on plea from XIII Corps, who wished to retain what Leese termed, "the most experienced armoured brigade in Italy."(20)

Stymied on all fronts, Burns assisted by helpful suggestions from Leese, came up with an inspired bit of ad hocery. For 5th Armoured Division he fashioned a new 12th Infantry Brigade under Brigadier Dan Spry comprising the Wetminsters and two "created" battalions - the PLDGs converted from recce to infantry and the Lanark and Renfrew Scottish, under Lt Col W.C. Dick, from the 89th and 109th Batteries of the Corps' LAA Regiment. The regiment's third battery, the 35th, was switched to the new traffic control organization. While the result did not quite equal the biblical loaves and fishes it was a marvelous bit of improvisation which was to prove its worth on the Gothic Line. On the down side the new brigade would inevitably demand additional infantry reinforcements and casualty replacements and these, since D-Day, were becoming a very scarce commodity. They were to become more so in the near future.

Canadian Troops in the narrow streets of Italy. (DND)

THE ITALIAN CAMPAIGN

CHAPTER VII

THE GOTHIC LINE AND AFTER

Now thrive the armourers, and honour's thought
Reigns solely in the breast of every man
    Shakespeare *King Henry V*

To The Gothic Line

With Rome fallen, the Continent invaded and Russian hordes pouring to the Oder, a less resolute foe than the Germans would be forgiven for cutting their losses in Italy and withdrawing to the Alps. But once again the Germans showed that they were made of sterner stuff.

To protect the Valley of the Po the Germans, in 1943, had begun the construction of a new defensive line, originally named Apennine, then Gothic (by which name it will be known here) and finally Green Line. It stretched from Pisa to Rimini. From early 1944 the defences were vastly upgraded with *Panzerturm* (emplaced tank turrets) and fortifications on all key approaches, including the mountains - an area the Germans had neglected, to their regret, on the Gustav/Hitler Lines. The line was fronted by a four mile wide belt of cleared area laden with demolitions, mines and wire. In advance of the Gothic the Germans built several intermediate lines the principal being the Albert - Frieda centered on Lake Trasimeno, between Rome and Florence, the site of a notable victory by Hannibal over Rome in the Third Century BC. Kesselring ordered his Army Group C to hold this line.

While the Canadian Corps revamped and regrouped, the 1st Canadian Armoured Brigade was attached to XIII Corps in its northward advance. On 21 June the Ontario Regiment supported the 78th division's attack near Chiusi by Lake Trasimeno.(1) In four days of hard slogging the Ontarians destroyed five enemy tanks and earned a message of praise from the corps commander. The Three Rivers Regiment, in its turn, supported the British 4th Division whose inexperience in working closely with armour was soon evident. In ten days the Three Rivers tankers suffered their highest losses to date - 26 tanks and 94 men and accomplished little.

At the Arezzo Line protecting Florence it was the turn of the Calgary Tanks. They once more supported the 8th Indian Division in advancing southwest of that city. The advance was another exercise in frustration against German rearguards, mines and demolitions. The Three Rivers took over on 27 July and pushed to the Pesa River. By 3 August the Indians and Canadians had cleared the south bank of the Arno as the New Zealanders and South Africans entered Florence.

After recouping in the Volturno Valley 1st Canadian Division relieved the New Zealanders in and around Florence. This was a quiet sector but sniping, shelling and patrols cased considerable losses. On 8 August the division moved to Perugia having fulfilled a deception role in Florence. While this was happening the Allies in Italy lost seven divisions including the entire CEF along with the Canadian/American Special Service Force to the South of France in Operation "Dragoon".

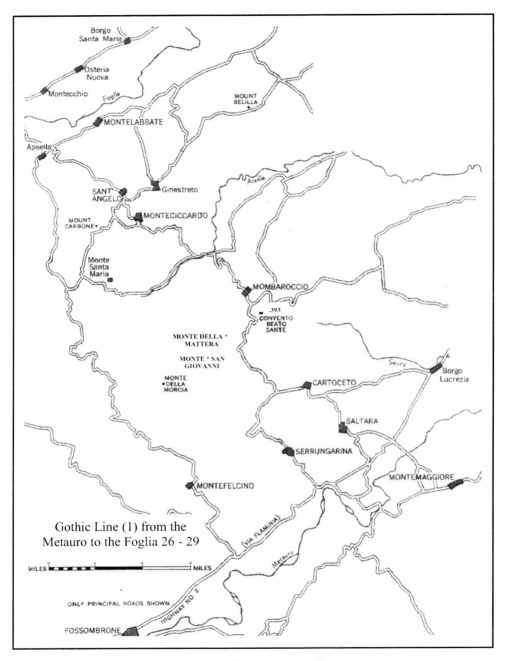

Gothic Line (1) from the Metauro to the Foglia 26 - 29

Operation Olive - Preparations

With the loss of over one-quarter of his force to the main event in Northwest Europe Alexander decided that his best chance of keeping pressure on the enemy was to advance centrally with the 5th and 8th Armies on a general line Florence - Bologna. To deceive the enemy he would feign an amphibious landing in the Genoa area and an attack on the Adriatic side. For the latter he had the Polish Corps advance on Ancona and tried to simulate Canadian presence there.

Sir Oliver Leese, despite a previous appreciation by his staff which opted against an Adriatic venture, prevailed upon General Alexander to switch the 8th Army effort to that coast. His reasoning appears to have been that his troops and equipment were not geared to a mountain campaign while the Adriatic flats appeared to offer his army a chance to exploit its overwhelming preponderance in armour and artillery. Graham and Bidwell offer the additional reason that Leese, for personal reason, wished never again to have to operate shoulder to shoulder with Clark. The problems that XIII Corps were having in the central highlands provided him with an additional argument for the change.(2)

Typical of Sir Oliver Leese's style the decision, according to the British official historian General W. G. F. Jackson, "was taken without adequate staff examination... or sufficient time for senior commanders to probe the consequences of such a major change."(3) But rightly or wrongly the decision was taken and 8th Army prepared for the tremendous feat of crossing back over the Apennines to the Adriatic sector. D-Day for the forthcoming 8th Army operation was set for 25 August. Its code name was "Olive".

One thing that did go right in the preliminaries to "Olive" was the deception plan in switching the Army to the Adriatic. Following Diadem the Germans had been particularly concerned with the location of the Canadians whom they rightly viewed as shock troops. In July the COS German 10th Army had wondered, "If only I knew where the Canadians are."(4) While the COS LXXVI Corps, on learning of the Canadians appearance near Florence predicted, "One of these days the Canadian Corps is going to attack and then our center will explode."(5) He was correct about the looming Canadian attack and its effect but wrong about the location. Between 5 and 20 August the Canadians along with most of the 8th Army moved over the Apennines to the Adriatic. It was a remarkable logistical achievement as was the gaining of the hoped-for deception. The move completed, the Canadian Corps took over a four mile front along the River Metauro on the Polish left flank.

The German Defences

On the 8th Army front the German 10th Army (General von Vietinghoff) deployed ten divisions in LXVI Panzer Corps on the coast and LI Mountain Corps on the hilly inland area. Two divisions were held in Army Reserve.

The Gothic Line in this sector was powerful, well prepared and some ten miles deep. A strong outpost line was based on the Metauro River. Behind this was the "Vorfeld", a four mile deep scorched-earth area heavily wired, mined and riddled with demolitions. The main defensive line, based on the River Foglia, contained the usual German bag-of-tricks of pill boxes, registered killing grounds, dug-in tank turrets with mines and wire in profusion. The mine fields contained a high percentage of anti-tank mines with a delay mechanism and anti-personnel mines of the hard to detect wooden *schu* and Bouncing-Betty types.

GAUDEAMUS IGITUR

The Allied Plan

General Alexander's stated intention was to drive the enemy out of the Apennines position and exploit to the lower Po. 8th Army on the Adriatic would take Ferrara and Ravenna while the 5th Army in the centre would wait until 8th Army had drawn in the German reserves. Then it would attack on an axis Florence - Bologna

For its attack, 8th Army had eleven divisions. II Polish Corps of two divisions was on the coast with the Canadian Corps, also of two divisions, on their left flank in the lowlands. The powerful British V Corps of five divisions (4th, 46th, 56th, 4th Indian and 1st Armoured) was to the Canadian's left in the hill country. X Corps, of only the 10th Indian Division, provided the link-up with 5th Army to the west. 2nd New Zealand Division was in reserve. The British XIII Corps of 1st British, 8th Indian, 6th Armoured and 6th South African was attached to 5th Army.

On the coast, the Polish Corps was to take Pesaro and would then be squeezed out of the line. Inland the Canadians were to drive in the German outpost line then break through the main Gothic Line and extend to the sea. The V British Corps (Lt Gen C.F. Keightly) was to attack through the hill country to the Rimini - Bologna road then turn west on Bologna thus menacing the German rear.

The Canadian Corps was tasked with attacking up a corridor some ten miles wide between the sea and the Apennine foothills. For this Lt Gen Burns devised a four phase attack plan. In Phase I the 1st Division would cross the Metauro River and establish a deep bridgehead on the north side. Phase II involved an advance of ten miles by both divisions to the main Gothic Line on the Foglia River. En Route they had to clear the 1200 foot high Mombaroccio Ridge. Phase III called for the breaking through of the Gothic Line. The final phase envisaged exploitation to Rimini, the Romagno and beyond.

The Canadians Break the Gothic Line

As the 8th Army prepared to assault the Germans began an undetected thinning out of their outpost line to the Mombaroccio position south of the Arzilla River. The 1st Canadian Division silently crossed the Metauro with 1st and 2nd Brigades leading. The subsequent artillery bombardment - a series of timed concentrations on suspected enemy positions rather than the previous wasteful creeping barrages- began at midnight. By first light on 26 August, against light opposition, the division had captured the towns of Serrungarina and Saltara and established a brigehead some three thousand yards deep. Churchill tanks of the British 21st Army Tank Brigade moved across in support.

Throughout 26 August First Division, flanked by the British 46th Division on the left and the Poles on the right, continued to advance against increasing opposition. Determined sub-unit attacks were required to secure Montes della Mattera and San Giovanni and Point 393. The Canadians, unaware, advanced under the most interested gaze of Prime Minister Winston Churchill who, accompanied by General Alexander, had crossed the Metauro and arrived unannounced at the RCR forward headquarters. In his memoirs Churchill recounts his relish at seeing action taking place but makes no specific mention of being with the Canadians.(6) The previous night he had however telephoned General Burns to wish him good luck and to express his hope that the troops would have a hot meal before kicking off.(7)

THE ITALIAN CAMPAIGN

The advance continued on the 27th against the usual thorough German rearguard actions of demolitions, minefields, pre-registered shelling and long-range small arms fire. It was not until evening that the Arzilla River, backed by the Monteciccardo - Ginestreto Ridge, was reached. It took a further day's spirited fighting to cross the Arzilla, clear the ridge and advance to the Foglia where the main enemy defences began. The Germans were still not convinced that the Adriatic push was the main event although they were getting concerned. Their COS 10th Army commented, "if they really are Canadians... it will be a true major operation."(8)

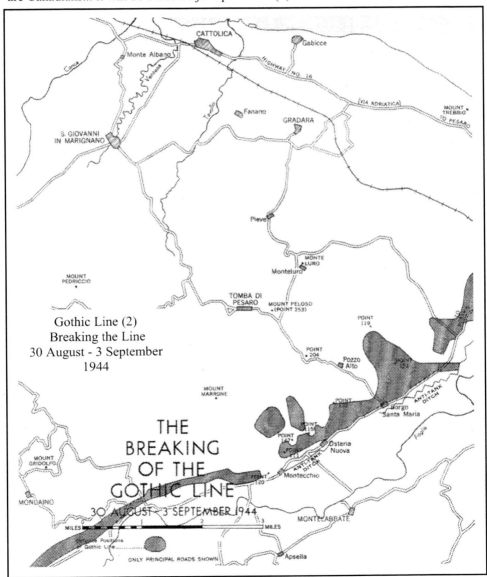

Gothic Line (2)
Breaking the Line
30 August - 3 September 1944

GAUDEAMUS IGITUR

This assessment was soon confirmed when a copy of General Leese's pre-battle Order-of-the-Day was captured by the Germans who swiftly reacted. The 1st Parachute and 98th Infantry Divisions reinforced the hard-pressed 71st while the 26th Panzers were soon brought up followed by the 27th and 29th Panzer Grenadiers.

When patrols indicated that the Germans behind the Foglia seemed unprepared Burns decided to gate-crash the line. He brought 5th Armoured up on the left of 1st Division and at noon on 30 August he attacked with 11 Brigade of the Armoured Division on the left and 1st Division's 3rd Brigade on the right. The initial objectives were Montecchio and Point 120 to the Cape Bretons, Points 111 and 147 to the Perths, Osteria Nuova to the PPCLI and Point 133 to the West Novas. Three days of bloody battle were to follow.

On 5th Armoured's front the Cape Bretons were repulsed from Point 120 but the Perths brilliantly took Point 111 and with it the honour of being the first Allied unit to break into the Gothic Line. The Irish Regiment of Canada then moved forward through the gap made by the Perths. During the night of 30/31 August the New Brunswick Hussars, despite traffic jams at the Foglia, came over in support. The Irish and Hussars attacked at noon on the 31st and won a magnificent victory capturing Montecchio and 250 prisoners.

On the right, on 1st Division's sector, things got off to a rather shaky start. Both the PPCLI (attached to 3rd Brigade for the operation) and the West Novas entered a large minefield east of Osteria Nuova. The field was thick with the dreaded "S" (Schrapnellminen) - the "Bouncing Betty"- and the new wooden, hence hard to detect, Schu anti-personnel mines. As the two battalions struggled amidst the mines the enemy machine gunners opened up. At dawn on the 31st the West Novas tried again and, caught in another minefield, were repulsed after suffering 80 casualties. But the Patricias, exploiting the success of 11 Brigade on their left and supported by a squadron of Churchills of the 48th RTR, attacked in mid-afternoon and brilliantly captured Points 115 and 133 along with 200 prisoners, many from the vaunted 1st Paras.

Back on 11th Brigade's sector a squadron of the 8th Hussars advanced from Montecchio towards Monte Marrone but were initially repulsed. The Cape Breton Highlanders then came up with another squadron of Hussars and advanced through a sea of defence works, including a number of emplaced tank turrets, to take the hill. The Perths and BC Dragoons passed through and attacked west of Pozzo Alto towards Point 204 located on a spur leading to Tomba di Pesaro. When the Perths were held up by a pocket of paratroops backed by heavy artillery and mortar fire the BCDs plunged on alone. Under a hail of anti-tank, mortar and artillery fire the Dragoons stormed and captured Point 204 at a cost of 30 tanks and 44 personnel casualties including their redoubtable CO Fred Vokes, brother of the General, who was killed. As darkness fell the victorious BCDs were relieved by the Lord Strathconas and Perths who, during the night, beat off a succession of strong counter-attacks by the Paras. Lt Col WW Reid, CO of the Perths, although wounded, then led a tank hunting team in routing the Germans and capturing two SP guns. He won a well deserved DSO. When daylight came the bodies of 40 enemy dead were found surrounding the position.

By midnight on 31 August the Canadian Corps had broken into the Gothic Line to a depth of over two miles on a one mile front. Ahead loomed the heights of Monte Luro - Tomba di Pesaro. The next day, on 1st Division's front, the R 22e R with a company of Carleton and Yorks captured Point 131, the high ground by Borgo Santa Maria. The

THE ITALIAN CAMPAIGN

Seaforths took Pozzo Alto and drove for Point 119.

On 11th Brigade's sector the newly converted Princess Louise's Dragoon Guards under Lt Col W. Darling, supported by Lord Strathcona's Horse, stormed Monte Peloso. Under a withering wall of fire infantry and tanks thrust forward until at the foot of the objective only 40 PLDGs remained. The Strath's tanks took over and charged the crest as the Plugs struggled to keep pace. When they at last secured the crest only 15 of Darling's men were left. Reinforcements arrived during the night but still left the force under 100. It had been a superb but bloody achievement, won at a cost of 130 casualties. Darling won the DSO. The Irish and 8th Hussars then clinched things by passing through the PLDG at dusk, and capturing 70 enemy en route, before seizing Tomba di Pesaro. On 1st Div's front the Loyal Edmontons captured the formidable 950 foot high Monte Luro, which was studded with defensive works, in a surprisingly easy fight.

It had been a magnificent achievement for Burns and his Canadian Corps, won, unfortunately, at a cost of 900 casualties. The breaking of the Gothic Line in such a brilliant manner may have been the Canadian's finest single action of the entire war. General Sir William Jackson, the official British historian and one sparing in his praise, wrote, "31st August was a highly successful day for 1st Canadian Corps...its infantry and tank co-operation working well, both of its divisions made steady progress....By the end of the day...Green I (had been) successfully breached."(9) Jackson was even more fulsome in his praise of the Canadian actions over the next two days - "1st and 2nd September were proud days for 1st Canadian Corps...every man sensed that he was writing an important page in Canadian history."(10) And write it they did - unhappily very few Canadians today know anything about it. It says something of Canadian priorities, and sentiments, that one of the proudest episodes in Canadian history is today virtually ignored by its citizens.

With the Gothic Line broken by the Canadians the way seemed open for exploitation to Rimini and beyond. In spite of the difficulties being experienced by the powerful Vth Corps the Canadian successes led to the impression that a break out was imminent. Indeed the V Corps Operation Order of 2 September stated, "The enemy have been badly mauled by I Canadian Corps and...there is the possibility of a break through on that front."(11) But the Vth on the left were still hung up in the mountains. Its 1st Armoured Division, held too far back, had not crossed the Metauro.(12) The Poles were a spent force and the victorious Canadians were like a boy with both hands in the cookie jar - they had used both of their divisions in breaking the line and had no reserves left to exploit. Leese's bungling of the initial force composition and the handling of reserves brought the chickens flocking home to roost.

On the V Corps front Lt Gen Keightley tried mightily to take Coriano the key to the Second Green Line. His 46th Division had been dragged along by the Canadian advance but still lagged. On its left a gap was created which Keightley plugged with the 56th Division which failed to take Monte Gemmano, the hinge on which V Corps hoped to swing through the Second Green Line. In an unfortunate assessment Maj Gen Hull, Commander of 1st Armoured Division, was told to pass through a gap created by V Corps and pursue the enemy. But this depended on 46 Division taking Coriano Ridge which they had failed to do. With his Lorried Infantry Brigade still far behind Hull hurried into the attack with only his 2nd Armoured Brigade. On 3 /4 September, in a scene reminiscent of its Western Desert battles, 2nd Armoured Brigade attacked Coriano into a setting sun against an unlocated enemy and suffered a bloody defeat. The Brigade's

GAUDEAMUS IGITUR

three armored regiments lost 70 tanks in the process.

While Keightley struggled and Leese dithered Maj Gen Vokes organized a force commanded by British Brigadier Dawnay comprising his 21st Army Tank Brigade, with the Royal Canadian Dragoons and two companies of R22er under command and 2nd Brigade in support, to drive on Cattolica and the Adriatic and cross the River Conca. This mission Dawnay brilliantly accomplished though not in time to trap the retreating remnants of the German 1st Parachute Division.

On 2 September Lt Gen Burns went to HQ 8th Army to report. General Alexander was with General Leese and both seemed greatly pleased and surprised at the speed of the Canadian advance. On the spur of the moment an impressed Alexander recommended Burns for the DSO. It appeared to Burns that the two British Generals had vastly upgraded their appreciation of his capabilities. Indeed they were soon to give him the British, and other, formations that, not so long ago, they said he could not handle. Alas, too late the phalarope! Had they done so at the outset the 8th Army might now be at the Po.

It now became evident that Coriano, which lay in V Corps sector, would have to be taken before any northward advance could be resumed. On 4 September the 5th Canadian Armoured Brigade and their Motor Battalion advanced one - half mile towards Besanigo Spur. The next day the Cape Bretons and Irish completed the capture of the spur. On the right the 1st Division took Santa Maria and the Palazzo Ceccarini. But all of these were negated by the failure of the British 1st Armoured Division at Coriano.

General Leese now decided to halt operations and reorganize prior to resuming the attack. But already the autumn rains, which turn fields into liquid bogs and peaceful streams into raging torrents, were beginning to pour down. On 6 September Leese, in a major *volte face* from his post-Liri vow, placed the British 4th Infantry Division and 25th Army Tank Brigade (less one regiment) under Burns' command alongside the previously allocated Greek Mountain Brigade. The powerful 2nd New Zealand Division was slated to follow.

On the other side the Germans, resilient as always, had bent but not broken. The 10th Army's von Vietinghoff and 76th Corp's Traugott Herr kept pulling rabbits from the hat. The 98th Division sent one regiment to augment the 1st Parachute, and the rest to aid the 71st Division in blocking the British 46th Division west of Coriano. While the 278th Division stopped the 56th British the remnants of the 5th Mountain held Gemmano. The formidable 26th Panzer and 29th Panzer Grenadiers prevented V Corps from securing the Canadians' vulnerable open left flank as the 162nd Division was hurled in the path of the advancing Canucks. In this crisis von Vietinghoff, in conversation with Kesselring, paid tribute to the Canadians, "I am told that the 5th Canadian Armoured Division was excellent…though not strong in numbers' the Canadians are right good soldiers."(13) High praise indeed from such a distinguished source.

General Leese's new plan called for Keightley's V Corps to capture Coriano and I Canadian Corps to cross the Marano River and advance to the Marecchia on the San Fortunato - Rimini line. The attack was set for 12/13 September. But before it could be launched Burns, at the behest of Hoffmeister and with Keightley's concurrence, saw Leese and obtained agreement to critically change the plan. Under this change the Canadian 5th Armoured would assault and capture Coriano from the east while V Corps attacked the outlying ridges leading to Coriano from San Clemente in the west. At this stage Alexander judged the time to be ripe for Clark's 5th Army to begin its advance on the central front.

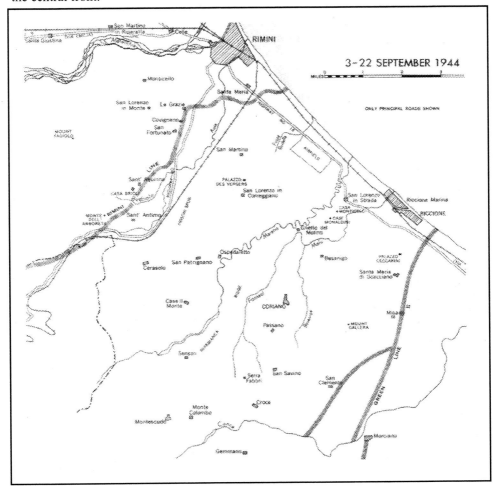

Gothic Line (3) and Coriano

For this critical operation Lt Gen Burns ordered an elaborate eight - phase attack in which Hoffmeister's 5th Armoured would capture Coriano. The 4th British Division would then pass through and advance in parallel with the 1st Canadians to cross the Marano, break the Rimini Line and advance over the Marecchia River. The Greek Brigade was to advance along the coastal flank aimed at Rimini.

The assault on Coriano opened at 2300 hrs on 12 September with the Vth British Corps attacking the south end of the ridge. Then at 0100 hrs on 13 September the Canadian 5th Armoured struck from the east. Both attacks were supported by all 700 guns of the 8th Army. 5th Armoured's attack was led by 11 Brigade's Perth Regiment on the left and the Cape Breton Highlanders right. The attack was spectacularly successful and by dawn the ridge had fallen. The Canadian Irish and 8th Hussars then assaulted the village of Coriano. In bloody fighting the Irish cleared the village, captured 60 prisoners and drove the remaining defenders helter - skelter to the south. The Irish were somewhat miffed to see the retreating Germans - some 800 in number - stream straight into the hands of V Corps who bagged the lot.

Coriano was yet another magnificent Canadian victory, won at a cost of 200 casualties. In the opinion of Lt Gen Burns " the taking of Coriano… was the most effective divisional operation carried out while I was commanding the Corps. The importance of the objective…the way the fight developed according to plan, and the final success combined to give it a completeness which was not often attained…"(14) General Leese was laudatory, "It was a hard fight and a decisive action in the battle."(15) And the Germans, this time the COS of 76 Corps, again paid the Canadians a grudging tribute, " Enemy armored formations, particularly Canadian tanks, no longer sensitive to artillery fire but carry on even under heaviest fire concentrations."(16)

But once more the Germans plugged the gap, bringing in three new divisions from the north.

They were additionally aided by the rains which turned the little Fornaci stream into a river and blocked the advance of the British 1st Armoured. The British 4th Division also found the going to be tough, being delayed a day in passing through 5th Armoured by heavy shelling. Burns then passed the exhausted 5th Armoured into reserve to rest and recuperate.

To Rimini and the Romagna

When on 25 August the Canadian Corps started its spectacular battle to break the Gothic Line few would have guessed that the hardest fighting would come after the line had been broken and Coriano taken. But that is exactly what happened. The week long slugging match which followed between 14 and 22 September was to be the hardest battle and result in the highest Canadian casualties of any action they fought in the entire Italian campaign. The key Canadian objective was San Fortunato ridge which lay broodingly behind the Ausa River controlling access to Rimini, the Marecchia and the plains beyond. But before San Fortunato could be attacked the Corps had to clear the San Patrignano - Cerasolo feature on the left and the San Martino - San Lorenzo ridge on the right.

The attack opened on the morning of 14 September with 4th British Division directed on San Patrignano and 1st Armoured Division of V Corps advancing on its left. On its right the 3rd Brigade of 1st Canadian Division crossed the Marano with the West Novas and R22er moving on the San-Lorenzo - San Martino ridge. On the extreme right of the Corps the Greek Brigade pushed north along the coast supported by New Zealand tanks and a motor company, two platoons of the Sask LI and with the RCDs in reserve.

Both battalions of Third Brigade had a rough reception from the 26th Panzer Grenadiers on the San Lorenzo ridge. The West Novas and a squadron of 12 RTR were stopped short of their objective with heavy casualties and most of the tanks knocked out. It was much the same with the Van Doos on the right who were held up short of San Martino by withering fire from their objective and from San Lorenzo. The Quebecois suffered 100 casualties in this action. Third Brigade tried again at 0830 hrs on 15 September. Supported by a fresh squadron of 12th Royal Tanks the West Novas, who had been twice repulsed in futile attacks made during the night, battered their way

THE ITALIAN CAMPAIGN

against bitter opposition into San Lorenzo. With the Royal Tanks stymied by deadly anti-tank fire the Scotians brought up their battalion anti-tank guns and systematically blasted the enemy from their positions. By 1830 hrs the heavily fortified village was theirs.

Further north the R22eR reopened their drive on San Martino by capturing the huge 700 room Palazzo des Vergers. At 1500 hrs they began to assault along the ridge to San Martino. With most of their supporting tanks knocked out C Company charged the village behind the heroic leadership of Sergeant Yvon Piuze. With the company pinned down Piuze and two companions raced ahead into a wall of fire. When his comrades fell Piuze charged on alone firing a Bren Gun as he plunged into the German position. Miraculously he succeeded in wiping out two enemy machine gun posts in succession before being killed while attacking a third. Piuze was recommended for a richly deserved Victoria Cross but failed to get it due to bungled action by higher command. Inspired by Piuze's heroism C Company captured San Martino. Unfortunately Piuze's, and C Company's, heroics were cancelled out that night when a botched change-over with the Seaforths resulted in the German paratroopers sneaking back into San Martino and re-establishing their position which they held for two more days. The Seaforths, Van Doos and 48th Highlanders were all repulsed in bloody attempts to bypass the village, suffering over 200 casualties in the process.

Things were not going any better elsewhere. On the Corps' left the British 4th Division, after initial success was stopped at San Patrigano. While on the Fourth's left the 1st Armoured and 56th Infantry Divisions of V Corps were falling behind in the rugged Apennine foothills. And on the extreme right the Greek Brigade with its New Zealand and Canadian support elements was blocked at Rimini Airfield. The airfield was finally taken in a brilliant but bloody action by the Royal Canadian Regiment which suffered 90 casualties.

On 17 September Burns pressed Vokes and Dudley Ward (Commander 4th Division) to cross the Ausa the next day. Ward, sensing that the enemy to his left was weakening, agreed. But Vokes' approach was still blocked by the paratroops in San Martino and he would need to mount a major preliminary operation before he could tackle the Ausa. His plan called for 2nd Brigade to clear San Martino to enable 3rd Brigade to advance to the Ausa on the left. First Brigade would continue its advance on Rimini. Things got off to a shaky start when 2nd Brigade's Loyal Edmontons got trapped in a gully which had been pre-registered as a killing ground. In two hours they lost 60 men and had to be withdrawn under a smoke screen. But, with the enemy pre-occupied by the Loyal Eddies, the PPCLI blasted their way to within 200 yards of the vital Rimini rail line. Half of the Patricia's infantry and their supporting British tanks became casualties but they had got behind, and unhinged, the enemy who withdrew during the night. The Carleton and Yorks then advanced to the Ausa.

On the night 18/19 September 3rd Brigade, with the Hast PER under command, crossed the Ausa under artificial moonlight. The engineers, working furiously, carved the Ausa's banks and erected an ARK Bridge(17) over which the 48th RTR trundled across. The West Novas and Hasty Ps reached the Rimini - San Martino railway line but could not force the ridge beyond. Taking 60 prisoners, but losing 65 men and all but three of their tanks, the Canadian attack stalled. The British 4th and 1st Armoured Divisions were having equally sticky times at Sant Aquilina and Monte dell' Arboreta.

Vokes ordered a new assault on San Fortunato Ridge that night, 19/20 September.

GAUDEAMUS IGITUR

Third Brigade was to attack frontally while the Second would infiltrate the northern part of the ridge and take San Lorenzo and Le Grazie. It would be no easy task as 76 Panzer Corps had reinforced the heavily fortified ridge with eight battalions.

Frontally the R22er, supported by the 145th RTR, attacked at last light and by midnight had taken the Villa Belvedere on the crest. The 22nd took over 200 prisoners and counted over 50 enemy dead. They then pursued the defenders to the west. Meanwhile 2nd Brigade's infiltration attack was a spectacular success. The Loyal Eddies advanced at 2100 hrs and after a wild melee reached the crest and wiped out a strong counter attack and a Tiger tank. By 0430 hrs they were secure in San Lorenzo where the Seaforths took over and passed San Fortunato village. By 0600 hrs they took La Grazie and before the day was out had captured over 200 Germans. The Hasty Ps captured an additional hundred. With the capture of Palazzo Paradiso by the Van Doos the entire San Fortunato Ridge was now in Canadian hands as the enemy hastily withdrew over the Marecchia.

Under driving rains the Princess Pats and a squadron of 48th Royal Tanks bypassed Monticello, which was defended by Tiger tanks of the 26th Panzer Grenadiers, and reached the Marecchia River by midnight. By noon on 21 September the entire battalion was across and into the Romagna. In the Churchillian-like prose of the official British historian, "8th Army at last saw the 'promised land' through sheets of sleeting rain as it crossed the wide bed of the Marecchia river to enter the flat Romagna on 21st September."(18)

On the Corps' right the 48th Highlanders took Celle as the Germans evacuated Rimini. Rimini was assigned to the Greek Brigade which miffed the Canadians who felt the prize was theirs. But it was a well merited award to the Greeks who had fought so well in support of the Canadian flank and had suffered over 300 casualties. On the Corps' left flank the 4th Division crossed the Marecchia on 22 September and reached Highway 9 - the Rimini - Bologna road. The capture of San Fortunato ridge by the Canadians enabled V Corps to advance and 1st Armoured also crossed the Marecchia. On that day the 5th Canadian Armoured took over from the 4th British and the 2nd New Zealanders relieved the Canadian 1st. Operation Olive was over!

L'Envoie

By any yardstick Canada's greatest achievement of the entire Italian Campaign, and arguably of the entire war, was its magnificent breaking of the formidable Gothic Line, followed by the storming of Coriano and San Stefano and the advance to the Romagno. To the senior British commanders, and to the official British historian, it was an astounding performance. Under the command of a colorless leader who had been disliked by his subordinates and mistrusted and unwanted by his British superiors the small, two-division, Canadian Corps achieved spectacular successes. Sandwiched between the tired Polish Corps on the coast and the six-division strong British V Corps (really a small army) to the west the Canadian Corps had been assigned a secondary role in support of the expected massive V Corps offensive. Just the opposite happened.(19)

While V Corps became bogged in the mountains and its 1st Armoured Division floundered the Canadian Corps surged forward. First by driving in the outpost line Green I, then closing up to and smashing the main line Green II, capturing Coriano and San Stefano and forcing the Marecchia the Canadians opened the door to the Po. Great as were these successes they could have been even greater had General Leese overcome his mistrust of Lt Gen Burns at an earlier stage and given him the tools to finish the job. But too late were these resources allotted, by which time they had been wasted elsewhere until the autumn rains and "General Mud" made their allotment irrelevant.

Ironically the belated allotment of additional formations to, and the belated conversion of General Leese from adversary to cheerleader of, Lieutenant-General Burns may have contributed to Burns' downfall. When General Richard McCreery, himself categorized by Mark Clark as a "feather duster", succeeded Leese in command of 8th Army in November he would force the replacement of Burns for what he led himself to imagine was the latter's lack of drive and ruthlessness in handling his new formations. McCreery, who had been detached from the 8th Army for many months, appears to have been ignorant of Burns' personal achievements and of the singular achievements of the Canadian Corps. In fact, nearly uniquely in the annals of the Italian Campaign, Burns' planning and direction of the Gothic and Coriano battles had gone almost exactly as planned. His management and direction of his two Canadian, and later one British, divisional commanders had been authoritative and impressive, yet sensitive, and crowned with success - in short, just what a commander should be. Like Currie in the First World War his very real achievements were subsumed in the public consciousness by impressions foisted by others. *Sic Transit Gloria!*

Sir Oliver Leese, to his very great credit, did a personal *volte-face* and was most generous in his praise. In a signal to Burns he stated, "You have won a great victory. By the bitterest fighting since El Alamein and Cassino you have beaten eleven German divisions and broken through into the Po Valley. The greatest part of the German armies in Italy were massed against us and they have been terribly mauled. I congratulate you and thank you all."(20) To each of Burns' units he signaled, "Well done Canada." Had Leese remained in command of 8th Army Burns' star could conceivably have shone brightly. But, as noted above, it was not to be. Unfortunately the change did Leese himself no good. Sent to command British land forces in Southeast Asia he repeated his insensitive handling of subordinates by attempting to fire the revered Slim and was himself sacked.

Alas, the great victory had come at a terrible price From the start of "Olive" the 8th Army had suffered 14,000 casualties of which one-third - 4,500 - fell to the Canadians, who made up only one-fifth of the total force. But the Corps had taken all of its objectives along with 2,500 prisoners and killed far more. Its old adversary the German LXVII Corps had been savaged and suffered 14,000 casualties which it could ill afford. Battalions in the 10th German Army were now reduced down to 250 men each.

But the sword cut both ways and the heavy casualties which the Canadians suffered in Italy and concurrently in Northwest Europe brought on a reinforcement and, at home, a conscription crisis. The British, suffering equally, were forced to reduce their infantry battalions from four to three companies each and to disband several brigades. Also disbanded was the disappointing British 1st Armoured Division whose armored brigade was added to the 78th Division. And still the rains poured down.

The Valley of the Po

The Po Valley had been the holy grail towards which the Allied armies had struggled for over a year. Its flat plain beckoned their massive armored divisions to be cut loose and run wild to Venice and the Alps. But like so much else in this frustrating campaign the promise was to be better than the fact. Much of the Romagna was reclaimed marshland, drained by a vast network of ditches and banked canals. The clay soil, like clay everywhere, turned into a morass when rains combined with off-road vehicle traffic. In the rainy season, which was now in full swing with a vengeance, the only practical vehicle travel was on the few and indifferent metalled roads. The fields were mainly orchards, interspersed with wired trellises and stone farmhouses which the enemy turned to his defensive advantage. And the many steams, rivers and end-canals flowed into the Adriatic at right angles to the Allied line of advance.

In preparation for the advance General Leese assigned to the Canadian Corps the ancient Via Adriatica, now Highway16, through Ravenna to Ferrara. V Corps was assigned Highway 9, the Via Emilia, as its axis of advance. Lt Gen Burns, in turn, allocated Highway 16 to the New Zealand Division and gave 5th Armoured the tough task of advancing between Highways 9 and 16. The New Zealanders kicked off on 22 September but were soon held up on the Canale Viserba. 5th Armoured had slow going passing through 4th Division's bridgehead and only cleared it on the 23rd. Its vanguard 12th Brigade had to fight to clear Casale, Variano and San Vito but reached and crossed the Uso River on the 25th. In these seemingly minor actions the Brigade lost 275 men. Inland the British Vth Corps kept pace with the Canadians.

On 27 September Hoffmeister passed 11 Brigade through to the Fiumicino. One company of the Irish Regiment smartly crossed the river but no tanks or anti-tank guns were able to follow. The next morning the enemy counter-attacked with tanks and infantry and much of the Irish company, lacking anti-tank defences, was overrun. An attempt to reinforce the Irish was thwarted by heavy rains which made the Fiumicino virtually impassable. The New Zealanders were similarly stymied and for ten days the 8th Army advance remained stalled.

At this juncture Lt Gen Sir R.L. McCreery, formerly commanding X Corps in Clark's 5th Army, succeeded General Leese in command of the 8thArmy. On 8 October McCreery initiated a regrouping to try and get the Corps onto better ground. The 1st Canadian Division was to take over Highway 9 from V Corps while the 2nd New Zealand moved left to take over from 5th Armoured. All three of Burns' divisional commanders, including the New Zealanders, voiced their concerns over trying to operate in the terrible prevailing conditions. Burns, who on the Liri had been criticized for not backing his divisional commanders, passed these views on to McCreery. McCreery, trying to put his stamp of authority on 8th Army, took Burns' intervention in the wrong way. Instead of ascertaining the facts, or taking account of Burns previous superb exercise of command, McCreery quite wrongly made up his mind that Burns lacked the moral toughness to force his subordinates to perform unpleasant actions. The episode, which was to lead to Burns subsequent dismissal, speaks volumes for McCreery's own inadequacies in the exercise of higher command. Two days later McCreery, finally twigging to the fact that V Corps had much better ground on which to operate, gave the main thrust to that corps with the Canadians in a flank protection role. The fact that this showed that Burns had been right only stiffened the small-minded McCreery in his resolve to sack him.

Back on the battlefield, the 1st Brigade of 1st Division hustled rearguards of the 90th Panzer Grenadiers from the Scolo Rigossa canal and Bulgaria village. At Bulgaria the Hasty Ps, supported by Strathcona tanks which had daringly crossed the canal on an ancient shaky bridge, wiped out the German defenders and took 55 prisoners at a cost of 30 casualties. Second Brigade then took over to cross the next river the Pisciatello - probably the ancient Rubicon which Caesar crossed to fame and power. On the 18th the Loyal Eddies, now under Lt Col J.R. Stone, pushed across and secured a small bridgehead supported by Churchills of the 12th RTR which, with a mixture of guts, initiative and deserved good luck, forded the river against engineer advice to come to the aid of the Eddies. The joint force captured 55 Germans and suffered 35 casualties. The 1st Canadian and 2nd New Zealand Divisions then pursued the retreating Germans to the next river, the Savio, while the Carleton and Yorks and British 46th Division combined to take Cesena. To protect his right flank Burns formed an *ad hoc* Cumberland Force under the commander of 5 CAB comprising the GGHG, BCD, 27 Lancers, Greeks and New Zealanders which kept pace to the Savio.

The Savio was a major river the crossing of which Vokes assigned to the 2nd Brigade. On 20 October the PPCLI managed to get one company across where it came under heavy fire and repeated attacks. The next evening the Seaforths and Loyal Edmontons crossed behind the fire of eight artillery regiments and all the mortars and MMGs of the Saskatoon Light Infantry who fought as a complete unit for the first time. The Seaforths got two companies across in rapid order and cleared numerous enemy positions taking over 50 prisoners. The Edmontons initially ran into difficulties but reinforced their assault companies and soon had a viable bridgehead.

To combat the swarming enemy tanks the Seaforths organized a tank hunting platoon of four PIAT groups. That night using a combination of PIAT bombs, Hawkins grenades and LMGs they wreaked havoc on the enemy. The tank-hunters destroyed a staff car, an SP gun and a Panther tank, drove off others and killed or routed a number of supporting infantry. For this action Pte E.A. Smith was awarded Canada's third, and last, Victoria Cross of the Italian Campaign. The next morning the Seaforths captured another Panther and cleaned the enemy out of the bridgehead taking 150 prisoners.

Although 2nd Brigade had established a mile wide and deep bridgehead its battalions were soon isolated by the raging Savio. To relieve the pressure Vokes ordered 3rd Brigade to cross at Borgo di Ronta. It was a mistake. The West Novas got two companies across but these were heavily counter-attacked and lacking support were forced back. At this juncture McCreery told Burns to cease his efforts as the Germans were being unhinged by the advances of V Corps and the 5th Army in the west. The Canadians then conformed and followed the retreating Germans eight miles to the Ronco. On 28 October the Canadian Corps passed into Army reserve and moved to the Rimini area to rest and recuperate.

Actions Away From the Line

While the Canadians reorganized and rebuilt their seriously diminished and sapped battalions a conscription crisis raged at home. The Defence Minister J.L. Ralston had visited the Canadians in Italy and Northwest Europe in September to see for himself how bad the reinforcement situation really was. On his return to Canada Ralston precipitated a cabinet crisis, resigned and was succeeded by Andy McNaughton who failed to find enough volunteers to fill the bill. Despite fearing a Quebec backlash Mackenzie King reluctantly bowed to overwhelming public and military opinion and obtained approval to send the NRMA (National Resources Mobilization Act) conscripts ('Zombies' as they were popularly called) overseas. In the end little backlash occurred and nearly 13,000 conscripts were sent overseas of whom only 2,500 actually reached combat units. These served well and 330 became casualties including 70 dead. None reached Italy.

The period out of the line was a tough time for the Canadians whose rapidly diminishing ranks were only partly filled with replacements, many of whom were raw recruits often poorly trained. After the euphoria of late summer when the war's end had seemed near morale naturally suffered following the high casualties of the Gothic period and the prospect of another dreary, wet, miserable winter in the line.

Near the end of October Burns was summoned by General McCreery and told of his dismissal. The reason given, as previously stated, was Burns' perceived lack of ruthlessness in dealing with subordinates. And since McCreery was himself a ruthless man there was some truth in this. But given Burns' record and the fact that he consistently outshone most British Corps Commanders it seems unlikely that he would have been summarily dismissed had he enjoyed strong Canadian backing. Indeed, McCreery and his predecessors all treated the gloomy, pessimistic and non-driving Freyberg with kid gloves. And Monty himself backed down when Crerar threatened to call on government intervention. It seems likely that McCreery took action after learning of consultations with Ralston during the latter's visit and in the knowledge of the early antipathy of Vokes and, to a lesser extent, Hoffmeister towards Burns. A prime suspect in tipping off McCreery would be Desmond Smith, Burns' own Chief-of-Staff who was vehement in his dislike of Burns and had been sounded out by Ralston in September. Smith long proclaimed his innocence in back-stabbing his own commander but the evidence is far from clear. Burns himself was strangely muted in his wartime memoirs. It is a matter that deserves further study.

Burns was replaced by Lt Gen Charles Foulkes late of 2nd Corps in Northwest Europe. George Kitching became Foulkes' COS while Vokes and Maj Gen Harry Foster of 4th Armoured Division in Northwest Europe switched commands. Whether this latter, seemingly pointless, move had anything to do with confusion between Vokes and Foulkes, as has sometimes been suggested, is unclear. But from Vokes' viewpoint the move was just as well as he disliked Foulkes even more than he disliked Burns.

To The Santerno

In order to keep up the pressure and prevent the Germans from withdrawing more troops to the Northwest Europe front Alexander planned a new offensive in which 5th and 8th Armies were to take Bologna by a pincers movement. Once this was accomplished, and the stage set for a major offensive in early 1945, Alexander would put operations on hold while preparing for the final drive. But before this pincer operation could start 8th Army would have to advance to the Santerno River, its jump off line for Bologna. General McCreery called for the Canadian Corps, on the Army's right flank, to capture Russi and cut Highway 16 thereby isolating Ravenna. It would then turn through Lugo to establish a bridgehead over the Santerno at Massa Lombarda. The Canadian operation was code-named "Chuckle". It was to be anything but.

For this operation the Corps had to cross seven watercourses of which two, the Lamone and the Senio, were full blown rivers. Lt Gen Foulkes committed both of his divisions from the outset, 1st left and 5th right. The start line was the Montone which was to be secured by the 10th Indian Division. 1st Division was to capture Russi and cross the Santerno. 5th Armoured would take San Pancrazio and Godo, cut Route 16 and capture Ravenna. On 1 December the Canadians moved into the Indian bridgehead near Casa Bettini. The offensive began at 0930 hrs the next day with the West Novas and R22er of 3rd Brigade in the van. Against light opposition the West Novas took Russi that night with the Van Doos keeping pace to the west. By the morning of 4 December Third Brigade closed up to the Lamone.

On 5th Division's front the vanguard 12th Brigade, led by the PLDG, were initially held up along the Montone. The situation was restored by the Westminsters who crossed the Montone in a smart operation killing six enemy and capturing 17. They then took San Pancrazio on 3 December and moved on Piangipane five miles to the north. Crossing several minor waterways en route the Westminsters reached the Godo - Ravenna road and ambushed an enemy convoy killing ten Germans, capturing 23 and knocking out two tanks and three half-tracks. It had been a magnificent show at a cost of seven men. The Westies then went on to capture Piangipane on 4 December. At this juncture the PLDGs and BCDs, supported by Porterforce and Italian partisans, captured Ravenna. The city, now a provincial capital, had once been the Imperial seat of the West Roman Empire and contained many historic buildings. It was to be the most important city to be captured by the Canadians in Italy. By the morning of 6 December Fifth Armoured held a five mile front on the Lamone.

On 1st Division's front (temporarily commanded by Brigadier Desmond Smith awaiting Foster's arrival) came a bungled and unnecessary change over between First and Third Brigades, due in equal parts to errors by Smith and Third Brigade's Bernatchez. This resulted in First Brigade being thrust hastily and ill-prepared into a poorly reconnoitred crossing of the Lamone which ended in a bloody schemozzle. Prior to a short preliminary bombardment the Hasty Ps moved close to the river bank and were decimated by their own artillery firing short. Forty-eight Hasty Ps were killed or wounded and the remainder so disorganized that their part in the crossing was temporarily scrubbed.

Things initially went better with the RCR's crossing although one platoon was wiped out by devastating enemy mortar fire. Three companies got over and moved inland and at dawn linked up with those of the Hasty Ps who had reorganized and crossed later. Suddenly out of the fog the RCR were hit by a powerful SP-gun supported counter-attack which struck from the shelter of a railway embankment. The enemy hit the Royal Canadians at their weakest point and made fast progress. Lacking tanks or anti-tank guns the remnants of the two Canadian battalions fought a rearguard action back across the Lamone. Together they had suffered 165 casualties.

Harry Foster arrived to take over the Division the next day and in connivance with Foulkes sacked the First Brigade's Allan Calder, by far the least culpable of the three brigadiers involved, along with the commanding officers of the RCR and Hast PER. These disgraceful sackings were typical of the manner in which Foulkes and Foster seemed to think that lashing out at any subordinate without ascertaining the facts indicated a strong command grip. In fact it just magnified their own command flaws. To add insult to injury Desmond Smith, one of the real culprits of the debacle, was rewarded by being given command of Calder's brigade.

By 10 December Foulkes had prepared for a new crossing of the Lamone. Meanwhile the British 46th Division of V Corps, whose initial shortcomings had been exposed at the Gothic Line, proved to be a fast learner and bloodily defeated a strong German attack at Faenza.

For the new attack 1st Division would cross the Lamone where it had previously failed while 5th Armoured would cross at Villanova. Once across both divisions would push on to the Senio. Although the Senio was only four miles away to get there would force the Canadians to cross four more watercourses - the Fossos Vetro and Vecchio, the Naviglio Canal and the Fosso Munio. Each was a prospectively strong defensive position. On the night of 10 December the Canadians gate-crashed the Lamone. This time it worked in spades. 5th Division's 11 Brigade kicked off first at 1930 hrs in a silent crossing led by the Cape Breton Highlanders who took Villanova and 45 prisoners and the Perth Regiment who captured Borgo di Villanova to the south. The Westminsters and Irish followed and driving off enemy counter-attacks pushed through to cross Fosso Vetro and reach the Fosso Vecchio by noon on the 11th. The Irish took 50 prisoners and knocked out an equal number.

First Division's 3rd Brigade, with the 48th Highlanders under command, crossed in assault boats under artificial moonlight following an imaginative high-angle artillery bombardment. The guns paused half-way into their program then suddenly resumed catching scores of just re-emerged Germans in the open. Brigadier Bernatchez, atoning for his change-over muddle, sent three battalions across in the first wave - 48th left, West Novas centre and Carleton and Yorks right. The assault was brilliantly successful and by dawn 3rd Brigade, with light casualties, had established a large and secure bridgehead. The Germans hastily retreated behind the Naviglio which they strongly defended with the fresh 98th Division and the special Kesselring Machine-Gun Battalion.

The Naviglio

Lt Gen Foulkes planned another two division crossing for the Canale Naviglio. Although no one knew it at the time it was to be the last full-scale battle by the Canadian Corps in Italy. The operation started at last light on 12 December. On the left 1st Division's 1st Brigade, with the Carleton and Yorks under command, started things off. At 1900 hrs Brigadier Desmond Smith sent the Carletons across. Although Smith had, once more, allotted too little time for reconnaissance and orders(21) the gallant New Brunswickers got over in style. The lead companies quickly cleared the canal's far bank at Bagnacavallo taking 45 prisoners. Smith then reinforced the bridgehead with the remaining Carletons and three companies of the Hastings and Prince Edwards who had not yet fully recovered from their mauling on the Lamone.

At dawn the expected tank-led enemy counter-attack hit with savage fury. Lacking armour, but well supported by the divisional artillery, the Carleton and Yorks doggedly fought back but were eventually pushed into a small toe-hold on the Naviglio. The Hastings and Prince Edwards once more suffered badly. Most of two companies were overrun, the remainder regrouped around a single bankside farm house. The situation was critical when the BCDs were finally able to get a few tanks across. The first few tanks over were standard Shermans whose short-barreled 75s were at a great disadvantage against the enemy's Panthers - but were murderous against the German infantry and SP guns. Then at 1500 hrs the Dragoons brought across two Fireflies - Shermans with long-barreled 17 pounders - and the day, and the bridgehead, was saved. The Carletons whose staunch defence had saved the bridgehead suffered 35 casualties, the unfortunate Hastings and Prince Edwards twice that number.

Desmond Smith then sent over the Loyal Edmontons, supported by BCD tanks, to restore the bridgehead. For once enough time had been allowed for recce and orders and the Loyals went in well prepared at 1600 hrs. The Seaforths followed and aided by artificial moonlight the bridgehead was restored. The enemy, whose armour could be heard milling about all night, attacked at dawn. First Division's artillery again came to the fore pounding the enemy at every turn and slaughtering German infantry in the open. At day's end two Tiger and four Panther tanks lay brewing outside the Seaforth's perimeter and enemy dead littered the area. The Eddies, at a cost of 50 casualties, captured 90 Germans and killed or wounded as many.

5th Division's attack by 12 Brigade had not gone as well. The Lanark and Renfrew Scottish were stopped on the Naviglio's near bank and fought a furious small arms and grenade battle throughout the night. At the end they had suffered 110 casualties with nothing to show for it. The dismounted Princess Louise Dragoon Guards on their right suffered even worse. Two companies (or squadrons as they were still termed) managed to fight their way across the canal but were caught in murderous cross fire and driven back with 90 casualties including a number taken prisoner.

Thwarted on his own front 5th Division's commander Bert Hoffmeister, with the initiative which was becoming his hallmark, arranged to pass his division through 1st Division's bridgehead. On the 14th the Westminsters started through. Well supported by Strathcona tanks and Air Force Kittyhawks they ruthlessly winkled out the enemy along the canal capturing over 100 prisoners. The Lanark and Renfrew followed up and captured Osteria. The bridgehead was now wide and deep but the walled town of Bagnacavallo remained in German hands, its defenders protected behind thick stone barriers. The 17 pounders of the 7th Anti-Tank were brought up to destroy the church towers that the Germans were using as OPs. The 48th Highlanders then slowly moved against the Fosso Vecchio behind a series of artillery stonks.

Maj Gen Foster now ordered First Brigade to cross the Fosso Vecchio. For this operation Desmond Smith again called on the Royal Canadians and the Hastings and Prince Edwards. Perhaps he had little choice but after the hard fighting through the Gothic and the crushing reverse on the Lamone both battalions were nearly worn out. The Hasty Ps - the stars of countless bygone battles - were in particular at the end of their tether. They managed to stagger to the Fosso Vecchio and were stopped. The RCR did little better, only one company getting across. Heroism abounded - a Private Otis duplicating Smokey Smith's bravery in using his PIAT with cool disregard for his own life by destroying one tank, hitting another, destroying a section of infantry and then carrying a wounded man to safety. Others have won the Victoria Cross for less, but Otis settled for a DCM. In the end the RCR lost 70 men for no positive gain.

Foulkes tried again that night employing both his divisions. On the left the 2nd Brigade's Patricias and Loyals attacked silently at 2000 hrs on 19 December. They once more did a superb job. Against strong defences and vicious counter-attacks they surged ahead, infiltrating, clearing, destroying. By the afternoon of the 20th they had taken all their objectives and over 200 prisoners but at the terrible cost of 150 casualties.

On the right 11 Brigade sent in the Perths and Irish who had to attack over a flat, featureless, waterlogged plain to reach the canal. Both battalions were initially stopped by heavy aimed fire along the Fosso Munio. Then a company of Perths infiltrated the enemy defences to capture their objective the Casa della Congregatione before dawn. The enemy, as usual, counter-attacked with armour supported fury that morning. The Perths fought back repulsing a succession of attacks as the exhausted engineers struggled to build a crossing for the tanks. Shortly after noon they succeeded and Strathcona tanks fought their way forward to the relief of the gallant Perths. By 1530 hrs, at a cost of 80 Perths and 42 Irish, the battle was won. This dogged action unhinged the entire German defences in that sector. They evacuated Bagnacavallo and made a fighting withdrawal. On 21 December 3rd Brigade closed up to the Senio and Operation "Chuckle" was finally over.

It had, once more, been a bloody success. In twenty days the Canadians had broken three major, and several minor, heavily defended water lines and advanced nine miles battling for every yard. They had captured nearly 1,700 Germans, killed or wounded many hundreds more, and forced him to bring in reserves he could not afford. But the butcher's bill was again heavy and grim. The Canadians had 2,550 casualties of which 550 were fatal. The poor bloody infantry had, still again, been stretched to the limit. There was pathetically little left.

The Last Hurrah

During Operation "Chuckle" General Alexander called off his offensive for the winter. This decision was partly engendered by a severe reverse suffered on 5th Army's front but mainly because of the abominable weather and terrain. With it came a change in high command. General Alexander was promoted to Field Marshall and replaced Maitland Wilson as Supreme Commander Mediterranean Theatre. Mark Clark in turn replaced Alexander in command of 15th Army Group and General Truscott was brought from France to replace Clark at 5th Army. The changes, as usual, brought with them their kindergarten level of juvenile bickering and backbiting. Clark who disdained the British and the 8th Army publicly raked his British commander of XIII Corps over the coals. He denigrated what he claimed was a British lack of drive and avoidance of danger while claiming the glory. He ridiculed General McCreery as "a washout - a feather duster." McCreery for his part later claimed to have had only two problems in Italy and they were Mark and Clark.(22) The Germans, without bickering, also made changes. Kesselring moved to Germany to become Commander-in-Chief West and was replaced by the always able von Vietinghoff. Traugott Herr was promoted from LXXVII Corps to command the 10th Army.

For the Canadians winter was mainly a miserable routine of First World War type static warfare along the dreary Senio punctuated by an effort to give each unit a good Christmas break. For this period the Corps was temporarily reunited with 1st Armoured Brigade. The "static" period also marked a return to the previous winter's routine of endless tiring, and oft times harrowing, patrolling.(23) Although there was benefit to be had when patrols were ordered for some specific purpose such as gaining or denying information, they were ordered all too often simply "to keep the troops on their toes" or "to dominate No-Man's Land" the end result of which was simply to exhaust already over-fatigued troops. To all infantrymen, but especially the subalterns and NCOs who because of limited numbers seemed to always be detailed for patrol, the duty was distasteful and nerve-wracking in the extreme.

The Canadians did fight one last major battle in Italy, or more properly two simulta-

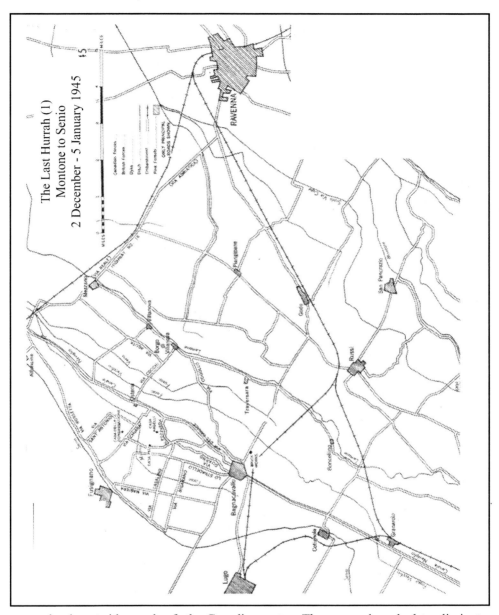

neous battles at either end of the Canadian sector. These were launched to eliminate German footholds below the Senio. On the left the Germans held a salient protruding from Cotignola to Granarolo. On the right, in the waterlogged flats below Lake Comacchio, they held a series of canal bank positions extending from the coast inland to Alfonsine.

Lt Gen Foulkes assigned the Granarolo operation to 1st Division who would co-operate with the flanking 56th (Dick Whittington) Division. Harry Foster in turn gave

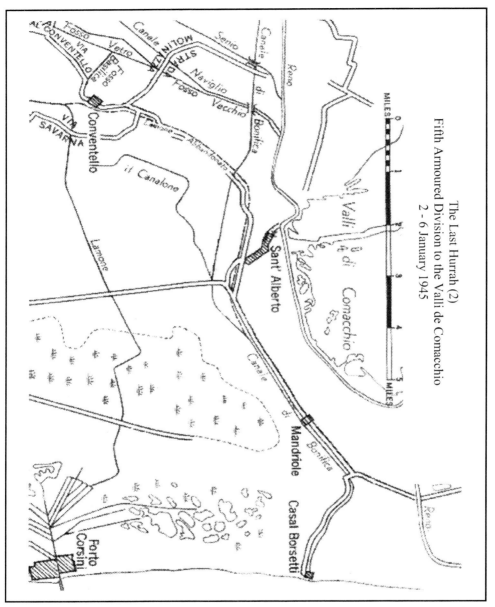

The Last Hurrah (2)
Fifth Armoured Division to the Valli de Comacchio
2 - 6 January 1945

the task to Pat Bogert's Second Brigade. The operation, which started with a diversionary attack by the Royal 22nd near Bagnacavallo, went off like clockwork. On the afternoon of 3 January, 1945 The Princess Pats attacked south of Granarolo, caught the enemy by surprise and captured 55 Germans and an SP gun. The Seaforths moved behind Granarolo after dark allowing the Loyal Edmontons to capture the town on the 4th. This was the cue for the British V Corps part of the operation which went just as well. Assaulting in Kangaroo APCs the 56th kept pace along the Senio.

THE ITALIAN CAMPAIGN

For a loss of only 30 men Second Brigade had scored a notable victory described by Bogert, its commander, as "one of the neatest battles this brigade has ever had."(24) In light of the many brilliant actions fought by this superlative formation there may have been a bit of hyperbole in Bogert's remarks - but just a bit!

Fifth Armoured Division was assigned the operation against the Comacchio Flats and it did equally well against a considerably tougher foe. The area was defended by the 721st Jager Regiment with one battalion in the Lamone - Vecchio gap south of Conventello, a second on the marshes to the coast and a third west of the Fosso Vecchio. Another regiment was in reserve near Bonifica. Unlike 2nd Brigade's comparatively trouble free performance at Granarolo, Hoffmeister realized that his assignment would call for a deft use of all of his resources. He first called upon 11 Brigade to capture the key bottleneck between Conventello and the Fosso Basilica. Once secure 5th Armoured Brigade would pass through to cross the Canale di Bonifica and capture Sant' Alberto on Lago Comacchio. The armored brigade planned to overcome the marshy ground by utilizing the frozen conditions and by fitting some of its tanks with grouser track extensions to better distribute the tank's ground pressure.

At 0500 hrs on 2 January, 1945 under artificial moonlight and a heavy artillery program the assault battalions - Perths left and Irish right - moved forward with a squadron of the 8th New Brunswick Hussars. The battalions advanced swiftly and efficiently taking one farmhouse strongpoint after another. With daylight fighter-bombers of the Desert Air Force arrived to strafe targets ahead of the advancing infantry. By mid-afternoon the two battalions were on their objectives - Conventello and the defile - having killed or wounded scores of enemy and captured seventy-five.

Hoffmeister now unleashed his armour with the BCDs advancing on the Via Savarna and the 8th Hussars going cross-country. Halted by Panther and SP fire from behind a ditch the tankers called upon the Cape Breton Highlanders who roared up in Bren Gun Carriers at dusk. At dawn the enemy counter-attacked and were driven back by the Breton boys. The tanks then took over and rapidly drove on repelling weak German armored elements en route. They were finally stopped by a deep and wide canal over which the Germans had blown the crossings. The armour leaguered for the night as the Perths arrived in front of the Bonifica.

At 0430hrs on the 4th the Germans mounted an exceptionally strong and well supported counter-attack by a composite battle group of four battalions from the 16th SS Panzer Grenadiers, 26th Panzers and 114th Jager Division. The attack, behind a heavy artillery bombardment, hit near the Fosso Basilica where the Westminsters and 1st King's Royal Rifle Corps of the attached British 9th Brigade waited. The Germans managed to get within 500 yards of the Lamone before being bloodily repulsed by massive artillery fire and superb small arms shooting by the Westminsters and Rifles. At dawn the Irish and New Brunswick Hussars counter-attacked and mopped up the remaining enemy as the Desert Air Force blasted their rear along the Fosso Vetro. With light casualties to themselves the defenders captured 200 and killed or wounded a like number.

To the north the BCDs, Perths and Cape Bretons methodically fought and cleared their way over, through and around enemy posts, water obstacles and wire strewn vineyards to take Sant' Alberto early on 5 January. The Canadians then tidied up the front clearing the Reno River west to the Vecchio and moving east to the coast where they met the British 12th Lancers advancing north under Canadian command.

Hoffmeister's final battle in Italy had been a superb triumph for his generalship and

GAUDEAMUS IGITUR

for all-arms and joint-service co-operation. In five days the Mighty Maroon Machine and its supporting cast had defeated eight battalions, taken 600 prisoners, killed and wounded hundreds, destroyed many Panther tanks, SP and other guns, captured all its objectives and totally liquidated the enemy east of the Senio. Both 8th Army and 15th Army Group were impressed. The demanding and hard-to-please McCreery praised the "splendid fighting spirit and great skill" shown by the two Canadian divisions. And the equally difficult Mark Clark sent to General Foulkes, "My sincere congratulations on the successful attacks by your troops during the past few days. The operation was thoroughly planned and executed. Despite strong enemy resistance and counter-attacks Cdn Corps and 5th Corps pressed forward taking a heavy toll of enemy dead and many prisoners."(25) It was a magnificent tribute to a magnificent final act. And for the Canadians in Italy it was the last hurrah!

Operation Goldflake

Having campaigned long and hard with the British to get first a division and then a corps into action in the Mediterranean the Canadian government and high command from at least mid-1944 had begun to campaign equally hard to reunite its army in Northwest Europe. It was the sort of thing to drive Churchill, Brooke, *et al* (already embroiled with Australia in similar contretemps) to utter distraction and to provide hidden grist for their diaries. Resistance to the move came on a number of counts: the further undesirable reduction of strength in Italy, shipping shortages and even a minor brouhaha over the possible, if highly implausible, use of Canadians in the Balkans. But despite whatever irritation the Canadian lobbying was causing them, both the Prime Minister and CIGS Brooke, to their very great credit, did all they could to satisfy the Canadian request. The matter was finally settled at a Chiefs of Staff meeting in Malta when, en route to the Yalta Conference, General Brooke proposed and FM Alexander accepted the move of the Canadians to "France". General Marshall tipped off Lt Gen Foulkes on the news and formal authority was issued by the British War Office on 5 February, 1945.

The move which would be made from Leghorn and Naples to Marseilles and thence to Holland was an administrative masterpiece as the Canadians were spread over half of Italy - 1st Division on the Senio, 5th in reserve along the coast, Headquarters at Ravenna, 1st Armoured Brigade with 5th Army and bits and pieces everywhere else. But it all went amazingly swift and well and by 28 February the 5th Armoured Division, now reorganized as a "normal" armored division (with its 12th Brigade disbanded), entered the line south of Arnhem. First Armoured Brigade soon followed suit. Last to go was First Division. Its 3rd Brigade left the Senio line on 27 February and joined the Canadian Army in the Rhineland on 3 April. On 13 April I Canadian Corps, reunited with 1st Canadian Army, was ready for its final operation, the liberation of Holland.

Epilogue

Historians and participants have long debated the many arguments put forth as the strategic requirements for fighting the Italian Campaign: to tie down German forces; to aid the Russians, to knock Italy out of the war; to do something between North Africa and D Day; to enter Europe via the "soft underbelly" and the Lubljana Gap; to provide

THE ITALIAN CAMPAIGN

bomber bases; to secure the Balkans; etc., etc. Whatever the merits or demerits of these arguments there can be no doubt that the 22 month Italian Campaign, the longest undertaken by the western Allies during the war, was a mighty campaign in every respect and was, in the end, completely victorious. A total of 26 nations fought on the Allied side and suffered 321,000 casualties. The enemy, before his final mass surrender, lost 658,000.

Until they left Italy, two months before the end, the Canadian First Division was the longest serving Allied division in the theatre. Some 93,000 Canadians served in Italy of whom over 26,000 - more than 25% - became casualties. Canadian formations fought in the vanguard of 8th Army from the outset and spearheaded some of its greatest battles - Sicily, the Reggio landing, the Moro, Ortona, the Liri, the Hitler, Gothic and Rimini lines, Coriano, the Lamone, the Senio. Their armored brigade supported British formations at Cassino, Florence and with the 5th Army. They participated in two great assault landings - Pachino in Sicily and Reggio in Italy - leading the final Allied return to mainland Europe. They were always victorious.

The two Canadian divisions and the armored brigade were probably the finest formations in the Canadian Army. They considered themselves the best in the world.(26) And with some justification. Many historians place the German 1st Parachute Division at the top of the list and it was certainly superb. Yet whenever it met the 1st Canadian Division - as it often did as the Germans sought to counter the best with the best - the Canadians emerged victorious. On the few occasions that the Germans fought on the wrong side of a water barrier without their tanks or anti-tank guns they complained of this lack for their defeat. Yet such unsupported actions were all too often par for the course for the Canadians who were nevertheless expected to prevail and they usually did.

The German command itself considered the Canadians to be elite troops - not only from their reports, some of which have been quoted before, but also from the fact that, as noted above, they sought to place their best divisions opposite the Canadians whenever they could. Of the twenty different divisions which the Canadians faced in Italy only one or two could be considered sub-standard. At least four of the very best - the 1st Parachute, 26th Panzer, 28th and 90th Panzer Grenadier - were placed opposite the Canadians again and again., surely the ultimate appraisal. The Germans also nervously searched for the appearance of Canadians in the line as harbingers of an impending offensive, and they were usually right.

Although most Canadians were happy to leave the miseries of Italy to rejoin their brethren in Holland they were thereby denied the reward and glory of participating in the final victory. Like Enna, Messina, Rome and Rimini the prizes for their victories too often went to others. But by helping to liberate Holland from its bonds they earned the eternal thanks and gratitude of that marvelous country. And that is the ultimate and most satisfying reward of all.

The North Nova Scotia Highlanders landing at Bernieres-sur-Mer. (NAC PA 122765)

Canadian troops disembark at low tide later in the day. (DND)

THE NORTHWEST EUROPE CAMPAIGN

CHAPTER VIII

NORMANDY - FROM D - DAY TO CAEN

I will lay odds that ere this year expire,
We'll bear our civil swords and native fire
As far as France - I heard a bird so sing,
Whose music to my thinking pleased the king !

Shakespeare *King Henry V*

To Overlord

There are a handful of pivotal battles whose names still resound with the informed public as marking high-water turning points in the Second World War. France 1940, the Battle of Britain, Pearl Harbour, Midway, Stalingrad, El Alamein and Hiroshima are on everyone's list, as is D-Day the 6th of June, 1944. But while the first seven doubtless were key turning points it is moot whether or not D-Day deserves this august rating. Certainly from a western Allied viewpoint it does, but on the grander canvas perhaps not. For by this date the fate of Germany was already ordained. The Russians, victorious at Kursk, were rapidly closing up to the Oder, while in Italy only the forthcoming autumn rains would prevent the Allies from pushing to the Alps and beyond and entering Germany via the "soft underbelly" as Mr. Churchill was fond of saying. Meanwhile the RAF and USAAF were ravaging Germany from end to end in a bombing campaign that Air Marshal Sir Arthur Harris argued could win the war on its own.

But all of this is to quibble as, from the western perspective, D-Day was truly a most momentous event. It marked the return of the western armies to the "real" mainland Europe after four long years and once ashore these armies sealed the German fate. Much bitter fighting remained but the march of the Allied armies from east, west and south was thereafter inexorable. It all started eighteen months before.

The Casablanca Conference of January 1943 decreed that a plan be made for an Allied invasion of northern France. For this purpose an inter-Allied planning staff was formed in London under British Lt Gen Sir Frederick Morgan who was appointed Chief-of-Staff (COSSAC) to the, as yet unnamed, Supreme Allied Commander. As the appointment of US General D.D. Eisenhower as the Supreme Commander was delayed until the Cairo Conference of December 1943, Morgan and staff were obliged to plan on their own. Normandy, near the limit of range for UK based fighters, was chosen as the invasion site over its nearest competitor the Pas de Calais where defences were heavier and German reserves and fighter airfields were closer. Elaborate deception plans, which proved to be surprisingly effective, were put in train to convince the enemy that the Pas de Calais or Norway were the real targets. An enormous bombing campaign targeted all likely areas and the rear communications network. Based on the experiences of Dieppe, Sicily and Italy new landing craft and techniques were developed along with a whole train of specialized assault equipments such as swimming (duplex-drive (DD)) tanks, SP Artillery, armoured engineer equipments, flame throwers and a range of amphibious craft.(1)

GAUDEAMUS IGITUR

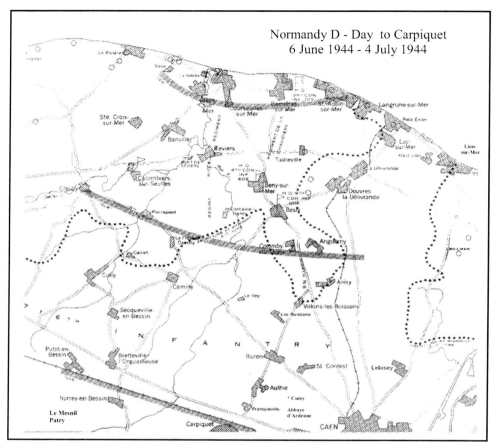

Normandy D - Day to Carpiquet
6 June 1944 - 4 July 1944

When Eisenhower was appointed Supreme Commander, General B.L. Montgomery was brought from Italy in January 1944 as his ground forces commander for the opening phase of the invasion. Montgomery, as was his want, started by belittling Morgan's plan, although he ended up by retaining much of it in principle. He did however considerably augment the size of the invasion force. He also commenced a series of briefings of senior commanders to put his personal stamp on things.

The Enemy Defences

Since 1942 the Germans had been progressively increasing and strengthening their defences in the west. Harbours were defended and all likely landing beaches covered by gun emplacements, strong points, minefields, wire and anti-landing craft devices of obstacles and mines. By June, 1944 the Germans had 58 divisions in the west under Field Marshal Gerd von Rundstedt, Commander GHQ West. Under him Field Marshal Erwin Rommel commanded Army Group "B" with the 7th Army in Normandy and Brittany and the 15th from the Seine to Holland. Army Group "G" consisted of the 1st Army of five divisions along the Bay of Biscay and the 19th Army of eight divisions on the Mediterranean. Netherlands Command had four divisions.

THE NORTHWEST EUROPE CAMPAIGN

Rommel, based on his experience, wanted to place his armoured divisions well forward in order to hit the enemy immediately on landing. The more conservative Rundstedt preferred to group most centrally from whence they could massively attack the main enemy landings once identified. In the end a poor compromise was adopted with two armoured divisions held close to what turned out to be the actual invasion beaches. Four of the ten remaining armoured divisions could only be released by order of Wehrmacht Headquarters in far-off Berlin.

The actual coastal defences were manned by infantry divisions of varying effectiveness. All were backed by a formidable array of machine guns, mortars, artillery, anti-tank and anti-aircraft guns and self-propelled (SP) weapons. Many of the coastal weapons were housed in massive concrete emplacements thickly surrounded by wire and mines. In what was to become the British/Canadian beachhead the Germans had 13 infantry battalions supported by 250 artillery pieces and 50 SP anti-tank guns. The principal immediate armoured forces were the 21st Panzer and 12th SS Panzer divisions. The sector was commanded by the LXXXIV Corps under General Dollmann's 7th Army. The Canadian assault area was manned by the 716th Infantry Division.

The Allied Plan

For the invasion General Montgomery's 21st Army Group included the US 1st Army under General Omar Bradley of two assault and four follow-up divisions and Lt Gen Miles Dempsey's 2nd British Army of three assault (including one Canadian) and three follow-up divisions. One British (including a Canadian parachute battalion) and two American airborne divisions would land in advance of the seaborne assault. The invasion force was to be progressively augmented to some 24 divisions by the third week after D-Day.

In addition to massive pre-invasion attacks by RAF Bomber Command and the US 8th Air Force, over 100 fighter squadrons were assigned to protect the invasion force and 35 were available for direct air support. Naval support was provided by some 250 vessels ranging from battleships to special gun and rocket firing landing support craft.

The planned invasion area extended some 50 miles from the Orne River on the left to halfway up the Cotentin Peninsula on the right, equally divided between the two assault armies. On the US sector Bradley assigned "Utah Beach", north of the Carentan Estuary to Lt Gen Collins VII Corps with the 4th US Infantry as the assault division. Lt Gen Gerow's V Corps was to land on "Omaha Beach", adjacent to the British 2nd Army, with the veteran 1st US Infantry Division in the van. Each US corps had two follow-up divisions. The 82nd and 101st Airborne Divisions' drop zones were both in the VII Corps sector north of the Douve River.

Dempsey's 2nd British Army assigned the eastern sector to Lt Gen J.T. Crocker's I Corps with the 3rd British Division landing at Lion-sur-Mer ("Sword Beach") and the 3rd Canadian Division between St Aubin and Courseulles ("Juno Beach"). The 51st Highland Division was the Corps' follow-up formation. On 2nd Army's right Lt Gen Bucknall's XXX Corps would land on "Gold Beach" near Arromanches with the 50th Northumbrian Division. The 7th Armoured and 49th West Riding divisions comprised Bucknall's follow-up force. The 6th British Airborne Division, including the 1st Canadian Parachute Battalion, was assigned drop zones east of the Orne River on the extreme left flank of the invasion front. The five British/Canadian assault beaches

("Gold" and "Juno" each with two, "Sword" with one) were all about a mile wide with gaps of up to five miles between them. A ten mile gap separated the British and US beaches.

Drawing on shortcomings exposed at Dieppe the 79th British Armoured Division of specialized armoured assault equipments (the "funnies") would support each of 2nd Army's sectors by breaching obstacles, destroying strong points and clearing lanes off the beaches. Also profiting from Dieppe special Contact Detachments from the reconnaissance regiments were to provide radio communications directly to divisional headquarters from each landing beach thus giving commanders unfiltered, real-time information with which to operate. Beach Groups of pioneers, Royal Marines and, in the Canadian Sector, special battalions of the Royal Berkshire and King's Regiments provided landing assistance, traffic control, casualty clearance and prisoner collecting on the beaches. All of these were important elements to a successful invasion but, as Wellington observed on the eve of Waterloo, in the final analysis it all depended on "that article"- the ordinary soldier of the combat arms. He - the infantry private, tank trooper and engineer sapper - rather than the statesmen, generals and gilded planners held the success or failure of "Overlord" in his hands.

The Canadian Assault Force

In mid-1943 the 3rd Canadian Infantry Division (Maj Gen R.F.Keller) and 2nd Canadian Armoured Brigade (in Normandy Brig R.A.Wyman) were designated as the Canadian assault formations and began special training. This included embarkation, debarkation and landing drills, field firing, mine clearance, cliff and obstacle scaling. In early 1944 assault landing exercises were held near Portsmouth. New equipments included Duplex-Drive (DD) swimming tanks, Fireflies (Shermans with 17 pounders), Priests (SP 105mm guns), flame throwers and improved 6 pdr A tk ammunition. The Fireflies and 6 pdr ammunition were to result in initial unexpected bad consequences through unfamiliarity although both would soon prove their worth. By mid-May 1944 the training ended and the assault formations were confined to secure areas where they were briefed in detail on their tasks.

The invasion, code-named "Overlord", was critically dependent on weather and tides which severely limited the choice of suitable dates. Finally, after one delay and with the Met forecast still dicey and the window of opportunity vanishing, General Eisenhower bit the bullet and ordered D-Day for the 6th of June,1944. H-Hour for the Canadian Sector was 0730 hrs at which time the tides should be covering the mined beach hedgehogs for a safer run-in of the landing craft. The airborne troops were to be dropped much earlier - starting at 0100 hrs for the 6th Airborne and its Canadian paratroops.

The Canadian assault landing area, code-named "Juno", stretched for some four miles from St. Aubin-sur-Mer on the left to Vaux on the right. "Juno" was divided (from left to right) into "Nan" (sub-divided into Red, White and Green) and" Mike" (sub-divided into Red and Green) beaches. The 8th Canadian Infantry Brigade (8 CIB) (Brig K.G. Blackader) was assigned "Nan" (less Green) and 7th Brigade (7 CIB) (Brig H.A. Foster) "Nan Green" and "Mike". The 8CIB assault units were as follows: "Nan Red" - The North Shore Regiment (NSR) (Lt Col D.B. Buell). "Nan White" - The Queen's Own Rifles of Canada (QOR of C) (Lt Col J.G. Spragge). Follow-up battalion - Le Regiment de la Chaudiere (R de Chaud) (Lt Col J.B. Mathieu). Supporting Armour

THE NORTHWEST EUROPE CAMPAIGN

- 10th Armoured Regiment, The Fort Garry Horse (FGH) (Lt Col R.E. Morton). 7 CIB units were: "Nan Green" - The Regina Rifle Regiment (RRR) (Lt Col F.M. Matheson). "Mike Red" - The Royal Winnipeg Rifles (RWR) (Lt Col J.M. Meldram). "Mike Green" - C Company The Canadian Scottish Regiment (C Scot R) (Lt Col F.N. Cabeldu). Follow-up Battalion - C Scot R less C Coy. Supporting Armour - 6th Canadian Armoured Regiment, The 1st Hussars (1H) (Lt Col R.J. Colwell).

The 9th Canadian Infantry Brigade (9CIB) (Brig D.G. Cunningham) was the divisional reserve. It consisted of: The Highland Light Infantry of Canada (HLI) (Lt Col F.M. Griffiths), The Stormont, Dundas and Glengarry Highlanders (SD&G) (Lt Col G.H. Christiansen) and The North Nova Scotia Highlanders (NNSH) (Lt Col C. Petch). The 27th Armoured Regiment, The Sherbrooke Fusiliers (SF) (Lt Col M.B. Gordon) provided tank support. Divisional units included: The 7th Reconnaissance Regiment, The 17th Duke of York's Royal Canadian Hussars (7 Recce) (Lt Col T.C. Lewis) and The Cameron Highlanders of Ottawa (MG) (CH of O) (Lt Col P.C. Klahn). Artillery units were the 12th, 13th, 14th Field (all SP), 3rd Anti-Tank and 4th Light Anti-Aircraft Regiments RCA.

On the extreme left of the Canadian sector the 48th Royal Marine Commando were to land behind the NSR on "Nan Red" and turn east to link up with 3rd British Division who would be landing at Lion-sur-Mer (Sword Beach). This link-up was a vital element in subsequent Canadian battle plans.

The Landings
Nan Red and White

Despite the massive air and naval preparatory bombardments and run-in covering fire many of the beach defences on 8th Brigade's assault front were largely untouched. (2) To add to the problems of the assaulting infantry the DD tanks of the supporting Fort Garry Horse, instead of swimming ashore with the first wave, were brought in on their landing craft and only came into action after the infantry had crossed the beach and were fighting in the villages.

The North Shore Regiment landed at St. Aubin-sur-Mer at 0800 hrs. Its "A" Company on the flank managed to charge across the beach, clear its front and dash behind the village at a cost of 25 casualties. "B" Company assaulting the village head-on was itself caught in the flank by a determined 100 man enemy company firing from a huge concrete blockhouse and surrounding trenches. "B" Company then divided with two platoons continuing on to clear the town while the third, assisted by Fort Garry Shermans and Royal Marine Centaur tanks, tried to storm the blockhouse. The blockhouse continued to frustrate the attackers until the "funnies" of 79 Armoured came to the rescue. An AVRE (Armoured Vehicle Royal Engineers) mounting a petard launcher moved up and blasted several shots at the blockhouse. The huge petards (nick-named "coal scuttles") cracked the concrete walls and killed half the defenders. The rest, severely concussed, stumbled out into captivity. The assault had cost "B" Company 65 casualties - over half its strength.

With the beach defences surmounted the North Shores moved swiftly inland past their initial objective ("Yew") and into Tailleville. Here they collided with the headquarters and reserve company of the 2nd Battalion 736th Regiment. A stiff battle raged all afternoon and ended with the victorious North Shores and Garrys capturing the

GAUDEAMUS IGITUR

village and 60 prisoners.

The Royal Marine Commandos came ashore while the North Shores were still engaging the bypassed enemy bunkers. They became embroiled in the battle and suffered severe casualties before things settled down enough for them to turn eastward to effect their mission of linking with the British 3rd Division. The Marines eventually effected a tenuous link-up along the beach but inland a worrying gap yawned between the two 3rd Divisions which German armour was preparing to exploit. An initial panzer probe was beaten back by British armour and anti-tank guns but the gap remained. Apparently neither the commanders of the British 1st Corps nor 3rd Division appreciated the continuing problem and, without informing the flanking Canadians, moved their right hand brigade over to the left flank to join with the embattled 6th Airborne Division. While in the fog of battle the move probably made tactical sense for the moment it nullified a next-day pre-planned move by the British on St. Contest to cooperate with a Canadian drive on Carpiquet. This annulment and the failure to notify the Canadians was to play a tragic role in tomorrow's battles.

The Queen's Own Rifles landed at "Nan White" at Bernieres-sur-Mer. The landing was opposed by a company manning nine concrete emplacements containing 50mm guns and machine guns backed by the superb German mortars and artillery, all of which seemed to have escaped the pre-landing bombardment. "A" Company QOR, landing to the west of the village, moved quickly inland and joined in clearing the town. "B" company landed 250 yards east of its planned run-in, just enough to place it directly in front of the main enemy casement. Taking heavy casualties but pepper-potting forward in text-book "fire and movement" the Queen's Own got behind the concrete bunker and, aided by Fort Garry tanks, blasted in and the enemy surrendered. The action, brilliant as it was, cost "B" Company over 65 casualties. The reserve QOR companies then dashed through and moved quickly to report line "Yew". Barney Danson, later to be Canadian Minister of National Defence, and who was soon to lose all three of the close friends who landed with him, was one of the QOR of C platoon commanders whose company got troops ashore through fire and confusion and onto its objective that day. Another was CSM Charley Martin who was to become a legend within and without his battalion.

8th Brigade's reserve battalion, the Chaudieres, landed at 0900 hrs while the Queen's Own were still battling in Bernieres. But by now the engineers with the superb beach organization had made several good exits from the beach and through the seawall into the town. The lack of this had been one of the problems which had doomed Dieppe to failure and on which corrective action had been taken to the benefit of "Overlord". Through these gaps the Chauds accompanied by FGH Shermans and SP Priests plunged inland. By mid-afternoon they had overrun an artillery battery and captured Beny-sur-Mer. They then pushed on to Basly and patrolled as far as Colomby-sur-Thaon.

This dispassionate, bare-bones outline does scant service to the troops involved in the D-Day landings. Indeed it is probably impossible to describe the tensions within each soldier as he bobbed, seasick, wet with the huge splashes of exploding shells and detonating mines in a tiny landing craft while bullets pinged off the bow, waiting in dazed hebetude for the craft to finally beach. Then the ramp crashes down - hopefully in water not over one's head. If lucky the soldier can make a clear dash from the craft, but all too often he must clamber over the bodies of comrades in front, shot down as the ramp fell. The wade through the surging water, already turning red from the blood of hit infantrymen, is an agonizing slow motion exercise in Hell. Then the beach and the dash to the seawall as friends fall around one and enemy machine gunners sweep the beach in enfilade. Only another combat infantryman can begin to comprehend, however dimly, the gut-wrenching, throat-drying, heart-pounding terror that was their constant companion on that terrible day. That they did it at all is a wonder. That they did it so magnificently is to their, and their country's, everlasting honour.

"Nan Green"

The Regina Rifles of 7 Brigade came ashore at Courseulles-sur-Mer, possibly the most heavily defended part of the Anglo-Canadian, and perhaps entire, D-Day front. In the words of Major C.S. Tubbs, OC "C" Company, "Half a dozen machine gun posts were embedded along the 500 yard stretch of beach. Two concrete gun casements stood one on either side of the Seulles River's mouth. At the eastern end of the strongpoint a third casemate housed another gun. A warren of trenches connected all of these positions which were sited primarily to bring enfilade fire along the beach, rather than firing seaward. Six anti-tank and four field guns provided support."(3) And the ubiquitous German mortar teams had pre-registered the beach area with great precision.

The Reginas, supported by a squadron of DD tanks of the 1st Hussars, landed with great panache, with "B" Company left and "A" right. In Major Stu Tubbs' words again, "The theme was to crash the beach and go like stink."(4) The battalion transport officer, and soon to be OC "D" Company, Captain G. Brown put it thus: "It is probably as well we didn't know what was ahead of us. Experienced troops would have been more cautious. A landing like ours calls for initiative and dash, not intelligent caution, if it is to be successful. Ignorance was bliss."(5)

"B" Company made good progress crossing the beach under heavy fire and were soon clearing the town. "A" Company on the right suffered heavy losses in landing and was held up by withering fire from a large casemate on the right flank. This vital strongpoint was finally knocked out through an extraordinary act of heroism by Lt. W. Grayson and a handful of his platoon of "A" Company. Grayson received the MC. He deserved a VC for without his deed of reckless daring not only the Regina's landing but also that of the Winnipeg's would have been in extreme peril. "A" Company, now reduced to just 40 men, then fought their way inland. Some of the Rifles, their bangalores lost, were held up by a thick belt of barbed wire interspersed with mines. Again it was "funnies" to the rescue. A flail tank of the 79th Division materialized and ploughed through the wire detonating a mine en route. The Reginas charged through the gap and into town.

"C" and "D" companies followed 15 minutes later. "C" got ashore and into Courseulles without too many unpredicted problems. But it was quite another story with "D" Company. Two of its landing craft, caught on a rising tide, struck mines some 200 yards out killing the company commander, battalion signals officer and many others. Only 49 men of "D" Company , now commanded by a lieutenant, survived to work their way inland. Despite heavy casualties the "Johns", as they were universally known, and their escorting tanks cleared Courseulles and advanced inland to Reviers and Fontaine Henry hard by their intermediate report line "Elm". By this time their accompanying Hussars squadron had lost half its tanks.

GAUDEAMUS IGITUR

"Mike Beach"

Landing to the west of the River Seulles, which the Germans had flooded, The Royal Winnipeg Rifles, "the Little Black Devils", came ashore on the extremely open "Mike Red" beach where many of the obstacles and bunkers had been little touched by the covering bombardment. Fortunately one of the most dangerous had received a direct hit from naval gunfire and the Reginas had taken care of another.

The supporting 1st Hussars tanks were held up on landing and until they arrived it was touch and go. "B" Company was landed in front of a very heavily defended area but fought its way inland with great determination and heavy casualties. By the time it had cleared pill boxes and obstacles and worked its way inland it was down to one officer and 30 men. "D" Company landed to the west and after crossing several flooded ditches captured La Valette and with the remnants of "B" moved on to take Graye-sur-Mer.

"A" and "C" companies followed up and passed through while the assault companies were still winkling-out the enemy from near the beach. "C" Company took Banville while "A" assisted the Can Scots in capturing St-Croix-sur-Mer. The Winnipegs then moved on to Creully on the inter-divisional boundary where, as planned, they contacted the "Geordies" of the British 50th Division. They went on to secure report line "Elm" before last light.

"Mike Green"

"C" Company The Canadian Scottish landed on "Mike Green" on the extreme west of the Canadian landing sector. Due to observation aided by the flat open ground its primary objective, Le Chateau Vaux area, had received a severe pounding from the navy and the principal strong point had been knocked out. The company assaulted the chateau and after a short fight forced the surrender of its defenders.

The remaining Can Scots came ashore and joined up with "C" near St. Croix. The full battalion then pushed on and after some stiff engagements took Colombiers-sur-Seulles before crossing "Elm" and advancing to Pierrepont, Cainet and Camilly some six miles inland. They completed a fine day's work by contacting the Reginas at La Fresne on their left and the Winnipegs at Creully on their right. The Canadian Scottish had captured over 200 prisoners and killed or wounded scores more at a cost of 87 casualties to themselves. Although high their casualties were the lowest suffered by the three western regiments on that "longest day".

The Reserve Brigade

While the 7th and 8th Brigades were fighting their way inland the reserve 9th (Highland) Brigade, with its 27th Armoured Regiment, The Sherbrooke Fusiliers, started coming ashore about 1100 hrs at Bernieres in 8th Brigade's sector. The Highland battalions landed with bicycles to speed their drive inland but heavy congestion on the beach and the masking of underwater obstacles by the rising tide slowed things considerably. It was mid-afternoon before the brigade got clear of Bernieres and 1800 hrs before reaching its assembly area at Beny-sur-Mer. The North Novas and Sherbrookes pushed on to Colomby-sur-Thaon and Villons-les-Buissons where they had a stiff fight to clear out the enemy before last light.

End of the Longest Day

Although no German armour had yet been encountered and the ways to Caen and Carpiquet (the respective final objectives of the British and Canadian 3rd Divisions) seemed relatively open, the Commander Ist Corps, Lt Gen Sir John Crocker, wisely decided to hold for the night along the general line of "Elm". The day's brilliant successes masked the immense congestion and confusion on the beaches and time was needed to sort things out. In particular the artillery had to be positioned, the tanks replenished, tank and personnel casualties replaced and the beaches put in order for the orderly receipt and transmission of everything.

Although the main force held up along line "Elm", one troop of the 1st Hussars moved three miles south to cross the Caen-Bayeux railroad thus becoming the only sea-landed unit on the entire Allied front to reach its final objective on D-Day.(6) The troop was later brought back to the main Forward Defended Locality (FDL). Although this was a one-off effort it shows what might have been possible had Lt Gen Crocker opted for a "Hell for Leather" all-night advance on D-Day rather than the more prudent course actually adopted. Conjecture aside, the 3rd Canadian Infantry Division had performed admirably in its baptism by fire. Although its one day casualties of 940 (340 killed) were less than feared beforehand they were still a very considerable number.(7)

By nightfall some 75,000 British and Canadian and 60,000 American troops were ashore and 23,000 more had arrived from the sky. On the British/Canadian front over 900 tanks, 5000 other vehicles, 600 field, anti-tank and anti-aircraft guns and 4000 tons of stores had been landed. The Allies were there to stay.

Of more immediate concern were the wide gaps that still existed between units and formations despite the odd contact patrol that had been made. The gap between the British and Canadian 3rd Divisions of from two to four miles was particularly disturbing. This was exacerbated when Headquarters I Corps and 3rd British Division changed pre-arranged contact plans on D-Day without informing the affected Canadians. At the last minute they switched the British 9th Brigade, which was to have provided linkage, from the division's right flank to the left. The resultant gap and with it the failure to fully cooperate with the planned next day's Canadian advance was to have near catastrophic results. Why Crocker's experienced Corps staff did not tidy up the coordination aspects of this change is a mystery and is another example of the unforeseen perils that bedevil the best laid plans in the crucible of war.(8)

The Germans had initially been uncharacteristically slow in reacting to the invasion. This was partly due to Allied deception measures, partly to air interdiction and partly due to the absence, for one reason or another, of key German commanders. They soon took steps to correct these things and although they still feared a "real" invasion on the Pas de Calais the Germans were soon taking energetic steps to drive the "little fish" ,as Colonel Kurt Meyer termed them, back into the sea. Rommel and other commanders hurried back and against the British/Canadian sector were preparing to launch the 21st Panzer Division east of Caen and the 12th SS Panzer Division west of that city. The Panzer Lehr Division was also working forward. And in the air the Luftwaffe began their nightly attacks on the beach head.

GAUDEAMUS IGITUR

The Death Ride of the North Novas

Due to congestion on the beach and sporadic nearby fighting the North Nova Scotia Highlanders (NNSH), along with the rest of 9 Brigade, had a rough time getting through Bernieres. And once in the open they had some spirited encounters before reaching the Anisy - Les Buissons - Caen road. It was midnight before the regiment had assembled and dug-in. They then passed a fitful night of alarms and excursions against German patrols and marauding half-tracks. In these ongoing encounters since leaving the beach the North Novas had acquitted themselves very well - destroying 17 half-tracks and other vehicles and killing many enemy.

The Corps' plan for 7 June was for the 3rd British Division to take Caen while the Canadians took Carpiquet and its airfield. Maj Gen Keller, GOC 3CID, in accordance with pre-planning, directed that Brig Cunningham's 9th Brigade capture the Canadian objective. Cunningham held his Orders Group (O Gp) at 0500 hrs on 7 June. He was unaware of the precise plans of 3rd British Division and was certainly unaware of their change of plan for the linking flank. But, as previously arranged, he expected the British 3rd to parallel his advance by attacking at dawn along a line Cambes - St Contest on the left flank of 9 Canadian Brigade. Cunningham assigned the vanguard of his advance to the North Novas supported by tanks of the Sherbrooke Fusiliers and other detachments.

Despite having passed a disturbed night the North Nova Battle Group was in high spirits as they kicked-off at 0740 hrs from Villons-les-Buissons. The Vanguard, under Maj J.D. Learment was organized in the standard "advance to contact" formation which the Scotians had often practised with the Sherbrooke Fusiliers. First was an advanced guard of the Fusiliers' light Stuart tanks, then "C" company NNSH in Universal (Bren Gun) Carriers followed by a platoon of Camerons' MMGs', a troop of SP anti-tank guns of 3rd Anti-Tank Regiment, a section of assault pioneers and four six-pounders of the unit's A tk Platoon. Behind the Vanguard the other three companies rode on the tops of the Shermans of the Sherbrooke Fusiliers. At this stage everything seemed right on.

Unfortunately four things conspired to upset "the best laid plans of mice and men." First and foremost, the 12th SS Panzer Division had concentrated around the intervening Abbaye d' Ardenne where Colonel (later Major General) Kurt Meyer's 25th SS Panzer Grenadier Regiment had deployed two battalions of infantry and one of tanks. Meyer also had excellent observation over the entire area from the Abbaye tower. Second the 3rd British Division's parallel and flank protecting advance, compounded by the unannounced switch of its right brigade, was stopped in its tracks. Its attack by 185 Brigade only got as far as Lebisey Woods and, much later in the day, part of 9 Brigade only reached Cambes. This failure by 3rd British Division, coupled with poor coordination by Headquarters Ist Corps, left the Canadian brigade's critical left flank wide open to an enemy riposte from St Contest. It was an opportunity any German commander, especially the thrusting Meyer, would rush to exploit. Thirdly, and crucially, the supporting 14th Field Regiment (whose SP guns had a range of only 10,500 yards) was mired at Beny, just out of range of Authie, the Highlanders' intermediate objective. Thus the artillery regiment had to make a critical move forward while the Highlanders were already on the march. Then when the guns reached their new position at Basly they came under fire from Germans still holding out in a bypassed strong point. And, if these were not enough, the naval forward fire controller lost communications with the sup-

THE NORTHWEST EUROPE CAMPAIGN

porting warships. Naval gunfire could have totally dominated any enemy threat from St Contest. Alas, the guns were to remain silent.

These things unknown to them the highly trained NNSH Battle Group advanced with great elan, knocking out two 88s, three half-tracks and many infantry en route. Despite a temporary ambush of NNSH Battalion Headquarters the troops pushed on. At 1150 hrs they reached Buron which was defended by a strong enemy force. At the same time heavy fire was poured into the column's open flank from St Contest which the British 3rd had been expected to neutralize.

Chivvied by Brigade, which was in turn pressed by Division and Division by Corps, the Vanguard bypassed Buron and headed for Authie leaving Buron to the follow-up companies - all perfectly in accordance with time honoured battle procedure. Meanwhile the Stuarts of the Sherbrooke Fusiliers reached Franqueville. Then all hell broke loose.

With the Highlanders still out of range of their artillery, both of their flanks exposed to thin air and their companies strung out Meyer struck. In the face of savage enemy fire, and a tank - led counter from St Contest, the Highlanders quickly regrouped. The Vanguard was ordered to defend high ground behind Authie with "B" Company moving to the left and "A" to the right of that village. The battle quickly degenerated into a melee. "B" Company could not get past Buron so the Vanguard and "A" were ordered back. But it was too late. "A" Company was overrun while the survivors of the Vanguard "C" worked their way back. The enemy then launched a savage attack around Buron and overran part of "D" Company before a counter-attack by the Sherbrookes and M10 tank destroyers, now finally and excellently supported by artillery, drove them back in disarray. The surviving North Novas were then withdrawn to a Brigade "fortress" at Les Buissons held by the SD&G and HLI. The severely mauled Germans did not dare to re-enter Buron for another day. For their part the widely dispersed Canadian division lacked the resources to take the village in the brief window of opportunity available.

Thus ended the attempt to storm Carpiquet by a coup-de-main. Few at the time realized that a full month would elapse before the next attempt, on what was planned as the D + 1 objective, would be made. The attempt had been a bloody failure in which the North Novas had suffered 242 casualties, 84 of them fatal. And some 20 of the prisoners which they lost were summarily executed by their SS captors. The Sherbrooke Fusiliers lost 21 tanks and 60 men.(9) But they had destroyed over 30 German tanks plus a number of scout cars, half-tracks, SP guns and many enemy soldiers. Most significantly the savage battle had completely blunted any immediate attempt by the enemy to destroy the invaders. This important aspect of the battle's outcome is overlooked by armchair critics whose fixation with what went wrong totally blots out the positive results. Perhaps the worst result was the loss of a very fine regiment. Although the North Nova Scotia Highlanders were to fight many more tough, valiant and often successful battles they never regained their superb cutting edge D-Day form. Indeed they came to be considered almost a hard-luck regiment.

Brig Cunningham has been severely criticised for sending a regiment off into the blue without tidying up all of his support, flanks and rear as Monty would be want to do. But that is hindsight generated hogwash. The Canadians, along with the rest of the invasion force, were under extreme pressure from within and above to get onto their final objectives without delay. And on the morning of 7 June the prizes of Carpiquet and Caen were well worth the risks. Had any of the four bad-luck elements described above not happened the gamble could have worked and the Normandy campaign possibly shortened by a month. It failed, but so did Balaclava which is best remembered for the heroism of the Light Brigade rather than the command blunders. So too should the death ride of the North Novas.

For decades after the American Civil War its Confederate survivors lamented the failure of Longstreet to come up at Gettysburg. We may in turn lament that the 3rd British Division did not come up at St Contest. But of such things - "for want of a nail" - are battles won or lost. And the Canadians would win nearly all of them from here on in.

Holding the Line

While the North Novas were preparing on the morning of 7 June for their ride of destiny the rest of 3rd Canadian Division was advancing to its final post-landing positions. The left of the line lay anchored on Villons-les- Buissons. On the right the Winnipegs rapidly advanced across the Caen - Bayeux railway, line "Oak", and occupied Putot-en-Bessin. Somewhat worryingly flanking patrols revealed that the 50th Division had not reached the pre-arranged contact point at Brouay so the gap on the Canadian right remained open. The Reginas also moved rapidly from Le Fresne-Camilly to line "Oak" with "C" Company taking up a very advanced and exposed position at Norrey-en-Bessin south of the railway line. Battalion Headquarters and "A" and "B" Companies were at Bretteville-l'Orgueilleuse with "D" Company being relocated to Cardonville mid-way between Norrey and Bretteville. The Canadian Scottish and 1st Hussars were in brigade reserve with one company and one squadron detached to cover the brigade's left flank which now lay exposed following 9 Brigade's failure to advance the line to Authie.

Following his repulse of 9 Brigade on 7 June, Colonel Kurt Meyer directed his attention to 7 Brigade's advanced salient between Rots and Le Mesnil-Patry with Major Stu Tubbs' isolated "C" Company, RRR, at Norrey as the first target. Several initial probes were made against Norrey - some inadvertent and some planned with the results being the same in either case. Tubbs' company coolly knocked out a number of troops and vehicles and sent the enemy reeling back to Le Mesnil-Patry. The next day a strong German infantry force again attacked Norrey behind a heavy mortar barrage. Tubbs' company decisively threw them back, aided by excellent artillery defensive fire tasks. The retreating Germans left over 25 dead behind. "C" Company continued with its aggressive defense, ambushing and capturing five half-tracks and several other vehicles and bagging the crews. Ominously, several of the prisoners came from the Panzer Lehr Division an indication that despite near total Allied control of the air fresh German armour was reaching the battlefield.

On 8 June the German 12th SS Division made a determined effort to drive a wedge through the Canadian position and, as Kurt Meyer put it, "chase the little fish into the sea." 3rd Battalion of the 26th Panzer Grenadiers moved straight up route D83 and was heavily engaged by the Regina's "C" Company(10). They veered off towards Villeneuve and Cardonville as Norrey held firm.

The Germans had better luck, albeit temporary, on the Canadians' right where the Royal Winnipeg Rifles held Putot-en-Bessin. The "Little Black Devils" had several strikes against them. One, over which they had no control, was the weak strength of their rifle companies as a result of heavy D-Day casualties. Another, over which they certainly did have control, was the poor siting of their company localities which was engendered in part by concern over the open right flank and in part by trying to cover all of a very strung-out village. Equally critical, for whatever reason - concern for the civilians or because of ingrained training habits - the Rifles did not occupy the strong stone Norman houses. Instead they opted to defend the village from two-man slit trenches dug into flat, open ground, many with poor fields of fire because of their close proximity to surrounding wheat fields and a railway embankment which gave the enemy a protected, covered approach. The Winnipegs placed their "A" Company at the railway bridge with "C" to the east. "D" Company was further east in higher ground with good fields of fire and with FOO and mortar support. Battalion Headquarters and "B" Company were sited north of the village.

At 1000 hrs the 2nd Battalion 26th Panzer Grenadiers attacked. On their first attempt they were beaten back by fire from the 24th Lancers supporting the 50th Division on the right flank. The Germans then turned their attention east - approaching the Winnipegs under cover of the railway line. Suddenly, behind a violent concentration of artillery and mortar fire and supported by four SP guns, they broke from the wheat fields right on top of the unfortunate "A" Company before the latter could do more than take up arms. The company was overrun almost at once. The Panzer Grenadiers then turned on the isolated "C" Company with similar results. Things were much different when they tried to close with "D" Company. From well sited positions with good fields of fire and calling on artillery and mortar support "Dog" Company repulsed the enemy's advance. Battalion Headquarters and the remains of "B" Company then joined up with "D" and called for tank support which, at that stage, could have had a decisive influence on the battle. Unfortunately this could not be readily provided as the supporting Hussars, reduced through combat to two squadrons, were trying to cover the Brigade's open left flank.

Brig Foster then ordered a squadron of Hussars to join the Canadian Scottish and directed the Can Scots to restore the situation. To fill the left flank gap the Divisional Commander Maj Gen Keller ordered 8 Brigade to slip to the right to fill this threatened position. A potentially dangerous thrust by German tanks into the gap was thwarted when the reinforced and regrouped Sherbrooke Fusiliers trundled into position and drove them off.

Lt Col Cabeldu's Can Scots started their attack at 2030 hrs behind the thunderous artillery support of the 12th and 13th Field Regiments and the 4.2 inch mortars and MMGs of the Camerons of Ottawa. A squadron of Hussars hurried over and married-up with the infantry en route. This squadron covered the Scots' dangerous right flank as the battalion's Carrier Platoon covered the other. Advancing into a hail of fire the Scots crashed into Putot forcing the enemy into full retreat. Heroism abounded in that attack. By his personal dash and example Major Plows, leading "A" Company and carrying the remnants of "D" along with him, hurtled into the enemy and routed them. He deserved the VC and got nothing. Lt Bernie Clarke, whose heroism and initiative on D-Day had knocked out a key pill box and captured 50 prisoners did it again at Putot. He lead a rare and wild bayonet charge that overran three machine gun posts, killed many and captured another 18. Clarke who clearly deserved the VC - twice - was wounded the next day and also got nothing. Two of his NCOs - Cpls Mitchell and Courtney, the latter killed leading a charge, also displayed heroism of a high order and went unrewarded.(11)

In this decisive and brilliantly fought action the Canadian Scottish suffered 45 killed and 80 wounded. The Winnipeg Rifles had nearly twice as many including 64 taken prisoner of whom 45 were murdered in cold blood on SS orders. But that is another story. This one ends with the fact that the first German attempt to throw back the Canadians and penetrate to the sea had ended in failure. Putot was firmly in Canadian hands and Norrey stood strong and defiant athwart the enemy's desired line of advance. But despite suffering a bloody nose the Germans were not about to give up so easily. They had further strings to their bow and the Regina Rifles would be their target.

Bretteville and Cardonville

The battle of Bretteville l' Orgueilleuse on 8/9 June 1944 is a proud Regina Rifles battle honour and the tale of that battle - where enemy tanks were destroyed and their attack beaten off at the very door of battalion headquarters (BnHQ) - has long been a part of Canadian military lore. And the epic defence of Norrey-en Bessin a mile or so away by the Regina's "C" Company is also a cherished event with military historians. But almost unknown to Canadians, and until recently virtually unrecorded, the equally heroic battle of Cardonville by the Rifle's "D" Company has escaped the historians' purview. This should change and Cardonville should now take its place to complete the trilogy of magnificent feats of arms performed by the Reginas on those momentous dates.(12)

On the morning of 8 June "D" Company had been drawn back from its dangerously advanced position en route to Carpiquet and replaced the RWR's Carrier Platoon at La Ferme de Cardonville, roughly half way between Norrey and Bretteville. The farm buildings, located just off the Paris-Cherbourg railway line, consisted of a solid two story stone house and assorted outbuildings all surrounded by a high stone wall. A small apple orchard lay just north of the wall. A country road to Bretteville passed close by the eastern wall and tall grain fields billowed across the tracks.

The Reginas were dog tired when they took over the farm from the Winnipeg's Carrier Platoon - they had been constantly fighting, marching and digging since landing on D-Day. And they were under the strain of almost constant sniping, machine gunning and mortar fire. Nevertheless they set about preparing the farm for defence as best they could. Unlike the unfortunate Winnipegs at Putot they decided to defend primarily from within the walls instead of digging in outside. The Company Commander, Capt Gordon Brown, placed his headquarters and two platoons within the walls with the third platoon, two 6- pounders of the Anti-Tank Platoon, the attached FOO and company vehicles in the orchard. They were warned of a likely impending attack and watched in horror as the Winnipegs at Putot, only a mile west, were overrun. However they were cheered on by the magnificent counter-attack by the Canadian Scottish which restored the situation.

About midnight enemy tanks started passing close by the farm en route to Bretteville oblivious to the presence of "D" Company. Incredibly the tanks were not accompanied by infantry. Communications, as happened so often in that war, were now inoperable between the forward companies and battalion headquarters. "C" Company at Norrey and "D" at Cardonville now hunkered down to meet the expected assault.

Shortly thereafter some 22 Panther tanks rumbled into "A" Company and Bn HQ at

THE NORTHWEST EUROPE CAMPAIGN

Bretteville igniting a wild midnight melee. Using PIATs, Hawkins Grenades, 6-pounders and small arms the Reginas battled back as the tanks roared and fired. Tracers and flares lit the night sky and fires raged everywhere. In a hectic life-or-death struggle the Regina's PIAT/Grenade teams knocked out five Panthers, a light tank, an armoured car and even a Volkswagon. The CO, Lt Col Matheson, with his Sten gun personally accounted for a German motorcyclist who had injudiciously ventured too far forward. The "Johns" lost many men, seven carriers and two 6-pounders. But they had held firm and stopped in its tracks a full fledged German armoured drive to the sea. As the sky lightened around 0300 hrs the Germans, ever fearful of Allied rocket-firing Typhoons and Thunderbolts, grudgingly withdrew. Three Canadian tanks appeared at this juncture to nip at their heels.

As the Bretteville battle wound down the returning Panthers surrounded "D" Company's orchard. The company commander was contemplating a desperate "sticky-bomb"(13) attack when violent firing erupted and the enemy tanks smashed into and around the orchard crushing slit trenches, vehicles and 6-pounders and machine-gunning everything above and below ground. One Panther partly broke into the walled compound before withdrawing under a fusillade of fire - perhaps fearful of being trapped as his comrades had been at Bretteville. Shooting and fires raged everywhere. The rapidly lighting sky finally convinced the tanks to withdraw toward Mesnil while they still could.

Respite was short lived for the embattled "D" Company who were now out of communication with everyone except "C"(14) and, eerily, with an English speaking German who had tapped into the Regina's telephone lines. "Dog" Company was soon under infantry attack as waves of Panzer Grenadiers charged the farm. The enemy closed right up to the walls and were repulsed again and again in bitter hand-to-hand fighting. Valour came from many sources including the OC and his CSM Jim Jacobs who was everywhere encouraging, firing, organizing and from the 2IC Dick Roberts and Sgt Gardiner who did likewise. An unnamed rifleman positioned a Bren gun at an upper window and wrought havoc on the enemy while a Cameron's machine gunner took his Vickers outside the walls and coolly blasted an enemy group firing from a wood. Just when things seemed darkest, communications were suddenly re-established with the hitherto embattled BnHQ. Capt Brown was at long last able to call down effective artillery and mortar fire on enemy strong points and advancing troops and the exhausted and now disheartened enemy finally and reluctantly wound down their attack. It had been a near run thing.

It had also been a night and day of confused horror for the determined Regina Johns but in the end they had prevailed against some of toughest and best troops in the world. It is scant exaggeration to say that the gallant stands of Matheson's men probably prevented a German breakthrough to the beach and a splitting of the bridgehead in two. This opinion is echoed by German historian and former 12 SS officer Hubert Meyer who is quoted in Terry Copp's excellent , *Guide to the Battlefields of Normandy,* "Four attempts to capture Norrey, a cornerstone of the Canadian defence, had failed. Together with Bretteville, the village formed a blocking position. Therefore, repeated efforts were made via different approaches to take these positions. They failed because of insufficient forces, insufficient preparation due to real or imagined time pressures, and, not least of all because of the bravery of the defenders..."(15)

But the Germans were not quite done yet. Repulsed at Norrey, Bretteville and

GAUDEAMUS IGITUR

Cardonville and thrown out of Putot the 12th SS took one last crack at Norrey. As the SS attacked over the open fields they blundered into a minefield and were caught in a hail of fire. With incredible timing, and luck, a mixed bag of reinforcing Canadian armour - 1st Hussars and Garrys - appeared and caught a column of enemy tanks in the flank. In minutes the Canadians had destroyed six Panthers without loss to themselves. Other Panthers brewed in the minefield as the enemy again beat a sullen retreat to lick its wounds

Although much sporadic fighting remained the Canadians settled down to closing the gaps between salients, absorbing reinforcements and getting ready for the next phase. With one exception they would consolidate their present positions for the rest of the month while Allied attempts were made elsewhere. In the west the rapidly expanding US 1st Army pushed steadily through the Cotentin peninsula with Cherbourg falling at month's end.

Meanwhile the British 2nd Army made two major attempts to break out around Caen. The first of these, from 11 to 15 June, was an imaginative attempt by Montgomery to encircle Caen using his veteran former 8th Army divisions.(16) The left hook by Ist Corps directed the 51st (Highland) Division through 6th Airborne's bridgehead east of the Orne towards Cagny. The right hook by XXX Corps sent 7th Armoured Division (the Desert Rats) through 50th Division on Tilly and Villers Bocage. The left hook by the Highlanders failed within hours and they linked up with 6th Airborne. The right by 7th Armoured started with great promise but at Villers Bocage its lightly armoured Cromwells and supporting Royal Rifles infantry were destroyed in a series of superb defensive traps sprung by a handful of Tiger tanks under the legendary Captain Wittman.(17) It was the foretaste of many similar bitter pills to be swallowed by 21 Army Group over the next two months.

A second major British offensive near the end of the month was the start of a series of attacks which, it was hoped, would culminate with the fall of Caen. In Operation "Epsom", starting on 26 June, five British divisions of the newly operational VIII Corps comprising the 15th, 43rd, 49th, 50th and 11th Armoured divisions were to attack south against Villers Bocage, Fontenay, Cheux, Verson and Hill 112. In Phase II, 4-6 July, code named "Windsor", the Canadians were to take Carpiquet. Finally, in Operation "Charnwood" Caen was to fall to a combined attack by the British 3rd and 59th and Canadian 3rd Divisions. More on these later but first the Canadians were to make one more ill-advised attack in support of a British tidying-up advance to Audrieu and Tilly-sur Seulles.

Le Mesnil Patry - 11 June 1944

This action started as the Canadian part of a pincers to squeeze out the salient between XXX Corps and I Corps on the Canadians' right flank. Maj Gen Keller assigned the operation to Brig Wyman's 2nd Armoured Brigade on a hurry up basis as Keller himself was being pushed by Lt Gen J. Crocker to get going. As so often happens when things start off half-cocked they end up in disaster. There was actually no real need for a panic attack but as the German Hubert Meyer sardonically noted in relation to SS attacks on Norrey real or, in this case, imagined time pressures resulted in insufficient preparation.

Wyman used his own 1st Hussars along with the attached Queen's Own Rifles for the operation. The objective was Cheux south of the Fontenay-Marcelet road. Starting from the Regina's firm base at Norrey the battle group would first need to eliminate the enemy at Le Mesnil Patry before turning onto the high ground south of Cheux. The first blunder occurred, in line with Hubert Meyer's wry observation,(18) when on 11 June Ist Corps suddenly advanced the date of the operation from the 12th to the 11th. Because of this unnecessary change Wyman's command was left with no time for reconnaissance or even to devise a proper artillery fire plan - steps absolutely necessary before attacking a strongly defended position which Le Mesnil was known to be. Lamentably it was to be a theme that was to be repeated time and again in Normandy - troops hurried into attack without proper preparation because of higher command insistence that the operation start at some unrealistic time on the basis of the flimsiest reason or, more usually, none at all.

The plan, such as it was given the conditions, called for "D" Company QOR and the Hussars to crash Le Mesnil Patry from whence "A" Company would advance to secure the road junction a half mile beyond. The infantry would ride into action on the backs of the Hussars' tanks. No one clearly knew what the artillery was supposed to do. The advance began at 1430 hrs on 11 June and was a costly failure. "D" Company, mounted on tanks, only advanced some 300 yards before coming under a torrent of fire from Le Mesnil and the flanking tall fields of wheat. Within minutes half the company and half the tanks had become casualties. "A" Company tried to pass through and met a similar grim fate. The attack ground to a bloody halt. Whatever the attack lacked it wasn't courage. Individual acts of heroism abounded.

One small group under a wounded Lt George Bean with Sgt S. Scrutton, seven men and two tanks somehow made it to the end of Le Mesnil. Here they wrought havoc on the enemy with Bean and Scrutton locating targets and directing tank fire onto them. Bean was wounded twice more and when the tank wireless failed Sgt Scrutton took over and remounted the survivors and roared back to friendly lines. From the small party two were killed, two wounded and one missing. Bean, who was yet another who rated the VC, at least received an MC. Sgt Scrutton got a well deserved Military Medal.

With "D" Company and "B" Squadron of the Hussars virtually wiped out and "A" Company severely mauled the operation was called off. On the withdrawal they came under severe shelling which some believed came largely from our own guns. The cost was high. The Queen's Own had 55 killed, 60 wounded and 11 captured. The Hussars lost 70 men and 35 tanks - nearly half their entire war casualties. But the Germans also suffered. They lost at least a dozen tanks, several anti-tank guns and scores of troops. Six of the Canadian prisoners, mostly wounded, were later murdered by their captors.

The action accomplished nothing although higher command tried to put a brave face on things by claiming, perhaps partly correctly, that the battle had pre-empted another enemy attack on 7 Brigade and had materially assisted XXX Corps in its attack. In the event offensive action by the Germans now ceased and the Canadians settled down to regroup and rebuild for the next big push

Carpiquet

After failing to encircle Caen on 11-14 June the British 2nd Army planned a much larger operation, code named "Epsom", set for 25-28 June. This had the same objective as before, the encirclement of Caen, but this time the push would chiefly be made from the west with much larger forces and a more complex plan. XXX Corps was to start by seizing the high ground between Fontenay and Rauray preparatory to VIII Corps attacking south to secure a firm base between the Orne and the Odon. At this point the 11th Armoured Division was to establish itself astride the Caen-Falaise road. Once this happened Phase II called for I Corps to capture Carpiquet with 3rd Canadian Division while the Highland Division swept from the Orne bridgehead west of Caen to complete the encirclement.

Although the British initially made good gains, finally taking the elusive Cheux and crossing the Odon, they were stopped short of Evercy and Hill 112 and the attack ground to a halt. The resulting huge salient alarmed the Germans and drew all but one of their available armored divisions to the Caen front. Montgomery later claimed that this was all part of the unfolding of his master plan to let the Americans run free in the west. The gigantic size and ambitious objectives of "Epsom" and later "Charnwood" and "Goodwood" lead one to suspect this to be just another Montyism in which *ex post facto* he claims that the meager results were just as planned despite the fact that his own pre-battle orders stated otherwise.

With Phase I of "Epsom" stalled Phase II was cancelled. However the Ist Corps' Lt Gen Crocker decided to go ahead with the Canadian attack on Carpiquet which was rescheduled for 4 July under the code name "Windsor". This rather inexplicable decision by Crocker does nothing for his reputation as a planner. "Windsor" would precede the massive and decisive "Charnwood" assault on Caen by only three days and would place the Canadians in a narrow salient open to fire from three sides and subject to undivided German attention. In fairness to Crocker perhaps he felt that "Windsor" would ease things for "Charnwood" but with hindsight it is clear that there was no reason to launch it except as an integral and same-dated part of "Charnwood".

The task of taking Carpiquet was given to 8 Brigade with the Royal Winnipeg Rifles and Fort Garry Horse under command. Massive support was provided including 10 regiments of artillery, Flails, Crocodiles and AVREs, two squadrons of Typhoons and the nine 16 inch guns of the battleship Rodney. Much was expected of this support - far too much considering the enemy's massive dug-in concrete blockhouses, trench systems and hidden support weapons. Most were to be virtually untouched by the ensuing bombardment. The assault area was almost suicidal - the four attacking battalions had to cross a mile of open ground to close with the enemy. And every possible approach had long been ranged and registered by the excellent German artillery and mortars and covered by machine and anti-tank guns firing on fixed lines. Mines and wire were in profusion.

The attack plan was, of necessity, fairly simple. Starting from near Marcelet to the west the North Shores left and Chaudieres right, accompanied by Fort Garry tanks, would attack along the general axis of Route 9 and capture Carpiquet village. The Royal Winnipeg Rifles and Garry tanks would attack about a mile to the south to seize the airfield's hangars. At this juncture the Queen's Own were to push through the town to capture the control buildings east of the airfield. The Brigade's left flank was covered by the Sherbrooke Fusiliers while the 43rd (Wessex) Division was to protect the open right flank by occupying Verson to the south.

Things went bad even before H-Hour. In a tactic they were to employ again and again German wireless intercepts of Canadian radio traffic correctly divined the Assembly Area as woods near Marcelet and had them heavily shelled. The attack started

THE NORTHWEST EUROPE CAMPAIGN

behind the thunderous artillery bombardment of eight artillery regiments firing a block barrage 400 yards thick which lifted 100 yards every three minutes. The Germans also correctly divined this and fired their own defensive fire tasks just behind the blocks to great effect. The Canadian infantry tried to minimize this by leaning closely on their own barrage but suffered heavy casualties. Somehow, drawing on superhuman inner effort, the North Shores and Chauds reached the town where they were held up by a storm of fire from virtually intact bunkers. The heavy pre-assault firing of Typhoon rockets and Rodney's 16 inchers had had very little effect. Crocodile flame-throwers came to the rescue and the depleted infantry pressed on.

On the right flank the Winnipeg's advance took them south of the rigidly timed block barrage and their tanks were held back. Overcoming numerous enemy posts en route and under murderous artillery and mortar fire the Black Devils finally reached and, after bitter fighting, cleared the first hangar. However under withering fire from bunkers and flanks and artillery and mortars the Rifles could not go on even with the tardy arrival of six tanks. They were forced to withdraw halfway back to Marcelet.

The Queen's Own then took over on the left and promptly encountered a huge bunker which neither Crocodiles nor AVRE petards could crack. The riflemen finally took it by pouring oil and petrol into the ventilators and igniting the mix. Sixteen of 28 defenders died in the bunker, 12 surrendered. The RWR made a fresh assault on the hangars to the east but were again repulsed. They were ordered back after dark as was the flanking Wessex Division in the now exposed Verson.

The three battalions of 8 Brigade and the Fort Garrys formed a stronghold in Carpiquet village and over the next three days fought off repeated counter-attacks and held firm. The MMGs and mortars of the Camerons of Ottawa were particularly valuable in helping 8 Brigade prevail in this grim contest of endurance and guts. The Germans finally gave up attacking but intensified their shelling of the nearly surrounded Canadians.

The battle of Carpiquet was a bloody action that need never have been fought as Operation "Charnwood" to start on the 6th would overrun all of the adjacent area. Canadian casualties were high - some 130 for the New Brunswickers and Manitobans, somewhat less for the QOR and Chauds. The Fort Garrys lost a dozen tanks and many men. Carpiquet was loudly criticized as a Canadian failure by some senior British officers who had totally unrealistic expectations of what the Rodney and massed artillery could accomplish. At the very worst the battle could be deemed only a partial failure as Carpiquet village had been taken and held against vicious resistance. The failure, if indeed there really was one, lay with Lt Gen Crocker and his Ist Corps staff for ordering such a needless and suicidal attack. But Crocker, who was neither fool nor uncaring of his men, had his reasons, probably the aiding of "Charnwood", which hindsight should not belittle. And, on any score, no one could find any fault with the Canadian infantry who, in a replay of the First Day on the Somme, advanced a mile over open ground under murderous fire against a fanatical foe. That they were successful on the left and nearly so on the right is a testimony to valour of the highest order. Few could have done as much - no one could have done more.

The final word goes to the Canadian historian Terry Copp who wrote, "Carpiquet, like a number of other battles fought by British Second Army in June and July, illustrates a fundamental criticism that has been directed at Montgomery's conduct of the campaign in Normandy, Too often, it is argued, Second, Second Army committed a

GAUDEAMUS IGITUR

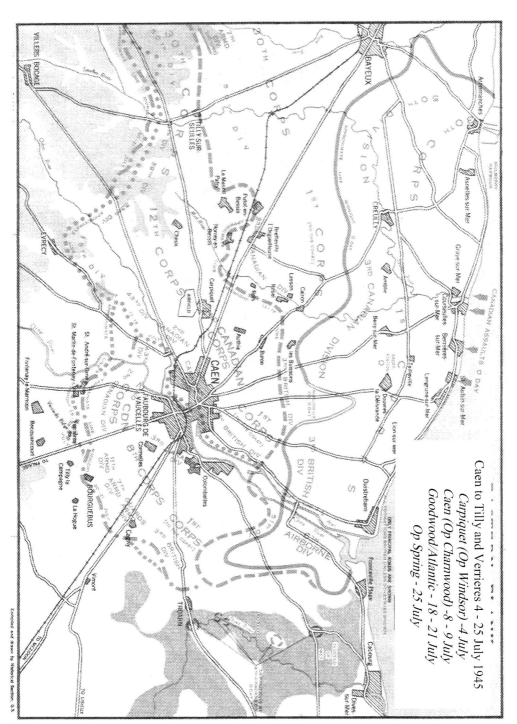

Caen to Tilly and Verrières 4 - 25 July 1945
Carpiquet (Op Windsor) - 4 July
Caen (Op Charnwood) - 8 - 9 July
Goodwood/Atlantic - 18 - 21 July
Op Spring - 25 July

THE NORTHWEST EUROPE CAMPAIGN

brigade resources of the Army should have been brought to bear....There was no easy answer to the problem....The bitter complaints of battalion commanders who cursed limited attacks because they allowed the full weight of German artillery to be brought to bear on a small section of the front are hard to argue with, but no one wanted to attack without the largest possible measure of artillery support."(19)

Caen

Operation 'Charnwood" the final assault on Caen was undertaken by Ist British Corps under Lt Gen J. Crocker commencing at 0420 hrs on 8 July 1944. The operation involved three divisions - the 3rd British on the left, the newly arrived 59th (Midland) in the center and the 3rd Canadian on the right. The attacking divisions started from an arc some three miles from Caen and would be required to take a number of intervening villages before the final push. The two British divisions were to start first with the Canadians soon joining.

The attack was to be backed by the usual vast artillery and naval firepower and strong air support. The latter included an attack by 450 heavy bombers on the evening before the local D-Day. Because of the danger to friendly forces the bombers, which carried a huge weight of explosives, had to bomb several miles in rear of the front lines, including the outskirts of Caen. Although they put on a marvelous show, greatly heartening the waiting and watching infantry, the result was disappointing. The bombing was too far back to discomfit the German combat troops, although no doubt the rear area services were severely shaken. But worse, the bombing killed a large number of French civilians and reduced many buildings to rubble, thereby impeding the Allied advance.

The Canadian part of the operation was divided into four phases. Phase I was to commence with the capture of Buron and Gruchy by the 9th (Highland) Brigade. In Phase II that Brigade's North Novas would take Authie (their ill-fated objective of D+2) and Franqueville while the SD&Gs advanced on the Chateau de St Louis. At this stage 7 Brigade was to pass through and capture Cussy and the Abbaye Ardenne. Finally Phase IV would see the capture of Caen by all three brigades led by the 8th from Carpiquet and the 9th from Cussy - Abbaye Ardenne. The Canadian attack started at 0730 hrs and once again the enemy poured fire into the Assembly Area, Forming Up Place, Start Line and en route to the objective.

Moving closely behind their own massive barrage the Highland Light Infantry of Canada with "A" Squadron Sherbrooke Fusiliers hammered their way into Buron in an epic all day battle that, for sheer savagery, ranks with any fought in the European Campaign. The tale of that battle has been faithfully and meticulously recorded by Capt Snowie and should be read with pride by all Canadians.(20) The Germans resisted fiercely with everything in the book as casualties to men and tanks soared. Of myriad acts of heroism that day one merits particular note. Corporal Wenzel aggressively led his small section into the teeth of the enemy position as his men dropped around him and he himself was wounded. Wenzel's tiny group knocked out several key enemy posts permitting the advance to continue. Then, with his section destroyed, the wounded Wenzel, still firing, advanced alone into the heart of the enemy defences where he was killed. The gallant corporal was recommended for the Victoria Cross but, as happened so often to Canadians, the recommendation was denied. And since he had been killed he was ineligible for a lesser decoration and so received only a Mention in Dispatches.

GAUDEAMUS IGITUR

Only recently has the ban on the posthumous award of lesser decorations been rescinded - too late to honour so many deserving dead of the Second World War.(21) The HLI finally prevailed and with a reinforced "A" Squadron of Sherbrookes beat off a succession of enemy counter-attacks. Buron had been the battalion's first major action and was their Calvary - the magnificent victory had cost them an appalling 260 casualties.

The companion attack on Gruchy by the Stormont, Dundas and Glengarry Highlanders and "B" Squadron Sherbrookes went well until the attackers came under withering fire from the enemy's principal anti-tank and machine gun belt. Things were touch and go until the 7th Cavalry, in the form of the Scout Troop of the 7th Canadian Reconnaissance Regiment, charged into the fray under the inspired leadership of its commander Lt Ayer. The troop's thinly armed carriers roared past the Glens and into the midst of a dug-in enemy company. Firing machine guns and dropping grenades on the startled Germans Ayer's gallant charge saved the day. The enemy was overrun, 30 prisoners were taken and dozens were killed or wounded. The Glens stormed close behind and in savage fighting cleared the town by mid-morning.

Due to heavy resistance in Gruchy and especially Buron, where the enemy mounted a violent counter-attack, the Phase II attack by the North Novas and Glengarrys could not get underway until 1430 hrs. The assault by the SD&Gs on the Chateau de St Louis went extremely well and by 1600 hrs the "Sand, Dirt and Gravel" boys had secured their objective. The North Novas were not so lucky. They were heavily shelled in Assembly Area and Start Line and mercilessly machine gunned en route. But excellent fire support from the Cameron's 4.2 inch mortars and Vickers guns and the scout cars of the 7th Recce, added to the sheer courage of the Scotians got them onto the objective and beyond.

The stubborn resistance at Phases I and II delayed the 7th Brigade attack until 1830. The Canadian Scottish, like the previous units that day, were caught by heavy fire as they moved up to the Start Line. As they began their attack they came under severe flanking fire from the village of Bitot which the 59th Division had not yet captured. With insouciant elan the Can Scots charged the last 100 yards as the barrage lifted and plunged into the enemy position. Then, to add to their problems, the Victorians came under fire from the Abbaye Ardenne which the Reginas had not yet silenced. The street fighting was bitter and grim. The 1st Hussars' tanks and Can Scots' PIAT teams operated to great effect, knocking out half a dozen enemy tanks and capturing another. By nightfall, at heavy cost, Cussy was theirs.

The Regina Rifles on the right, because of unreplaced casualties, were down to three effective companies. These had a tough time getting underway because the North Novas were still fighting in Authie, the Regina's Start Line. This forced the Rifles into an over hurried start - their brief, on the move, O Group was held at 1700 hrs which had been set as their H-Hour. As one result the artillery program ran on ahead. Their supporting tanks, which had to marry-up on the move, arrived late and got blasted by 88s from the Abbaye. As the crews bailed out they were machine gunned from a series of mounds halfway to the Abbaye. With their tanks knocked out and the artillery barrage far ahead the prairie boys, taking casualties at every turn, were on their own. Their advance led over a mile of flat, open ground. "B" Company fought its way to the mounds and was decimated, "C" and "D" passed through.

Stu Tubbs' superb "C" Company, the victors of Norrey, was shot to pieces and Tubbs himself lost a leg. "D" Company, now down to 60 men, continued on alone.

THE NORTHWEST EUROPE CAMPAIGN

Bereft of tanks, artillery and heavy mortars the Reginans charged the last 150 yards under the smoke screen of their own 2inch mortars. One platoon under Lt J. Mooney took off on a wide left hook and ran into a German 88 battery which they overcame after a brutal fight.(22) Only Mooney and a handful of his men survived. The remaining two decimated platoons staged a wild frontal assault through the wheat fields, destroyed the enemy in their trenches and closed up to the Abbaye walls. They occupied the Abbaye early the next morning, took over Kurt Meyer's private quarters, liberated his wine cellar and captured a disabled tank. The Saskatchewan men had fought a magnificent fight and won a decisive victory but at a cost of over 200 casualties - almost crippling to a unit that started the battle at two-thirds strength. But the positions on which the Germans had anchored their defences had been shattered and the way to Caen - that elusive target since D-Day now lay open.

The fall of Caen on 9 July was almost anti-climatic as the Germans had begun to withdraw from that ruined city the night before. On the left two companies of Glengarrys with two squadrons of Sherbrooke Fusiliers, and soon supported by North Novas and HLI, drove straight at the city from Franqueville. They brushed through minefields, anti-tank guns, rearguards and shellfire and were soon fighting their way against dwindling resistance into the center of the town. On the right the Chaudieres and Queen's Own finally cleared the airfield and the North Shores drove to the Odon under the admiring view of the GOC Wessex Division from a church tower near Verson.(23) The Battle of Caen cost the three assaulting divisions 3500 all ranks. The Canadian division lost 1200, more than on D-Day. But the Germans lost even more and the bastion of Caen had fallen.

Men of the Regina Rifles man a 3-inch mortar in Bretteville. (NAC PA 128794)

GAUDEAMUS IGITUR

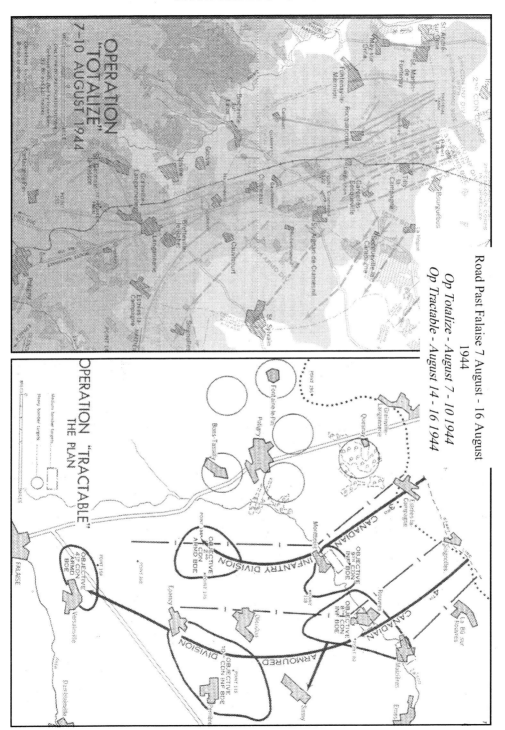

Road Past Falaise 7 August - 16 August 1944
Op Totalize - August 7 - 10 1944
Op Tractable - August 14 - 16 1944

THE NORTHWEST EUROPE CAMPAIGN

CHAPTER IX

THE ROAD PAST FALAISE

The thundering line of battle stands,
And in the air death moans and sings.
But Day shall clasp him with strong hands,
And night shall fold him in soft wings.
  Julian Grenfell. *Into Battle.*

Preparing the Next Stroke

With the fall of Caen, General Sir B.L, Montgomery set about planning the next step. This, in his view, would require the destruction of German armour, the capture of Falaise and, with the American 1st Army, the encirclement and elimination of the German 7th Army. His campaign started modestly enough on 10 July, the day after the capture of Caen, when 43 Division in Operation "Jupiter" seized Hill 112 which had been a thorn in 2nd Army's side since D+1. Then modesty was dropped, the next attempt was to be positively gigantic.

While preparations for this gigantic attempt were ongoing the Canadians were being augmented, first to corps and then to army strength. But since the Ist Canadian Corps was now serving in Italy the Canadian combat element of the 1st Canadian Army was to be limited to the IInd Canadian Corps for most of the duration of the war. Lt Gen H.D.G. Crerar established his Tactical Headquarters (Tac HQ) at Amblie in Normandy on 18 June but his Army would not become operational until late July. IInd Canadian Corps under Lt Gen G.C. Simonds opened its Tac HQ, also at Amblie, on 29 June and became operational on the Orne on 11 July. To complete the Corps the 2nd Canadian Infantry Division (2 CID) (Maj Gen C. Foulkes) and 4th Canadian Armoured Division (4 CAD) (Maj Gen G. Kitching) arrived in Normandy by mid-July.

General Montgomery stated that his policy was, "to draw the main enemy forces in to battle on our eastern (British/Canadian) flank, and to fight them there, so that our affairs on the western (American) front may proceed the easier."(1) Montgomery correctly assessed that only by keeping powerful, unremitting pressure on the enemy in the vital Caen/Falaise area could he prevent Rommel from grouping his armour for a concentrated thrust to sever the Allied line and penetrate to the sea. If this must mean a meat-grinder strategy of head-on attacks, as it surely would, so be it.

At the same time the beachhead was becoming exceedingly crowded making it also necessary for 2nd Army to advance to gain ground for the deployment of further divisions, rear installations and airfields. Having tried several times to break out on his western flank Montgomery now instructed Lt Gen Sir Miles Dempsey to attack with his 2nd Army east of the Orne from the bridgehead originally established by the 6th Airborne Division. For the attack, code named "Goodwood", Dempsey was to employ three massed armored divisions along with four infantry divisions in three corps including, for the first time, IInd Canadian.

Since the airborne bridgehead east of the Orne only measured some four by five miles, the decision to use this tiny plot as the springboard for such a massive attack was strange indeed. It meant that three armored divisions had to laboriously cross the Orne, one by one, then deploy and force through a two-mile wide bottleneck before fanning out south of Caen. The resulting congestion can only be imagined. Even given the poor communications which were then so prevalent, Montgomery and Company must have been aware of the horrible problems experienced on the Liri, in just such a situation, by Sir Oliver Leese less than two months before. But even without this example of "how not to do it" the selection seems odd indeed. The main attack was to be delivered by Lt Gen Richard O'Conner's VIII Corps which included all three armored divisions.(2)

Paralleling VIII Corps, the newly operational IInd Canadian Corps was to clear Caen's eastern suburbs, Colombelles and Faubourg de Vaucelles then attack south through Giberville and St Andre-sur-Orne. The Canadian part of "Goodwood" was code named Operation "Atlantic" which, although no one suspected it at the time, was to be only the opening act in a quadripartite series of increasingly desperate efforts to take Falaise. "Goodwood" was to be preceded by a massive attack by heavy bombers on the flanks and deep rear of the line of attack.

The massed tank attack on 18 July was spearheaded by the 11th Armoured Division closely followed by the Guards Armoured with the veteran 7th Armoured to exploit and break out. In the initial critical stages the armored divisions would have to "run the gauntlet" down a narrow corridor covered by a line of fortified villages which, it was hoped, would be neutralized on the left by the 3rd and 51st Divisions and on the right by the Canadian Corps. Once past the bottleneck the armored divisions were to fan out with the 11th to Fontenay-le-Marmion and Falaise, the 7th to Cramesnil and St Sylvain and the Guards to Cagny and Vimont. En route to their objectives the tanks had to cross two railway embankments which would silhouette their soft underbellies to the enemy's waiting anti-tank guns. And if the armour somehow could overcome all of these they still had to face the formidable line of Bourguebus Ridge where the Germans had massed no less than seventy-eight 88mm anti-tank guns. All-in-all the plan for "Goodwood" was not one that a staff college student would wish to submit to a glowering directing staff if he had any hopes of a decent graduation.

As at Caen the massive aerial bombardment wrought havoc in the rear areas but left the forward troops and the vital gun line shaken but ready for action. The armoured divisions charged mightily but were destroyed in a cauldron of fire from 57 and 75mm PAKs, deadly 88s and the hull-down Mark IVs, Panthers and Tigers of the German armoured divisions. 11th Armoured alone lost 130 tanks, the others only slightly less.

The mighty armoured assault of "Goodwood" thus came to a crashing halt although Mongomery at first refused to admit this. Instead he signaled to his CIGS, Sir Alan Brooke, "Operations this morning a complete success" and "Situation very promising and it is difficult to see what the enemy can do about it."(3) We have just seen what they could and did do about it on the VIII Corps front. Now it was the turn of the Canadians.

Operation "Atlantic"

8th Brigade opened the Canadians' attack at 0615 hrs on 18 July by moving on Colombelles, the north east quarter of Caen across the Orne. On the left the Queen's Own made excellent progress moving through more open ground against the 16th Luftwaffe Division who were still stunned by the bombardment. By last light, after a half-days' street fighting, the Toronto battalion captured Giberville. Together with its supporting squadron of 1st Hussars the QOR had killed some 200, captured 600 and knocked out a number of anti-tank and machine gun posts at a cost of 79 casualties. It was a most promising beginning.

Alas, on the right things did not go as well. After an initial rapid advance the Chaudieres were halted at the Colombelles Chateau by a group of fortified strong posts. The ensuing bitter fighting, with no room to manoeuvre, resulted in heavy casualties and a telescoping of the follow up North Shores and 9th Brigade. The defenders of the Chateau and nearby iron works were finally overcome after a set piece attack with heavy artillery support. By nightfall the North Novas and HLI of 9 Brigade had penetrated into the northern reaches of Vaucelles.

Sizing up the situation, Simonds and Keller ordered 7 Brigade to make a crossing of the Orne to the south directly from Caen into Vaucelles. Guided by French Resistance citizens of Caen the Regina Rifles worked their way through that city's rubble-blocked streets and located an undefended, partly demolished, bridge over the Orne. Using this bridge and some boats the Reginas crossed the river and, with text-book house clearing drills, soon overran Vaucelles. Following closely the divisional engineers erected a Bailey bridge over which tanks and support weapons soon rumbled across.

Lt Gen Simonds now decided to insert the newly arrived 2nd Division, the veteran formation of Dieppe, into the fray with the task of clearing the Louvigny triangle west of the Orne. The operation was assigned to 4th Brigade's Royal Regiment of Canada (RR of C) (Lt Col J.C.H. Anderson). The fighting was bitter and lasted throughout the night. Louvigny fell the next morning but by then Simonds had already decided to make his next effort east of the Orne.

On the afternoon of 19 July the British 7th and 11th Armoured Divisions attacked towards Hubert-Folie and Verrieres Ridge. The 5th Canadian Infantry Brigade of 2nd Division was to parallel the British advance and take Fleury-sur-Orne, Point 67 and Ifs. The attack began at 1300 hrs amid initial costly confusion when Le Regiment de Maisonneuve (R de Mais) (Lt Col H.L. Biasiallon) was caught in its own supporting artillery fire while crossing the Start Line. The follow up companies and a squadron of Sherbrookes took over and secured Le Haut by 1630 hrs. Here the Calgary Highlanders (Calg H) (Lt Col D.G. MacLauchlan) passed through and captured Point 67. The Black Watch (BW) (Lt Col S.S. Cantlie) was directed on Ifs which it took at midnight. 5th Brigade then spent the rest of the night beating off enemy probes and platoon size counter-attacks. With the coming of dawn Maj Gen Foulkes could be well satisfied with the performance of his division in its first blooding since Dieppe.

The British armour again achieved only mixed results at heavy cost. The 11th Armoured took Bras and Hubert-Folie but lost a further 65 tanks and was relieved on these positions by the 3rd Canadian Infantry Division on the 20th. The veteran 7th Armoured continued to labour. It finally succeeded in occupying Bourguebus but failed to clear Verrieres the original German gun line. Here occurred one of those maddening mix-ups which all too often plague attempts to relieve one formation with another in the heat of battle and result in the loss of a glittering opportunity.(4) Having secured Bourguebus the 7th Armoured overlooked Verrieres Ridge with a strong force of tanks and infantry. A modicum of daring and initiative should have prompted the 7th to rush and secure that vital ridge while the enemy was still off balance. At the very least, prudence, and the need to keep up the pressure, should have encouraged it to hold fast and provide powerful fire support while 2nd Canadian Division passed through to attack and clear the ridge and surrounding villages. Instead, for whatever reason (probably because of pre-conceived, inchoate plans and Simonds' arrogant belief that he could do better) it did neither. Incredibly, after a quick meeting between Simonds and Lt Gen R. O'Connor, Commander VIII Corps, 7th Armoured was withdrawn leaving the field to the hastily arriving Canadians and to the rapidly regrouping Germans. Unfortunately this failure of command - for that is what it was - was all too often to be the hallmark of British and Canadian (and Simonds in particular) command in Northwest Europe. Time and again they would fail to seize the moment, and the prize, opting instead for the laborious teeing-up of a formal, artillery dependant, attack while the moment vanished. It is difficult to believe that Patton or almost any German general would fail at such a moment.

But the comedy of errors did not end there. Before the changeover took place the 4th County of London Yeomanry, a unit of 7th Armoured, had moved west from Bourguebus along Verrieres Ridge and circled Beauvoir Farm. With a minimum of infantry support the Yeomanry could have taken Verrieres village. But this golden opportunity was thrown away by the over-formal relief of 7th Armoured by the Canadians and was absolutely squandered by Simonds and Foulkes who, ignoring the fact that the British controlled the ridge, included it in a pre-attack artillery barrage which required the British to abandon their position and withdraw north-east.

The Canadian generals had a number of sensible options. The most sensible of these was to ask O'Connor to have 7th Armoured secure the ridge pending a Canadian pass-through. Only ignorance of the facts or Simonds' overweening arrogance, each equally culpable, would have rejected this option. If, for some reason, 7th Armoured lacked infantry for the job a modicum of inter-corps liaison could have obtained Canadian infantry to assist. They were certainly ready at hand. One or two battalions of either 8th Brigade at Hubert-Folie or the 5th overlooking Fleury and St Andre could have been hurried forward in support. Instead 2nd Division laid on a formal, artillery heavy, frontal attack using 6th Brigade which had to be brought forward from far in the rear. Then, having thrown away the chance for a rapid coup-de-main in favour of a deliberate attack, but belatedly recognizing the need to gain the ridge before the Germans reinforced it, the Canadian generals substituted unwarranted haste for measured speed in hustling the struggling 6 Brigade into premature action. Once again would haste translate into waste - this time the needless waste of hundreds of Canadian youth.

Although the leapfrogging of 6 Brigade past the 5th had formed part of Foulkes' plan an unforeseen and large widening of the front made it necessary for 6 Brigade to attack with all three of its battalions up. To create a reserve Brigadier Young was given the Essex Scottish (Essex) (Lt Col B.J. MacDonald) from 4 Brigade. Warned of this move only at 0200 hrs the Essex had to laboriously night- march forward from Caen to arrive at their FUP at 1130 hrs dog-tired with little sleep and even less to eat. The assaulting Fusiliers Mont-Royal (FMR) (Lt Col J.G. Gauvreau) were also exhausted after an all-night march and unfed when they were ordered forward just as they were to breakfast. Not the ideal way for a new formation to make its battle debut.(5)

Young's plan called for the FMR on the left to take Verrieres via Beauvoir and Troteval Farms. The South Saskatchewan Regiment (SSR) (Lt Col F.A. Clift) in the center was to capture the ridge while the Queen's Own Cameron Highlanders of Canada (QOCH of C) (Lt Col J. Runcie) on the right had St Andre as its objective. The Essex were to follow the SSR and hold the high ground between Verrieres and St Andre. The

THE NORTHWEST EUROPE CAMPAIGN

FMR and Camerons were each supported by a squadron of Sherbrooke Fusiliers with the third squadron in reserve. This meant that the South Saskatchewans in the vital center role lacked direct tank support. Each battalion had a troop (4 guns) of the 2nd Anti-Tank Regiment in Direct-Support.(6)

The attack was supposed to start at 1200 hrs by which time the battalions would have left their FUPs and be shaking out to cross the Start Line. For various reasons - bad flying weather, the need to allow time for recce and to ensure the withdrawal of British armour - H Hour was postponed to 1500 hrs. To the unfed troops, tired from being force marched into action, this classic example of "hurry up and wait" was compounded when the Germans, as was their wont, pounded the troops in their unprotected FUP. And, of course, the delay gave the alert enemy further precious time to reinforce the ridge. So what could have been a virtual walk in the park a few hours earlier was turning, thanks to senior officer bungling, into yet another costly frontal attack.

On the left flank the FMR, starting from Ifs, had to advance almost two miles to reach their objective Verrieres village. En route they would need to clear both Beauvoir and Troteval farms. Initially, against the shell shocked 272nd Division, the advance went well, trenches were cleared and a number of prisoners (150 before the operation ended) were taken. At the farms the Fusiliers encountered the main enemy defences, stiffened by the arrival of troops from the 1st SS Panzer Regiment. In attempting to bypass the partly cleared farm buildings the Fusiliers were caught in the flank and rear by the SS and by heavy artillery and mortar fire. The supporting Sherbrooke tanks knocked out two Panthers but lost several Shermans in return. Then communications failed, the FOO was killed and the FMR were forced to consolidate around the farms. Lt Col Gauvreau's battalion had performed extremely well and despite taking severe casualties was to hold onto the farms against intense enemy pressure. So if it could not be said that the left had attained total victory at least it had made a reasonable start.

Not so the center. Here the South Saskatchewans were expected to advance two miles through waist high wheat fields to their objective - a track on the far slope of the ridge. The Saskatchewans, attacking without tank support, leaned close onto their barrage and moved rapidly ahead. Eliminating stiff opposition and trying to outpace the German defensive fire the prairie battalion reached its objective at 1700 hrs with only moderate casualties. It was now dangerously far ahead of its flanking battalions. The SSR called forward their anti-tank guns which, in the absence of tank support, were an absolute necessity. Meanwhile, brigade headquarters, believing that the South Sasks were firm on their objective, ordered the Essex Scottish to move forward. If everything was going well ahead it was the correct procedure. However if the forward battalion was not firmly established the center would have both feet off the ground at a critical juncture. Unfortunately it was the latter which came to pass.

Before the SSR had time to dig in on the exposed forward slope, where the high grain fields had given way to a low pea field, they were violently hit by a half-dozen tanks attacking from the open left flank supported with deadly effect by heavy artillery and mortar fire. Caught in the open the lead company was ordered back into the grain fields for protection. In so doing they suffered heavily including the critical loss of their PIAT teams and wireless. As German tanks roamed at will through the grain fields, running down and machine gunning the near defenceless infantry, the Acting CO, Major G.R. Mathews, called for tank support. Then he and his IO were themselves killed and communications with brigade failed. As the OC "B" Company, Major J.S.

Edmondson, rallied the remnants of the scattered battalion the unit's anti-tank guns rushed forward to support. Most were caught coming forward in the open and destroyed before they could even unlimber and get into action. Throughout all this horror a violent rainstorm swept the area negating air cover and observed ground supporting fire alike. Fighting from the grain fields the Saskatchewan's few remaining PIATs destroyed one enemy tank and damaged another as the commanders of both "A" and "C" Companies were killed.

Edmondson with all his rear-link communications gone, including the vital artillery link, took stock of the perilous situation of his shattered battalion. The CO, two company commanders and scores of other officers and men were dead or wounded while the survivors lay scattered in the overrun wheat fields without anti-tank protection. He decided that a withdrawal was the only option.

As the South Saskatchewans pulled back, understandably in some confusion, the Essex Scottish moved up in support. As the Essex were halfway up the slope they too were caught in devastating aimed fire before they could dig-in or even adopt a proper defensive position. The Essex, taking heavy casualties, were shaken when the Saskatchewan survivors surged through their position. As confusion reigned the Essex too lost all their communications. As losses mounted the lead company, with all its officers and most of its NCOs now casualties, attempted to withdraw and leaderless there was a lack of control.

As the CO of the Essex sought to regain control two companies held throughout the long night with enemy tanks churning all around. By morning battalion headquarters, "C" Company and part of "D" were cut off. The situation was finally stabilized with the arrival of a fresh squadron of 1st Hussars and only restored when the Black Watch were launched in a counter-attack behind heavy artillery support. The attempt in the crucial center had thus become a bloody shambles.

The Cameron Highlanders on the right would also attack over open ground to St. Andre-sur-Orne. They were supported by a tank squadron, albeit much reduced, of Sherbrooke Fusiliers. As happened so often in the past, and was to happen again and again, the Germans quickly determined the Cameron's Assembly Area, FUP, SL and routes forward and brought heavy fire onto them. Although the Winnipegers soon lost their command vehicle, OC Headquarters Company, IO and rear-link they managed to maintain communications. Moving steadily under heavy fire and heavy rain the Camerons rooted out fanatical opposition taking a number of prisoners. As they reached the orchards around St. Andre enemy resistance intensified and it took the Highlanders until the next day to secure the hamlet. In the counter-attacks which inevitably followed the Manitobans beat back everything, their PIATs knocking out two tanks. And St. Andre was theirs.

Operation "Atlantic" which had started with such high hopes ended in bitter disappointment for both IInd Corps and 2nd Division. That division, in its first major operation since the disaster at Dieppe, had suffered a sobering 1150 casualties, mostly by 6th Brigade on the last day. The Saskatchewans and Essex each lost about 250, over half their combat strength.

Their were many reasons for this reversal of fortune - the bad weather which precluded ground and close air support; the (once again) failure of communications and thus of on-call support; the lack of tanks in the critical center; the timely arrival of the veteran SS regiment; and, above all, the totally unjustified decision to delay operations which were on the brink of success in order to relieve the British VIIIth Corps by Simonds' Canadians. Some criticism could be leveled at green troops being hurtled into a firestorm but too much should not be made of this. Nothing could save unsupported infantry, no matter how veteran, when caught in the open, as were the SSR. Perhaps more experienced troops would have got their anti-tank weapons up faster, but perhaps not. And perhaps veteran troops, as 2nd Division would rapidly become, would have stood firm when, leaderless and under a storm of fire, the Saskatchewans retreated through the Essex. But this is conjecture and in no way should the combat troops, who suffered appalling casualties, be faulted for what was in truth a failure of command.

But it had been by no means a one sided battle. The German defenders had been roughly handled, their First SS Panzer Corps was now exhausted and in desperate need of reinforcements. The Germans described the fighting as tough and bitter - a grudging compliment to the freshly blooded Canadians. But the ridge remained in enemy hands and much grueling fighting would be needed to break through to Falaise. And it would fall to the Canadians to do it.

Operation "Spring" - 25 July 1944 - The Plan

General Montgomery was understandably upset at the failure of his mighty armoured assault in "Goodwood". Eisenhower, goaded by his deputy and virulent Montyphobe Air Marshall Tedder, voiced his surprise and disappointment. A lesser egotist than Montgomery might have shrunk from the criticism of first being too cautious up to Caen and then too rash now. But though Monty may have lacked many fine qualities self-confidence was not one. On 22 July he issued a new directive with the stated aim of drawing enemy panzers to the Caen area to aid the US breakthrough in the west where St. Lo had already fallen. Not content with just aiding Bradley, Montgomery planned a new colossal crack south of Caen which he expected would lead to the fall of Falaise and victory on the eastern flank.

His plan called for the Canadian Corps to attack on 25 July and seize the "Goodwood" objectives from Tilly-la Campagne to May-sur-Orne. XII British Corps would then attack west of the Orne followed by the Canadian and VIII Corps driving on Falaise leading to an armoured breakthrough on 3 or 4 August. The operation was codenamed "Spring".

Lt Gen Simonds' plan for his Corps in "Spring" envisaged a three phased attack using both Canadian infantry divisions, two armored brigades (one Canadian) and two attached British armoured divisions. In Simonds' Phase I the 3rd Canadian Infantry Division would take Tilly while the 2nd would tackle May-sur-Orne and Verrieres Ridge. In Phase II 2nd Division was to advance to Fontenay-le-Marmion and Rocquancourt, 7th Armoured to Cramesnil and 3rd Division to Garcelles-Secqueville. In Phase III the Guards Armoured Division was to advance to Cintheaux and Bretteville-sur-Laize.

This seems a very large and powerful force totaling some 28 infantry battalions and 12 regiments of armour and if employed en masse would have constituted an overwhelming hammer. But under the plan devised by Simonds and his divisional and brigade commanders this massive asset was to be fed into the battle in dribs and drabs. Phase I, always a critical stage, was to be mounted by only four battalions and two armoured regiments on a four mile front. Since the assault element of each battalion only numbered some 300 - 400 men they would be called upon to attack dug in defenders who were superior in numbers. And these defenders comprising the severely weakened but resilient 272nd Division and battle groups of the 1st and 9th SS Panzer and 2nd Panzer Divisions were the very troops to take full advantage of this incredible opportunity.

Why the generals so grossly violated the principle of war of Concentration of Force is pure conjecture. Perhaps they wished to avoid the mistakes of "Goodwood" although the circumstances were entirely different. More likely they were unused to handling such a massive force so reverted to doing things as they had always practiced before on much lower levels. Or perhaps they shrank from the risk of imperiling their operation if things went wrong. In which case they should have heeded Montrose's warning that, "He either fears his fate too much, or his desserts are small; who dares not put it to the touch to win or lose it all."

Due to weather induced delays to Bradley's west flank offensive the great American break-out at St. Lo would now take place on the same day, 25 July 1944, as the start of Operation "Spring". The results were to be quite different.

The Left Flank - Tilly - la - Campagne

Third Division's part in Operation "Spring", the capture of Tilly-la-Campagne on the Corps' left flank, was spearheaded by the North Nova Scotia Highlanders of 9 Brigade. Starting from Bourguebus the Highlanders would have to advance over a mile through open grain fields under enemy observation. To screen their advance H hour was set for 0330 hrs - just before dawn. Artificial moonlight (searchlights beamed off low cloud) would come on at H hour, ten minutes after the artillery bombardment had commenced.

But before the North Novas attacked Les Fusiliers Mont - Royal were to clear the enemy from around the intermediate Troteval Farm. The clearing operation was undertaken by a composite FMR company under Major J. Dextraze, later to be commander of the post-war armed forces. Supported by Sherbrooke tanks, artillery and mortar fire "J Dex" command executed a classic and totally successful pincers attack starting at 2000 hrs on the 24th. But this brilliant action was to give the show away.

Alerted by the Troteval action the Germans divined the oncoming attack and once again correctly determined the likely Assembly Areas, FUPs and SLs. But this time they added a new wrinkle. As the NNSH moved up they were bombed by German aircraft and suffered casualties before taking additional punishment from guns and mortars. At H hour the Novas crossed the Start Line but the searchlights failed to come on. Shortly thereafter the Highlanders were informed that 2nd Division's attack was delayed, leaving their right flank exposed. For the unfortunate victims of a similar gaffe at Buron it was, in a later vernacular, "déjà vu all over again". To compound their problems as the troops were half way to Tilly the searchlights suddenly came on. Because of an unpredicted ground mist this created a light-beam dispersion which illuminated the attacking Canadians rather than the defending Germans. Enemy machine gunners blasted the Highlanders who sought protection from view, if not fire, in the tall grain.

As "C" Company reached the edge of Tilley, "B" and "D" ran into the enemy's main defences. In savage fighting which cleared most of the enemy trenches the "D" Company officers were killed and their platoons badly cut up. Two NCOs fought their way to the objective but when surrounded with no friendly forces in sight they retired with the company's survivors to a covered position. "B" Company collided with two dug in tanks. The company's PIAT crews destroyed one but the other with infantry support decimated the attackers. Lt Col Petch then ordered "A" Company forward but it too ran into a killing zone and took up positions near "C" Company as dawn broke. With communications spotty at best the survivors beat off all German attempts at counter-attacks. A squadron of Fort Garrys was called forward to assist. During the O Group to plan their action a mortar bomb killed three of the squadron's officers.(7) The squadron then made three gallant attempts to aid the Maritimers but all were repulsed with the loss of eleven tanks. The North Novas suffered 140 casualties, including 61 dead. In the six weeks since D Day this unfortunate unit had lost 850 men.

The Centre - Verrieres - The Triumph of the Rileys

On the left of 2nd Division, adjacent to, but a mile away from, 3rd Division's North Novas, 4 Brigade prepared to attack Verrieres village. The attack would be undertaken by the Royal Hamilton Light Infantry (Lt Col J.M. Rockingham)(8) with the Royal Regiment of Canada to pass through and secure the ridge as a firm base for exploitation by the 7th Armoured Division. The FMR were to secure the Start Line for the Rileys as they had done for the 3rd Division at Troteval.

Finding that the enemy still dominated his Start Line, and unable to locate the FMR, Rockingham sent his "C" Company forward to do the job. "C" Company cleared the SL in fine fashion, its PIAT crews hitting two tanks and forcing the rest to withdraw. Despite the fact that this operation delayed them by 20 minutes the RHLI attacked under intense fire and after a wild charge reached the village. In furious platoon, section and individual fighting Rocky's men cleared Verrieres and surroundings just after dawn. Casualties were heavy but as officers fell their NCOs took over and kept up the momentum of the attack.

As dawn broke a troop of the 2nd Anti-Tanks' 17 pounders spotted a group of enemy tanks on the Riley's flank and promptly destroyed four of them. The FOOs, now able to identify targets, called down artillery fire on enemy strong points many of which were hidden in haystacks. Despite all of this the determined Germans were still able to mount heavy tank supported counter-attacks. The RHLI fought back with furious resolve, their six pounders and PIATs bagging several Panthers. As the enemy struck again tanks of the 1st Royal Tanks of 7th Armoured Division came to the aid of the beleaguered Light Infantry. Throughout hours of desperate fighting the RHLI and 1st RTR, aided by artillery and rocket firing Typhoons threw back the attacks and held firm to Verrieres. It had been an heroic battle and would become a proud battle honour, but again the price was high. By day's end the victorious Royal Hamiltons had suffered 175 casualties, 50 of them killed.

Lamentably the follow-up attempt by the Royal Regiment of Canada and the 7th Armoured Division to take Rocquancourt ended in failure. While the battle for Verrieres still raged the RRof C were ordered forward with the 1st Royal Tanks to advance in parallel on their right. H Hour was 0600 hrs. Because of the ongoing battle for Verrieres Lt Col J.C. Anderson had to swing his battalion, with a squadron of 1st Hussars, wide of the village as his pre-arranged supporting artillery fire plunged on far ahead.

Under intense fire the Royals crossed the ridge at 0900 hrs and advanced into a veritable maelstrom. Well camouflaged tanks, SP guns, mortars and machine guns of the

GAUDEAMUS IGITUR

2nd Panzers, backed by a rejuvenated 272nd Infantry Division, sprang a classic trap. "C" Company was boxed-in in a wheat field and cut to pieces, only eighteen survived, many including most of the wounded were made prisoner. The remaining Royals pulled back and dug-in on the rear slope from where they beat off a German counter-attack. On the right flank the 1st RTR could do no better and moved back to support the Royals and Rileys in holding Verrieres. So the center ended in something of a stand-off.

The Right Flank - St Andre - St Martin - May

On the right flank Brigadier W.J. Megill's 5th Brigade started under several severe handicaps. The first of these was the terrain. From the brigade's Start Line through the twin villages of St Andre-sur-Orne and St Martin-de-Fontenay to the sloping, coverless ground south to May-sur-Orne the attackers would be wide open to observed enemy fire. Accordingly the attack would be made at night, under artificial moonlight. However, unappreciated by the Canadian staffs, a warren of mine shafts and tunnels in the area gave the enemy a secure, covered way to move and hide his troops. A second handicap faced by Megill was that one of his battalions, Le Regiment de Maisonneuve, had been so depleted that it had been withdrawn into divisional reserve with no replacement provided. Finally, there was the problem of ensuring a secure Start Line something Simonds had specifically demanded and everyone had agreed. Megill wanted Les Maisonneuves returned for this task Foulkes refused but placed 6 Brigade's Camerons under 5 Brigade in lieu. All fine and large except that the Camerons were under strength, dog-tired and fully committed in trying to hold and clear St Andre, their objective from Operation "Atlantic". Foulkes, who seems to have had little concept of the principle of Concentration of Force, compounded the problem by reserving Megill's Black Watch for Phase II leaving that unfortunate Brigadier with only one battalion, the Calgary Highlanders, for Phase I.

Megill's plan made the best of a very bad situation. The already over-committed Camerons, on the evening of 24 July, were to clear St Andre and St Martin as the Calgary's SL for their assault on May-sur-Orne starting at 0330 hrs on 25 July. At first light the Black Watch alone would start Phase II by attacking through May up the slope of Verrieres Ridge to Fontenay-le Marmion. A tall order for a brigade let alone one battalion. With all the troops allocated to Simonds for "Spring" it seems as maddening to us today as it must have seemed to Megill at the time that such a crucial operation should be mounted on a shoestring - and a badly frayed shoestring at that.

As might have been expected things got off to a bad start. It took the under strength, battle weary Camerons most of the night to clear the enemy from St Andre and St Martin. But even then determined pockets of infiltrating Germans would pop up from the ruins in flank and rear and start things all over again.

The Calgary Highlanders (to become renowned as the Calgary Hooligans) moved up by night suffering from the by now *de rigeur* lacing of Assembly Area and FUP by German artillery and mortars with the added fillip of strafing by German aircraft which, grounded by day, emerged to activity by night. The Calgarys were 15 minutes late crossing the SL even as the Camerons struggled to secure it. As they moved swiftly trying to catch up to their barrage the Calgarys were fired on by enemy popping up from the underground quarry shafts. "C" Company was held up for two hours dealing with a series of machine gun nests. All the officers of "B" Company became casualties so the company carried on under its sergeant-major and NCOs. By mid-morning - some six hours later than planned - "C" Company finally reached the northwest edge of May-sur-Orne where it was held up. "B" Company trying to come up in reserve mistook its location in the dark and in error cleared St Martin thinking it was May. The Phase II Start Line was thus far from secure.

Meanwhile the Black Watch had left their Assembly Area at Beauvoir Farm and by 0530 hrs - their planned H Hour - they were still strung out along a hedgerow leading to St Martin. They came under intense fire and both the CO and senior major were killed. The Watch retired to St Andre to reorganize and revise plans for their delayed Phase II attack which would now be led by their new acting CO Major F.P. Griffin. Griffin consulted with Brigadier Megill who, unusual for Canadian commanders at this stage, had come right up front to find out for himself. Further delays were required for reconnaissance and the preparation of a new fire plan, during which time the IO of the Black Watch made two sorties into May (the Calgary's Signals Sergeant had done the same the night before). H-Hour was finally set for 0930 hrs - in broad daylight. "B" Squadron 1st Hussars was placed in support of the Watch.

Behind an artillery barrage the Black Watch advanced in an unwavering line with rifles at the high port into a hail of fire in the finest tradition of their regimental ancestors at Ticonderoga.(9) At an early stage the battalion's rear link was destroyed and in short order the FOOs lost communication with the guns, as a result the artillery barrage inexorably ran on far ahead of the advancing infantry. From the moment it crossed the Start Line the battalion was raked by well aimed mortar fire and was taken in the front and flank by machine gun and rifle fire from concealed positions. Over the crest additional machine gunners waited backed up by SPs and tanks many hidden in haystacks or in hull down positions.

Major Griffin gallantly took his place at the head of his magnificent command, directing and encouraging as his men fell around him. The battalion now reduced to perhaps 60 men crested the ridge, still trying to hold formation, and was decimated. Major Griffin was among those killed at the end still facing the front. His valour that terrible day was worthy of the VC, but again nothing was done. Of some 350 infantrymen who assaulted only 25 returned. The Royal Highland Regiment, as the Watch were entitled, suffered a staggering 307 casualties of whom 123 were killed, 101 wounded and 83 prisoners, one-third wounded. The supporting Hussars lost six tanks and all officers but one.

The charge can best be described, in a mixture of awe and wonder, by the German commander defending as, "soldiers marching upright holding rifles across their breasts in readiness as if on the drill square....Despite strong fire on them...scarcely anyone looked for cover....No sign of panic despite their visible losses...they kept marching upright. "It was "most impressive and perplexing." And finally, "The attack of the Canadians faded out before the ridge as actually there was nobody left. It had been sheer butchery."(10) Meanwhile "the enemy (Canadian) artillery had fired 3 to 4 kilometres to our rear." In the words of the observer of a similar doomed charge, that of the Light Brigade at Balaclava, "C'est magnifique, mais cela n'est pas la guerre."

But the day's carnage had not yet run its course. As the Black Watch literally disintegrated under fire the Calgary Highlanders were dislodged from their precarious foothold at May. Ordered to regroup in the factory of St Martin, the Calgarys, due to an error in order transmission, possibly by a Liaison Officer, assembled instead at St

GAUDEAMUS IGITUR

Andre. The Germans, using the factory tunnels, promptly reoccupied the factory and mine shafts. An abortive attempt by the Maisonneuves to restore the situation ended in failure and a further 52 casualties. The frustrating day's work cost the Calgarys 172 officers and men.

After several more orders and counter-orders Simonds, in consultation with Dempsey, called off the battle. The bloody operation of 25 July had cost the Canadians 1450 casualties - their heaviest one-day losses, Dieppe excepted, of the entire war. Casualties of another ilk included the sacking of 9 Brigade's Brigadier Cunningham and two of his battalion commanders, Christiansen of the Glengarries and Petch of the North Novas. And Operation "Spring" became perhaps the most critiqued, and criticized, Canadian operation of the war.

A "Spring" Assessment(11)

The most obvious error emerging from "Spring" was the astonishing failure by Simonds to make full and concerted use of the massive resources available to him. This has been likened, perhaps uncharitably, to prostate trouble - a full and bursting bladder resulting in only a few droplets at the front end. Although he had been allotted four and two-third divisions (or equivalent), comprising 28 battalions, 12 tank regiments, plus MG, recce and armoured car units, his attacks were delivered successively by only a handful of single, often widely spaced, battalions. Of these, four battalions and one tank regiment attacked individually in Phase I, one battalion in Phase II and one committed as a forlorn hope after Phase II was lost. Of the two armored divisions at his disposal Simonds used only a single armored regiment.

Admittedly no commander is going to commit everything in the first phase when substantial forces will be needed for following phases. But to start by using only one-seventh of your resources and then dwindling these to one- twenty-eighth is palpably wrong. This predilection for small attacks, powerfully supported on narrow fronts, seems to have become a fixation not only with Simonds but with Canadian commanders everywhere.(12)

Nor did bad generalship end with Simonds. Foulkes reworked the Corps plan without consulting his brigadiers and launched the critical right flank attack with a brigade from which one battalion had been removed and another was already fully committed - leaving only a single battalion to do a brigade's job. He gave his subordinates assurances of support from other divisions without ascertaining that the support was not, in fact, forthcoming. Once battle was joined he became a mere conduit for orders from Corps and confined his interventions, until too late, to exhorting fully committed subordinates to get going. Neither Foulkes nor his brigadiers, with the shining exception of Megill, went forward in person to ascertain the true facts. Young of 6 Brigade, completely ignorant of the problems his Camerons were having in St Andre, blithely asserted that the Start Line was secure when a minimum of personal reconnaissance would have shown just the opposite.

Brigadier Megill, the sole bright spot among Canadian commanders that day, was appalled by the plan for "Spring" which, in his words, "seemed to have been prepared by someone who could not read a contour map and had never seen the ground."(13) Throughout he tried to keep a grip on things by going forward to see for himself and to try and secure flank cooperation and support. Pity that in this he was almost alone.

THE NORTHWEST EUROPE CAMPAIGN

Command, control and communications (C3) are indispensable keys to successful operations, along with good intelligence. However in 1944 the essential link in this triumvirate -communications - ranged from poor to non-existent. Companies were soon out of radio touch with each other and with battalion. Battalion rear links with brigade often vanished at crucial times and even brigade rear links to division were iffy. The tank nets were often good as were the artillery links until, as so often happened, the FOO or his signaller or his wireless set became a casualty. Much reliance was placed on line, indeed the Calgary's Signal Sergeant preceded his unit into May for this purpose, and too little on liaison officers, runners or back-up wireless such as the recce point detachments which were provided on D-Day. As a result battalion HQ, brigade, division and corps were often left in the dark with no or, what is worse, wrong information.

The failure, with the notable exceptions of J Dex at Troteval and Rocky at Verrieres, to ensure the security of Start Lines was a classic example of compounded bungling. Everyone, from Simonds down, stressed the necessity of this yet failed to follow through - substituting wishful thinking and wrong assumptions for ascertaining the facts with the result that attacking battalions were blasted before they could get started. Plenty of uncommitted units could have been found for this absolutely crucial task - from 7 or 8 Brigades of 3rd Division or even from the British armored divisions. Instead the Canadian commanders left this job to the weakened FMR, whose ad hoc company at Troteval had to be gerrymandered together and whose second company earmarked for Verrieres was never found, and to the Camerons on the right who were already in over their heads at St Andre.

To their shame both Simonds and Foulkes tried to blame the troops for what was their own failure of command and intelligence. In particular the division and brigade commanders should have positively confirmed whether St Andre and St Martin were secure and, if not, to have taken proper steps to ensure this. Secondly, intelligence and staff at all levels were remiss in not appreciating the problems posed by the mine shafts and tunnels and taking steps to counter these. Finally provision and resources should have been made to mop up behind the lead companies. The battalions lacked the means to deal with front, flanks and rear simultaneously and their ingrained battle drills encouraged them to bypass strong points and get onto their objectives ASAP. They were thus vulnerable to enemy pockets popping up behind them. This problem was well known but little was done about it.

One final and, to the Canadians, deleterious result of "Spring" was that Montgomery, noting that six of ten German panzer divisions were concentrated south of Caen, concluded that further large scale efforts in that sector were unlikely to succeed. Since 2nd Army's western flank, hinged at Caen, was already swinging south in keeping with the Americans' break out at St Lo, Monty decided to switch his main effort there. Accordingly all three British armored divisions were sent west of the Orne to spearhead 2nd Army's drive on Caumont in Operation "Bluecoat". The newly activated 1st Canadian Army would thus take over east of the Orne without recourse to these prized armoured assets.

The Interregnum

A number of events, some momentous, took place between Operation "Spring" and the start of the next major Canadian offensive in early August. On the German side von Rundstedt had been replaced by von Kluge, Rommel had been seriously wounded in an air attack and a failed bomb attempt on Hitler's life resulted in savage reprisals against those, including generals, suspected of connection with the attempt. On the western front, in Normandy on 25 July, Bradley's 1st American Army had broken out at St Lo in Operation "Cobra". By 30 July Avranches had fallen - an advance of 40 miles and von Kluge rushed his panzers west for a last throw of the dice to avert disaster.

On the eastern flank 1st Canadian Army, under Lt Gen H.D.G. Crerar became operational on 23 July and was given command of Lt Gen J.T. Crocker's Ist British Corps of the 3rd, 49th and 51st British infantry and 6th Airborne divisions. The IInd Canadian Corps remained with Dempsey's 2nd Army until the completion of "Spring" when it would pass to Crerar's command. Crerar, through no fault of his own, started off on the wrong foot. On the day he took command Crerar was subjected to one of Montgomery's famous, fatuous, and patently false put downs, "Harry made his first mistake on taking command and his second after lunch." Then John Crocker, who had snidely denigrated the Americans in Tunisia before his own Corps bogged down on Green and Longstop Hills, tried to push his insubordination on Crerar who sought to have him sacked. The incident brought out another twisted side of Montgomery's personality. Although Monty could, with relish, insult both subordinates and superiors he could not bear to see a row between subordinates. He accordingly hurried to smooth things over between his two generals. To the credit of both Crerar and Crocker they put the incident aside and Crocker became a loyal and most effective subordinate of Crerar during the long months to come.

Following Operation "Spring" IInd Canadian Corps passed under Crerar's command and with it came two fresh, and green, armored divisions - the 1st Polish and 4th Canadian. 4th Canadian Armoured, the "Green Machine", was newly commanded by Maj Gen George Kitching and while well trained it had never exercised under Kitching and, because of the exigencies of the D-Day preparations, had not participated in a divisional exercise for five months. The arrival of the new divisions gave Simonds the chance to relieve the weary 3rd Canadians, who had been in continuous action for 55 days and desperately needed R and R. 4th Armoured Division, consisting of the 4th Canadian Armoured Brigade (4CAB) (Brig E.L. Booth) and 10th Canadian Infantry Brigade (Brig J.C. Jefferson) took over the left of the Corps sector.

On the operational side the Canadians made a number of small, company or battalion sized attacks most of which fizzled out for lack of strength. On 28/29 July Les Maisonneuves attacked St Martin's Church and were repulsed. Two days later an FMR company again under the redoubtable J. Dextraze took the church in a brilliant attack. They were preceded by an equally brilliant effort by the Essex Scottish who redeemed their "Atlantic" debacle by taking a well defended farm between Verrieres and Tilly. Tilly however stayed out of the Canadians grasp. On 1 and 2 August both the Calgarys by day and Lincoln and Wellands by night were rebuffed in attempts to seize that elusive village. Similar small probes on May-sur-Orne and La Hogue failed. Finally on 4 August the Camerons and engineers captured the factory and its tunnel heads but attempts to destroy them were only partly successful and the exposed force was withdrawn.

These small operations and especially the failed attacks on Tilly were further evidence, if any was still needed, of the wasteful futility of mounting footling, small company or single battalion attacks. The Canadian generals had yet to learn that it is better to use a sledgehammer on a fly than a flyswatter on an elephant. The fortified villages, such as Tilly that the Germans fashioned out of the strong Norman buildings, were nearly impervious to field artillery fire but would have made excellent targets for Bomber Command or the heavy artillery of AGRA. But no one seems to have thought of it.

The American Breakout

Operation "Cobra" was transformed into a full scale breakout on 1 August when General George S. Patton's newly arrived 3rd US Army was turned loose from Avranches. Omar Bradley the commander of the new US 12th Army Group, with the agreement of Eisenhower and Montgomery, changed the US drive's direction from Brittany to the east, via Le Mans and Argentan, to trap the German 7th Army between the US 12th and British 21st Army Groups.

It was a move that caught Montgomery, who always claimed that operations went exactly as he had molded them, wrong footed. Only days before he had switched his own emphasis and all British armored divisions to his, and the American's, inner or hinge flank His powerful 2nd British Army was now deeply embroiled far to the west in Operation "Bluecoat's" drive past Caumont. To provide the eastern arm of the pincers to entrap the German army he would now have to rely on Crerar's Canadians and especially the IInd Corps of two battle weary infantry divisions and two green armored divisions. Even Monty could not claim that he had planned it that way.

In early August von Kluge, desperately aware of the danger the American breakout posed, tried to disengage his armored divisions from the eastern Caumont - Falaise front to mount an eight panzer division attack against the American hinge at Mortain. The heavy attacks of Operations "Spring" and "Bluecoat", where Dempsey was now assaulting Mont Pincon, thwarted his plan and he could only scrape together four divisions for Mortain. Here the German attack foundered on superb defensive fighting by the US 30th Infantry and 3rd Armoured Divisions, excellent artillery support and well controlled tactical air sorties. Von Kluge had shot his bolt and now Patton could run riot. But to trap the Germans he needed the cooperation of Montgomery's 21 Army Group. As early as 29 July Crerar had instructed Simonds to draw up plans for a major attack on Falaise in great strength and with maximum air support. It was code named Operation "Totalize".

Operation "Totalize" 7 - 13 August
The Plan

Having observed the annihilation of the British tank attacks in Operation "Goodwood", and the difficulties experienced by his own infantry divisions in "Atlantic" and "Spring", Simonds made two key decisions to ensure the success of "Totalize". And this time his decisions were both sound and innovative. The first of these was to attack at night to protect his armour. While night attacks with infantry were certainly not new, large scale armoured attacks at night were a major departure from standard British/Canadian practice. His second idea, in order to counter enemy fire en route to the objective, was to mount as many of his infantry as possible in armoured carriers. For this he had the units' own limited number of Universal (Bren Gun) Carriers plus the scout cars of the Recce Regiments and motor battalions. These were neither enough nor entirely suitable. So, in a brilliant innovation, he had Priest self-propelled gun carriers, which the artillery had discarded in favour of towed 25 pounders, converted into armored personnel carriers. Simonds was able to procure and convert some 75 of these APCs, dubbed Kangaroos or unfrocked Priests, which with the other carriers were enough to lift two brigades.(14)

For air support Simonds would use British heavies the night before the attack to hit the first line of enemy defences and American bombers the next day to hit the second. Fighter-bombers would provide close air support. The attack would be supported by 360 guns which would only open up after the attack began. This staggered use of supporting fire was another innovative departure from previous norms.

The APC mounted force would attack in a closely packed four column phalanx with tanks, flails and AVREs leading the way. Direction would be maintained by artificial moonlight, special navigation and taping parties, colored star shells and Bofors guns firing tracer along the flanks. Dismounted infantry would follow to mop up and reinforce.

"Totalize" was to be conducted in two phases advancing on either side of the Caen-Falaise highway. Phase I would break through the main enemy defences anchored on Verrieres Ridge and seize the high ground Cramesnil - Bretteville-sur Laize. In Phase II the two armoured divisions would smash through behind the day bombardment of American bombers to secure the Laison Valley and hopeful Falaise.

For Phase I on the left one APC mounted brigade of the Highland Division and the 33rd British Armoured Brigade would drive south, bypassing the defended village Tilly, to take Cramesnil Spur. The rest of the division, following on foot and in soft vehicles, would eliminate the bypassed enemy at La Hogue, Secqueville, Tilly and Garcelles. On the right of the highway the 4th Brigade of 2nd Canadian Division mounted in APCs would be supported by the divisional 8th Recce Regiment and the 2nd Canadian Armoured Brigade. Their objective was the area Bretteville - Cintheux - Hautmesnil. On the Corps' far right the dismounted 6th Brigade would capture the bypassed Rocquancourt, Fontenay and May-sur-Orne. H hour for the attack was 2300 hrs on 7 August.

The Canadian attack would be opposed by the German 89th and 272nd Infantry Divisions, the 12th SS Panzers, a flak-cum-anti-tank division and much of the 101st Heavy Tank (Tiger) Battalion under the legendary Captain Michael Wittman who had personally accounted for a reputed 143 tanks on both the eastern and western fronts.

Operation "Totalize" - Phase I

Promptly on schedule 1000 heavies of RAF Bomber Command dropped 3,500 tons of bombs on the flanks of the Corps' lane before obscuring smoke and dust forced the cancellation of the programme. At 2330 hrs behind a rolling artillery barrage the armoured columns surged forward, severely hampered by the billowing dust thrown up by their tracks. However despite some understandable misdirections and vehicles getting hung up on obstacles the attack was a huge success and a vindication of Simonds' bold planning. The Royal Regiment of Canada captured its objective of Gaumesnil by dark. The Royal Hamilton Light Infantry secured the quarry area near Caillouet after dawn and promptly dug in. With the aid of a squadron of Sherbrooke tanks they beat off a strong tank supported German counter-attack. The Essex Scottish encountered enemy tanks en route and lost direction only reaching their objective of Caillouet by mid-morning. They finally captured the village with an APC charge supported by Sherbrooke tanks. East of the road the Highland Division was equally successful although their follow-up infantry had tough fights for La Hogue and Tilly.

The follow up attacks by 6 Brigade on the bypassed German strong points met with mixed results. Brigadier Young decided to attack with all three of his battalions at once to use surprise in lieu of artillery which would not initially be available to him. He did however have the 4.2 in mortars and MMGs of the Toronto Scottish as well as each battalion's own support weapons, plus tanks of the 1st Hussars.

Fontenay and May-sur-Orne had been only partly touched by the air bombardment and artillery programme and would be tough nuts to crack. However Rocquancourt on 4 Brigade's center line had been heavily shelled before being bypassed by the mounted brigade. Here the South Saskatchewans assaulted with great dash and rapidly reached and cleared the village capturing a number of dazed defenders in the process.

The Camerons had a much rougher time. From their Start Line to Fontenay-le-Marmion the battalion had to advance over 3000 yards without artillery or tank support. until after first light. They suffered serious casualties in the advance and on the objective including the CO, his replacement and two company commanders. With artillery finally available the FOO was wounded and a bombardier took over as heavy fighting raged through the morning. Sizing up the situation, Brigadier Young decided to pry open Fontenay from the east flank. Accordingly he ordered the South Saskatchewans to attack westward and clear the ridge between Rocquancourt and Fontenay. The South Sasks with two troops of 1st Hussars tanks did this in grand style totally routing the enemy and taking 250 prisoners. The Camerons captured another 80 and Fontenay, that elusive objective of previous battles, was finally in Canadian hands. The Camerons suffered 120 casualties throughout. The comparatively easy manner in which the Saskatchewans, by attacking from the flank, had overrun a strong enemy position which had defied all previous attacks delivered frontally raises the question of why Canadian commanders seemed so reluctant to try the indirect approach when the potential results were so great. But for whatever reason it was seldom tried.

If further proof of the difficulty of frontal attacks was needed it came in the form of the final attempts to capture May-sur-Orne another of the frustratingly elusive goals left over from Operation "Spring". The task was given to Les Fusiliers Mont Royal who encountered a very sticky wicket. Once more a furious battle developed around that bitterly contested village and even with belatedly available artillery support the Fusiliers could not force an entry. Finally, in the early afternoon, with the aid of tanks, artillery and especially Crocodile flame throwers the FMR blasted their way into and through the town. At long last May too had fallen.

Despite the bloody struggle on the right flank Phase I of Simonds' attack had been a brilliant success, completely overrunning the very strong German defences and pushing forward four miles. The wisdom of using APCs was evident in the comparative casualties. The mounted, and protected, 4th Brigade had only 63 casualties including an incredibly low 7 dead. By contrast the foot slogging, and unprotected, 6th Brigade lost 210 men in attacking bypassed towns. As the morning fog lifted it was time for the eagerly awaited Phase II. And the Germans would have to defend against it without the near mythical Captain Wittman who finally came to the end of his nine lives that morning being killed either by a gunner in a Canadian tank or by a British anti-tank gun.

Operation "Totalize" - Phase II

In his preparations for Phase II Simonds made two major mistakes - one through changing his original plan, the other through not changing his original plan. Simonds had first intended to open Phase II with only the 4th Canadian Armoured Division attacking astride the Caen - Falaise highway with the Polish Armour held back for exploitation. At the last minute he changed his mind and inserted the 1st Polish Armoured Division onto the left of the highway, thus squeezing the 4th Armoured into a narrow corridor on the right. Both the Canadian's Kitching and the Pole's Maczek were somewhat discombobulated by this 11th hour change of heart which carried such potentially serious consequences.

The second and far more serious error was Simonds' failure to follow up his glittering Phase I success by not scrapping his original Phase II set-piece plan and instead sending his armour Hell-bent for Falaise at once. For whatever reason, and there were many, Simonds decided to stick with his original plan which meant a substantial delay in ground operations while the troops waited for the American heavy bombers to come from England and bomb far ahead of the current front lines. He made one minor concession to speed by moving up the air attack from 1400 to 1230 hrs but the damage was done and the momentum gained in Phase I was irretrievably lost. The German general Kurt Meyer could only watch in delighted amazement as Canadian tanks milled about in rear instead of thrusting forward, thus giving the Germans just the time they needed to reorganize their defences. As Meyer so trenchantly put it, "An armoured attack which is divided into phases is similar to a cavalry attack which is interrupted by a pause for feeding."(15)

Just as Phase II got under way a comedy act worthy of Laurel and Hardy developed over the village of Gaumesnil. This village was to have been taken by 4 Brigade that morning, an event that was delayed when the attacking Royal Regiment had to pull back for the American bombing. Since Phase II had now started 2nd Division thought that 4th Armoured would overrun Gaumesnil en route to Bretteville. On the other hand the GOC 4th Armoured thought that the village was still 2nd Div's responsibility. While Kitching and Foulkes were still doing their Alphonse - Gaston act the Royals went ahead and took the place to permit the 4th's lead unit, the Grenadier Guards, to get going.

A fumbling attack by a squadron of Grenadier Guards, led by the same Ned Amy who had displayed such dash outside Ortona the previous December, resulted in the loss of four tanks and a narrowing of the divisional front to a few hundred yards. While division and brigade screamed exhortations to "push on", "bypass" and "move fast" the Grenadier's CO, Lt Col W.W. Halpenny, continued his leisurely promenade. After several hours he had advanced only a half-mile - less than the South Sasks had done on foot at Rocquancourt.

Finally a bright spot! While bypassing Cintheaux, one of Halpenny's troop commanders, Lt I.P. Phelan, noted the flash of a gun. Phelan returned fire with HE and killed the crew of an 88. He then charged the position and knocked out three 20 mm and three 88mm guns before dismounting and capturing 31 prisoners, three more 88s and a

20mm. Fifteen enemy had been killed. It was a brilliant action but about the only bright spot in the Guards' performance that day.

It took until 1800 hrs before the Argyll and Sutherland Highlanders (A&SH) (Lt Col J.D. Stewart) and a squadron of the South Alberta Regiment (SAR) (Lt Col G.D. de S. Wotherspoon) took Cintheaux and 40 prisoners. The Argylls would go on to capture Hautmesnil that evening and the quarry along with 25 more prisoners the next morning. Since several hours of daylight remained after the capture of Hautmesnil one would expect that Halpenny would finally shake his torpor and get cracking. Wrong again! While Kitching at division and Booth at brigade, getting more apoplectic by the moment, screamed, "Forward", Halpenny calmly decided to go back to Gaumesnil to leaguer for the night.(16)

Apologists for Halpenny have tried to explain that leaguering was SOP for armoured regiments at night and that his unit was doing as well as anyone else. While it was true that the Poles, who had run into 20 Panthers at the outset and been badly shot up, and 5 Brigade at Bretteville had done no better, it is difficult to excuse Halpenny's catatonic performance on that critical day. It is also hard to imagine that Patton, or Rommel, or Meyer, or for that matter Vokes or Hoffmeister would have acted in such a leisurely way and let opportunity slip away.

It is even possible that the schemozzle that followed could be laid at Halpenny's doorstep. Simonds and Kitching, both furious at 4th Division's slow and clumsy progress, resolved to attack that night giving Halpenny Force the limited objective of Bretteville-le-Rabet. The point was given to the fresh, but untried, British Columbia Regiment (BCR) (Lt Col D.G. Worthington) with the Algonquin Regiment (Algn R) (Lt Col A.J. Hay) under command. Worthington's task was to bypass Bretteville and seize the key Hill 195 some two miles further south.

Meanwhile Halpenny Force started at 0330 hrs. One-half mile from the objective the Lake Superior Regiment (L Sup) (Lt Col R. A. Keane) dropped off the tanks and deployed for battle. Bitter fighting followed at first light with the Guards showing much more dash and initiative than on the previous day and the Lake Superiors performing some of their more heroic actions of the war. Fighting continued through the morning when Bretteville and 200 prisoners fell to the Lake Sups.

The BCR/Algn group took off while fighting still raged around Bretteville. To avoid entanglement there Wotherspoon swung wide to the left around the place. This manoeuvre threw the battle group somewhat off track at the outset. Encountering numerous obstacles and enemy posts en route, and anxious to avoid Halpenny's errors and thus keep going and not be held up, Worthington's force drifted further southeast instead of southwest. Inexplicably they failed to notice that they had not crossed the Falaise road, which they would have to do to get to Point 195. As dawn broke they came under heavy fire and regrouped at what they thought was their objective, Point 195. In fact they were some two miles to the east, in the Polish sector. All day long as brigade and division frantically searched for them, and Worthington called for defensive fire around Point 195, the Germans alternately attacked and mercilessly shelled the BCRs and Algonquins. By days end, except for a handful who worked their way back, the force was destroyed. Worthington was among the dead.

At 0700 hrs on the 9th Worthington had erroneously reported that he was on his objective Point 195. Kitching, pleased that things had gone so well, arranged for the Corps Armoured Car Regiment (12th Manitoba Dragoons) to sweep the division's right flank. They were followed by the 3rd Division in the mop-up role. Becoming suspicious that events were not as reported, Kitching ordered that a battle group of the Governor Generals Foot Guards (GGFG -an armored regiment despite the title) (Lt Col M.J. Scott) and Algonquins with MMGs, anti-tank guns, flails and mortars close up to Point 195. It took several agonizing hours for the group to assemble and it did not get going until 1500 hrs. Artillery support was not available and the group soon ran into trouble, was stopped and lost 14 tanks.

With his armoured brigade seemingly unable to get untracked, Kitching turned to his infantry, instructing Brig Jefferson to clear southwest from Bretteville. Jefferson gave the job to the Lincoln and Welland Regiment (Linc & W) (Lt Col J.G. McQueen) and a squadron of South Albertas. By 1800 hrs the group, after a stiff fight, cleared Grainville - Langannerie. By last light they were at the spur leading to Point 195. Late on the 9th Jefferson ordered the Argylls to take over. In a brilliant two mile night advance over difficult terrain the Argylls, with excellent navigation, hit their objective bang-on as dawn broke. After a short scuffle which netted a few prisoners they dug in and by mid-morning were joined by a squadron of Canadian Grenadier Guards' tanks.

Against the inevitable heavy counter-attacks the Argylls and Grenadiers held firm although the battles cost the Guards 16 tanks and 35 men. With German resistance stiffening the 3rd Division was brought up. An attack by the Queen's Own and North Shores on Quesnay Wood reached, but failed to hold, the objective. The two units took 200 casualties for no gain. On 10 August with the Poles on the left, 4th Armoured on the right and 3rd Infantry in the center all stalled. Operation "Totalize", which had started with such promise, came to a fizzling end.

"Totalize" - An Assessment

"Totalize" had been a bittersweet victory but a victory nevertheless. In three days IInd Canadian Corps had broken the enemy's strong main defences below Caen and advanced nine miles. They had killed, wounded and captured thousands of the enemy and destroyed a large number of tanks, guns and other equipment. But though they had broken in, they had not broken out and Falaise remained a taunting will-of-the-wisp before them. By the yardstick of previous Anglo-Canadian efforts it had been a magnificent success. But the public had a new yardstick now - the breathtaking advances of the Americans in the west. And armchair critics, regarding their small-scale newspaper maps from the comfort of their parlours, would compare the long, broad sweeping American arrows with the Lilliputian Anglo-Canadian inching and tsk-tsk in disapproval. But to the troops burying their dead, evacuating their wounded, replacing 40% tank losses and trying to integrate raw reinforcements for the next holocaust it was enough that they - for the moment - were still alive.

The APC and infantry attacks of the first phase had been brilliantly conceived, brilliantly conducted and brilliantly successful. The subsequent armour heavy attacks of Phase II had been disappointing. Although they had come near to reaching the Corps' pre-planned minimum final objectives they had not achieved decisive success. Their attacks had been marred by far too much caution on the first day and, in an effort to avoid this, by the BCDs rashly bashing on without due diligence into oblivion that night. Had the two roles been reversed things may have gone quite differently.

There were many reasons by which crowning success had been turned into suffocating frustration. Simonds' errors in cramming two divisions into the space for one and, above all, his maddening pause, and loss of momentum, to permit a relatively ineffectual air attack have been noted. Once more communications had been a bug bear, although much better than in previous operations. But response times and reactions had been abysmally slow as witness the critical hours lost as the GGFG battle group tried to get its act together and move on. Kitching has been roundly criticized for his role but given the narrowness of the sector Simonds gave him his scope for sweeping manoeuvre was severely constrained and admonishing subordinates to get cracking in the heat of battle yields diminishing returns. The armoured divisions still had to learn when to be bold and when to be prudent and not to get the two mixed up. They would have precious little time to get ready for the next big push. Operation "Tractable" was due to open on 14 August.

Operation "Tractable" - 14 - 16 August 1944

By 13 August the XV Corps of Patton's racing 3rd Army had reached Argentan, some 20 miles south of Falaise and on the boundary between the 12th US and 21st British Army Groups. The two towns marked the open end of a huge horseshoe shaped pocket stretching 30 miles to the west with the German 7th and 2nd Panzer Armies inside and trying to get out. The Allies hoped, indeed expected, to trap the Germans inside by linking up near Trun between Falaise and Argentan. To avoid a collision between the British/Canadians moving south and the Americans moving north Patton instructed his lead Corps to advance slowly towards Falaise. He was overruled by Bradley, Commander 12th Army Group, who ordered him to halt at the inter-group boundary.

Bradley seethed at the slowness of the Canadian advance and suggested that Montgomery substitute his veteran British divisions for the task. He did not know, and of course Montgomery did not elucidate, that several weeks earlier Monty had moved the bulk of his Army Group, some nine divisions, to the west. They now laboured slowly south through bocage country in Operation "Bluecoat" and were consequently pushing at exactly the wrong end of the pocket. Montgomery also did not advise Bradley that his so-called veteran divisions were doing no better, and often worse, than the three battle weary Canadian divisions. So instead of rapidly switching his three armoured divisions back to the Caen - Falaise front where they might have played a decisive role in closing the pocket Monty did nothing of the sort. Nor did he recommend a change in the Army Group boundaries to permit Patton to close the gap. Instead he contented himself by issuing a directive on 11 August requiring the Canadians to bypass Falaise and link up with the Americans at Argentan while the British would take Falaise.

With his 1st Canadian Army now operational and responsible for the Caen - Argentan front, Lt Gen H.D.G. Crerar ordered his single Canadian Corps, the IInd, to "dominate the communications centered on the North, East and South of Falaise, in order that no enemy may escape."(17) While his four exhausted and casualty depleted divisions were granted a few days to rest, regroup and rebuild after "Totalize", Simonds planned his next blow, Operation "Tractable" due to start on 14 August.

"Tractable" - The Plan

Simonds planned "Tractable" as a daylight repeat of "Totalize" with a comprehensive smoke program to replace darkness in masking the force from the expectant enemy. His plan called for the APC mounted 8th Brigade and the 4th Canadian Armoured Brigade to form the eastern flank of the armoured phalanx while the 9th Brigade and 2nd Armoured Brigade would form the western. The armoured brigade would lead each column. Each armoured column was to bypass strong points and keep driving south to clear the Laison valley. The 10th Brigade of 4th Armoured Division and the 7th Brigade of 3rd Division were to advance on foot behind the armour and clean out bypassed enemy. Exploitation would then be made to Trun and a link-up with the Americans. The two divisions of the British Ist Corps, the 49th and 51st, were to keep pace on the Canadians' left flank.

The left column would rapidly close to the Laison, which was not believed to be much of an obstacle, effect bounce crossings and advance on a general axis of Route 91 to Versainville overlooking Falaise. The right column was to bypass Quesnay Wood, which would be dealt with by air, cross the Laison at Montboint and secure the high ground near Soulangy. In the exploitation phase the Armour would bypass Falaise, leaving it to the 2nd British Army, and charge on to Trun and Argentan to close the pocket. H Hour was 1145 hrs on 14 August.

Meanwhile on the right 2nd Division had been working its way south against the German 271st Division. Moulines and a large bag of prisoners were taken on the 12th. The next day the Calgary Highlanders took Clair Tizon, just six miles from Falaise, and forced a bridgehead over the Laize River. The quickly reacting Germans brought up a battle group of the 12th SS and managed to contain the bridgehead.

Despite the, to be charitable, decidedly mixed results of the heavy air bombing in "Totalize" Simonds ordered it up again for "Tractable" and timed it to begin after the troops had crossed the Start Line. Also prior to the operation Simonds gathered his divisional commanders and after castigating them for their perceived slowness in "Totalize" demanded all-out speed in "Tractable". But the gremlins still lurked to sabotage his hopes.

With sheer bad luck, the day before the operation a lost scout car of the 8th Recce stumbled into enemy lines and was blasted. Upon examination a complete outline of the planned attack was found on the dead body of the car's commander. It is doubtful that this find was much of a bonanza to the enemy as at this stage he was so depleted as to be unable to make any grand counter. Nevertheless to be forewarned is to be forearmed and the enemy, at the very least, was able to mitigate the worst effects of the bombing and to mass what resources he could find along the line of the Laison.

The Mad Charge

At 1145 hrs on the 14th the mighty phalanx of armour and APCs kicked off in what came to be called, "The Mad Charge".(18) Smoke and dust soon covered the columns making navigation a nightmare and adding churning chaos to the charge. Both columns reached the Laison in jig time only to find, neither for the first nor last occasion, that intelligence had erred and the river, despite its shallow depth, could only be crossed with great difficulty. While the tanks thrashed about looking for fords, fascine carrying Churchills of the 79th Armoured finally rumbled up and crossings were made. Strangely enough, no one in 4th Armoured or IInd Corps seems to have thought to include Ark Tanks, which had been so successfully used in Italy, in their order of battle, resulting in

THE NORTHWEST EUROPE CAMPAIGN

a further loss of precious time.

Those units such as Recce and Motor battalions which were equipped with more lightly armoured vehicles than those of the tank regiments fared much better in effecting crossings of the river. The 4th Division's Motor Battalion, The Lake Superior Regiment, crossed quickly and raced on to Perrieres conducting crisply executed dismount and take-out actions against anti-tank and machine gun posts en route. They were soon joined by troops of the BCR and later by the CGG. One company of the Lake Sups then moved on to cut the Falaise - St Pierre road.

The 7th Reconnaissance Regiment also crossed quickly and took Point 160 where they were joined by Fort Garrys and 1st Hussars in seizing their high ground objective. The two armored regiments, despite their problems at the river, had a tanker's dream that day. The Hussars captured several hundred enemy, destroyed eight field guns and six 88s. But their own losses were so high that two squadrons had to be temporarily amalgamated into one.

The APC mounted infantry relieved the armour on the Laison and set about mopping up. Considerable opposition was met and at Chateau d' Assy the Glengarrys had to use carrier mounted "Wasp" flame throwers to winkle out the enemy. The foot slogging 2nd Division kept pace on the right taking La Cressoniere and La Chesnaie. On the ground things seemed to be going reasonably well.

But from the air disaster struck again. A few of the 800 heavy bombers mistook their target areas and rained havoc in the Canadian's rear and on the right flank south of Quesnay. Due to some inexplicable staff snafu the bomber crews had not been informed that yellow smoke, flares and panels indicated the location of friendly troops. Worse still the bomber target makers for the day were also yellow. The results were predictable. The Royals lost 56 men and 24 key vehicles plus mortars, machine and anti-tank guns and much needed wireless sets. The South Saskatchewans, other 2nd Division units and the Poles also took a pounding. The only compensating element to this schemozzle was that Air Marshall Coningham had come forward with Simonds' Colonel GS, R.W. Moncel, in a de-turreted Staghound to see the show and had to take cover in a quarry as the bombs rained down. Moncel likened it to being in a coal cellar at delivery time.

That evening the 7th Brigade came forward to relieve the 2nd Armoured on high ground between Potigny and Olendon. After a six mile march the RWR and Can Scots secured the hill by night. The next morning the Winnipegs and 7th Recce took Soulangy while the Can Scots were sent against Point 168. Well placed German anti-tank guns prevented the supporting 1st Hussars from moving with the infantry so the Canadian Scottish attacked on their own. After another of their epic battles the Scots took the hill but suffered 130 casualties, their highest one day total in Normandy.

Two other significant events marked the 14th of August. First of these was the loss of Brigadier Booth, commander of 4th Division's Armoured Brigade (also numbered 4th) along with several of his staff and critically important command tanks. This resulted in 4th Armoured operating rudderless at a crucial stage of the battle. For a variety of reasons, some of which could have been obviated by better battle procedure, several hours passed before Lt Col Scott of the Foot Guards took command of the brigade. His command was short lived as Scott himself became a casualty. This resulted in further delays in the exercise of effective command before Robert Moncel was dispatched from Corps HQ to take over 4th Armoured Brigade.

The second significant event was another change of plan by General Montgomery.

GAUDEAMUS IGITUR

His original plan to have 2nd (British) Army take Falaise was placed in jeopardy by stout German resistance against that Army's advance. The nearest British divisions to Falaise - the 53rd (Welsh) and 59th (Midland) - were being blocked by stubborn fighting from the German 89th and 271st Divisions. Accordingly Montgomery ordered the 1st Canadian Army to take Falaise as well as to swing left to Trun. It was certainly a good command decision by Montgomery and illustrated his hands-on grip of the action, although critics might carp that he should have planned it that way at the outset and allocated to Crerar the resources necessary to do the job. Be that as it may, the problem was now in Crerar's hands and the Canadians would have to adjust in mid-battle. They would also have to do it with the formations that they had. Simonds, the Corps Commander responsible, decided to use 3rd Infantry and 4th Armoured Divisions in the original left hook role north-east of Falaise while 2nd Infantry Division was assigned the difficult job of taking that city - the birthplace of William the Conqueror.

Tractable - the Finale

While 3rd Division struggled around Hill 168 and Soulangy, 4th Armoured Division on the left was also running out of momentum. On the 15th the Argylls took Perrieres, which had been reached on the first day, and with the help of the 17 pounders of 3rd Anti-Tank knocked out two tanks and captured 20 men. Meanwhile the Algonquins spent most of the day taking and retaking Epanecy aided, amid a fog of confusion, by the Lincoln and Wellands.

Early on the 15th Simonds shuffled his formations moving the Poles from Quesnay to the left flank. On 4th Division's front the headquarters of its 4th Armoured Brigade was still somewhat shaky as its lost command vehicles had not yet been replaced and the double loss of its commanders precluded a firm grip from the top. Nevertheless before the wounded acting Brigade Commander, Lt Col Scott, was evacuated he ordered his two Guards Regiments and the weak BCRs to take their final objective, the high ground above Falaise. After the frustration of a refueling/replenishment delay the regiments moved off in fits and starts ,under effective fire from camouflaged, hull down enemy tanks they could not see, groping for a way forward. Before them was a flat open plain fully dominated by the enemy. Meanwhile one regiment of the division's artillery was now out of range while the other was on the move. In the confusion the Guards first reported their objective taken then after another delay cancelled this over-optimistic erroneous report. A seething Kitching and fuming Simonds were not amused. The Germans had once more somehow managed to mass the tanks and anti-tank guns they had left around the Canadians' final objective. By last light the tank regiments of 4th Armoured Division were reduced to little more than 20 tanks each.

Since leading his 4th Armoured Division into Operation "Totalize" Maj Gen Kitching had done his best to ginger his subordinates and keep momentum going but a number of things had conspired against him. Several of these were imposed from above including the delays to employ heavy bombers in comparatively ineffective roles and the squeezing of the division into a regimental front. From his subordinates came Brigadier Booth's unfortunate choice of selecting the tentative Halpenny to lead the opening charge which resulted in a creeping stop-and-go when speed was of the essence. Nor could Kitching be held directly responsible for the blundered loss of one-third of his armour and half the Algonquins when Worthington's command went astray. But he could perhaps have been more effective in finding out where they really were. Kitching started "Tractable" with drive and dash until an intelligence failure resulted in congestion, confusion and delay on the Laison. Finally his armoured brigade lost control when it lost in succession two commanders and its command vehicles at a critical stage of the battle. Despite these things Kitching himself could have done more. He could, for example, have taken a page from the German book and led from the front. But he, like most Canadian generals of the era, chose instead to direct from the rear via demands and exhortations on the basis of scanty, misleading and conflicting information and poor communications. As a result "Tractable" had now run out of steam and would soon come to an end.

Simonds was already working on a new plan and, as the 15th ended, 2nd Division took the high ground above Falaise. Simonds' orders on 16 August called on 2nd Division to take Falaise and the 3rd to relieve the 4th in its present location. The 4th and Polish Armoured Divisions were then to swing wide to close the Falaise gap at Trun and link up with the Americans at Argentan. And, as the Canadians battled towards Falaise and Patton was running wild, Allied forces landed in the south of France in Operation "Dragoon" and prepared to move north. It seemed that indeed the war might end in '44. But first there was work to do.

Falaise - 16-18 August 1944

Maj Gen Kurt Meyer entrusted the defence of Falaise to Kampfgruppe Krause - yet another of those improvised and highly effective battle groups which the Germans seemed to conjure out of nothing like a magician pulling rabbits from a hat. Krause's command only numbered some 200 comprising the remnants of the 1st/26th Panzergrenadiers, the 12th SS patrol company, several Tigers of the 102nd Panzers and two Pak 75s. At first blush this seems a mismatch when pitted against a Canadian brigade. But not necessarily so since the brigade would normally attack with two battalions each with two companies up - meaning four companies in the assault. And at this stage of prolonged operations the battle weary companies could only muster some 70 to 90 men each. Also the Canadians would be attacking in the open against a hidden, dug-in enemy fighting behind strong stone buildings and supported by tanks superior to anything the Allies could muster. When one recalls the success that a single company of Reginas, without tanks, had against a much stronger attacking enemy force at Cardonville the odds at Falaise suddenly even up.

Maj Gen Foulkes gave the task of capturing Falaise to Brigadier Young's 6th Brigade supported by the two remaining and amalgamated tank squadrons of Sherbrooke Fusiliers. The brigade would attack from the northwest with the South Saskatchewans left, the Queen's Own Camerons right and Les Fusiliers Mont-Royal in close reserve. H Hour was set for 1300 hrs on the 16th but congestion and the assembly of marching troops pushed this back to 1500 hrs.

On the left the Saskatchewans and their accompanying Sherbrookes came under fire from two Tigers and dug-in Grenadiers on the outskirts of the town. After a fire fight and the loss of two Shermans the prairie boys drove the Germans back into Falaise. Here the skillfully dug-in Germans knocked out three more tanks but the Canadians relentlessly pressed on and drove the enemy back into their interior defences of fortified

GAUDEAMUS IGITUR

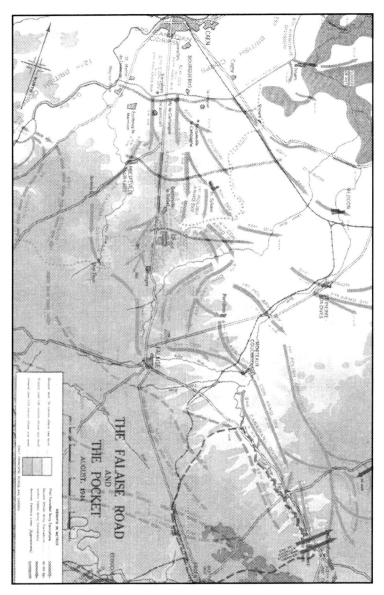

The Falaise Gap 17 - 21 August 1944

stone houses. After one repulse the South Sasks regrouped and advanced into town fighting grimly for every house and yard. After driving the enemy from his intended final position in the railway station the exhausted, but triumphant, Saskatchewans dug-in on the road to Trun at 0300 hrs on the 17th.

On the right the Camerons were initially thwarted trying to cross the River Ante. Under heavy fire and with supporting armour held up, the Camerons only forced their entry into town at 0200 hrs on the 17th. Against furious resistance the Manitobans pushed right through Falaise and on to St Clair, a mile to the east where they dug-in.

THE NORTHWEST EUROPE CAMPAIGN

Within Falaise the Germans still stubbornly clung to their keep in the Ecole Superiore, a large stone building surrounded by a thick stone wall. Les Fusiliers Mont-Royal were brought up and a frantic battle ensued. Twice repulsed the determined French-Canadians stormed the building at 0200 hrs on the 18th while undergoing a rare attack by German aircraft. By dawn it was all over. A very few prisoners were taken, German dead lay everywhere.

At long last Falaise, that almost mystical, elusive city which had been the Holy Grail of 21 Army Group for so long was in Allied hands. It was now a ruined prize bought with the blood of thousands of young Canadians. Krause's battle group had put up a fanatical, skillful resistance but in two days they had been bested and destroyed by a small force of equally brave, dauntless and determined Canadian amateurs. The historian James Lucas has made a study of the actions of 17 German battle groups on all fronts during the Second World War.(19) Although the thrust of the study, taken from the German perspective, is on the superb performance of the Kampfgruppen, it is significant that only in the Falaise battle were the Germans constantly routed from one strong position after another in such a short time. 2nd Division and 6th Brigade can be very proud of their fine actions in this epic battle.

Closing the Gap - 16-21 August 1944

Even as 2nd Division was battering ever forward to clear Falaise, Simonds put in play his plan to close the Falaise Gap - the mouth of a pocket now some 12 by 35 miles brimming with the shattered elements of 21 German divisions. Montgomery meanwhile changed the inter-Group boundary so that the Americans could move to Chambois the new proposed junction. Possibly fed up with Montgomery's slowness and Bradley's interference Patton had already stripped his XV Corps of two divisions, sending them eastward. Then Bradley changed responsibility for the Argentan front from Patton's 3rd to Hodges 1st Army necessitating the replacement of Heaslip's XV Corps by Gerow's Vth. The reshuffle resulted in the Americans wasting most of the 17th and in their 90th Division getting locked in a see-saw battle for Bourg - St Leonard in the best tradition of 21 Army Group. At the same time the British Ist Corps of Crerar's Army attacked north-east towards Lisieux (home of St Therese) and Livarot.

Simonds moved the 1st Polish Armoured Division to the Corps' left flank where it seized crossings over the Dives River at Jort. The 12th SS' Kurt Meyer countered by sending yet another of his ad hoc battle groups to that area where they blocked the Poles throughout the day. On the right 4th Armoured Division, preparing to cross the Ante east of Falaise sent the Argylls to Damblainville and the Algonquins to Couliboeuf. Both crossings were secure by last light on the 16th.

On the 17th the Poles were held up at Norrey-en-Auge after a disappointing advance. Within 4th Armoured Division its 10th Infantry Brigade tried to move south of Damblainville but came under heavy fire with traffic congestion blocking the crossing. Kitching, seizing control, switched his division east to the Couliboeuf crossing. The move, which required traffic control of the highest order, was made in the face of a number of monumental traffic jams. By 1600 hrs 4th Armoured Brigade, with the Grenadier Guards in the van, had crossed and charged forward to seize Louvieres-en-Auge only two miles north of Trun. Here their progress was blocked by yet another conjured up German battle group. Montgomery, whose own battles were marked by extreme caution and who was four headquarters removed from the action, was miffed at what he perceived to be the slowness of the Canadian advance.

Simonds, with his 4th Armoured at the gates of Trun, redirected the Poles to Chambois which they were told to take that night. But orders are one thing and translating them into action quite another. It took the Poles until the 18th to get their advance going. They then had to fight a series of furious actions with enemy parties who were escaping down the Trun - Les Champeaux road. Progress was slow. On the morning of the 18th the 4th Armoured Division captured Trun and blocked the German escape route to Vimoutiers. Simonds now ordered that division to advance down the Trun - Chambois Route D13 to Moissy. The Poles were ordered to take Mount Ormel and Chambois and link with the Americans.

"C" Squadron South Albertas under Major David Currie, a former garageman from Moose Jaw, with a company of Argylls advanced on St Lambert-sur Dives where they were held up by 88mm fire which knocked out several tanks. The Germans continued to pour through the Chambois gap as the South Albertas and Argylls battered ahead. On the morning of the 19th Currie's men against desperate opposition captured two-thirds of St Lambert knocking out two tanks - one by determined infantrymen using grenades. At 1100 hrs a large German convoy which was trying to squeeze through St Lambert bumped Currie's position and was destroyed under a hurricane of fire.

The other SAR Squadrons took up positions in an arc behind St Lambert from where they could better cover the field .They were joined by Currie's FOO whose high OP enabled him to bring devastating fire, including several "Mike" targets, onto the fleeing enemy. The RAF and USAAF also had a field day strafing inside and outside the pocket - occasionally targeting Canadians and Poles in error. The enemy in turn desperately shelled and mortared St Lambert and, at one stage, managed to cut off "B" Squadron SAR to the east. At 1800 hrs Currie breathed a little easier when he was reinforced by a company each of Argylls and Lincoln and Wellands.

At Trun the Lincs and Winks with a squadron of South Albertas, New Brunswick Rangers machine gunners and a troop of SPs repulsed repeated attacks by frantic German units, sub-units and unorganized rabble trying to break out. By last light they had taken 500 prisoners and killed hundreds more. As the enemy continued to squeeze past Trun and St Lambert Kitching was strangely inactive. The armoured regiments of 4 Brigade, which could have played a decisive role at the front, remained harboured out of contact waiting to be moved up to plug the gap. Kitching, out of personal touch and depending on the usual melange of conflicting SITREPS, seems to have failed to appreciate the vital need to plug the gap and held back waiting for things to develop. The fluidity and confusion of the multiple actions apparently caused him to misread the true nature of the battle. Thus when 4th Brigade was finally ordered into action its tanks were sent north-east towards Vimoutiers instead of south-east to St Lambert, Moissy or Chambois. In fairness to Kitching there were substantial bodies of enemy outside, as well as within, the pocket to which the Poles at Maczuga could attest and which a commander would ignore at his peril. But Simonds had tasked Kitching with closing the Trun - Chambois gap which could have been much better accomplished by massing his three armored regiments behind the Dives to cover the many holes in the front held by the South Albertas and supporting infantry companies. It was just the sort of role that German tankers would beg to have and of which they would make the most.

On the 19th the Poles finally forced their way to Coudehard and at 1930 hrs a regiment tentatively entered Chambois and linked, albeit tenuously, with the Americans. The bulk of the division dug-in to the north. And the enemy still held crossings over the Dives at St Lambert and Moissy.

Early on the 20th, as 9 Brigade moved on Trun, the Germans began their major break-out attempt concentrating on the St Lambert - Chambois sector. As the remains of 5th Panzer and 7th Armies attacked from the south, the 2nd Panzer Corps struck from the west isolating the Poles on Hill 262, named by them Maczuga (the Mace) and adjacent hills. The Poles fought fanatically and were most effectively aided by the medium guns of the Canadian AGRA, directed by Captain Pierre Sevigny, later to become a Canadian cabinet minister.

The attacks on St Lambert renewed with increasing violence as the retreating enemy hurled themselves again and again at Currie's small command. As dusk descended on the 20th the Germans made a last frenetic attack on his position and were stopped dead in their tracks. In the words of Currie's citation, "Seven enemy tanks, twelve 88mm guns and forty trucks were destroyed, three hundred Germans killed, five hundred wounded and two thousand one hundred captured. Major Currie then promptly ordered an attack and completed the capture of the village thus denying the Chambois - Trun escape route to the remnants of two German armies."(20) With all his officers killed or wounded and with virtually no sleep Currie, over three days of constant action, directed, encouraged, cajoled and led his men inspiring them by his personal courage and example to, in the words of Kipling, "hold on when there is nothing in you, Except the Will which says to them: 'Hold on!'"(21) Currie received a well merited VC, incredibly the only one awarded to a Canadian in Normandy.

Meanwhile 3rd Division had been ordered forward to join the 4th. The Royal Winnipeg Rifles, Stormont, Dundas and Glengarry Highlanders and Camerons of Ottawa relieved the Lincolns and Wellands in Trun and were promptly into action. On the 21st they fought a pitched battle against attacking escapees. The Camerons' Vickers Guns, in particular, had a field day mowing down the attackers in heaps. For a time the adjacent village of Magny was lost but, with their last-gasp attack destroyed, the enemy surrendered in droves. Lt Gen Menny, commanding the 84th Division, was among the captives.

2nd Armoured Brigade was now placed under 4th Division to augment its battle-depleted armoured brigade while 9 Brigade was temporarily placed under 10 Brigade's Brig Jefferson. Kitching, somewhat belatedly, ordered the 5th Anti-Tank Regiment to create a screen across the division's front to be backed up by the 1st Hussars and South Albertas, later augmented by the HLI of C. The screen was commanded by the 5ths Lt Col Douglas Harkness who was yet another to enter the Federal cabinet after the war.

On the 20th Maj Gen Kitching, awakening to the true needs of the battle, cancelled 4th Armoured Brigades' move to Vimoutiers and directed it to the south. Brig Moncel, the brigade's fourth commander in only one week, was ordered to both aid the hard pressed Poles on Maczuga and to finally seal the Gap by occupying positions behind the Trun - Chambois road. Why Kitching had not ordered this last mission two days before is a mystery and one which probably contributed to his later sacking. Partly due to this tardiness the Germans would later claim that up to 40% of their troops who were still in the pocket on the 20th managed to make their escape. But thousands did not.

On the 21st the Grenadier Guards and Governor General's Foot Guards blasted their way through to relieve the Poles on Maczuga by mid-afternoon. The BCR (The Duke of

Connaughts) advanced past the Guards and reached Mont Ormel by last light. Finally on this day the Highland Light Infantry of Canada and 1st Hussars attacking with strong artillery support reached Chambois by last light after very severe fighting and linked up with the Poles still holding out there. At long last the Falaise Gap was truly closed.

Normandy in Review

Although one major battle remained to be fought by the Canadians in what is geographically a part of Normandy - La Foret de la Londe - for all intents and purposes the Normandy campaign ended on 21 August when the Canadians closed the Falaise Gap. "Apres cette le deluge" as Allied armies roared roughshod over France and Belgium to the borders of the Reich.

The Canadians, despite some subsequent criticism - none directed at the troops - could look back with proud satisfaction on a job in Normandy very well done. In a 77 day campaign, fought for the first 42 days by just one division, the next 21 by two and the final 13 by three the Canadians had played a lead role greatly transcending their small size. From start to finish they had been the spearhead of many of the most vital battles and advances undertaken by the Anglo/Canadian Army Group. They had again and again faced and defeated the cream of the German army. It is noteworthy that of the 12 divisions of 21 Army Group in Normandy the 3rd Canadian Division suffered the heaviest casualties and the 2nd Canadian, which only came into action after Caen, the second heaviest of the entire campaign.

One notes with pride that on D-Day the 3rd Canadian Division assaulted one of the most heavily defended beaches outside of, and perhaps including, Omaha. They brilliantly overcame savage resistance and by nightfall had penetrated farther inland than anyone else. They were the first Allied sea-landed division to seize their final objectives.

Although unknown outside of Canada, and scarcely known within, the brilliant and victorious stand of the 3rd Canadian Division at Norrey, Bretteville and Cardonville in the first week prevented the Allied bridgehead from being cut in two by powerful enemy attacks. Thereafter the division mounted an heroic attack over open ground at Carpiquet and decisively defeated the enemy in savage battles at Buron and Abbaye Ardenne to finally force his withdrawal from Caen.

With 2nd Division now in the line the newly activated IInd Canadian Corps mounted a series of intense attacks around Verrieres Ridge culminating, with the arrival of 4th Armoured Division, in two brilliant Canadian conceived and executed APC mounted attacks which broke the main enemy line. This was followed by a superb street fighting battle resulting in victory at Falaise and an unimaginably violent and successful struggle to close the Gap at Trun and St Lambert.

The true measure of the valour of the Canadian soldiers can only be appreciated, and then only dimly, by standing on the old German defence lines and looking back up over the long stretches of naked landscape over which the Canadians had to advance, shelled and machine gunned at every step, to close with and defeat the enemy. The task was even more daunting when, through casualties and constant action (56 days for 3rd Division), the battalions routinely had to commence each action at two-thirds battle strength which rapidly diminished thereafter. That they succeeded at all is a wonder. That they succeeded so well almost defies belief. And it was only the beginning.

THE NORTHWEST EUROPE CAMPAIGN

CHAPTER X

THE CHANNEL PORTS AND THE SCHELDT

My God! Did we really send men to fight in this?

Lt Gen Kiggell (Haig's COS) on viewing for the first time
the sodden Passchendaele battlefield (Attributed)

The Pursuit to the Seine

As the Allies tightened their noose on the Falaise Pocket General Montgomery, on 20 August, issued his directive for the next phase - the advance to the Seine and beyond. As long as the Pocket remained Montgomery directed that the Americans from the south and Canadians from the north would keep the "bottle tightly corked" while 2nd British Army moved "eastwards up the bottle" preparatory to breaking out. Crerar's 1st Canadian Army was only to withdraw the "cork" on Montgomery's order when the Pocket had been cleared. It would also develop a thrust on Lisieux and Rouen and when the Pocket was eliminated would cross the Seine and clear the Havre peninsula. As the Americans drove to Louviers and Elbeuf the British 2nd Army was to rapidly advance to cross the Seine and Somme and destroy the enemy in the Pas de Calais.

On 22 August with the Falaise Pocket eliminated the 1st Canadian Army began its drive to the Seine. Simonds had already prepared for this by sending 2nd Division to take Vimoutiers on the 21st and Orbec on the 22nd. The next day the 3rd and 4th Canadian Divisions moved east as the Polish Division went into reserve to recoup. On the left flank of the Canadian Army the strong Ist British Corps of four divisions, which had been little engaged in the Falaise battles, moved on Honfleur, Pont L'Eveque and Lisieux.

On 26 August the Lincolns and Wellands met the Americans at Elbeuf, with the US forces then moving east. The Lincolns and SAR occupied Criquebeuf and crossed the Seine at 1700 hrs that day. The next day 10 Brigade engaged in stiff fighting at Igoville and Sotteville against the 17th Luftwaffe Division which was protecting the withdrawal of the German main forces. On 30 August the 9th Canadian Brigade entered Rouen.

Meanwhile 2nd Division had come a cropper. As it advanced on the Seine it collided with the fresh 331st German Infantry Division which was covering the approaches to Rouen from the Foret de la Londe. Faulty intelligence led Maj Gen Foulkes to believe that the forest was only lightly held. Events were to show how wrong he was. The 4th Brigade entered the forest from the south and the 6th from the west and north. The enemy were skillfully dug in and well supported by the superb German mortars. With bad weather limiting air support and artillery fire comparatively ineffective in the woods the infantry struggled forward against an enemy they could not see. Trying to keep direction and pinpoint an elusive enemy in a gloomy, dripping woods made for a miserable and costly campaign.

For three days 2nd Division struggled in vain. Then on the night 28/29 August the bulk of the enemy slipped across the river with the rearguard escaping on the 30th just before 3rd Division captured Rouen and blocked any further withdrawal. 2nd Division

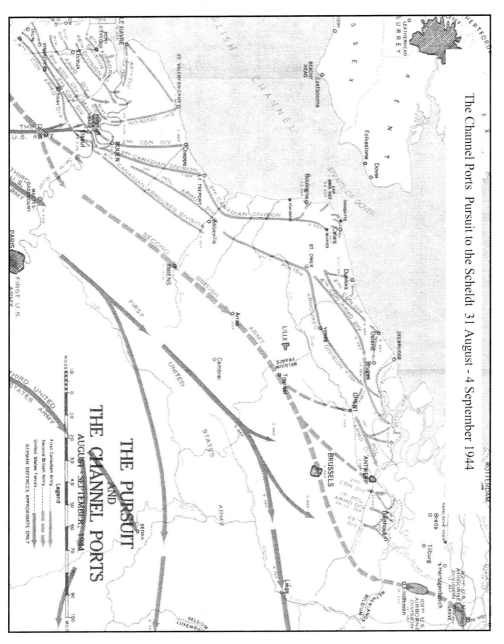

suffered 580 casualties in what many critics have said was a battle that should never have been fought. With hindsight this may be right. The forest should probably just have been screened with one of the independent national brigades attached to 1st Army while 2nd Division bypassed to Rouen. But battles are not fought with hindsight and here Foulkes, with the information available to him, took what he believed to be the appropriate action.

It turned out wrong but once the troops were committed deep in the forest it would have been most difficult to extract them and try something else. But for the weary troops it had been a bloody, dreary battle with little of the exhilaration of victory at the end. And more of its ilk were to follow.

The Race To The Rhine

As August turned to September the end of the war in Europe seemed tantalizingly near. While the 1st Canadian Army worked its way up the Channel coast, the British 2nd drove on Belgium, the US 1st on Aachen and the Ardennes, the US 3rd on Metz and the Saar and the newly arrived US 7th (soon to be joined by the French Army "B" in the new 6th Army Group) advanced on the Belfort Gap. Alas, as so often in war, what was to have been the end of the affair turned into an affair without end.

On Sepember 1st Montgomery was promoted to Field Marshal paving the way for the elevation of his Army commanders, Crerar and Dempsey, to General.(1) However his promotion was bittersweet for, in accordance with long standing arrangements, he now had to step down as land forces commander, a position to be directly assumed by Eisenhower. Montgomery's parish was now restricted to 21 Army Group. He relinquished his land forces command with little grace and less tact and continued to bombard Eisenhower with unsolicited advice and uncalled for criticism. His peremptory request to assume de facto command of Hodges' 1st US Army was just as peremptorily denied.

One of Montgomery's suggestions cum demands was that Eisenhower virtually ground the rest of his command and give Monty the resources and go-ahead to plunge onto Berlin via the Munster - Osnabruck axis. Montgomery's rationale to run things his way (apart from his normal egotism) was that until the Channel ports were opened the AEF, still being supplied from Normandy, lacked the resources to operate more than one Army at a time. Eisenhower, for a variety of good reasons, demurred and authorized a broad front advance on Germany by all his armies.(2) He also impressed upon Montgomery the need to open the port of Antwerp at an early date.

Montgomery did however wrest from Eisenhower an agreement to enable him to first launch a joint airborne operation on the northern axis Eindhoven - Nijmegan - Arnhem to bounce the Rhine and advance into Germany. The Combined Chiefs of Staff, meeting in Quebec in early September, agreed to an initial northern approach. However they specifically emphasized the need to open the north-west ports, particularly Antwerp and Rotterdam, before bad weather set in.(3)

The Approach to Antwerp

With the crossing of the Seine 1st Canadian Army's task, in accordance with Montgomery's directive of 26 August, was to take Le Havre, Dieppe and destroy all enemy in the coastal belt up to Bruges. Lt Gen Crerar assigned the Havre operation to Crocker's Ist British Corps which being on the coastal flank was well positioned for the role. IInd Canadian Corps was directed on Le Treport, Dieppe and a crossing of the Somme at Abbeville.

On 1 September the 2nd Canadian Division returned in triumph to Dieppe to the tumultuous welcome of the townspeople. In a like manner the 51st Highland Division entered St Valery-en-Caux where the original division had been destroyed in 1940. The taking of Dieppe and Crerar's decision to briefly rest the weary 2nd and 4th Divisions resulted in yet another petulant row with Montgomery. Possibly due to a signals mix-up Crerar attended a victory parade in Dieppe when Montgomery had demanded his presence at a conference with the Americans. Although the conference did not touch on any matter affecting the Canadians, Montgomery was furious with Crerar for failing to show and called him on the carpet. Montgomery's tirade only ended when Crerar stated that they should take the matter up with their respective governments. At this Monty, ever the bully, backed down and, over Crerar's objections, considered the matter closed.

On the battlefield the 2nd British Army on the Canadian's right, with no intervening Channel ports to worry about, made spectacular advances. Against negligible opposition they captured Amiens on 31 August along with the Commander and Headquarters of the 7th German Army. On 3 September the Guards Armoured captured Brussels and the next day the 11th Armoured entered Antwerp and found the docks intact. The British now had their eyes firmly fixed on the east and a drive into Germany. No one, including Lt Gen Brian Horrocks whose troops took Antwerp, seems to have known, or ignored it if they did, that Antwerp could not be used until its approaches guarding 50 miles of channel to the sea had been cleared of the enemy.

The Germans alone seemed to have been aware of this and desperately strove to extricate their 15th Army north into Walcheren and the Scheldt approaches. Montgomery and others in the higher command knew what the Germans were trying to do from ULTRA intercepts (4) and air reconnaissance. But believing in the prospects for success of their forthcoming drive into Germany they were not overly concerned with backwater Antwerp and left to the air forces the interdiction of the northward retreating Germans. Montgomery also felt that the ports of Dieppe, Boulogne, Calais and Dunkirk could support his northern thrust. He was quite content that the rest of the AEF might have to be grounded to serve his purpose. He was also mistaken. Dieppe could only handle 1000 tons a day, Dunkirk was bypassed and Boulogne, although captured on 22 September, was only cleared for shipping on 12 October, long after "Market Garden" - the airborne thrust to break into Germany - had failed.

Both the XXX Corps' Horrocks and Maj Gen Roberts, whose 11th Armoured took Antwerp, later bitterly lamented not receiving information or direction to close the Scheldt and stymie the German withdrawal. As Horrocks, who was excluded from the ULTRA chain (5) later wrote ,"If I had ordered Roberts to bypass Antwerp and advance only fifteen miles north-west, in order to cut off the Beveland isthmus, the whole of this force which played such a prominent part in the subsequent fighting, might have been destroyed or forced to surrender."(6) Horrocks, who had also been fixated on the Rhine, afterwards believed that the Battle of Arnhem was lost on 4 September by the failure to seal the Scheldt.

One general who did know what the Germans were doing, or at least after the war claimed that he knew, was Simonds. According to him he urged Crerar to ignore the Channel ports for the nonce and send IInd Corps on Breskens thence east along the Scheldt River to Antwerp thus trapping the 15th Army. Crerar, who was operating under firm instructions from Montgomery to capture the Channel ports before tackling the Scheldt, declined. Simonds blamed Crerar's Dieppe dust-up with Montgomery, in which he had been accused of failing to follow orders, for his reluctance to broach

THE NORTHWEST EUROPE CAMPAIGN

Monty on the matter. If so, it was yet another instance where Montgomery's penchant for hectoring his subordinates had backfired. Regardless of who was at fault it certainly was not the Canadian soldier but it was he who would pay with his blood for a failure of higher command.

The Channel Ports

Le Havre -- Operation "Astonia" 10 - 12 September 1944

The capture of Le Havre had long been assigned to Lt Gen Crocker's Ist British Corps of the 1st Canadian Army. That excellent Corps, located on the Army's left flank, had not been involved in closing the Falaise Gap and was thus reasonably fresh and able to plan ahead. They were ready and able. Crocker's leading units closed up to the port on 2nd September and he began thorough preparations for its capture.

Staring on 5 September the Navy, featuring the twin 15 inch guns of the monitor HMS Erebus to be joined by the eight 15 inch guns of HMS Warspite, bombarded the city's defences. On the same date Bomber Command commenced the first of three heavy raids on the port and gun areas in which some 4000 tons of bombs were dropped.

On 10 September Ist Corps opened its land offensive from the east with the 49th and 51st Divisions, two tank brigades, 79th Division "funnies", eight heavy and medium AGRA Regiments and a squadron of Canadian Kangaroos. Crocker's attack was brilliantly successful. At noon on 12 September the garrison surrendered. At a cost of only 338 casualties the Corps had captured a good sized port and 11000 prisoners. Unfortunately, due to extensive demolitions, the docks were only opened to shipping on 9 October when they were allocated to the US Armies as a supply base.

Boulogne - Operation "Wellhit" 17 - 22 September

In a signal to Crerar on 6 September, Montgomery acknowledged that, "Antwerp may be unusable for some time as Germans are holding islands at mouth of Scheldt." and he urged Crerar on the early capture of Boulogne.(7) In fact Crerar had already directed 3rd Division to begin preparations to take the city and on 5 September the division had closed up to the city's outer defences. It was soon apparent that a major assault would be necessary and this could not begin until the heavy supporting weapons could be moved the 160 km north from Le Havre once that city had fallen.

On 13 and 15 September Montgomery further clarified matters by ordering the capture first of Boulogne, then Calais, the masking of Dunkirk and then devoting "the whole energy of the Army" to enable full use to be made of Antwerp.(8) While 3rd Canadian Division concentrated on Boulogne and Calais the Polish Armoured Division on the Army's right flank took Ypres and Roulers on 7 September. On The Poles left the 4th Canadian Armoured Division crossed the Ghent canal and fought a series of actions and took many prisoners around Moerbrugge. Meanwhile after resting and refitting at Dieppe the 2nd Division moved on Dunkirk and Ostend. On 12 September the Corps Armoured Car Regiment led 4th Brigade and 4th Armoured Division in the capture of the lovely medieval city of Bruges.

Boulogne had been designated a fortress by the Germans and was strongly fortified on the landward side as well as mounting powerful coastal defences. It was defended by a force of 10,000 commanded by the formidable Lt Gen Heim, formerly COS to the

GAUDEAMUS IGITUR

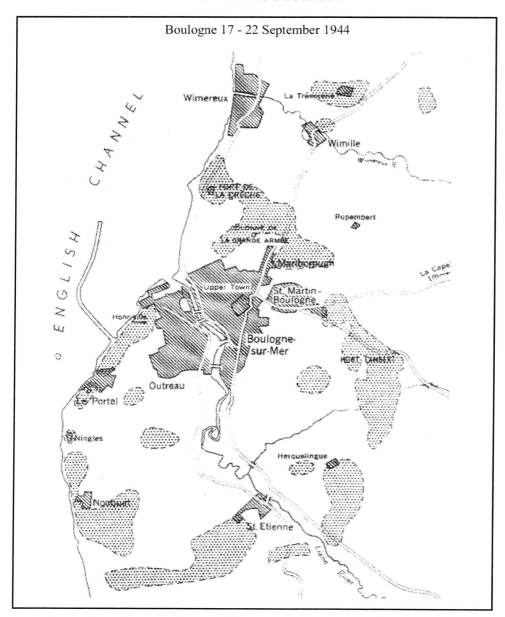

Boulogne 17 - 22 September 1944

legendary Heinz Guderian. Boulogne thus promised to be a tougher nut to crack than Le Havre yet Crerar was only able to provide one division to take both it and Calais. Maj Gen Dan Spry, who had succeeded the wounded Keller in command of the 3rd Division, decided to attack Boulogne with 8 and 9 Brigades supported by the AGRAs, armour and Funnies while 7 Brigade masked Calais. Once Boulogne was taken 8 Brigade and the supporting arms would be rushed to Calais to assist 7 Brigade to capture that prize.

THE NORTHWEST EUROPE CAMPAIGN

The fortress of Boulogne was protected by a semi-circle of very heavily fortified and defended strong points. From north to south these were the Fort de la Creche, St Martin, Mont Lambert, Herquelingue, St Etienne and Nocquet. Behind these were other strong points especially Buttercup and Portel with the immensely strong Citadel standing in the upper town. Some mile and one-half to the north the strong points of Wimereux, La Tresorerie and Wimille provided powerful flank protection.

Maj Gen Spry's plan called for 9 Brigade under Brig J. Rockingham to attack from the east below Route N42 while 8 Brigade attacked north of that road. Both brigades would advance to the Liane River which flowed south-north through the city before emptying into the harbour. 9 Brigade would then cross the river and clear the left bank while 8 Brigade was to turn north to capture Fort de la Creche, La Tresorerie and Wimereux. Once again the assault troops were to be carried in APCs and be supported by tanks, artillery and the specialized armour of 79 Division. In view of the strength of the enemy Maj Gen Spry established a Phantom force based on the divisional Machine Gun Battalion, the Ottawa Camerons, to feign an attack from the south. The attack was scheduled for the morning of 17 September.

The key to the enemy defences was perceived to be the heavily fortified and dominating Mont Lambert. Thus prior to the ground assault the hill was to be attacked by nearly 700 heavies of Bomber Command. However to ensure safety the assaulting troops had to be 2000 yards back of the bomb line which would, as in the past, provide ample time for the German defenders to emerge and engage the attackers. To overcome this the Air Force devised a simple ruse. After bombing the aircraft would circle back in a simulated run with bomb doors open to deceive the enemy into staying under cover while the attackers closed up. The ruse worked as planned.

At 1000 hrs with the real bombing finished the heavies commenced their dummy run. As the enemy took cover the APC mounted attackers - North Novas and Glengarrys - with Engineer AVREs, Flails and Fort Garry tanks charged forward. Once more the air bombing proved a mixed blessing. While it had a demoralizing effect on the pinned down attackers it caused few casualties or material damage. But worse, as at Caen, the concentrated bomb cratering impeded the tanks and APCs to such an extent that halfway up the hill the North Novas and Glens had to "de-pouch" and assault on foot. Neither the tanks nor AVREs nor Flails could get through. Nevertheless the Scotians and Glens fiercely pressed on eliminating some 20 enemy posts en route to the summit. Once the engineers had gapped the minefield and the AVREs had filled a few craters the Crocodile flame throwers arrived and greatly helped in reducing the many pill boxes.

While the North Nova Scotia Highlanders battled to clear Mont Lambert the Stormont, Dundas and Glengarrys forced their way to the Liane. It took them most of the night to hammer through the rubble choked streets against furious German counter attacks. The next morning the battalion faced the daunting task of storming the castle-like, stone walled Citadel. With incredible timing a local Frenchman appeared and guided the Canadians to a secret tunnel leading to the Citadel's interior. As Churchill tanks raked the walls with fire and the AVREs blew charges against the entrance gates the Canadians emerged from the tunnel behind the defenders. The stunned enemy surrendered, yielding over 200 prisoners.

8 Brigade on the Division's right battled its way into town led by the Queen's Own Rifles and Chaudieres as the North Shore Regiment attacked Le Tresorerie. By nightfall

the North Shores captured Le Tresorerie as the Queen's Own reached the harbour and the Chaudieres advanced on Fort de la Creche. The Rifles and Chauds were held up throughout the 20th. Then on the 21st, behind a superb attack by 75 medium bombers, the two battalions closed right up to the fort. The next morning under a hurricane of fire from all weapons of the infantry supported by tank and anti-tank guns blasting at point blank range the 500 man garrison surrendered.

On the left 9 Brigade crossed the Liane under supporting fire from the infantry's own mortars, PIATs and machine guns. The HLI, at a cost of 65 casualties and four Flail tanks, established a bridgehead through which the SD and Gs attacked to clear Outreau and Buttercup Hill. Another 200 prisoners passed into Canadian hands. The Canadian Highland Brigade spent the 20th and 21st in winkling the stubborn defenders from the town and dock as the enemy retreated into the heavily fortified Le Portel. At 1400 hrs on 22 September 9 Brigade attacked. Within two hours the fort fell, Lt Gen Heim surrendered and 3rd Division secured Boulogne. A total of 9500 prisoners were captured by the Canadians.

Led by Montgomery, the staffs at 21 Army Group and SHAEF were critical of the perceived slowness of the Canadian capture of the town. The six-day battle was unfavorably compared with I Corps' brilliant two day victory at Le Havre. But, as usual, the criticism was shallow, uninformed and completely unfounded. Against Le Havre the British employed two full divisions, four heavy bomber attacks, strong naval, including battleship and monitor, firepower and much stronger tank and artillery support. When the enemy commander was wounded the garrison soon packed it in. However at Boulogne the Canadians had only two brigades - one-third the size of the Havre attackers. They also lacked naval assistance and had less air, tank and artillery support. The Boulogne garrison, which actually outnumbered the attackers, fought from strong fixed defences and led by a tough and resolute general battled to the bitter end. And it was this latter factor which marked the main difference between the two battles. This is attested to by the fact that the two brigades at Boulogne suffered 650 casualties, almost twice the number lost by two full divisions at Le Havre. And this in no way detracts from the truly magnificent British capture of Le Havre.

Having said this, it is difficult to believe that Lt Gen Simonds could not have assembled a stronger force to take Boulogne. Part of the answer of course lay with the many other tasks facing him, notably Calais, Cap Gris Nez, Dunkirk and the Scheldt. But the suspicion remains that Simonds underestimated the enemy's resolve. And his predilection with using only part of the force available is a recurring theme in Simonds' battles. At Boulogne, at the very least, 7 Brigade could have been added leaving the screening of Calais to Recce, armoured car and Allied contingents. But all of this is to quibble. By any yardstick the capture of Boulogne was, at the divisional, brigade and battalion levels, soundly planned and brilliantly executed. It resulted in a great victory against a tough, skillful and bravely determined foe. It is a proud battle honour and the story should take its place in a well recorded, and remembered, Canadian history.

Operation "Market Garden" 17 - 25 September 1944

While the bitter battle for Boulogne still raged momentous events elsewhere on 21 Army Group's front stole the headlines with the promise of a spectacular victory and even an early end to the war. This was Montgomery's airborne/land attack over the

THE NORTHWEST EUROPE CAMPAIGN

Meuse and the two Rhine channels of Waal and Neder Rijn aimed at Nijmegan, Arnhem and the Munster triangle, code named "Market Garden". Once again Monty started full of confidence, proclaiming that "Our real objective is the Ruhr." Once again he was to be disappointed.

"Market Garden" saw the dropping of Lt Gen Browning's I British Airborne Corps of the US 82nd and 101st and British 1st Airborne Divisions at Grave, Nijmegan and Arnhem to secure crossings over the Meuse, Waal and Neder Rijn Rivers. Brian Horrocks XXX Corps, led by the Guards Armoured Division, was to rapidly advance north along the airborne axis to secure and connect the three airheads while VIII and XII Corps widened the corridor. XXX Corps had only to advance 65 miles from the Escaut to Arnhem. The possibilities glittered.

From the start things faltered. Strong German resistance, blown bridges and contested crossings seriously delayed XXX Corps. The American drops at Grave and Nijmegan were successful but at Arnhem a combination of factors, especially the designated dropping of the division too far from the objective and the unexpected presence of German armour, frustrated the operation and led to its failure. On 21 September Horrocks ordered the survivors of the British 1st Airborne to be withdrawn over the Neder Rijn. This hazardous water crossing withdrawal was undertaken by four field companies of engineers including the 20th and 23rd Canadians manning storm and assault boats. In the end 2400 men were evacuated, most by the Canadian storm boats. The Canadians suffered eight casualties, five fatal. Their commander received the DSO for a fine night's work.

There were many reasons for the failure, all copiously documented elsewhere.(9) One of these was doubtless the ponderous and cautious relief operation conducted by Lt Gen Brian Horrock's XXX Corps - a hallmark of British and Canadian commanders in North-west Europe of whom Horrocks was probably the most gifted. As the distinguished British General David Fraser put it, "It is difficult to imagine that a Rommel or a Patton on the Waal on 19th September 1944 could not have reached the Arnhem bridge - somehow."(10)

Of greater puzzlement is why Montgomery chose such a difficult, multi-river approach in the first place, rather than the more direct and obvious drive over the Rhine near Wesel - which was in fact the route actually used the next year. Some analysts have argued that the main reason was to exploit a gap between the German 15th Army withdrawing northward and the 7th withdrawing eastward although Allied generals were seldom this perspicacious. Others have claimed that the direct route was not used because the heavy anti-aircraft defences ringing the Ruhr, including the Wesel area, would have seriously threatened the airborne approach. Perhaps there is some truth to both, or perhaps the real reason lies elsewhere - locked forever in Monty's crypt.

Calais - Operation "Undergo" 25 September - 1 October 1944

From Cap Gris Nez to Calais 13 miles to the east the Germans had established ten batteries of heavy guns to control the narrow English Channel. The batteries were well guarded by strong landward defences. Additionally, the approaches to Calais were protected by large areas of marsh and flooded ground. The center of the city was covered by an outer ring of forts lining a network of canals. A bastioned wall and moat secured the central citadel. From Cap Blanc Nez, seven miles west, to Calais the

GAUDEAMUS IGITUR

Germans had constructed strong defensive keeps at Noires Mottes, Belle Vue Ridge, Coquelles and Vieux Coquelles. Minefields and wire covered a series of concrete anti-tank and machine gun pillboxes behind which the strong 7500 man garrison resolved to fight to the end.

On 5 September the 7th Recce Regiment later joined by the Toronto Scottish machine gunners formed a 20 mile screen around the Cap and Calais. On the 16th the Royal Winnipeg Rifles and Regina Rifles supported by 1st Hussars tanks and artillery attempted to rush the Cap but were repulsed. The two rifle regiments then left for the attack on Calais and the 7th Recce resumed their screen.

For the attack on Calais Maj Gen Spry used the 7th and 8th Infantry and 2nd Armoured Brigades supported by the Flails, AVREs and Crocodiles of the 31st British Tank Brigade, Kangaroo APCs and several field and medium artillery regiments including those of the 51st Division. Due to supply problems, which the capture of the Channel ports was expected to alleviate, the rest of that fine division lay temporarily immobilized at Le Havre. Spry's plan called for 7 Brigade to capture Belle Vue, Coquelles and Calais town while 8 Brigade took out Escalles, Cap Blanc Nez and Noires Mottes. 9 Brigade was tasked with the separate action of capturing the batteries at Cap Gris Nez. Until this was done the port of Boulogne could not be used. A smoke screen was to shield Calais from the guns at Cap Gris Nez.

The land attack was preceded by three massive bomber assaults. The first of these was marred by a series of Headquarters "channel of communication" turf wars which resulted in an air attack on Boulogne's Fort de la Creche being cancelled in error with a subsequent day long postponement in the Fort's capture. Despite the intermediate foul-ups at SHAEF, HQ 84 Group and HQ 2nd TAF, Harris' Bomber Command did its job with excellent results. The second bomber attack on 24 September was again marred by headquarters' SNAFUs which led to the air attack being launched without Flak suppression resulting in the loss of eight out of 188 aircraft. On 25 September - Calais' D-Day - 900 aircraft took off but only 300 bombed with again excellent results.

At 1015 hrs on 25 September, following the air bombardment, the assault troops went in behind the flails of 31st Armoured. By evening the Chaudieres captured Cap Blanc and 200 prisoners while the North Shore were surrounding Battery Lindemann at Noires Mottes. Fighting interspersed with negotiation continued throughout the night and in the morning the Noires Mottes garrison of 285 and Lindemann's three great guns fell to the Canadians.

On the right the Winnipegs met stiff resistance at Vieux Coquelles but managed to capture the enemy positions by last light. When the Reginas, with a company of the Royal Montreal Regiment, were held up at Belle Vue, Brigadier Spragge sent the Canadian Scottish on a wide flanking via Sangatte and the coast to Fort Lapin. The next day 7th Brigade followed an attack by 190 bombers to close up to the city's inner defences but with strong resistance Fort Lapin, Bastion 11 and Les Barques still held out.

On 27 September after a further air bombardment the Can Scots, tanks and Crocodiles captured Fort Lapin and put two companies across the water defences behind Bastion 11. Still Bastion 11 and the Citadel held out and the two companies were cut off for 48 hours. The Winnipegs had an equally tough fight at Fort Nieulay where pill boxes were skillfully built into the fort's walls. Finally, with the aid of flame throwers, the Little Black Devils prevailed and several hundred Germans surrendered. The Regina Rifles on the right flank kept pace over flooded lowlands to penetrate to the factory area

THE NORTHWEST EUROPE CAMPAIGN

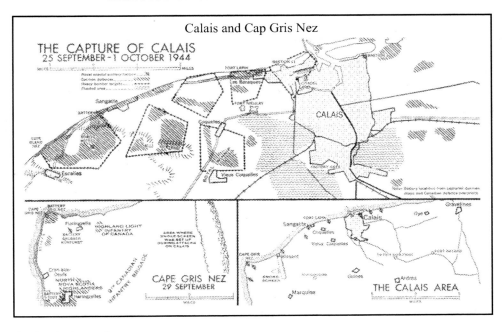

in the city's southern quarter.

By September 27 following yet another Bomber Command attack the garrison was reeling. Maj Gen Spry called on the Germans to parlay. The Germans agreed and Spry ordered a cease fire. At the meeting on the 29th the Germans stalled but a 24 hour truce was agreed to permit the evacuation of some 20,000 French civilians. When the truce expired 7 Brigade advanced against crumbling opposition. As the Can Scots took Bastion 11 and the Citadel the Reginas and Winnipegs moved steadily through the town as thousands of Germans retreated before them right into the waiting arms of the Queen's Own and Camerons. At 1900 hrs the German commander surrendered to the Camerons and after a night of sporadic fighting the city was completely cleared by 0900 hrs on October 1st. A total of 7500 prisoners were taken at Calais. Canadian casualties were a surprisingly light 300.

The Cap Gris Nez battle by 8 Brigade again featured some excellent work by Bomber Command which mounted two very accurate attacks. The North Novas on the left had as their objectives the Battery Todt and the German HQ at Cran-aux-Ouefs. The HLI had Batteries Grosser Kurfurst and Gris Nez. The attack was supported by the 1st Hussars and the Flails, Crocodiles and AVREs of 31st Brigade plus field and medium artillery.

The attack started at 0645 hrs on 29 September. As Flails beat through minefields and AVREs filled the craters the HLI moving closely behind the barrage captured Grosser Kurfurst and four huge guns by 1030 hrs and Battery Gris Nez and its three guns by mid-afternoon. On the left the North Novas made equal progress, employing novel petard cum grenade attacks on the massive armoured gun emplacements. By midmorning Battery Todt fell soon joined by the Headquarters at Cran. At a cost of only 42 casualties the two battalions captured 1600 prisoners and 15 great guns. For the first time in four years the English port of Dover was freed from the constant threat of shelling from the German cross-channel guns. The Canadians also played their part in freeing England from the ordeal of flying bombs (V-1s) when they overran the bomb launching sites between Dieppe and Dunkirk.

The September battles for the Channel ports yielded 30,000 prisoners, many enemy dead and the capture of Le Havre, Boulogne, Cap Gris Nez and Calais. But the extensive damage to the ports led to their remaining closed to shipping for several weeks. Critics have argued that the month taken to reduce the Channel ports could better have been spent by merely masking the ports and proceeding to the early clearance of the Scheldt and the opening of Antwerp. They may well be right but at that time the Allied gaze was fixed firmly on the Rhine and the Ruhr rather than on resupply. Montgomery himself had ordered the early capture of "one good Pas de Calais port" before tackling the Antwerp approaches while he launched his massive stroke to Arnhem and the Munster triangle. When that grand gamble failed priorities suddenly changed and the Canadian Army was directed to clear the Scheldt and open the great port of Antwerp as a top priority.

The Scheldt - 16 September - 8 November 1944
Geography and Defences

The Scheldt derives from two long narrow inlets cutting south-eastward from the North Sea below the Maas Estuary. The top inlet, the East Scheldt, cuts between the islands of Schouwen and Tholen to the north and Walcheren and the Bevelands to the south. The West Scheldt enters south of Walcheren Island and South Beveland penninsula becoming the tidal Scheldt River 15 miles north of Antwerp. To its south on the mainland is a flat area between Zeebrugge and the Scheldt River of which the western half came to be called the Breskens Pocket.

Nearly all of the Scheldt lies within the Netherlands although the Dutch part of the Breskens Pocket is only from five to ten miles deep. The whole comprises waterlogged, canal laced, heavily diked flatlands much of which in 1944 was flooded or a sea of mud. Travel off the roads, which usually ran along the tops of dikes, was difficult for infantry and nearly impossible for vehicles.

With the fall of Antwerp the Germans, keenly aware of the need to deny the Allies the use of that great port, had decided upon a plan of defence based on Walcheren, the Breskens, South Beveland and the approaches to the east. To this end they spent most of September withdrawing their 15th Army under General von Zangen into the Scheldt fortress. By 23 September they were in position with one division in the Breskens Pocket, one in the Beveland peninsula and strong forces to the east below the Maas River. Walcheren Island was protected by a large number of heavy guns in huge concrete emplacements, mostly grouped along the west coast.

The Plan and Preliminary Operations

On 14 September Field Marshal Montgomery issued orders mainly covering 2nd Army's operations towards Arnhem. He instructed the 1st Canadian Army to capture

THE NORTHWEST EUROPE CAMPAIGN

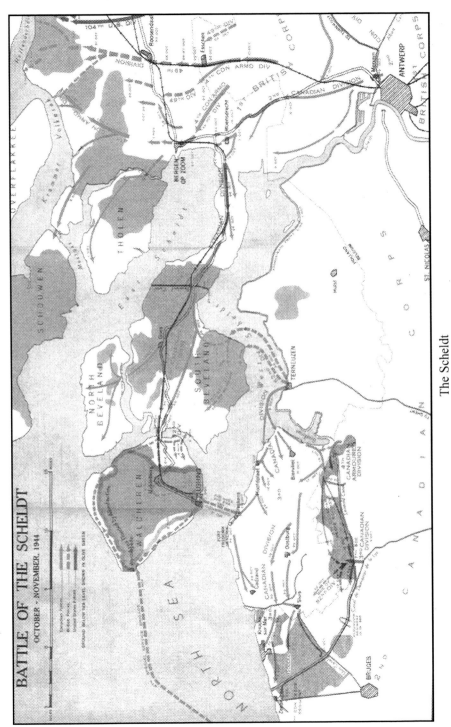

The Scheldt
6 October - 6 November 1944

GAUDEAMUS IGITUR

Boulogne and Calais and then clear the Scheldt. He promised Crerar the use of airborne troops for Walcheren and heavy bomber support throughout. The Canadian Army was to relieve the British 2nd around Antwerp on the 17th and operate northwards on an axis Breda - Utrecht - Amsterdam - Rotterdam. Finally, still believing that 21 Army Group would make the main thrust north of the Ruhr on Berlin, he instructed the Canadian Army to move on Bremen and Hamburg on the left flank of 2nd Army's main thrust. Much of this of course was never to come about.

Even before receiving this instruction the Canadian Army's two armoured divisions - the 1st Polish and 4th Canadian - had been pushing north of the Ghent canal. The Poles were to clear the area between the Terneuzen Canal and the Scheldt. The 4th Canadians were directed west of the canal from Moerbrugge to Breskens. After heavy fighting the Poles captured Terneuzen on 20 September. 4th Armoured advancing against the main enemy force in the Breskens Pocket was not so lucky.

First they had to cross the Leopold Canal. An attempt by the Algonquins to cross near Moerkerke gained only a tenuous bridgehead under constant fire with no further crossing feasible. After beating off a succession of attacks and suffering 158 casualties the Algonquins were withdrawn. 4th Armoured Division now angled right via Maldegem to Watervliet and the Braakman Inlet. 1st Canadian Army was now about to begin the Scheldt campaign in earnest.

The Eastern Approaches

On 16 September the 2nd Canadian Division relieved the 53rd (Welsh) Division in Antwerp where the Germans still held the northern outskirts and the line of the Albert Canal. It was a surreal existence where troops in rotation could leave the battle front and take a tram to the downtown pleasures of a city largely untouched by war. On the 19th Crerar ordered IInd Corps to advance north on Roosendaal and Bergen op Zoom and then swing west to clear South Beveland and Walcheren. On the 24th the Ist British Corps arrived from Le Havre where it had been grounded while Market Garden absorbed all available supplies. Ist Corps took over the right of the Canadian front, flanking Dempsey's 2nd Army. Since supplies still had to come from far back in Normandy all things, including artillery ammunition, were in very short availability throughout Crerar's Army.

Because a direct push into the northern Antwerp suburbs promised costly street fighting, Maj Gen Foulkes, GOC 2nd Division, decided on an outflanking to the east. This option carried its own problems as it would require crossing both the Albert and Antwerp-Turnhout Canals. Reconnaissance revealed that at Wyneghem a partially intact 90 foot lock gate offered the hazardous chance of a crossing of the Albert. After midnight on 22nd September an eight man patrol of the Calgary Highlanders, under Sgt C. Crocket, worked its way along the narrow gate finishing with a hair raising inching along an eight-foot section of 6 inch pipe and a strand of wire. As the patrol reached the far bank it was challenged by a German sentry whom Crocket dispatched with a knife. As Crocket's patrol scrambled to join him a German machine gun swept the lock, killing the last man. The Sergeant then swiftly led his patrol in storming two enemy machine gun posts knocking both out and killing the crews. A company of Calgarys then followed and with further reinforcements, including the Maisonneuves, spent a wild day beating back enemy counter attacks while the engineers struggled to complete a bridge by last light. With the Albert breached the enemy hastily retired behind the Antwerp - Turnhout Canal, allowing the 49th Division to make an unopposed crossing further down. The rapid dislodging of the enemy from the Albert was due almost entirely to Crocket's heroic action. He was recommended for the VC but, as with so many other Canadians, Montgomery peremptorily downgraded it to "a very good DCM."

Taking advantage of the Calgary's success to cross the Albert unopposed the British 49th Division rapidly closed up to the Antwerp - Turnhout Canal. In a brilliant manoeuvre the British division feigned at one place and crossed at another. By the time the enemy reacted the "Polar Bears" had two brigades across and defeated all enemy attacks taking 800 prisoners in the process. It was a tribute to imaginative planning and textbook execution - something all too uncommon among 21 Group commanders.

Meanwhile 2nd Canadian Division, without subterfuge of any sort, was unsuccessful in trying to cross at Lochtenberg to the west. At this juncture Crerar, with a second corps now available to him, made the British Ist Corps responsible for operations northeast of Antwerp and placed the 2nd Canadian and 1st Polish Divisions under Crocker's command. Crocker did not disappoint - his adroit handling of his Corps yielded excellent results over the next month. With his timely reallocation of duties complete Crerar, suffering from severe dysentery, was evacuated to England. Simonds assumed temporary command of 1st Canadian Army and Foulkes of II Corps. Brig R.H. Keefler assumed temporary command of 2nd Division.

Just when it seemed that Crocker might quickly clear the eastern approaches to the Scheldt Monty changed things again, albeit not without reason. To permit 2nd Army to operate southeast from Nijmegen he directed that the Canadian Army protect the 1st's right flank by advancing its right formation - the Ist Corps - northeast along a line Tilburg - s'Hertogenbosch. Before turning his attention eastward Crocker wisely directed that 2nd Canadian Division abandon its attempts to cross the Antwerp - Turnhout Canal at Lochtenberg and to cross via 49 Division's bridgehead. Crocker's skilled direction paid dividends

Advancing from the 49th bridgehead 5th Brigade's Black Watch quickly took St Leonard. Then the Maisonneuves, Calgary Highlanders and Fort Garrys, after a hard fight, cleared Brecht on October 1st. This loosened the enemy's grip around Antwerp and 4th Brigade pushed into Merxem. Then 6th Brigade took over and the South Sasks and Camerons captured Brasschaet on 2 October and Cappellen on the 4th. The 4th Brigade passed through and after a sharp battle the Essex Scottish took Putte. The Brigade kept up the pressure and advanced to within three miles of Woensdrecht the gateway to the Beveland Peninsula. At this point 2nd Division reverted back under command of IInd Corps.

Woensdrecht

Woensdrecht was the cork in the bottle neck of South Beveland Peninsula and the way to Walcheren. The Germans were determined to hold it at all costs to keep communications open between 70th Division within and LXVIIth Corps outside the Beveland bottle. The Canadians were equally determined to cork the bottle and seal it off.

On 7 October while 6 Brigade held the Division's right flank angling back some 20 miles to Turnhout, 5 Brigade, supported by the 4th, was ordered to capture Woensdrecht.

GAUDEAMUS IGITUR

As the Calgary Highlanders battled their way into Hoogerheide the Maisonneuves on the right were held up short of the Hoogerheide - Huijbergen road. The Calgarys who took 60 prisoners in their drive were turned east to take the Maisies' objective in the flank. As they were preparing for this move Dutch civilians reported that a large tank led German force was assembling at Bergen op Zoom to attack them.(11) This was part of Battle Group Chill mainly comprising the 6th Parachute Regiment which, after halting the Poles on the Army's right, were now directed on Woensdrecht.

While the Germans were cranking up their riposte the Canadian's own attacks were floundering. The Black Watch had been repulsed at Korteven and the Calgarys were battling for their lives in Hoogerheide. Supported by the Fort Garrys the "Hooligans" threw back attack after attack, destroying three enemy tanks in the process. The German official battle report testifies to the bitter, no-holds-barred, see-saw battle between their Combat Group Heydte and the Canadians. On their left the Royal Regiment was halted short of the highway to Beveland. Keefler ordered 5 Brigade to do the job via Woensdrecht Station. The operation was code named "Angus". Few Canadian operations were to engender such bitterness.

Brigadier Megill's plan called for the Black Watch to attack over a thousand yards of flat, water soaked beet fields absolutely devoid of cover against an unlocated enemy. At first light on Friday the 13th the Black Watch attacked with two under-strength rifle companies. Because of the boggy polder the supporting tanks could not advance with the infantry and a morning fog negated long range support. The 42nd advanced into a hail of artillery and mortar fire and into the enfilade fire of skilfully sited machine guns firing on fixed lines. Bloodily repulsed in their attack the tired Black Watch were ordered to attack again in the afternoon. Again they were shot to pieces and after midnight Megill called off the attack and withdrew the tattered battalion. Woefully under strength when the battle began the battalion had almost ceased to exist. It had suffered 145 casualties of which 56 were killed, 62 wounded and 27 missing. It had indeed been "Black Friday" for that unfortunate unit. And on their right 4th Brigade was beating back a succession of savage attacks and also suffered severely.

On 16 October 4th Brigade's Royal Hamilton Light Infantry supported by a squadron of tanks, 170 guns and the MMGs and mortars of the Toronto Scottish attacked Woensdrecht before first light and within an hour had gained the town. At 1030 hrs the German paratroops, supported by tanks and SP guns and personally led by Colonel von der Heydte, attacked. In short order they overran one company and were onto the second when its commander called for artillery fire onto his own position, which was answered in spades. The Rileys' veteran CO, Lt Col Denis Whitaker, upped the call to a Victor Target - every gun in the Corps. The resulting cascade of shot, shell and HE caught the enemy in the open and utterly obliterated the attack. But the Germans were not finished yet and for the next five days they attacked, shelled and mortared the Canadians. At a cost of 167 casualties the Rileys prevailed. Help was soon to come from outside but in the meantime 2nd Division was paying the price in blood for the failure of Mackenzie King's government to provide an adequate stream of trained reinforcements to the fighting volunteers. It was a shameful period of political infamy.(12)

THE NORTHWEST EUROPE CAMPAIGN

The Breskens Pocket - 6-31 October 1944

The clearing of the Scheldt actually involved five quite distinct and overlapping mini-campaigns. The first of these, from roughly 16 September to 16 October, involved the clearing of the land approaches to South Beveland. The second, from 22 September to 9 November, comprised the right flanking actions of I British Corps in advancing from the Albert Canal to the Maas. The third, from 6 to 31 October, was the battle for the Breskens Pocket. The fourth, from 29 October to 2 November, saw the clearing of South Beveland and the Walcheren Causeway. The final episode, the capture of Walcheren Island, lasted from 1 to 8 November. Having discussed the first two, we now return to the third of these, the battle for the Breskens Pocket.

The Breskens Pocket, situated between the Leopold Canal, the Braakman Inlet and the North Sea, protected the southern land flank of the Scheldt. Known by the enemy as "Isabella" or "Scheldt Fortress South" it had been fortified before the war and was now strongly defended by the 68th Infantry Division, heavily laced with Eastern Front veterans, under the skilful and determined command of Maj Gen K. Eberding. Isabella's flat, saturated polder country had been considered by the pre-war Belgians to be unsuitable for military operations. Now flooded by the Germans and under a soggy, dripping October sky it was more unsuitable than ever. The only "dry" approach was from the east below the Braakman Inlet. It was anything but an appetizing dish to set before the Canadians.

The Breskens pocket had been sealed off from the east when the Poles reached Terneuzen on 20 September. Realizing that the waterlogged, reclaimed polder of the Pocket was unsuitable for armour Simonds gave the job of clearing it to the 3rd Canadian Infantry Division which at that time was heavily involved with the Channel ports. In early October with the Channel ports, save Dunkirk, now secure the 3rd Division moved north to take over from 4th Armoured Division along the Leopold Canal. Simonds planned on crossing the canal south of Aardeburg with two brigades. When the enemy's attention and reserves had been fixed by this force the third brigade would assault his rear from the Braakman Inlet. The initial crossing of the canal was to be made by 7th Brigade which was required to move the 90 miles north from Calais after the capture of that port on 1st October. This left the embattled 7th precious little time for planning and reconnaissance. The section of the canal chosen for the crossing was 90 feet wide and highly diked on each bank. The enemy was dug in on the reverse bank of his dike. Since they would be virtually impervious to artillery fire the assault would be made behind the massed firing of 17 Wasp flame throwers. It was expected that the flaming liquid would roll down the dike into the enemy trenches.

In assault boats laboriously carried forward by the North Shore Regiment the assault battalions - Reginas left, Can Scots right - launched into the canal at 0530 hrs on 6 October. On the extreme left, northeast of Moerhuizen, a company of the Royal Montreal Regiment, temporarily exchanged from its Army Headquarters defence duties with a company of Reginas, crossed successfully. On the far right both Can Scots' companies landed unopposed at Oosthoek. But in the centre the Regina's company was delayed in its launching while the brief effect of the flamethrowers passed. When the company finally launched the enemy had re-emerged and cut the unprotected Rifles to pieces. The Regina's follow up companies then had to be boated across into the tiny bridgehead secured by the Royal Montrealers. The enemy counter attacks were swift and his mortar and machine gun fire deadly. By last light the RMR company virtually ceased to exist and 7 Brigade held only two tenuous and isolated bridgeheads which could not be linked.

The ensuing five days in the Regina's slender bridgehead could best be characterized by Bernard B. Fall's description of action in another, later war as "Hell in a Very Small Place".(13) Pinned to a narrow, muddy canal bank, soaking wet, totally sleep deprived and physically exhausted the Regina's riflemen fought an endless succession of section and individual battles against a fanatical enemy sometimes located only ten yards away. Co-ordinated company or even platoon actions were almost impossible.(14) Individual riflemen might throw 25 grenades a night at the enemy, only to be answered by a shower of potato-mashers - the German's cylindrical, stick-handled and most effective grenade. Any attempt by the enemy, in his turn, to mount a company sized attack was destroyed by the accurate and constant Canadian artillery fire - joined, weather permitting, by fighter-bombers. Only on the right, in the Can Scots bridgehead, was movement possible which the Victoria boys exploited by taking Moershoofd. And by one of the ironies of the Gods of War it was only by the Regina's dike-sized foothold that a bridge could be built and this could not be done until the bridgehead could be much enlarged.

To effect this enlargement Brigadier Spragge decided to land the Royal Winnipeg Rifles in the Canadian Scottish bridgehead and attack west to link with the Reginas. At 0445 hrs on 7 October, as the Winnipegs were crossing, a savage attack hit the Can Scots "C" Company and overran two platoons. The third platoon under Sgt A. Gri and Company HQ under Capt R. Schjelderup fought back from farm buildings killing many enemy before they were overwhelmed. Schjelderup and Gri were captured but later made a daring escape in mid-winter and rejoined their regiment. Both were decorated for their conduct. The Winnipegs once across joined in counter-attacking the enemy, killing many and freeing some prisoners.

The westward advance of the Little Black Devils along the canal bank was slow and bloodily contested. Only on the 9th was contact made with the Reginas and for three days the combined battalions struggled to enlarge the bridgehead. On the 13th at long last a bridge was built and tanks of the British Columbia Regiment - the Duke of Connaught's Own - moved across. The bridgehead was now secure and as 9 Brigade attacked from the rear the enemy's iron grip on the Leopold Canal was broken.

The Amphibious Outflanking

Following the capture of Cap Gris Nez Brigadier Rockingham's 9th Brigade had been selected to perform the waterborne assault on the rear of the Breskens Pocket. After two days of training at Ghent with LVTs (Landing Vehicles Tracked) Rocky's brigade on 7 October set sail down the Terneuzen Canal. They were slated to cross the mouth of the Braakman Inlet and make a stealth landing at 0200 hrs on 8 October. Difficulties in passing the locks on the Terneuzen Canal caused the operation to be delayed by 24 hrs.

After midnight on 9 October the LVTs set out with the Highland Light Infantry and North Nova Scotia Highlanders aboard. The HLI were landed two kilometres west of the Braakman, the NNSH nearer to Hoofdplaat. The operation caught the enemy by surprise and there was little initial opposition. Before noon the LVTs had shuttled over

THE NORTHWEST EUROPE CAMPAIGN

the rest of 9 Brigade. Maj Gen Eberding now reacted violently calling on his divisional reserve and the coastal guns at Flushing and Breskens to engage the Canadians. He also ferried two companies of infantry and combat engineers over from Walcheren to add to his defenders.

As enemy resistance stiffened Hoofdplaat only fell to the SD&G Highlanders on 10 October with Biervliet taken by the HLI the next day. At this juncture Maj Gen Spry wisely decided against reinforcing 7 Brigade's bridgehead on the Leopold and sent 8 Brigade to reinforce the 9th on the north coast of the Pocket. But it was to be far from a cakewalk.

The advancing Canadians were faced with the Hobson's Choice of trying to slosh through the sodden, often flooded, beet fields or attack along the tops of the dikes which gridded the polder. The German machine guns were skilfully sited to cover either option. The advance thus became a dreary battle of attrition in which each enemy post had to be eliminated one-by-one. Casualties were appalling, most to rifle or machine gun fire in contrast to other battlefields where mortar and shellfire casualties predominated. The high proportion of fatal casualties, nearly 50%, was also exceptional. Then the weather cleared slightly allowing the air force to come in support of the struggling infantry. 2nd TAF eagerly took the challenge and flew 1300 sorties to the end of the campaign.

On October 14th the 4th Armoured Division crossed to the south of the Braakman Inlet and linked up with 8 Brigade on the 18th. As 8 Brigade closed in on Oostburg and 9 Brigade on Breskens the long suffering and exhausted 7 Brigade was relieved on the Leopold by the 157th Brigade of 52nd (Lowland) Division. Ironically the 52nd was a mountain division which henceforth was to do most of its fighting in muddy flatlands, sometimes even below sea level. Under command of 3rd Canadian Division the Lowland Brigade met up with the 17th Canadian Hussars at Aardenberg squeezing the enemy between a line of Breskens - Schoondijke - Sluis - Zeebrugge and the North Sea.

Then more frustration! 9 Brigade's attacks on Breskens and Fort Frederik Hendrik were delayed when many of its supporting AVREs and Flails, which were closely grouped for replenishment, were blown up when an ammunition truck in their midst detonated an influence mine (one which only detonates after a set number of vehicles have tripped it).

The unknown sapper who set the mine's trip mechanism set better than he ever could have dreamed. As if this were not misfortune enough bad weather in England prevented the hoped for bomber support for the attack.

Finally at 1000 hrs on 21 October the Glengarrys attacked Breskens. When his main approach was held up Lt Col Roger Rowley sent one company looping behind the enemy via the top of a sea wall. Using a small kapok floating bridge they crossed the flooded anti-tank ditch and punched into town. Under fire from the heavy guns of Walcheren Rowley's men battled through the streets and with the timely help of Crocodile flame throwers completed the capture of Breskens by midnight. The Germans in the pocket were now isolated from Walcheren.

Schoondijke fell to the HLI after a fierce battle on the 25th. On the same day the North Novas persuaded the garrison of Fort Frederik Hendrik to surrender under pain of annihilation. Meanwhile 7 Brigade had been reinserted into the battle along the north coast and rapidly advanced westward. The powerful bastion of Oostburg fell to the Queen's Own Rifles after a brilliant outflanking attack.

GAUDEAMUS IGITUR

An attempt by the enemy to establish a new line between Cadzand and Zuidzande collapsed under 7 Brigade's relentless coastal drive. On the 30th 8 Brigade closed up to the enemy's final line along the Uitwaterings Canal. 9 Brigade now took over and crossed the canal in two places. On the south flank the Chaudieres also seized a bridgehead by improvising an Ark bridge from a dumped carrier, timbers and steel beams. The horror of the Breskens Pocket ended on 1 November with the capture of Knocke by the HLI and the surrender of Maj Gen Eberding to the North Novas.

Few battles have been fought under such appalling conditions. That they prevailed against an extremely tough enemy of equal strength is a testimony to the valour, determination and resolution of the sodden, dog-tired, constantly attacking Canadian infantrymen. And to the brilliance of Simonds' right hook over the Braakman. Armchair generals may scoff that the capture of the pocket took three weeks. Anyone who viewed that flat, flooded, killing-ground battlefield would wonder that its capture was possible at all. And it was again *les glorieux* of 3rd Division who did it .

South Beveland and the Causeway - 24 October - 2 November 1944

While the 3rd Division still grimly battled for the Breskens Pocket the 2nd faced its own Hell on South Beveland which, like Breskens, was polder country virtually devoid of cover. On 24 October 4 Brigade began its advance up the neck of the peninsula. It had been Simonds' intention to catch the defenders, the strong 70th Division, in a pincers with 5 Brigade providing the southern arm via an amphibious crossing from Terneuzen to Beveland near Oudelande. But with 5 Brigade still getting sorted out after Woensdrecht, Simonds replaced it with the 156th Brigade of the Lowland Division which was still under command of IInd Corps. It speaks volumes on the complete confidence, co-operation and operational consonance that existed between the British and Canadians that a UK Brigade could be inserted into a Canadian division in the midst of a battle without skipping a beat.

After the Royal Regiment had forced the eastern neck of the peninsula Brigadier Cabeldu attempted to rush an infantry/tank column to the Beveland Ship Canal at the western end of the neck. The narrow bowling alley approach coupled with mud and strong German defences behind mines and anti-tank guns thwarted this effort so Cabeldu reverted to infantry attacks in small bites. His brigade then mounted a succession of night outflanking manoeuvres which unseated the enemy with Krabbendijke falling on the 26th.

6 Brigade took over in the north as the Lowland Brigade landed on the south of Beveland and rapidly advanced to Hoedekenskerke. On the 27th all three battalions of 6 Brigade closed up to the canal. On the right the Camerons were repulsed with all but one of their assault boats sunk. However in the centre, after being stopped once, the South Saskatchewans crossed on two broken road and rail bridges and seized a small bridgehead which they held against several counter-attacks. In the south Les Fusiliers Mont-Royal staged an evening approach through waist-deep water and then scrambled across the canal locks. Catching and routing the enemy from the rear the Fusiliers took 120 prisoners. By noon a bridge was completed and the rest of the division stormed across.

On the right coastal flank a squadron of the 8th Recce, by dint of some daring initiative by Major R. Porteous and timely advice from the Dutch underground, staged an ad hoc water crossing to North Beveland and closed in on its garrison. Supported by the mortars and MMGs of the Toronto Scottish the squadron hammered the defenders. At this point some skilful trickery by Lt Col B.M. Alway, CO of the 8th Recce, including a non-firing, deck-top pass by a squadron of Typhoons bound for Walcheren, resulted in the surrender of all 450 men of the North Beveland garrison. By this time on the 29th two brigades of the Lowland Division had crossed over to South Beveland and met up with the 4th Canadian Brigade at Gravenpolder. When the 5th Canadian Brigade captured Goes the enemy abandoned Beveland and slipped across the causeway into their final stronghold of Walcheren.

Walcheren is connected to South Beveland by a 1000 metre long, 40 metre wide road, rail and bike-path causeway, absolutely devoid of cover. On either side are treacherous mud flats which flood at high tide. The causeway was mined and under direct enemy fire. Half-way along it the enemy had blown a huge water-filled crater. Its crossing would be a most tricky undertaking.

A series of unfortunate on-again, off-again decisions and indecisions by the Corps Commander, Maj Gen Foulkes, and Brigadier Keefler, the acting 2nd Division Commander, led to that division being tasked with securing a bridgehead over the causeway through which the 52nd Division would pass. The 52nd would then clear Walcheren in conjunction with sea-borne landings. Thus was launched one of the most controversial and ill-starred, yet heroic and indomitable, actions fought by the Canadians since Dieppe. It has been likened in futility and irresponsibility to the Charge of the Light Brigade some 90 years earlier. The number of assaulting troops involved , some 600, were about the same but the parallel ends there. The Light Brigade charged into disaster and history due to incredible bungling in conception and ordering. The 5th Canadian Brigade's series of charges were the result of commanders, after careful consideration, finding no other viable alternatives within the time allowed. They were wrong but had no way of knowing this at the time.

On 31 October Brigadier Megill of 5 Brigade directed that the Black Watch try to rush the causeway while the Calgary Highlanders prepared for an assault water crossing of the tide-flooded mud flats that night. Starting at mid-day "C" Company of the Black Watch courageously advanced down the causeway under heavy fire. Seventy-five yards from the Walcheren side they were halted by a hail of shot and shell. At this crucial juncture the engineers determined that high tide was insufficient to enable assault boats to carry the Calgarys over the mud flats as planned while the flats at low tide would not support amphibious vehicles. Megill now appeared to have no option but to order the Black Watch to hold fast while the Calgarys and Maisonneuves passed through to establish a bridgehead. The Calgarys would have the first crack.

Whatever his reservations Major Ellis, the Calgary's acting CO, planned on forcing a bridgehead some 1000 yards deep around the end of the causeway. Since this could only be done with maximum firepower he ordered up all the support he could muster - medium and field artillery, 4.2 and 3 inch mortars, Bofors Guns and MMGs. The mortars in particular were expected to be useful in containing the enemy dug-in on the dike's far banks. At midnight on 3 October the Calgarys started down the causeway behind heavy supporting fire. The lead company was halted by the usual deadly German defensive fire made more lethal by the narrowness of the open approach. The company withdrew to the crater while Ellis teed up a new attempt.

At 0605 hrs on 1 November, under heavy fire, "D" Company reached the end of the causeway and launched an assault on a key road block - just about the time that British commandos commenced an assault landing on the opposite side of Walcheren. "D" Company took 14 prisoners and consolidated while "A" and "B" companies came across to enlarge the bridgehead. "C", the reserve company, was pinned down on the causeway.

"A" and "B" companies were also under extreme pressure, holding out behind the dike at the edge of the mud flat. Unfortunately, neither for the first nor last time, wireless failure and casualties to the runners resulted in a lack of effective covering fire just when it was most needed. Only heroic action by Sergeant Laloge of "D" Company, at the end of the causeway, prevented a breakthrough. Casualties to officers were so heavy that the Brigade Major George Hees, another future Cabinet Minister, volunteered to take over "A" Company with a FOO as his 2IC.(15) As German attacks and fire intensified there was grave danger of the forward companies being cut off so "A" and "B" were ordered back behind "D" Company. Brigadier Megill now ordered Le Regiment de Maisonneuve to pass through the Calgarys and re-establish the bridgehead to enable the Lowland Division to take over in accordance with pre-planning. Then at midnight Keefler at 2nd Division HQ changed the plan again. The Maisonneuves would now be relieved by the 157th Lowland Brigade at 0500 hrs. This meant that only a one company bridgehead would be in place when the change over took place.

The Maisies started across at 0400 hrs on 2 November into the same inferno of fire that had so decimated the Black Watch and Calgary Highlanders. When "D" Company reached the end of the causeway enemy fire had reduced its strength to about 40 - the size of a normal platoon. It was to be "D" Company's finest hour. Against all odds they captured the anti-tank gun which so dominated the causeway then moved on under heavy fire to take their stone house final objective. With dawn came further confusion. Instead of the Lowland Division, a platoon of Germans trying to withdraw to Middleburg appeared behind the Maisies and were promptly engaged. As an RAF Typhoon destroyed an approaching enemy tank, Pte Carriere of the R de Mais used his PIAT to destroy a 20mm gun which had been effectively engaging the Montrealers.

At 0600 hrs the Glasgow Highlanders of 157 Brigade started across. The horror of that crossing has been vividly described in their divisional history and can be applied in spades to the Canadians who had done it several times before - and while the enemy defences were intact.(16) One platoon of Scots finally reached the Maisonneuves but heavy fire prevented the latter from leaving. In the end both Maisies and Glaswegians were withdrawn under cover of a smoke screen to behind the Glasgow companies holding the causeway. Although Walcheren would not fall for another six days to a combined commando and Lowland attack, for the Canadians the Battle of the Scheldt was over.

Typically it had ended much as it had started - in controversy. The commander of the 52nd Division, Maj Gen E. Hakewill-Smith, had from the outset been opposed to the idea of a frontal assault down the causeway and had been appalled at the terrible bloodbath suffered by 5th Brigade in its attempts. He wanted to find a better way for his Lowlanders to cross and was threatened with a sacking by Maj Gen Foulkes, the acting Corps Commander, if he did not get cracking. And Hakewill-Smith did find a better way but not before his Glasgow Highlanders had endured the same charge into Hell as had 5th Brigade.

On the night of 1 November an engineer recce party of the 52nd Division, possibly acting on Dutch advice, found a path through the Slooe Channel mudflats some two miles south of the causeway. Along this path on 3 November the Cameronians and Highland Light Infantry of the 156th Brigade picked their way across to outflank the enemy defences and link up with the Glasgow Highlanders at the causeway. It was a brilliant coup and showed what could be done with intelligent pre-planning. And vindicated once more the adage that, "Time spent on reconnaissance is seldom wasted."

Walcheren and the Right Flank

Apart from artillery located at Breskens and some engineers and medical staff no Canadians participated in the final clearing of Walcheren. This operation too was clouded with controversy especially related to the flooding of the island, the cancelled use of paratroops and the provision of bomber support. The final assault was launched on 1 November (as the Canadians crossed the causeway) by the British 4th Special Service Brigade which was sea landed at Westkappelle and by 155 Brigade and No.4 Commando crossing from Terneuzen to Flushing.

Although the always co-operative Sir Arthur Harris had been ready to provide Bomber Command support to the Canadians as required, a layer of intervening headquarters now blocked the previous direct relationship between Crerar and Harris. Requests now had to be filtered through 21 Army Group and SHAEF. At SHAEF the meddlesome Air Chief Marshal Tedder, Eisenhower's deputy, belittled what he wrongly thought was the Canadian Army's over reliance on air power and was instrumental in complicating, misinterpreting and refusing requests for bomber support. As a result the formidable forts and heavy guns on Walcheren were largely untouched.

This lack of air support contributed to the near disaster which befell 4 Special Service Brigade on its landing. The naval fire support squadron was severely shot up - losing 18 of 25 craft and 298 sailors. The commandos also suffered heavily in landing and owed much of their ultimate success to the fact that one of the enemy batteries ran out of ammunition. After six days the commandos and Scots succeeded, after much hard fighting, in clearing the island. And on 28 November the first convoy sailed through the Scheldt to Antwerp.

While IInd Canadian Corps was still battling in the Breskens Pocket and on the approaches to Walcheren the Ist British Corps, comprising the 49th British, 4th Canadian Armoured and 1st Polish Armoured Divisions and 2nd Canadian Armoured Brigade, was joined by the 104th US Division (Terry Allen's "Timber Wolves") - the only time a US division fought under Canadian Army command. In a long series of actions Crocker's Corps protected both the right flank of the Canadian Army and the left flank of the British 2nd Army. From 16 October to 10 November it advanced from Antwerp to the Maas and captured the cities of Bergen-op-Zoom, Roosendaal and Breda and closed up to the Moerdijk. The line reached would be held by 1st Canadian Army throughout the coming winter

The Scheldt - An Assessment

The Scheldt Campaign provided no end of lessons, second guessing, recriminations and muttering in the ranks. Which is a pity because for a major campaign fought with such limited resources the outcome was an indisputable success. The official British history of the Northwest European Campaign puts it thus: "the First Canadian Army had been wholly responsible for the land operations in the coastal area, culminating in....the clearance of both banks of the Scheldt estuary and the freeing of Antwerp's port....they had advanced from the Seine to the Scheldt and the Maas, capturing the ports of le Havre, Dieppe, Boulogne, Calais and Ostend.....they had taken 68,000 prisoners.....they had themselves suffered 17,000 casualties....The part they played in the Allied actions of those months was outstanding."(17)

However on the command level errors abounded. First on the part of Lt Gen Horrocks for not sealing off the Scheldt approaches when he had that glittering chance in September. Then Montgomery ensured a bloody campaign when he initially ignored the Antwerp approaches and focused on the Rhine and Ruhr. He then compounded this error by equivocating in his instructions to Crerar, first ordering him to concentrate on the Channel ports then belatedly demanding the clearance of Antwerp. Even when the Scheldt battle was in full flight Monty could not resist putting his spoke in the wheel by reversing himself on the use of heavy bombers and paratroops to aid Crerar and by changing the priorities of Ist British Corps resulting in the bloodletting at Woensdrecht and a week's delay in clearing the Scheldt. Eisenhower's skirts were not clean in this matter either. After acquiescing in Montgomery's eastern thrust he only started to give priority to Antwerp on 9 October -16 days after the Arnhem operation had ended. Having finally ordained Antwerp as Priority One he then undercut his own position by denying Crerar the use of airborne troops (which were essentially to remain unused until March 1945). He also weakly let his deputy so muddy up air request channels and Bomber Command support as to seriously jeopardize the Walcheren operation.

Eisenhower never bothered to visit First Canadian Army to see for himself what was going on.(18) To be charitable, he may have wished to not be seen as interfering in Montgomery's conduct of operations But Ike was, after all, the Supreme Commander and it was his duty to find first hand the nature of the problems which affected his directives. Had he done so he might have made a much better job of allocating priorities. Instead, in the run-up to the Scheldt, he denied Crerar the critical supply and transport needed while frittering these resources away on Montgomery's Arnhem, Bradley's Lorraine and Patton's Moselle ventures.

Field Marshal Sir Alan Brooke was one of the few who recognized the error at an early date. On 5 October he wrote in his diary that Montgomery's strategy was faulty in not concentrating on Antwerp instead of Arnhem - although his prescience is dimmed somewhat by making his entry two weeks after Arnhem had failed.(19) One wonders what he would have written had Arnhem succeeded? Furthermore Brooke himself failed to pursue his views and appears not to have insisted that full resources be allotted to the opening of the Scheldt. In his own memoirs, long after the event, Montgomery admitted that he made a bad mistake in underestimating the difficulties in opening the Antwerp Approaches.

Blame for the perceived slowness in opening the Scheldt has been dumped on Crerar and his Canadians. They were the wrong targets. The true culprits were Ike, Monty, Tedder, Brereton (commander airborne forces) and even Brooke. The thrusting Horrocks escapes the list because his "error" was made without his knowledge of the facts, due in part to his exclusion from the ULTRA list. It is ironic that Churchill's fear of compromising ULTRA by restricting the recipients was frequently negated by his own habit of "spilling the beans" in insecure trans-Atlantic telephone conversations

THE NORTHWEST EUROPE CAMPAIGN

with Roosevelt.

But all of this too is hindsight. In September, after the total defeat of the Wehrmacht in Normandy and the exhilaration of the ensuing wild hayride to the French borders, the imminent defeat of Germany seemed certain. The Saar and Ruhr appeared open and helpless - just one push and it would be over. In such circumstances it would have taken a very cautious and weird general to turn his back on these glittering opportunities and focus on backwater Antwerp - which would have guaranteed a prolongation of the war in the west. Never mind that it all turned out that way in the end. The chance for early victory on the Rhine then loomed large and had to be taken.

On the national Canadian level the Channel ports and Scheldt seemed to the Canadians to be a relegation of their part in the war to secondary status. While the other armies enjoyed the glamour and headlines of rapid advances and prime chances the Canadians were given the stodgy clean-up jobs on flank and rear. In his highly critical book on Canadian command in Normandy, John English has suggested that had the Canadians done better in Normandy they might have been rewarded with the glamour thrust on Brussels and Antwerp.(20) Since the Canadians only comprised one-quarter of the British/Canadian force, had one-third of the armour, had already spearheaded the advance to Falaise and were already on the Army Group's left flank the conjecture is a non-starter even ignoring British national pride, which cannot be ignored.

The Channel ports and Scheldt provided further dreary examples of the predilection of Canadian commanders with spreading their resources too thinly and failing to give priority to the principle of concentration of force. The pint-sized forces employed at Boulogne, Calais, Breskens, Beveland and the Causeway foredoomed these efforts to long and costly battles. Admittedly this was not all the Canadians' fault - the initial grounding of all of Ist Corps, then the Highland Division, deprived Crerar of critically needed forces. And much of his force was further drained away by Mongomery's charging Crerar with far too large a right flank clearance and protection role while the main Scheldt effort was run on a shoestring. Here, once more, Crerar's run-in with Montgomery over the Dieppe ceremony, on veiled charges of insubordination, caused the Canadian to accept an unrealistic assignment rather than insisting that his Army should tackle the Scheldt alone and leave Breda, Roosendaal, the Maas and flank protection to Dempsey's Army.

But all of this aside, the Canadian commanders had a genius for downloading a divisional attack to a single brigade which in turn entrusted things to a single battalion which, all too often, ended up attacking with two companies. Thus what was supposed to be a powerful divisional attack ended up as a desperate struggle forward of around 200 men - rapidly dwindling to merely double figures.

Canadian tactics frequently were just variations of, "high diddle-diddle, right up the middle" even when other options were available. The headfirst debacle on the Leopold Canal was redressed by the brilliant outflanking at the Braakman, but Woensdrecht and the Causeway were examples of the head-butting tactic writ large. Even admitting that Woensdrecht was compounded by Monty's fiddling with I Corps' thrust lines more could have been expected of HQ 2 Division. Too little attention was paid to the value of the Dutch underground and local citizenry in gaining intelligence and finding ways around. The Causeway is the text-book example of this. After shattering itself in head-long rushes down a thousand yard dike into the mouth of Hell, 5th Brigade saw what Dutch intelligence and a little ingenuity could do when the Lowland Division waded

GAUDEAMUS IGITUR

across the Slooe Channel virtually unopposed.

The final fault lay with the reinforcement problem - a predictable result of Mackenzie King's refusal to impose conscription and the failure of Canadian generals and staff to properly comb the vast number of rear echelon troops in England and Canada in order to find combat reinforcements. The result was that units, after their initial action, were chronically under strength. The replacements were never enough to cover battle casualties and normal wastage.

But even had a good reinforcement stream been provided, which never happened, the long periods in constant action by the Canadians meant an inevitable decline in combat efficiency. Following a significant period of action a unit needs to be taken out of the line and brought up to strength and given time to integrate and train its new men and sub-units before going back into battle. Thereafter, when a unit is in the front line, reinforcements, even if properly trained, can only be effectively absorbed up to a point. If casualties can be minimized, say under 20%, and sufficient junior officers, NCOs and "old sweats" survive new trained replacements can be gainfully accepted. But when casualties soar and most officers and NCOs go down, and when reinforcements are not well trained, the result is a dramatic drop in combat effectiveness. It was a problem that was never solved and all too often a unit was forced to commence an action at three-quarter strength or less, rapidly dropping to less than half. The problem was particularly acute in the late autumn of 1944 The rebuilding of units in Italy and Northwest Europe after the major battles of the spring and summer had drained the Canadian pool of trained reinforcements. The titanic and wasting battles of the fall in both theatres resulted in such critical manpower shortages that it brought on the conscription crisis which severely threatened government solidarity and effectiveness at home. Meanwhile bases in Canada and England were full of able bodied soldiers who were destined never to see action.

But none of this can in any way detract from the unbelievable courage, resolution and determination displayed by the Canadian combat soldiers on the Leopold, the Albert, the Bevelands and the Causeway. Their magnificent and victorious actions wove a proud, crimson panel into the tapestry of Canadian history. All the more pity that so few Canadians, especially young Canadians, are even dimly aware of it.

Men of the Regina Rifles in action At Calcar, Germany, 16th. February, 1945.

(NAC PA 177577)

THE NORTHWEST EUROPE CAMPAIGN

CHAPTER XI

THE RHINELAND

Hard pounding this, gentlemen;
Let us see who will pound the longest.

Wellington, at Waterloo (attributed)

The Winter Front 8 November 1944 - 8 February 1945

Following the Scheldt operation, Montgomery reshuffled his 21st Army Group. While the British 2nd Army mounted an offensive to clear the enemy from the west side of the Meuse (the Flemish Maas) the 1st Canadian Army was entrusted with defending the 135 mile front along the Maas from the Scheldt to the Rhineland. On the left Lt Gen Crocker's Ist British Corps manned the line from the North Sea to Maren above s'Hertogenbosch. His 52nd Division remained at Walcheren while the south bank of the Maas was held by the 1st Polish and 4th Canadian Armoured Divisions. The 12th Manitoba Dragoons, the IInd Corps Armoured Car Regiment, patrolled between Schouwen Island and Moerdijk.

On the right IInd Canadian Corps held the Reichswald front with the 2nd and 3rd Canadian Infantry Divisions. Nijmegan Island, between the Waal and the Neder Rijn, was initially manned by the 50th Northumbrian and US 101 Airborne Divisions. At the end of November these were relieved by the 49th West Riding and 51st Highland Divisions with the 101st returning to the Americans and the long, and valiant, serving 50th following the 59th into disbandment. The Germans faced the Canadian Army with General Student's Army Group H whose 25th Army fronted I British Corps and 1st Parachute Army was opposite the IInd Canadian.

The static battlefield permitted the Canadian divisions to hold their fronts with two brigades each while the third, in rotation, rested and trained. The divisions were thus slowly built back to strength and efficiency again. Although static the front was by no means quiet, punctuated by exhausting patrolling, digging, wiring, shelling and sniping. Of course static is a relative term and the constant patrolling and shelling resulted in not insignificant casualties. The three months on the Maas resulted in 683 Canadian casualties, an average of over 225 a month. So much for "Im westen nichts neues" (All Quiet on the Western Front.)

The Germans eventually flooded Nijmegan Island forcing the shrinking of the Allied bridgehead which then was held by 49 Division alone. A unit of the German 7th Parachute Division attacked while this contraction was in progress but was beaten back by the 49th who killed 60 and captured 100 at a loss of 200 to themselves. The Germans also made numerous attempts, including the use of midget submarines, to destroy the three bridges at Nijmegan. Their frogmen blew a gap in the road bridge which was soon repaired while floating mines damaged an army laid barge bridge. The midget submarines were spectacularly unsuccessful, many being sunk by Canadian artillery and anti-tank guns.

There were a number of shuffles of senior Canadian commanders in this period. In early November Crerar returned from convalescence in the UK to resume command of the 1st Canadian Army and receive promotion to General. Lt Gen Simonds reverted to the command of IInd Corps while Maj Gen Foulkes, the acting Corps Commander on the Scheldt, was promoted to Lt Gen and replaced E.L.M. Burns as Commander of I Canadian Corps in Italy. Maj Gen A.B. Matthews was promoted to command 2nd Division. Finally there was a switch of divisional commanders. H.W. Foster moved to command 1st Division in Italy while Chris Vokes came from the 1st to replace Foster in command of 4th Armoured.

Preparing for '45

As the Scheldt campaign was winding down FM Montgomery was looking ahead to 1945 and the final battles to destroy Nazi Germany. On 2 November 1944 he issued a directive which inter alia instructed the 1st Canadian Army to plan for the dual tasks of offensive operations southeast from Nijmegan between the Rhine and the Meuse and northwards across the Neder Rijn to secure the high ground between Arnhem and Apeldoorn and a bridgehead over the Ijssel.

On 7 December Montgomery telephoned Crerar to confirm 1st Canadian Army's responsibility for the first part of his directive - the clearing of the west bank of the Rhine. For the operation Crerar was assigned Lt Gen Horrocks' XXX Corps of one armoured and four infantry divisions. The attack, code named "Veritable", was scheduled for 1 January 1945 or soon thereafter. On 16 December Monty confirmed his instructions in writing and took the opportunity to brashly declare that the enemy could no longer mount major offensive operations.(1) The Field Marshal topped his string of wildly wrong predictions this time, for on this very day von Rundstedt opened his famed Ardennes offensive - the "Battle of the Bulge" - with two panzer armies.

Apart from causing Operation "Veritable" to be delayed by over a month the Ardennes battles only indirectly affected the Canadian Army. As a precaution Montgomery took back XXX Corps to be prepared to counter any enemy advance over the Meuse. He also instructed Crerar to make preparations in case German Army Group H might attempt to aid von Rundstedt by attacking from the north. Although not part of the 1st Canadian Army, the Canadian Parachute Battalion was brought over from England with 6 Airborne Division to provide a blocking force in case the Germans broke clear of the American lines. None of these eventualities came about as the Americans, after initial serious reverses, held at the Elsenborn Ridge, Bastogne and elsewhere and as the German panzers ran out of fuel the US 1st and 3rd Armies mounted massive counter attacks and restored the situation. By 7 February it was all over.

Kapelsche Veer   26 - 30 January 1945

While the "Bulge" was still being eliminated, and before "Veritable" could get underway, the Canadian Army had to mount a clearing-out action which although small in size was to be bloody and controversial. Since the Scheldt battles the Germans had retained possession of a small island, Kapelsche Veer, in the Maas north of Tilburg where Crerar had his Army Headquarters. In anticipation of the success of the Ardennes offensive von Rundstedt had alerted Army Group H to be prepared to attack from the north in a classic pincers. As part of this action General Student strengthened the Kapelsche Veer outpost with a strong and well dug-in reinforced company supported by SP guns, artillery, mortars and machine guns from across the Maas. In the event the Ardennes action petered out but not so Kapelsche Veer.

Realizing the potential threat posed by the island, Lt Gen Crocker ordered the Polish Armoured Division, in whose sector Kapelsche Veer lay, to eliminate the enemy holding it. On 30 December the Poles made their first attack and were repulsed with the loss of nearly 50 men. On 6 January they attacked again and after some initial small success were again driven off with a further loss of 120. Crocker now ordered the 47th Royal Marine Commando to do the job. On the night of 13 January the Marines attacked from both flanks. They too were repulsed with heavy casualties. Crocker now turned to the 4th Canadian Armoured Division under the newly arrived Chris Vokes.

4th Armoured's operation, code named "Elephant", called for masking the island with smoke while a 60 man canoe party approached the north harbour and simultaneous attacks were launched from south and west. The initial silent attack was to be made by the Lincoln and Wellands of 10 Brigade At 0745 hrs on 26 January two companies landed on the east flank but were held up by heavy fire when the smoke screen partly failed. The canoe party, caught in ice floes, abandoned the harbour landing and joined the eastern landed companies. In the face of heavy counter attacks the eastern force was withdrawn by noon. "B" Company, landed to the west held firm. Brig Jefferson now decided to reinforce "B" company with a company of Argyll and Sutherland Highlanders and a troop of South Alberta's tanks.

On the 27th the Lincolns and Argylls started working their way slowly around the island in a pincers movement as the enemy fiercely resisted from interconnected machine gun posts dug into the canal banks. German attempts to reinforce the island and counter-attack were annihilated by the Canadian artillery using proximity fused air bursts. It took the combined Lincs and Argylls another three days of savage fighting but on the night of 30 January the remaining Germans evacuated the island.

It had been a bloody show. The victorious Canadians suffered 235 casualties. They captured 35 prisoners and counted 145 enemy dead while the German commander of the 6th Parachute Division later reported 300 to 400 battle casualties and another 100 to frostbite. Perhaps even worse from a Canadian viewpoint was a further erosion of the soldiers' faith in their higher commanders. Both the Lincolns and Argylls were incensed at their senior officers, especially Maj Gen Vokes, for committing "them to a battle that could only be won at a price no combat soldier thought worth paying".(2) Kapelsche Veer would go down alongside Le Mesnil Patry, Carpiquet, Fontenay, Woensdrecht and the Causeway as Canadian Second World War equivalents of the Somme and Passchendaele as blundered exercises in futility.

Operation "Veritable" 8 February - 10 March 1945

Operation "Veritable" by 1st Canadian Army of 21 Army Group was intended to clear the west bank of the Rhine north of the Ardennes as a prelude to crossing that river and slicing into the heartland of Germany. Similar operations were to be conducted south of the Ardennes by the US 6th and 12th Army Groups. Because of the flooded state of the Maas and the possibility of further flooding if, as was highly likely, the Germans blew the dams the preferred line of advance for 21 Army Group was down the gap between the Rhine and the Maas. While 2nd British Army held the line of the Maas and

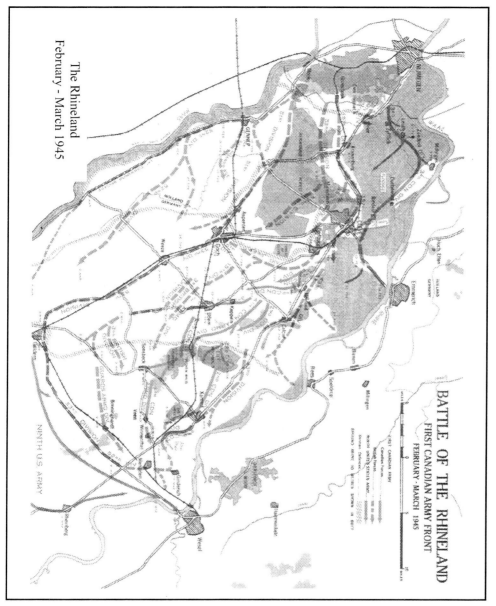

prepared for the Rhine crossings the Canadian Army would clear between the two rivers by advancing south from Nijmegan in concert with an attack northward by the US 9th Army advancing north from the Roer River.

Between the flood plains of the Rhine and Maas, only six miles wide in the north but broadening to the south, the country featured rolling farmland interspersed with huge planted state forests - first the Reichswald, then Moyland Woods, the Hochwald, Balberger and Tuschen Walds and lesser woods. Several small to medium sized towns lay

THE NORTHWEST EUROPE CAMPAIGN

in the path of the Canadian advance - Cleve (home of Anne, Henry VIII's fourth wife), Goch, Calcar, Udem, Xanten, Kevelaer and Geldern - most were fortified, all were to be bitterly fought over.

The sector also held the northern end of the once formidable Siegfried Line, the Reich's "West Wall". Three main lines of defences lay athwart the Canadians' axes of advance. First, a strong system to the west of the Reichswald and down the east bank of the Maas. Then the Siegfried Line proper, three miles further back, based on the fortified town of Goch. Finally came the Hochwald Layback from Geldern to Rees. The initial defences were manned by LXXXVI Corps of General Alfred Schlemm's 1st Parachute Army which had the 84th Division blocking the northern six-mile entrance gap, backed by the 276th Division with two reserve divisions close at hand.(3) Schlemm correctly forecast that the Allies would assault southward between the two rivers but he was held back and denied resources by his superiors who feared a *schwerpunkt* elsewhere.

Because of the narrowness of the front before Cleve Crerar proposed to open the attack with one reinforced corps and introduce a second later on. For a number of reasons, including strong hints from Montgomery, Crerar selected the British XXX Corps under the cool, confident and sometimes flamboyant Brian Horrocks to open the assault. The main attack was to be launched south-eastward between the Nijmegan - Krefeld road and the Maas where the going was expected to be better. Here Horrocks would initially deploy three infantry divisions, the 15th, 51st and 53rd from a start line between Wyler and Mook. The terrain north of the Krefeld road was, or soon would be, flooded and hence unsuitable for major operations. Here Horrocks employed the Canadian 3rd Division to guard his left flank and clear the waterlogged west bank of the Rhine as far as Cleve and Emmerich.

The start line was to be secured by seven battalions of the 2nd Canadian Infantry Division, already in place. The remaining two battalions of that division would operate in support of 15th Scottish Division on the left of the main thrust. They were to capture the key fortified village of Wyler and clear the Krefeld road to Kranenburg at which point they would be squeezed out of the line and released for the next stage.

"Veritable"-the Opening Phase 8 - 21 February

The opening drive by XXX Corps involved the breaching of the Siegfried Line, the clearance of the Reichswald, the capture of Cleve and the fortified villages of Goch and Calcar. Thereafter II Canadian Corps would pass through, or join, XXX Corps and clear the Hochwald, capture Geldern and close to the Rhine at Wesel. The attack was preceded on the night of 7/8 February by massive Bomber Command raids on Cleve and Goch. A minor controversy arose over the bombing of Cleve where an all HE raid devastated the town (it later claimed to be the most completely destroyed town in Germany) creating rubble and craters which made entry difficult. Horrocks claimed that he had requested only an incendiary raid. Bomber Command claimed, and delivered, otherwise.(4)

At 1030 hrs on 8 February "Veritable" began behind the heaviest artillery programme by the British/Canadian armies to date with over 1000 guns involved. The heavy bombardment completely stunned the defending 84th Division and the first objectives quickly fell. By first light on the 9th all three British assault divisions had closed up to the main enemy position.

Canadian infantry participation was initially more limited. To the left of 15 Division the Calgary Highlanders advanced through Vossendaal to the Krefeld road where they split their line of advance. One company turned south to link up with the Scottish Division at Kranenburg. Two companies moved north on Wyler but were halted by a concealed minefield covered by heavy fire. Lt Col Ellis quickly regrouped his battalion and assaulted anew. By 1830 hrs the strongly fortified hamlet of Wyler was captured along with 285 prisoners. The Calgarys lost 67 men. The Maisonneuves, attacking further south, captured Den Heuvel and Hochstrasse.

The enemy's blowing of the dikes and flooding the land between the highway and the Rhine turned into a two-edged sword. While they did succeed in flooding XXX Corps' main supply route (MSR) they also flooded their own anti-tank ditches, minefields, wire and trenches between Cleve and the Rhine. To overcome this flood-land the Canadians would put to very good use the specialised vehicles and tactics they had developed on the Scheldt.

The Canadian 3rd Division opened its assault at 1830 hrs on the 8th under the eerie glow of artificial moonlight. Except on the extreme right the Canadians rode into battle in the Buffaloes which had proven so indispensable at Breskens. On the right the foot-slogging Regina Rifles, supported by tanks of the British 13th/18th Hussars, captured the Quer Damm and the fortified village of Zyfflich. Using Buffaloes the Canadian Scottish captured Niel but only after the Buffalo carrying Tactical Bn HQ had been hit by a Panzerfaust killing several officers and wounding the CO and seven others. On the left the North Shores took their objective and many prisoners after most of their officers became casualties when the OC Buffalo squadron, showing admirable initiative, assumed command of the assault companies and led the troops to victory.

On the main front a driving rain and General Mud combined to slow the pace of advance to that of sodden infantrymen struggling through bog under constant fire. Behind them the maddeningly familiar pattern of route congestion and traffic chaos again took over with thousands of vehicles of different formations struggling and slithering to grind forward on the few barely usable roads.

Featuring heroic battling by 44th Armoured Brigade, Gordon Highlanders and King's Own Scottish Borderers, supported by the 6th Guards Tank Brigade, the 15th Division fought its way toward Cleve. As Schlemm hurried his 7th Parachute Division forward the Scots reached the town and prepared to clear it the next day.

At this point misleading reports amid the fog of war caused Lt Gen Horrocks to understand that the 15th Division had secured Cleve. Anxious not to lose the momentum of the advance, as had happened so often before, the thrusting Horrocks ordered the 43rd Wessex to pass through to Goch and Udem. With Cleve not in fact taken this resulted in the superimposing of the two divisions along one road largely under water. The 43rd then joined the 15th in fighting amid the ruins of the shattered Cleve as Schlemm hurried his only armoured reserve, the XLVII Panzer Corps of two divisions, to the Reichswald front. After bitter fighting Cleve was cleared by 12 February. Although the West Wall was now breached it would take a further week of unremitting struggle under the most miserable conditions of weather and terrain to advance just five more miles. As the 15th and 43rd Divisions lurched toward Moyland and the Highland Division penetrated south, the 53rd Welsh Division struggled through the heart of the Reichswald against determined opposition. The Reichswald was to be a charnel grounds for the 53rd. In ten days they suffered nearly 5000 casualties - almost half of their total losses in the entire Northwest European Campaign.

With the flooded Roer preventing Simpson's 9th US Army from pushing northward in Operation "Grenade" von Rundstedt finally accepted the fact that "Veritable" was indeed the main Allied threat. He now belatedly released to the embattled 1st Parachute Army the new divisions which Schlemm so desperately needed for the vital defence of the outer Reich. Meanwhile the 3rd Canadian Division sloshed through the flooded Alter Rhein to capture Donsbruggen in conjunction with 15th Division. By midnight on the 11th the SD&G Highlanders took the fortified hamlet of Rindern, a key anchor of the West Wall. On the 12th the HLI captured Duffelward and Wardhausen. On 14 February 9th Brigade cleared, if that word can be applied to its submerged condition, the Emmerich - Cleve road thus ending the waterborne portion of "Veritable" which earned for 3rd Division the sobriquet of "Water Rats".

Moyland Wood 16 - 21 February 1945

By 14 February the assault divisions of XXX Corps were finally clear of the Reichswald and Cleve was in their grasp. But the continual rain, mud, flooding and rear area traffic congestion made re-supply a nightmare and precluded any lightning armoured advance. The delayed effects of the Ardennes offensive had repaid the enemy in unforeseen ways. Had Crerar as planned been able to start his offensive in early January the cold weather and frozen ground would have minimized flooding and given the tanks solid footing. Now everything was mud-stuck and the American 9th Army offensive remained stalled.

Thus, as Horrocks introduced the 52nd Lowland Division into the southern flank of his widening front, Crerar brought up Simonds' IInd Corps on Horrocks' left. Crerar's plan was to attack with every division he could get forward and thus stretch the enemy to the limit of his endurance and reserves. IInd Corps, with 2nd and 3rd Canadian Infantry Divisions, 2nd Armoured Brigade and 46 Brigade of 15th Division, would advance from Cleve on Udem. XXX Corps was directed on the axis Goch - Weeze - Kevelaer. The Guards, 11th and 4th Canadian Armoured Divisions were in reserve for exploitation or reinforcement as required. As a first step II Corps had to clear Moyland Wood and XXX Corps the fortified town of Goch.

On 13 February the 15th Scottish Division advanced along the Cleve - Calcar road to within two miles of Moyland when it became embroiled in a bitter battle for a long, narrow woods of the same name. In three days of "the worst experience they had endured since the campaign began"(5) the Scots had only taken half the woods and then withdrew leaving many of their dead behind.(6)

On 16 February 7th Canadian Brigade was ordered to take over from the weary Scots and take Moyland Wood. The first to try were the Regina Rifles who bogged down with heavy casualties on the same lateral road killing ground that had stopped the Scots. However at the same time the Canadian Scottish had bypassed south of the wood to the farmsteads of Heselerfeld and Rosskamp. Here Acting Corporal P. Katchanoski assumed command of his platoon when his officer and sergeant became casualties and organized and led its defence in beating off numerous counter-attacks over a 72 hour period. His award of the DCM was extremely well earned. Meanwhile the Royal Winnipeg Rifles captured the village of Louisendorf in a brilliant Kangaroo mounted attack supported by tanks of the 3rd Scots Guards who later in April were to liberate the notorious Belsen Concentration Camp.

On the 18th as the 6th Parachute Division relieved the 116th Panzers in Moyland Wood the Reginas tried again, this time from the south. Against fanatical opposition and heavy shelling from across the Rhine the Reginas managed to batter their way onto the central crest which was seized by a single platoon under Lt W.L. Keating. Under intense pressure the platoon held on and beat off a series of counter-attacks until relieved five hours later. Keating's MC was most deserved. By now the gallant Rifles had suffered over 100 casualties. The next day a casualty weakened company of the Can Scots was directed into the southeast corner of the woods and was virtually destroyed. Although the failures at Moyland were not solely his fault, Brigadier Spragge bore the onus and was replaced temporarily by the Regina's Lt Col Gregory and later by Brig T.G. Gibson.

At 1000 hrs on 21 February the Royal Winnipeg Rifles, supported by a squadron of Sherbrooke Fusiliers and twelve Wasp flamethrowers, began a methodical block-by-block clearing of the woods. Unlike the earlier attacks on the wood the Winnipegs were well supported by artillery, mortars, anti-tank and machine guns and for the first time in many days the weather permitted good support from RAF Typhoons. Despite severe casualties which reduced one company to 40 men and another to only 25 under an NCO the Winnipegs doggedly and valorously kept charging forward and eventually prevailed. The final charge by "D" Company owed much of its success to its commander Major L.H. Denison who by personal example and leadership kept it going "through Hell and high water" onto the objective and led its defence through a long night against heavy counter-attacks. He received the DSO.

The six day battle for Moyland Wood cost 7 Brigade 480 casualties of which the Winnipegs suffered 183 (mostly on the last costly day), the Can Scots 163 and the Regina Rifles 134. In some ways it resembled the Foret de la Londe in being an unwanted impediment to the real operation further on followed by an underestimation of the problem and going at it in a piecemeal, under-funded way. But no one could gainsay the valour of the troops - the ordinary frightened, miserably uncomfortable, bone-tired, combat infantrymen - who somehow found the strength and raw courage to stumble forward again and again into the mouth of Hell to confront an enemy he could not even see. And incredibly in the end he succeeded. The 6th Paras withdrew from the wood to behind the Calcar line and early the next day the Maisonneuves of 2nd Division entered Moyland village.

To Goch and Calcar

While 7 Brigade was still clawing its way into the maw of Moyland Wood, 4 Brigade of 2nd Division was straining to cut the Calcar - Goch road and secure the high ground beyond as a springboard for Simonds' next push. At 1200 hrs on 19 February, behind a thunderous rolling barrage from 14 field regiments supported by seven medium regiments and two batteries of heavies, 4 Brigade charged forward in Kangaroos. The attacking Royal Hamilton Light Infantry and Essex Scottish were each supported by a squadron of Fort Garry Horse plus the heavy mortars and MMGs of the Toronto Scottish. Several tanks and APCs bellied up in the soft ground while mines and an anti-tank screen behind the Goch - Calcar road knocked out a further eleven tanks and seven

APCs. Both battalions got onto (Essex) or very near (RHLI) their final objectives and dug-in preparatory to the sure-to-come counter-attack. The Essex were the first to be hit in mid-afternoon but by 1630 hrs had repulsed the enemy and consolidated their position. One hundred prisoners taken were from the fresh 12th Parachute Reconnaissance Battalion, an unpleasant harbinger of things to come.

At 2000 hrs battle groups from the 116th Panzers and the newly arrived Panzer Lehr Division launched ferocious attacks against both Canadian battalions. On the left two companies of the RHLI were overrun and the enemy penetrated to battalion headquarters before being stopped by artillery fire which the Rileys called down on their own position. The fighting raged all night but morning found the Hamiltonions the masters of their position which was ringed by enemy dead and the hulks of seven knocked out panzers.

The Essex faced a similar maelstrom of attacks during which the enemy penetrated behind them and destroyed all but the basement of the house holding battalion headquarters. Undeterred Lt Col J. Pangman continued to control his battalion from the basement as enemy tanks roamed about. At this stage Brig Cabeldu requested an additional battalion as a reserve and received the Camerons from 6 Brigade. He then ordered the Royal Regiment of Canada to reinforce the Essex. The Royals moved up to the besieged battalion headquarters that night and relieved it in the morning. They then pushed on to the Essex' original final objective only to find that there "A" Company under Maj K. MacIntyre, and now down to 35 men, still held out despite being cut-off for 48 hours.

With the Royals fully committed to relieving the Essex, Brig Cabeldu's wisdom in securing an additional battalion became manifest when the Panzer Lehr attacked the RHLI in force. As Lt Col Whitaker's men battled for their lives Cabeldu sent the Queen's Own Camerons and a squadron of Fort Garrys to their aid. A troop of self-propelled 17 pounders of the 18th Anti-tank Battery joined the fray and knocked out seven Panthers. At the end of the day the Panzers gave up the struggle and withdrew leaving behind scores of dead along with eleven brewed-up tanks and six 88mm SP guns. The two day battle to secure a start line had cost the Canadians 400 casualties.

Operation "Blockbuster" 22 February - 11 March 1945

It had taken XXX Corps two weeks of slogging through mud, flood and sheeting rain to reach the Calcar - Goch line. With the flooded Roer and raging Maas securing flank and rear the Germans had developed their layback position and brought nine of their best divisions to man the 20 mile front. The strongly defended layback stretched from the Rhine opposite Rees across the Hochwald and Balberger Wald to Geldern in the south.

For his final phase, code named Operation "Blockbuster", Crerar would attack on the left with the IInd Canadian Corps of the Canadian 2nd and 3rd Infantry and 4th Armoured Divisions and 2nd Armoured Brigade. They would be backed by the British 43rd Wessex and 11th Armoured Divisions. Horrocks' XXX Corps of the 3rd, 15th, 51st, 52nd, 53rd and Guards Armoured Divisions would advance between the Canadians and the Maas.

Simonds' plan called for 2nd Division to open the attack on 26 February in the north to enable 4th Armoured to push south on Udem. Then 3rd Division would attack the heavily fortified towns of Keppeln and Udem while 11th Armoured was to swing south

GAUDEAMUS IGITUR

of Udem to Kervenheim. At this stage 4th Armoured, via the Hochwald Gap, and 11th Armoured, south of the Balberger Wald, would advance on Xanten and Wesel.

On 25 February, while Simonds was getting ready, receding waters and clearing weather on the Roer allowed Simpson to finally begin his drive northward. With the enemy fully occupied in the north the US 9th Army of three Corps moved rapidly against light opposition. Not so lucky were Horrocks' 15th and 53rd Divisions who, from 22 to 25 February, attacked south to Weeze at a cost of 900 casualties. General Schlemm, as yet unperturbed by the American advance, deployed a mighty force to thwart Crerar's obviously forthcoming attack. Von Luttwitz' XLVII Panzer Corps defended the high ground between Calcar and Udem with the 6th Parachute and 116th Panzer Divisions and 7th Parachute Regiment. Meindl's IInd Parachute Corps of the 7th and 8th Parachute, 15th Panzer Grenadier and 84th Infantry Divisions held from Udem to Weeze. Below Weeze LXIII and LXXXVI Corps deployed south to Roermond. In the northern half of the Hochwald Layback, which the Germans termed the Schlieffen Position, Schlemm had massed fifty 88mm guns to back up extensive minefields. Counting support from across the Rhine Schlemm had call on some 1000 artillery and 700 mortar pieces which was the heaviest concentration that the Western Allies had faced in the war.

As 2nd Division moved up to the attack in a steady, bone-chilling rain the Germans, as so often before, accurately estimated the locations of the Canadian FUPs and relentlessly shelled and mortared them. Then as 4 Brigade secured the Start Line of the Goch - Calcar road, preparatory to the 0430 H Hour, the enemy, at 0400 hrs with exquisite timing, hit the RHLIs, who were defending the left of the SL, with an infantry/tank attack. The Rileys held and with tank and artillery support beat off this spoiling attack just in time.

At 0415 hrs on 26 February 600 guns opened up as the infantry shook out preparatory to hitting the Start Line. At H Hour - 0430 hrs - while 5 Brigade held the high ground above Calcar all three battalions of 6 Brigade attacked line abreast. The Cameron Highlanders on the left and South Saskatchewans on the right were mounted in Kangaroo APCs while les Fusiliers Mont-Royal in the centre rode on the tanks of the Fort Garry Horse. Each attacking battalion was supported by a squadron of the Sherbrooke Fusiliers.

The South Sasks and FMR reached their objectives before dawn and deployed to meet the enemy's counter-charge but on the left the Camerons were stymied by mud, mines and heavy fire. After the briefest of checks, which caused the artillery barrage to run on ahead, the Camerons switched their axis to follow the FMR. When their Commanding Officer, Lt Col E.P. Thompson, was killed by a sniper they were led and inspired by the incredible daring and leadership of Major David Rodgers the OC "A" Company. As his APC neared the objective it came under extremely heavy fire from two adjacent houses that the enemy had turned into a strong point. Ignoring the fire that hailed off the armoured sides of his APC, Rodgers jumped out and all by himself charged the houses clearing each in turn killing four, wounding others and capturing twelve. His company, inspired by his example then charged and swept their final objective. After directing the reorganization of his company Rodgers, disturbed by the lack of higher direction, went to Battalion HQ to find what was happening. He found it a complete shambles with the CO dead, the IO wounded, communications gone and the headquarters pinned down by heavy direct fire. With only his batman in support

THE NORTHWEST EUROPE CAMPAIGN

Rodgers charged the enemy stronghold house, smashed open the door and dashed inside clearing it room by room. When his Sten gun ran out of ammunition he completed the clearance with his pistol killing nine and capturing twelve. Rodgers returned to the headquarters, put it back in operation and assumed command of the battalion pending the arrival of the Second in Command. He then, despite continuing enemy fire, visited each company in turn, reorganizing, encouraging, adjusting fire plans and exercising effective command until later relieved by the Battalion 2IC. Unbelievably, the recommendation that Rodgers receive the Victoria Cross was turned down and he received only a DSO. Of all the many deserving Canadians rejected for the VC the incredible rebuffing of Rodgers tops the list.

One Canadian who did actually receive the VC that day was Sgt Aubrey Cosens of the Queen's Own Rifles. The Rifles as part of 3rd Division's 8 Brigade were attacking on the right of 2nd Division to clear a ridge overlooking Keppeln. Their advance was up a mile long muddy slope which formed a serious impediment to tank movement and made walking difficult. On the outskirts of the hamlet of Mooshof "D" Company was held up by heavy fire from three fortified buildings. The lead platoon now under Sgt Cosens suffered severely and after beating off an enemy counter attack was reduced to just five men. At this critical juncture a 1st Hussars tank miraculously appeared which Cosens, under fire, mounted to direct the tank's gunfire onto the hidden enemy. While so mounted Cosens saw a group of enemy paratroops preparing to attack and directed a charge which dispersed them. Still on the exposed outside of the tank he ordered it to ram the first farm building, jumped off and single handed cleared the building killing or capturing all of the enemy. From a second cleared building Cosens ordered the tank to cover him as alone he charged across a road under fire, burst into the last building and cleared it by himself. In his one-man wrecking operation Cosens killed over twenty enemy and captured another twenty. After reorganizing the tiny remnants of his platoon his charmed career came to an end as he was killed by a sniper. His VC was very well merited as was Rodgers' non-VC. Incredibly it was to be the hard-fighting 3rd Division's only VC of the entire war. And this for the division with some of the most heroic exploits, superb achievements, longest periods in action and heaviest casualties of all the formations in 21 Army Group.

Despite Cosens' heroics the Queen's Own and Chaudieres were slowed by heavy fire from both flanks and the village of Keppeln. That village, which the North Shores were to take when the flanks were cleared, was defended by a strong force of paratroopers supported by tanks and SP guns. Any delay there would seriously compromise 9 Brigade's forthcoming assault on Udem. And since the North Shores' advance was to be made down a bare forward slope 1500 yards long the prospects were most daunting. But for a change sound thinking prevailed. Between them Brigadier Roberts, Lt Col F. White of the 1st Hussars and the North Shores' John Rowley concocted a plan which, though fraught with peril, was the only one feasible if 3rd Division's momentum was not to be lost.

After plastering the village with a battery of heavy (7.2 inch) artillery, followed by a conventional barrage, a squadron of Hussars carrying two platoons of North Shores charged down the slope with all guns blazing. Behind them two armoured infantry companies and three Wasp flamethrower carriers struggled to follow. At least half a dozen Hussars' tanks were brewed up by enemy tank fire or mines and others bogged in the mud. But they diverted the enemy's attention just long enough to permit the infantry and Wasps to come in on the flank. The flamethrowers routed the enemy armour as the infantry and five surviving Hussars tanks cleared the village. By 1700 hrs Keppeln belonged to the North Shores and 9 Brigade could pass through to assault Udem.

The situation was now ripe for Simonds to insert the 4th Armoured Division - the Green Machine - into the fray. Organized into five infantry/tank battle groups the division began its attack through churning, track-clogging clay. They were faced by a determined enemy liberally equipped with tanks, anti-tank guns and Panzerfausts fighting from behind extensive minefields. It took two hours to advance 500 yards - a far cry from the envisaged mighty mailed fist charge and it was dusk before the ridge above Keppeln was reached. The Governor General's Foot Guards and Lake Superiors then mounted a brilliant night attack to clear the ridge as 9 Brigade assaulted Udem. Early on the 27th both the town and ridge were in Canadian hands as the 43rd Wessex took Calcar. The opening round had been very costly with over 1000 casualties and 100 tanks lost. And the Hochwald loomed ahead.

The Hochwald 27 February - 3 March 1945

The final German defensive position before the Rhine at Wesel was a five mile long ridge with the Hochwald on the north and the Balberger Wald on the south. In between a rail line ran through the Hochwald Gap, the entrance of which was blocked by a small hill, Point 73 - the "Albatross". The Hochwald Layback which faces the Calcar Ridge across 1600 yards of open valley was defended by the remains of four parachute divisions well supported by tanks, SP Guns and anti-tank defences.

Before first light on 27 February the Calgary Highlanders of 2nd Division crossed the Start Line to assault the edge of the Hochwald at its mid-point while the Algonquins and South Albertas of 4th Armoured Division attacked the "Albatross". Despite murderous defensive fire which inflicted heavy casualties the Calgarys reached the forward edge of the Hochwald by 0900 hrs and by mid-afternoon were dug-in on their final objectives.

The attack of the Algonquins and SAR got off to a bad start when a tank squadron carrying a company of infantry bogged down before even reaching the Start Line. Attacking without them the remainder of the battle group got to the base of the "Albatross" but because of the missing company and squadron lacked the strength to take the hill. The attackers then became the attacked as the beleaguered Algonquins and South Albertas came under a murderous sheet of fire and were forced to beat off several counter attacks.

In an unreconnoitered and unwise attempt at outflanking the position Brig Jefferson sent "A" squadron of the Albertas and the Algonquin Carrier Platoon straight into an ambush sprung by 88s and Panzerfausts. Every tank and all but one carrier were destroyed leaving the Algonquins' right flank seriously exposed. An attempt to push the Argyll and Sutherlands through The Gap was thwarted and the troops were forced to dig-in 500 yards short of their objective. To the north, on 5 Brigade's front, attempts by the Black Watch and Maisonneuves to exploit the Calgary's earlier success also went unfulfilled. It was evident that a much bigger grouping would be needed to force The Gap and clear the Hochwald Layback. But what Maj Gen Vokes came up with was not much bigger than what had been tried, and found wanting, before.

The next crack would have 10 Brigade clear the Tuschen Wald which formed a northern arm of the Balberger Wald protruding into the Hochwald Gap. 4th Armoured Brigade was then to smash through to secure a small woods, code named "Weston", some 2000 yards beyond. The attack started in promising fashion. At 0300 hrs oh 28 February, behind another thunderous artillery barrage, the Argyll survivors charged "Albatross" and by dawn captured it along with 70 prisoners. They moved on to a lateral road running through the middle of the Hoch and Balberger Walds and dug in. The battalion spent the rest of the day enduring ceaseless artillery and mortar fire and a succession of tank led counter attacks. As casualties mounted re-supply and casualty evacuation had to be done by tanks running the gauntlet to keep the Highlanders in action. An attempt by the Lincoln and Wellands to force the Tuschen Wald south of the railway line met with failure.

With "Albatross" taken the Canadian Grenadier Guards, their tank strength down to half the nominal number, and the Lake Superior Motor Battalion passed through the Argylls to attack "Weston." The tank going was so abominable that only ten tanks in the two leading companies reached the Start Line. After advancing some 1000 yards the Guards lost a further seven tanks and the attack sloshed to a halt. In 48 hours of fighting the Grenadiers lost four Commanding or Acting Commanding Officers to wounds.

Meanwhile to the south XXX Corps was getting up a head of steam and cracking forward on a broad front while the American 9th Army was rapidly pushing northward against dwindling opposition. The brilliant Schlemm was now fighting what amounted to a war on three fronts. Most generals facing such a hopeless situation would either throw in the towel or seek the quickest way out, but Schlemm was anything but an ordinary general. Already fully committed he somehow was able to scratch together a few regiments to hurl against the Americans. But no matter how potentially dangerous were the XXX Corps and American advances the real and present danger was on the front of IInd Canadian Corps where a break through could cut off his entire army. So Schlemm dipped into his final reserve and sent his last two parachute battalions against the Canadians. Everything, on both sides, was now in the shop window.

In this setting Simonds directed 2nd Division to clear the Hochwald while the 3rd attacked Balberger et al. Accordingly on March 1st the 4th Brigade attacked to the left of 5 Brigade to seize the north half of the Hochwald. The Essex Scottish, supported by tanks of the Sherbrooke Fusiliers, seized the edge of the forest after taking heavy casualties and hung on against the patented German knee-jerk counter attacks. In this battle Major F. Tilston, twice wounded in the assault, on arriving on the objective moved about in the open, ignoring enemy fire, to organize the defence of his rapidly diminishing platoons. When ammunition ran low Tilston made six trips through bullet swept ground to bring bandoliers of ammunition to his troops. Hit yet again he reorganized the defence of his company and insisted on giving clear orders for its continuing defence before accepting any medical treatment. For his heroism, which cost him both legs, Major Tilston received the Victoria Cross.

On the 2nd the Royal Hamilton Light Infantry advanced on Marienbaum while 6 Brigade began pushing through the southern half of the Hochwald. On 3 Division's front, south of the railway line, the Chaudieres were first stopped but attacked again to finally grab the eastern half of the Tuschen Wald. The Queen's Own and North Shores then passed through to clear the Balberger. Slowly but surely the enemy's grip on the Hochwald was loosening but still refused to let go.

As 2nd Division pushed through the Hochwald 4th Armoured Brigade made yet another try to capture "Weston." The Armoured Brigade had the will and the spirit but after ten days of continuous action losses in men and equipment had dangerously sapped its strength. The companies of the Motor Battalion were at one-third strength while the armoured units had half their required complement of tanks. On 1st March a sadly depleted force of Grenadier tanks and Lake Superior infantrymen again set out. En route all of the tanks were knocked out or bellied up in the mud. Alone the rapidly diminishing Lake Sups kept going. Somehow, through a supreme effort of will, what was left of "C" Company got onto the objective and into some farm buildings where they were surrounded and mercilessly pounded. On the 2nd the Algonquins and Governor General's Foot Guards made two desperate efforts to get through to the Superiors but each time were repulsed with heavy losses. Before they could try again eight surviving Lake Superiors struggled back led by Sgt C. H. Byce who had taken command after all the officers had become casualties and led his men out killing or wounding 20 Germans as they came. The rest of "C" Company, after the most heroic defence against hopeless odds, had been wiped out.

During March 3rd the 6th and 8th Brigades completed the clearing of the Hochwald and Balberger. The next day 5 Brigade advanced without meeting the enemy. The bloody battle for the Hochwald was finally over. Meanwhile on the Canadians' left the 43rd Division approached Xanten while to the south 11th Armoured Division entered Sonsbeck.

The Wesel Bridgehead 3-10 March 1945

As General Schlemm desperately sought to stem the rapid American advance from the south and the more methodical Anglo/Canadian drive from the north and west he was subjected to a barrage of orders from Hitler which forbade him to either retreat across the Rhine or blow the Rhine bridges. Hitler's orders had by now lost all sense of reality - he placed higher priority in moving coal barges up the Rhine and inland canals to the North Sea than in saving Schlemm's army to fight east of the Rhine. Schlemm finally withdrew to a bridgehead from opposite the Ruhr in the south to Geldern then north to Xanten. He was determined to keep the Wesel crossings open.

On 4 March Crerar directed II Canadian Corps to drive through Xanten and Veen to Menzelen and Wesel. XXX Corps was directed to sweep through Geldern, Issum and Alpen to Wesel. As Horrocks relentlessly swung against bitter fighting towards Bonninghardt and the Americans increased speed, the Canadian Corps fought yet another series of exhausting battles against a fanatical enemy. On 6 March the 2nd Division started toward Xanten while 3rd Division moved through Hammerbruch Spur, cleared Sonsbeck and linked up with the British 3rd Division. 4th Armoured division then moved east on Veen. That day Schlemm finally received permission to withdraw over the Rhine by 10 March. He began thinning out his rear areas but maintained magnificent control on the front lines.

It took 4th Armoured Division three days - from 6 to 9 March to capture Veen in a series of brutal attacks. First the Argylls and South Albertas took a crack. Then the Algonquins and Lincoln and Wellands with BCR and South Alberta tanks had a go - casualties were heavy but they kept pressing. Before Veen was cleared the Algonquins and Canadian Grenadier Guards looped around that village to attack Winnenthal. Aided by a company of Lake Superiors and flame throwers the Canadians, within 24 hours,

THE NORTHWEST EUROPE CAMPAIGN

took the town and 125 prisoners. It had been another gruelling battle for 4th Armoured and Xanten, in German legend the home of Siegfried, promised more of the same for the 2nd Division.

Xanten 8 - 10 March 1945

Advancing north of the Nijmegan -Xanten road the British 43rd Division came within two miles of Xanten on 5 March. At the same time 2nd Division moved to secure the villages of Roschhof and Birkenkampshof. On 7 March Simonds directed the 43rd Division to seize Luttingen, clear the northern part of Xanten above the railway line and capture Beek. 2nd Canadian Division was to clear the south half of Xanten and the high ground along the Alter Rhein. Before dawn on 8 March, once more in a driving rain, the Wessex and 2nd Canadians attacked behind a strong artillery barrage. In the north the Wessex, by dint of superb sub-unit tactics and excellent use of 79 Division's "funnies", got into Xanten by noon. This despite the fact that their artillery barrage, as happened so often before, rolled merrily on ahead when the infantry were first checked at an anti-tank ditch. South of the main road 4th Brigade led 2nd Division's assault with the Essex and RHLI supported by tanks of the Sherbrooke Fusiliers and Flails and Crocodiles of 79 Division. By noon the Essex reached the outskirts of Xanten. However on the right the RHLI had come a cropper. At a huge crater blocking the road the Germans, with superb patience and courage, executed a classic ambush. After allowing the lead Hamilton companies to pass through they sprang the trap and cut them off as artillery, mortars and machine guns decimated the Canadians. One company was surrounded and lost a number of prisoners, two others suffered heavy casualties including both company commanders killed.

On the sound principle of reinforcing success Brigadier Cabeldu passed the Royal Regiment through the Essex to keep pace with the Wessex in clearing the town. By mid-afternoon Xanten was cleared. The 43rd Division then swerved to take Beek and fought a bloody battle for Luttingen. At this juncture Maj Gen Matthews, Commander 2nd Division, ordered 5th Brigade to attack through Xanten to the Alter Rhein. The brigade responded in high style. At 2245 hrs on the 8th the Maisonneuves, supported by tanks and flails, thundered down the main Nijmegan road to capture a firm base on the high ground south of Beek, capturing 120 prisoners in the process. The Black Watch then passed through half-way to Birten. 6th Brigade's South Saskatchewans and Fusiliers Mont-Royal, operating in support of 5 Brigade, executed a classic pincers to clear Die Hees Wald. Before dawn on 9 March the Calgary Highlanders captured the high ground dominating Birten and the Winnenthaler Canal. The leap-frogging continued in fine sequence, this time with the Maisies again in the lead. As the regiment was preparing for a canal crossing a prisoner indicated that a large force of enemy paratroops was assembling in a woods to repeat the cut-off manoeuvre that had dry-gulched the RHLI. Forewarned and forearmed the Maisonneuves called up tanks, Crocodiles and Wasps and launched a pre-emptive strike on the ambushers who rapidly became the ambushees. The attack by the Maisonneuves completely routed the enemy and netted 200 prisoners.

At this the Calgary Highlanders took over and crossed the canal against no opposition sending patrols off towards Wesel. Simonds hoped to be able to bounce the Wesel bridges thereby pulling off a Remagen above the Ruhr. But it was not to be. Early on the 10th as the Calgarys were preparing for a mad dash to Wesel loud explosions indicated that they were too late - the bridges had been blown.

The coup-de-grace was administered from the west and south. In a brilliant series of actions XXX Corps' Welsh Division overran Issum against tough opposition as the Guards Armoured Division took Bonninghardt in what they called one of the stiffest battles ever fought by the division. The Guards then cut the Xanten - Rheinberg road. Keeping pace the Lowland Division surged through Menzelen to Ginderich where on the 10th they met patrols from the Calgarys. With most of the Germans long evacuated across the Rhine the US 16th Corps on 11 March captured Fort Blucher, opposite Wesel, along with a few stragglers thus eliminating the last German position on the Lower Rhine. The Battle of the Rhineland was finally over.

Rhineland Epilogue

The month long battle of the Rhineland was one of the grimmest and toughest of the entire war. Nature and a skilled and determined enemy ensured that every battle, save the opening day's break-in, had been paralysingly slow and bitterly contested. A series of "what ifs" conspired to make it so. First of these, of course, was the month's delay in launching "Veritable" caused by the German Ardennes offensive which substituted mud and floods for frozen vehicle-friendly ground. Second was the flooding of the Roer. The delay this imposed on Simpson's Operation "Grenade" enabled the German Schlemm to overwhelmingly concentrate against the 1st Canadian Army. Third was the abominable weather which not only turned the ground soldiers' world into a charnel house of horror but deprived the Allies of their trump card - overwhelming air power. Fourth was the area selected by the Allies for the battle - a narrow 6 to 15 mile wide rectangle from which manoeuvre was excluded and only headlong butting was possible. Despite the flooded Maas it must somehow have been possible to assault cross it at some place, say Afferden or Well, and take the enemy in the rear. It should at least have been tried.

Having said all this, and despite the constraints against him, Crerar directed an admirable battle. In marked contrast to previous Canadian predilections with narrow front nibbling, Crerar sought to keep major pressure on the enemy from flank to flank of his widening front. His handling of his two corps, the IInd Canadian and XXX British, displayed just enough deft touch to ensure that his Corps Commanders, Simonds and Horrocks, received the direction, resources and support needed without imposing on them undue interference or demands.(7) The gifted Horrocks in particular responded admirably to Crerar's generalship and, with the single exception of the mix-up at Cleve, directed his divisions about the sodden Rhineland with the adroit touch of a chess grandmaster moving his pieces relentlessly to "Check".(8)

Simonds was somewhat more constrained in that he normally had only four divisions as opposed to the eight that were available at one time or another to Horrocks. Nevertheless one again gets the nagging impression that, as at The Falaise Gap, Operation "Spring" et al, he did not fully exploit the resources available to clobber the enemy with overwhelming force. The Hochwald is a classic example where he started with nibbling attacks by two weakened and widely dispersed battalions of different divisions instead of hitting the forest in force with two full brigades as he was later forced to do to gain success.

The accountants' tally starkly showed the grim reality of the terrible month long battle. The British and Canadians lost 15,600 men - 5650 of them Canadian. Together they had captured 22,000 Germans and killed or seriously wounded as many more. General Eisenhower, who strange for a supreme commander rarely visited the Canadian Army during the European campaign, was fulsome in his praise for the conduct of the Rhineland battles. In a letter to Crerar he wrote, "…to express to you personally my admiration for the way you conducted the attack by your Army beginning on February 8….Probably no assault in this war has been conducted under more appalling conditions of terrain than has this one. It speaks volumes for your skill and determination and the valor of your soldiers, that you carried it through to a successful conclusion."(9)

But the final word goes to General Sir David Fraser, "It had been as hard fighting as any phase in the North-West European campaign, fought in the inhospitable winter of the lower Rhineland, on a narrow front where the only tactic was to apply massed artillery fire and batter at a stoutly defended door. Veritable held few surprises. It could not be assisted by mobility or manoeuvre. Veritable was a killing match; slow, deadly and predictable. It was the last of its kind."(10)

The South Alberta Regiment in their Sherman tank on the move to Veen, Germany, 7th. March, 1945. (NAC PA 113677)

GAUDEAMUS IGITUR

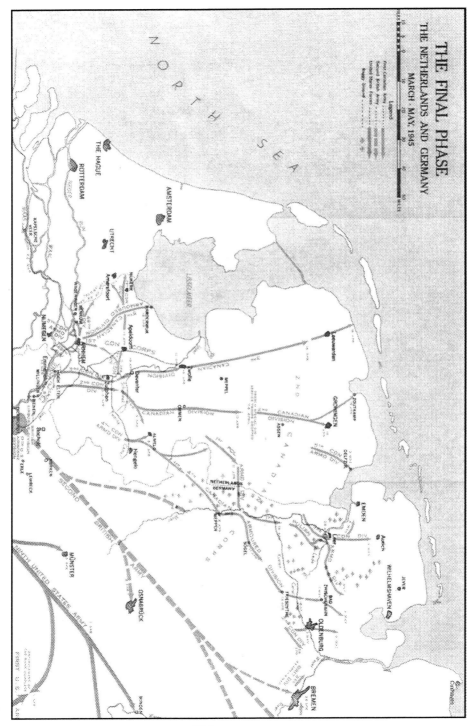

Holland and Germany 23 March - 4 May 1945

THE NORTHWEST EUROPE CAMPAIGN

CHAPTER XII

FROM THE RHINE TO THE NORTH SEA

One more river and that's the river of Jordan
Just one more river and that's the river to cross.

Afro-American Spiritual

Preparing for the Rhine

While 1st Canadian Army's Operation "Veritable/Blockbuster" was still in bloody progress the 2nd British Army was preparing for the next, and hopefully final, phase - the Rhine crossing and beyond. For such a major and symbolical operation it was inevitable that it would give rise, once again, to an international and senior command level spat. This time the argument developed on two planes - the location of the main thrust and the question of a unified ground forces commander for the northern arm. The British, who were the main proponents of the single as opposed to multi-front thesis, wanted the main thrust to be made north of the Ruhr and under British command. Montgomery naturally proposed himself as the supreme northern commander.(1)

Eisenhower, while paying lip service to the idea of northern thrust primacy, directed that two major thrusts be developed. North of the Ruhr Montgomery's 21 Army Group would cross between Wesel and Emmerich. South of the Ruhr the Americans were to cross between Mainz and Karlsruhe. The American 9th Army would come under 21 Army Group for the initial phase. And Eisenhower quashed once and for all Montgomery's *idee fixe* of a supreme land commander.

Meanwhile events elsewhere were forcing everyone's hand. On 7 March, while "Blockbuster" was still grinding on, the US 1st Army in a brilliant coup seized intact the Ludendorff Bridge over the Rhine at Remagen and began clearing a massive bridgehead between Bonn and Coblenz. Then on the night of 22-23 March Patton's 3rd Army bounced the Rhine south of Mainz. Montgomery's mighty orchestration of a northern *schwerpunkt* began, more and more, to take on the role of second fiddle.

Field Marshal Montgomery had originally targeted his Rhine crossing, code named "Plunder", for 31 March. But the progress of operations elsewhere prompted him to advance his timetable, first to 24 March and finally to the 23rd. The 21 Army Group crossing would be made by two armies - the 2nd British in the north at Rees and Wesel and the US 9th in the south at Rheinberg. The intial role of the Canadian Army was simply to hold the line of the Rhine/Maas from Emmerich to the sea and to secure the Nijmegan bridgehead. Once the crossing was successful the 2nd British and 9th American Armies would drive on Hamm, Munster and Henglo into the interior of Germany while 1st Canadian Army would head in the opposite direction to capture the Dutch cities of Deventer and Zutphen preparatory to crossing the Ijssel River to Apeldoorn and the surrounding high ground. Thus while the American and British Armies had the main and satisfying task of plunging deep into Germany the Canadian Army was given the decidedly less glamorous and secondary role of tidying up the rear. Montgomery, to his credit, did however ensure that Canadian formations would be

GAUDEAMUS IGITUR

attached to the British 2nd Army to participate in the Rhine crossing and beyond.

Operation "Plunder" 23 March 1945

General Sir Miles Dempsey's 2nd Army planned to cross the Rhine on a two corps front. XXX Corps under the renowned Horrocks was assigned the northern crossing at Rees while Lt Gen Neil Ritchie's (2) XII Corps would cross on the right flank at Wesel adjacent to the American 9th Army. XXX Corps, consisting of the British 3rd, 43rd, 51st, 11th Armoured and 3rd Canadian Divisions, chose the 51st Highland to make the initial assault crossing. With perceptive consideration for Canadian sensibilities Horrocks placed 9th Canadian Brigade under the Highland Division for inclusion in the assault. On 20 March, in anticipation of further operations east of the Rhine, IInd Canadian Corps was placed under command of 2nd Army.

Horrocks planned to obtain a lodgement between Rees and Haldern to permit bridging the Rhine. 9th Canadian Brigade was to follow the left flank brigade of 51 Division and then turn left to a line Dornick - Vrasselt. The rest of 3rd Canadian Division would then cross to advance on Emmerich. The assault would be preceded by massive air strikes, the largest concentration of artillery used by the West in the entire war and a concentrated airborne drop. The airborne assault, code named "Varsity", was to be onto high ground east of the Rhine by the US 18th Airborne Corps of two divisions - the 17th US and 6th British Airborne Divisions. The 1st Canadian Parachute Battalion, now under Lt Col Jeff Nicklin the former Winnipeg Blue Bomber footballer, would drop as part of 6th Airborne.

The German First Parachute Army, still reeling from "Veritable", was charged with holding the Rhine between Emmerich and Krefeld with the LXXXVI and IInd Parachute Corps facing the British 2nd Army. North of Emmerich, in the proposed Canadian sector, XLVII Panzer Corps of Army Group H was in reserve with the 116th Panzer and 15th Panzer Grenadier Divisions. Alas, the once vaunted First Parachute Army, now commanded by General G. Blumentritt in succession to the brilliant Schlemm who had been wounded, had suffered so heavily west of the Rhine that its IInd Corps now had fewer men than a normal division. Tanks and guns were in very short supply and air support was now virtually non-existent.

The assault crossing which began at 2100 hrs on 23 March behind monumental air and artillery support, and "pepperpot" direct firing, was a complete success. Using Buffaloes, stormboats, DUKWs, D-D tanks, and even naval landing craft, the initial waves landed within ten minutes of launching. Despite meeting stiff opposition at Speldrop the Highland Division soon outflanked Rees and bridging commenced. Ritchie's XII Corps at Wesel was equally successful.

At 0425 hrs on 24 March the Highland Light Infantry of Canada, under Lt Col P.W. Strickland, crossed in Buffaloes under command of the Highland Division's 154 Brigade and moved to an Assembly Area northwest of Rees. The 154th were having a sticky time at Speldrop where parts of its Black Watch were trapped and to add to their woes their divisional commander was killed. The Canadian HLI was then ordered to capture Speldrop and relieve the Black Watch. After very heavy fighting which lasted into the 25th the Canadians captured Speldrop, eliminated the enemy and relieved the Watch. The action cost the HLI 33 casualties.

At 1000 hrs on the 24th Operation "Varsity" began with an awesome display of 1590 aircraft and 1335 gliders. Despite heavy anti-aircraft fire the airborne corps reported success by noon with the 17th US firm below Diersfordt and Isselrott and the 6th British around Hamminkeln. The 1st Canadian Parachute Battalion dropped as part of 3rd Parachute Brigade at Diersfordt Wood. Their story will be told later in this volume. Here we note that despite dispersion and considerable opposition they were everywhere successful. The Canadians lost 65 men of whom 23, including their CO, were killed. One of their number, Corporal F.G. Topham, won the Victoria Cross for his valour that day.

To Emmerich and Beyond

On 24 March the rest of 9 Brigade, reinforced by the North Shore Regiment, crossed the Rhine and joined up with their vanguard HLI. That night Rockingham's 9th Brigade relieved the 154th with the task of breaking out of the pocket formed by the Alter Rhein. The operation called for the capture of Grietherbusch, Bienen and Millingen. On 29 March 9th Brigade came under command of 43 Division which had crossed as part of Horrocks' plan to expand his bridgehead to three divisions with 3rd Canadian left, 43rd centre and 51st right. Unfortunately, as seemed to happen so often, this alignment placed the Canadians against the enemy's heaviest defences along the Alter Rhein. Here the Germans, taking advantage of the strong defensible position, had brought up the 15th Panzer Grenadier Division which, although just a shadow of its once proud self, was still capable of tenacious resistance.

On the left of 9 Brigade, which was also the left of the entire Allied Expeditionary Force, the Stormont, Dundas and Glengarry Highlanders captured Grietherbusch. But in the centre the hard luck North Nova Scotia Highlanders came up against the main Panzer Grenadier defences at Bienen. Attacking on March 25 over open ground, as they had so often before, the North Novas were soon pinned down under heavy fire. That afternoon, as General Horrocks watched, the Scotians mounted a new attack supported by tanks and Wasps. By last light they had broken through to the edge of Bienen at the terrible cost of 114 casualties of whom 43 were killed. The HLI then took over and by noon the next day, still against bitter resistance, had cleared the town. The way was now open for the North Shore Regiment to attack Millingen on the Emmerich - Wesel railway line. Despite the death in action of their CO, Lt Col J.H. Rowley, the New Brunswickers cleared the town by mid-afternoon. All of the initial Canadian objectives had now been taken.

The Canadian bridgehead rapidly expanded with the Canadian Scottish of 7 Brigade arriving to augment the 9th. On the 27th the remainder of 7 Brigade came across along with 3rd Division Headquarters, now under Maj Gen R.H. Keefler. At 1700 hrs 3rd Division took over the left of the Allied line, still under command of XXX Corps. The next day, with the arrival of the rest of 8 Brigade, Horrocks handed command of 3rd Division to Simonds' IInd Canadian Corps. The whole operation had gone remarkably well with Canadian and British battalions and formations being employed and interchanged without distinction as to nationality. In just a few days the 9th Brigade had smoothly passed from the 51st to the 43rd to the 3rd Canadian Division, from the XXXth to the IInd Canadian Corps and from the British to the Canadian Army. It was the last time that Canadian formations served under a British corps headquarters. But the proud British/Canadian link was to remain, with the 49th West Riding Division staying with 1st Canadian Army to the end.

GAUDEAMUS IGITUR

On 28 March, with the Rhine crossings everywhere successful, Field Marshal Montgomery issued a new directive to his three Army Commanders.(3) In it he expressed his intention of driving hard for the Elbe to gain quick possession of the North German Plains. His plan called for the US 9th Army to advance on Magdeburg while the British 2nd Army moved on Hamburg. The 1st Canadian Army was to open supply routes through Arnhem and clear Northeast Holland, the coast towards the Elbe (with 2nd Army help) and finally West Holland. This may have been Montgomery's idea but Eisenhower thought otherwise.

Upon receiving a copy of Montgomery's directive Eisenhower issued his own plans which, to the chagrin of the British, changed the final objectives and gave the principal role to the Americans. He first told Montgomery that Bradley's 12th Army Group would make the main offensive east of the Rhine and that the 9th Army would revert to Bradley after the Ruhr was cut off. Then, without reference to the British, he informed the Russians that the AEF would advance on the lines of Erfurt - Leipzig - Dresden and Regensburg - Linz, leaving Berlin to the Soviets. This effectively placed the British in a supporting role - hardly surprising since the Americans had four times the British battlefield strength. Ike's actions effectively undercut Montgomery, no doubt to the satisfaction of Bradley, Patton, Marshall and the American public. It brought a storm of protest from Churchill but with President Roosevelt dying - he had less than two weeks to live - his complaints fell on deaf ears and the Eisenhower strategy was confirmed.

In view of Ike's decision, Montgomery on 5 April issued his ultimate directive for future operations.(4) 2nd Army would now secure the Weser and capture Bremen preparatory to crossing the Aller and Leine rivers and advancing over the Elbe. 1st Canadian Army's tasks were to:
   a) Clear western Holland with one corps of at least two divisions, a task of secondary importance if resources were insufficient for other tasks;
   b) Clear northeast Holland and the North Sea coast up to the Weser;
   c) Advance with one armoured division on the axis Almelo - Neuenhaus - Meppen - Sogel - Friesoythe - Oldenburg to protect 2nd Army;
   d) Finally, advance from Bremen toward Hamburg protecting 2nd Army and clearing the Cuxhaven peninsula.

Emmerich and Beyond

Before 1st Canadian Army could take over operations east of the Rhine it would be necessary for IInd Canadian Corps, still under command of 2nd Army, to clear Emmerich and open a supply route for the Army. Since 2nd Division, followed by the 4th, would only cross the Rhine on 28 - 29 March the Emmerich show fell naturally to 3rd Division which was in position.

Maj Gen Keefler directed that 7 Brigade capture the much destroyed Emmerich while 8 Brigade was directed to clear the commanding Hoch Elten feature some three miles to the northeast. 7th Brigade's attack opened on the night of 27 - 28 March with the Regina Rifles clearing Dornick and the Canadian Scottish capturing Vrasselt on the railway line. Both units reached the outskirts of Emmerich where they ran into strong opposition from the German 6th Parachute and 346th Divisions. During the night of 28 - 29 March the Reginas and Can Scots, assisted by tanks of the Sherbrooke Fusiliers and flame throwing Crocodiles of the Fife and Forfar Yeomanry, pushed on against savage resistance. The operation required crossing the Landwehr Canal by the Scots and vicious house to house fighting by the Reginas who slogged doggedly forward through the 29th. The Royal Winnipeg Rifles entered the fray on the northern part of the town beating back a strong German counter-attack on the 30th. The Victoria Scots then surged forward to capture the cement works west of the city as a firm base for 8 Brigade's attack on Hoch Elten. The successful but brutal three-day battle cost the Western Brigade 175 casualties, one-third fatal.

8 Brigade began its attack on the key Hoch Elten feature on the night 30 - 31 March with Le Regiment de la Chaudiere heading for the village of Elten on the left flank and the Queen's Own Rifles advancing on the woods and high ground to the right. The Hoch Elten feature had been subjected to extremely heavy aerial and artillery bombardment in the preceding days which eased 8 Brigade's task. Both battalions captured their objectives by last light on the 31st. Meanwhile against somewhat lesser opposition Rockingham's 9th Brigade captured s'Heerenberg and Stokkumer Bosch to the north.

The newly arrived 2nd Division wasted no time in getting cracking with its vanguard 6th Brigade and the Divisional Recce Regiment pushing eight miles inland to capture Etten, Silvolde and Terborg on the 31st. The next day 5 Brigade charged on another five miles to Doetinchem. The Corps' 18th Armoured Car Regiment and 4th Division's South Albertas patrolled deep to the Northwest on the same day.

The Battle of Emmerich - Hoch Elten had been very well executed by Maj Gen Keefler, his three brigadiers and the units concerned. The fact that four of the units involved selected this battle from among all others as one of the ten to be emblazoned on their colours attests to its importance and difficulty.

First Canadian Army Operations

At midnight on April 1st the 1st Canadian Army became operational east of the Rhine assuming command of IInd Corps which was already in action there. On that day also Ist British Corps reverted under command of 2nd British Army having served continuously with the Canadian Army since Normandy. It had been a long and winning association bringing honour and pride to both nations. In its place below Arnhem was the Ist Canadian Corps recently arrived from Italy. April 1st was also noteworthy as the date on which the 1st and 9th US Armies met at Lippstadt completing the encirclement of the Ruhr. They were to cut the pocket in two on the 8th and complete its liquidation on the 18th capturing the entire Army Group B of the 5th Panzer and 15th Armies amounting to 317,000 prisoners. Its commander, the brilliant Field Marshal Model the victor of so many similar sweeping encirclements on the Eastern Front, committed suicide on the 21st. The encirclement and elimination of the huge Ruhr pocket was one of the great, spectacular Western successes of the entire war but has been largely subsumed by the other great events then being enacted on various fronts. The great victory was also an indication of the now total domination of the western front by US forces, a domination which was enhanced by the reversion of 9th Army to US Command.

While the Americans majestically swept forward on many axes on their "German hayride" to the Elbe, Bavaria and Czechoslovakia and the British advanced on Bremen/Hamburg and the Baltic, the Canadian Army turned to the more pedestrian, if highly important, tasks of clearing Holland and the North Sea coast. Operations were faithfully conducted pursuant to Montgomery's directives of 24 and 28 March. Although much

more complicated and jumbled in practice these operations may conveniently be considered in three segments as follows :
- a) Western operations between Emmerich and the Ijssel Meer comprising the crossing of the Ijssel River and the capture of Zutphen, Deventer and Apeldoorn followed by the capture of Arnhem and closure to the Grebbe Line.
- b) The liberation of eastern Holland and drive to the North Sea.
- c) The northwestern drive across Germany to Emden, Oldenberg and Bremen.

These operations, especially the first two, were hampered to a considerable extent by a desire to minimize casualties and damage to the valiant and long suffering Netherlanders. Indeed it was finally decided, partly for military reasons and partly humanitarian, not to proceed with a major advance into Holland west of the Ijsselmeer. But, unhampered by such considerations, the armchair strategists, comfortably ensconced at home and deriving their information from small-scale newspaper maps, could be forgiven for unfavourably comparing the Canadians' slow advances into Holland with the spectacular broad-arrow charges of the British, and especially American, forces clear across Germany. But in the end it was the Canadians who emerged the real winners. For by clearing eastern Holland and accepting the surrender of all German forces in western Holland the Canadians had the great honour of freeing that wonderful country and earning the everlasting thanks and remembrance of its people. It is an association that its Canadian liberators treasure to this day.

To Western Holland

After clearing the Hoch Elten feature IInd Corps split its advance along two axes. While the 2nd and 3rd Infantry Divisions moved northwest to the Ijssel River, Zutphen and Deventer, 4th Armoured moved northeast on an axis Lochem - Hengelo - Borne. The inter-Army boundary was a line Ruurlo - Borculo - Delden - Borne, below which the British were pushing on Bremen and Hamburg.

On the northeast axis 2nd Division started on 2/3 April with a lightning advance of 20 miles to the Twente Canal. The Royal Regiment cracked smartly across capturing a company of engineers preparing field defences which they did not have time to man. A company of the Royal Hamiltons followed to enlarge the bridgehead. Despite heavy shelling the Canadian engineers soon had rafting in progress and on the 3rd had so rapidly ferried across the Fort Garrys, 8th Recce and 2nd Anti-Tank that the Germans thought they were being overwhelmed by amphibious forces. To the east at Delden 4th Armoured was equally successful but that is a later story.

On 2nd April Lt Gen Simonds had considered using 2nd Division to "tap out" Zutphen (where in 1586 a wounded and thirsting Sir Philip Sidney gained romantic immortality by giving his water bottle to a wounded private soldier because, "thy necessity is greater than mine"). But 2nd Division's rapid push northward, coupled with Zutphen's reluctance to capitulate led him instead to order 3rd Division to take both Zutphen and Deventer some ten miles to the north.

On 5 April the initial advance on Zutphen was led by 9 Brigade which had to fight some pitched battles against the 361st Volksgrenadier Division to clear the water protected approaches to the town. 9 Brigade then moved north to cover 7 Brigade's attack on Deventer while 8 Brigade assaulted Zutphen from the east. The North Shores were initially held up in the north of the town but the Chaudieres, despite severe opposition, made excellent progress in the south. Reinforced by the North Shores the Chauds rapidly penetrated the city and by midday on the 8th the entire town was in Canadian hands. For their brilliant action the Chaudieres received "Zutphen" as an emblazoned battle honour - the only Allied infantry regiment to be so honoured.

7 Brigade's 9 April attack on Deventer went like clockwork. While 9 Brigade crossed the Schipbeek Canal and advanced north, 7 Brigade turned west on Deventer with the Royal Winnipeg Rifles and a company of the Queen's Own on the left and the Canadian Scottish right. The town was well protected by waterways and the troops had tough slogging but kept going. Tanks of the Sherbrooke Fusiliers thwarted an attempted tank led enemy counter attack before it could gather momentum. The Germans tried to stem the western Canadians along an anti-tank ditch but resistance crumbled as the Regina Rifles passed through the Winnipegs during the night. Within 24 hours Deventer had fallen with the considerable assistance of the Dutch underground. 7 Brigade suffered 125 casualties but captured 500 prisoners.

Operation "Cannonshot" - 1st Division Over the Ijssel

The capture of Zutphen and Deventer set the stage for the Canadian Army to execute Field Marshal Montgomery's prime directive to it of opening a supply route to the northwest through Arnhem. General Crerar planned to implement the directive in two stages. First, to cross the Ijssel and capture Apeldoorn and the surrounding high ground. Then to attack north from the Nijmegan salient across the Neder Rijn to Arnhem.

The first of these stages was entrusted to Simonds' IInd Corps using the 1st Canadian Division in its initial operation since coming from Italy. All eyes were on the Red Patch Devils to see if their brilliant successes in hilly Italy could be repeated in the flat, waterlogged Netherlands. The Red Patches did not disappoint. The operation, code named "Cannonshot", was launched by 2nd Brigade on 9 April by crossing the Ijssel between Zutphen and Deventer. H Hour was 1630. Behind a strong artillery bombardment and smoke screen the assault battalions, Seaforths left and PPCLI right, crossed the river in Buffaloes. The Seaforths, meeting weak opposition, smashed forward and consolidated on their final objective by 1750 hrs. The Princess Pats met somewhat stiffer opposition but by 1800 hrs, after routing the enemy and knocking out a captured French tank which the Germans were using, they too reorganized on their objective. Despite heavy enemy shelling, which Canadian counter-battery operations had been unable to suppress, the hard driving engineers, at a cost of 17 casualties, completed a bridge and two rafts by 0200 hrs on the 12th.

On 12 April the 1st and 3rd Brigades crossed over and advanced on Apeldoorn under heavy artillery and mortar fire. Here the CO of the 48th Highlanders, Lt Col D.A. Mackenzie, was killed - on the same date that President Roosevelt died at Warm Springs Georgia.

Operation "Anger" - The Capture of Arnhem

Arnhem had first been the object of Allied intentions in September 1944 in the failed Operation "Market Garden." Thereafter came a series of on again - off again plans to take the city which were deferred for many reasons, especially the demands of operations elsewhere including the Ardennes, "Veritable" and "Plunder". Nevertheless Headquarters 1st Canadian Army had long prepared outline plans for the operation, code named "Anger" which were later passed to Lt Gen Foulkes' Ist Corps for study and implementation. Foulkes' more detailed planning also metamorphosed through alterations and dithering before crystallizing, on 27 March, in a three phased plan. Phases 1 and 2 involved the clearing of the Nijmegan "island" by the British 49th and Canadian 5th Armoured Divisions. Then 49 Division would capture Arnhem after a bounce crossing at Oosterbeek on the city's western flank.

49 Division began clearing the island in Operation "Destroyer" on 2-3 April, joined by 11 Brigade of 5th Armoured Division to the west. Against minimal opposition, but a huge number of mines and craters, the island was cleared on 3 April. The only real fighting was experienced by the Perth Regiment which, with little difficulty, beat off two enemy counter-attacks. Then, typical of the fumbling that seemed to haunt all things related to Arnhem, the operation was put on hold for a further ten days. Only after the 1st Canadian Division had crossed the Ijssel, as previously noted, did Foulkes finally turn 49 Division loose, but not before once more monkeying around with the plans. In this seemingly unnecessary change the attack, which was launched on 12 April, came from the east across the Ijssel and not from the south over the Neder Rijn. The ease with which the West Riding Division, aided by Canadian tanks, engineers and artillery, captured Arnhem makes one wonder why all the previous fooling-about and needless dithering? It was not Foulkes' finest hour although he seemed to have a penchant for such things. In the event the British division captured the city and 600 prisoners with minimal loss to themselves.

The long overdue capture of Arnhem did not put paid to the high command frittering and foozling which plagued actions along the Neder Rijn. On 5 April Montgomery stated that following the fall of Apeldoorn and Arnhem the Canadians would clear all of West Holland. Crerar and his subordinates at once put matters in train to this effect. Then on 12 April the Field Marshal made a *volte face* and decided against the liberation of West Holland. Instead the Canadians would now clear north-eastern Holland and the Emden - Wilhelmshaven "peninsula" and dominate the Weser below Bremen and the Elbe below Hamburg.(5) Until the main eastern tasks were finished operations in the west would be limited to what the two divisions could accomplish with only their own resources. Accordingly on 15 April the ever cautious Foulkes cancelled the West Holland operation and directed that, "I Cdn Corps will clear enemy from Western Holland between the Ijssel and the Grebbe Line."(6) The desperate plight of the Dutch civilians in West Holland was well known but it was hoped to provide aid by other means such as air drops and Red-Cross convoys.

Apeldoorn and Operation "Cleanser"

With 1st Canadian Division reverting to Ist Corps on 13 April Lt Gen Foulkes issued new orders to his command. On the left the British 49th Division would advance to the Grebbe Line via Renkum, Bennekom and Ede clearing the north bank of the Neder Rijn en route. 1st Division would capture Apeldoorn and advance through Voorthuizen and Barneveld to the Grebbe. Since 1st Division was facing stiff opposition and the 49th very little, Foulkes, in Operation "Cleanser", had 5th Armoured Division drive northward from Arnhem behind the enemy lines to the Ijsselmeer along the axis Barneveld, Voorthuizen, Putten. The 1st Canadian Armoured Brigade, less several detached squadrons, would hold the Nijmegan "island" as far as Tiel along with two Belgian battalions and a composite force under the 7th Anti-Tank Regiment. To the west the south bank of the Rhine and the Scheldt islands was held by elements of the Netherlands District.(7)

On the left the 49th Division, after a pause to permit the 5th Armoured to pass through, began its advance supported by the Ontario Regiment and the Calgary Tanks. After several sharp skirmishes, especially at Ede the division took Wageningen and Bennekom on the 17th. Here they were ordered to stand fast to facilitate political approaches with the dual aims of supplying the Dutch civilians and preventing the enemy flooding of the countryside.

On the right flank, on 13 April, 1st Division after crossing the Ijssel and routing the German 162nd Naval Infantry Regiment met surprising opposition from the 361st Volksgrenadier Division. Maj Gen Harry Foster directed his 1st Brigade and tanks of the 1st Hussars north of Apeldoorn and sent the 3rd Brigade to the south. Strong opposition was expected along the Apeldoorn canal covering approaches to the city. Meanwhile, in compliance with the directive to open the Arnhem - Zutphen communications corridor Foster sent the 2nd Brigade and Three Rivers tanks south to contact the 49th Division at Dieren and Eerbeek. In so doing 2nd Brigade crossed the Apeldoorn Canal and began bridging, thus pre-empting 8th Brigade's assault crossing of that barrier.

On the evening of the 16 April 1st Division closed up to the pleasant city of Apeldoorn with its Dutch Royal summer residence at Het Loo while 5th Armoured cut it off from behind. With help from the Dutch underground the RCR secured vital lock gates and the eastern edge of the city by 0430 hrs on the 17th. The Hasty Ps and 48th Highlanders then seized Het Loo and the north-west of the town as the enemy fled. The West Novas completed the occupation of the city from the south. The citizens of Apeldoorn tumultuously welcomed their Canadian liberators with an emotional outpouring of joy. Although considered a minor blip in the grand scheme of the European War finale and totally subsumed by the wide swaths being cut across Germany by the Russians, US and British the Ijssel Meer operation had been a stern test. In seven days from 11 to 17 April the 1st Canadian Division had suffered 506 casualties but it had captured 2600 prisoners, liberated large chunks of the Netherlands and won the grateful, enduring thanks of the wonderful Dutch people.

Operation "Cleanser" - 15-18 April.

5th Armoured's drive northward from Arnhem to the Ijsselmeer was conducted under a severe time stricture as the division was slated to be moved to support IInd Corps in northeast Holland after the 17th. Hoffmeister's plan called for his advance to be led by the 5th Armoured Brigade (Brig I.H. Cumberland). At 0630 hrs on 15 April the advance kicked off with the 8th Princess Louise's Hussars advancing on the left on Deelen and the British Columbia Dragoons on the right on Terlet. The BCDs main problem was the terrain as they lost only one tank to enemy action. The 8th Hussars lost two but overran and captured the headquarters of the German 858th Grenadier Regiment in Deelen.

At noon the Strathconas passed through the Hussars and reached Otterloo at last light. Early on the 16th they cleared Otterloo and headed for Barneveld where they had a short fight and lost two tanks. By nightfall they were at Voorthuizen as the Hussars, GGHGs and 11 Brigade passed Lunteren to the south. Meanwhile the BCDs on the right swept directly to Voorthuizen thus blocking any attempt by the German 6th Parachute

GAUDEAMUS IGITUR

Division to withdraw that way.

Alarmed at the loss of Apeldoorn and 5th Armoured's drive through their rear the Germans made frantic attempts to break out. On 17 April some 600 - 900 enemy under the 952nd Volksgrenadier Regiment made a dash at Otterloo where 5th Armoured had its headquarters along with the 17th Field Regiment and a battery of 3rd Medium. Hoffmeister countered by placing the Irish Regiment to cover the eastern approaches. At midnight the enemy struck the village igniting a wild night-long melee with the embattled gunners firing over open sights and fighting as infantry. At daybreak the Irish with Wasps and a troop of tanks routed the enemy who left 100 dead behind. The Canadians suffered 47 casualties, over half by the 17th Field who also lost three guns.

While the Battle of Otterloo was in progress the Cape Breton Highlanders took Barneveld paving the way for the drive to the Ijsselmeer. On the left the Strathconas and a company of Westminsters headed for Nijkerk but ran into tough opposition and lost three tanks before being diverted to support the 8th Hussars' drive on Putten. The Hussars experienced hard fighting losing 14 tanks and 18 men. Meanwhile the BCDs and a company of Westminsters cleared Voorthuizen.

While 5th Armoured pushed north the 1st Infantry Division advanced west from Apeldoorn. On the 17th the two divisions linked up at Barneveld. Early the next day the Hussars and Westminsters, aided by the Dutch Resistance, captured Putten as the Hussars Recce Troop reached the Ijsselmeer. By the afternoon of the 18th the Straths, BCDs, Perths and Dutch resistance cleared the port of Harderwijk - just too late to prevent the escape of a sizeable part of the German 6th Paras.

On 19 April 5th Armoured handed over operations to 1st Division and started their move to the northeast. In four days of excellent actions in Operation "Cleanser" the Mighty Maroon Machine advanced 40 miles, took half a dozen towns, captured 1800 prisoners, killed hundreds more and closed to the Ijsselmeer. Its own casualties amounted to 76 men and a score of tanks.

On 22 April, as 1st Division closed up to Amersfoort and the Grebbe Line and 49th Division kept pace to the south, Field Marshal Montgomery, in conformity with the wishes of General Eisenhower the Supreme Commander, issued his final directive of the campaign.(8) This directed that the Canadian Army not operate west of the present line pending further orders. Ist Canadian Corps would thus finish out the war in a static mode along the Grebbe Line while arrangements were made to bring food to the starving Dutch. However secondary this operation in Western Holland may have seemed to the outside world to the Ist Canadian Corps and the Dutch civilians it was <u>the</u> war. Since entering Northwest Europe the Corps had liberated all of the Netherlands southeast of the Ijsselmeer and taken 8860 prisoners. It had fought the good fight to the end.

To bring relief to the trapped civilians a special Headquarters Netherlands District, under British Maj Gen Galloway, had been formed within 1st Canadian Army. The valiant Netherlanders would have preferred the Allies to have attacked and destroyed the hated enemy in Western Holland, but for reasons beyond Canadian control this was not to be. On the political front Churchill and Eisenhower feared that an offensive into West Holland, with its concomitant air and artillery strikes, could inflict unacceptable casualties and damage on the civilian population. They also feared that an attack might prompt the Germans to blow the dikes and return much of the countryside to its 17th Century salt water state. On the military side Montgomery believed that victory elsewhere would lead to the bloodless early relief of the Dutch - which is pretty much what

THE NORTHWEST EUROPE CAMPAIGN

happened. And the demands of other critical fronts would prevent him from giving Lt Gen Foulkes the resources needed for a rapid, surgical conquest of West Holland.

After much talking and dithering between Allied and enemy civilian and military commanders and the Dutch Government-in-Exile relief finally started on 29 April when RAF Bomber Command, later joined by the US Air Force, began dropping food to the Dutch cities. On 2 May a safe land route was finally established between Arnhem and Utrecht enabling Allied lorries to bring in supplies at the rate of 1000 tons a day.

From Emmerich to the Sea

While Ist Corps, through no fault of its own, was engaged in on-again, off-again actions south of the Ijsselmeer, IInd Corps was marching northward to the sea. After crossing the Twente Canal in early April the 2nd and 3rd Divisions, later joined by 5th Armoured, drove rapidly to clear the northeast Netherlands. Meanwhile 4th Armoured Division, soon to be joined by the Polish Armoured Division, advanced north-eastward across Germany toward Wilhelmshaven and Bremen.

On 2nd Division's front its 6th Brigade reached the Schipbeek Canal on 6 April. Although the enemy had blown the only bridge the Camerons were soon across and advancing on Holten. To assist the overall advance two small airborne drops had been considered - "Amherst" in the east and "Keystone" in the west. In the event only "Amherst", involving small, section-size, bodies from the 2nd and 3rd French Regiments de Chasseurs Parachutistes and the 1st Belgian Paras, went ahead. The general task of these small bodies was to seize bridges on IInd Corps' line of advance and to secure airfields at Steenwijk. The drops were made on the night 7/8 April and over the next two days small groups of paras moved about destroying communications and harassing the German withdrawal. On 9 April the first groups were relieved by the Corps' 18th Armoured Car Regiment at Meppel and by the Poles at Coevorden. At Spier embattled groups of 3 RCP were saved in the nick of time by the sudden arrival of scout cars of the 8th Recce. It is difficult to assess the value of the parachute drops, which failed to take the airfields, but they doubtless contributed to the rapid Canadian advance. Their brief actions cost the paras 91 casualties.

2nd Division continued its rapid northward thrust led by the 8th Recce with the 1st Armoured Cars (Royal Canadian Dragoons) providing flank protection. On 12 April Les Fusiliers Mont-Royal captured the canal bridge at Beilen with a brilliant, deep outflanking sweep. 4 Brigade passed through and the next day captured Assen with another smartly executed cut-off move. The action netted 600 prisoners and throngs of cheering civilians who by now had become a most gratifying feature of every liberated town. On the afternoon of the 13th the Brigade reached the outskirts of the provincial capital of Groningen whose rich history encompassed membership in the important Middle-Age Hanseatic League. Here the enemy, including Dutch SS Troops, staged a determined defence. In order to save civilian lives the Canadian attackers refrained from shelling the city. This forbearance greatly complicated their task, already made difficult by numerous interlacing canals - a feature of many Dutch towns.

In bitter hand-to-hand fighting the Royal Regiment and Royal Hamilton Light Infantry cleared the southern quarter of the city aided by a brilliant dash by the Essex Scottish to capture an intact bridge. 6 Brigade passed through on the night 15/16 April and relentlessly pushed northward. At this juncture Maj Gen Matthews sent 5 Brigade crashing into the city from the west to clear the northern parts. Operations were hampered by Dutch civilians constantly thronging the streets to cheer on their Canadian liberators. But these brave civilians also shared in the conquest of the city by guiding and informing the troops. Their assistance was particularly valuable in aiding the Camerons to cross the Van Starkenborgh Canal and get a damaged lift bridge into operation. This action on 16 April completed the liberation of the city. In a superbly controlled four-day battle 2nd Division cleared an important city with minimum cost to the inhabitants and captured 2400 prisoners. The division's own casualties were 209.

While Groningen was being liberated the Royal Canadian Dragoons captured Leeuwarden and reached the North Sea above Dokkum and Zoutkamp. This concluded a brilliant 16 day, 120 mile advance by the valiant 2nd Division during which they fought several stiff battles, crossed and bridged numerous watercourses, liberated many towns and captured over 5000 prisoners. It was a fitting triumphal march for this once hard luck division which had fought and suffered so grievously in Normandy, the Scheldt and the Rhineland.

Not to be outdone Keefler's 3rd Division kept pace on the left of the Second. After clearing Deventer on 11 April the vanguard 9th Brigade dashed northward in a motley collection of tanks, armoured gun tractors and carriers, heading for Leeuwarden. Battles were fought against weak enemy resistance at Zwolle, Meppel and Steenwijk. Everywhere the Canadians were greeted by delirious, cheering, flower-throwing crowds of civilians. And again the civilians aided the soldiers including helping to construct an ad-hoc bridge at Akkrum using a barge as the base. The divisional 7th Recce Regiment (17th Duke of York's Royal Canadian Hussars) raced on to Leeuwarden only to find the RCDs had beaten them into the town.

Swinging west the Highland Light Infantry reached the Friesland coast of the North Sea at Harlingen, storming the town and capturing 400 prisoners. Keeping pace the Queen's Own and North Shores of 8 Brigade captured Makkum and the eastern end of the great causeway across the throat of the Ijssemeer. Between 15 and 18 April the entire Friesland coast, except for a pocket at Delfzijl, was in Canadian hands. In its 26 day, 115 mile advance the 3rd Division had fought numerous battles, liberated scores of towns, crossed and bridged 30 canals and captured 4600 prisoners. It had been a magnificent achievement.

Keefler's men had little time to savour their victorious advance as they were hustled east to relieve the Polish Division west of the Ems below Delfzijl. In a brief operation, before again being switched, the Canadian Scottish and Sherbrooke Fusiliers fought a very tough battle on 21/22 April to capture Wagenborgen at a cost of 65 men. The division then turned the Delfzijl pocket over to the newly arrived 5th Armoured Division before heading east across the Ems estuary below Emden.

The Delfzijl Pocket - 23 April - 2 May 1945

After completing Operation "Cleanser" in style Hoffmeister's 5th Armoured Division had been hurried north to relieve the 3rd Division below Delfzijl. Hoffmeister was charged with clearing the enemy from west of the Ems estuary and controlling the Fresian coast. To fulfil this task he would first have to eliminate the Delfzijl Pocket.

Located on the Ems estuary, Delfzijl was well protected by the terrain. The city, a second class North Sea port, was behind a large flooded area. The surrounding country was flat, wet and laced with canals and ditches, reducing vehicle movement to the few existing roads. There was very little cover. Defended by 1500 soldiers and marines operating from concrete emplacements and an extensive barbed wire protected trench system, Delfzijl was covered by emplaced batteries at Emden, Borkum Island and the Dollart Peninsula. Recognizing that this would be primarily an infantry operation Hoffmeister placed the 11th Lorried Infantry Brigade east of the port and 5th Armoured Brigade to the west. The attack would be coordinated with 3rd Division's operations east of the Ems.

Brigadier Johnston, Commander 11 Brigade, began 25 April by constricting the perimeter with advances by the Irish Regiment and Westminsters from the east, the Perths from the west and the British Columbia Dragoons from the south-west. The Irish made steady progress advancing north from Wagenborgen to Heskeves, a mile east of Delfzijl, by the 30th. With little cover, terrible terrain, mines, demolitions and constant shelling the going was necessarily slow. The Westminsters, also continually shelled, cleared all ground to their left save for the Dollart Peninsula. On the 29th the Perths and BCDs captured Marsum. Just getting there had been a nightmare for the Perths who struggled for four days to advance two miles along the coast from Holwierde. During these four hellish days the Perths suffered 78 casualties.

On 29 April the Cape Breton Highlanders relieved the Perths and moved forward to capture Uitwierde half way to Delfzijl. At mid-morning on the 30th the Cape Bretons began their final attack through miserable going against wire, mines, MG posts on the dikes and four large concrete bunkers. The next day they and the Hussars captured the town. On May 2nd the Irish passed westward to eliminate the Weiwerd - Farmsum redoubt. The 5th Division captured 4150 of the enemy in this their final action of the war. Their own casualties were 236. In the light of operations elsewhere and the rapid approach of final German capitulation there is doubt as to why it was necessary to have the Delfzijl battle at all. Nevertheless, once this very difficult and controversial operation was entrusted to Hoffmeister's 5th Armoured that superb division completed an extremely difficult action in fine fashion - as it had in each of its battles since the Melfa in far-off Italy almost two years before.

To Bremen and the Jade

While Ist Corps engaged in its frustrating limited operations south of the Ijsselmeer and was denied the chance of liberating West Holland IInd Corps had the much more satisfying task of rapidly freeing eastern Holland and overrunning northwest Germany as far as the Weser. The rapid advance of 2nd and 3rd Infantry Divisions to the Frisian coast has been described. And while this was in progress the armoured half of IInd Corps - 1st Polish and 4th Canadian Armoured Divisions - drove hard for Emden, Oldenburg and Wilhelmshaven.

After crossing the Twente Canal on 4 April Maj Gen Vokes' 4th Armoured Division advanced to the northeast on a general axis Almelo - Emlichheim - Meppen - Oldenburg. On 6 April the 4th Armoured Brigade reached the Ems while the 10th Infantry Brigade ran into surprisingly stiff opposition at Wierden. It would take them three days to clear the area. With the Argylls in the van 4th Armoured Brigade crossed the Ems, captured Meppen and many prisoners and ploughed ahead. Because of the flat, boggy ground the armour could seldom deploy far from the roads leaving the infantry to once more bear the brunt.

The Lake Superiors and Lincoln and Wellands fought a stiff battle for Sogel on 9 and 10 April driving back several determined counter-attacks. At nearby Borger the Canadian Grenadier Guards lost three tanks in supporting the Lake Sups. The division rapidly thrust for Friesoythe which the Argyll and Sutherlands captured in a beautifully executed right hook with the Lake Superiors providing the frontal screening force. The Argylls' CO was killed by some bypassed enemy at Friesoythe leading to rumours that he had been shot by a civilian sniper. Unhappily, in reprisal, a large part of the town was burned by the enraged Canadians.

As the Canadian Armoured Division closed on the vital city of Oldenburg another squabble developed over bomber support. On April 14th the Canadian Corps Headquarters requested that Oldenburg be subjected to a heavy bombing raid. After ponderous forwarding through parallel Army and Air Force channels the proposal was approved using medium instead of heavy bombers. Once again Eisenhower's air marshals - this time Coningham - messed things up, cancelling the 17 April raid while the bombers were actually en route to the target. Coningham apparently had the mistaken, and in the event irrational, impression that SHAEF had forbidden such raids as our troops might need the buildings after the war. At Canadian insistence the attack finally went in and proved most effective.

Before the Canadians could get into Oldenburg they had to cross the formidable 100 foot wide Kusten Canal which had actually been first reached by 10th Infantry Brigade before it was relocated elsewhere. After taking Friesoythe on the 14th the 4th Armoured Brigade tried to get to and over the canal but was thwarted by sodden tank-poor ground and demolitions on all feasible approaches. The only course now open to Vokes was an assault crossing of the canal followed by time consuming bridging and rafting. Because of the terrible ground Vokes decided to cross below Bad Zwischenahn followed by a thrust south-east to Oldenburg. The Germans apparently thought likewise as the crossing area was defended by two battalions of marines plus elements of 7th Parachute Division under HQ 2nd Parachute Corps. The attack was entrusted to the 10th Brigade.

At 0100 hrs on 17 April the Algonquin Regiment crossed in assault boats. They were supported by fire from tanks of the BCRs, machine guns of the New Brunswick Rangers and divisional artillery. The assault was successful and the Algonquins consolidated around a bridgehead some 350 yards deep and 1500 wide. Heavy enemy shelling and mortaring hampered attempts at bridging and the German marines put up a strong resistance, mounting an SP supported counter-attack at last light. The Algonquins held, the attackers were driven off and two companies of Argyll and Sutherlands arrived to secure the bridgehead. On the 18th more enemy attacks were decisively beaten back by the Argylls as a company of Lincoln and Wellands came across to widen the bridgehead to enable the 8th Field squadron RCE to commence rafting and the 9th to start bridging. By morning on the 19th tanks of the BCR were across.

On 21 April 10 Brigade advanced to the Aue River. The terrain north of the Kusten Canal was absolutely appalling with the few roads rapidly deteriorating into the surrounding swamp. The entire resources of 4 Division's engineers was required to keep a few roads barely operable. Thus denied proper tank support the infantry paid the price in blood. In the week since storming the canal, 10th Brigade's infantry suffered 400 casualties resulting in rifle companies reduced to 50 - 60 men each - half the required strength and dangerously low for ongoing operations. Fortunately with the conscription crisis resolved and zombies finally available the reinforcement of battalions now proceeded at a steady, albeit barely adequate, pace.

On 25 April Moncel's 4th Armoured Brigade, with the Lincolns and Argylls under command, took over the advance on Bad Zwischenahn with flank protection from the Corps Armoured Car Regiment (12th Manitoba Dragoons), 10 Brigade and attached Royal Marines. The South Alberta Regiment advanced below Oldenburg.

This day, 25 April, also marked the final bomber attack of the war by RCAF squadrons. 6 (RCAF) Group was part of a force of 480 heavies that bombed coastal defences on Wangerooge Island covering the approaches to Willhelmshaven, the Weser and Bremen. SHAEF wished to avoid a repeat of Antwerp where the port had been taken but the approaches left untouched. Despite heavy and accurate bombing and the killing of 300 people, the concrete emplaced guns were relatively unscathed and soon back in action. The raid cost seven aircraft of which an astounding six, including four Canadian, were lost in collisions. Twenty-eight Canadian and 20 British and Free French airmen were lost. Bomber Command only launched three other raids in the war - to Berchtesgaden, Norway and Kiel while turning its full weight to Oprations "Manna" - the supply drops on Holland and "Exodus" -the repatriation of prisoners of war. Strangely, the last Bomber Command casualties of the war, over Kiel on 2/3 May, also occurred by collision when two aircraft of 199 Squadron collided on the bomb run.

On the ground the enemy, as he had done throughout the war, conducted a skilful defence behind myriad mines, craters and road blocks all covered by heavy, well controlled fire. Under these trying conditions it took 4th Armoured until 28 April to close up to Bad Zwischenahn. On 30 April the Argylls and Grenadier Guards' tanks outflanked the city to the west and reached the town's northern lake. Meanwhile the Lincolns and Wellands fought into the town from the east. That night the enemy decamped and Vokes' preparations to move on Oldenburg were thwarted by a Corps change of plans.

The Ems and Leda

While 4th Armoured Division in the east was struggling "through mud and blood to the green fields beyond" the three other divisions of the corps were battling valiantly elsewhere. After operating west of the Ems the Polish Armoured Division was switched east of that river and against considerable opposition fought its way to the Kusten Canal and south of the Leda.

On the 19th Field Marshal Montgomery issued his final directive to the Canadian Army. Since the US 18th Airborne Corps had been added to 21 Army Group for the advance to the Baltic the Canadian Army was no longer required east of the Weser.(9) Accordingly Crerar's operations would be limited to the area between Emden and Wilhelmshaven and the Frisian Islands. By the same token Monty's own wings had been somewhat clipped. On 6 April he had taken one last crack at enhancing his role in the final push by requesting that Eisenhower allot him ten US Divisions for an advance to Lubeck and Berlin. Eisenhower had finally had enough of his difficult subordinate and crisply replied "...you have the role of protecting Bradley's northern flank (on the latter's main thrust to Leipzig). It is not his role to protect your southern flank. My directive is quite clear on this point."(10) Eisenhower also clamped down on the 9th Army's Simpson who, after crossing the Elbe, asked for permission to drive for Berlin -

a scant 50 unprotected miles to the east. Ike forbade any further eastward advance directing his subordinates north to Lubeck and south to the (non-existent) German National Redoubt in Bavaria.

Back on the Canadian front, Lt Gen Simonds on 22 April sent the Poles eastward towards Moorburg to assist 4 Division around Oldenburg. The Polish role east of the Ems was now given to 3rd Division. 4th Armoured Division was directed north via Mollburg and Varel to the Jade. 2nd Division, in a remarkable 48 hour switch from the left of the line to the right, came up between Oldenburg and Bremen. To fill in the Canadians' extreme right flank at Bremen the British 3rd Division was temporarily added to Crerar's Army but took little part in the final Canadian battles.

With the Poles headed east the task of capturing Leer, at the junction of the Ems and Leda Rivers, fell to Keefler's 3rd Division. Although Leer was comparatively lightly defended by the enemy it was well protected by its twin river barriers. Accordingly Keefler opted to attack the town in a three phase amphibious Operation "Duck" "H" hour was set for 0500 hrs on 28 April with Rockingham's 9th Brigade to lead the charge.

Behind a heavy Typhoon rocket attack and a 35 minute artillery bombardment the North Nova Scotia Highlanders got smartly across the Leda and into Leer. The Highland Light Infantry attacked from the east into the town's centre. Only to the west was there trouble when the Stormont, Dundas and Glengarry Highlanders came under heavy fire while crossing and lost two assault boats and 15 men. They also penetrated into Leer when operations were halted for the night. On the 29th in tough street fighting Rocky's men cleared the town. Their casualties, for what was a very well planned and fought battle, totalled 70 which some might consider light for such a vital operation. Those unfortunate to be one of the 70, and those who fought with them, would certainly think otherwise.

The Final Battles

With the fall of Leer operations in the west of the IInd Corps sector moved rapidly to their denouement. 7 Brigade swiftly cleared the area around Leer with the Canadian Scottish capturing Loga to the east. Keefler now directed 8 Brigade to force the Ems - Jade canal with 7 Brigade to pass through and capture Aurich. 9 Brigade was directed at Emden. On 4 May, as the curtain rang down on the war in 21 Army Group's area, 9 Brigade was five miles from Emden and closing fast while 8 Brigade was negotiating the surrender of Aurich. To the east the divisional 7th Recce Regiment reached the Ems - Jade Canal at its mid-point with the road to Wilhelmshaven virtually clear.

In the centre the Poles plugged on to Astederfeld while 4th Division, reinforced by the Corps' Armoured Car Regiment, two Belgian Regiments and 2nd Armoured Brigade (less two regiments) took Grabstede and Bekhausen just five miles from the elusive Jade. The Argylls of 10 Brigade reached Mollberg as the cease fire kicked in.

Oldenburg and the Weser

On 19 April 2nd Division had been brought in on the left of 2nd Army's 43rd Division to clear the west bank of the Weser in support of XXX Corps assault on Bremen. The division was then directed to advance northwest to capture Oldenburg. On 22 April 6th Brigade moved into Kirchhatten where it ran into stiff resistance from an ad hoc battle

THE NORTHWEST EUROPE CAMPAIGN

group formed from an NCOs School. Strong counter-attacks, directed especially against the Camerons, were beaten back over the next two days.

4th Brigade now took over and in hard fighting captured Kirchhatten and Nuttel and reached the Oldenburg - Delmenhorst road on the 25th as the British fought into adjacent Bremen. On the Corps' right flank 5 Brigade pushed north from Delmenhorst and under constant shelling and machine gun fire captured Hude and kept going. In three days, as the end of the war approached, the Brigade lost 130 men, 54 by the Maisonneuves - hardly the finish the troops were hoping for. On 28 April 4 and 6 Brigades headed for Oldenburg as 5 Brigade pushed to the Weser and northeast. On 3 May 2nd Division entered Oldenburg to find that the enemy had slipped out during the night. The division then slogged into Butjadingerland, the sodden peninsula between Jade and Weser, as at 0800 hrs on 5 May 1945, the war in Northwest Europe ended. While the soldiers involved, and most others, would not agree, in one sense the war ended a day too soon - thereby denying the Army the honour of capturing Wilhelmshaven which would have been the crowning achievement in a long, bloody and victorious campaign. But that is to quibble, what they did accomplish brought honour enough.

Finale

Since March the Germans had been putting out clandestine feelers to end the war in the west. But as Russia was excluded the western Allies rebuffed these unofficial soundings. Then on 30 April the German Fuhrer Adolf Hitler committed suicide to be succeeded by Admiral Donitz and negotiations became real. On 2 May the German forces in Italy surrendered and on 3 May an official delegation representing Field Marshal E. Busch, commanding German forces facing 21 Army Group, arrived at Montgomery's Headquarters in Luneburg Heath. At 1830 hrs on 4 May the German delegation - Admirals von Friedeburg and Wagner, Generals Kinzel and Paule - and Field Marshal Montgomery signed the formal instrument of surrender of "all German forces in Holland, in north-west Germany, including all islands, and in Denmark...." All hostilities would cease at 0830 hrs on 5 May.(11)

General Crerar's first official notification came in a telephone call from Brigadier Belchem of Montgomery's Headquarters at 1255 hrs on 4 May. Belchem asked that the forthcoming attacks not be made on Aurich and Jever but the Canadians could continue with the improvement of positions. At 2035 hrs Crerar heard from the BBC by radio of the official surrender. It was not until 2050 hrs that official word was received from Montgomery's Headquarters. The Germans in south Germany soon followed suit and on 7 May, at Reims, General Jodl surrendered all German forces to General Eisenhower, Supreme Commander AEF, effective 8 May 1945. The instrument was ratified at Russian Headquarters in Berlin on 9 May, the same date that bypassed garrisons in the Channel Islands and Dunkirk surrendered.

From the crossing of the Rhine, if not before, it had been apparent to friend and foe alike that the end of the war was near. But the German soldier, faithful to the end, kept fighting to the last. Indeed the official casualty lists show that the Canadians suffered 60 casualties (20 fatal) on 4 May and 10 (3 fatal) on 5 May.(12) While it is awful to die or be maimed any time there is something particularly appalling in being killed or wounded on the war's last day. May they rest in peace.

The end of the war was greeted with relief rather than celebration by the battle weary

Canadians. On 9 May General Crerar sent a message to his command "From Sicily to the River Senio, from the beaches of Dieppe to those of Normandy and from thence through northern France, Belgium, Holland and north-west Germany, the Canadians and their Allied comrades in this army have carried out their responsibilities in the high traditions which they inherited....Crushing and complete victory over the German enemy has been secured. In rejoicing...we shall remember the friends who have paid the full price for the belief...that no sacrifice in the interest of the principles for which we fought could be too great."(13)

Messages of congratulations came to the Canadians from many including Field Marshal Montgomery who on 5 May sent the following: "My dear Harry I feel that on this day I must write you a note of personal thanks for all that you have done for me since first we served together in this war. No commander can ever have had a more loyal subordinate than I have had in you. And under your command the Canadian Army has covered itself in glory....I want you to know that I am deeply grateful for what you have done. If ever there is anything I can do for you, or for your magnificent Canadian Soldiers, you know that you have only to ask. Yrs always Monty."(14) It was a well deserved tribute but Monty, ever being Monty, was much later to gratuitously tell a Canadian commodore that Crerar was quite unfit for higher command and that Simonds, Monty's protégé, was the only Canadian worthy of the honour.(15) This typical Monty denigration says more about the Field Marshal's quirky character and unreliable pronouncements than about Crerar's command abilities - for which the record speaks for itself.

Crerar's Canadians, often pitifully few, under strength and given the most terrible assignments had indeed covered themselves in glory. And of course magnificent victory was bought at a frightful cost. From the Rhine crossing on 24 March to final victory on 5 May, just a month and a half, the Canadian Army suffered 6298 casualties. Their losses for the entire eleven month Northwest Europe campaign were 44,339 of whom over 11,000 were fatal. Allied formations, principally British, who served in 1st Canadian Army, suffered a further 23,000 casualties. To paraphrase Kipling, "If blood be the price of [victory] Lord God we have paid in full."(16)

I will close this episode on a personal note. In the small prairie town I came from there was naturally much rejoicing from parents, and other next-of-kin, when the end of the war came and their loved ones had survived. One such family, the Allens, were especially happy as all four of their sons had enlisted and miraculously survived. Or so they thought. Several days after the end of the war came a telegram informing them that their son Kenneth had been killed in action - one of the unfortunate last. Ken had been my public school deskmate for several years. He was one of four boys, out of a dozen or so in my class of '43, all of whom enlisted, to be killed in the war - a classroom fatality rate of over 30%. *Sic Transit Gloria.*

The Northwest Europe Report Card

In eleven months of almost continual action the Canadians had indeed, to use Monty's phrase, covered themselves in glory. From first to last - from D-Day to the Baltic (17) - they had spearheaded some of the most climactic battles of the entire campaign. Landing in the face of some of the heaviest opposition they made the deepest penetration of any Allied division on D-Day and were the first to reach their final D-

THE NORTHWEST EUROPE CAMPAIGN

Day objectives. Their heroic defensive battles around Bretteville thwarted the major enemy attack to cut the bridgehead and reach the coast. Their costly victories at Buron, Cussy, Authie and Abbaye Ardenne led directly to the long-sought capture of Caen. The terrible grinding battles of Operations "Spring", "Totalize" and "Tractable" led to brilliant success at Falaise and the closing of the pocket at St Lambert. The capture of the Channel ports and Scheldt were absolutely vital to the maintenance of all subsequent Allied offensives. The Rhineland battle, in which eight British divisions served under Canadian command, was a triumph of that command and of the valour of the three Canadian divisions involved. So too were the subsequent battles of the Rhine, Holland and Northwest Germany. At war's end it was a Canadian battalion which, with British Armour, made the deepest penetration of any Commonwealth unit, forestalling the Russians at Wismer on the Baltic.

This record is all the more astonishing when considering that out of 90 Allied Divisions on the Continent only five, indeed until the last month only three, were Canadian. It is little appreciated that the Canadians achieved so much with so little - with only one division to the capture of Caen, just two to August then only three until the Rhineland was cleared. Only in the final few weeks, with the arrival of the Ist Corps from Italy, did the full Canadian content of five divisions come into play. Until the final phase the Canadian Army was augmented by Allied formations, usually one Polish division and on occasion French, Belgian, Netherlands and once even an American division. But it was the magnificent British divisions which provided most of the augmentation. Ist British Corps fought continuously under Canadian command from the formation of 1st Canadian Army to victory in the Rhineland. In the Rhineland Campaign Horrock's XXX Corps provided most of the divisions involved. And one British Division - the 49th West Riding - was a proud part of Canada's Army to the very end. But despite these superb Allied contributions the few Canadian divisions played a leading, often spearhead, role in each of the Army's battles.

During its operations the Canadian Army met and defeated 60 enemy divisions and was consistently and deliberately opposed by many of the finest formations in the German Army - a true tribute indeed. Against die-hard opposition the Army still took 192,000 prisoners while losing only 2200 themselves - an incredible statistic. But the last word will go to General Eisenhower. In his final report on the campaign the Supreme Commander highlighted three episodes as being the most decisive in ensuring victory. These three were the Normandy beaches, the Falaise pocket and the battles west of the Rhine in early 1945. In each of these battles the Canadians played a most important part. Quite a record for a force which numbered at most 4 ½ % of all the combat formations involved in the "crusade in Europe."

GAUDEAMUS IGITUR

CANADIAN PARACHUTE OPERATIONS

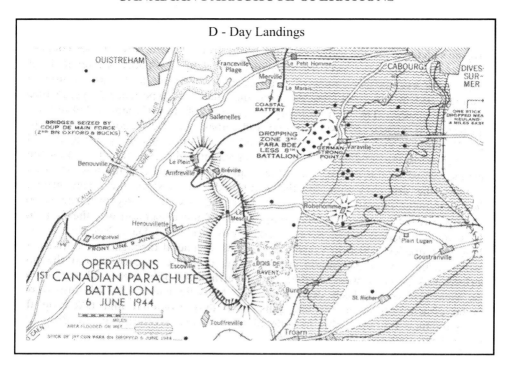

D - Day Landings

PARATROOPS - SPECIAL FORCES and CANLOAN

CHAPTER XIII

FIRST CANADIAN PARACHUTE BATTALION

Give my heroes kind wind and fair weather;
Let no parachute sidle or slump.
For tonight we go warring together
And my soul will be there at the jump.

WAAF   G.D. Martineau   A Parachute Packer at Ringway   1944

Backdrop

In June 1940 at the height of Britain's darkest hour - France fallen, the Dunkirk army saved but toothless, air raids mounting and a German invasion expected - Prime Minister Winston Churchill issued yet another of his endless stream of memoranda. This one had nothing to do with any of the above crises. Instead it called for the establishment of a corps of parachutists. Churchill, with his blotting paper mind which absorbed but seldom mastered the minutiae of the day, had long been impressed by the pre-war manoeuvres of Russian paratroops and by the wartime exploits of German airborne troops in Holland and especially Eben Emael. He wanted Britain to have some of the same perhaps as a rapid defence force now, perhaps as airborne commandos later.

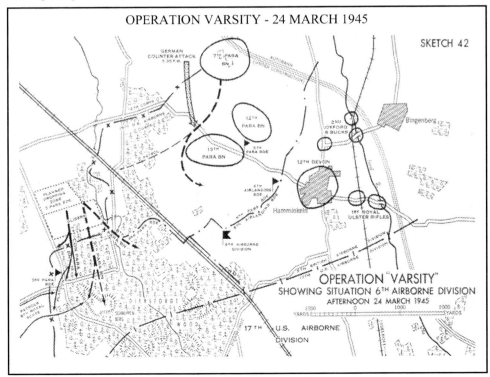

GAUDEAMUS IGITUR

Having pressed the button Churchill turned to other matters. The RAF, taking up the cause, established a parachute training centre, called the "Central Landing School" at Ringway, the airport of Manchester. Staffed jointly by the air force and army the School was allocated six old Whitley bombers and little else. An army major and air force squadron leader were appointed joint commanders. Little by little with volunteer troops and using air force ground officers as the parachute experts the force progressed. The experts wanted to use Bristol Bombays with side doors as the jump aircraft but were overruled and forced to use the unsuitable Whitleys with their hole-in-the-floor exits. Initial training jumps were made from baskets suspended below tethered blimps which were cold, windy, bumpy and airsickness inducing. And since they lacked a slipstream the jump started with a terrifying 150 foot vertical gravity drop before the parachute canopy opened.

After many alarms and excursions and the boredom of endless waiting the paratroops mounted their first operation in February 1941 against a water aqueduct in Apulia, southern Italy with the Whitleys flying from Malta.(1) Extraction of the small 40 man force was to be by submarine. The drop went surprisingly well with only minor glitches and the aqueduct was blown. Then everything went wrong with the operation degenerating into something of a harlequinade and the force was captured. But it was a start and a reasonably good one.

In November 1941 the parachute arm gained status with the appointment of Maj Gen F. Browning as GOC Airborne Forces. They were to never look back as increasingly successful or strategically important operations against Bruneval, Tunisia, Cos/Samos, Sicily, Taranto, South France, Normandy, Arnhem, the Ardennes, the Rhine, Wismer and Greece followed in growing strength and success throughout the war. In several of these operations formed bodies of Canadian paratroops were to play a full role.

The First Canadian Parachute Battalion

In 1941 with things going from bad to worse for the Allies worldwide the possibility of enemy, especially Japanese, forces landing in North America could not be ruled out. Indeed in June 1942 the Japanese occupied Attu and Kiska in the US Aleutians and, Midway apart, appeared virtually unstoppable. Canadian authorities had already taken steps to protect both coasts with substantial numbers of troops and air bases. Then on 1 July 1942 a further step was taken with approval for the formation of a Canadian parachute battalion. Its original duties were conceived as home defence for the recapture of airfields and reinforcements for remote areas.

The battalion was raised during the late summer of 1942 and included some 85 officers and men who had already qualified as paratroops in the UK. Since Canada as yet had no parachute training facilities the unit was sent to the US School at Fort Benning GA for this purpose. The US period featured extensive physical training, parachute ground school, jumps from the Mock Tower, High Tower (a version of the Coney Island attraction) and finally side door parachuting from C-47 Dakota aircraft.

As 1942 drew to a close and the threat of an invasion of Canada receded to near zero the original role for the Parachute Battalion, which had now completed its training in the US, also largely evaporated. But by good fortune the British at that time were in the process of raising a second airborne formation, the 6th Airborne Division under Maj Gen R.N. Gale, and the Canadian Parachute Battalion, under Lt Col G.F. Bradbrooke, was offered and accepted into this formation.(2) The battalion arrived in Britain on 28 July 1943 and moved to Salisbury Plain where it became a unit of the 3rd Parachute Brigade under Brigadier S.J. Hill. It was a marvellous, symbiotic union with the gifted Hill proving again and again that he was the ideal fighting commander to lead the high spirited Canadians.(3)

Hill's 3rd Parachute Brigade consisted of the 1st Canadians, the 8th (Midland) and the 9th (Home Counties) Battalions. The rest of the infantry component of the division comprised the 5th Parachute Brigade of the 7th (Light Infantry), 12th (Yorkshire) and 13th (Lancashire) Battalions and the 6th Air Landing (Glider) Brigade of the 2nd Oxfordshire and Buckinghamshire Light Infantry (Ox and Bucks), 1st Royal Ulster Rifles and 12th Devons. There was also the 22nd Independent Parachute Company.

On arrival in the UK the Canadians underwent further training to bring the unit in line with British practices. All ranks re-qualified as jumpers at Ringway and took specialist and junior leader training with emphasis on marksmanship. The RAF units assigned to airborne duties also required extensive training and practice. Two RAF wings, numbers 38 and 46, comprising 15 squadrons and 425 aircraft - Stirlings, Halifaxes, Albermarles and Dakotas - were allocated to the task. All aircraft were fitted with a special short range radio, Rebecca II, to home in on Eureka Beacons which were to be used by pathfinders to mark the drop zones. The training period culminated on 24 April with a three division Exercise "Mush" which was the dress rehearsal for their forthcoming role in the invasion.

The Airborne Plan For D-Day

In the original concept it was proposed that an airborne division be dropped on Caen just ahead of the sea borne landings. Given the vulnerability of lightly armed airborne troops against armour that idea was dropped. Under the revised plan three airborne divisions - two US and one British - would be dropped just prior to the landings to secure the flanks of the invasion force. The US 82nd and 101st Divisions would drop on the Cotentin Peninsula and secure the right flank behind the American beaches. 6th Airborne Division was to secure the left flank northeast of Caen and seize the high ground and key bridges and junctions in the area Benouville - Varaville - Troarn.

6th Division's detailed plan called for pathfinders from each battalion and the independent company to drop at 0020 hrs on 6 June and mark the three drop zones of K (Cuverville), N (Ranville) and V (Varaville) while a *coup-de-main* glider force of the Ox and Bucks seized two key bridges over the Orne and the Canal de Caen. Thirty-five minutes later, at 0055 hrs the two parachute brigades would drop to secure the dropping zones and other key locations. The Air Landing Brigade, less the *coup-de-main* party and one battalion which was to arrive by sea, would land in the afternoon. The commandos of Lord Lovat's 1st Special Service Force were to land by sea and link-up with the paratroops on D-Day.

Maj Gen Gale gave 5 Brigade plus the *coup-de-main* gliders the task of capturing the bridges at Benouville and linking up with 3rd British Division, the left-hand formation of the Allied sea assault force. This link-up mission was to have unforeseen and most unfortunate consequences on 3rd Canadian Division's forthcoming advance on Carpiquet. As previously noted, concern over the airborne link-up caused Lt Gen Crocker to switch the right hand brigade of the British 3rd Division to the left flank adjacent to 6th Airborne thus resulting in a gap between the British and Canadian 3rd Divisions. The failure of 3rd British Division to secure this gap played a major role in the destruction of 9 Canadian Brigade's D+1 advance on Carpiquet.

3rd Parachute Brigade to which the Canadians belonged had a somewhat more roving mission than had the 5th. Its tasks were to destroy a coastal battery at Merville and bridges over the Dives and Divette Rivers and secure the Sallenelles - Troarn ridge. Within the Brigade plan the Canadian Battalion had several missions. "C" Company, selected for the pathfinder role, was to mark and secure the Canadian Drop Zone V and destroy a bridge at Varaville on the Divette. "B" Company and a section of engineers would destroy the bridge at Robehomme on the Dives. "A" Company was to protect 9 Battalion's assault on the Merville Battery. Once these missions were accomplished the battalion would occupy an area around Le Mesnil crossroads (4) on the right flank of the Brigade sector.

The 1st Canadians in Action

At 2300 hrs on 5 June the main body of the 1st Canadian Parachute Battalion took off from Down Ampney in 29 Dakotas, three of which towed gliders with jeeps and heavier equipment. Their destination was Drop Zone V in Normandy in the area defended by the 711th German Infantry Division. Due to a series of mishaps, which are an unfortunate ingredient of every war, the Canadian pathfinders of "C" Company, who had earlier dropped from Albermarles, lost most of their Eureka marking equipment in the swampy ground. The problem was compounded by dark foggy conditions which prevented the visual identification of landmarks and by some pilots, in trying to avoid AA fire, mistaking the Orne River for the Dives. As a result the Canadians, who dropped between 0100 and 0130 hrs on 6 June, were scattered over an area ten times larger than planned with two sticks dropped four miles off target. Due to this resulting wide dispersion within and between sticks and their separation from one another by woods and marshes some 85 Canadians were unable to link up and were taken prisoner. The battalion also lost most of its mortars and MMGs which, lowered beneath the jumpers on ropes, disappeared into the marsh. The lightly armed crews, bereft of their principal weapons, were formed into an ad hoc mobile reserve.

Despite these misadventures the Canadians took all their objectives. "C" Company, after attempting to mark their landing zone, destroyed a bridge over the Divette and attacked a heavily defended strong point west of Varaville. Assisted by elements of 3rd Brigade HQ and the 3rd Parachute Squadron RE the under strength Canadians fought a bitter battle for the strong point. It was finally taken at 1030 hrs along with 42 prisoners and heavy casualties to both sides. The company, under heavy artillery and mortar fire, held Varaville until relieved by Lovat's commandos that afternoon. It then withdrew to the pre-planned battalion defensive area at Le Mesnil. Three Canadians were decorated for this action - two MMs and one MC.

"A" Company suffered the worst dispersion on dropping and by 0630 hrs only 22 all ranks had managed to make it to the company RV. As a result by the time they arrived to cover 9 Battalion's attack on the Merville Battery the Home Counties battalion had successfully completed the job. Both groups then moved to their pre-arranged defensive positions. "B" Company was also badly dispersed but managed to collect 35 of their own troops and 25 from assorted other units in time to successfully blow the bridge at

Robehomme. That this was done despite the absence of the engineers responsible, and after having to scramble about to locate explosives from various sources, speaks volumes for the training, adaptability and initiative of the parachutists in action. "B" Company held the high ground around Robehomme against numerous enemy probes and collected a further 90 friendly parachutists from various units who dribbled in during the day. On D+1 the company, of which over two-thirds of its number belonged to other units, fought its way back to the battalion area near Le Mesnil.

By this time 3rd British Division had made firm contact with the 6th Airborne and opened land supply lines from the beaches. Three commandos, three glider battalions and the light tanks of the Division's Recce Regiment arrived to augment Gale's formation which now had more infantry than a standard division but was weak in armour, artillery and heavy support weapons.

The Defensive Battle East of the Orne

Supported by naval gunfire and 3rd Division's artillery the troops of 6th Airborne fought a number of spirited actions in holding the left of the Allied line from east of the Orne. On 8 June the German 346th Division, spearheaded by two Panzer Grenadier battalions, mounted a series of attacks on the 1st Special Service and 3rd Parachute Brigades with the Canadian Battalion in the forefront. The Canadians had by now collected four of their mortars and these, taking a leaf from the German book, bombarded likely enemy forming-up places and inflicted considerable casualties. Supported by medium tanks and SP guns the Germans attacked "B" and "C" Companies .and were bloodily repulsed. One enemy tank succeeded in penetrating the battalion perimeter before being driven off by PIAT fire. Under Captain R.R. Griffin "B" Company counter-attacked and drove the enemy out of his forward positions and hung on there against severe opposition. Griffin won the MC and four other Canadians won MMs for this action

On June 10th the enemy mounted a heavy attack on the 9th Parachute Battalion at Le Plein and the salient between the 9th and the Canadians. It was beaten back with heavy casualties to the enemy. On the 11th the 153rd Brigade of the Highland Division arrived to help defend the Airborne Division's bridgehead and promptly learned just how rugged things were in that area. The 5th Black Watch was sent to 3rd Airborne Brigade to plug the gap at Breville between the 9th Paras and 1st Commando. They attacked Breville on the 11th and again on the 12th and were bloodily repulsed each time. On the second occasion, on 12 June, the enemy violently counter-attacked and after driving back the Scots attacked the 9th Paras. The situation for the Home Counties battalion was exceedingly grim when the Brigade Commander James Hill arrived on the scene personally leading "C" Company of the 1st Canadians in a wild attack. The Canadians succeeded in driving back the enemy, retaking much of the overrun terrain and stabilizing the situation - just in time. This spirited action enhanced the reputation of both Hill and his Canadians and further strengthened the bond between the two.

Skilfully analysing the situation, Maj Gen Gale made his riposte. Appreciating that the enemy 346th Division having been continually in action for 6 days, suffered considerable casualties and had just committed to the attack, Gale believed they would not be adequately prepared to face a rapid Allied counter. Determined to strike while the iron was hot he called on his last reserve the under strength 12th Paras, together with a company of Devons, a squadron of 13/18 Hussars tanks, backed by five artillery regiments and attacked Breville at 2200 hrs that night, June 12th. In ferocious fighting in which the 12th and Devons lost 175 men Breville was captured, the gap closed and the Airborne bridgehead secured.

The arrival of the rest of the Highland Division on the Airborne's flank enabled Gale to rotate his tired Brigades in relief. During this time the 1st Canadians received 100 non-parachutist infantry reinforcements. The Canadian battalion then engaged in the normal harrowing defensive actions of digging, wiring, patrolling and night alarms and excursions while their brethren of the 1st Canadian Army battered their grim and bloody way down the road to Falaise. As the noose tightened on the Falaise gap the Airborne Division prepared to return to a war of movement on the flank of the Canadian Army as it moved northward.

The Advance to the Seine

On 17 August with the fall of Falaise to the Canadian Army and the start of the battle of the Falaise Gap, Lt Gen Crocker's Ist British Corps of the 6th Airborne, 49th and 51st Divisions began its advance to the Seine. For this operation 6th Airborne was reinforced by the 1st and 4th Special Services Brigades plus Belgian and Dutch units. It was a most formidable infantry force but was woefully deficient in transport and supporting arms. However the chief problem facing Maj Gen Gale was the marshy terrain and the three intervening rivers before the Seine - the Dives, the Touques and the Risle.

While the Glider Brigade, Belgians and Netherlanders cleared the enemy from along the coast the two parachute brigades and the commandos advanced along the axis Troarn - Pont l' Eveque - Pont Audemer. By the evening of 17 August the Canadian parachutists had cleared the Bois de Bavent and bumped the enemy at Plain Lugan. Brig Hill now ordered them to capture four bridges over the Dives east of Goustranville. They attacked at 2200 hrs on 18 August and by midnight had overrun two strong points and captured their objectives and 150 prisoners. Captain John Clancy and Sgt W. Green of "A" Company won the MC and MM respectively for this action.

The Division continued its advance for another week. Then on 30 August, when reaching the mouth of the Seine, it was withdrawn first into Army Reserve and then returned to England to prepare for further airborne tasks. During their three months of action the 1st Canadian Parachute Battalion had performed most effectively but at a high cost. The battalion with a posted strength of under 450 had suffered 357 casualties. Over half of these - 235 - were lost in the first two weeks when the fate of the airborne bridgehead still hung in the balance. It is also significant that of 87 men taken prisoner 85 were lost as a direct result of individuals being dropped widely dispersed on D-Day and were picked off singly while trying to rejoin their unit. Thereafter over 2 and ½ months, despite fighting a series of very tough offensive and defensive battles, mounting endless patrols and advancing from Orne to Seine they lost only two more prisoners. This raw statistic speaks volumes for the valour, determination and endurance of Canada's proud paras.

The Ardennes

After returning to England on 7 September the 6th Airborne Division embarked on a

PARATROOPS - SPECIAL FORCES and CANLOAN

strenuous training program preparatory to its return to action featuring street fighting and a practice drop over the Thames which simulated the Rhine. On 16 December Field Marshal Montgomery issued a pre-Christmas directive to his command in which he confidently and boldly proclaimed that the enemy could no longer "stage major offensive operations."(5) The Field Marshal, as was his want, then ticked off his reasons to prove that the Germans could not mount an armoured offensive. For neither the first nor last time the arrogant Monty was wrong as on that very day the Germans launched a massive armoured attack in the Ardennes. Two German Panzer Armies - the Fifth and Sixth - caught the Allies napping with a sudden lunge aimed at cutting the Allied armies in half and capturing Antwerp. By 24 December they had inflicted 80,000 casualties, including 8000 prisoners, on the US 1st Army before being blocked by determined American resistance at Elsenborn Ridge and Bastogne. By then the mighty German drive had run short of petrol and lost its steam, but not before forcing the Allies to make hasty counter moves including ordering up the 6th Airborne Division from England. This time the Division came as ordinary infantry by ship, rail and truck rather than by air.

The 1st Canadian Parachute Battalion embarked on 24 December for Belgium. They were to spend a dreary Christmas and a further ten days in the town of Rumes before moving to the front near Rochefort on 5 January 1945. Advance elements of the division including 5 Brigade had actually reached the front on New Years Day. By then the German advance had been halted by US forces and the Canadians were not heavily engaged being principally involved in endless patrolling in the bitter cold winter. The adjacent 5th Brigade was not so lucky being required to attack the villages of Bure and Wavreille resulting in a violent three day battle. Although ultimately successful the 7th and 13th Parachute Battalions suffered 190 casualties. Thereafter in cold and drifting snow the division remained in an aggressive defensive posture until being relocated at the end of January to an area along the Maas between Venlo and Roermond in Holland.

The Canadian battalion, along with the rest of the division, spent their time defending and patrolling along the Maas. There were several patrol clashes resulting in casualties to both sides but in the main the Canucks suffered more casualties from accidents and weather than from battle. After two cold and miserable months in the Ardennes and along the Maas, while great battles raged in the Rhineland, the division returned to England on 25 February 1945 to prepare for their next great challenge - the over-the-Rhine drop. In anticipation of this operation the division left much of its transport in Belgium, to be brought forward when needed.

Operation "Varsity" - 24 March 1945

On the night of 23 March 1945 Montgomery's 21 Army Group, now spearheaded by Dempsey's 2nd British Army, crossed the Rhine near Wesel in a massive assault code named "Plunder". The assault which was led by the 51st Highland and 15th Scottish Divisions and 1st Commando Brigade, with Canada's 9th Brigade under the 51st Division, was everywhere successful.

At 1000 hrs on 24 March the airborne half of the operation, code named "Varsity" began with the drop of two airborne divisions - the 17th US and 6th British - over the Rhine. The airborne operation was under 18th US Airborne Corps commanded by US Lt Gen M. Ridgeway. Maj Gen Gale had left 6th Airborne to become Deputy Commander of 1st Allied Airborne Army (never operationally employed as such). His successor at the 6th Airborne was Maj Gen E. Bols. Lt Col J.S. Nicklin, a former star lineman with the Winnipeg Blue Bombers, was the new commander of the Canadian Parachute Battalion. The role of 18th Airborne Corps was to drop on important high ground east of the Rhine, disrupt the enemy's defence of Wesel and assist the advance of Dempsey's ground troops as they attacked eastward from the Rhine.

The tactics of the Airborne Army had come a long way since Normandy. The D-Day drop had been marred by a number of factors. For starters it had been a night drop in advance of the sea landings which, coupled with inappropriate tactical loadings and groupings and insufficiently trained aircrew, resulted in large troop dispersions, intermingling of units and sub-units and enemy reactions not bothered by a ground advance. The Arnhem drop was also flawed but for different reasons. Not the least of these was an attempt to drop too far from the objective and group at a distance before moving on. "Varsity" corrected these errors in several ways. First, it was a daylight operation which permitted close formation flying and visual identification of landmarks resulting in the dropping of troops in tight groupings. This of course pre-supposed total control of the air, which at that stage of the war the Allies certainly had. Secondly, the drop followed, rather than preceded, the land forces' water crossing which permitted the paras to give full rein to their forte of causing confusion and obstruction in rear of the land battle. Finally the troops were dropped in tight tactical groupings on or near to their objectives instead of trying to form up miles away as at Arnhem.

Maj Gen Boles planned on maximising the airborne advantage of speed and surprise by dropping the entire division close together in two small areas within the space of ten minutes. In this he was greatly aided by having the American 9th Troop Carrier Command who were adept at flying in tight formation. The American Dakotas flew in three lanes with aircraft in four sections of three planes in closely following "V"s. For their part the paras optimised the tactic by allotting companies to lanes instead of to consecutive aircraft as heretofore. Thus units and sub-units would drop close together without the confusing intermingling of Normandy and Arnhem.

The drop was preceded by days of aerial and ground bombardment on clearly defined areas. But again, as with the D-Day landings, the results of this massive expenditure of firepower were disappointing with key enemy batteries north and east of the dropping zone left relatively unscathed.

The Airborne Operation

18th Airborne Corps concentrated its drop in a tight five by three mile grouping within three to five miles of the Rhine between Xanten and Wesel The US 17th Airborne Division was allotted the southern sector nearest the Rhine with 6th British Airborne Division's area adjacent to the north. 6th Airborne was allocated five dropping zones west of the Issel River between Bingenberg and Schneppenberg. 3rd Parachute Brigade under the redoubtable Hill was to land on the northwest corner of the Diersfordt Wald and secure the Wald and the Schneppenberg feature. 5th Parachute Brigade under Brig Poett was to be dropped northwest of Hamminkeln and secure the main road. The 6th Air Landing Brigade under Brig Bellamy was assigned three glider landing zones around Hamminkeln. They were to eliminate the enemy from that area and capture bridges over the Issel. Division Headquarters and the Light Airborne Regiment RA were assigned a zone in the centre of the divisional area

The division, in 1500 aircraft and 1330 gliders, took off from England at 0700 hrs on 24 March in perfect weather but on arriving over their objective three hours later found it covered in a thick haze from the ground bombardment and the burning town of Wesel. 3rd Parachute Brigade, including the Canadians, arrived nine minutes early causing a premature halt to the covering artillery bombardment. The paratroops were met by heavy fire from light anti-aircraft guns and small arms from the woods. Although the drop was comparatively accurate a number of jumpers, inevitably, came down in trees on the edge of the woods where they were hung up and became easy targets for the German defenders. Lt Col Jeff Nicklin, the Canadians' CO, was one of these unlucky soldiers who were shot dead as they dangled helpless from their chutes. Ironically Nicklin barely escaped a similar fate in Normandy, as a company commander, when his chute caught on the edge of a building where he hung until rescued. The odds of this happening twice in a row are vanishingly small but long odds seem to pay off more frequently in bad situations than in good. The ex-footballer Nicklin was the prototypical swashbuckling paratrooper and loss of his ilk, as with USMA's great end John Trent in Korea, are especially poignant.

Within the hour 8th Parachute Battalion secured the dropping zone against heavy opposition. 9th Battalion and the Canadians then attacked the Schneppenberg feature and captured it along with all of their other objectives by early afternoon. In so doing they killed or captured hundreds of the enemy. By 1500 hrs they made contact with patrols of the 8th Royal Scots of the 15th Division, thus achieving the first link-up with the advancing 2nd Army.

The Canadians, along with their British comrades of the 8th and 9th Paras, had performed beautifully and taken all their objectives ahead of schedule But it had been a tough fight in which they suffered 65 casualties including 23 killed. The Brigade as a whole lost 270 men mostly by the unfortunate 8th Battalion. The Division sustained a whopping total of 1078 casualties, 350 fatal. But, as in Normandy, they had been spectacularly successful. And for this they were to be rewarded by being placed in the vanguard of 2nd Army's advance to the Baltic.

One of the heroes of the day was Corporal F.G. Topham, a medical orderly of the 1st Canadians. Over a period of six hours, although himself painfully wounded, he continually risked his life by again and again rescuing wounded jumpers under fire. For this he was awarded the Victoria Cross - the last to be won by a Canadian in Northwest Europe.

The Race to the Baltic

On 27 March 1945 6th Airborne Division came under command of VIIIth British Corps as the vanguard of 21 Army Group's advance to the Baltic. The division was assigned a general axis of Erle, Lembeck, Osnabruck, Hannover, Celle, Luneburg, Wismar. The start of the long 300 mile march to the Baltic coincided with the final phase of Operation "Varsity" when 5 Brigade, after a tough battle, took Erle. For the advance the division was supported by the Churchill tanks of the 4th Grenadier Guards (6th Guards Tank Brigade), two regiments of field and one of medium artillery, SP anti-tank guns and three RASC transport platoons.

On this date also 3rd Brigade took Lembeck in a savage battle with a Panzer Grenadier training battalion. The assault was led by the 8th and 9th Parachute battalions with the Canadians, now under Lt Col G.F. Eadie, in the follow-up and mop-up role. Over 300 prisoners were taken in this well executed operation. Mounted on the backs of the Grenadier's tanks the Canadians took over the lead and headed for a bridge over the Ems at Greven. At 2130 hrs the Canadians dismounted three miles from Greven and advanced rapidly on foot to the town. Two violent explosions followed in the darkness which led the rest of the brigade to fear the worst for the Canadians. But at 2300 hrs the Canadians reported that the bridge was captured intact. When 9 Battalion came up in support they found the town strewn with dead Germans killed by the Canadians. They also found that the Canucks, in the darkness, had captured the wrong bridge over a dry wadi with the Ems bridge further on. This was blown in their faces but by 0730 hrs the next day a crossing was effected. On 1 April the Canadian battalion crossed the Dortmund - Ems canal and took Ladbergen after a stiff fight. The pace of advance was such that the 70 miles from Greven to Minden (site of a major British victory in the Seven Years War)(6) was covered in 36 hours with numerous skirmishes en route.

5 Brigade then took the van and crossed the Weser, capturing the important airfield at Wunsdorf after another hard fight. On 7 April they captured the important bridges at Bordenau and Neustadt. Unhappily the latter bridge was skilfully blown as they crossed killing 22 paratroopers of 12 Battalion and wounding many more.

On 9 April the Canadians, once more in the vanguard, were called upon to go to the rescue of a troop of the division's 6th Airborne Armoured Recce Regiment which was holding a bridge at Ricklingen north of Hannover. This action was well described by their Brigade Commander Brig Hill, "Having marched 20 mi over very bad rds the day before, they [the 1st Cdn Paras] marched a further 14...and were then called on to put in an aslt on a small village. This they successfully did. Meanwhile an SOS had been sent out for them to try and rescue a small recce det which was holding an important br just to the south (sic) of Hannover. In order to do this the leading company of the battalion doubled pretty well non-stop for two miles with full equipment and stormed the bridge over an extremely open piece of ground under fire from three or four S.P. Guns without turning a hair. They got the bridge intact but the Reconnaissance Regiment had been unable to hold out."(7)

Brig Hill was not the only one impressed by this action. In the history of the "6th Guards Tank Brigade" the author at page 157 reports admiringly on a Canadian Sergeant's orders to his section as, "I guess we gotta get this bridge and if we hit anything, don't you guys sit around. Let's go."(8) They did and the Germans fled. Such off-the-cuff orders would never rate a "pass" at Staff College but they epitomized the "Git there fustest with the mostest" drive of the Canadians in the best mode of Confederate general Nathan Bedford Forrest.(9) And they invariably worked.

The advance resumed. On the 14th the paratroops took the beautiful, and comparatively intact, medieval town of Celle. On 17 April they cleared Riestedt near Uelzen where the KOSBs of 15th Division had such a difficult street fight. The 21st found them at Kolkhagen. On the 29th the Scottish Division secured a bridgehead over the Elbe near Lauenberg below Hamburg through which the 6th Airborne passed to resume the vanguard. On the 1st of May 6th Airborne Division again came under command of the XVIIIth US Airborne Corps. The British division was now given the mission of reaching the Baltic with all speed to forestall the Russians, who were advancing in the opposite direction, from moving on the Danish peninsula. In contrast to the bitter battles being waged by the Canadian Army west of the Weser, The British 2nd Army now advanced unopposed. The Germans here realized it would be better to be taken by the Western Allies than the Russians.

Accordingly on 2 May the Canadians, now supported by, and riding on, the Shermans of "C" Squadron the Royal Scots Greys, set off at top speed in "the Grey's longest charge." They reached Wittenburg in the morning and refuelled at Lutzow. All resistance collapsed and as the Germans surrendered in droves they were merely pointed to the rear and sent on. On the evening of May 2nd the Canadians, careening along on the rocking backs of the Grey's racing tanks, reached Wismer on the Baltic. They arrived just hours ahead of the Russians who, appearing that night, were chagrined to discover that they were stopped by a Canadian manned barrier. Wismer was the most easterly point reached by any Commonwealth troops in the theatre and the place where 21 Army Group first made contact with the Red Army. The 1st Canadian Parachute Battalion and the gallant Scots Greys could be well satisfied that they were the ones who did it.

Epilogue

It is difficult to separate the achievements of the 1st Canadian Parachute Battalion from those of the entire 6th Airborne Division and especially from its sibling battalions of the 3rd Parachute Brigade. So while acknowledging that most objectives were attained in company with their British brethren there are some specifics which merit recounting.

Note has been made of the fact that the 6th Airborne Division was the first Allied formation to attain all of its D-Day objectives, a proud distinction in which the Canadian battalion fully shared. Of the Canadians' own four D-Day objectives they achieved the main three with flying colours. The only one in which they fell somewhat short - covering the 9th Battalion's attack on the Merville battery - was due to the excessive dispersal in dropping of the company responsible and British speed in taking the battery before the Canadians could assemble.

An airborne division is deficient in many of the requirements of defence, especially tanks, artillery and heavy weapons. Despite this the 6th Airborne held and gradually widened its Orne bridgehead from D-Day to the August break-out. In this staunch defence the Canadian battalion was instrumental in defeating two heavy enemy attacks. And, led personally by their English brigadier, they mounted a brilliant counter-attack which blunted a critically dangerous German drive.

With the closing of the Falaise Gap in mid-August the Airborne Division played its full part in Ist Corps' advance to the Seine despite their lack of tanks, transport and heavy support. In this advance the Canadians routed a strong enemy force, cleared the Bois de Bavent and Plain Lugan and captured key bridges over the Dives.

6th Airborne Division's role in defending against the German Ardennes offensive was limited as was the Canadian part. Nevertheless the parachute battalion was the only Canadian unit to participate in that famous battle and performed well under terrible conditions of climate and terrain.(10)

In its drop over the Rhine in support of 21 Army Group's water crossing the Airborne Division profited from a number of tactical improvements to its D-Day operation. Landing by day after the water crossing had begun the division and its Canadians landed in tight sub-units and quickly achieved all of their objectives although at considerable cost. In this operation the Canadians won their last VC of the European war.

GAUDEAMUS IGITUR

Partly in recognition of its excellent performance on the Rhine the Airborne Division was placed in the vanguard of 21 Army Group's race to the Baltic. And once more the Canadian battalion participated with distinction. In a wild hayride of nearly 300 miles the Canadian paras fought several stiff battles and secured a number of key locations en route. The piece-de-resistance came on the last dash when the Canadians, riding on the backs of Royal Scots Greys' tanks, reached Wismer on the Baltic forestalling by just a few hours a Russian advance to the Danish peninsula. The war ended with the Canadians and Greys as the most advanced troops in all of 21 Army Group.

They had fought a magnificent fight in six separate scenarios. From Normandy to the Baltic the 1st Canadian Parachute Battalion had attained many significant victories but at a high cost. From a war establishment of under 450 they suffered 496 casualties, 125 fatal. Their valour and the admiration of their comrades and country had been bought in blood. But they had done themselves and their country proud indeed.

1st SPECIAL SERVICE FORCE ITALY 1943 - 1944

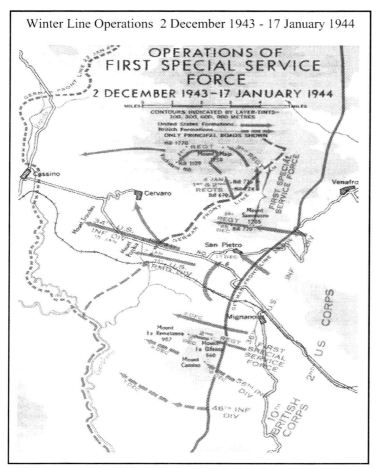

PARATROOPS - SPECIAL FORCES and CANLOAN

CHAPTER XIV

THE FIRST SPECIAL SERVICE FORCE

We few, we happy few, we band of brothers;

Shakespeare, *King Henry V*

Background

The First Special Service Force grew from a most unlikely source - the fertile mind of a rather odd Englishman, the psychologist Geoffrey Pyke. Pyke sought fruition for his theory of an over snow vehicle that could swan about the glaciers of Norway, Italy and the Carpathians manned by a few skilled soldiers wreaking havoc on key installations as German ski troops floundered after them. Pyke's somewhat off-the-wall ideas eventually received the sympathetic hearing, if not backing, of Prime Minister Winston Churchill and his head of Combined Operations Lord Louis Mountbatten - both of whom shared a predilection with weird ideas for conducting operations in secondary theatres by unconventional means. Since the development of such a vehicle was, at that time, beyond British resources Mountbatten turned to US General George C. Marshall for help.

Marshall accepted the idea in April 1942 and directed the design and production of such a vehicle and the assembly and training of a small group of men to utilize it.(1) The twin tasks were assigned to Lt Col Robert T. Frederick, a coast artillery officer on the staff of US Army Headquarters. Frederick set about the task with boundless energy. He assigned the vehicle design to the Studebaker automobile company(2) and activated an old National Guard facility, Fort William Henry Harrison in Montana, as the base where the troops would be assembled and trained for their special mission. For want of a better title Frederick named the new unit "The First Special Service Force" (1 SSF). Their wartime deeds were to earn them the sobriquets of "The Devil's Brigade" or "The Black Devils". Lord Mountbatten, with Churchill's blessing, proposed that Canadian troops be added to the force. After consultations all around Canada agreed to participate.

Since the force was designed for a special semi-commando type of operation Frederick tailored its organization accordingly. The force with Frederick as the commander comprised three regiments each commanded by a colonel. Each regiment had two battalions under lieutenant-colonels each of three companies of three platoons of two sections. Regimental strength was originally 32 officers and 385 men, later increased to 575 all ranks. The original intention was that American and Canadian personnel strengths would be about the same. But when the force size was suddenly increased the Canadian quota remained, pegged by Ottawa. Thus the personnel ratio came to be about 65% American to 35% Canadian.

GAUDEAMUS IGITUR

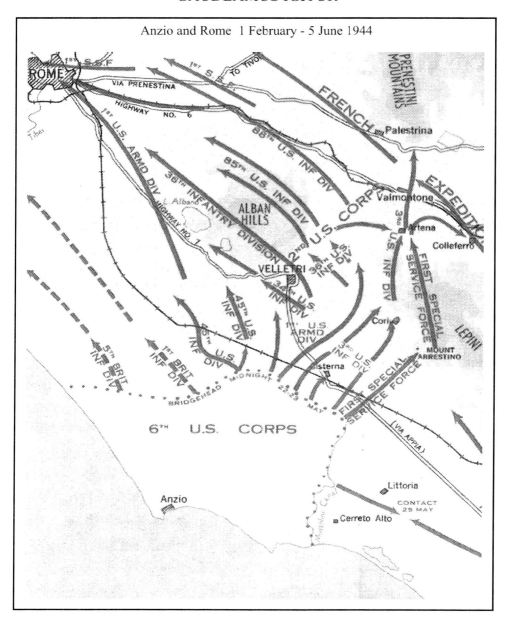

Anzio and Rome 1 February - 5 June 1944

Canadian Participation

On 26 June 1942 the Canadian Prime Minister Mackenzie King approved Canadian participation.(3) Acting with wartime haste, National Defence Headquarters on 14 July authorized the posting of 47 officers and 650 other ranks to the new unit. The Canadians were originally entitled the 2nd Canadian Parachute Battalion, a name changed in

PARATROOPS - SPECIAL FORCES and CANLOAN

May 1943 to the 1st Canadian Special Service Battalion. Lt Col J.G. McQueen was appointed Canadian commander and was originally the Force Executive Officer (XO). McQeen broke his leg in a parachute training jump and was invalided out. He was replaced as force XO by an American.

Other officers came from a variety of sources with many of the other ranks selected from volunteers for parachute training. Canadians and Americans were distributed without distinction throughout the Force. The Force dressed in American uniforms with crossed arrows as their badge. Their shoulder patch was a red arrowhead with a horizontal "USA" over a vertical "CANADA".

Force Mission

From the outset it had been envisaged that the Force, using their special over-snow vehicles, would operate as semi-commandos attacking vital installations in the enemy's rear. The hydro-electric systems of Romania, Italy and Norway were favoured objectives since all were fed from high mountain dams with the water carried to generators via long and vulnerable penstocks. Special explosives were developed for this task which were to prove their worth in many other theatres. The mission resulted in the force being trained as paratroopers, demolition experts, skiers, mountaineers and commandos. A high level of individual skill, fitness, endurance and initiative was demanded.

Colonel Frederick long favoured Norway as the theatre of operations for a number of reasons: clearly definable and vulnerable objectives; a friendly populace; terrain which favoured Force tactics; and better prospects of getting troops in and out. In the end it was rejected because serious damage to the hydro-electrical system would likely cause far more harm to the civilian population than to the enemy. With the ice-field mission scrapped so too went the Force's requirement for an over-snow vehicle. Ironically it was solely for the employment of such a vehicle that the Special Service Force was raised in the first place.

With the Force's *raison d'etre* now rejected Col Frederick cast about for new tasks. In the course of this quest his command moved to the eastern states and practiced sea borne operations in Virginia and special operations in Vermont. While at Fort Ethan Allen in Vermont the Force was suddenly warned for active service and boarded troop trains for embarkation ports. Everyone below field officer rank assumed they were headed east for Europe. They were nonplussed when at Albany the trains turned west. At midnight on 3 July 1943 they debarked at San Francisco's Angel Island.

Kiska

Japan had initiated the Pacific War on 7 December 1941 with a brilliant surprise attack on Pearl Harbour in which much of the US Pacific Fleet was disabled. This was followed three days later with the sinking of the Prince of Wales and Repulse off Malaya. With the arena largely cleared of opposition the Japanese then set about achieving one of the most remarkable series of sweeping advances and crushing victories in the annals of war. Hong Kong fell in December, Singapore in February 1942, the Philippines in May, preceded by the Dutch East Indies, Guam, Wake Island and numerous other Pacific Isles. From Thailand they commenced a deep advance into Burma.

GAUDEAMUS IGITUR

Although the reeling Allies did not know it at the time, by mid-May 1942 the Japanese had attained all of the objectives for which they went to war. These were the destruction of the US and British Pacific fleets, the enlargement of Japanese hegemony to encompass a "Greater East Asia Co-Prosperity Sphere" giving them access to oil, other raw materials and markets and providing them a hoped-for impregnable defensive ring. While they had no real intention of invading North America or Australia the Japanese had a little tidying-up to do before they felt secure. In the south this involved the taking of Fiji, Samoa, New Hebrides (Vanuatu), New Caledonia, Solomons and New Guinea. In the east and north they aimed for Midway and the Aleutians.

Here, for the first time, they came a cropper. On 4-8 May in the indecisive Battle of the Coral Sea the Japanese were checked in their attempt to take New Guinea.(4) The eastern thrust ended in disaster for the Japanese at the climactic Battle of Midway on 3-6 June 1942, one of the truly decisive battles in history. But while Midway was getting underway the northern arm of the Japanese eastern pincers attacked the Aleutian Islands which extend some 1760 km southwest from the Alaska Peninsula across the North Pacific.

Although forewarned by intelligence intercepts Admiral Theobald's US North Pacific force bungled the interception of the Japanese force which proceeded to blast the US base at Dutch Harbour and occupy the western Aleutian Islands of Attu and Kiska. With Midway lost the Japanese made no serious efforts to extend their Aleutian operations. Nevertheless, these engendered a series of air and naval clashes over the next year, These culminated, on 11 May 1943, in the storming of Attu by the US 7th Infantry Division.(5) In savage fighting and at a cost of 1700 casualties the Americans secured the island on 2 June. The Japanese lost 2380 dead and 28 prisoners. More importantly the Americans recovered a nearly intact Zero fighter from the Attu bogs from which subsequent analysis enabled the Allies to, at long last, find a way to counter this legendary fighter. Kiska, however, remained a thorn in the North American side.

At the Washington "Trident" Conference of May 1943 the Joint Chiefs of Staff authorized an attack on Kiska. The operation was under the overall control of Admiral Kinkaid USN, reporting to Admiral Nimitz the C in C Pacific. The detailed attack plan was the responsibility of Lt Gen Buckner USA with Maj Gen Corlett as Task Force Commander. A Canadian brigade, the 13th, under Brig H.W. Foster took part in the operation as did one bomber and two fighter squadrons RCAF.(6) However this account deals only with the 1st SSF.

On 9 July 1 SSF boarded two Liberty ships at San Francisco as part of Amphibious Task Force No. 9. The SSF comprised 177 officers and 2283 men of whom 42 and 552 were Canadian. The 1st and 3rd Regiments were commanded by Americans, Canadian Lt Col D.D. Williamson commanded the 2nd. Five of the six battalions were commanded by Canadians: Majors (later Lt Cols) Becket, Akehurst, MacWilliam, Gilday and Bourne. While the force was at sea the Allies landed in Sicily and, off the Solomons in the Battle of Kula Gulf (one of the epic "Slot" battles), the US cruiser "Helena" was sunk.(7) The 1st Special Service Force, originally scheduled for assembly off Adak, was diverted by its Colonel to Amchitka where it landed on 24 July 1943.

The plan for Kiska called for a landing on the Southern Sector (Quisling Bay) on D-Day, August 15, by the 1st Regiment SSF and the 17th and 87th US Infantry Regiments. On D+1 a landing would be made on the northern coast (Witchcraft Point) by the 3rd SSF, the Canadian 13th Brigade and US infantry. The 2nd SSF Regiment under Canadian

PARATROOPS - SPECIAL FORCES and CANLOAN

Lt Col Williamson formed part of the reserve and was to be ready to parachute into the Northern Sector if called on.(8) To the chagrin of the Special Service Force other elements of the Kiska force were liberally equipped with the Weasel amphibious tracked vehicle while the SSF - the progenitors of the Weasel - went without.

The Kiska Operation

The actual operation turned, in the end, into something of a fiasco. Following the loss of Attu and the abandonment of any idea of an eastward move the Japanese decided on 21 May to evacuate the Kiska garrison. Initial attempts were made by submarine and some 800, mainly civilians, were removed in this way. But the use of submarines was abandoned after four were lost to the US navy or to the hazards of Aleutian navigation and surface vessels were substituted. An initial attempt on 17 July failed due to bad weather. But on 28 July two cruisers and six destroyers entered Kiska in a thick fog and loaded the entire remaining garrison. Some 5183 servicemen and civilians were boarded in under an hour and dashed safely home. It was an incredible performance achieved, despite a strong US naval blockade, by equal parts of superb Japanese seamanship, foggy weather and sheer luck. Just prior to the attempt US aircraft reported radar contact with unknown vessels off Attu and part of the blockading force took off in a fruitless search. This was followed by a US Navy refuelling operation 100 miles from Kiska which drained further forces from the area.

The blockade turned into near farce on 27 July when US radar detected what appeared to be enemy vessels on their screens. A US battleship task force engaged these targets by radar controlled fire, expending a prodigious amount of ammunition. It transpired that this "Battle of the Pips" resulted from ghost radar returns from distant islands.(9) Subsequent air and naval reconnaissance revealed no real activity on Kiska, although there were occasional reports of minor gunfire which may have been the result of delayed action charges set by the enemy before departure. More tellingly no radio or radar signals were detected after 28 July.

Despite the lack of evidence of a Japanese presence the attacking force exercised considerable prudence as the enemy was well known to "play possum" for long periods. Some thought that the enemy had withdrawn into the interior to conduct a final defence. In the event the landings on 15 and 16 August went ahead as scheduled and were, of course completely successful. But it was something of an embarrassment for a force of 34,000 to attack an empty island. Although most of the invading force, including the Canadian 13th Brigade, were to stay on the island for many months the 1st Special Service Force was withdrawn by the end of August. There were fresh tasks ahead.

Italy - The Winter Line

As the Kiska operation ground to a halt the Allied leaders were meeting at the First Quebec Conference, 11 - 24 August 1943. Here discussions centered on how to exploit the successes in Sicily via Italy and on the coming invasion of France from both north and south. Lord Louis Mountbatten, who had first backed the creation of the SSF, learned that it was now unemployed in Kiska and suggested it be sent to the Mediterranean for employment in Italy, Dalmatia or elsewhere in the Balkans. The Conference agreed and the Arrowheads were hurriedly extracted from Kiska and in rapid order relocated first to Camp Stoneham CA then Fort Ethan Allen VT and finally Camp Patrick Henry at Norfolk VA.

On 28 October 1943 1 SSF embarked at Newport News aboard the Empress of Scotland (nee Japan) en route to Africa, arriving at Casablanca on 5 November. It was immediately sent by rail to Oran. On 19 November the unit sailed for Italy where it occupied the Italian Artillery School barracks at Santa Maria north of Naples and came under command of the US 5th Army.

Following its Salerno landing in September the 5th Army had cleared Naples and slowly pushed north over the Volturno River coming up against the German Winter Line. Here the 5th Army's General Mark Clark assigned the British X Corps the task of clearing Monastery Hill, Monte Camino and forcing the lower Garigliano. The US IInd Corps was against the Monte la Difensa - Monte Maggiore massif on the eastern ridge of the Camino heights. IInd Corps had been bloodily repulsed in its initial efforts to take the Massif.

On 26 November the 1st Special Service Force was placed under command of Maj Gen Walker's 36th (Texas) Division - the heroes of the movie "A Walk in the Sun"- which had suffered severely at Salerno and the Volturno. Just two days before 5th Army had issued Operation Directive No. 11, the plan for Operation "Raincoat", in which the British X Corps would seize Mt Camino and the US IInd La Difensa - Mt Maggiore. These operations were preliminary to seizing the Mignano Gap and the Liri Valley.

La Difensa - 2 - 8 December 1943

The 36th Division Plan called for the 1st SSF to capture Monte La Difensa (Hill 960) and la Remetanea (Hill 907) while the British were clearing Camino (Hill 963) and 36 Division the Maggiore Heights. The terrain was such that both La Difensa and Camino would have to be taken together as the enemy on one would render the other untenable. The attacks took place at the same time as the Sangro - Moro - Ortona battles were being fought on the other side of Italy. The common denominator between the two fronts was the incessant rain. All during November divisions of the 5th Army had struggled against stiffening German resistance in this area. Attacks by the US 3rd and 36th Divisions and the British 56th Division and 201st Guards Brigade had made only minimal gains.

Colonel Frederick assigned the initial phase to Canadian Col D.D. Williamson's 2nd Regiment, possibly because they had fretted in reserve at Kiska. But for whatever reason it was a good choice. On the eve of the attack, during a light-hearted discussion on the relative order of US and Canadian decorations, Canadian Lt Col T. MacWilliam who would lead the assault battalion of 2nd Regt. opined that he only wanted a long service medal. Alas, his service and life were to last only another 36 hours.(10)

Arriving at their debussing point at 2100 hrs on December 1st the 2nd Regiment slowly worked its way forward through a light rain and deep, clinging mud to the flank of Mt Difensa. In pitch darkness they scrambled up the very steep slope often having to resort to the use of climbing ropes. It took two hours for MacWilliams' 2nd Battalion to climb to its assault position. At 0300 hrs they moved off reaching the crest an hour and a half later.

Attacking No. 1 Company left, 2 centre and 3 right the battalion lost cohesion in the craggy going and heavy enemy fire. But this was exactly the sort of combat for which the Force had long trained as its platoon and section leaders smoothly took over as the situation demanded. As dawn illuminated No. 2 Company on the crest six enemy MG posts opened up on them from caves. Three section sergeants at once improvised a pincers attack and eliminated two of the posts as a lieutenant and two men of No. 1 Company nailed a third. When the OC of No. 1 Company was killed by a German carrying a white flag his enraged company cleared out all nearby enemy.

By 0700 hrs the 2nd Regiment was in control of La Difensa with the enemy retreating to nearby Mt Remetanea (Hill 907). As the company began moving out a mortar salvo crashed in killing Lt Col MacWilliam and a sergeant and wounding two others. The battalion XO took over 2nd Battalion as Col Frederick called a temporary halt to re-supply and re-ammunition the Force. This was a difficult and gruelling job involving six hours of man-packing and clambering up very steep slopes.

At 0830 hrs the British reported the capture of Monte Camino, although they were soon to be driven off, while 36 Division cleared lesser hills. On La Difensa the Special Service Force had done an excellent job - capturing 35 and killing over 100 while driving a reinforced battalion off the hill. Meanwhile heavy German fire played havoc in the rear areas inflicting severe casualties on the Force's reserve 1st Regiment.

The Arrowheads spent the 4th on aggressive patrolling clearing the enemy from the spurs and saddles leading to Remetanea. A prospective German counter-attack was broken up by fire directed from La Difensa. With the British 56th Division again attacking the Monastery from which they had twice been driven, Col Frederick ordered 2nd Regiment to take Remetanea by day. The 1st Battalion, reinforced by a company of the 3rd Regiment, led off and was stopped on the saddle half-way to the objective.

At mid-afternoon the 2nd Battalion tried its luck and was fiercely engaged by enemy defending from two knolls. The positions were finally carried after a determined attack by No. 5 Company of the 2nd Battalion. With half his platoon killed or wounded and he himself severely wounded, Lt Boyce, an American, heroically charged and eliminated the enemy positions before being killed. After being reinforced by the 1st Battalion the 2nd Regiment held the saddle overnight. At dawn on the 6th the 1st Battalion charged and cleared Monte la Remetanea and swiftly patrolled to Rocca d' Evandro. The next day they linked up with the British 56th Division who had retaken Monte Camino for good.

The 1st SSF spent December 7th in extremely aggressive patrolling against dug-in machine guns and infiltrating snipers. One four man patrol under Lt Atto from Montreal wiped out four pockets of snipers with Canadian sergeants Brotherton and Keleher killing nine Germans and Atto taking two prisoners. On the return in dense fog Atto became separated from his patrol but continued on with his two prisoners and eliminated a further enemy post capturing five more. He returned with seven prisoners covered by his now empty pistol.(11)

On the 8th the 1st Regiment completed the operation by attacking and taking Hill 604, capturing seven enemy and killing 25. The massif was now totally in Allied hands. As the Force completed its brilliant work on La Difensa - Remetanea torrential rains started to flood the Rapido and Garigliano Rivers. Kesselring then ordered his Germans back over the rivers while they could still be crossed.

The 1st Special Service Force was relieved by the 142nd Infantry Regiment on the 9th and passed into reserve. They had done an excellent job but at the steep price of 400 battle casualties including 81 dead or missing. On the 10th Col Frederick received glowing letters of congratulation from Lt Gen Mark Clark Commander 5th Army and from Maj Gen G. Keyes Commander II Corps.(12) The tributes were well earned.

Monte Majo

Before the Winter Line could be secured and the Mignano Gap opened it would be necessary to clear the Monte Majo massif some six miles east of Cassino. As a preliminary to this the Force was required to capture Hill 670 a lower spur of the Sammucro feature previously captured by other 5th Army formations. The capture of Hill 670 was entrusted to US Colonel A.C. Marshall's 1st Regiment.

Marshall's attack commenced on Christmas Day and was spearheaded by Canadian Lt Col Akehust's under strength 2nd Battalion. As the battalion approached the Start Line a mortar round hit the command post killing the adjutant and another man and wounding Akehurst. Col Marshall then personally took charge of the battalion as the attack went in under heavy fire. Thanks largely to the heroism of two company commanders - Capt McCall who remained in action despite a neck wound and Lt Smith who was killed - the battalion took the objective by 0700 hrs. The attack cost the 1st Regiment 65 casualties with the 2nd losing another 12 in a support role.

On January 1st 1944 the SSF kicked off against Monte Majo. The operation started with the 1st and 2nd Regiments advancing on the valley town of Radicosa and the intervening Hills 670 and 775. On 4 January Colonel Walker's 3rd Regiment, with battalions commanded by Canadians Gilday and Bourne, swung northeast on a wide outflanking manoeuvre. Colonel Frederick now directed Walker to take Monte Majo flanked on the left by the 1st Regiment's advance on Monte Vischiataro (Hill 1109).

Lt Col Gilday's 1st Battalion of the 3rd Regiment led off and worked its way up the slopes under heavy fire. Under appalling conditions of terrain and weather Gilday's men led the 3rd to the crest of the formidable 1259 metre Mt Majo where they held on for three days beating off a succession of enemy attacks. Meanwhile the flanking 1st Regiment met considerable resistance which threatened its advance on Vischiataro. Accordingly, after dark on 7 January, they were brought over to Mt Majo in order to attack Mt Vischiataro from the northern flank. Attacking westward Marshall's 1st Regiment took Hill 1270 then swung south on Mt Vischiataro which fell with surprising ease. For the next week the Force cleared enemy snipers and rearguards from the barren, frozen slopes while other 5th Army formations attacked on either flank. By 15 January enemy resistance ceased east of the Rapido.

It had been a terrible campaign in brutally cold weather over treeless, snow-covered crags in the face of gale-like winds. Getting supplies up and casualties out required super human effort. Frostbite was endemic. Over half the Force's strength became casualties through battle, exposure, frostbite and fatigue. The six week campaign cost the Canadian contingent a further 70 casualties and by the end of January only 350 remained. This draining of strength was exacerbated when, under an impending reinforcement crisis, National Defence Headquarters temporarily halted the movement of Canadian replacements to the Force. It was in this weakened state that the 1st Special Service Force embarked on its next mission - Anzio.

PARATROOPS - SPECIAL FORCES and CANLOAN

Anzio

With the Allies everywhere bogged down along the Italian Winter Line the Supreme Commander of the theatre, General Harold Alexander, planned a new offensive on the western Italian front. In conjunction with an attack on Cassino Clark's 5th Army was to land at Anzio, 35 miles south of Rome, and advance on the Alban Hills to cut off all German forces to the south. Prior to this operation the British Xth Corps on 17 January attacked across the Garigliano and secured a bridgehead after bitter fighting. German reserves were hurried to meet the threat leaving the Anzio area defended by a single battalion and three engineer companies. The Allied strategy thus worked to perfection but its implementation was to be something else again.

On 22 January 1944 the US VI Corps under Maj Gen J.P. Lucas launched Operation "Shingle"- the landing at Anzio. The move caught the Germans somewhat by surprise as, despite ample previous proof to the contrary, they still credited the Allies with possessing a daring and initiative hitherto absent in the extreme. They thus expected that any landing would be made north of Rome, possibly around Leghorn, and seriously jeopardize the entire German position in Italy. The Allies were once more to disappoint them, and themselves.

Alas, as with so many Allied ventures, the operation was hurriedly planned and timidly executed. In the words of the historians Calvocoressi, Wint and Pritchard, "The initial landings were practically unopposed and a daring commander might have made a dash for Rome ....But General Lucas ... a man of pessimistic temperament on discovering no Germans in his path behaved as though there were. Kesselring was given ample time to organize a defence and seized it. By the end of the week the expedition was in trouble."(13)

The landings were led by the US 3rd and British 1st Divisions and three Ranger battalions. They were rapidly followed by the US 45th Infantry and 1st Armoured Divisions, the 504th Parachute Regiment, the British 56th Division and other elements. When Lucas finally tried to advance he was stopped cold. The rapidly reacting Germans poured reserves, including von Mackensen's 14th Army, into the area and began to energetically attack the Allies.

Lucas' VIth Corps rapidly passed from the offensive to the defensive and was frequently only saved from disaster by allied air and naval support.(14) An attempt by 3rd Division on 27 January to enlarge the beachhead to the east resulted in the annihilation of the attached 1st and 3rd Ranger Battalions. The troops in the beachhead, now some 30 miles wide by 15 deep, were stretched to the limit. The bulk of the Corps was positioned on the dangerous left flank from Nettuno west facing the main enemy lines of advance. The eastern flank was less vulnerable being somewhat shielded by the Pontine Flats, reclaimed by Mussolini from marsh into farmland, which retained dangerously high water tables. The Mussolini Canal running south - north from near Cerreto Alto to Highway 7, the ancient Via Appia, provided a formidable obstacle to tanks. Lucas, lacking sufficient divisions, temporarily assigned the canal area to the 39th Combat Engineer Regiment.

Into this situation on 1 February came the 1st Special Service Force which had been hurriedly withdrawn from IInd Corps control and shipped to the beachead. Frederick its commander had recently been promoted to Brigadier. Lucas replaced the engineers with Frederick's force to which he attached the 460th Field Artillery Battalion, the 160th

Field Battery and a company of tank destroyers. The SSF was assigned seven miles of the eastern sector - about one-quarter of the entire line - a frontage normally assigned to at least a division. The Force was woefully under strength. Only the 3rd Regiment was up to strength, the other two were reduced to one battalion each. Frederick placed the strong 3rd Regiment along 4½ miles of the dangerous left flank. Three companies of the 1st Regiment covered the next 2½ miles to the canal's mouth. 2nd Regiment was held in reserve as the main raiding force.

The ground on the east flank precluded major operations by either side but that did not hold back the Special Service Force. Its initial task was to restore Allied supremacy along the Mussolini Canal and drive the enemy back from its outpost and observation line. This the Force did in fine fashion, sending patrols deep into enemy territory. They soon moved right across the canal to stay. The next three months were spent in increasingly larger raids and in establishing defences along the canal embankments. On 18 February the SSF routed an attack by two companies of infantry and a company of tanks. The enemy withdrew leaving behind three wrecked tanks and 25 dead. A week later another attack on the 3rd Regiment was again roughly repulsed.

On the last night of February No 2 Company of the 1st Regiment under Capt McCall, one of the heroes of Hill 670, with the point led by US Lt G. Krasevac and Canadian S/Sgt S. Wright executed a brilliant trap. By night's end McCall's men had taken 111 prisoners, 35 by Wright, at a cost of only two wounded. Then on 15 April three companies of the 2nd Regiment supported by tanks of the 1st Armoured Division plus armoured cars and a platoon of M10 tank destroyers made a three pronged drive over the canal at Strada Litoranea, Cerreto Alto and a beach lockhouse. The attack was superbly executed with 60 prisoners taken and half as many killed for a loss of one man and two tanks. Similar successful raids, albeit with somewhat less spectacular results, followed and always the Force kept up the pressure.

Despite steady attrition from shelling, patrolling and sickness the Force was substantially reinforced when 400 Rangers were transferred into the 1st Regiment. Then on 9 May the Force was suddenly replaced along the perimeter by the 36th Combat Engineers and withdrawn to the centre of the beachhead. Big events were happening along the Adolf Hitler Line on the main Italian front and a link-up between the VI and IInd Corps was eagerly anticipated. And, in a change of heart, the Canadian authorities decided to again reinforce the Force's Canadian contingent, sending 255 specially selected troops to Anzio. Casualties in the beachhead had, because of the nature of the fighting, been comparatively modest totalling 384 of whom 54 were killed, 51 missing and 279 wounded. The Canadian share was 117, roughly proportional to its strength.

The Fall of Rome

With the Hitler Line to the south being breached by both the 5th and 8th Armies, the VIth Corps in the beachhead, now under Lt Gen Truscott, prepared to go over to the offensive and hopefully trap the German forces below Rome. The offensive was code named "Buffalo". The plan called for VI Corps to drive north through the Velletri gap into the Valmontone plain and cut Highway 6. The Corps' left flank of the British 1st and 5th and US 1st Armoured and 45th Infantry Divisions was to clear the Alban Hills and advance to the Tiber River. The US 3rd Division was to capture Cisterna and drive on Valmontone. The 1st Special Service Force was to advance on the Corps' right flank

PARATROOPS - SPECIAL FORCES and CANLOAN

on a line Monte Arrestino - Artena and Segni. The 34th and 36th Divisions were in reserve to exploit any breakthrough and clear Velletri.

Despite General Alexander's instructions calling for 5th Army to advance inland to trap the Germans retreating before the 5th and 8th Armies, Mark Clark had other ideas. His eyes were firmly fixed on Rome thus creating yet another endless controversy between the generals. When the US IInd Corps linked up with the bridgehead from the southern front Clark directed Truscott's VI Corps north towards Rome instead of east to Valmontone. The German 10th and 14th Armies seized the opportunity to escape north past the Tiber. So once again, as so often before, the Allies blew a glittering opportunity to secure a meaningful and decisive victory.

The US IInd Corps was leaving Terracina on 22 May when the Special Service Force was preparing to kick off along the Cisterna Canal. The 1st Regiment with a battalion from the 2nd plus armour and M10s would lead the advance with the 3rd keeping pace on the flank. The 100th (Nisei) US Infantry Regiment covered the right flank while an ad hoc Pollock Force from 3rd Division advanced on the left. When 1 SSF would reach the Rome - Naples railway line they were to be relieved by the 34th Division and then move on Mt Arrestino.

At 0500 hrs on 23 May the US IInd Corps advanced behind strong artillery and mortar support. By 1000 hrs under heavy fire the Force crossed Highway 7 and cut off Cisterna, as the inevitable German counter-attack hit back behind a dozen Tiger and Panther tanks. Two companies of the 1st Regiment were badly cut up and forced to withdraw. US air, artillery and armour finally stopped the enemy along Highway 7, but it was now apparent that the advance to Rome would be anything but a walk in the park. The force was relieved that that night to regroup for the next phase, just as IInd and VIth Corps finally joined up near Borgo Grappa.

At 0700 hrs on 25 May the SSF, with the 3rd Regiment leading, advanced on Mt Arrestino. That hill fell the next day along with the town of Cori as the Force headed for Artena south of Valmontone. They arrived just as 3rd Division took the town. On 28 May the SSF was directed east to secure the important railway junction of Colle Ferro. Under heavy fire, resulting in severe casualties, the Force pushed on beating off a strong enemy attack en route. Colle Ferro fell on June 2nd as Frederick's troops made contact with the French Expeditionary Force advancing from the Liri Valley.

On 3 June HQ IInd Corps allotted an ad hoc armoured group called Force Houze to the SSF and gave the combined force the task of leading the drive on Rome. They started their advance at 0915 and by nightfall were only ten miles from the Eternal City. Before midnight 2nd Regiment, under Canadian Lt Col Akehurst, and the 3rd headed for the Rome suburbs to secure key bridges over the Tiber. Patrols entered Rome early on June 4th but met strong enemy resistance. The final attack committed all three Regiments of the Force - 2nd and 3rd from the east and the 1st from the south. In this action Col Marshall, the fine commander of the 1st Regiment, was among those killed. 3rd Regiment then completed the capture of the bridges and Rome was theirs. As the troops celebrated their huge victory over the next 48 hrs they learned that on June 6th the Allies had landed in Normandy. Rome and Italy then rapidly faded to the back pages of the public conscience. But the losses remained to be counted. The breakout battle and capture of Rome had cost the Canadians in the Force 185 casualties.

As the 1st SSF rested, regrouped and prepared for operations into Tuscany they, as is the lot of an elite force, were transferred once again. Italy began to fade from their

screen as they were assigned to the reactivated 7th Army under Lt Gen A.M. Patch, the victor of Guadacanal, for a forthcoming invasion of southern France, code named "Anvil". At this time also Brigadier Frederick was promoted and left the Force, his successor being Colonel Walker of the 3rd Regiment. Upon leaving the 5th Army for the 7th the Force received a glowing letter of praise from the hard-to-please Mark Clark which read in part:
"It is with the deepest regret that I see the 1st Special Service Force leave the fold of Fifth Army....your Force has more than lived up to our expectations...although its reputation...had preceded it....The part played by your elite American - Canadian Force is so well known....The gruelling fighting ...on the main front in the dead of winter, the important part which you took in the establishment and in the defense of the beachhead during its historic four months' siege, the way in which your relatively small Force maintained an aggressive offensive on a front equal to that held by any full division, and finally your brilliant performance in the final breakout...which culminated in the capture of Rome have entered history and forged a bright new link....I was particularly happy to have ...your Force with its international composition...(it) symbolizes the efforts of the United Nations in this war, and gives promise for the more solid and permanent peace to follow....sincere congratulations for a job superbly executed..."(15)

La Côte d'Azure

In early July the Force moved to Santa Maria near Salerno to prepare for Operation "Anvil". General Patch planned to land his army on a broad front from Toulon to St Raphael with three infantry divisions, the SSF, French commandos and an airborne task force (Maj Gen Frederick's new command). The task of the 1st Special Service Force was to capture Les Iles d'Hyeres covering Toulon on the Army's left flank.

Since Les Iles were fronted by high rocky cliffs the landings would require special training in rock climbing. While this was in progress the Force's S2 (Intelligence Officer) - Lt Col Burhans, the author of the Force's history, made a daring reconnaissance of Les Iles in a British submarine. On 14 August, after staging on Corsica for two days, the Force embarked on the Canadian troopships Prince Henry and Prince Baudouin and several destroyers for the last major waterborne assault on Europe.

At 2300 hrs on the 14th, the first anniversary of its first operational landing in Kiska, the Force boarded their landing craft for the assault. Les Iles comprise two principal islands - in the east the six by one mile Ile du Levant and in the west the 2 1/2 by two mile Ile de Port - Cros. A further small island lies just to the west of Port Cros.

Colonel Walker decided to attack Levant in the south centre with the 2nd Regiment left and the 3rd right. The 1st Regiment would tackle Port Cros. After scrambling up 80 foot cliffs the Canadian Akehurst's 2nd Regiment proceeded rapidly inland across the island to Fort Arbousier taking out a number of positions and a score of prisoners. The 3rd Regiment landed equally well and headed off to clear the east of the island. Back in the west 2nd Regiment had a tough struggle to capture the small northern port of del Avis but succeeded when Canadian Lt Col Becket of the 3rd Regiment added one of his battalions to the fray.

The 1st Regiment on Port Cros had a stickier time as the enemy retired into a series of updated Napoleonic forts with 13 foot thick walls which proved impervious to both the navy's 8 inch shells and air force rockets. Two of these formidable star-shaped forts were taken through excellent sub-unit tactics. The third held out until help was received from the battleship HMS Ramilles which had been supporting the mainland invasion. Ramilles promptly put twelve 15 inch rounds into and through Fort del Eminence. Resistance ceased. With the islands all clear the Force moved to near Calvire on the mainland for their next assignment.

Patch decided to use his main force to thrust west through Toulon and Marseilles then turn north up the Valley of the Rhone to join with Patton's Third Army which had broken out of Normandy and started to run wild. He sent the 45th Division north through the mountains to Grenoble. Patch then assigned the 1st Special Service Force to Maj Gen Frederick's 1st Airborne Task Force with the mission of advancing east along the Cote d'Azure to the Italian border.

Subsequent operations comprised roughly three phases - the long advance up the coast against rearguards, demolitions and mines; the capture of the pre-war French casemates, the "Little Maginot Line"; and the holding of a line generally along the Italian frontier. The advance along the coast was a series of small actions, some very bloody, followed by the liberation of a town and a welcome by the local French authorities. In the latter of these the French Canadian officers of the Force were able to respond to mayoralty welcomes in French. The advance was greatly aided by the Force's ad hoc Cannon Platoon under Canadian Howie MacIntosh. MacIntosh had four 75 mm cannon mounted in half-tracks which proved invaluable in blasting strong points on the line of march. In succession the SSF secured such storied resort towns as St Tropez, St Raphael, Cannes, Antibes, Villeneuve, Nice, Monte Carlo and Menton.

At Menton, near the Italian border, the role changed somewhat. It was decided not to advance into Italy until the 15th Army Group, now under Mark Clark, drove north the next spring. The Force then engaged in taking out a large number of very formidable French border strong points which had routed the attempted Italian invasion of France in 1940. Fortunately the low-morale defenders were not up to the standards of the *poilu* of 1940 and most fell without too many problems. One, Fort Castillon on a high saddle well inland from Menton, did hold out for a month thereby frustrating Force attempts to bring relief to the French civilians in the inland town of Sospel. The Force also had a difficult time in reducing the enemy from ridges near Menton and they continued to endure sporadic enemy artillery fire throughout. A number of sharp actions resulted in the taking of numerous enemy prisoners but always at the cost of casualties to the Force. In these actions the SSF enjoyed excellent fire support from US destroyers and the French warship "Lorraine" lying offshore.

From mid-September the Force settled down to a holding role, with generally little opposition from the enemy apart from bursts of moderate to severe shelling. The Special Service men continued with their forte of vigorous patrolling resulting in a steady trickle of enemy prisoners. On 27 October 1944 the enemy abandoned the front and Fort Castillon fell at last. And finally an order was now received from Washington deactivating the Force once the present mission was ended. It soon did as on 28 November the 1st Special Service Force was relieved by the 100th (Nisei) Battalion of the 442nd Regimental Combat Team.

L'Envoi

On the afternoon of 5 December 1944 the 1st Special Service Force paraded for the

GAUDEAMUS IGITUR

last time on the Loup River flats near Villeneuve. After a chaplain's service the colours of the Force were lowered and cased. Then, in a scene reminiscent of the division of the Blue and the Grey at West Point at the outbreak of the Civil War, the six-hundred Canadians fell out. As their American comrades stood to attention with the positions vacated by the Canadians deliberately left blank, the Canadian contingent marched past under their own flag. The 1st Special Service Force had ended. The Canadians all left to join units of their army in Italy or Northwest Europe. Seven officers left for the 6th Airborne Division preparing for the war's last bash.

The Force's epitaph is summed up by writer Sholto Watt of the Montreal "Standard". "I can testify to their spectacular power and efficiency, their marvellous morale and their never failing spirit of attack. They were exactly what one would expect from North America's best - an inspiration to all and a terror to their enemy....Their legend a feat of arms which will remain celebrated in history...an example of international brotherhood which deserves enduring honour."(16) This accolade was echoed by a soldier of the US 3rd Division - one of the very best - who told the Army paper "Yank", "The First Special Service Force are the best god-damned fighters in the world".(17) Those who fought with them - or against them - would agree.

MajGen. G. Kitching, GOC 4th Armoured Division during the great Falaise Battles, at a post-war inspection of the Canadian Guards. The author is third from Kitching's right.

PARATROOPS - SPECIAL FORCES and CANLOAN

CHAPTER XV

CANLOAN

For he to-day that sheds his blood with me
Shall be my brother...
And gentlemen in England, now a-bed
Shall think themselves accurs'd they were not here
And hold their manhoods cheap whiles any speaks
That fought with us upon Saint Crispin's day.

Shakespeare *King Henry V*

Setting for CANLOAN

This recounting of the campaigns of the Canadian Army in the Second World War has perforce been confined to actions in which formed bodies of that army have participated. There were of course numbers of Canadian soldiers, both officers and men, who served with the armies of other nations, principally the United Kingdom or the USA. For example pre-war RMC graduates could opt for service with the British forces. Others joined for adventure or to escape the drudgery of the depression. During the war also small numbers were attached to other armies for battle experience of which attachments to the British 1st and 8th Armies in North Africa and the US 10th Army in Okinawa are the best known. Formed units of Canadian foresters, engineer tunnelers and intelligence teams also served apart from the Canadian army in places as diverse as the Ardennes, Anzio, Gibralter and South-East Asia. But unlike the many Canadians who served as a matter of course in squadrons of the RAF or ships of the Royal Navy it was unusual for soldiers to be so employed.

There was however one outstanding exception. Just prior to, and after, D-Day some 670 Canadian officers were loaned to the British Army for combat service. Some 50 of these were Ordnance (RCOC) but the rest - 623 - were to serve as junior infantry officers in assault battalions. They were code named CANLOAN and served magnificently, bringing great credit and honour to themselves, their British regiments and to Canada. Their record is well documented and presented by Wilfred I. Smith, himself a CANLOAN officer and former Dominion Archivist, in "Code Word CANLOAN."(1) Only a broad outline is recounted here.

Background

In the First World War Canada placed a Corps of four divisions in the field. To provide the steady stream of reinforcements needed once battle was joined and casualties soared entire battalions were recruited in Canada and sent overseas as full fledged units. Once in England most of the battalions were broken up. The other ranks and some junior officers went to France as reinforcements. The remaining officers were farmed out around England to training, administrative or supernumerary establishments while some were returned home. But as units kept arriving from Canada the pool of surplus officers mounted. While the combat units in France were prepared to accept a number of junior subalterns they naturally wished fill vacancies in the rank of captain and above through promotion from within their own ranks. The Canadian authorities sought ways out of this dilemma and discussions were held with Britain on using Canadian officers within British units. Eventually a number of these were "seconded" to British formations in a variety of functions although few ended up in combat units as the British battalions also wished to reward their own through promotion. The Second World War produced a somewhat similar situation though for vastly different reasons. The solution adopted was also vastly different and more satisfying to all concerned. The solution was code named CANLOAN.

In the Second World War Canada fielded a complete, if under strength, combat Army of five divisions and two armoured brigades. A further three divisions were held in Canada largely for defensive duties especially after Pearl Harbour raised the spectre of a possible Japanese lodgement on the west coast. In addition a large number of command, training, administrative, protective and other static units were formed throughout Canada all employing many officers.

Although the 1st Division went to England in 1939, to be followed by four other divisions, armoured brigades and a plethora of other units and establishments, they saw little action until 1943 when one division and a tank brigade fought in Sicily and Italy. It was only in 1944 that the remainder of the Army was committed to action. Meanwhile fresh batches of officers kept being appointed in Canada with little chance of early service overseas. Then from 1943 when the threat of an invasion of Canada vanished the three homeland divisions started to be run down and the reserve of surplus officers grew.

Meanwhile the British Army had been heavily, if spasmodically, engaged since 1939. Their normal battlefield manpower wastage was greatly exacerbated by the many defeats and wholesale losses of prisoners resulting from the debacles which plagued their early campaigns. These losses and the prospect of further large scale casualties in the forthcoming Italian, Burmese and Northwest European campaigns led the British authorities to seek an alleviation of their problem of a shortage of junior officers.

The CANLOAN Origins

Considerable confusion exists over the exact progenitor of the CANLOAN scheme. This is somewhat surprising given the scheme's short, precise and well documented existence and the fact that its historian was the respected former Dominion Archivist, the late Wilfred Smith. Some accounts credit the origin to Col J.L. Ralston the Canadian Minister of National Defence. Others credit meetings in Gibralter between Ralston and General Sir Ronald Adam, the British Adjutant-General and his Canadian counterpart Maj Gen H.F. Letson. There are several other claimants. All of which perhaps supports the aphorism that defeat is an orphan while success has many parents. For the CANLOAN scheme, with one important exception, was a resounding success. The exception was the comparatively low number of volunteers who ultimately served.

Whatever the origins, the principal engine for its implementation was the British Army's projected critical shortage of junior infantry officers for 1944. The Canadian problem was, of course, just the opposite - an embarrassing surplus which was expected to reach 2000 by April 1944. Thus in September 1943 the Canadian authorities

PARATROOPS - SPECIAL FORCES and CANLOAN

approached the British to see if the latter could accept surplus Canadian officers especially in the ranks of captain and above. The British response was that while senior officers were not required there was a critical need for junior infantry officers.

After a series of discussions between and within British and Canadian circles it was estimated that up to 2000 Canadian infantry subalterns, to which was later added 50 from the Ordnance Corps, would be available for loan to the British army. An urgent requirement was for 600 to be posted to units of 21 Army Group for the forthcoming invasion. On 16 February 1944 Col Ralston announced the implementation of the CANLOAN scheme.

The Implementation

On 10 February, just prior to Ralston's announcement, the Canadian Adjutant-General's branch issued a directive requesting that Military Districts be canvassed to provide volunteers for the programme. The required figures were for 1450 infantry and 50 ordnance officers. Volunteers were to be packaged in installments of 250 between March and May 1944.

The initial response was very good and it seemed for a time that the 1500 quota could readily be met. Large numbers of young subalterns were locked into frustrating training and administrative tasks in Canada with no prospect of getting overseas. They had been frustrated at every step in previous attempts to do so. These initial volunteers were eager for action and long months spent in sterile postings in Canada only increased their eagerness. Indeed anyone visiting the many training centres and units of the three home defence divisions could be forgiven for thinking that every officer in Canada was chomping at the bit to get overseas and into action. The final results - something less than 700 - was a sober revelation.

After the initial surge of volunteers the numbers dropped to near zero despite the best efforts of all concerned to get the stream flowing again. There were many reasons for this seeming lack of proper spirit. Some officers serving in formed battalions at home would be quite willing to go overseas with their own units but had no desire to go outside their own. Others for a variety of reasons, good and bad, were reluctant to be sent on their own to serve in the uncertainties of what to them seemed a foreign army. Others were happy to serve Canada but not the unloved and mistrusted Imperial England. Some had married and were persuaded not to leave their wives and families. Others after sober reflection simply did not wish to be shot at. While others had simply become too content with their comfortable Canadian billets and chances of promotion to exchange these for the uncertainties of unknown prospects abroad.

Thus it was with some embarrassment that in April 1944 Canadian Military Headquarters in London had to inform the British AG General Adam of the let down in volunteers and the capping of the scheme at under 700. Sir Ronald Adam, the very epitome of an officer and a gentleman, accepted the shortfall with good grace and understanding and expressed appreciation for the numbers that had volunteered.

The volunteers were assembled at Camp Sussex NB, under the aegis of Brigadier Milton Gregg VC, where they underwent the necessary training, indoctrination and documentation. Some 90 non-infantry officers were sent off to Brockville for a cram conversion course while the 50 ordnance officers were separately dispatched. The seconded officers were assigned special personal numbers prefixed CDN. Capt D.M.

GAUDEAMUS IGITUR

Findlay received the coveted number CDN/1. The first flight of 52 officers left for the United Kingdom on 29 March arriving on 7 April. Other flights followed in measured succession, the ninth and last leaving on 24 July after the invasion had taken place.

The reception of the Canadians varied from draft to draft but all were received with a warm welcome. The third draft which arrived at Leith Scotland was met with impressive pomp and circumstance by the Commander East Scotland District, the band of the Royal Scots, pipers of the King's Own Scottish Borderers and representatives of the Edinburgh messes, followed by receptions and tours. The processing of the new arrivals went exceedingly smooth with every effort made to send officers to their affiliated regiment or a regiment of their choice. Although Guards regiments were excluded from the scheme five Canadians were accepted into the elite Grenadier Guards at the request of the Commanding Officer 1st Battalion.

All the Canadian officers fitted in very smoothly into their new regiments. Some, such as those sent to Scottish, Welsh, Cornish, Yorkshire or Durham units had a few linguistic difficulties but these were soon overcome. Almost without exception the Canadians were very well received and immensely enjoyed their new units. The British units in turn were nearly universal in their ready and enthusiastic acceptance and absorption of "the colonials."

Into Action

By mid-May, a scant three weeks before D-Day, 500 Canadians had arrived and been sent either to the assault battalions of their regiments or to Reinforcement Holding Units (RHUs) to reinforce the battalions as casualties accrued. Over half of the CANLOAN officers who had arrived in the UK prior to D-Day were assigned to combat battalions - one officer was even commanding his own platoon of the King's Shropshire Light Infantry within 24 hours of docking in Scotland. Some battalions, lacking vacancies on their War Establishments, went to the extent of sending their own officers to RHUs so that the newly arrived Canadians could be accommodated. In his memoir, General Sir Ronald Adam the British AG commented warmly on the Canadians, "They were such excellent material that some units took them with them on D-Day leaving others (non-CANLOANS) to wait as reinforcements."(2) It was a generous tribute from a fine soldier.

Although the Canadians were accepted by their fellow British officers as "one of us" there was one distinction. Many Britons regarded the "colonials" as composite Red Indians / bushmen who relished action and thrived on patrolling. While this image did not fit most Canadians the perception remained and the CANLOAN officers certainly got more than their quota of patrols to lead.

Even before the CANLOAN officers got into action they suffered two serious casualties. One officer received a crushed spine on pre-invasion training but after months in hospital and his return to Canada he lived to fight another day. The other officer, Lt A. Crabb of the 1st Border Regiment, 6th Airborne Division, was killed by accident on the PIAT range on 5 June, the day prior to D-Day. He was the first of 128 fatal casualties that the CANLOAN officers were to suffer.

The first Canadian to be killed on D-Day was Capt J. McGregor a platoon commander of the 2nd East Yorks who died attacking a pillbox on the first afternoon. An indication of the ferocity of the action experienced by CANLOAN officers can be

PARATROOPS - SPECIAL FORCES and CANLOAN

gleaned from the experiences of the six Canadians who landed with assault battalions of 3rd Division (2nd East Yorks and 1st Royal Norfolks). Of the six, one was killed and one wounded on D-Day. Two were killed later, one of whom (Lt J. Laurie) was to win the MC before being killed only three weeks before the war's end. One other also won the MC and survived. Five Canadians also landed on D-Day with the 56th Independent Infantry Brigade attached to 50th Division. This fine brigade was later absorbed into the 49th Division, which was the only British division to serve continuously with the 1st Canadian Army from the Army's activation in July 1944 to the war's end. It was appropriate that the badge of this first class formation was, by coincidence, the polar bear.

In his excellent account of CANLOAN Wilfred Smith, writing of 3rd British Division's operations on D-Day, mentions that at day's end two brigades (8th and 185th) dug-in on Perriers Ridge to counter the German 21st Panzer Division while the 9th Brigade was moved to the right flank to cover the gap between the British and Canadian 3rd Divisions.(3) This account is at variance with Colonel Stacey's account in the official Canadian history (4) which has one battalion of 9 Brigade going to Lion-sur-Mer to assist the Royal Marines while the other two were sent to the division's left flank to assist 6th Airborne Division. Given the failure of 3rd British Division to mount an agreed attack St Contest on D+1, with disastrous results to 3rd Canadian Division's advance on Carpiquet, it would seem that Stacey's version is the correct one, but the matter is far from clear.

From D-Day to the Baltic

As the attacks on Caen ground on and the bitter beachhead battles of attrition raged more and more CANLOAN officers entered the fray. They were to participate, often with distinction, in all of 2nd British Army's battles to war's end. The list of these battles rolls like a film's credits and reads like a battlefield "who's who" - D-Day, Caen, Operations Epsom, Charnwood, Goodwood, Bluecoat, Totalize, Tractable, the Falaise Gap, the race to Antwerp, le Havre, Arnhem, Walcheren, Veritable, Plunder, Varsity and the advance to the Baltic.

Since in these battles the Canadians fought individually or in very small numbers in different battalions throughout the 2nd Army any recounting would merely parrot what is already written in fine style and detail in Wilfred Smith's "Code Word CANLOAN" and in the British Official and unit histories. Those wishing to learn more on this matter are referred to Smith's book which deserves wider Canadian recognition than heretofore. However one incident merits retelling here.

On 16 October 1944 Field Marshal Montgomery ordered a halt to offensive action in the Lowlands except for an advance westward through s'Hertogenbosch - Breda which was planned to cut off the Germans in southwest Holland. Three Divisions of XII Corps, the 7th Armoured, 15th and 53rd Infantry, all of which had CANLOAN content, were involved in this operation. As part of the advance the 6th Royal Welsh Fusiliers of 53rd Division mounted an attack towards Breda on 23 October. "A" Company of the Fusiliers was commanded by CANLOAN Captain R.G. Marsh. The regimental history of the RWF tells his tale: "A" Coy under Capt R.G. Marsh advanced along the s'Hertogenbosch road capturing many prisoners as they went. Reaching its objective it dug in in an area vital to the enemy. During determined enemy counter attacks a night and morning of fierce and bitter fighting ensued during which A Coy, under the magnificent and inspiring leadership of Capt Marsh, although completely cut off from the rest of the battalion, defied every effort to drive them from their position and inflicted heavy losses on the enemy. A Coy had infiltrated right into the main German position covering s'Hertogenbosch....Throughout the night A Coy was continuously attacked in a pitched battle of hand-to-hand fighting and direct enemy fire into Coy HQ by an SP gun. Inspired by the bravery of their gallant commander the coy hung on despite heavy casualties. Capt Marsh was severely wounded but refused to leave his post. At last about 1000 hours the gallant A Coy was relieved....A Coy's magnificent fight at Hintham added a new and well earned battle honour to...the Regiment. Unfortunately a heavy price was paid, Capt Marsh dying of his wounds shortly after his coy was relieved. In his death the Bn lost an officer of outstanding gallantry and merit whose cool bravery in action was an inspiration to his men. Capt Marsh was recommended for the Victoria Cross and received a posthumous Mention in Dispatches."(5) Seldom has the VC been awarded for a more valorous action. But in the end it was just another failed Canadian VC !

Although the CANLOAN infantry officers were intended for Northwest Europe four of their number served in Italy with the Royal Irish Fusiliers of the famed 78th Division. Of these one was killed in action, one was wounded and taken prisoner and one received a MID. Also not generally known, even to informed Canadians, is that 20 CANLOAN officers fought at Arnhem with 1st Airborne Division, mostly in the Air Landing (Glider) battalions. Only two of the Canadians were able to get out when that heroic but ill-starred operation failed. A further 23 CANLOAN officers were to serve in the 6th Airborne Division, which also included a Canadian parachute battalion.

The record of the "Gallant 600" is shown in the fact that they fought in all of 2nd Army's battles from first to last, sustained 75 per-cent casualties and won 100 awards for gallantry. In the words of British General Sir John Mogg who, as a Lieutenant-Colonel, "had the good fortune to have three CANLOAN officers in my battalion, each of whom served with great courage, distinction and loyalty, being completely integrated and staunch members of the 9 DLI team." Of the CANLOAN officers as a whole Mogg wrote that they earned "the respect, admiration and regard" of the British and Canadians "for their courage, sense of joyous comradeship, discipline and devotion to duty."(6) They wrote a proud chapter in Canadian history of which Canadians today should strive to learn more.

CHAPTER XVI

RESULTS AND CONCLUSIONS

And everybody praised the Duke,
Who this great fight did win.
But what good came of it at last?
Quoth little Peterkin.
Why, that I cannot tell, said he;
But 'twas a famous victory.

Robert Southey, *After Blenheim*

The Context

Any value judgement of what the Canadian Army did in the Second World War must be viewed from the perspective of the Canadian, indeed Western, peoples of that era. Present day Canadians, happily insulated by over half a century from the direct effects of war, may quite naturally be tempted to colour their judgments with visions of Viet Nam anti-war protests and a smug satisfaction that their leaders kept them out of the second Iraq war. The mantra that all war is evil and nothing can be worse is anthem enough.

Today's Canadians may be surprised to learn that their forefathers, still suffering from the trauma of the First World War, generally shared this pacific view until shortly before the outbreak of the Second. Then when concession after concession to Herr Hitler yielded only further Nazi aggrandizement the psyche of most Canadians, in common with that of most of the Empire and Commonwealth, snapped one hundred and eighty degrees to one of steely resolve to stop and eliminate the peril no matter what the cost. A nation of pacifists had come to realize that there comes a time when war can indeed be a lesser evil than standing meekly by while a rapacious monster swallows all around.

The majority of the Canadian youth of that era fully subscribed to this view and expected, and in turn were expected by their countrymen, to serve. Admittedly the average volunteer did not really comprehend what he was getting into and individual motives for enlisting widely varied. Nevertheless nearly all young men expected to serve and to serve until the end. The previous chapters testified as to how well they did their job.

The Military Lessons

Conventional wisdom would be inclined to say that not much that is relevant today emerged from a war that ended some sixty years ago. And in light of the tremendous technological advances since then, and their application in two Gulf Wars and Afghanistan, there is seeming merit to that reply. But a closer look at what, from a military sense, has transpired since the Second World War, and especially in the intervening "western" wars, would reveal that many of the lessons that emerged from that conflict

GAUDEAMUS IGITUR

are indeed relevant today.

The first of the major "western" wars fought since 1945 - the Korean War of 1950 - 53 - was a virtual replay of the Second World War. Indeed much in the "static" period of 1951 - 53 bore an uncanny resemblance to the First. To be sure there were improvements in communications, air support, casualty evacuation and infra-red devices but the war was fought in the time honoured manner of seizing and holding ground and destroying the enemy's forces in the process.

Vietnam, 1960-75, featured the massive use of air power, helicopter support and improved firepower and communications. But the first three of these turned out not to be decisive and the war was again fought mainly by infantry actions on the ground. Even the guerrilla aspect was not so different from that experienced in many theatres in WW2. The fourth of the advances noted above, that of communications, could even be considered to have had a negative impact as it led to an attempt to direct the war from Washington - with predictable lamentable results.

The Falklands War of 1982 featured major technological advances in satellite communications and air and naval actions. But the crucial land battles were decided once more by infantry fighting very much as they had fought some forty years before in the hills of Tunisia or on the road to Falaise.

But, say you, fast forward to the wars in the Gulf, Afghanistan and Iraq of the 1990s and early 2000s. These wars were truly different - fought and won by massive and incredibly precise air strikes, smart bombs, superb missile and fire control systems, night vision, global positioning and satellite control. No "Up guards and at 'em" there. (1) Well, yes and no. Certainly these marvellous things were used to great effect but there were a number of qualifying factors. For starters, all of these wars were fought against foes who were decidedly less than resolute, especially in the Gulf and Iraq. When in the Gulf the enemy tried to employ his outdated armour he was bested not by air strikes alone but also by superb Allied tank fighting. And despite massive air strikes the second Iraq War was decisively won on the ground by armoured columns that would not have seemed too strange to the Desert Rats, Afrika Korps or Panzer Group Kleist of 1941-42.

Afghanistan is a special case. Here the foe, at least on paper, appeared formidable, having given the Russians a black-eye in the previous decade. While smart bombs and precision strikes were certainly effective the war was actually decided by two other factors. The first of these was the existence on the ground of a strong army of Northern Afghans who had already fought the Taliban to a standstill. This army was able to exploit US air power to win victories, and make advances, that astounded the Americans and went too far and too fast for the latter's taste. And second, once more, was the crucial use, effectively aided by helicopter lift, of small unit combat infantry actions. The prestigious journal *Foreign Affairs* contains a definitive article by Professor Stephen Biddle in which this thesis, on the key role of infantry in Afghanistan, is convincingly demonstrated.(2)

So if there are still time honoured lessons to be gleaned from the Second World War what are they? The following sections will attempt to make this case.

RESULTS AND CONCLUSIONS

Generalship

A recurring theme in the previous chapters has been the perceived ordinary performance of Allied, especially British/Canadian, generals when compared with the high standards of their adversaries. In a number of places we have complained that the Allied generals seemed overly detailed in planning, overly rigid in execution and lacked grip and flexibility once battle commenced. We have criticized those instances where Canadian generals seemed fixed on trying to manage a battle by pre-arrangement then leaving things to drift and failing to take immediate advantage of those golden opportunities which a fluid battle fleetingly offers. We have taken pains to point out those times when, with a few shining exceptions, Canadian brigadiers and above stayed remote from the front lines and tried to divine the progress of a messy battle from late, incomplete and misleading scraps of information. Too rarely did these commanders do what was *de rigueur* among German generals - stay forward and personally see and direct operations as they unfolded.

These are certainly not new lessons, indeed Wellington attributed his early successes in battle to leading from the front. Of the depressing Netherlands campaign of 1794-95 he wrote, "The real reason why I succeeded in my own campaigns is because I was always on the spot - I saw everything and did everything myself."(3) His Second World War counterpart would be the brilliant German Erich Von Manstein.(4)

Our generals seemed not to be of this mold. Yet, paradoxically despite these shortcomings, the Canadian generals directed their troops to victory after victory. They may have lacked the elan and professional competence of their German adversaries but they nearly always prevailed against them. The reasons commonly advanced for this often simply stress the Allies' overwhelming preponderance of men, equipment, air and naval support and technology. But that was only the global picture and on the ground things were often quite different. In too many of his battles the Canadian soldier fought an enemy of equal strength who possessed greatly superior tank and anti-tank guns, superb machine guns, mortars and artillery fighting from hidden defensive positions surrounded by wire and mines and often sited behind a river barrier. Despite this the Canadians nearly always won.

To continue to win against such odds the Canadian generals clearly had to be doing something right. An examination of their battles leads to a number of conclusions and a number of common threads all pointing to why they succeeded. They usually based their actions on sound appreciations and planning with a clear understanding of what their troops were expected to accomplish and assembled the right mix of men, equipment, arms and ammunition to do the job. Their tactics, if pedestrian and sometimes over rigid, were designed to win behind an overwhelming density of artillery, well led infantry, meshed supporting arms and an iron determination to succeed. This refusal to accept failure and to keep pushing until victory was won became the hallmark of Canadian generals as illustrated by Ortona, the Hitler and Gothic lines, the four great battles from Caen to Trun, the Scheldt and Rhineland. It was not simply a case of butting ahead with the same failed plan as was the case too often in the First World War. Instead the Canadian generals would seek a new point of attack as in the Liri Valley and before Ortona or a whole new approach as in the dash to Adrano and the deep outflanking at Breskens.

And, perhaps surprisingly in the light of our previous chiding of the generals for lack of imagination, they often enough exhibited a considerable degree of innovation as did Simonds in his plans for "Totalize" and "Tractable", his use of Jock Columns and his deft touch in the final days. Assoro is another shining example but even in the misery of Kapelsche Veer, the use of canoe parties was imaginative thinking and Hoffmeister's battles often displayed this quality in full measure.

We have sometimes tended to denigrate our generals for battering at a closed door behind masses of artillery but the tactic worked! And these were the tactics which the Soviets, with indifferent troops, employed in their Eastern Front victories and which led us to view the Soviet military with such awe in the post-war years. It was the tactic which the often colourless Crerar used to great advantage in Operation "Veritable" where he deliberately exerted maximum pressure on the enemy, from one end of the line to the other, by "putting everything in the shop window". For this he earned both the encomium of his brilliant British subordinate Horrocks and total victory.

Post-war Doctrine

The tactical thinking of the Canadian Army in the immediate post-war years, then commanded by General Foulkes, profited greatly from the lessons of the war. The combat arms practised integrated all-arms mobile battle groups in the German model using advanced Sherman tanks, de-turreted Sherman APCs and imaginative fire plans meshing artillery, mortars, machine guns, flame throwers and close air support. A new generation of officers and NCO's emerged imbued with the all-arms spirit. For the infantry paratrooping became the norm. It seemed the dawn of a new era.

All of this came to virtual standstill with the onset of the Korean war where events and terrain conspired to return things to a near First World War model. The static Korean front of 1951-53 led to a stifling of generalship as commanders at all levels, profiting from fixed lines and enhanced communications, tended to run things by telephone from far in the rear. Following Korea, until the introduction of the lightly armoured M113 APC in the late 1960s, the infantry reverted to movement in highly vulnerable ¾ ton trucks and infantry - tank tactics suffered accordingly.

The army was seldom tested defensively in the Second World War. Its major defensive battle took place just after D-Day in the linked defences of Putot, Norrey, Cardonville and Bretteville. The last three named defences were based on companies fighting from built up area stone buildings and walls and were highly successful. At Putot the infantry fought in the relative open from a series of isolated and poorly sited slit-trench company localities and the result was a near disaster illustrating the folly of such dispositions. Probably because stone buildings are a rarity in Canada, and wide open training areas the norm, the Putot example was the one adopted in post-war training. Lip service was paid to such time honoured requirements as reverse slopes, mutual support based on defiladed automatic and anti-tank weapons and interlocking fields of fire. But in practice companies were usually sited out of effective defensive support range of one another. Platoons usually adopted a straight-ahead defensive posture with little thought to mutual support with others. As a result Putot was repeated on Hill 187 in Korea.(5)

In the Second World War the Germans were masters at mounting immediate counter-attacks, with whatever was at hand, before the attackers could get set defensively or properly site their anti-tank weapons. The British/Canadians eschewed this highly effective tactic in favour of the laid-on, set-piece deliberate counter-attack. This

RESULTS AND CONCLUSIONS

tactic worked at Putot but was a near failure in Korea. On the Hook in late 1952 the British Black Watch were heavily attacked at night and partly overrun. 3 PPCLI from the reserve were ordered to mount a full scale counter-attack at first light. By the time the attack finally got underway the enemy had withdrawn of his own volition and the chance to roughly handle him was gone. At Hill 187 in May 1953, despite ample pre-warning that something was up, the Canadian commanders allowed a single company of 3 RCR to be attacked at night in isolation and partly overrun. No counter-attack was even attempted and the enemy was allowed to withdraw with the spoils of war.

At no time did the British/Canadians develop the rapid riposte used so successfully by the Germans everywhere and by the Japanese in trouncing a succession of stodgy British attacks in the early Arakan battles. As a result great opportunities were lost to catch the attackers in flank and rear and turn defeat into victory.

The Generals

Although this section deals mainly with Canadian generals the seamless integration of Canadian and British formations in the war requires that attention also be paid to the British generals under, or with, whom the Canadians served. And any list of British commanders must start with that strange, enigmatic, showman Field Marshal Bernard Law Montgomery.

The Field Marshal certainly had his share of peculiar personality traits driven by an overweening ego. But given that his professional inter-war career was spent in the company of often inept and uninspiring fellow officers it is small wonder that he developed a sometimes dogmatic and unyielding certitude towards those around him. Despite, or perhaps because of, these traits he was very often right and nearly always successful. Unfortunately this cut both ways as his fondness for proclaiming that battles went exactly as he had planned them paid him a disservice in overlooking his actual flexibility in adapting his plans as the battle progressed. In Sicily when his much trumpeted east coast push stalled he adroitly shifted first to the Canadian flank and then gave the final prime role to Patton's Americans.

Normandy went just about the way Montgomery said he planned it although not always the way he appeared to try to execute. His initial grand plans to encircle Caen were excellent in concept as was his all-or-nothing tank attack of "Goodwood" albeit the latter was marred by a poor choice of terrain. His closing of the Falaise Gap was initially hampered by his unfortunate decision to concentrate the British armour at the wrong flank but he recouped by adroitly altering Army objectives in the heat of battle. Montgomery's preparation and launching of the Second army from Normandy to Antwerp was well done.

Although much criticized for failing to give priority to the opening of Antwerp his decision to instead gamble at Arnhem was the correct one at the time. Thus despite his many faults Monty, unlike the First World War's Haig, emerged from final victory with esteem and honour and it is hard to argue with results.

The Army Commanders

Since many of the battles in Italy and Northwest Europe were fought at the corps or divisional levels it is difficult to assess the performance of the Army Commanders, especially as they often laboured under Monty's steely overview. Leese, who was a very good Corps Commander in Sicily, bungled his two major battles as Army Commander in Italy before being bundled off to Burma where he totally blotted his copy book. His successor McCreery's major action affecting the Canadians was his controversial sacking of Burns right after the latter had won the 8th Army's greatest victory in Italy up to that time. Dempsey performed quite well in command of the British 2nd Army and made few mistakes. He deserves an above average passing grade.

General Crerar who took command of the 1st Canadian Army in Normandy was almost invisible, except for a soon resolved spat with Lt Gen Crocker, until the Falaise Gap was closed. His unfortunate dust-up with Montgomery over the Dieppe aftermath may, if one is to believe Simonds, have led to early missed opportunities on the Scheldt. Crerar's one great battle "Veritable", in which he commanded most of the British and Canadian divisions, was very well conducted, earning the praise of both Eisenhower and Horrocks. One could argue that his last over-the-Rhine campaign was pursued with insufficient vigor. But neither, Monty's post-war denigrations to the contrary, did he make any real mistakes. A solid passing grade.

The Corps Commanders

Horrocks emerged as 21 Army Group's star performer as crowned by his post-Falaise dash to Antwerp and his masterful handling of XXX Corps in "Veritable". Yet his halting attempt to relieve Arnhem was most hesitatingly conducted. Flamboyant and extroverted, he was a soldier's general - fulsome in praise when merited and able to ginger the best out of his subordinates which, after all, is the hallmark of a true leader. He earns a very high rating.

Crocker started on the wrong foot under Crerar in Normandy and played only a minor role until the Gap was closed. His subsequent attack on Le Havre was brilliantly planned and brilliantly executed. On the Scheldt he conducted his east flank operations with a deft hand and was rewarded with a string of successes which stamped him as above average.

Foulkes did not start too well. As a divisional commander his performance on Operation "Spring" was poor. As a Corps Commander he was only fair on the Scheldt but did well in Italy and late Holland. He thereby received the command of the post-war Canadian army.

Simonds was a Monty acolyte and an enigma. Cold and ruthless he blew hot and cold. His division did very well in Sicily but it was here that Simonds devised the artillery heavy piecemeal frontal attacks that were to stultify the tactics of the Canadian Army thereafter. His concepts for "Totalize" and "Tractable" were brilliant but his conduct of each was flawed. His stint as an Army Commander on the Scheldt was good. As a Corps Commander for the final push he did very well in East Holland, somewhat less well in the drive for the Jade. He was considered by Montgomery to be Canada's best general..

The much maligned Burns was just the opposite of Horrocks. Dour, unsmiling, unloved by superiors, peers and subordinates alike. He fought two major battles in Italy - in the Liri Valley and on the Gothic Line - and clearly won them both. Allotted only a subordinate role on the Gothic Line he succeeded so brilliantly that his became the main

RESULTS AND CONCLUSIONS

thrust and was singled out for praise by the official British historian. His Gothic Line battles were the 8th Army's greatest achievements to that time and possibly Canada's greatest victories of the war. Sacked at the moment of victory because of palace intrigue he never received the honours he earned. Since here he is rated for achievement and not personality he receives an "A".

The Division Commanders

Chris "throw in another battalion" Vokes was blunt and thrusting, if unimaginative. Doggedly victorious at Ortona and the Hitler Line he was in turn triumphant and flawed. His brusque manner turned off his subordinates in Northwest Europe. But throughout it all he was a winner. .

Keller was maligned by the McKenna brothers and not admired by his Corps Commander for his command in Normandy. But, despite the ill-considered opinions of others on Carpiquet, his division was brilliantly successful. Had Keller not been wounded he may have truly blossomed.

Kitching was thrown into the Normandy cauldron with two strikes against him - poor tasks from his Corps Commander and poor performances by his subordinates. His division certainly underachieved but much of this was the fault of his brigadiers and unit commanders. But he failed to light a fire under his subordinates and his handling of the Falaise Gap battles was poor - an incorrect allocation of resources to tasks and a remote and poor control of events. Under other circumstances he may well have done better but sadly must be judged on what he did and failed to do.

Keefler under-performed with 2nd Division on the Scheldt but succeeded very well commanding 3rd Division in East Holland. A late comer he finished with a good reputation..

Matthews did well in East Holland and fairly well on the approaches to the Jade. Another late comer he also gets a good grade.

Foster did very well commanding 7 Brigade in Normandy but was just fair in succession to Kitching with 4th Armoured Division. He started off-base in Italy but finished well in West Holland. .

Hoffmeister was Canada's best general of the war. After a hesitant start on the Liri he never made a meaningful mistake. His performances on the Gothic Line, the Romagno, Coriano and Holland were magnificent. He well merits an "A+".

Communications

Communications, that often criticised wartime bugbear, materially improved postwar. Hardware especially advanced although skilled usage sometimes lagged. At company level the fixed-channel # 26 set was a boon as platoons and company could now readily converse. The battalion to company set still required tedious tinkering and fiddling and its bulk made the signaller a marked target. The rear-link to Brigade featured the monster 19 set, designed for tank use. It required very skilful operation - a commodity often in short supply.(6) And unfortunately good communications sometimes resulted in commanders far in the rear trying to control things that should have been left to the officer on the spot.(7)

Wireless security remained an ongoing problem and led to constant low grade security contretemps, despite the fact that the Germans had derived much of their intelligence, such as the location of Assembly Areas and FUPs, simply by monitoring the location and volume of traffic. Post-war security resulted in some ridiculous situations such as a division - brigade link being tied up for two hours in the passage and reception in Slidex (low grade cipher) of a long bomb-line with resulting errors, queries and re-transmissions as the battle roared on far ahead.

Honours and Awards

The Canadian handling of the award of decorations ranged from hit and miss to poor.

Commanders who were only too eager to secure a meaningless DSO for themselves were strangely reluctant to fight for honours for their men. The constant failure of valorous Canadians to receive the Victoria Crosses they so clearly won is a disgrace and has been a constant theme in this book. For a Corps to receive only three VCs for the entire two year Italian campaign, involving some of the hardest and most successful battles anywhere, is an absolute farce. As is only one for Normandy and three for the rest of Northwest Europe. Contrast this with the *five* awarded to a single British regiment - the Royal Norfolks - in the same war. No doubt the Norfolk awards were merited but no more so than that earned, but not received, by a dozen Canadians. An even worse example is that of the Lancashire Fusiliers of the First World War who won 18. Six of these were issued to the Regiment to be distributed *as it saw fit* to members of the battalion who had landed at "W" Beach in Gallipoli - an absolutely ludicrous way to award decorations. No doubt that "W" Beach was a brutal experience, but no more so than any of the six Canadian assault battalions experienced on D-Day where nary a single VC was awarded.(8)

The stupid regulation which precluded the posthumous award of lesser decorations than the VC has now been rescinded but too late to recognize the many dead Canadians who earned them. The awarding of lesser decorations was also hit and miss. The company of Regina Rifles that stormed the Abbaye Ardenne received nothing simply because its officers were too involved in ongoing operations to have time to write them up. The same for the brilliant victory at Assoro, It is to be hoped that this sort of nonsense will never be repeated.

L'Envoie

But enough of this nay saying! Let us end the book by accentuating the positive and recap what the Canadian soldiers actually did in this great war. Never mind that it has all been said earlier in previous chapters. For those who only want the 60 second sound bite they can get it just by reading the opening section and this last one. For lovers of real beer it will point them to further research. And for Canadians at large just read this section and rejoice in the truly incredible things that your grandfathers dared to do. Gaudeamus Igitur!

RESULTS AND CONCLUSIONS

Background

In assessing the magnitude of what our soldiers did one must bear in mind the incredibly small numbers of Canadian formations in relation to their Allies in each theatre and what they accomplished with so few troops. For example, in Sicily Canada fielded only a single division, in Italy until past Ortona only the same division plus an armoured brigade. The great battles of the Hitler and Gothic Lines, in which Canada shone, were fought with only two divisions plus the brigade - out of some thirty that the Allies had in that theatre. In Northwest Europe Canada fielded only five divisions - indeed from just one to three until nearly the last month - out of a total of 90 Allied divisions. Yet they were constantly in the vanguard. At the war's end General Eisenhower enumerated the three major campaigns fought in the entire European Theatre as the D-Day landings, the Falaise Pocket and the west bank Rhineland battles of 1945. In each of these, despite their small numbers, the Canadians played a major role.

Hong Kong (December 1941).

Two Canadian infantry battalions participated out of the eight available for the defence of Hong Kong. After the mainland was lost a single Canadian battalion - the Royal Rifles of Canada - provided virtually the only coherent fighting force for the Island's Eastern Brigade which bore the brunt of the Japanese attacks. Almost devoid of transport or support weapons this single battalion, for nearly a week without respite, constantly defended, counter-attacked and withdrew to the next position over some of the most difficult terrain anywhere. Totally exhausted at the end of this ordeal they still somehow found the inner strength to stay in action as a viable force right up to the Island's surrender.

In the Canadian commanded Western Brigade several battalions, in one form or another, were available and all fought well. Of these, the Winnipeg Grenadiers distinguished themselves in the defence of Wong Nei Chong and in several heroic counter-attacks, in one of which a Grenadiers' Sergeant-Major won the VC.

With his headquarters overrun the Canadian Brigadier Lawson could have done as have countless others in his position and surrendered with honour. Instead he chose to go outside to fight it out and was killed in the attempt. Even the Japanese were impressed. It is also noteworthy that the only two battles in all of Hong Kong where the Japanese reported meeting heavy resistance were fought against the Canadians.

Dieppe (August 1942).

This controversial operation was poorly planned at the higher levels and was inadequately supported in execution. Despite this the two Canadian brigades attacked again and again over open beaches into murderous fire. The fact that nearly one-quarter of the landed Canadians were killed and one-third wounded speaks volumes for their valour in a hopeless cause.

GAUDEAMUS IGITUR

Sicily (July-August 1943).

The 1st Canadian Infantry Division emerged as the best British/Canadian, and perhaps Allied, division in the Sicilian Campaign. At the outset they were allotted a secondary role in mountainous terrain in support of the planned major push up the east coast. When the coastal drive faltered the Canadians took over the main event. Constantly attacking over appalling terrain the Division was brilliantly successful - against some of the cream of the German Army. Its incredible capture of the heights of Assoro was the stuff of legend.

Italy (1943-44).

Selected as one of two divisions to lead the Allied return to mainland Europe the 1st Canadians fought their tortuous way through the mountainous toe of Italy to capture Potenza and help in the relief of Salerno. Sent to the Adriatic front they emerged as the star of Montgomery's ill-fated winter campaign succeeding in the brutal battles of the Moro and Ortona as the rest of the 8th Army faltered.

United with 5th Canadian Armoured Division, under Ist Canadian Corps, the 1st Division moved west over the Apennines in the Spring of 1944 and participated in the crucial Liri Valley campaign where they spearheaded the breaking of the Hitler Line. Meanwhile 1st Canadian Armoured Brigade fought alongside other formations of the 8th Army on the Liri and in the advance to Florence.

Switched again to the Adriatic front the Ist Canadian Corps under Lt Gen Burns was allocated a supporting role in breaking the Gothic Line to the five-division strong V Corps' main effort. The roles soon reversed as Burns' Canadians broke the Green, Gothic and Rimini Lines, captured Coriano and led to the threshold of the Po Valley thus guarantying the success of next spring's final offensive. It was perhaps Canada's greatest single victory of the war.

Northwest Europe (1944-45).

3rd Canadian Division was selected as one of the five Allied divisions to spearhead the D-Day assault. Landing on Juno Beach against ferocious opposition the 3rd Canadians penetrated the farthest inland of any sea-landed Allied division on D-Day and were the first to capture all their D-Day objectives. Thwarted in a bold attempt to seize Carpiquet the Division then fought a superb defensive battle at Norrey - Cardonville and Bretteville preventing the enemy from driving to the coast and splitting the Allied beachhead.

In July the Division fought a savage series of battles at Authie, Buron and Abbaye Ardenne opening the door to Caen which they captured alongside the British. Joined by 2nd Canadian Division under IInd Canadian Corps they fought a series of bloody battles around Verrieres Ridge - Tilly-la-Campagne. IInd Corps, now comprising the 2nd and 3rd Canadian Infantry, the Polish and 4th Canadian Armoured and the 51st Highland Divisions, then fought two imaginative APC mounted battles which broke the enemy's main defences and led to the capture of Falaise in a brilliant action by 2nd Division. Against frantic enemy resistance the IInd Canadian Corps finally closed the Falaise Gap

RESULTS AND CONCLUSIONS

and linked up with the Americans.

In the break-out from Normandy the Canadians were assigned the difficult coastal flank in which they were required to capture the fortified ports of Le Havre, Boulogne and Calais and the cross-channel guns and flying bomb sites at Cap Gris Nez and Pas de Calais. This was followed by the terrible Scheldt battles of the autumn 1944 fought over appallingly difficult polder and mud terrain in cold, rain-sodden weather. Their victory was a triumph for the raw courage and incredible endurance of the individual Canadian combat soldier.

Early 1945 found the 1st Canadian Army conducting its greatest battle of the war - the brutal slugging match of Operation "Veritable" in which most of the British and all of the Canadian divisions in the theatre fought under Canadian command. The month long battle, one of the most difficult of the war, ended with the elimination of the enemy west of the Rhine and was included in Eisenhower's list as forming part of one of the three key battles of the entire European campaign.

The European war's final phase gave the Canadians their proudest role - the liberation of the wonderful Netherlanders from four years of Nazi yoke. This campaign forged a bond between our two peoples which has endured ever after. And this is surely something in which we can all rejoice.

Separate note must be made of the exploits of the 1st Canadian Parachute Battalion of 6th Airborne Division who dropped on D-Day, securing all their objectives and playing a key part in holding the Orne bridgehead before advancing to the Seine. After brief service in the Ardennes they dropped over the Rhine and with 6th Airborne Division led the advance of all Commonwealth forces to the Baltic and a link-up with the Russians.

Meanwhile 600 junior Canadian officers were attached to British infantry battalions for the Invasion. Fully integrated they fought with bravery and distinction in every one of the British 2nd Army's battles on the Continent, including Arnhem.

Finally a special bow to the battalion plus of Canadians who joined with their American cousins in the splendidly unique Canada/USA Special Service Force which fought with distinction on the Italian Winter Line, at Anzio, led the capture of Rome and participated in the liberation of southern France.

In Memorium

On the memorial to the 14th Army at Kohima are engraved the words which can be applied to all of the youth of the Commonwealth who gave their lives in the Second World War. They are also a fitting tribute to those of whom this book is written.

> *When you go home tell them of us and say*
> *For your tomorrows we gave our today.*

REFERENCE NOTES

Chapter I - Overview and Setting

1. Denis Winter, *Haig's Command,* (St. Ives, Penguin, 1991) pp. 78-79. The caption to the illustration reads in part, " From Spring 1917 to the Armistice, the Canadian

Corps was the most effective fighting force in Haig's Army..." Winter was an Australian and not likely to lightly give such an accolade to another national force.

See also J. Morris, *Farewell the Trumpets,* (Bungay Suffolk, Penguin, 1979) p. 213. Morris, an Englishman, writes: "most people agreed, for instance, that the Canadians were the best troops on the western front..." This sentiment was echoed several times by another English writer, and Great War infantry subaltern, R. Aldington in his novel, *Death of a Hero.* Incidentally, Aldington"s short story, *At All Costs,* included in E. Hemingway, *Men at War,* (Berkley, Crown, 1942) pp. 133-147, remains the most gripping and realistic account of the trench life of an infantry officer in the First World War.

2. Winter, *op cit,* pp. 270-271. Winter remains one of the few historians to give Currie his just due. Astonishingly, Currie is frequently totally omitted from otherwise comprehensive and authoritative reference works dealing with the World Wars. An example is the otherwise superb, *The Encyclopaedia of Twentieth-Century Warfare,* N. Frankland, ed, (New York, Crown, 1989) which includes hordes of lesser known generals down to divisional level but makes no reference at all to Currie.

Users of the Internet are also short-changed. The website *www.world war1.com* gives an overly-glowing account of Australia's Monash and a decidedly perfunctory one of Currie. This is an area Canadian historians should set out to correct.

3. Winter, *op cit* pp.265, 289-290.

4. Cole and Priestley, *An Outline of British Military History,* (London, Sifton Praed,1937) pp.377-378. Although the victory at Amiens was almost entirely a Canadian and Australian triumph the authors never mentioned either in their account of the battle, simply referring to "the British Army" or to "Rawlinson's Fourth Army". They do, however, conclude that Amiens was "the most brilliant British victory of the war" (but see also Winter's award of this accolade to Drocourt-Queant - another Canadian success). In their otherwise excellent book Cole and Priestly seem to have been perversely determined to deny the Canadians their just due - never mentioning their critical roles at the Somme, Passchendaele, Amiens, Hindenberg Line, Arras, Cambrai or Mons. They grant the Canadians only second billing for Vimy and of their magnificent stand at 2nd Ypres the authors sourly remark that the Germans "allowed themselves to be held up by the Canadians..."(p.322).

5. Winter, *op cit,* p271.

6. See D. G. Dancocks, *Sir Arthur Currie,* (Toronto, McLelland Stewart,1988) for an account of this sordid affair.

7. Although the turning points are often taken as Stalingrad, Alamein and Guadalcanal the "turns" were by no means uniform or evident. The Marines at Tarawa could be forgiven for seeing little light at the end of the tunnel in mid 1943. While in Burma the British continued to remain stalled and mauled through most of that year. In Russia the decisive turn only came in July 1943 when the Germans lost their last throw of the victory dice at Kursk. And, of course, no Canadian who fought in Italy or Northwest Europe would concede that his battles could even be remotely considered as mop up operations.

8. The " November Handicap" and the "Dash to the Wire" were two of many wry sobriquets which the British soldier attached to the headlong "flaps" of the Desert Army in 1941-42.

9. The value of seasoning can be overstated as battle survivors frequently tend to grow more cautious and less daring as the campaign stretches on with no immediate end in

RESULTS AND CONCLUSIONS

sight. Certainly the resounding success of the D Day assaults owed much to the "hell for leather" dash of well trained but battle raw troops for whom the realities of grinding attrition had not yet become apparent. Gordon Brown, a former Commanding Officer, also makes this point in his segment of the chapter on the Regina Rifles in *We Were There*, Vol. 2, J. E. Portugal ed, (Royal Canadian Military Heritage Society,1998).

10. The growing unease that ordinary Canadians felt over this situation was encapsulated by the then popular CBC radio show *The Happy Gang*. During the war the "Gang" did their bit by inserting patriotic routines into their acts, one such being a parody on *Barnacle Bill The Sailor*. This skit ended with Bill saying something like, "Now I've got to hurry and get to Berlin and give those Nazis a sock on the chin." Increasingly, as the war dragged on with no Canadian land participation, the Gang changed the ending first to "...get to Berlin or others will get there *before I get in*." And finally, in utter frustration, to "...get to Berlin or the Russians will take it *before we begin*."

11. David Day, *The Great Betrayal, Britain, Australia and the Onset of the Pacific War 1939-42*,(New York, Norton,1989). Day describes how the British leaders, once their pre-war promises to defend Australia with a fleet based in Singapore had proven hollow, severely criticised Australia for withdrawing troops from the Middle East for its own defence and for other deemed shortcomings . Although the fall of Singapore was due largely to the failings of the British command (both grand and theatre strategic and theatre tactical) Churchill, at p. 292, blamed the Australians as primarily responsible. Eden, Cadogan, Hardy and Pownall all weighed in with similarly off-base comments at various times.

12. The remark was made during one of Pearson's superb seminars for graduate students in International Affairs at Carleton University in 1970/71. The "Carleton Clubbers" refer to the pre-eminent Tory club in St. James. Balliol is one of Oxford's more tony colleges.

13. The Normandy episode of the TV series *The Valour and the Horror* made much of Keller's alleged leadership and drinking problems at the expense of a meaningful appraisal of Canada's achievements in the campaign.

14. Perhaps not totally forgotten. Wartime histories point to Tobruk being garrisoned by the inexperienced 2nd South African Division. In fact the majority of the garrison was British with the main German breakthrough made against the 11th Indian Brigade. Tobruk's fate was sealed through the ineptitude of the commander of the reserve and counter-attack force. The South Africans were only peripherally engaged until after the battle was lost.

15. The section on the Italian Campaign in *The Encyclopaedia of Twentieth Century Warfare*, *op cit*, was written by General Sir William Jackson the British official historian for the Mediterranean and Middle East. At p. 222 Jackson, inexplicably for an official historian, writes: "...Montgomery did not cross the Sangro until December 1, and was then defeated in the battles of Orsogna *and Ortona* (my italics) December 4-28." Orsogna, attacked by the New Zealanders, was indeed a defeat but Ortona was a magnificent Canadian victory. The current Canadian government must have paid more attention to Jackson than the facts judging by the shameful way they "supported" the effort by Canadian veterans to hold a reunion in Ortona over Christmas 1999 and erect a monument to the battle. Much credit goes to Canadian veteran Tojo Griffiths for guiding the reunion to a resounding success .

16. Colonel C.P. Stacey, *Official History of the Canadian Army in the Second World*

GAUDEAMUS IGITUR

War, Vol. I " Six Years of War". (Ottawa, Queen's Printer, 1955) , Appendix A, Table 2. John Ellis, *On The Front Lines,* (Toronto, Wiley, 1991), Appendix. These give rounded percentages of POWs to total casualties as follows: US 11, UK 35, Australia 48, New Zealand 33, South Africa 54, India 51 and Canada 8 1/2. Ellis concludes that this indicates a truly remarkable reluctance by Canadians to "throw in the towel".

Chapter II - Hong Kong

1. Through innuendo and selective scene setting the Hong Kong TV episode of *The Valour and the Horror* could lead those unfamiliar with the facts to wrongfully conclude that the Canadians had participated in the Gin Drinkers/Shing Mun fiasco and in the initial defence of the Island's invasion beaches. The actual principal battles and deeds of the Canadians and Brigadier Lawson were largely ignored.

2. D. Day, *The Great Betrayal, Britain, Australia and the Onset of the Pacific War 1939-42* (New York, Norton, 1988) A well researched account of the British - Australian interplay regarding the unfulfilled promise of the protection of Australia by a British fleet and the guaranteed defence of Singapore in exchange for large Australian overseas commitments. As Day put it: " Churchill's grand promises (were) long on generalities and short on specifics" as a result of which "Australia ... took it at face value, handing over men and equipment in exchange for a blank cheque of doubtful value that could only be banked after the bailiffs had already broken down the front door." pp. 75-83.

3. All of the Western powers, in the face of overwhelming evidence to the contrary, believed the Japanese serviceman to be a weak-eyed, second-class, unthinking automat led by officers with little initiative. Examples abound : For Air Chief Marshall Sir R. Brooke-Popham C-in-C Far East see: O. Lindsay *The Lasting Honour* (London, Hamish Hamilton, 1978) p.18; For Maj Gen A. Grasett, *Ibid* p.3; For Maj Gen C.M. Maltby see T. Ferguson *Desperate Siege: The Battle of Hong Kong* (Toronto, Doubleday,1980) p.32; For British ex-pats generally see: *Ibid* p.25.

Tactical intelligence was equally deplorable. Believing their own wishful thinking the Allies were repeatedly nonplussed and routed when the Japanese employed night assaults, outflanking manoeuvres and pepper-pot attacks - something all armies are trained to do as a matter of course. And completely blind to copious evidence from China and Manchuria the Allies were all too often panicked by the mere appearance of a few mediocre Japanese tanks - often attacking straight down a main road. See D. Fraser *And We Shall Shock Them* (London, Cassell, 1999) pp.184-189

The story was the same concerning equipment. For whatever reason (probably none at all) the Allies believed the Japanese air arms consisted only of obsolete types manned by inferior crews. The famed Zero (Mitsubishi A6M "Zeke") thus came as a total surprise, despite copious prior evidence, and achieved such ascendancy over the mediocre Allied aircraft of the day that it became clothed in the myth of near invincibility. N. Gunston *Fighting Aircraft of World War II* (London, Salamander,1988) pp.266-267

4. T. Ferguson, *Ibid* p.24 ;p.27.

5. Prior to the Canadian's arrival the Hong Kong Garrison under Maj.Gen. C.M. Maltby (successor to the Canadian ex-pat Maj.Gen A.E. Grasett) comprised the 2nd Royal Scots, 1st Middlesex, 5/7 Rajput, 2/14 Punjab; two coastal (8th and 12th),one anti-aircraft(5th) regiments and one defence battery (965) Royal Artillery; 1st Hong

RESULTS AND CONCLUSIONS

Kong and Singapore Royal Artillery; two fortress companies Royal Engineers and the Hong Kong Volunteer Defence Corps including infantry and artillery.

The artillery was a decidedly mixed bag: twenty-nine fixed coastal pieces of 9.2, 6, 4.7 and 4 inch calibre; eight 18 pounder and 2 pounder beach defence guns; fourteen heavy and two light anti-aircraft guns and mobile artillery of twelve 6 inch; eight 4.5 inch, eight 3.7 inch and four 60 pounders. Ammunition was limited - only 25 rounds per fixed gun for land targets and 70 rounds 3inch mortar per battalion

On 8 December 1941 the naval force consisted of the old destroyer *Thracian* ,several gunboats and some motor torpedo boats. The air force had two Walrus amphibians and three obsolete torpedo bombers. C.P. Stacey, *Six Years of War* (Ottawa, Queen's Printer, 1955) pp. 456-457.

6. W.S. Churchill, *The Grand Alliance* (Boston, Houghton Mifflin,1951) p.177. Churchill was originally adamantly opposed to the proposed reinforcement of Hong Kong, writing : "This is all wrong....there is not the slightest chance of holding Hong Kong or relieving it....Instead of increasing the garrison it ought to be reduced to a symbolical scale." Later he (in his words) "allowed myself to be drawn from this position, and...two Canadian battalions were sent as reinforcements."

7. Stacey, *op cit* ,pp 451-455.

8. Stacey, *ibid,* p. 440.

9. Stacey, *ibid,* p.458.

10. The line was on commanding high ground but lacked depth and faced considerable dead ground. Its defences had been started three years earlier, abandoned, then restarted with the change of plan on the Canadians' arrival. Due to the line's ten mile length the three manning battalions were widely dispersed in a series of platoon localities. The Royal Scots had one reserve company, the Rajputs one as brigade reserve and the Punjabs one for the brigade screen then reserve. In the event none of these available companies were used for counter-attack. The entire line was supported by only four troops of mobile artillery - a mixed bag of 6, 4.5 and 3.7 inch.

11. A. Horne, *To Lose a Battle,*(Harmondsworth, Penguin,1979), p. 332.

The incomplete line of pillboxes defending the Meuse at Sedan was methodically destroyed by flat trajectory fire directed at embrasures by anti-aircraft guns manhandled to the opposite bank. This came as a shocking surprise to the French command despite the fact that the Germans had rehearsed this exact tactic against pillboxes of the old Czech frontier defence line a year earlier - all of which had been reported in detail by the French Military Attache. There is no evidence that the British were similarly surprised at Hong Kong. However there is also no evidence that they gainfully employed the nineteen months since Sedan to revamp their beach defences to prevent such an occurrence.

12. A quick reconnaissance by Colonel Doi led him to decide on an immediate attack on Shing Mun, even though the redoubt lay in another regiment's assigned sector - something absolutely anathema to British tactical concepts. His Third Battalion attacked at midnight and after some sporadic severe fighting soon captured the entire position. Stacey, *op cit,* p.465.

13. Like the Belgians at Eben Emael almost two years previous, the Hong Kong commanders seem to have given little thought at what to do in the event that the enemy got onto the redoubt. Consequently they did little to effectively assist the redoubt's manning platoon which was soon eliminated. Matters were not helped when the

redoubt's platoon commander initially positioned himself in the artillery observation post leaving his sergeant to lead the defence of the platoon.

According to Ferguson , *op cit,* p.71, the Punjab's commanding officer requested permission to counter-attack but was denied by Brigadier Wallis. Subsequently, at Golden Hill, Wallis tried to get the CO Royal Scots to counter-attack but the latter declined! *Ibid,* p.79. While Stacey, *op cit,* p.465, has Wallis and Maltby "discussing" the mounting of a counter-attack but deciding against this because the reserves were too far away, the ground too broken and the situation unknown - an incredible admission of the failure of command.

Shing Mun had offered possibilities of the classic defensive tactic of fighting from tunnels and pillboxes while friendly artillery and machine gun fire raked the position and its approaches. The British did however learn. Twelve years later in Korea the Duke of Wellingtons brilliantly fought just such a battle on The Hook and were completely successful.

14. Stacey, *op cit,* p.467. It was perhaps not quite so easy. At Golden Hill the Scots redeemed some of their lost reputation by putting up a stiff, albeit unsuccessful , fight.

15. The British command seems to have been particularly incensed at the actions of some other ranks of the Royal Rifles in defending the officers mess at Stanley. While the facts are murky they do speak volumes on the colonial mind set of the era - a theme later rehashed in the film *The Guns of Batasi.*

16. Stacey, *op cit.* p.481. Also noteworthy, Churchill's *The Grand Alliance,* which devotes only two pages of generalities to the battle for Hong Kong, singles out Lawson's last action for special praise. Churchill *op cit,* p.635.

17.The gun was a 70mm Battalion Gun Type 92 which looked odd but was highly successful, combining mobility with firepower and could be manhandled by its crew over almost any terrain. It was issued to all infantry battalions and could be employed in direct fire or as a gun/howitzer. Like the Japanese 50 mm light spade-baseplate mortar (the so-called "knee mortar") the gun came as yet another nasty surprise to the Allies.

18. Fraser, *op cit,* p.183.

19. Stacey, *op cit,* pp. 438-439.

20. The existence of good counter-attack plans does not, in itself, mean too much. Six months later at Second Tobruk the reserve commander made six detailed counter-attack plans. In the event, despite many opportunities to do so, none were used. M. Carver, *Tobruk* (London, Clowes, 1964).

21. Perhaps indicative is the fact that the Royal Scots earned 38 battle honours in the Second World War but were not awarded the honour " Hong Kong" although they received the broader "South East Asia 1941". D. Henderson, *The Scottish Regiments* (Glasgow, Harper Collins,1996) p.167.

Chapter III - Dieppe

1. The 907 Dieppe dead comprised over 18% of the 4963 embarked force from just an 11 hour battle. The percentage of dead among those who actually landed is much higher. The 1154 wounded amount to a further 23%, giving a total dead and wounded percentage of 42% of those who embarked and over 50% of those who actually landed. The equivalent figures for the 1976 strong Canadian Hong Kong contingent is 15% killed, 25% wounded and 7% died in captivity. Total dead were thus 22%.

RESULTS AND CONCLUSIONS

The November 1943 Tarawa operation is the closest Pacific equivalent to Dieppe in force strengths and battle ferocity. Tarawa cost the 2nd US Marine Division some 1500 total casualties from an estimated 5000 who landed on the first day (the Canadian Dieppe equivalents were 2061 from some 4000 - 4500 who landed). The entire three day Tarawa (Betio) battle cost the Marines 3070 casualties from an undetermined number put ashore. Both battles are equivalent studies in courage.

2. Following Dunkirk the British contemplated returning a "Second BEF" to the Continent comprising all of the fully formed divisions in the UK, which meant in effect only the 52nd Lowland and 1st Canadian. To these would be added whatever remained of the 1st Armoured Division already fighting in France. After some uncertainty it was decided to join with the French in defending a "Brittany Redoubt". Accordingly the 1st Canadian Division commenced preparations and on 11 June the 1st Canadian Infantry Brigade embarked, arriving in Brest on 12 and 13 June. Chaos reigned and the Canadian brigade was dispatched in penny packets by road and rail to various places between Laval and Le Mans - far in advance of the proposed redoubt.

The French situation rapidly deteriorated, leading to an armistice, and on 14 June the force was ordered back It re-embarked on 17 June taking, over considerable opposition from the movement control staff, all of its guns and other key equipment but leaving behind (unnecessarily so in Canadian opinion) most of its transport.

3. The Commandos, a name derived from Boer raiding parties in the last South African War, started as Independent Companies of Infantry, then Special Service Battalions and finally as Commandos under a Combined Operations Headquarters initially headed by the renowned Admiral Sir Roger Keyes. In late 1941 Keyes was succeeded by the newly promoted Vice Admiral Lord Louis Mountbatten a cousin of the king.

4. Long after the event Mountbatten claimed that his idea for a double envelopment of Dieppe was rejected by the Chiefs of Staff (COS) in favour of a frontal attack. Mountbatten said that he only agreed to this if a "sufficiently strong aerial bombardment " was provided to support the frontal attack. In fact the idea of heavy bombing and the use of paratroops had been cancelled by early June, a decision to which Mountbatten made no demur. Likewise Gen Montgomery, who was present when the decision to cancel the bombing was made, disclaimed all knowledge of the decision and said he would have opposed it. There is no record that the COS were at all involved. As to the supposed double encirclement, the left (Puys) pincer would still have been impractical. Whitehead et al, *Dieppe 1942*, publisher unknown, p41 and B. Greenhous, *Dieppe, Dieppe*, Editions Art Global Inc, Montreal,1992,. P 54 and p 57.

5. In typical Monty fashion he initially bypassed McNaughton and broached the idea with Lt Gen H. Crerar the Corps Commander.

6. The Canadian disappointments included: Trondheim, April 1940, cancelled before embarkation; Brittany Redoubt, June 1940, Canadian brigade withdrawn before seeing action; Defence of Britain, 1940/41, no enemy invasion; Spitsbergen, August 1941, no enemy encountered; Hardelot Commando raid, April 1942, Canadian participants were not landed.

7. C.P. Stacey, *Six Years of War*, Queen's Printer, Ottawa, 1955, pp 352-358.

8. This was the Commando's belief. The Germans reported the explosion was caused by an air strike. In either case the result was spectacular. Greenhous, *op cit*, p 84.

9. Equally important was the need to effectively screen off the headlands from the beach by keeping them constantly smoked out. As Lt Col Labatt, CO RHLI, noted

"After the smoke had come down and while it was thick, enemy firing faded to almost nothing... As the air cleared... fire became very much brisker." Greenhous, *op cit*, p 140. To maintain a smokescreen would have required equipping the destroyers and gunboats with ammunition specific to the task. The attempt to use Boston bombers in the smoking role was only adequate for the task of smoking off the entire beach for the initial landings. Thereafter the requirement was for constantly applied pinpoint smoking of specific targets. It was not provided.

10. The PIAT (Projector Infantry Anti-Tank) began replacing the Boys Anti-tank Rifle in 1941. It is not clear if the Canadian units at Dieppe had been so equipped. A much maligned weapon, the PIAT was actually very effective inside 100 yards and could fire with less effect up to 350 yards. Primarily an anti-tank and anti-bunker weapon it could also fire HE and smoke and in the hands of a skilled operator it could function in the platoon mini-artillery role.

11. One or two landing craft commanders later claimed that after the initial wave of soldiers suffered heavy casualties there was some reluctance on the part of others to follow and they had to be urged off. Apart from the natural tendency to hesitate before charging into a killing ground the overwhelming majority of troops did simply rush ahead. Capt G.A. Browne, a FOO with the RRof C, testified that "The Royals in my ALC [assault landing craft] appeared cool and steady... they gave no sign of alarm... small arms fire was striking the ALC and there was a not unnatural split-second hesitation.... But only a split-second. The troops got out onto the beach... fast... across the beach to the wall and under the cliff."
Greenhaus, *op cit*, pp 88-90. Stacey, *op cit*, p366.

12. Capt Browne reported "In five minutes they were changed from an assaulting Battalion on the offensive to something less than two companies... being hammered by fire they could not locate." Stacey, *op cit*, p 365.

13. Another problem with Catto's decision to try and link with the Essex Scottish was the existence of the intervening Dieppe Harbour which extended inland for over a mile to the River Arques. However had the Essex succeeded in clearing the town the harbour-waterway could probably have been readily crossed on its several sluice gates and bridges.

14. Ironically one of the RN officers who criticised the Royals for lack of dash displayed only a modicum of that quality himself. When ordered to evacuate Blue Beach he only tentatively approached the beach under fire and did not land, reporting : "Could not see... Blue Beach owing to fog and heavy fire.... Nobody evacuated." Stacey, *Op Cit*, p 367.

15. Stacey, *Op Cit*, p 392.

16. The original plan called for the entire force to withdraw through Dieppe town but the failures at Red and White beaches rendered this impossible. Fortunately for the Pourville force some of the landing craft intended for Red Beach went to Pourville instead. This materially aided the Pourville evacuation to the detriment of the troops at Red.

17. Note has already been taken of the decision not to land tanks at Pourville partly because of the erroneous assumption that the River Scie was a major obstacle. But even had it so been, it was no reason not to provide the Pourville force with the tank support necessary to help them achieve their own objectives.

18. A. Robert Prouse, *Ticket to Hell Via Dieppe*, Von Nostrand Rheinhold, Toronto,

RESULTS AND CONCLUSIONS

1982, p 12.

19. Stacey, *Op Cit*, pp 391-373.

20. Major E. Magnus, a Canadian Staff Officer reported: " The information Combined Operations had was scanty. It was based on aerial photographs and on pictures...of Dieppe before the war. There was very little basic defence information. There were a lot of assumptions." Whitehead, et al, *Op Cit*, p 41.

21. Brian Loring Villa, *Unauthorized Action, Mountbatten and the Dieppe Raid*, Oxford University Press, Toronto, 1989.

22. Villa, *Op Cit*, pp 19-35.

23. Winston S. Churchill, *The Hinge of Fate*, Houghton Mifflin, Boston, 1950, pp 509-511.

24. Colonel John Hughes-Wilson, *Military Intelligence Blunders*, 1999.

25. Saul David, *Military Blunders*, 1997.

26. Greenhaus, *Op Cit*, p 152.

27. Lord Lovat, the commander of the supremely successful No 4 Commando commented "the top brass survived the post-mortem by finding a convenient scapegoat in Gen. Hamilton Roberts ... a fighting soldier who carried out the orders he was given and acted like a gentleman in accepting his dismissal in silence without protest." Greenhaus, *Op Cit*, pp 10 and 149.

28. Singapore was an exception as it was a defensive land battle. But the Island's numerous 9.2 and 6 inch guns, supplemented by two much ballyhooed 18 inch guns taken from the old battle cruiser "Furious", proved virtually useless against land targets.

29. Lt Col Gordon Brown, in relating the crucial Bretteville - Cardonville battle of June 1944, describes how his company fought a desperate struggle against successive savage German attacks without being able to contact his supporting guns, heavy support weapons or battalion headquarters - which was less than a mile away. Indeed at one stage his best communication was with a German soldier who had tapped into his lines. J. Portugal, *We Were There, The Army - 2*, Royal Canadian Military Institute Heritage Society, 1998, pp 833-839.

30. A lesson which was well learned and applied thereafter. For example, the success of the Regina Rifles in storming the beach at Courseulles-sur-Mer on D-Day owed much to the valorous initiative of Lt W. Grayson in assaulting and clearing a key enemy pill box that imperilled the landing. Portugal, *Op Cit*, pp 868, 869, 897.

31. Churchill, *Op Cit*, p 511.

Chapter IV - Sicily

1. The First Canadian Tank Brigade became the First Canadian Armoured Brigade on 26 August 1943, although the units only received their new designation in November. For uniformity of nomenclature, and because the Brigade never fought together as such in Sicily, the designations "Armoured" and "CAB" have been used throughout. Similarly although the Edmonton Regiment only received the title "Loyal" in October the designation "Loyal Edmonton Regiment" has been used throughout.

2. D'Este Carlo, *Bitter Victory*, Collins, Toronto, 1988, P 31, quoted British Brigadier Ian Jacob: "The US regarded the Mediterranean as a kind of dark hole, into which one entered at one's peril."

3. D'Este, *Op Cit*, p 47, quotes British CIGS Sir Alan Brooke's assessment of Admiral Mountbatten as "Quite irresponsible, suffers from the most desperate illogical brain and is always producing red-herrings", and "a man of intense enthusiasm ... and an immense ego." The British commanders seem to have had a penchant for denigrating one another (and everyone else). Admiral Cunningham considered General Alexander as "totally unfit for the job." While General Montgomery was even more scathing in writing that Alexander had a "limited brain" and "could not make up his mind" or "give clear and concise orders" and that "the higher art of war is beyond him." D'Este, *Op Cit*, pp 340-341.

4. D'Este, *Op Cit*, p 171.

5. D'Este, *Op Cit*, p 170.

6. The monitor supporting the Canadians was HMS "Roberts". "Erebus" and "Terror" (the names carried by Franklin's ill-fated ships) supported the British. Each mounted two 15 inch guns. Farley Mowat, *And No Birds Sang*, Toronto, McClelland &Stewart, 1979, pp 74-75, credits the "Roberts" with mounting four 16 inch guns.

7. The US DUKW, known as the "Duck", was an amphibious vehicle based on the GMC 6x6 truck fitted with a boat-like hull for buoyancy. Its name came from the GMC designators of "D" - model year 1942, "U"- amphibious, "K" - all-wheel drive, "W" - twin rear axles. Over 21,000 were produced during the war and were used in all theatres.

8. For the comic-opera capture of d'Havet see Daniel G. Dancocks, *The D-Day Dodgers*, Toronto, McClelland & Stewart, 1991, pp 45-46.

9. D'Este, *Op Cit*, p 328.

10. Dancocks, *Op Cit*, pp 54-55. Montgomery was also to play the role of conciliator in Normandy when Canadian Lt Gen H.D.G. .Crerar wanted to sack his British Corps Commander Lt Gen J.T. Crocker and was dissuaded by Monty.

11. See D'Este, *Op Cit*, Appendix L for a full account of the Montgomery - McNaughton fiasco.

12. Mitcham, Samuel G. and von Stauffenberg, Friedrich, *The Battle of Sicily*, New York, Crown, 1991, pp 134-143 and 158.

13. Saunders, Hillary St George, *The Red Beret*, London, Joseph, 1950, pp 128-129.

14. Nicholson G.W.L., *The Canadians in Italy*, Ottawa, Queen's Printer, 1956, p 100.

15. D'Este, *Op Cit*, p 404.

16. This is the version given by Dancocks, *Op Cit*, p 62, which seems to be based in part on Graham's own evidence. The author Farley Mowat, who took part in the venture, credits Tweedsmuir with devising the plan. It is likely that both versions are partly right.

17. For many years during and after the war the Canadian infantry battalion establishment made no provision for a battle staff to assist the CO in his wartime function of forward command. The Adjutant, who was the CO's chief staff officer in peacetime, was often relegated to "A" Echelon in wartime to run the unit's personnel and administration. This often resulted in the IO becoming a battle ADC to the CO to the detriment of his intelligence and scout and sniper duties. Some battalions still used the Adjutant to run the Command Post (CP) while others appointed an officer, often OC Support Company, as "Battle Adjutant." The CP staff typically comprised the Battle Adjutant, IO, Signals Officer, one or two support platoon commanders and sometimes the RSM. Since ad hocery reigned no two units functioned in quite the same way and inefficiency

RESULTS AND CONCLUSIONS

and lapses in procedure often followed. Incidentally Mowat's appointment as IO helps to explain why he survived the war. Very few rifle platoon commanders were to do so unscathed.

18. Mowat, Farley, *The Regiment*, Toronto, McClelland & Stewart, 1955, p 84.

19. Mowat, Farley, *And No Birds Sang*, Op Cit, pp 128-130.

20. Duffy himself was to eventually command the regiment after the war in its Militia guise.

21. Nicholson, *Op Cit*, p 106.

22. According to General Rodt, Commander 15th Panzer Grenadiers, the stiff German resistance in Leonforte was due in part to the Canadians having shot some prisoners in view of the Germans. Mitch am and von Stauffenberg, *Op Cit*, P 194.

23. See Chapter XVI for a discussion on the seeming inequity in the award of VCs and other decorations. Maj Gen Simonds, who had no problem with accepting a DSO for himself although he was rarely under aimed fire, had much more stringent standards concerning awards for lower ranks as he stated: "If decorations are distributed too freely they lose their value in the eyes of the Army ... and to the recipients." Dancocks, *Op Cit*, p 72. Apparently the holus-bolus issue of DSOs, CMGs and CBEs to generals and other senior officers was not considered to be too free a distribution - although awards to these officers certainly had little value "in the eyes of the Army."

24. Simonds aped his mentor Montgomery by insisting on getting a good night's sleep almost regardless of the situation. While this is acceptable practice for an Army Commander who is several levels removed from the actual fighting it is certainly much less so for a Divisional Commander who should be exercising hands-on control of any major action. It is hard to imagine the German's Rommel, Meyer, Schmalz, *et al*, sleeping during a battle under their aegis, except to snatch a few minutes here and there as exhaustion demanded and the situation permitted.

25. The term "divisional attack" conjures up images of a massive crack by a good portion - at least four to six battalions - of the division simultaneously assaulting the enemy with strong tank and artillery support. But as developed by Simonds and refined by Vokes a Canadian "divisional" attack too often meant a succession of individual brigade attacks within which individual battalions successively attacked. Thus at any one time the attack amounted to merely a one battalion thrust probably led by just two rifle companies, or little more than 200 men from a divisional strength of over 15,000. This tactic was repeated so frequently in Italy as to draw comment from General Sir William Jackson, the British Official Historian, as what he perceived to be the Canadian norm. Lamentably, Simonds was to repeat this method in Normandy and was to push it to ridiculous lengths in the great battles leading to Falaise where the zenith was reached in Operation "Spring."

26. After the war Bell-Irving became Lieutenant-Governor of British Columbia. The Seaforths collectively seem to have done well Post-Bellum. Hoffmeister became president of MacMillan Bloedel as later did Robert Bonner another Seaforth, who was also at one time BC's Attorney-General.

27. Among the many aphorisms of Napoleon his admonition to his Marshals to "Ask of me anything but time" still rings true today.

28. More correctly it marked the end for the division and the Three Rivers Regiment of 1 CAB. The other two major units of the armoured brigade, the Ontario and Calgary Regiments, had landed at Syracuse on 13 July as part of the Army Reserve. On 21 July

they were assigned to XIII Corps, first supporting 5 Division on the Dittaino then the 51st Division in its advance along the eastern slopes of Mt Etna. On 11 August the units were withdrawn to Army Reserve and were reunited as an armoured brigade.

29. The joint planning staff originated under Eisenhower's headquarters, later being absorbed into Alexander's 15th Army Group Headquarters.

30. Bradley, Omar N and Clay Blair, *A General's Life,* New York, Simon and Schuster, 1983, pm 167.

31. Loss is a relative term as two of the ships, Queen Elizabeth and Valiant, which were audaciously attacked in December 1941 by Italian frogmen in Alexandria harbour, were eventually repaired. Another, the carrier Eagle, which was sunk by the submarine U73 while ferrying aircraft to Malta was not part of Cunningham's command but was lost in his area of responsibility. The Barham which was sunk with heavy loss of life off Sollum by the U331 in November 1941 was both part of Cunningham's command and a total loss.

32. Dancocks, *Op Cit,* p 96.

33. The full text of Leese's gracious comments are given in Nicholson, *Op Cit,* p 179. To a Canadian they still make most satisfying reading.

Chapter V - From Reggio to Ortona

1. The British divisions selected for the move were the 50th and 51st Infantry and the 7th Armoured. All had fought under Montgomery at Alamein and in the long advance to Tunisia. They were expected to spearhead 21 Army Group's advance through Northwest Europe but their performances in that theatre seldom reached Alamein levels.

2. G.W.L. Nicholson, *The Canadians in Italy,* Queen's Printer, Ottawa, 1957, p 189.

3. Nicholson, *Op Cit,* p 228.

4. N. Hamilton, *Master of the Battlefield,* Hamish Hamilton, London, 1983, p 62.

5. J.W. Pickersgill, *The Mackenzie King Record,* Vol.1, University Press, Toronto, 1960, pp 520 and 558-607.

6. D.G. Dancocks, *The D-Day Dodgers,* McClelland & Stewart, Toronto, 1991, pp 132-133. The opposition, widespread among British commanders and staff, was spearheaded by Alexander who signalled to the CIGS, Sir Alan Brooke, "We already have as much armour in the Mediterranean as we can usefully employ in Italy .... I do not want another Corps Headquarters at this stage."

7. A mistake the Canadians belatedly tried to rectify by attempting, in May 1944, to reunite the Canadian Army by withdrawing the two divisions from Italy. They were not to be able to do so for another year. C.P. Stacey, *The Victory Campaign,* Queen's Printer, Ottawa, 1960, p 647.

8. Jock Columns were named after Maj Gen J.C. (Jock) Cambell VC who, as Commander 7th Armoured Division's Support Group in 1940-41, organized mixed all-arms columns to harass the enemy in the Western Desert. He won the VC at Sidi Rezegh and was killed the next year.

9. Nicholson, *Op Cit,* p 247.

10. Dancocks, *Op Cit,* p152

11. Ortona certainly deserved this rating, but the Canadian Department of Veteran's Affairs apparently had a short memory. When in the late 1990s veteran Ted Griffiths, who fought as a tanker at Ortona, tried to organize a joint reunion of Canadian and Ger-

RESULTS AND CONCLUSIONS

man participants at Ortona, the Department sniffily turned him down. Griffiths, undeterred, lined up the finances and organization through his own energy and the reunion went ahead. It was a great success.

12. Mouse holing involves breaking, or blowing, holes in building walls and gaining access via a covered approach without the added hazard of trying to enter through a door or window.

13. The Canadian Veteran's Affairs Department was not alone in failing to notice what the Canadians achieved at Ortona. The British Official Historian (General Sir William Jackson) wrote that Montgomery "was defeated in the battles of Ortona and Orsogna, December 4-28", Noble Frankland. Ed. *The Encyclopedia of Twentith Century Warfare,* Mitchell Beazley, New York, 1989, p 222. It was an uncharacteristic slip-up by Jackson. He was to be lavish in his praise for the Canadian victories on the Gothic Line in late 1944 - another glorious achievement that Canadians know little about.

14. Nicholson, *Op Cit,* p 328.

15. *Ibid,* pp 338 - 339.

16. *Ibid, p 339.*

Chapter VI - From Winter to Diadem

1. J. Ellis, *On The Front Lines,* John Wiley, London, 1991, pp 53 - 57, describes the attitude towards patrolling of the soldiers who actually had to do the job.

2. Anzio is another forgotten battle as far as Canadians are concerned, something that Chapter XIV of this work tries to rectify. Few realize that a battalion of Canadians fought there as part of the US/Canada Special Service Force. Even fewer know that a troop of the 1st Canadian Drilling Company RCE served at Anzio from 26 March to 6 May in the construction of underground headquarters.

3. A.Bryant, *Triumph in the West,* Greenwood, Westport, 1974, p 116.

4. The CEF - Corps Expeditionnaire Francais - was commanded by General Alphonse Juin. It comprised the 1st French Motorized Infantry Division, 2nd Moroccan Infantry Division, 3rd Algerian Infantry division and 4th Moroccan Mountain Division. The North African Goums had the reputation of raping their prisoners.

5. The artillery barrage, the name derived from its resemblance to water flowing over a river barrage, is essentially a line of controlled fire designed to move ahead of, and protect, attacking infantry. They are timed to move forward at the expected pace of the infantry, such as 100 yards every three minutes. In practice such coordination is seldom attained and bogged infantry watch in frustration as the barrage rolls its inexorable way far into the distance. Barrages come in a variety of forms - timed, rolling, step, block, even defensive. They are very wasteful as much of the fire falls on empty ground. Increasingly they were replaced by timed concentrations on likely enemy positions with times and targets adjusted as necessary by Forward Observation Officers (FOOs) accompanying the infantry.

6. Artillery targets are identified by the number of guns assigned to them. Most common are Troop (four guns), Battery (eight - the standard immediate support for a battalion) and Mike (a regimental target of 24 guns). Less common because they take needed support from other formations are Uncle (all guns in the division), Victor (all guns in the Corps) and William (all guns within range).

7. Mowat, *The Regiment, Op Cit, p 189.*

8. Dancocks, *Op Cit,* pp 261 - 262.

9. Nicholson, *Op Cit,* p 462.

10. In battle procedure the Assembly Area is where the various units and sub-units get together and assemble for the coming action. It should be well back out of the view and direct fire of the enemy. Here final preparations are made and orders given and a hot meal can be provided. The Forming Up Place, as the name implies, is where the attacking troops and tanks shake out into the formations with which they will attack. It must be close to the front but out of view of the enemy. Little time should be spent here. The Start Line is a well defined line such as a road or stream where the troops begin their actual attack on the enemy. The lead troops cross it at H-Hour and all timings for supporting fire are based on this time.

11. Canadian divisions wore rectangular identifying shoulder patches dating from the First World War. 1st Division wore red, 2nd blue, 3rd French Grey, 4th green and 5th maroon. The divisional route signs bore the colour patch plus arrows pointing to the up route or the down. The Highland Division's route signs had a red HD on a blue background, resulting in their being known as the "Highway Decorators".

12. The M3 Stuart light tank was nicknamed "Honey" by the British because its many features, including reliability, maintenance and crew comfort, were so superior to contemporary British light and cruiser tanks.

13. Perkins clearly deserved the VC. Some claim that he did not simply because two VCs could not be awarded for the same action - a patently ridiculous idea as Dieppe showed. The full story of Perkin's daring-do is in the Canadian Military History Vol. 2, No 1, Crossing the Melfa River, p35

14. See David Fraser, *And We Shall Shock Them,* Cassel, London, 1999, p 290.

15. Fraser, *Op Cit,* p 141.

16. Dancocks, *Op Cit,* p 288 and Nicholson, *Op Cit,* pp 450 - 453.

17. E.L.M. Burns, *General Mud,* Clarke Irwin, Toronto, 1970, p 162.

18. D. Graham and S. Bidwell, *Tug of War,* St. Martins, New York, 1986, p 294

19. The 61st Infantry Brigade (The Rifle Brigade) was added to the British 6th Armoured Division and the 24th Guards Brigade (one of the few formations to do well in Norway 1940) went to the 6th South African Armoured Division. After the break-up of 1st Armoured Division, following the Coriano debacle, its 2nd Armoured brigade wet to the 78th Division.

20. Nicholson, *Op Cit,* p 465.

Chapter VII - The Gothic Line and After

1. Chiusi was known in Roman times as Clusium, a name familiar to every schoolboy of my era from the opening lines of Macaulay's epic poem *Horatius,* "Lars Posena of Clusium, By the Nine Gods he swore...."

2. Graham and Bidwell, *Op Cit,* p 348.

3. General Sir William Jackson, *The Mediterranean and the Middle East, Vol VI, Part II,* HMSO, London, 1987, pp 124 - 125.

4. Nicholson, *Op Cit,* p 488.

5. Nicholson, *Op Cit,* p 470.

6. Winston Churchill, *Triumph and Tragedy,* Houghton Mifflin, London, 1953, p 121.

7. Burns, *Op Cit,* p 182.

8. Dancocks, *Op Cit*, p 312.
9. Jackson, *Op Cit*, p 243.
10. Jackson, *Op Cit*, p 246.
11. Jackson, *Op Cit*, *p 250.*
12. One reason that 1st Armoured had been held so far back was that Leese, to his credit, was trying to avoid the congestion that had plagued the Liri show. But had he been less stubborn at the outset and given 1st Armoured to Burns rather than Keightley it could have been deployed much earlier with far happier results.
13. Graham and Bidwell, *Op Cit*, p 347.
14. Burns, *Op Cit*, p 194.
15. Nicholson, *Op Cit*, p 537.
16. Nicholson, *Op Cit*, p 536.
17. The ARK was a turretless Churchill tank with folding ramps. It was to be driven into a stream or small ravine as an improvised bridge for the rapid passage of armour. Sometimes for deeper ravines one ARK would be driven on top of another. When standard ARKs were not available turretless Churchills without ramps were used in lieu.
18. Jackson, *Op Cit*, p 237.
19. Jackson, *Op Cit*, p 305, wrote, "The fault in casting stemmed directly from Leese's vision of the armoured battle which he wanted to fight. He chose the right man in Keightley to lead the 5th Corps but the Corps Staff and three of its divisions (1st Armoured, 46th and 56th) were not such happy choices."
20. Burns, *Op Cit*, *p 207.*
21. To ensure that sufficient time is allowed commanders and staffs are supposed to make a "Time Appreciation". This starts with "H" hour and works back, allotting time from the bottom-up for each preliminary action - section, platoon, company and battalion recces and orders, liaison, moves to and action in the Assembly Area, FUP, SL, etc. This is followed by a "Warning Order" giving such things as task, earliest time of move, RV and time of O Group and administrative instructions. However all too often because of the real or assumed pressure of events, or exhortations from above, everything gets compressed. Usually the first thing to go is proper reconnaissance, this despite the aphorism that "Time spent on reconnaissance is seldom wasted." But in the heat of action, especially when there may be a chance to bounce the enemy before he is ready, things get rushed. Illustrating once more Napoleon's direction to his Marshals, "Ask of me anything but time."
22. Graham and Bidwell, *Op Cit*, pp 367-380.
23. British/Canadian patrols were of three main types :"Reconnaissance" by usually just two or three persons to gain information by stealth. "Fighting" by anything from a section to a platoon to get something, often a prisoner, by a sudden assault on an enemy post. "Standing" of anything from two men to a platoon to either give early warning or to deny an enemy approach as an "Ambush Patrol." The two or three man standing patrols were dubbed "Listening Posts" by the US forces. Frequently in the First World War, less frequently in the Second, "snatch" patrols to grab a prisoner would be made by two to four men.
24. Nicholson, *Op Cit*, p 646.
25. Nicholson, *Op Cit*, p 651.
26. Dancocks, *Op Cit*, p 426.

GAUDEAMUS IGITUR

Chapter VIII - Normandy - From D-Day to Caen

1. "Funnies" was the collective nickname of the myriad specialized assault equipments most frequently operated by the 79th Armoured Division. Often based on the Churchill tank they included: Flail, Roller and Bangalore mine clearing tanks; AVREs (Assault Vehicles Royal Engineers) mounting Petards (Spigot mortar explosive launchers); Onion, Carrot and Goat demolition placers; CDLs (Canal Defence Lights - turret searchlights); Fascine and mat layers; ARK (Armoured Ramp Carrier) mobile bridging tanks. Other specialized equipments included: DD (Duplex-Drive) swimming tanks; Crocodile flame throwers; DUKW, Weasel and Buffalo and LTV amphibious vehicles.
2. The Royal Marine Commandos were especially critical of the meagre results of the naval bombardment. LT Col N.R. Moulton of 48 RMR noted "the much vaunted pre - H-hour bombardment on our beach [Nan Red] was almost completely ineffective" and "There was a serious failure of the Intelligence Services to discover...the true nature of the German beach defences....The existence of strong points not being realized, nothing much was done to neutralize them..." *We Were There*, Vol 4, P1666. A Royal Navy after battle report estimated that of 106 gun positions, pillboxes, Tobruk bunkers, etc studied only 14% had been put out of action by naval gunfire. *We Were There*, p 1668.
3. *We Were There*, pp 906-07.
4. *Ibid*, p 907,
5. *Ibid*, p 893.
6. Of all Allied formations only 6 Airborne Division attained all its objectives on D-Day. Stacey, C.P., *The Victory Campaign : Operations in Northwest Europe, 1944-1945*, Ottawa, Queen's Printer, 1960.
7. A poignant reminder of these casualties is shown in a photo in *The Canadian Summer* of Lt R.R. Smith of the Regina Rifles briefing seven of his NCOs on their D-Day tasks. Five of the seven were to be killed in action. McAndrew, Graves and Whitby, *Normandy 1944 The Canadian Summer*, Art Global, Montreal, 1994, p 23.
8. Much confusion exists over what went wrong with the proposed coordination between the two 3rd Divisions on D+1. The original plan called for the British 9th Brigade to seize the high ground around St Contest and contact the Canadian left. Its second task, which would have detracted from the first, was to attack Caen from the West if 185 Brigade was unsuccessful in attacking from the North. Neither task came about. One battalion of 9 Brigade was sent to assist the Royal Marines who were in trouble at Lion-sur-Mer. The other two were sent to assist 6 Airborne Division on their division's left flank. In the event none of the British 9th Brigade's battalions were seriously in action on D-Day. To compound matters 185 Brigade, acting on sketchy information, also sent one of its battalions to the left flank - leaving the expected full-scale attack on Caen to be made by only a single depleted battalion which was bloodily repulsed. The upshot, in the words of the official Canadian historian, was that "the possibility of establishing contact with the Canadians went by the board." And the next day's Canadian advance was thereby imperilled.

The Commander 3rd British Division may have felt that 9 (Br) Brigade's task could be assumed by the 4th Special Service Brigade whose task was to clear the coast between the British and Canadian 3rd Divisions and capture Lion. But both 48 RMC at St Aubin and 41 at Lion suffered heavy casualties and stalled making it necessary to land 46 RMC and bring back a battalion of 9 (Br) Bde to assist. The gap between the two 3rd

RESULTS AND CONCLUSIONS

Divisions thus remained huge. Fortunately tanks of the Staffordshire Yeomanry and SP Anti-tank guns were in position to block an attempt on 7 June by 21st Panzer Division to reach the coast through the gap. But the critical area around St Contest remained firmly in German hands and was to play a crucial role in thwarting the Canadians' D+1 advance. Stacey, *Op Cit,* pp 114-116.

9. Just before D-Day the armoured regiments received Sherman "Firefly" tanks mounting 17 pounder guns to be distributed one per troop. At Buron malfunctions occurred with this gun until crews discovered they had to bleed the recoil mechanism to eject empty shell casings. It seems incredible that such a critical operation was not drummed into the crews beforehand. McAndrew, et al, *Op Cit,* p 51.

10. In a situation eerily similar to the Firefly problem, new higher muzzle-velocity ammunition was issued to battalion 6 pounder Anti-tank guns prior to the invasion. The higher velocities required less lead of crossing targets. At Norrey the NCO commanding "C" Company's attached six-pounders was either unaware of, or had forgotten, the change and missed two easy crossing targets. The error if repeated elsewhere could have had serious consequences, pointing again to the need to strongly emphasize such things.

11. See *We Were There, Op Cit,* pp 1943-44 and 1960-61 for a dispassionate account of the heroism displayed by Plows, Clarke, Mitchell and Courtney in this battle.

12. Gordon Brown's gripping account of the Battle of Cardonville is at *We Were There, Op Cit, pp 833-859.*

13. The "sticky bomb" was a short-handled anti-tank grenade coated in a sticky substance that an intrepid infantryman was expected to place on a tank's engine cover where it would adhere and detonate some seconds after the handle was released. Stories, probably apocryphal, abounded of unfortunate soldiers who, in bringing the bomb back to swing it onto the tank, stuck it to their own back pack with predictable terrifying results.

14. When Brown phoned Stu Tubb to enquire what they should do about the prowling Panzers, Tubb calmly replied "There is not much we can do, is there?" The reply is noteworthy for two things. First , is Tubb's incredible calmness in crisis - one good reason why his company did so well at Norrey. Second, is the strange fact that the infantry companies had taken such meagre preparations against just such an eventuality, despite the fact that exactly this type of enemy tank-led response had long been expected. Experience from North Africa, Italy and training should have resulted in forearming the companies with copious PIATs, Hawkins grenades, sticky bombs and 6- pounder teams against this sort of thing, while providing ample long-range tank and anti-tank support. *We Were There, Op Cit,* p 839.

15. Terry Copp, *A Canadian's Guide to the Battlefields of Normandy,* Wilfred Laurier University, Waterloo, 1994, pp 74-76.

16. These three, the 50th Northumbrian, 51st Highland and 7th Armoured Divisions, had all won high reputations in North Africa although their lustre had been somewhat dimmed in Tunisia and Sicily. Sent to Northwest Europe to spearhead the invasion they never regained their previous and expected high levels of performance. The 50th was to be disbanded at year's end due to manpower shortages.

17. Henry Maule, *Caen The Brutal Battle and Breakout from Normandy,* David and Charles, Trowbridge, 1988. P 22. Captain Wittman, who had attained near legendary status among friend and foe alike, was eventually killed in battle near Falaise by either

British M 10s or Canadian tanks. The dispute over "who did it" is the Second World War's equivalent of the First's controversy between Canada's Roy Brown and Australian infantry over who got the Red Baron.

18. Copp, *Op Cit*, pp 74-76.
19. Copp, *Ibid*, p 86.
20. J. Allan Snowie, *Bloody Buron*, Boston Mills, Erin, 1988.
21. See the RUSI Journal, Vol. 144, No.1, 1999 and related issues for articles by Brig Stuart Ryder, former Director of Honours and Awards, on the revamping of British awards to include, *inter alia*, the posthumous award of all decorations.
22. The fight was so severe that a German officer wrote an account of the gallant action his battery had fought against "the Regina Rifles". He did not realize that his battery had been overrun by a single under strength platoon. *We Were There, Op Cit*, p 930.
23. Reginald H. Roy, *1944 The Canadians in Normandy*, Macmillan, Toronto, 1984, p 61.

Chapter IX - The Road Past Falaise

1. Roy, *Op Cit*, p 67.
2. O'Connor had a rather remarkable career. After leading the Western Desert Force to a smashing victory at Sidi Barani in December 1940 he was captured during Rommel's first offensive into Cyrenaica in April 1941. Imprisoned in Italy he escaped amid the confusion of the Italian surrender in September 1943. He returned to England and was rewarded by Brooke with command of VIII Corps for the coming invasion.
3. Maule, *Op Cit*, p 93.
4. The results were similar to those that were to befall 1st Division at the Gothic Line in Italy that September, where a bungled changeover between R22er and Seaforths lost a promising chance and resulted in much further bloodshed.
5. Contrast this with the prescient wisdom of Winston Churchill (a battalion commander of the Royal Scots Fusiliers in the First World War). On phoning Burns to wish him well on the eve of the Gothic Line battle Churchill admonished him to ensure his troops went into battle with a hot meal inside them.
6. The descending hierarchy of support was : Under Command, In Direct Support, In Support and In Location. Apart from indicating the degree of priority call the various levels carried certain degrees of authority to move, or administer, the supporting units with variations such as "in location and under command for move." The most significant difference probably related to the artillery where a battery would be in Direct Support of a battalion and therefore at their priority call. The rest of the artillery regiment would be In Support and thus available unless tied up in active support of other units.
7. One of the Fort Garry casualties was Lt Jim Milner a cousin of the author's wife. He lies in the Canadian cemetery at Beny Sur Mer with so many of his comrades.
8. After a brilliant career in the Second World War Rockingham was called back from civilian street to be the first commander of 25 Brigade in Korea. He was later the first and only commander of the short-lived peacetime 1st Canadian Division. Here he earned the sobriquet of "Roaringham."
9. The parent British Black Watch, formed in 1725, was sent to North America in 1756 to participate in the French and Indian wars. In July 1758 under General Aber-

RESULTS AND CONCLUSIONS

crombie they moved against French held Fort Ticonderoga in upstate New York. The French, under Montcalm, defended the fort from behind a barrier of abbatais (cut-down interlacing trees with the broken branches facing the enemy). The Highlanders launched their multiple attacks with the claymore without waiting for orders or artillery fire and were cut to pieces under murderous fire. They lost 650 out of 1000 men.

10. McAndrew, et al, *Op Cit,* p 126. The German General Kurt Meyer held similar views. In a post-war interview with Lt Col Jack Donahue, a Canadian Army Public Relations Officer, Meyer expressed outrage at what he perceived to be the senseless manner in which young Canadians were sent to their slaughter in this battle. Conversation with Donahue, Kingston, 1956.

11. For an excellent analytical account of Operation Spring see the Canadian Military History journal, Volume 1, Numbers 1&2, Autumn 1992, Terry Copp, *Fifth Brigade at Verrieres Ridge.*

12. One of the principal protagonists of successive single battalion divisional attacks was Maj Gen Vokes as exemplified by his Gully (December 1943) and Liri (May 1944) battles in Italy.

13. Canadian Military History, *Op Cit,* Autumn 1992, p 61.

14. These APCs were able to carry over a section each with excellent protection and performance. They were briefly copied in Canada after the war using de-turreted Shermans then in abundance. The result was an excellent vehicle and led to the development of some very effective infantry/tank battle group tactics which lamentably went by the board with the onset of the Korean War. It was not until the late 1960s that Canada again acquired an APC in the guise of the much battle-inferior M 113.

15. Roy, *Op Cit,* p 195.

16. Leaguering was a standard and necessary armoured corps post-battle operation in which the unit/sub-unit would withdraw to a protected locality to refuel, rearm and replenish - actions which were seldom possible in the FDLs. The tanks, then less effective at night but vulnerable to infantry tank-hunting teams, would also often leaguer overnight for protection and move back to their battle positions at first light.

17. Roy, *Op Cit,* p 235.

18. Maule, *Op Cit,* p 144.

19. James Lucas, *Battle Group,* Cassell, London, 1993, pp 143-155.

20. Roy, *Op Cit,* p 306.

21. Rudyard Kipling,*If-Rewards and Fairies,* Macmillan, London, 1932, pp 175-176.

Chapter X   The Channel Ports and the Scheldt

1. Crerar was actually promoted on 16 November 1944 after his return from convalescence at the end of the Scheldt campaign.

2. The reasons for Eisenhower's decision were many and valid - including pressure from his own generals Bradley and Patton who had succeeded so brilliantly in Normandy while Montgomery dithered. But the decisive influence came from General Marshall who because of the overwhelming preponderance of US forces in Europe quite rightly demanded that the US dictate the Strategy.

3. Stacey, *Op Cit,* p 331.

4. ULTRA was super-secret information obtained from breaking enemy codes at the British Code and Cipher School at Bletchley Park in Buckinghamshire. The list of

recipients of the information, which was tightly controlled by Churchill himself, was limited to a small circle of senior politicians, commanders and select staff officers.

5. Below 21 Army Group Headquarters only the two army commanders plus Simonds, as Crerar's deputy, were privy to ULTRA.

6. Brian Horrocks, *Corps Commander*, Sidgwick & Jackson, London 1977, pp 80-81.

7. Stacey, *Op Cit*, p 329.

8. Stacey, *Op Cit*, p 336.

9. Hilary St. George Saunders, *The Red Beret*, Michael Joseph, London, 1950, pp 255-278. Noble Frankland, *Op Cit*, p 39. Fraser, *Op Cit*, pp 347-348.

10. Fraser, *Op Cit*, p 397.

11. See *Canadian Military History*. Vol. 4, No 1, p 6, for a mild implied criticism of the failure of the Canadians to amply use the Dutch underground.

12. Dancocks, *Op Cit*, pp 348-352 and 373-379.

13. Bernard B. Fall, *Hell in a Very Small Place*, Lippincott, New York, 1967.

14. Ellis, *Op Cit*. p 73.

15. Although the incident reflects credit on Hees personally it illustrates the inchoate state of battle procedure then in effect. As BM Hees should have been at Brigade HQ minding the store while his brigadier could have been forward to direct operations.

16. Williams, *Op Cit*, p 141.

17. Ellis, Major L.F., *History of the Second World War, Vol 2 - Victory in the West*, HMSO, London, 1962, p 128.

18. Not quite true. Eisenhower did pay a visit to the Polish Armoured Division near Breda on 29 November 1944 but this was more in the nature of a photo-op than on military matters.

19. FM Lord Alanbrooke, *War Diaries 1939-1945*, Weidenfeld &Nicolson, London, *2001*, p 600.

20. John English, *The Canadian Army and the Normandy Campaign, A Study of Failure in High Command*, New York, Praeger, 1991.

Chapter XI The Rhineland

1. C. P. Stacey, *Official History of the Canadian Army in the Second World War Volume III, The Victory Campaign*, Ottawa, Queen's Printer, 1960, pp 439-440.

2. Terry Copp, *The Battle for Kapelsche Veer*, Legion Magazine, May/June 2002, pp 33-35.

3. In his excellent account based on his service as a staff officer at 1st Canadian Army Headquarters, Jeffery Williams has Schlemm commanding the Fifth Parachute Army. J. Williams, *The Long Left Flank*, Stoddart, Toronto, 1988, pp 185 and 198. However both the Canadian Official History and the West Point Atlas identify the formation as the First Parachute Army which is the designation used here.

4. Martin Middlebrook, *The Bomber Command War Diaries*, Penguin, London, 1990, p 661.

5. The History of the 15th Scottish Division as quoted in Stacey, *Op Cit*, p 482.

6. See Gordon Brown's account of the demoralizing effect on relieving troops when the dead of the relieved unit/formation are left lying about uncollected and unburied. Canadian Military History, Vol. 6, No 1, *The Battle of Moyland Wood*, p 101

7. Contrast Crerar's effective generalship in "Veritable" with his own catatonic

RESULTS AND CONCLUSIONS

performance up to Falaise. Also contrast it with Montgomery's slow and indecisive directions to Crerar over Antwerp and with Monty's later meddling interference which deprived the Canadian Army of the use of I Corps during the crucial attempt to seal off Beveland.

8. In his memoirs Horrocks paid this tribute to Crerar "General Crerar...in my opinion has always been much underrated, largely because he was the exact opposite of Montgomery. He hated publicity but was full of common sense and always prepared to listen to the views of his subordinate commanders. Every day after the battle started he would fly over the front...in a small aircraft, and then come to see me wherever I might be." Horrocks, *Op Cit*, p 188.

9. Stacey, *Op Cit*, p 524.

10. Fraser, *Op Cit*, p 390.

Chapter XII - From the Rhine to the North Sea

1. When Churchill tried to finesse Alexander into the role of ground forces commander, by having him replace Tedder as Eisenhower's 2IC - a move the Americans rejected - Montgomery opposed the proposal. In his view no other British general should get the job if he could not have it.

2. Ritchie had an interesting up - down - up career. In 1941 as Deputy Chief of the General Staff Middle East in Cairo he was plucked by Auchinleck to replace Cunningham as commander 8th Army after the "Crusader" fiasco. Lacking command experience and with Auchinleck constantly looking over his shoulder he too failed and was sacked after the debacle of 2nd Tobruk. For most generals that would have been the end of the road. But Ritchie had a friend and champion in Brooke who gave him a second chance as a corps commander in Northwest Europe where he succeeded. After the war he retired to a civilian position in Canada and became a popular and excellent guest lecturer at the Canadian Army Staff College in the 1950s.

3. Stacey, *Op Cit*, p 539.

4. Stacey, *Op Cit*, p 548.

5. Stacey, *Op Cit*, p 572.

6. Stacey, *Ibid*. The Grebbe was a pre-war line of fortifications based on the Eem and Grebbe rivers from which the Dutch had unsuccessfully attempted to hold up the German invasion in 1940.

7. The name was something of a misnomer as the combat elements holding the Scheldt Islands and the Neder Rijn included the 4th Commando, 116th Royal Marine Commando and 33rd Armoured Brigades plus Dutch and Belgian units.

8. Stacey, *Op Cit*, p 587.

9. The addition of 18 Corps to 21 Army Group would place the Canadian Parachute Battalion and the rest of 6th Airborne Division in the vanguard of Montgomery's push to the Baltic.

10. Stacey, *Op Cit*, p 563.

11. D.C. Watt, *How War Came*, Cox and Wyman, Reading, 1990, p 2.

12. Stacey, *Op Cit*, p 611.

13. Stacey, *Ibid*.

14. Stacey, *Op Cit*, p 612.

15. Williams, *Op Cit*, p

GAUDEAMUS IGITUR

16. R. Kipling, *Rewards and Fairies*, MacMillan, London, 1932, pp 175 - 176.

17. The Canadians who advanced to the Baltic were with the 1st Canadian Parachute Battalion of 6th Airborne Division. See Chapter XIII.

First Canadian Parachute Battalion

1. The official reason for this choice of target was to deny water to southern Italy and to spread alarm and despondency among the people. The real reasons were probably to test the paratroops against what was hoped to be a soft target and to give employment to bored troops.

2. Maj Gen R.N. Gale, Commander 6th Airborne Division, described the fact that a Canadian parachute battalion was to join his division as "grand news indeed." Hilary St. George Saunders, *The Red Beret*, Michael Joseph, London, 1950, p 52.

3. Brigadier Hill was certainly the right man to lead the Canadians. In action he personally led a company of Canucks in a decisive counter attack. Back in England between operations he amicably resolved a sit-down strike by the Canadians over poor food. In the advance to the Baltic he led from the front. So great was the bond between Hill and his Canadians that at war's end the Canucks refused to let the train carrying them homeward leave until they had all shaken Hill's hand. Post-war Hill attended virtually every reunion of the 1st Canadian Parachute Battalion until well into his 90s.

4. Not to be confused with Le Mesnil-Patry the site of the bitter battle fought by the QOR of C and 1st Hussars on 11 June 1944.

5. Stacey, *Op Cit*, pp 439-440.

6. The battle of Minden was launched by mistake by six British battalions who being told that the order to advance would be "By the beat of a drum" misinterpreted it to mean "at" the beat and proceeded to advance over a field full of wild roses at unbroken French cavalry - an unheard-of manoeuvre in those days. They were victorious, resulting in one of the great victories of the Seven Years War. Ever after, until the battalions lost their identities in the 1968 mergers, they celebrated Minden Day by wearing roses on their hats and bedecking their colours and drums with roses.

7. Stacey, *Op Cit*, p 604.

8. Reported in Stacey, *Op Cit*, p 604.

9. Forrest, one of the outstanding generals of the Civil War actually said, "Get there first with the most men" but his phrase, like Wellington's "Up guards and at 'em", was embellished in the telling. After a remarkable wartime career Forrest sullied his reputation by taking a leading role in the Ku Klux Klan.

10. This is not strictly true. Several companies of No. 1 Canadian Forestry Group had been operating in the Ardennes when the Germans attacked and had to take up defensive positions before being withdrawn.

Chapter XIV - The First Special Service Force

1. R.D. Burhans, *The First Special Service Force*, Metheun, Toronto, 1981, pp 1-10.

2. The Studebaker Company eventually developed the excellent M-29 C Weasel amphibious tracked vehicle for this purpose. Ironically the Weasel was never to be used by the Special Service Force. However it was much used by others in all theatres - in-

RESULTS AND CONCLUSIONS

cluding the Canadians in the Scheldt and Rhineland.

3. C.P. Stacey, *Six Years of War,* Queen's Printer, Ottawa, 1955, pp 104-108.

4. Coral Sea was the first naval battle in history in which the opposing fleets did not come into direct contact. It was fought entirely by carrier aircraft and the result was something of a stand-off. The Americans lost one fleet carrier (Lexington), a destroyer and an oiler and had a second carrier (Yorktown) damaged. The Japanese lost only the light carrier Shoho and had the fleet carrier Shokaku damaged. But the Japanese were thwarted in their drive on New Guinea and the battle deprived them of a carrier force that might have turned the tide at Midway.

5. Nicknamed "the Sight-Seeing" because of their wide ranging Pacific employment - USA, Attu, Hawaii, Kwajalein, Leyte, Okinawa.

6. The 13th Brigade comprised The Canadian Fusiliers, Winnipeg Grenadiers (reconstituted after Hong Kong), The Rocky Mountain Rangers, Le Regiment de Hull, a company of The Saint John Fusiliers, 24th Field Regiment RCA, 46th Light Anti-Aircraft Battery, 24th Field Company RCE and 25th Field Ambulance.

7. Considerable popular myth credits the Helena with carrying the five Sullivan bothers to their doom (the incident which inspired the movie "Saving Private Ryan"). In fact the Sullivans were lost eight months earlier aboard the cruiser Juneau off Savo Island.

8. Burhans, *Op Cit,* pp 67-68.

9. Stacey, *Op Cit,* p 503.

10. Burhans, *Op Cit,* p 18.

11. Burhans, *Op Cit,* pp 121-122.

12. Burhans, *Op Cit,* pp 124-125.

13. P. Calvocoressi, G. Wint, J. Pritchard, *The Penguin History of the Second World War,* Penguin, London, 1995, pp 533-534.

14. The comments of Calvocoressi, et all, *ibid,* and Churchill, Bryant, *Op Cit,* p 116, notwithstanding. Although Lucas certainly lacked a flaming offensive spirit, in fairness to him he did have some legitimate reason for caution. With the rest of 5th Army hopelessly bogged down along the Rapido his force would have been dangerously exposed and on its own had it made a premature dash on Rome. Given the rapid German reaction to the landing his Corps could have been destroyed in detail had it left the security of its air and naval protected beachhead.

15. Burhans, *Op Cit,* p 250.

16. Burhans, *Op Cit,* pp 299-300.

17. Burhans, *Op Cit,* p 298.

Chapter XV - CANLOAN

1. Smith, Wilfred I., *Code Word CANLOAN,* Dundurn Press, Toronto,
2. *Ibid,* p 54.
3. *Ibid,* p 64.
4. Stacey, *Op Cit,* pp 114 - 116.
5. Smith, *Op Cit,* p 180.
6. *Ibid,* Forward.

GAUDEAMUS IGITUR

Chapter XVI - Results and Conclusions

1. This phrase was widely attributed to Wellington at Waterloo. He denied using it suggesting, with unconscious pomposity, that instead he may have said, "Stand up Guards". Richard Holmes in his excellent biography of the Iron Duke quotes him as saying, "Up Guards! Make ready! Fire!" Holmes R., *Wellington,* Harper Collins, London, 2003, p 249.

2. Biddle Stephan, *Afghanistan and the Future of Warfare,* Foreign Affairs, New York, March/April 2003, pp 31 - 46.

3. Holmes, *Op Cit,* p 32.

4. Von Manstein, Erich, *Lost Victories,* Henry Regnery, Chicago, 1958 is an excellent account of pro-active generalship which should be required reading for all budding commanders.

5. The precursor of Putot was Shing Mun Redoubt in Hong Kong where the planners, the staff, the Royal Scots and the Brigadier in command made just about every error in the book in planning and executing its defence. They totally eschewed mutual support, interlocking fields of fire, artillery DFs on the redoubt and any thought of immediate counter-attack, with predictable results.

The worthy successor to these fiascos was Dien Bien Phu, Viet Nam in 1954. Although the French command committed mistakes of every kind and level - strategic, intelligence, tactical, planning and execution, only one is considered here - the siting of battalion localities out of support range of on another. As a result, one of the two northern battalion positions fell the first night and the other, held by Foreign Legionnaires, fell the next. Only then did the French pull into a tight cluster around the centre where they held out for two months.

6. The 19 Set's propensity to fade with range resulted in some anomalous receptions, reminiscent of the classic, "Am going to advance send reinforcements" being received as, "Am going to a dance send three and four pence." In the 1960s, Canadian officers in a remote East African station, which had run out of coffee ("kahawa" in Swahili), were pleased when the Signals Centre announced the receipt of a message over the 19 Set stating, "Kahawa arriving aircraft 0900 hrs tomorrow." On the morrow everyone was nonplussed when the aircraft arrived bearing not coffee (kahawa) but the Defence Minister who was named Kawawa. The Minister was less than thrilled to be met by the Quartermaster-Sergeant and a truck instead of by the CO and a Guard of Honour.

7. In Korea in early 1953 the Firm Base of an Australian patrol was overrun at night and a fighting patrol was sent down to restore matters. Instead of letting the patrol commander do his job his company commander attempted to direct things from his CP far in the rear without a view of the ground. Using a 26 Set in clear language he so misdirected things that everyone within range was able to pinpoint every move of the patrol and the location of every Aussie body recovered. All concerned were lucky that the enemy failed to react.

8. The most flagrant example of the mass dispensation of VCs was the award of nine to the single company which defended Rorke's Drift in the Zulu Wars. In the twin, but losing, battle at Isandlhwana a further two were awarded to officers leaving the scene to save the colours - hardly the stuff of VC merit.

While things were much more stringent in the Second World War there were still questionable incidents such as the posthumous award of the VC to an officer in Somali-

APPENDICES

land who was later found to have been taken prisoner and was alive and well.

Also strange was the award of posthumous VCs to both the pilot and navigator of a Battle light bomber which was shot down while attacking a bridge near Maastricht during the German breakthrough in May 1940. The aircraft was one of a group of five which made the dangerous attack. Four were shot down with the loss of all crew while the fifth was badly damaged and was only nursed back to base after the pilot had ordered his crew to bail out over friendly territory. While there is no doubt that the recipients were very brave to make the suicidal attack, there was no evidence to distinguish their valour from that of the crews of other lost aircraft, or indeed the heroic surviving pilot who made the same attack and somehow managed to save his crew and eventually even his aircraft. One also wonders why VCs were given to two of the three crewmen while the third received nothing at all - he may, after all, have been the bravest of the three.

None of this is intended in any way to diminish the worthiness of those who received the decoration, only to show that the award was crucially dependent on how the recommendation was made and how it was supported at higher headquarters. Lt Col Jim Stone was fond of recounting how he convinced the Seaforth's CO to recommend Smokey Smith for the VC, instead of a lesser decoration, and that time it worked.

Appendix 1
Order of Battle (Arms Units Only)
First Canadian Army

(Dates start from operational entry in theatre and end with termination of war in Europe) *
Gen H.D.G. Crerar   (23 Jul-26 Sep 1944 and 9 Nov 1944-8 May 1945)
Lt Gen G.G. Simonds (Acting 27 Sep-8 Nov 1944)

GHQ and Army Troops 25th Canadian Armoured Delivery Regiment (The Elgin Regiment)
1st Army Group, RCA - 11th Army Field, 1st, 2nd, 5th Medium Regiments RCA
2nd Army Group RCA - 19th Army Field, 3rd, 4th, 7th Medium, 2nd Heavy Anti-Aircraft Regiments RCA
1st Rocket and 1st Radar Batteries RCA
1st Army Engineers RCE
1st Army Signals RCCS
HQ Defence Battalion (Royal Montreal Regiment)
Ist Canadian Corps (Italy 1 Feb 1944 - 12 Feb 1945 - NWE 13 Feb - 8 May 1945.)
Lt Gen H.D.G. Crerar (1Feb - 19 March 1944)
Lt Gen E.L.M. Burns (20 Mar - 5 Nov 1944)
Lt Gen C. Foulkes (10 Nov 1944 - 8 May 1945)
Corps Troops
1st Armoured Car Regiment (The Royal Canadian Dragoons)
7th Anti-Tank, 1st Light Anti-Aircraft (Lanark and Renfrew Scottish), 1st Survey Regiments RCA
Ist Corps Troops Engineers RCE
Ist Corps Troops Signals RCCS
Ist Corps Defence Company (The Lorne Scots (Peel, Dufferin and Halton Regiment))
1st Canadian Infantry Division
Maj Gen G.G. Simonds (10 July -31 Oct 1943) Maj Gen C. Vokes (1 Nov 1943 - 8 Dec 1944)
Maj Gen H.W. Foster (1Dec 1944 - 8 May 1945)
* Dates of arrival main bodies sometimes shown in lieu of formation becoming operational.
Divisional Troops
4th Reconnaissance Regiment (4th Princess Louise Dragoon Guards) (10 Jul 1943 - 13 Jul 1944

and 12 Mar - 8 May 1945)
1st RCHA, 2nd Field, 3rd Field, 1st Anti-Tank, 2nd Light Anti-Aircraft Regiments RCA
1st Canadian Divisional Engineers RCE
1st Canadian Divisional Signals RCCS
The Saskatoon Light Infantry (MG)
1st Canadian Infantry Brigade
Brig H.D. Graham (10 Jul - 17 Dec 1943)
Brig D.C. Spry (18 Dec1943 - 12 July 1944)
Brig J.A. Calder (13 Jul - 8 Dec 1944)
Brig J.D. Smith (9 Dec 1944 - 8 May 1945)
The Royal Canadian Regiment
The Hastings and Prince Edward Regiment
The 48th Highlanders of Canada
2nd Canadian Infantry Brigade
Brig C. Vokes (10 Jul - 31 Oct 1943)
Brig B.M. Hoffmeister (1 Nov 1943 - 19 Mar 1944)
Brig T.G. Gibson (13 Apr - 6 Oct 1944)
Brig M.P. Bogert (7 Oct 1944 - 8 May 1945)
Princess Patricia's Canadian Light Infantry
The Seaforth Highlanders of Canada
The Loyal Edmonton Regiment
3rd Canadian Infantry Brigade
Brig M.H. Penhale (10 Jul - 11 Oct 1943)
Brig T.G. Gibson (12 Oct 1943 - 12 Apr 1944)
Brig J.P. Bernatchez (13 Apr 1944 - 8 May 1945)
Royal 22e Regiment
The Carleton and York Regiment
The West Nova Scotia Regiment
5th Canadian Armoured Division (Italy 10 Nov 1943 - 15 Feb 1945 - NWE 28 Feb - 8 May 1945)
Maj Gen G.G. Simonds (10 Nov 1943 - 29 Jan 1944)
Maj Gen E.L.M. Burns (30 Jan - 19 Mar 1944)
Maj Gen B.M. Hoffmeister (20 Mar 1944 - 8 May 1945)
Divisional Troops
3rd Armoured Reconnaissance Regiment (The Governor General's Horse Guards)
17th and 8th (SP) Field, 4th Anti-Tank, 5th Light Anti-Aircraft Regiments RCA
5th Canadian Armoured Divisional Engineers RCE
5th Canadian Armoured Divisional Signals RCCS.
5th Canadian Armoured Brigade
Brig G.R. Bradbrooke (10 Nov 1943 - 22 Feb 1944)
Brig J.D. Smith (23 Feb - 6 June 1944)
Brig I.H. Cumberland (7 Jun 1944 - 8 May 1945)
2nd Armoured Regiment (Lord Strathcona's Horse (Royal Canadians))
5th Armoured Regiment (8th Princess Louise's (New Brunswick) Hussars)
9th Armoured Regiment (The British Columbia Dragoons)
The Westminster Regiment (Motor)
11th Canadian Infantry Brigade
Brig G. Kitching (10 Nov 1943 - 13 Feb 1944)
Brig T.E.D'O. Snow (14 Feb - 23 Jun 1944)
Brig I.S. Johnston (24 Jun 1944 - 8 May 1945)
The Perth Regiment
The Cape Breton Highlanders
The Irish Regiment of Canada

APPENDICES

11th Independent Machine Gun Company (The Princess Louise Fusiliers)
12th Canadian Infantry Brigade (13 Jul 1944 - 12 Mar 1945)
Brig D.C. Spry (13 Jul - 12 Aug 1944)
Brig J.S. Lind (13 Aug 1944 - 12 Mar 1945)
4th Princess Louise Dragoon Guards
The Lanark and Renfrew Scottish Regiment
The Westminster Regiment (Motor)
12th Independent Machine Gun Company (The Princess Louise Fusiliers)
IInd Canadian Corps (11 Jul 1944 - 8 May 1945)
Lt Gen Simonds (11 Jul - 27 Sep 1944 and 9 Nov 1944 - 8 May 1945)
Maj Gen C. Foulkes (Acting 27 Sep - 9 Nov 1944)
Corps Troops
18th Armoured Car Regiment (12th Manitoba Dragoons)
6th Anti-Tank, 6th Light Anti-Aircraft, 2nd Survey Regiments RCA
IInd Corps Troops Engineers RCE
IInd Corps Troops Signals RCCS
IInd Corps Defence Company (The Prince Edward Island Light Horse)
2nd Canadian Infantry Division (11 Jul 1944 - 8 May 1945)
Maj Gen C. Foulkes (11 Jul - 27 Sep 1944)
Brig R.H. Keefler (Acting 27 Sep - 9 Nov 1944)
Maj Gen A.B. Matthews (10 Nov 1944 - 8 May 1945)
Divisional Troops
8th Reconnaissance Regiment (14th Canadian Hussars)
4th, 5th, 6th Field, 2nd Anti-Tank, 3rd Light Anti-Aircraft Regiments RCA
2nd Canadian Divisional Engineers RCE
2nd Canadian Divisional Signals RCCS
The Toronto Scottish Regiment (MG)
4th Canadian Infantry Brigade
Brig S. Lett (11 Jul - 18 Jul 1944)
Brig J. E. Ganong (3 Aug - 30 Aug 1944)
Brig F.N. Cabeldu (31 Aug 1944 - 8 May 1945)
The Royal Regiment of Canada
The Royal Hamilton Light Infantry
The Essex Scottish Regiment
5th Canadian Infantry Brigade
Brig W.J. Megill (11Jul 1944 - 8 May 1945)
The Black Watch (Royal Highland Regiment) of Canada
Le Regiment de Maisonneuve
The Calgary Highlanders
6th Canadian Infantry Brigade
Brig H.A. Young (11Jul - 25 Aug 1944)
Brig F.A. Clift (26 Aug - 29 Aug 1944)
Brig J.G. Gauvreau (30 Aug - 26 Oct 1944)
Brig R.H. Keefler (10 Nov 1944 - 22 Mar 1945)
Brig J.V. Allard (24 Mar - 8 May 1945)
Les Fusiliers Mont-Royal
The Queen's Own Cameron Highlanders of Canada
The South Saskatchewan Regiment
3rd Canadian Infantry Division (6 Jun 1944 - 8 May 1945)
Maj Gen R.F. Keller (6 Jun - 8 Aug 1944)
Maj Gen D.C. Spry (18 Aug 1944 - 22 Mar 1945)
Maj Gen R.H. Keefler (23 Mar - 8 May 1945)

GAUDEAMUS IGITUR

Divisional Troops
7th Reconnaissance Regiment (17th Duke of York's Royal Canadian Hussars)
12th, 13th, 14th Field, 3rd Anti-Tank, 4th Light Anti-Aircraft Regiments RCA
3rd Canadian Divisional Engineers RCE
3rd Divisional Signals RCCS
The Cameron Highlanders of Ottawa (MG)
7th Canadian Infantry Brigade
Brig H.W. Foster (6 Jun - 21 Aug 1944)
Brig J.G. Spragge (26 Aug 1944 - 20 Feb 1945)
Brig T.G. Gibson (24 Feb - 8 May 1945)
The Royal Winnipeg Rifles
The Regina Rifle Regiment
1st Battalion, The Canadian Scottish Regiment
8th Canadian Infantry Brigade
Brig K.G. Blackader (6 June - 28 Sep 1944)
Brig J.A. Roberts (30 Oct 1944 - 8 May 1945)
The Queen's Own Rifles of Canada
Le Regiment de la Chaudiere
The North Shore (New Brunswick) Regiment
9th Canadian Infantry Brigade
Brig D.G. Cunningham (6 June - 4 Aug 1944) Brig J.M. Rockingham (8 Aug 1944 - 8 May 1945)
The Highland Light Infantry of Canada
The Stormont, Dundas and Glengarry Highlanders
The North Nova Scotia Highlanders
4th Canadian Armoured Division (30 Jul 1944 - 8 May 1945)
Maj Gen G. Kitching (30 Jul - 21 Aug 1944)   Maj Gen H.W. Foster (22 Aug - 30 Nov 1944)
Maj Gen C. Vokes (1 Dec 1944 - 8 May 1945)

Divisional Troops
29th Armoured Reconnaissance Regiment (The South Alberta Regiment)
15th, 23rd (SP) Field, 4th Anti-Tank, 8th Light Anti-Aircraft Regiments RCA
4th Armoured Divisional Engineers RCE
4th Armoured Divisional Signals RCCS
4th Canadian Armoured Brigade
Brig E.L. Booth (30 Jul - 14 Aug 1944) Brig R.W. Moncel (19 Aug 1944 - 8 May 1945)
21st Armoured Regiment (The Governor General's Foot Guards)
22nd Armoured Regiment (The Canadian Grenadier Guards)
28th Armoured Regiment (The British Columbia Regiment)
The Lake Superior Regiment (Motor)
10th Canadian Infantry Brigade
Brig J.C. Jefferson (30 Jul 1944 - 8 May 1945)
The Lincoln and Welland Regiment
The Algonquin Regiment
The Argyll and Sutherland Highlanders of Canada (Princess Louise's)
10th Independent Machine Gun Company (The New Brunswick Rangers)

Independent Armoured Brigades

1st Canadian Armoured Brigade
Brig R.A. Wyman (10 Jul 1943 - 26 Feb 1944)
Brig W.C. Murphy (27 Feb 1944 - 8 may 1945)
11th Armoured Regiment (The Ontario Regiment)

APPENDICES

12th Armoured Regiment (Three Rivers Regiment)
14th Armoured Regiment (The Calgary Regiment)
2nd Canadian Armoured Brigade
Brig R.A. Wyman (6 Jun - 8 Aug 1944)
Brig J.F. Bingham (9 Aug - 8 Dec 1944)
Brig G.W. Robinson (9 Dec 1944 - 8 May 1945)
6th Armoured Regiment (1st Hussars)
10th Armoured Regiment (The Fort Garry Horse)
27th Armoured Regiment (The Sherbrooke Fusiliers Regiment)

Operational Canadian Units Under British/US Command

The Hong Kong Garrison
The Royal Rifles of Canada
The Winnipeg Grenadiers
Headquarters and Services

6th British Airborne Division
1st Canadian Parachute Battalion

79th British Armoured Division
1st Armoured Personnel Carrier Regiment

First Special Service Force (US/Canada)
1st Canadian Special Service Battalion

Nomenclature Appendix II

AA (Ack Ack)	- Anti-Aircraft
Acorn (nn)	- Radio name for Intelligence Officer
ADS	- Advanced Dressing Station - a forward medical facility
AEF	- Allied Expeditionary Force
AFV	- Armoured Fighting Vehicle
AGRA	- Army Group Royal Artillery - the artillery above divisional level including all medium and heavy guns
Algoons (nn)	- The Algonquin Regiment
APC	- Armoured Personnel Carrier
ARK	- A de-turreted tank fitted with a folding ramp superstructure which can be driven into small obstacles and used as a quick-order bridge for tanks and F Echelon vehicles.
Arm	- A weapon. Also the collective designation of the Army's five combat elements (armour, artillery, engineers, infantry and signals).
Army	- The land element of a nation's armed forces. Also a higher operational formation of two or more corps normally commanded by a general
Ashcans (nn)	- The Argyll and Sutherland Highlanders
Assembly Area	- The designated area behind the FDLs, out of enemy sight and normal fire zones, where different units and sub-units assemble before an offensive operation
A tk	- Anti-tank
AVRE	- Army Vehicle Royal Engineers - a specialized vehicle on a tank chassis used for a variety of assault engineer purposes
Bangalore Torpedo	- A fused pipe packed with explosives used to gap wire obstacles. Developed in Bangalore India.
Barrage	- A line of artillery fire timed to move just ahead of attacking infantry to neutralize the enemy. Includes creeping, rolling,

GAUDEAMUS IGITUR

	block, box and other types.
Battalion	- The standard self-contained infantry unit of some 800 men comprising a headquarters, four rifle companies, a support company with pioneer, A tk, mortar and carrier platoons and a headquarters company of the unit's transport, quartermaster and administrative services.
Bayonet	- A detachable blade or spike fixed to the muzzle of a rifle as a stabbing weapon. Developed in Bayonne France.
Bazooka	- The US 2.6 inch A tk rocket launcher, roughly equivalent to the PIAT. The name came from its resemblance to a "musical" instrument fashioned from a section of pipe and a funnel by Bob Burns, an Arkansas hillbilly entertainer of the 1930/40s, which he had dubbed "bazooka".
Boys A tk Rifle	- A .55 inch A tk rifle used by Commonwealth infantry before the introduction of the PIAT
Bren	- The standard Commonwealth light machine gun of .303 calibre with a 30 round magazine. Originally designed by Brno of Czechoslovakia and produced in England by Enfield, hence the acronym. Reliable, accurate and easily carried it was popular with the troops.
Bren Gun Carrier	- Early common name of the lightly armoured, tracked, universal carrier. Used by all Arms units, especially by battalion support platoons. Open-topped, rugged, reliable and well liked.
Brewed (up)	- A vehicle that had been hit and set on fire.
Brigade	- The lowest field formation comprising three infantry battalions or armoured regiments and commanded by a Brigadier.
Brigade Group	- A brigade augmented with its own armour, artillery, engineers and service sub-units and thus self-contained.
Buffalo	- The British/Canadian designation of the American LVT, a fully tracked amphibious vehicle.
CAB	- Canadian Armoured Brigade
Cab Rank	- Close support aircraft loitering near the front line for the immediate engagement of on-call targets. Inefficient because worthwhile targets seldom materialized before the short endurance of the aircraft dictated a return to base. Much favoured by the ground forces but intensely disliked by the air force, hence seldom used.
CAD	- Canadian Armoured Division
Calgary Hooligans (nn)	- The Calgary Highlanders
CANLOAN	- The scheme under which some 600 Canadian infantry and 50 ordnance junior officers were attached to British units.
Carrier (Universal)	- A small, lightly armoured, open-topped, tracked vehicle used mainly by the infantry as weapons carriers and for local reconnaissance but widely employed in other roles. Sometimes called a "Bren gun carrier".
CCS	- A medical Casualty Clearing Station.
CDL	- Canal Defence Light - the cover name for a tank, usually the obsolete Matilda or Grant, mounting a special turret fitted with a powerful searchlight to dazzle the enemy and illuminate targets at night. Often bounced the beam off low clouds to produce "artificial moonlight."
CIB	- Canadian Infantry Brigade
CID	- Canadian Infantry Division
Churchill	- The standard British medium/heavy tank from 1942.

APPENDICES

CO	- Commanding Officer
COS	- Chief-of-Staff
Colours	- The two (King's/Queens and Regimental) ceremonial "flags" unique to each unit carrying its principal badges and battle honours.
Concentration	- An artillery fire task on a single specific target.
Corps	- The generic arm or service (e.g. infantry, ordnance) to which a unit belongs. Also a higher field formation of two or more divisions commanded by a lieutenant-general.
Crocodile	- Churchill tank mounting a flame thrower.
DCM	- Distinguished Conduct Medal. For Other Ranks it rated just below the VC.
DD	- Duplex-Drive. A tank fitted with special floatation and control gear enabling it to "swim" into action.
Direct fire	-Where a visible target is engaged over open sights without elaborate computation by the gunners.
DR	- Dispatch Rider, normally motorcycle mounted.
DSO	- Distinguished Service Order for officers. For captains and below represents an "almost VC". For lieutenant-colonels and majors represents an excellent job under fire. For higher ranks was often awarded "with the rations".
DUKW (Duck)	- An amphibious truck (often a version of the GMC 6x6) fitted with a boat-like hull. D= 1942, U=amphibious, K= all-wheel drive, W= twin rear axles.
Dukes (nn)	- Duke of Connaught's Own Rifles (British Columbia Regiment). Also the British Duke of Wellington's Regiment.
Dustbin (nn)	- A huge cylindrical charge fired by a spigot mortar from an AVRE.
Echelon	- The vehicle and service element of a fighting unit. Divided into: "F" - the vehicles needed for the conduct of the battle; "A" (A1 & A2) - immediate battle support; and, "B" - none-combat services such as pay, records, personnel administration.
Fascine	- A bundle of sticks, etc., to fill craters, ditches and small streams. Often carried and placed by AVREs. Was also the symbol of Mussolini's fascists.
FDL	- Forward Defended Locality - the former "Front Line".
Firefly	- Sherman tank with a long barrelled 17 pounder. The Allies first effective counter to the powerful German tanks.
Fixed Lines	- The pre-set lines of fire on which a weapon is set in order to cover likely target areas when darkness or other conditions preclude visual sighting.
Flail tank	- A tank fitted with an extended rotating chain mounting to pound the ground to explode mines at a safe distance.
FOO	- Forward Observation Officer - an artillery officer who accompanies forward infantry and armoured units to direct fire onto targets of opportunity
Foot Pads (nn)	- The Governor General's Foot Guards.
Formation	- A higher grouping of two or more units, e.g. brigade, division.,corps.
FUP	- Forming Up Place where an attacking unit shakes out into its assault formation before crossing the Start Line.
GI	- Government Issue. Adopted by US soldiers as their nickname
GOC	- General Officer Commanding.
GGHG	- Governor General's Horse Guards. The acronym is translated as "Good God How Gorgeous" by themselves and "…How Gruesome " by others.

GAUDEAMUS IGITUR

Green Patch	- The 4th Canadian Armoured Division.
GSO	- General Staff Officer. GSO 1 is a lieutenant-colonel, GSO 2 a Major and GSO 3 a captain.
H Hour	- Time from which an operation begins. Formerly Zero-Hour.
Harbour	- A secure area behind the FDLs where armoured units could re-ammunition and re-supply after an action.
Hawkin's Grenade	- A small anti-tank grenade carried by combat units for their immediate close-in protection.
HLI	- Highland Light Infantry.
IO	- Intelligence Officer.
Jeep	- The ubiquitous ¼ ton general purpose (GP) vehicle originally developed by Willis for the US Army. Named by the GIs, as a corruption of GP, after a small, cat-like, forecasting creature of that name in the comic strip "Popeye". "Popeye" also gave the nickname "Wimpy" to the RAF's Wellington bomber (after J. Wellington Wimpy, a friend of Popeye.)
Johns (nn)	- The Regina Rifles.
Kangaroo	- A Ram tank with the turret removed to create an APC.
Knee-Mortar (nn)	- The Japanese 50-mm light mortar Type 89 which had a small semi-cylindrical baseplate instead of the cumbersome tripod bases of contemporary light mortars. The GIs who thought it could be braced on the knee for firing learned otherwise. The design was soon copied by the Allies.
Lake Soups (nn)	- The Lake Superior Regiment.
Leaguer	- Similar to vehicle harbour.
Lincs and Wincs (nn)	- Lincoln and Welland Regiment.
LOB	- Left out of battle. A small number of key members kept out of a forthcoming action to enable a smooth continuum in the event that the principals become casualties.
LOC	- Line of Communication.
LMG	- Light Machine Gun, for Canadians the Bren.
Loyal Eddies (nn)	- The Loyal Edmonton Regiment.
M 10	- A self-propelled 17 pounder Anti-Tank gun mounted on an open-topped tank chassis.
MC	- Military Cross - Formerly restricted to junior and Warrant Officers, now open to both officers and Other Ranks.
MM	- Military Medal. The equivalent of the MC for Other Ranks.
The Maisies (nn)	- Le Regiment de Maisonneuve. Also, because they were brigaded with two Highland battalions, sometimes called " The Maisonneuve Highlanders"
Medium Artillery	- Corps or AGRA artillery with guns between 4 inch (field) and 7.2 inch (heavy) calibre. For Canadians normally 4.5 or 5.5 inch.
MG/MMG	- Machine Gun/ Medium Machine Gun ; for Canadians the latter was the water-cooled Vickers.
MG 42	- The standard German MMG with a high cyclic rate of fire. A superb weapon that was much feared.
Mighty Maroon Machine	- The 5th Canadian Armoured Division.
Mike Target	- An artillery target engaged by all 24 guns of the regiment.
Mark IV	- The standard German medium tank of the middle-war period. Armed with a 75 mm gun the Mk IV was in service to the war's end.
Mortar	- Smooth bore high angle weapons. Used by infantry in Canadian Army - Company mortar was 2 inch, battalion 3 inch and

APPENDICES

	Support Battalions used 4.5 inch models.
MSR	- Main Supply Route.
NCO	- Non-Commissioned Officer.
North Novas	- North Nova Scotia Highlanders.
No. 36 Grenade	- Standard segmented Canadian hand grenade.
O Gp	- Orders Group - a meeting where key personnel are given orders for a forthcoming action.
Panther	- Standard German battle tank of late war period. Heavily armoured with long barrelled 75 mm gun. Very effective.
Panzer	- German armoured entity.
Panzerfaust	-German disposable, short range, hand-held, anti-tank weapon. Roughly equivalent to US bazooka.
Princess Pats (nn)	-Princess Patricia's Canadian Light Infantry. Although the Princess preferred the use of this nickname the Regiment, somewhat pedantically, opted to call themselves "Patricia's".
Petard	-The large 215 mm mortar bomb fired by an AVRE, informally called the "Dustbin."
PIAT	- Projector Infantry Anti-Tank. The standard Canadian hand-held anti-tank weapon.
Pioneers	- Field engineers integral to infantry battalions. Also special British construction units.
Priest	-The US SP field gun - similar to Canadian Sexton.
RAP	- Regimental Aid Post.
R Gp	- Reconnaissance Group (Recce Group).
Red Patches	- 1st Canadian Infantry Division.
Regiment	- In US and German armies is a brigade size formation. In Commonwealth usage equates with a battalion sized unit.
Rileys (nn)	- Royal Hamilton Light Infantry.
Salvo	- Operation where a group of guns fire together on one target.
SAR	- South Alberta Regiment.
Schmeiser	- Standard German sub-machine gun. Called the "Burp Gun" because of its high rate of fire.
Sand, Dirt and Gravel (nn)	- The Stormont, Dundas and Glengarry Highlander (SD&Gs)
Seagull	- The Adjutant, who, like the bird, had a propensity for dumping on his junior officers.
Sherman	- Standard Allied medium tank.
Shrapnel	- A shell casing filled with ball-bearing like projectiles and a burster charge, fused to fire the projectiles forward in a cone. Lethal against troops in the open but ineffective against entrenchments. It failed to cut the German wire before the attack on the Somme. Invented by Henry Shrapnell RA in 1793 the name is erroneously used to refer to any HE shell splinters.
Slit Trench	- Small two-man fighting trench. Also "Fox Hole".
SP	- Self-Propelled, usually refers to artillery.
SL	- Start Line. A recognizable linear feature, such as a road, which is at right angles to the line of attack. Crossed by the leading troops at H Hour, from whence the timing of an operation begins.
STEN	- Standard Commonwealth sub-machine gun.
Stonk	- Artillery concentration on a single target.
SUNRAY	- Wireless name for commander. His 2IC was "SUNRAY MINOR".
Stuart	- The US M3 light tank, widely used by the Western Allies, often in

GAUDEAMUS IGITUR

	the Recce role with the turret removed. Nick-named "Honey".
TCV	- Troop Carrying Vehicle.
Tiger	- German heavy tank with an 88 mm gun. Much feared.
Uncle Target	- A target engaged by all guns of the divisional artillery.
VC	- Victoria Cross.
Victor Target	- An artillery target engaged by all guns of the Corps.
Weasel	- The US M29 tracked light amphibious vehicle. Originally developed in 1942 by Studebaker to meet the requirements of the Can/USA Special Service Force. It was never used by that force but was extensively used by others including the Canadians from the Scheldt onward.
West Novas	- The West Nova Scotia Regiment.
Whiskey (William) Target	- An artillery target engaged by all guns within range.
Wireless	- Radio.
WNG O	- Warning Order to alert subordinates to a forthcoming operation. Usually followed by an O Gp.
Zombie (nn)	- A Canadian conscripted under the National Resources Mobilization Act and required to serve only in Canada. A shortage of volunteers to replace battle casualties eventually resulted in some 10,000 being required to serve overseas.

Sources and Bibliography

Alan Brooke, FM, Lord, *War Diaries 1939-1945*, Eds, A. Danchev & D. Todman, Weidefeld & Nicolson, London, 2001.

Biddle, S., *Afghanistan and the Future of Warfare*, Foreign Affairs, New York, March/April, 2003.

Bryant, A., *Triumph in the West*, Westport, Greenwood, 1974.

Burhans, R., *The First Special Service Force*, Toronto, Metheun, 1981.

Burns, E.L.M., *General Mud*, Toronto, Clarke Irwin, 1970.

Canadian Military History, Wilfred Laurier, Waterloo, Vol. 1, No's 1 & 2, Vol. 2, No 2, Vol. 4, No 1, Vol. 6, No 1, Vol. 7, No 2.

Calvocaressi, P., Wint, G., Pritchard, J., *The Penguin History of the Second World War*, London, Penguin, 1995.

Copp, T., *The Fifth Brigade at Verrieres Ridge*, Canadian Military History, Vol. 1, Nos. 1&2.
 -*The Brigade, The Fifth Canadian Infantry Brigade, 1939-45*, Stony Creek, Fortress, 1992.
 -*A Canadian's Guide to the Battlefields of Normandy*, Waterloo, Wilfred Laurier, 1994.
 - *The Battle for Kapelsche Veer*, Legion Magazine, May/June, 2002.

Copp, T., and Vogel,R., *Maple Leaf Route : Caen*, Alma, Maple Leaf Route, 1983.
 - *Maple Leaf Route : Falaise*, Alma, Maple Leaf Route, 1983.
 - *Maple Leaf Route :Antwerp*,Alma, Maple Leaf Route, 1984.

Coyle, B., *War on Our Doorstep*, Surrey, Heritage House, 2002.

Churchill, W.S., *The Hinge of Fate*, Boston, Houghton Mifflin, 1950.
 - *The Grand Alliance*, Boston, Houghton Mifflin, 1951..
 - *Triumph and Tragedy*, Boston, Houghton Mifflin, 1953.

Dancocks, D., *The D-Day Dodgers*, Toronto, McClelland and Stewart, 1991.
 - *Sir Arthur Currie*, Toronto, McClelland and Stewart, 1988.

Day, D., *The Great Betrayal, Britain, Australia and the Onset of the Pacific War 1939-42*, New York, Norton, 1989.

APPENDICES

D'Este, Carlo, *Bitter Victory,* London, Collins, 1988.
Eisenhower, D.D., *Crusade in Europe,* Garden City, Doubleday, 1948.
Ellis, L.F., *Victory in the West - The Official History of the British Army in the Second World War, Vol. 2,* London, HMSO,1962.
Ellis, J., *On the Front Lines,* Toronto, Wiley, 1991.
English, J.A., *The Canadian Army and the Normandy Campaign : A Study of Failure in High Command,* New York, Praeger, 1991.
Esposito, V.J., Ed, *The West Point Atlas of American Wars, Vol. 2,* New York, Praeger, 1959.
Ferguson, T., *Desperate Siege : The Battle of Hong Kong,* Toronto, Doubleday, 1980.
Frankland, N., Ed., *The Encyclopedia of Twentieth Century Warfare,* New York, Mitchell-Blazely, 1989.
Fraser, D., *And We Shall Shock Them,* London, Cassell, 1999.
Frost, C.S., *Once a Patricia,* St, Catherines, Vanwell, 1988.
Graham, D. and Bidwell, S., *Tug of War,* London, Hodder and Stoughton, 1986.
Greenhaus, B., *Dieppe, Dieppe,* Montreal, Art Global, 1992.
Gunston, N., *Fighting Aircraft of World War II,* London, Salamander, 1988.
Hamilton, N., *Master of the Battlefield,* London, Hamish Hamilton, 1983.
Henderson, D., *The Scottish Regiments,* Glasgow, Harper Collins, 1996.
Horne, A., *To Lose a Battle,* Harmondsworth, Penguin, 1979.
Horrocks, B., *Corps Commander, X*
Jackson, W.G.F., *The Mediterranean and the Middle East, Vol. VI, Part II,* London, HMSO, 1987.
Lindsay, O., *Their Lasting Honour,* London, Hamish Hamilton, 1978,
Lucas, J., *Battle Group,* London, Cassell, 1993.
Manstein, Erich von, *Lost Victories,* Chicago, Henry Regnery, 1958.
Maule, H., *Caen The Brutal Battle and Breakout From Normandy,* Trowbridge, David and Charles, 1988.
McAndrew, Graves, Whitby, *Normandy 1944 The Canadian Summer,* Montreal, Art Global, 1994.
Mitcham, S.G., Von Stauffenberg, F. *The Battle of Sicily,* New York, Crown, 1991.
Middlebrook, M., Everitt, C., *The Bomber Command War Diaries,* London, Penguin, 1990.
Montgomery B.L., *Memoirs,* London, Collins, 1958.
Mowat, F., *And No Birds Sang,* Toronto, McClelland & Stewart, 1979.
 - *The Regiment,* Toronto, McClelland & Stewart,1955.
Nicholson, G.W.L., *The Canadians in Italy,* Ottawa, Queen's Printer, 1957.
Pickersgill, J.W., *The Mackenzie King Record, Vol. 1,* Toronto, University, 1960.
Potugal, J., Ed., *We Were There, The Army,* Royal Canadian Institute, Heritage Society. 1998.
Prouse, A.R., *Ticket to Hell Via Dieppe,* Toronto, Von Nostrand Rheinhold, 1982.
Roy, R., *1944 The Canadians in Normandy,* Toronto, MacMillan,1984.
Saunders, H., St. G., *The Red Beret,* London, Michael Joseph, 1950.
Smith, W.I., *Codeword CANLOAN,* Toronto, Dundurn,1992.
Snowie,J.A., *Bloody Buron,* Boston Mills, Erin, 1988.
Stacey, C.P., *Six Years of War,* Ottawa, Queen's Printer, 1955.
 - *The Victory Campaign : Operations in Northwest Europe, 1944-45,* Ottawa, Queen's Printer, 1960.
Swift, M., Sharpe, M., *Historical Maps of World War II,* London, PRC, 2000.
Williams, J., *The Long Left Flank,* Toronto, Stoddart, 1988.
Winter, D., *Haig's Command,* St. Ives, Penguin,1991.

GAUDEAMUS IGITUR

INDEX

Aachen 183
Abbaye d'Ardenne 136, 147 - 149
Abbeville 40, 183
Adam Gen R. 272, 273
Adrano 55, 62, 63, 64
AFHQ 71
Agira 55, 59, 61
D'Aguillar, Cape 15
Akehurst Lt Col J.F. 260, 264, 267, 268
Albatross (Pt 73) 218
Albert Canal 194
Albert - Frieda Line 101
Alexander FM Sir H. 46, 50, 51, 53, 58, 59, 65-68, 71, 76, 89, 97, 99, 100, 103, 104, 108, 120, 124, 265, 267
Algiers 47, 49
Allard Lt Col J.V. 86
Allen Maj J. 93
Allfrey Lt Gen C.W. 79, 87
Alter Rhein 221, 227
Amblie 151
Amiens 1, 184
Amy Maj N. 81, 168
Anagi 97
Anderson Lt Col J.C. 153
Andrews Lt Col J.G. 27
Anger Op 231
Angus Op 196
Ante R 176
Antwerp 183 passim
Anvil Op 268
Anzio 7, 43, 88, 89, 264 passim
Apeldoorn 225, 230, 231, 233
Aquino 93, 94, 97
Arbousier Ft 268
Ardennes 183, 250
Argentan 165, 171, 175, 177
Arezzo Line 101
Arielli R. 87
Arnhem 189, 228, 231, 232
Arno R. 101
Arques-la-Bataille 26, 31
Arrestino Mt 267
Arzilla R 104, 105
Aspromonte 72
Assen 235
Assoro 42, 55, 57, 58, 67
Astonia Op 185
Atella 76
Atlantic Op 152, passim, 160, 164
Atto Lt 263
Attu 260
Aue R. 238
Augusta 47, 49, 51
Aurich 240
Ausa R 110, 111
Authie 137, 138, 147
Avaranches 164
Ayer Lt 148

Bad Zwischenahn 238, 239
Balberger Wald 215, 216, 218, 219
Baltic 254
Bari 76
Barneveld 234
Basly 136
Bastogne 251
Bayeux 135
Baytown Op 71

Bean Lt G. 143
Beauvoir Farm 154, 155, 161
Becket Lt Col R.W. 260, 268
Bekhausen 240
Beilen 235
Belfort Gap 183
Bell-Irving Maj H. 61
Bennet's Hill 17
Berry-Sur-Mer 132
Bergen-Op-Zoom 194
Berlin 239
Bernatchez Brig P. 54, 90, 91, 117, 118
Berneval 26, 28, 36
Bernieres-Sur-Mer 132, 134
Beveland 192, 194, 200
Biasiallon Lt Col H.L. 153
Bienen 227
Bingeberg 252
Birkett Lt G.A, 16
Biscari 47
Bishop Maj W.A. 14
Blackader Brig K.G. 131
Blackshirt Militia 72
Blackwood Lt T.A. 17
Blue Beach 26, 29, 30, 31
Bluecoat Op 163, 165
Blumentritt Gen G. 226
Boa Vista 13
Bols Maj Gen E. 252
Boforce 75
Bogert Brig M.P. 54, 75, 123
Bois de Bavent 250
Booth Brig E.L. 50, 63, 164, 169, 173
Boulogne 184 passim
Bourguebus 152, 153, 154, 158
Bourne Lt Col J. 260, 264
Bowman Capt A. 17
Boyce Lt W. 263
Braakman Inlet 197, 198, 199
Bradbrooke Lt Col G.F. 246
Bradley Gen O.N. 3, 51, 53, 65, 66, 129, 158, 164, 171, 177, 204, 228, 239
Brant Pte J. 52
Breda 275
Bremen 228, 230, 232, 235, 240
Brereton Lt Gen L.H. 204
Breskens 184, 192, 194, 197, 199
Bretteville 140, 141
Bretteville-sur-Laize 157, 166, 170
Breville 249, 250
Brimstone Op 47
Broadhurst AM Sir H. 66
Brooke FM Sir A. 46, 77, 100, 124, 152, 204
Brooke-Popham ACM Sir R. 11
Brotherton Sgt W. 263
Brown Lt Col G. 133, 141
Browning Lt Gen Sir F. 189, 246
Bruneval 24
Brussels 184
Bucknall Lt Gen G. 129
Buckner Lt Gen S.B. 260
Buffalo Op 266
Bulge The 208
Burhans Lt Col R. 268
Burns Lt Gen E.L.M. 8, 88, 90, 92, 95, 97, 98, 99, 100, 104, 106-111, 113, 114, 116, 208
Buron 137, 147, 148
Butler Mt 15, 16

INDEX

Cabeldu Brig F.N. 129, 139, 215, 221
Caen 3, 4, 43, 135, 136, 144, 145, 147, 149, 150, 152, 157
Caillouet 166, 167,
Cairo Conf. 98
Calabria 47, 49, 72
Calais 185, 187, 190
Calcar 214, 215, 216, 218,
Calder Brig A. 118
Calpe HMS 36
Caltagirone 49, 51, 52
Cambrai 1
Cameron Mt 17
Campbell Capt A. 56
Camino Monte 262, 263
Canadian Corps 1
Canal du Nord 1
Canicatti 49
Canloan 271 passim
Cannes 269
Cantlie Lt Col S.S. 153
Cap Gris Nez 187, 190
Cardonville 138, 139, 140, 141, 142
Carpathians 257
Carpiquet 3, 128, 132, 135, 136, 137, 144, 145, 147
Carriere Pte J. 202
Casablanca Conf 48, 261
Casino 33, 34, 35, 40, 43
Cassino Monte 78, 88, 89
Castillon Fort 269
Castrovillari 74
Catania 47, 51, 53, 55, 59, 62
Catanzara 73
Catenanuova 62
Catto Lt Col D.E. 27, 30, 34
Causeway Bay 13
CEF 90, 92, 94
Celle 253, 254
Central Landing School 246
Centuripe 62, 63
Ceprano 95, 97
Cerreto Alto 266
Chambois 177, 178
Chamberlain Lt R. 87
Charnwood Op 142, 144, 146, 147
Cheux 142
Chiang Kai Shek 11
Christenson Lt Col G.H. 131, 162
Chuckle Op 119
Chung Hum Kok 16
Churchill W.S. 11, 18, 24, 39, 46, 68, 71, 76, 89, 104, 127, 204, 228, 234, 257
Cider 79 passim
Cintheux 157, 166, 168
Cisterna Canal 267
Clair Tizon 172
Clancy Capt J. 250
Clark Gen M. 71, 76, 88, 89, 94, 97, 103, 113, 114, 120, 124, 262, 264, 265, 267
Clarke Lt B. 139
Cleanser Op 233
Cleve 211, 212
Clift Lt Col F.A. 154
Cobra Op 164, 165
Coleman Capt R. 58
Colleferro 97, 267
Collins Lt Gen J.L. 129
Colombelles 152, 153
Colombiers-Sur-Seulles 134
Colwell Lt Col R.J. 131
Comacchio Lake 121, 123
Compobasso 77, 78

Coningham AVM A. 49, 50, 66, 67, 173, 238
Conrath L Gen P. 48, 53
Conventello 123
Coriano 107, 108, 109, 110, 113
Corlett Maj Gen 260
Courseulles-sur-Mer 129, 133
Cosens Sgt A. 217
COSSAC 127
Costa dell'Ambra 50
Cote d'Azure 268
Couliboeuf 177
Crabb Lt A. 274
Cramesnil 157, 166
Crapuzza 60, 61
Crerar Gen H.D.G. 3, 27, 76, 88, 99, 116, 151, 164, 165, 171 174, 177, 183, 184, 195, 203, 205, 208, 211, 213, 220, 223, 231, 241, 242,
Creully 134
Criscina Mt 62
Criquebeuf 181
Crocker Lt Gen J. 4, 5, 129, 135, 142, 144, 147, 164, 185 203, 207, 209, 247, 250
Crocket Sgt C. 194, 195
Crowe Lt Col R. 50, 60
Cumberland Brig I. 99, 233
Cunningham Adm A.B. 48, 64, 65, 66
Cunningham Brig D.G. 131, 136, 137, 162
Currie Maj D.V. 178, 179
Currie Gen A. 1, 2
Cussy 147, 148
Cuverville 247

Damblainville 177
Danson Lt B. 132
Darling Lt Col W. 107
Dawnay Brig D. 108
D-Day 127 passim
Defensa La 263
Delfzijl 236, 237
Delmenhorst 241
Dempsey Gen M. 3, 49, 66, 71, 76, 77, 78, 129, 151, 162, 164, 183, 205, 226, 252
Denison Maj L.H. 214
Destroyer Op 232
Deventer 225, 230, 231
Devil's Peak 13, 20
Dextraze L Col J. 158, 163, 164
Diadem Op 89, 98
Dieppe 7, 23 passim, 183, 184
Diersfordt 227, 252
Difensa 7, 262, 263
Dittaino R. 55, 57, 62
Dives R. 179, 248
Divette R. 248
Doi Col 13
Dornick 228
Dortmund-Ems Canal 254
Down Ampney 248
Dragoon Op 101, 175
Drocourt-Queant 1
Duck Op 240
Duffy RSM A. 56
Dunkirk 184
Dutch Harbour 260

East Brigade 15
Eberding Maj Gen K. 199
Edmondson Maj J.S. 155, 156
Eisenhower Gen D.D. 24, 47, 48, 49, 64, 65, 76, 88, 130, 157, 165, 183, 204, 223, 225, 228, 239, 241, 243
Elbe R. 239, 254

323

Elbeuf 181
Emden 230, 232, 237, 239, 240
Emmerich 226, 227, 228, 229, 235
Ems R. 237, 239, 240
Enna 49, 51, 54, 55
Epanecy 174
Ethan Allen Fort 259
Etna Mt 47, 59, 62, 64
Exodus Op 239

Falaise 4, 157, 166, 168, 171, 172, 173, 174, 175, 176, 177 181, 250
Faubourg de Vaucelles 152
Ferrara 104, 114
Findlay Capt D.M. 274
Fiumicino R. 114
Fleury-sur-Orne 153
Florence 101, 103
Foglia R. 104, 105, 106
FOO 36
Fontaine Henry 133
Foote Capt J.W. 36
Fontenay-le-Marmion 160, 167
Force 141, 65
Foret de la Londe 181
Fortore R. 77
Forrest Red 84
Fosso Basilicia 123
Fosso Munio 119
Fosso Vecchio 119
Fosso Vetro 123
Foster Maj Gen H. 116, 117, 119, 121, 208, 233, 260
Foulkes Lt Gen C. 116, 118, 121, 124, 151, 153, 160 162, 163, 175, 181, 194, 195, 201, 202, 208, 232, 235
Franqueville 137
Fraser Gen D. 17, 98, 99, 223
Frederick Maj Gen R.T. 257, 259, 262, 263, 265, 267
Frederik Hendrick Fort 199
Fries Maj Gen W. 48
Frisian Iles 239
Friesland 236
Friesoythe 238
Fronte Monte 61
Frosinone 78, 97

Gairdner Maj Gen C.H. 49, 64
Gardner Pte J. 51
Gap The 177
Gale Maj Gen R.N. 246, 247, 249, 250, 251
Gardiner Sgt J. 141
Galloway Lt Gen A. 234
Galloway Maj S. 84
Garigliano R. 76, 88, 262, 263
Gaumesnil 166, 168
Gauvreau Lt Col J. G. 154, 155
Gela 47, 49, 51, 64, 65
Geldern 215
Gerow Lt Gen L. 129, 177
Ghent 1934
Giarratana 51
Giberville 152
Gibson Brig T. 78, 89, 214
Gilday Lt Col T. 260, 264
Ginestreto 105
Goch 211, 214, 215, 216
Gold Beach 129, 130
Gold Flake Op 124
Goodwood Op 4, 151, 152, 157, 158
Gordon Lt Col M. 131

Gostling Lt Col A. 27, 32
Gothic Line 8, 76, 101, passim
Grabstede 240
Graham Brig H. 50, 52, 56, 57, 60, 78
Grainville 170
Grammichele 49, 52, 53
Granarolo 122, 123
Grayson Lt W. 133
Grazie Le 112
Grebbe Line 230, 234
Green Beach 26, 31
Green Line 101, 107, 112
Green Sgt W. 250
Gregg Brig M. 273
Gregory Lt Col A. 214
Grenade Op 213
Gresham Maj A. 16
Greven 254
Griffin Maj F.P. 161
Griffin Lt Col P.G. 96
Griffiths Lt Col F.M. 131
Grigas Pte J. 51
Groningen 235, 236
Gruchy 147, 148
Gully, The 79, 82, passim
Gustav Line 88, 89, 90, 92, 98
Guzzoni Gen A. 48, 65

Hakewill-Smith Maj Gen E. 202
Halpenny Lt Col W.W. 168, 169
Hamburg 228, 254
Hannover 253, 254
Hardgate Op 62
Harding Gen J. 89
Harkness Lt Col D. 179
Harlingen 236
Harris ACM A. 190, 203
Harrison Ft Wm Henry 257
Hautmesnil 169
d'Havet Maj Gen A. 51
Havre Le 185
Hees Maj G. 202
Heidrich Lt Gen R. 48
Heim Lt Gen F. 185, 188
Hennessy Col P. 11, 17
Herr Gen T. 120
Hill Brig S.J. 247, 249, 250, 252, 254
Hitler A. 38, 164, 241
Hitler Line 89, 90, 91, 93, 94, 98
Hoch Elten 228, 229
Hochwald 211, 215, 216, 218, 219
Hodges Lt Gen C. 183
Hoffmeister Maj Gen B. 76, 89, 95, 96, 99, 109, 114, 119, 123, 233, 234, 237
Hogue La 167
Home Lt Col W.J. 11, 15
Hong Kong 7 passim
Hoogerheide 196
Hopkins H. 24
Horrocks Lt Gen B. 184, 189, 204, 209, 211, 212, 213, 216, 220 226, 227
Hube Gen V. 48, 64
Hubert-Folie 153, 154
Hughes S. 2
Hughes-Hallett Capt J. 27, 36, 39
Hurricanes 28, 34
Husky Op 47 passim

INDEX

Ifs 153
Igoville 181
Ijssel (R.& Meer) 225, 230, 231, 232, 233
Ile du Levant 268
Ile de Port Cros 268
Ismay Gen H. 39
Ispica 51

Jackson Gen W.G.F. 103, 107
Jacobs CSM J. 141
Jade 240. 241
Jardine,s Lookout 20
Jasperson Lt Col F.K. 27
Jefferson Brig J.C. 50, 58, 164, 170, 179, 209
Jodl Col Gen A. 241
Johnson Brig I. 99, 237
Jubilee Op 24, 26, 35
Juin Gen A. 94
Juno Beach 129, 130

Kapelsche Veer 208, 209
Katchanoski Cpl P. 213
Keane Lt Col R.A. 169
Keating Lt W.L. 214
Keefler Maj Gen R.H. 195, 201, 202, 227, 228, 229, 236, 240
Keightly Lt Gen C. 104, 107, 108
Keleher Sgt J. 263
Keller Maj Gen R. 4, 130, 136, 139, 142, 153, 186
Kennedy Maj B. 56, 80
Keppeln 215, 217, 218
Kesselring FM.A. 48, 85, 108, 120, 265
Kincaid Adm T. 260
King W.L. Mackenzie 2, 3, 45, 46, 77, 115, 206
Kiska 259, 260, 261
Kitching Maj Gen G. 60, 87, 116, 151, 164, 168, 169, 170, 174, 175, 178, 179
Klaehn Lt Col P.C. 131
Kluge F.M. von G. 164, 165
Krasevac Lt G. 266
Krause Col 175, 177
Krefeld 211, 226
Kusten Canal 238

Labatt Lt Col R.R. 27
Laison 166, 172
Laloge Sgt 202
Lambert Mt 187
Lambert-sur-Dives St. 178, 179
Lamone R. 117, 118
Laurie Lt J. 275
Lauenberg 254
Law Maj A.T. 32
Lawson Brig J.K. 7, 11, 14, 16, 18, 21
Lebisey Woods 136
Leda 239, 240
Leer 240
Leese Gen O. 49, 55, 59, 63, 64, 66, 69, 76, 88, 90, 93, 95, 98, 103, 106, 107, 108, 110, 113, 114, 152
Leeuwarden 236
Leigh-Mallory AVM T.L. 27
Leighton Hill 16, 20
Lentini 53
Leonforte 49, 51, 53, 55 - 59
Leopold Canal 194, 197, 198
Levant Ile du 268
Lion-sur-Mer 131 passim
Liri Valley 78, 89 passim, 262
Lister Brig J.F. 99
Loshaw Sgt J.W. 94

Louvigny 153
Lubeck 239, 240
Lucas Maj Gen J.P. 265
Luneburg Heath 241, 253
Luro Mt 107
Lutzow 255
Lye Mun 19

Maas (Meuse) 207
Macdonald Lt Col B.J. 154
MacIntosh Lt H. 269
MacIntyre Maj K.W. 215

MacKenzie Lt Col D.A. 231
Maclauchlan Lt Col D.G. 153
MacWilliam Lt Col T.C. 260, 262, 263
Maczek Maj Gen S. 168
Maczuga 178, 179
Maggiore Mt 262
Mahony Maj J. 96
Majo Mt 264
Mann Brig C. 27
Mathieu Lt Col J.B. 130
Mathews Maj G.R. 155
Mathews Maj Gen A.B. 208, 221, 235
May-sur-Orne 160, 164, 167
McCall Capt G.N. 264, 266
McCreery Gen R. 113, 114, 115, 116, 120, 124
McGregor Capt J. 274
McLean Lt J. 81
McQueen Lt Col J.G. 170, 259
McNaughton Gen A.G. 2, 3, 25, 52, 116
McNaughton Spr M. 81
Meindl Gen E. 216
Megill Brig W.J. 161, 162, 196, 201
Melfa R. 95 passim
Meldram Lt Col J.M. 131
Menard Lt Col D. 27
Menny Lt Gen E. 179
Menton 269
Menzies Sgt R.W. 82
Meppen 237
Merville 248
Mesnil Le 248, 249
Mesnil Patry Le 138, 142, 143
Messina 47, 49, 52, 53, 59, 62, 64, 65, 71
Metauro 103 passim
Meyer Hubert 142, 143
Meyer Maj Gen K. 135, 136, 137, 138, 149, 169, 175, 177
Mignano Gap 262, 264
Millingen 227
Minden 254
Mitchell Cpl 139
Model F.M.W. 229
Moerbrugge 198
Moerdijk 203, 207
Moershoofd 198
Moissy 178
Mollberg 240
Moncel Brig R.W. 173, 179, 239
Montecchio 106
Montgomery F.M. B.L. 3, 4, 25, 45, 49 - 53, 55, 58, 59, 64-68, 73, 74, 76, 77, 86, 88, 116, 128, 129, 142, 144, 145, 151, 152, 157, 163-165, 171, 173, 174, 177, 181, 185, 189, 192, 204, 205, 208, 211, 225, 228, 229, 231-234, 239, 241, 242, 251, 275
Montone R. 117
Mooney Lt. J. 149
Mooshof 217
Morgan Lt Gen F. 127

325

Morning Glory Op 83
Moro R. 79
Mortain 165
Morton Lt Col R.E. 131
Mountbatten Adm L. 27, 39, 47, 257, 261
Mowat Lt F. 56, 94
Mussolini B. 47, 62, 71

Naples 73, 74, 76
Naviglio Canal 118, 119
Neder Rijn 207, 232
Nettuno 265
Nicklin Lt Col J.A. 252, 253
Nicholson Mt 17
Nijmegan 189, 207, 210, 232
Nissoria 55, 59, 60
North Sea 225
Norway 257, 259
Norrey 138, 140, 141, 142, 143, 148
NRMA 115

O'Connor Lt Gen R. 154
Odon R. 144
Oldenburg 230, 237-241
Olive Op 102, 103
Omaha Beach 40, 129
Orange Beach 26, 28, 29
Orange Blossom Op 83, 84
Ormel Mt 178
Orne R. 144, 151, 247
Orsogna 79 passim
Ortona 8, 79 passim
Osborne CSM J. 16
Osteria Nuova 106
Otis Pte H. 119
Otterloo 233, 234
Overlord Op 40, 88, 127 passim

Pachino 49, 50
Palm Villa 15
Palermo 47, 49, 53, 59, 64
Panaccioni 90
Pangman Lt Col J. 215
Parker Mt 15
Patch Lt Gen A.M. 268, 269
Patrick Henry Camp 261
Patton Gen G.S. 3, 48-51, 53, 59, 65, 66, 165, 169, 171, 204, 225
Passchendaele 1
Pearl Harbour 9, 259
Peloso Mt 107
Penhale Brig M. 50, 54, 62, 75, 78,
Perkins Lt E. 29, 96
Pesaro 104
Pescara 78
Petch Lt Col C. 131,159,162
Petit Appeville 31,32
Phillips Lt Col J.P. 27
Pisciatello R. 115
Plunder Op 225, 226
Pofi 97
Potigny 173
Pontecorvo 92-94
Port Cros Ile de 268
Porteous Capt A. 36, 43
Potenza 75, 76
Pourville 25, 26, 31, 36, 40, 41
Po Valley 101, 104, 113 passim
Powers Maj T. 60

Primosole Br. 53, 55
Prouse R. 34
Putot-en-Bessin 20, 138-140
Puys 25, 26, 28 passim
Pyke G. 257

Quatre Vents Farm 31-33
Québec Conf 261
Quesnay Wood 170
Quiberville 29
Quisling Bay 260

Radbergen 254
Ragusa 51
Raincoat Op 262
Ranville 247
Ralston J.L. 77, 116, 272
Ramilles HMS 268
Randazzo 47
Rapido R. 78, 263
Raphael St. 269
Ravenna 104, 114, 117
Red Beach 26, 30, 31, 33, 35, 36
Red Hill 15
Rees 225, 226
Regalbuto 55, 62
Reggio 72, 73
Reid Lt Col W.W. 106
Reichswald 207, 211
Remagen 225
Remetanea La 263
Reno R. 124
Repulse Bay 13, 15
Revisotto Mt 63
Rhine R. 183, 210, 225
Rhineland 207
Richardson Maj Gen A.A. 49
Richthofen FM von W. 48
Ricklingen 254
Ridgeway Lt Gen M. 251
Rimini 101, 104, 107, 110-112
Ringway 246, 247
Ritchie Lt Gen N. 226
Roberts Capt R. 141
Roberts Maj Gen J.H. 25, 27, 31, 35, 36, 40
Roberts Brig J. 217
Robehomme 248, 249
Rochefort 251
Rockingham Brig J. 159, 163, 187, 198, 227
Rocquancourt 159, 167
Rodgers Maj B. 216, 217
Rodt Maj Gen E. 48, 57
Roermond 251
Romagna 104, 110, 112, 114
Rome 7, 78, 88, 97, 267
Rommel FM E. 129, 164, 169
Roosevelt F.D. 9, 24, 205, 228, 231
Rots 139
Roundup Op 24
Rousseau Sgt J.P. 83
Rowley Lt Col R. 199
Rowley Lt Col J.H. 217, 227
Rutter Op 24, 26

Saane R. 25
Sacco R. 98
Salerno 43, 72, 74, 75, 262
Sallenelles 248
Salmon Maj Gen H.L. 46

INDEX

Salsa R. 63,64
Sangro R. 78, 79
San Stefano 62, 113
Sant Angelo in Teodice 90
Santa Maria 262, 268
Santa Teresa 62
Santerno R. 116, 117
Sardinia 47
Savio R. 115
Scheldt 181, 192, passim
Scie R. 25, 32
Scilli 51
Schlemm Gen A. 211, 212, 216, 219, 220, 226
Schmalz Col W. 53
Schneppenberg 252, 253
Scott Lt Col M. 170, 173
Schouwen 207
Scrutton Sgt S. 143
Seine R. 161, 250
Senio R. 116, 118
Shing Mun Redoubt 12, 19
Shingle Op 88, 265
Shoji Col 17
Sicily 45 passim
Siegfried Line 211
Simento R. 53, 55
Simonds Lt Gen G.G. 46, 54, 57, 59, 64, 66, 67-69, 75, 76, 78, 151-154, 160, 162, 163, 165-169, 174, 181, 188, 195, 197, 208, 216, 230, 231, 240
Simpson Lt Gen W.H. 213, 239
Sledgehammer Op 24
Slooe Channel 202
Smith Brig D. 99, 116-119
Smith Pte E. 115
Smith Maj H.A. 83
Smith Lt O.H. 264
Smith W.I. 271 passim
Snow Brig T.E. 99
Sogel 238
Somme R. 1, 181
Southam Brig W.W. 36
Southern Maj K. 113
Sonsbeck 220
Speldorp 226
Spragge Brig J.G. 130, 214
Spring Op 157, 158, 160, 162, 164
Spry Maj Gen D. 84, 86, 100, 186, 187, 190
Stalin J. 24, 47
Stanley Gap 13
Stanley Mound 14, 16
Sterlin Lt M. 81,82
Stewart Lt Col J.D. 169
Stockloser Capt W. 56
Stone Hill 15
Stone Lt Col J. 85, 115
Stoneham Camp 261
Strickland Lt Col P.W. 226
Studebaker 257
Student Col Gen K. 208
Sugar Loaf Hill 15, 16
Sutcliffe Lt Col J.L.R. 11
Sword Beach 129, 131
Syracuse 47, 49, 58, 64, 65

Tailleville 131
Taormina 62,
Taranto 75
Tedder AM A. 4, 5, 48-50, 65-67, 157, 203, 204
Teheran Conf 88
Termoli 77
Terneuzen 194, 197, 198

Theobald R Adm R.A. 260
Thompson Lt Col E.P. 216
Thracian H.M.S. 15
Tiber 267
Tilly-la-Campagne 4, 142, 157, 158, 165-167
Tilston Maj F.A. 219
Tobacco Factory 33, 34, 40
Tomba di Pesaro 107
Tommaso San 86
Topham Cpl F.G. 253
Torch Op 24
Torrice Crossroads 97
Totalize Op 165, 168, 170
Tower Hill 63
Tractable Op 41, 171, 174, 175
Trapani 47, 53, 64
Trasimeno Lake 101
Tresorie La 188
Triquet Maj P. 83
Troarn 247, 248
Troina 62-64
Tropez St 269
Trun 171, 172, 174 - 180
Truscott Lt Gen L.K. 66, 266, 267
Tubbs Maj C.S. 133, 138, 148
Tuschen Wald 218, 219
Tweedie Lt Col D. 54
Tweedsmuir Lt Col J. 56
Twente Canal 230
Ty Tam Tuk 15

Udem 215, 216, 218,
Uelzen 254
Undergo Op 189
Utah Beach 129

Valette La 134
Valguarnera 54, 55
Valmonte 97
Varaville 247, 248
Varel 240
Varengeville 26, 28, 29, 36, 41
Varsity Op 226, 251
Vasterival 28
Vaucelles 153
V C 16, 36, 43, 58, 81, 82, 96, 111, 133, 139, 143, 147, 161, 179, 195, 217, 219, 253, 276
Vecchio 123
Veen 220
Venlo 251
Veritable Op 211 passim
Verrieres 4, 153-155, 157, 159, 160, 163
Victoria 16
Vietinghoff Gen von H. 48, 72, 76, 96, 103, 108, 120
Villa Grande 83
Villa Rogatti 79 passim
Villapiana 75
Villeneuve 270
Villers Bocage 142
Villons-les-Buissons 135, 136, 138
Vimoutiers 178, 179, 181
Vimy Ridge 1
Vino Ridge 82
Vischiataro Mt 264
Vizzini 51, 52, 55
Vokes Maj Gen C. 50, 57, 61, 76-83, 86, 88-90, 92 - 95,99, 108, 111,116,169,208,209,218,237,239
Vokes Lt Col F. 96, 106
Volturno 76, 101
Voorthuizen 233

GAUDEAMUS IGITUR

Waal 207
Walcheren 42,43,184,192,194,199, 201,202, 203
Walker Maj Gen F.L. 262
Walker Col E.A. 264, 268
Wallis Brig C. 15, 16
Walsh Brig G. 80
Wan Chai 16
Wangerooge 239
Ward Maj Gen D. 111
Ware Lt Col C. 82
Weasel 261
Wellhit Op 185
Welsh Maj G.A. 58
Wenzel Cpl 147
Wesel 221, 225, 252, 253
Weser R. 232, 240, 241, 254
Westkappelle 203
Weston 219, 220
West Wall 211
Wetbob Op 24
Whitaker Lt Col D. 196, 215
White Beach 26, 33, 34, 35, 36,
White Lt Col F. 217
Wierden 237
Wilhelmshaven 232, 235, 237, 239

Wilson FM H. M. 120
Williamson Col D.D. 260, 262
Windsor Op 142, 144
Winter Line 262
Wismar 253, 255
Wittenburg 255
Wittman Capt M. 142, 166, 168
Woensdrecht 195, 196
Wong Nei Chong 13-16, 20
Wotherspoon Lt Col G.D.de S. 169
Worthington Lt Col D.G. 169, 174
Wright S Sgt S. 266
Wyman Brig R.A. 89
Wyler 211, 212

Xanten 216, 220, 221, 252

Yellow Beach 26, 28, 29
Young Maj C.A. 15
Young Brig H.A. 154, 162, 167
Young Gov. M. 17
Ypres 1

Zutphen 225, 230, 231